Think and Grow Rich

and

The Law of Success

In Sixteen Lessons

Start Publishing PD LLC

Cover art: Shutterstock/Taisiya Kozorez

Cover design: Jennifer Do

10 9 8 7 6 5 4 3 2 1

ISBN 979-8-8809-2327-4

Think and Grow Rich

and

The Law of Success

In Sixteen Lessons

by Napoleon Hill

Think and Grow Rich

Table of Contents

Foreword

What Do You Want Most?
Is It Money, Fame, Power,
Contentment, Personality,
Peace of Mind, Happiness?

The Thirteen Steps to Riches described in this book offer the shortest dependable philosophy of individual achievement ever presented for the benefit of the man or woman who is searching for a definite goal1. in life.

Before beginning the book you will profit greatly if you recognize the fact that the book was not written to entertain. You cannot digest the contents properly in a week or a month. After reading the book thoroughly, Dr. Miller Reese Hutchison, nationally known Consulting Engineer and long-time associate of Thomas A. Edison, said– "This is not a novel. It is a textbook on individual achievement that came directly from the experiences of hundreds of America's most successful men. It should be studied, digested, and meditated upon. No more than one chapter should be read in a single night. The reader should underline the sentences which impress him most. Later, he should go back to these marked lines and read them again. A real student will not merely read this book, he will absorb its contents and make them his own. This book should be adopted by all high schools and no boy or girl should be permitted to graduate without having satisfactorily passed an examination on it. This philosophy will not take the place of the subjects taught in schools, but it will enable one to organize and apply the knowledge acquired, and convert it into useful service and adequate compensation without waste of time. Dr. John R. Turner, Dean of the College of The City of New York, after having read the book, said– "The very best example of the soundness of this philosophy is your own son, Blair, whose dramatic story you have outlined in the chapter on Desire." Dr. Turner had reference to the author's son, who, born without normal hearing capacity, not only avoided becoming a deaf mute, but actually converted his handicap into a priceless asset by applying the philosophy here described. After reading the story, you will realize that you are about to come into possession of a philosophy which can be transmuted into material wealth, or serve as readily to bring you peace of mind, understanding, spiritual harmony, and in some instances, as in the case of the author's son, it can. help you master physical affliction. The author discovered, through personally analyzing hundreds of successful men, that all of them followed the habit of exchanging ideas, through what is commonly called conferences. When they had problems to be solved they sat down together and talked freely until they discovered, from their joint contribution of ideas, a plan that would serve their purpose. You, who read this book, will get most out of it by putting into practice the Master Mind principle described in the book. This you can do (as others are doing so successfully) by forming a study club, consisting of any desired number of people who are friendly and harmonious. The club should have a meeting at regular periods, as often as once each week. The procedure should consist of reading one chapter of the book at each meeting, after which the contents of the chapter should be freely discussed by all members. Each member should make notes, putting down *all ideas of his own* inspired by the discussion. Each member should carefully read and analyze each chapter several days prior to its open reading and joint discussion in the club. The reading at the club should be done by someone who reads well and understands how to put color and feeling into the lines. By following this plan every reader will get from its pages, not only the sum total of the best knowledge organized from the experiences of hundreds of successful men, but more important by far, he will tap new sources of knowledge in his own mind as well as acquire knowledge of priceless value *from every other person present.* If you follow this plan persistently you will be almost certain to uncover and appropriate the secret formula by which Andrew Carnegie acquired his huge fortune, as referred to in the author's introduction.

Tributes to the Author

From Great American Leaders

Think and Grow Rich was 25 years in the making. It is Napoleon Hill's newest book, based upon his famous Law of Success Philosophy. His work and writings have been praised by great leaders in Finance, Education, Politics, Government.

Dear Mr. Hill:– I have now had an opportunity to finish reading your Law of Success textbooks and I wish to express my appreciation of the splendid work you have done in the organization of this philosophy. It would be helpful if every politician in the country would assimilate and apply the 17 principles upon which your lessons are based. It contains some very fine material which every leader in every walk of life should understand. I am happy to have had the privilege of rendering you some slight measure of help in the organization of this splendid course of "common sense" philosophy.

Sincerely yours

(Former President and former Chief Justice of the United States):

Supreme Court of the United States Washington, D. C.

"By applying many of the 17 fundamentals of the Law of Success philosophy we have built a great chain of successful stores. I presume it would be no exaggeration of fact if I said that the Woolworth Building might properly be called a monument to the soundness of these Principles."– F. W. Woolworth: King of the 5 and 10 Cent Stores

"I feel greatly indebted for the privilege of reading your Law of Success. If I had had this philosophy fifty years ago, I suppose I could have accomplished all that I have done in less than half the time. I sincerely hope the world will discover and reward you."– Robert Dollar: A Great Steamship Magnate

"Mastery of the Law of Success philosophy is the equivalent of an insurance policy against Failure."– Samuel Gompers: Famous American Labor Leader

"May I not congratulate you on your persistence. Any man who devotes that much time . . . must of necessity make discoveries of great value to others. I am deeply impressed by your interpretation of the 'Master Mind' principles which you have so clearly Described."– Woodrow Wilson: a Former President of the United States

"I know that your 17 fundamentals of success are sound because I have been applying them in my business for more than 30 years."– John Wanamaker: a Merchant Prince

"I know that you are doing a world of good with your Law of Success. I would not care to set a monetary value on this training because it brings to the student qualities which cannot be measured by money, alone." – George Eastman: World's Largest Maker of Cameras

"Whatever success I may have attained I owe, entirely, to the application of your 17 fundamental principles of the Law of Success. I believe I have the honor of being your first student."– W.M.. Wrigley, Jr.: a Nationally Known Business Chief

Publisher's Preface

This book conveys the experience of more than 500 men of great wealth, who began at scratch, with nothing to give in return for riches except *thoughts, ideas* and *organized plans.* Here you have the entire philosophy of moneymaking, just as it was organized from the actual achievements of the most successful men known to the American people during the past fifty years. It describes *what to do*, also, *how to do it*! It presents complete instructions on *how to sell your personal services.* It provides you with a perfect system of self-analysis that will readily disclose what has been standing between you and "the big money" in the past. It describes the famous Andrew Carnegie formula of personal achievement by which he accumulated hundreds of millions of dollars for himself and made no fewer than a score of millionaires of men to whom he taught his secret. Perhaps you do not need all that is to be found in the book– no one of the 500 men from whose experiences it was written did– but you may need *one idea, plan or suggestion* to start you toward your goal. Somewhere in the book you will find this needed stimulus. The book was inspired by Andrew Carnegie, after he had made his millions and retired. It was written by the man to whom Carnegie disclosed the astounding secret of his riches– the same man to whom the 500 wealthy men revealed the source of their riches. In this volume will be found the thirteen principles of money-making essential to every person who accumulates sufficient money to guarantee financial independence. It is estimated that the research which went into the preparation, before the book was written, or could be written– research covering more than twenty-five years of continuous effort– could not be duplicated at a cost of less than $100,000.00. Moreover, the knowledge contained in the book never can be duplicated, at any cost, for the reason that more than half of the 500 men who supplied the information it brings have passed on.

Riches cannot always be measured in money!

Money and material things are essential for freedom of body and mind, but there are some who will feel that the greatest of all riches can be evaluated only in terms of lasting friendships, harmonious family relationships, sympathy and understanding between business associates, and introspective harmony which brings one peace of mind measurable only in spiritual values!

All who read, understand and apply this philosophy will be better prepared to attract and enjoy these higher estates which always have been and always will be denied to all except those who are ready for them.

Be prepared, therefore, when you expose yourself to the influence of this philosophy, to experience a *changed life* which may help you not only to negotiate your way through life with harmony and understanding, but also to prepare you for the accumulation of material riches in abundance.

The Publisher

Author's Preface

In every chapter of this book, mention has been made of the money-making secret which has made fortunes for more than five hundred exceedingly wealthy men whom I have carefully analyzed over a long period of years.

The secret was brought to my attention by Andrew Carnegie, more than a quarter of a century ago. The canny, lovable old Scotsman carelessly tossed it into my mind, when I was but a boy. Then he sat back in his chair, with a merry twinkle in his eyes, and watched carefully to see if I had brains enough to understand the full significance of what he had said to me. When he saw that I had grasped the idea, he asked if I would be willing to spend twenty years or more, preparing myself to take it to the world, to men and women who, without the secret, might go through life as failures. I said I would, and with Mr. Carnegie's cooperation, I have kept my promise.

This book contains the secret, after having been put to a practical test by thousands of people, in almost every walk of life. It was Mr. Carnegie's idea that the magic formula, which gave him a stupendous fortune, ought to be placed within reach of people who do not have time to investigate how men make money, and it was his hope that I might test and demonstrate the soundness of the formula through the experience of men and women in every calling. He believed the formula should be taught in all public schools and colleges, and expressed the opinion that if it were properly taught it would so revolutionize the entire educational system that the time spent in school could be reduced to less than half. His experience with Charles M. Schwab, and other young men of Mr. Schwab's type, convinced Mr. Carnegie that much of that which is taught in the schools is of no value whatsoever in connection with the business of earning a living or accumulating riches. He had arrived at this decision, because he had taken into his business one young man after another, many of them with but little schooling, and by coaching them in the use of this formula, developed in them rare leadership. Moreover, his coaching made fortunes for everyone of them who followed his instructions. In the chapter on Faith, you will read the astounding story of the organization of the giant United States Steel Corporation, as it 12 13 was conceived and carried out by one of the young men through whom Mr. Carnegie proved that his formula will work for all who are ready for it. This single application of the secret, by that young man– Charles M. Schwab– made him a huge fortune in both money and *opportunity*. Roughly speaking, this particular application of the formula was worth six hundred million dollars. These facts–and they are facts well known to almost everyone who knew Mr. Carnegie– give you a fair idea of what the reading of this book may bring to you, provided you *know what it is that you want*. Even before it had undergone twenty years of practical testing, the secret was passed on to more than one hundred thousand men and women who have used it for their personal benefit, as Mr. Carnegie planned that they should. Some have made fortunes with it. Others have used it successfully in creating harmony in their homes. A clergyman used it so effectively that it brought him an income of upwards of $75,000.00 a year. Arthur Nash, a Cincinnati tailor, used his near-bankrupt business as a "guinea pig" on which to test the formula. The business came to life and made a fortune for its owners. It is still thriving, although Mr. Nash has gone. The experiment was so unique that newspapers and magazines, gave it more than a million dollars' worth of laudatory publicity. The secret was passed on to Stuart Austin Wier, of Dallas, Texas. He was ready for it— so ready that he gave up his profession and studied law. Did he succeed? That story is told too. I gave the secret to Jennings Randolph, the day he graduated from College, and he has used it so successfully that he is now serving his third term as a Member of Congress, with an excellent opportunity to keep on using it until it carries him to the White House. While serving as Advertising Manager of the La-Salle Extension University, when it was little more than a name, I had the privilege of seeing J. G. Chapline, President of the University, use the formula so effectively that he has since made the LaSalle one of the great extension schools of the country. The secret to which I refer has been mentioned no fewer than a hundred times, throughout this book. It has not been directly named, for it seems to work more successfully when it is merely uncovered and left in sight, where *those who are ready*, and *Searching for it*, may pick it up. That is why Mr. Carnegie tossed it to me so quietly, without giving me its specific name. If you are *ready* to put it to use, you will recognize this secret at least once in every chapter. I wish I might feel privileged to tell you how you will know if you are ready, but that would deprive you of much of the benefit you will receive when you make the discovery in your own way. While this book was being written, my own son, who was then finishing the last year of his college work, picked up the manuscript of chapter two, read it, and discovered the secret for himself. He used the information so effectively that he went directly into a responsible position at a beginning salary greater than the average man ever earns. His story has been briefly described in chapter two. When you read it, perhaps you will dismiss any feeling you may have had, at the beginning of the book, that it promised too much. And, too, if you have ever been discouraged, if you have had difficulties to surmount which took the very soul out of you, if you have tried and failed, if you were ever handicapped by illness or physical affliction, this story of my son's discovery and use of the Carnegie formula may prove to be the oasis in the Desert of Lost Hope, for which you have been searching. This secret was extensively used by President Woodrow Wilson, during the World War. It was passed on to every soldier who fought in the war, carefully wrapped in the training received before going to the front. President Wilson told me it was a strong factor in raising the funds needed for the war. More than twenty years ago, Hon. Manuel L. Quezon (then Resident Commissioner of the Philippine Islands), was inspired by the secret to gain freedom for his people. He has gained freedom for the Philippines, and is the first President of the free state. A peculiar thing about this secret is that those who once acquire it and use it, find themselves literally swept on to success, with but little effort, and they never again submit to failure! If you doubt this, study the names of those who have used it, wherever they have been mentioned, check their records for yourself, and be convinced. There is no such thing as *something for nothing*! The secret to which I refer cannot be had without a price, although the price is far less than its value. It cannot be had at any price by those who are not intentionally searching for it. It cannot be given away, it cannot be purchased for money, for the reason that it comes in two parts. One part is already in possession of those who are ready for it. The secret serves equally well, all who are ready for it. Education has nothing to do with it. Long before I was born, the secret had found its way into the possession of Thomas A. Edison, and he used it so intelligently that he became the world's leading inventor, although he had but three months of schooling. The secret was passed on to a business associate of Mr. Edison. He used it so effectively that, although he was then making only $12,000 a year, he accumulated a great fortune, and retired from active business while still a young man. You will find his story at the beginning of the first chapter. It should convince you that riches are not beyond your reach, that you can still be what you wish to be, that money, fame, recognition and happiness can be had by all who are ready and determined to have these blessings. How do I know these things? You should have the answer before you finish this book. You may find it in the very first chapter, or on the last page. While I was performing the twenty year task of research, which I had undertaken at Mr. Carnegie's request, I analyzed hundreds of well known men, many of whom admitted that they had accumulated their vast fortunes through the aid of the Carnegie secret; among these men were: –

Henry Ford
William Wrigley Jr.
John Wanamaker
James J. Hill
George S. Parker
E. M. Statler
Henry L. Doherty
Cyrus H. K. Curtis
George Eastman
Theodore Roosevelt
John W. Davis
Elbert Hubbard
Wilbur Wright
William Jennings Bryan
Dr. Dmtid Starr Jordan
J. Odgen Armour
Charles M. Schwab
Harris F. Williams
Dr. Frank Gunsaulus
Daniel Willard
King Gillette
Ralph A. Weeks
Judge Daniel T. Wright
John D. Rockefeller
Thomas A. Edison
Frank A. Vanderlip
F. W. Woolworth
Col. Robert A. Dollar
Edward A. Filene
Edwin C. Barnes
Arthur Brisbane
Woodrow Wilson
Wm. Howard Taft
Luther Burbank
Edward W. Bok
Frank A. Munsey
Elbert H. Gary

Dr. Alexander Graham Bell
John H. Patterson
Julius Rosenwald
Stuart Austin Wier
Dr. Frank Crane
George M. Alexander
J. G. Chappline
Hon. Jennings Randolph
Arthur Nash
Clarence Darrow

These names represent but a small fraction of the hundreds of well known Americans whose achievements, financially and otherwise, prove that those who understand and apply the Carnegie secret, reach high stations in life. I have never known anyone who was inspired to use the secret, who did not achieve noteworthy success in his chosen calling. I have never known any person to distinguish himself, or to accumulate riches of any consequence, without possession of the secret. From these two facts I draw the conclusion that the secret is more important, as a part of the knowledge essential for self-determination, than any which one receives through what is popularly known as "education."

What is *education*, anyway?

This has been answered in full detail. As far as schooling is concerned, many of these men had very little. John Wanamaker once told me that what little schooling he had, he acquired in very much the same manner as a modern loco-motive takes on water, by "scooping it up as it runs." Henry Ford never reached high school, let alone college. I am not attempting to minimize the value of schooling, but I am trying to express my earnest belief that those who master and apply the secret will reach high stations, accumulate riches, and bargain with life on their own terms, even if their schooling has been meager.

Somewhere, as you read, the secret to which I refer will jump from the page and stand boldly before you, *if you are ready for it!* When it appears, you will recognize it. Whether you receive the sign in the first or the last chapter, stop for a moment when it presents itself, and turn down a glass, for that occasion will mark the most important turning-point of your life.

We pass now, to Chapter One, and to the story of my very dear friend, who has generously acknowledged having seen the mystic sign, and whose business achievements are evidence enough that he turned down a glass. As you read his story, and the others, remember that they deal with the important problems of life, such as all men experience.

The problems arising from one's endeavor to earn a living, to find hope, courage, contentment and peace of mind; to accumulate riches and to enjoy freedom of body and spirit.

Remember, too, as you go through the book, that it deals with facts and not with fiction, its purpose being to convey a great universal truth through which all who are ready may learn, not only *what to do, but also how to do it!* and receive, as well, *the needed stimulus to make a start.*

As a final word of preparation, before you begin the first chapter, may I offer one brief suggestion which may provide a clue by which the Carnegie secret may be recognized? It is this— *All achievement, all earned riches, have their beginning in an idea*! If you are ready for the secret, you already possess one half of it, therefore, you will readily recognize the other half the moment it reaches your mind.

The Author

Introduction

The Man Who "Thought" His Way into Partnership with Thomas A. Edison

Truly, "thoughts are things," and powerful things at that, when they are mixed with definiteness of purpose, persistence, and a *burning desire* for their translation into riches, or other material objects.

A little more than thirty years ago, Edwin C. Barnes discovered how true it is that men really do *think and grow rich.* His discovery did not come about at one sitting. It came little by little, beginning with a *burning desire* to become a business associate of the great Edison.

One of the chief characteristics of Barnes' Desire was that it was definite. He wanted to work with Edison, not for him. Observe, carefully, the description of how he went about translating his *desire* into reality, and you will have a better understanding of the thirteen principles which lead to riches.

When this *desire*, or impulse of thought, first flashed into his mind he was in no position to act upon it. Two difficulties stood in his way. He did not know Mr. Edison, and he did not have enough money to pay his railroad fare to Orange, New Jersey.

These difficulties were sufficient to have discouraged the majority of men from making any attempt to carry out the desire. But his was no ordinary desire! He was so determined to find a way to carry out his desire that he finally decided to travel by "blind baggage," rather than be defeated. (To the uninitiated, this means that he went to East Orange on a freight train).

He presented himself at Mr. Edison's laboratory, and announced he had come to go into business with the inventor. In speaking of the first meeting between Barnes and Edison, years later, Mr. Edison said, "He stood there before me, looking like an ordinary tramp, but there was something in the expression of his face which conveyed the impression that he was determined to get what he had come after. I had learned, from years of experience with men, that when a man really *desires* a thing so deeply that he is willing to stake his entire future on a single turn of the wheel in order to get it, he is sure to win. I gave him the opportunity he asked for, because I saw he had made up his mind to stand by until he succeeded. Subsequent events proved that no mistake was made."

Just what young Barnes said to Mr. Edison on that occasion was far less important than that which he thought. Edison, himself, said so! It could not have been the young man's appearance which got him his start in the Edison office, for that was definitely against him. It was what he thought that counted.

If the significance of this statement could be conveyed to every person who reads it, there would be no need for the remainder of this book.

Barnes did not get his partnership with Edison on his first interview. He did get a chance to work in the Edison offices, at a very nominal wage, doing work that was unimportant to Edison, but most important to Barnes, because it gave him an opportunity to display his "merchandise" where his intended "partner" could see it.

Months went by. Apparently nothing happened to bring the coveted goal which Barnes had set up in his mind as his *definite major purpose.* But something important was happening in Barnes' mind. He was constantly intensifying his *desire* to become the business associate of Edison.

Psychologists have correctly said that "when one is truly ready for a thing, it puts in its appearance."

Barnes was ready for a business association with Edison, moreover, he was *determined to remain ready until he got that which he was seeking.*

He did not say to himself, "Ah well, what's the use? I guess I'll change my mind and try for a salesman's job." But, he did say, "I came here to go into business with Edison, and I'll accomplish this end if it takes the remainder of my life." He meant it! What a different story men would have to tell if only they would adopt a *definite purpose,* and stand by that purpose until it had time to become an all-consuming obsession!

Maybe young Barnes did not know it at the time, but his bulldog determination, his persistence in standing back of a single *Desire,* was destined to mow down all opposition, and bring him the opportunity he was seeking.

When the opportunity came, it appeared in a different form, and from a different direction than Barnes had expected. That is one of the tricks of opportunity. It has a sly habit of slipping in by the back door, and often it comes disguised in the form of misfortune, or temporary defeat. Perhaps this is why so many fail to recognize opportunity.

Mr. Edison had just perfected a new office device, known at that time, as the Edison Dictating Machine (now the Ediphone). His salesmen were not enthusiastic over the machine. They did not believe it could be sold without great effort. Barnes saw his opportunity. It had crawled in quietly, hidden in a queer looking machine which interested no one but Barnes and the inventor.

Barnes knew he could sell the Edison Dictating Machine. He suggested this to Edison, and promptly got his chance. He did sell the machine. In fact, he sold it so successfully that Edison gave him a contract to distribute and market it all over the nation. Out of that business association grew the slogan, "Made by Edison and installed by Barnes."

The business alliance has been in operation for more than thirty years. Out of it Barnes has made himself rich in money, but he has done something infinitely greater, he has proved that one really may "Think and Grow Rich."

How much actual cash that original *desire* of Barnes' has been worth to him, I have no way of knowing. Perhaps it has brought him two or three million dollars, but the amount, whatever it is, becomes insignificant when compared with the greater asset he acquired in the form of definite knowledge that an intangible impulse of thought can be transmuted into its physical counterpart by the application of known principles.

Barnes literally thought himself into a partnership with the great Edison! He thought himself into a fortune. He had nothing to start with, except the capacity to *know what he wanted, and the determination to stand by that desire until he realized it.*

He had no money to begin with. He had but little education. He had no influence. But he did have initiative, faith, and the will to win. With these intangible forces he made himself number one man with the greatest inventor who ever lived.

Now, let us look at a different situation, and study a man who had plenty of tangible evidence of riches, but lost it, because he stopped three feet short of the goal he was seeking.

Three Feet From Gold

One of the most common causes of failure is the habit of quitting when one is overtaken by temporary defeat. Every person is guilty of this mistake at one time or another.

An uncle of R. U. Darby was caught by the "gold fever" in the gold-rush days, and went west to *dig and grow rich.* He had never heard that more gold has been mined from the brains of men than has ever been taken from the earth. He staked a claim and went to work with pick and shovel. The going was hard, but his lust for gold was definite.

After weeks of labor, he was rewarded by the discovery of the shining ore. He needed machinery to bring the ore to the surface. Quietly, he covered up the mine, retraced his footsteps to his home in Williamsburg, Maryland, told his relatives and a few neighbors of the "strike." They got together money for the needed machinery, had it shipped. The uncle and Darby went back to work the mine.

The first car of ore was mined, and shipped to a smelter. The returns proved they had one of the richest mines in Colorado! A few more cars of that ore would clear the debts. Then would come the big killing in profits.

Down went the drills! Up went the hopes of Darby and Uncle! Then something happened! The vein of gold ore disappeared! They had come to the end of the rainbow, and the pot of gold was no longer there! They drilled on, desperately trying to pick up the vein again— all to no avail.

Finally, they decided to *quit.*

They sold the machinery to a junk man for a few hundred dollars, and took the train back home. Some "junk" men are dumb, but not this one! He called in a mining engineer to look at the mine and do a little calculating. The engineer advised that the project had failed, because the owners were not familiar with "fault lines." His calculations showed that the vein would be found *just three feet from where the Darbys had stopped drilling*! That is exactly where it was found!

The "Junk" man took millions of dollars in ore from the mine, because he knew enough to seek expert counsel before giving up.

Most of the money which went into the machinery was procured through the efforts of R. U. Darby, who was then a very young man. The money came from his relatives and neighbors, because of their faith in him. He paid back every dollar of it, although he was years in doing so.

Long afterward, Mr. Darby recouped his loss many times over, when he made the discovery that *desire* can be transmuted into gold. The discovery came after he went into the business of selling life insurance.

Remembering that he lost a huge fortune, because he *stopped* three feet from gold, Darby profited by the experience in his chosen work, by the simple method of saying to himself, "I stopped three feet from gold, but I will never stop because men say 'no' when I ask them to buy insurance."

Darby is one of a small group of fewer than fifty men who sell more than a million dollars in life insurance annually. He owes his "stickability" to the lesson he learned from his "quitability" in the gold mining business.

Before success comes in any man's life, he is sure to meet with much temporary defeat, and, perhaps, some failure. When defeat overtakes a man, the easiest and most logical thing to do is to *quit.* That is exactly what the majority of men do.

More than five hundred of the most successful men this country has ever known, told the author their greatest success came just one step beyond the point at which defeat had overtaken them. Failure is a trickster with a keen sense of irony and cunning. It takes great delight in tripping one when success is almost within reach.

A Fifty-Cent Lesson in Persistence

Shortly after Mr. Darby received his degree from the "University of Hard Knocks," and had decided to profit by his experience in the gold mining business, he had the good fortune to be present on an occasion that proved to him that "No" does not necessarily mean no.

One afternoon he was helping his uncle grind wheat in an old fashioned mill. The uncle operated a large farm on which a number of colored sharecrop farmers lived. Quietly, the door was opened, and a small colored child, the daughter of a tenant, walked in and 23 24 took her place near the door.

The uncle looked up, saw the child, and barked at her roughly, "what do you want?"

Meekly, the child replied, "My mammy say send her fifty cents."

"I'll not do it," the uncle retorted, "Now you run on home."

"Yas sah," the child replied. But she did not move.

The uncle went ahead with his work, so busily engaged that he did not pay enough attention to the child to observe that she did not leave. When he looked up and saw her still standing there, he yelled at her, "I told you to go on home! Now go, or I'll take a switch to you."

The little girl said "yas sah," but she did not budge an inch.

The uncle dropped a sack of grain he was about to pour into the mill hopper, picked up a barrel stave, and started toward the child with an expression on his face that indicated trouble.

Darby held his breath. He was certain he was about to witness a murder. He knew his uncle had a fierce temper. He knew that colored children were not supposed to defy white people in that part of the country.

When the uncle reached the spot where the child was standing, she quickly stepped forward one step, looked up into his eyes, and screamed at the top of her shrill voice, *"My mammy's gotta have that fifty cents!"*

The uncle stopped, looked at her for a minute, then slowly laid the barrel stave on the floor, put his hand in his pocket, took out half a dollar, and gave it to her.

The child took the money and slowly backed toward the door, never taking her eyes off the man whom she had just conquered. After she had gone, the uncle sat down on a box and looked out the window into space for more than ten minutes. He was pondering, with awe, over the whipping he had just taken.

Mr. Darby, too, was doing some thinking. That was the first time in all his experience that he had seen a colored child deliberately master an adult white person. How did she do it? What happened to his uncle that caused him to lose his fierceness and become as docile as a lamb? What strange power did this child use that made her master over her superior? These and other similar questions flashed into Darby's mind, but he did not find the answer until years later, when he told me the story.

Strangely, the story of this unusual experience was told to the author in the old mill, on the very spot where the uncle took his whipping. Strangely, too, I had devoted nearly a quarter of a century to the study of the power which enabled an ignorant, illiterate colored child to conquer an intelligent man.

As we stood there in that musty old mill, Mr. Darby repeated the story of the unusual conquest, and finished by asking, "What can you make of it? What strange power did that child use, that so completely whipped my uncle?"

The answer to his question will be found in the principles described in this book. The answer is full and complete. It contains details and instructions sufficient to enable anyone to understand, and apply the same force which the little child accidentally stumbled upon.

Keep your mind alert, and you will observe exactly what strange power came to the rescue of the child, you will catch a glimpse of this power in the next chapter. Somewhere in the book you will find an idea that will quicken your receptive powers, and place at your command, for your own benefit, this same irresistible power. The awareness of this power may come to you in the first chapter, or it may flash into your mind in some subsequent chapter. It may come in the form of a single idea. Or, it may come in the nature of a plan, or a purpose. Again, it may cause you to go back into your past experiences of failure or defeat, and bring to the surface some lesson by which you can regain all that you lost through defeat.

After I had described to Mr. Darby the power unwittingly used by the little colored child, he quickly retraced his thirty years of experience as a life insurance salesman, and frankly acknowledged that his success in that field was due, in no small degree, to the lesson he had learned from the child.

Mr. Darby pointed out: "every time a prospect tried to bow me out, without buying, I saw that child standing there in the old mill, her big eyes glaring in defiance, and I said to myself, 'I've gotta make this sale. ' The better portion of all sales I have made, were made after people had said 'NO'."

He recalled, too, his mistake in having stopped only three feet from gold, "but," he said, "that experience was a blessing in disguise. It taught me to keep on keeping on, no matter how hard the going may be, a lesson I needed to learn before I could succeed in anything."

This story of Mr. Darby and his uncle, the colored child and the gold mine, doubtless will be read by hundreds of men who make their living by selling life insurance, and to all of these, the author wishes to offer the suggestion that Darby owes to these two experiences his ability to sell more than a million dollars of life insurance every year.

Life is strange, and often imponderable! Both the successes and the failures have their roots in simple experiences. Mr. Darby's experiences were commonplace and simple enough, yet they held the answer to his destiny in life, therefore they were as important (to him) as life itself. He profited by these two dramatic experiences, because he analyzed them, and found the lesson they taught. But what of the man who has neither the time, nor the inclination to study failure in search of knowledge that may lead to success? Where, and how is he to learn the art of converting defeat into stepping stones to opportunity?

In answer to these questions, this book was written.

The answer called for a description of thirteen principles, but remember, as you read, the answer you may be seeking, to the questions which have caused you to ponder over the strangeness of life, may be found in your own mind, through some idea, plan, or purpose which may spring into your mind as you read.

One sound idea is all that one needs to achieve success. The principles described in this book, contain the best, and the most practical of all that is known, concerning ways and means of creating useful ideas.

Before we go any further in our approach to the description of these principles, we believe you are entitled to receive this important suggestion.... *When riches begin to come they come so quickly, in such great abundance, that one wonders where they have been hiding during all those lean years.* This is an astounding statement, and all the more so, when we take into consideration the popular belief, that riches come only to those who work hard and long.

When you begin to *think and grow rich,* you will observe that riches begin with a state of mind, with definiteness of purpose, with little or no hard work. You, and every other person, ought to be interested in knowing how to acquire that state of mind which will attract riches. I spent twenty-five years in research, analyzing more than 25,000 people, because I, too, wanted to know "how wealthy men become that way.

Without that research, this book could not have been written.

Here take notice of a very significant truth, viz:

The business depression started in 1929, and continued on to an all time record of destruction, until sometime after President Roosevelt entered office. Then the depression began to fade into nothingness. Just as an electrician in a theater raises the lights so gradually that darkness is transmuted into light before you realize it, so did the spell of fear in the minds of the people gradually fade away and become faith.

Observe very closely, as soon as you master the principles of this philosophy, and begin to follow the instructions for applying those principles, your financial status will begin to improve, and everything you touch will begin to transmute itself into an asset for your benefit. Impossible? Not at all!

One of the main weaknesses of mankind is the average man's familiarity with the word "impossible." He knows all the rules which will *not* work. He knows all the things which *cannot* be done. This book was written for those who seek the rules which have made others successful, and are willing to stake everything on those rules.

A great many years ago I purchased a fine dictionary. The first thing I did with it was to turn to the word "impossible," and neatly clip it out of the book. That would not be an unwise thing for you to do.

Success comes to those who become *success conscious.*

Failure comes to those who indifferently allow themselves to become *failure conscious.*

The object of this book is to help all who seek it, to learn the art of changing their minds from *failure consciousness* to *success consciousness.*

Another weakness found in altogether too many people, is the habit of measuring everything, and everyone, by their own impressions and beliefs. Some who will read this, will believe that no one can *think and grow rich.* They cannot think in terms of riches, because their thought habits have been steeped in poverty, want, misery, failure, and defeat.

These unfortunate people remind me of a prominent Chinese, who came to America to be educated in American ways. He attended the University of Chicago. One day President Harper met this young Oriental on the campus, stopped to chat with him for a few minutes, and asked what had impressed him as being the most noticeable characteristic of the American people.

"Why," the Chinaman exclaimed, "the queer slant of your eyes. Your eyes are off slant!"

What do we say about the Chinese?

We refuse to believe that which we do not understand. We foolishly believe that our own limitations are the proper measure of limitations. Sure, the other fellow's eyes are "off slant," *because they are not the same as our own.*

Millions of people look at the achievements of Henry Ford, after he has arrived, and envy him, because of his good fortune, or luck, or genius, or whatever it is that they credit for Ford's fortune. Perhaps one person in every hundred thousand knows the secret of Ford's success, and those who do know are too modest, or too reluctant, to speak of it, because of its simplicity. A single transaction will illustrate the "secret" perfectly.

A few years back, Ford decided to produce his now famous V-8 motor. He chose to build an engine with the entire eight cylinders cast in one block, and instructed his engineers to produce a design for the engine. The design was placed on paper, but the engineers agreed, to a man, that it was simply impossible to cast an eight-cylinder gas engine block in one piece.

Ford said, "Produce it anyway."

"But," they replied, "it's impossible!"

"Go ahead," Ford commanded, "and stay on the job until you succeed no matter how much time is required."

The engineers went ahead. There was nothing else for them to do, if they were to remain on the Ford staff. Six months went by, nothing happened. Another six months passed, and still nothing happened. The engineers tried every conceivable plan to carry out the orders, but the thing seemed out of the question; "impossible!"

At the end of the year Ford checked with his engineers, and again they informed him they had found no way to carry out his orders.

"Go right ahead," said Ford, "I want it, and I'll have it."

They went ahead, and then, as if by a stroke of magic, the secret was discovered.

The Ford *determination* had won once more!

This story may not be described with minute accuracy, but the sum and substance of it is correct. Deduce from it, you who wish to *think and grow rich*, the secret of the Ford millions, if you can. You'll not have to look very far.

Henry Ford is a success, because he understands, and applies the principles of success. One of these is *desire*: knowing what one wants. Remember this Ford story as you read, and pick out the lines in which the secret of his stupendous achievement have been described. If you can do this, if you can lay your finger on the particular group of principles which made Henry Ford rich, you can equal his achievements in almost any calling for which you are suited.

You Are "The Master of Your Fate, the Captain of Your Soul," Because...

When Henley wrote the prophetic lines, "I am the Master of my Fate, I am the Captain of my Soul," he should have informed us that we are the Masters of our Fate, the Captains of our Souls, because we have the power to control our thoughts.

He should have told us that the ether in which this little earth floats, in which we move and have our being, is a form of energy moving at an inconceivably high rate of vibration, and that the ether is filled with a form of universal power which *adapts* itself to the nature of the thoughts we hold in our minds; and *influences* us, in natural ways, to transmute our thoughts into their physical equivalent.

If the poet had told us of this great truth, we would know *why it is* that we are the Masters of our Fate, the Captains of our Souls. He should have told us, with great emphasis, that this power makes no attempt to discriminate between destructive thoughts and constructive thoughts, that it will urge us to translate into physical reality thoughts of poverty, just as quickly as it will influence us to act upon thoughts of riches.

He should have told us, too, that our brains become magnetized with the dominating thoughts which we hold in our minds, and, by means with which no man is familiar, these "magnets" attract to us the forces, the people, the circumstances of life which harmonize with the nature of our dominating thoughts.

He should have told us, that before we can accumulate riches in great abundance, we must magnetize our minds with intense *desire* for riches, that we must become "money conscious until the *desire* for money drives us to create definite plans for acquiring it.

But, being a poet, and not a philosopher, Henley contented himself by stating a great truth in poetic form, leaving those who followed him to interpret the philosophical meaning of his lines.

Little by little, the truth has unfolded itself, until it now appears certain that the principles described in this book, hold the secret of mastery over our economic fate.

We are now ready to examine the first of these principles. Maintain a spirit of open-mindedness, and remember as you read, they are the invention of no one man. The principles were gathered from the life experiences of more than 500 men who actually accumulated riches in huge amounts; men who began in poverty, with but little education, without influence. The principles worked for these men. You can put them to work for your own enduring benefit.

You will find it easy, not hard, to do.

Before you read the next chapter, I want you to know that it conveys factual information which might easily change your entire financial destiny, as it has so definitely brought changes of stupendous proportions to two people described.

I want you to know, also, that the relationship between these two men and myself, is such that I could have taken no liberties with the facts, even if I had wished to do so. One of them has been my closest personal friend for almost twenty-five years, the other is my own son. The unusual success of these two men, success which they generously accredit to the principle described in the next chapter, more than justifies this personal reference as a means of emphasizing the far-flung power of this principle.

Almost fifteen years ago, I delivered the Commencement Address at Salem College, Salem, West Virginia. I emphasized the principle described in the next chapter, with so much intensity that one of the members of the graduating class definitely appropriated it, and made it a part of his own philosophy. The young man is now a Member of Congress, and an important factor in the present administration. Just before this book went to the publisher, he wrote me a letter in which he so clearly stated his opinion of the principle outlined in the next chapter, that I have chosen to publish his letter as an introduction to that chapter.

It gives you an idea of the rewards to come.

"My dear Napoleon:

"My service as a Member of Congress having given me an insight into the problems of men and women, I am writing to offer a suggestion which may become helpful to thousands of worthy people.

"With apologies, I must state that the suggestion, if acted upon, will mean several years of labor and responsibility for you, but I am enheartened to make the suggestion, because I know your great love for rendering useful service.

"In 1922, you delivered the Commencement address at Salem College, when I was a member' of the graduating class. In that address, you planted in my mind an idea which has been responsible for the opportunity I now have to serve the people of my State, and will be responsible, in a very large measure, for whatever success I may have in the future.

"The suggestion I have in mind is, that you put into a book the sum and substance of the address you delivered at Salem College, and in that way give the people of America an opportunity to profit by your many years of experience and association with the men who, by their greatness, have made America the richest nation on earth.

"I recall, as though it were yesterday, the marvelous description you gave of the method by which Henry Ford, with but little schooling, without a dollar, with no influential friends, rose to great heights. I made up my mind then, even before you had finished your speech, that I would make a place for myself, no matter how many difficulties I had to surmount.

"Thousands of young people will finish their schooling this year, and within the next few years. Every one of them will be seeking just such a message of practical encouragement as the one I received from you. They will want to know where to turn, what to do, to get started in life. You can tell them, because you have helped to solve the problems of so many, many people.

"If there is any possible way that you can afford to render so great a service, may I offer the suggestion that you include with every book, one of your Personal Analysis Charts, in order that the purchaser of the book may have the benefit of a complete self-inventory, indicating, as you indicated to me years ago, exactly what is standing in the way of success.

"Such a service as this, providing the readers of your book with a complete, unbiased picture of their faults and their virtues, would mean to them the difference between success and failure. The service would be priceless.

"Millions of people are now facing the problem of staging a comeback, because of the depression, and I speak from personal experience when I say, I know these earnest people would welcome the opportunity to tell you their problems, and to receive your suggestions for the solution.

"You know the problems of those who face the necessity of beginning all over again. There are thousands of people in America today who would like to know how they can convert ideas into money, people who must start at scratch, without finances, and recoup their losses. If anyone can help them, you can.

"If you publish the book, I would like to own the first copy that comes from the press, personally autographed by you.

"With best wishes, believe me,

"Cordially yours,

"Jennings Randolph"

Chapter One: Desire

The Starting Point of All Achievement: the First Step Toward Riches

When Edwin C. Barnes climbed down from the freight train in Orange, N. J., more than thirty years ago, he may have resembled a tramp, but his thoughts were those of a king!

As he made his way from the railroad tracks to Thomas A. Edison's office, his mind was at work. He saw himself standing in Edison's presence. He heard himself asking Mr. Edison for an opportunity to carry out the one *consuming obsession of his life*, a *burning desire* to become the business associate of the great inventor.

Barnes' desire was not a hope! It was not a wish! It was a keen, pulsating desire, which transcended everything else. It was *definite*.

The desire was not new when he approached Edison. It had been Barnes' dominating desire for a long time. In the beginning, when the desire first appeared in his mind, it may have been, probably was, only a wish, but it was no mere wish when he appeared before Edison with it.

A few years later, Edwin C. Barnes again stood before Edison, in the same office where he first met the inventor. This time his *desire* had been translated into reality. He was in business with Edison. The dominating *dream of his life* had become a reality. Today, people who know Barnes envy him, because of the "break" life yielded him. They see him in the days of his triumph, without taking the trouble to investigate the cause of his success.

Barnes succeeded because he chose a definite goal, placed all his energy, all his will power, all his effort, everything back of that goal. He did not become the partner of Edison the day he arrived. He was content to start in the most menial work, as long as it provided an opportunity to take even one step toward his cherished goal.

Five years passed before the chance he had been seeking made its appearance. During all those years not one ray of hope, not one promise of attainment of his *desire* had been held out to him. To everyone, except himself, he appeared only another cog in the Edison business wheel, but in his own mind, *he was the partner of Edison every minute of the time*, from the very day that he first went to work there.

It is a remarkable illustration of the power of a *definite desire*. Barnes won his goal, because he wanted to be a business associate of Mr. Edison, more than he wanted anything else. He created a plan by which to attain that purpose. But he *burned all bridges behind him.*

He stood by his *desire* until it became the dominating obsession of his life– and– finally, a fact.

When he went to Orange, he did not say to himself, "I will try to induce Edison to give me a job of some soft." He said, "I will see Edison, and put him on notice that I have come to go into business with him.

He did not say, "I will work there for a few months, and if I get no encouragement, I will quit and get a job somewhere else." He did say, "I will start anywhere. I will do anything Edison tells me to do, but before I am through, I will be his associate."

He did not say, "I will keep my eyes open for another opportunity, in case I fail to get what I want in the Edison organization." He said, "There is but *one* thing in this world that I am determined to have, and that is a business association with Thomas A. Edison. I will burn all bridges behind me, and stake my *entire future* on my ability to get what I want."

He left himself no possible way of retreat. He had to win or perish!

That is all there is to the Barnes story of success! A long while ago, a great warrior faced a situation which made it necessary for him to make a decision which insured his success on the battlefield. He was about to send his armies against a powerful foe, whose men outnumbered his own. He loaded his soldiers into boats, sailed to the enemy's country, unloaded soldiers and equipment, then gave the order to burn the ships that had carried them. Addressing his men before the first battle, he said, "You see the boats going up in smoke. That means that we cannot leave these shores alive unless we win! We now have no choice–we win, or we perish! They won.

Every person who wins in any undertaking must be willing to burn his ships and cut all sources of retreat. Only by so doing can one be sure of maintaining that state of mind known as a *burning desire to win*, essential to success.

The morning after the great Chicago fire, a group of merchants stood on State Street, looking at the smoking remains of what had been their stores. They went into a conference to decide if they would try to rebuild, or leave Chicago and start over in a more promising section of the country. They reached a decision–all except one–to leave Chicago.

The merchant who decided to stay and rebuild pointed a finger at the remains of his store, and said, "Gentlemen, on that very spot I will build the world's greatest store, no matter how many times it may burn down."

That was more than fifty years ago. The store was built. It stands there today, a towering monument to the power of that state of mind known as a *burning desire*. The easy thing for Marshal Field to have done, would have been exactly what his fellow merchants did. When the going was hard, and the future looked dismal, they pulled up and went where the going seemed easier.

Mark well this difference between Marshal Field and the other merchants, because it is the same difference which distinguishes Edwin C. Barnes from thousands of other young men who have worked in the Edison organization. It is the same difference which distinguishes practically all who succeed from those who fail.

Every human being who reaches the age of understanding of the purpose of money, wishes for it. Wishing will not bring riches. But desiring riches with a state of mind that becomes an obsession, then planning definite ways and means to acquire riches, and backing those plans with persistence which does not recognize failure, will bring riches.

The method by which *desire* for riches can be transmuted into its financial equivalent, consists of six definite, practical steps, viz:

First. Fix in your mind the exact amount of money you desire. It is not sufficient merely to say "I want plenty of money." Be definite as to the amount. (There is a psychological reason for definiteness which will be described in a subsequent chapter).

Second. Determine exactly what you intend to give in return for the money you desire. (There is no such reality as "something for nothing.)

Third. Establish a definite date when you intend to possess the money you desire.

Fourth. Create a definite plan for carrying out your desire, and begin at once, whether you are ready or not, to put this plan into action.

Fifth. Write out a clear, concise statement of the amount of money you intend to acquire, name the time limit for its acquisition, state what you intend to give in return for the money, and describe clearly the plan through which you intend to accumulate it.

Sixth. Read your written statement aloud, twice daily, once just before retiring at night, and once after arising in the morning. *As you read– see and feel and believe yourself already in possession of the money.*

It is important that you follow the instructions described in these six steps. It is especially important that you observe, and follow the instructions in the sixth paragraph. You may complain that it is impossible for you to "see yourself in possession of money" before you actually have it. Here is where a *burning desire* will come to your aid. If you truly *desire* money so keenly that your desire is an obsession, you will have no difficulty in convincing yourself that you will acquire it. The object is to want money, and to become so determined to have it that you *convince* yourself you will have it.

Only those who become "money conscious" ever accumulate great riches. "Money consciousness" means that the mind has become so thoroughly saturated with the *desire* for money, that one can see one's self already in possession of it.

To the uninitiated, who has not been schooled in the working principles of the human mind, these instructions may appear impractical. It may be helpful, to all who fail to recognize the soundness of the six steps, to know that the information they convey, was received from Andrew Carnegie, who began as an ordinary laborer in the steel mills, but managed, despite his humble beginning, to make these principles yield him a fortune of considerably more than one hundred million dollars.

It may be of further help to know that the six steps here recommended were carefully scrutinized by the late Thomas A. Edison, who placed his stamp of approval upon them as being, not only the steps essential for the accumulation of money, but necessary for the attainment of any definite goal.

The steps call for no "hard labor." They call for no sacrifice. They do not require one to become ridiculous, or credulous. To apply them calls for no great amount of education. But the successful application of these six steps does call for sufficient imagination to enable one to see, and to understand, that accumulation of money cannot be left to chance, good fortune, and luck. One must realize that all who have accumulated great fortunes, first did a certain amount of dreaming, hoping, wishing, *desiring,* and *planning* before they acquired money.

You may as well know, right here, that you can never have riches in great quantities, *unless* you can work yourself into a white heat of *desire* for money, and actually *believe* you will possess it.

You may as well know, also that every great leader, from the dawn of civilization down to the present, was a dreamer. Christianity is the greatest potential power in the world today, because its founder was an intense dreamer who had the vision and the imagination to see realities in their mental and spiritual form before they had been transmuted into physical form.

If you do not see great riches in your imagination, you will never see them in your bank balance.

Never, in the history of America has there been so great an opportunity for practical dreamers as now exists. The six year economic collapse has reduced all men, substantially, to the same level. A new race is about to be run. The stakes represent huge fortunes which will be accumulated within the next ten years. The rules of the race have changed, because we now live in a *changed world* that definitely favors the masses, those who had but little or no opportunity to win under the conditions existing during the depression, when fear paralyzed growth and development.

We who are in this race for riches, should be encouraged to know that this changed world in which we live is demanding new ideas, new ways of doing things, new leaders, new inventions, new methods of teaching, new methods of marketing, new books, new literature, new features for the radio, new ideas for moving pictures. Back of all this demand for new and better things, there is one quality which one must possess to win, and that is *definiteness of purpose,* the knowledge of what one wants, and a burning *desire* to possess it.

The business depression marked the death of one age, and the birth of another. This changed world requires practical dreamers who can, and will put their dreams into action. The practical dreamers have always been, and always will be the pattern-makers of civilization.

We who desire to accumulate riches, should remember the real leaders of the world always have been men who harnessed, and put into practical use, the intangible, unseen forces of unborn opportunity, and have converted those forces, [or impulses of thought], into sky-scrapers, cities, factories, airplanes, automobiles, and every form of convenience that makes life more pleasant.

Tolerance, and an open mind are practical necessities of the dreamer of today. Those who are afraid of new ideas are doomed before they start. Never has there been a time more favorable to pioneers than the present. True, there is no wild and woolly west to be conquered, as in the days of the Covered Wagon; but there is a vast business, financial, and industrial world to be remolded and redirected along new and better lines.

In planning to acquire your share of the riches, let no one influence you to scorn the dreamer. To win the big stakes in this changed world, you must catch the spirit of the great pioneers of the past, whose dreams have given to civilization all that it has of value, the spirit which serves as the life-blood of our own country— your opportunity and mine, to develop and market our talents.

Let us not forget, Columbus dreamed of an Unknown world, staked his life on the existence of such a world, and discovered it!

Copernicus, the great astronomer, dreamed of a multiplicity of worlds, and revealed them! No one denounced him as "impractical" after he had triumphed. Instead, the world worshiped at his shrine, thus proving once more that *"success requires no apologies, failure permits no alibis."*

If the thing you wish to do is right, and you believe in it, go ahead and do it! Put your dream across, and never mind what "they" say if you meet with temporary defeat, for "they," perhaps, do not know that *every failure brings with it the seed of an equivalent success.*

Henry Ford, poor and uneducated, dreamed of a horseless carriage, went to work with what tools he possessed, without waiting for opportunity to favor him, and now evidence of his dream belts the entire earth. He has put more wheels into operation than any man who ever lived, because he was not afraid to back his dreams.

Thomas Edison dreamed of a lamp that could be operated by electricity, began where he stood to put his dream into action, and despite more than ten thousand failures, he stood by that dream until he made it a physical reality. Practical dreamers *do not quit!*

Whelan dreamed of a chain of cigar stores, transformed his dream into action, and now the United Cigar Stores occupy the best corners in America.

Lincoln dreamed of freedom for the black slaves, put his dream into action, and barely missed living to see a united North and South translate his dream into reality.

The Wright brothers dreamed of a machine that would fly through the air. Now one may see evidence all over the world, that they dreamed soundly.

Marconi dreamed of a system for harnessing the intangible forces of the ether. Evidence that he did not dream in vain, may be found in every wireless and radio in the world. Moreover, Marconi's dream brought the humblest cabin, and the most stately manor house side by side. It made the people of every nation on earth back-door neighbors. It gave the President of the United States a medium by which he may talk to all the people of America at one time, and on short notice. It may interest you to know that Marconi's "friends" had him taken into custody, and examined in a psychopathic hospital, when he announced he had discovered a principle through which he could send messages through the air, without the aid of wires, or other direct physical means of communication. The dreamers of today fare better.

The world has become accustomed to new discoveries. Nay, it has shown a willingness to reward the dreamer who gives the world a new idea.

"The greatest achievement was, at first, and for a time, but a dream."

"The oak sleeps in the acorn. The bird waits in the egg, and in the highest vision of the soul, a waking angel stirs. *Dreams are the seedlings of reality.*"

Awake, arise, and assert yourself, you dreamers of the world. Your star is now in the ascendency. The world depression brought the opportunity you have been waiting for. It taught people humility, tolerance, and open-mindedness.

The world is filled with an abundance of *opportunity* which the dreamers of the past never knew.

A burning desire to be, and to do is the starting point from which the dreamer must take off. Dreams are not born of indifference, laziness, or lack of ambition.

The world no longer scoffs at the dreamer, nor calls him impractical. If you think it does, take a trip to Tennessee, and witness what a dreamer President has done in the way of harnessing, and using the great water power of America. A score of years ago, such a dream would have seemed like madness.

You have been disappointed, you have undergone defeat during the depression, you have felt the great heart within you crushed until it bled. Take courage, for these experiences have tempered the spiritual metal of which you are made—they are assets of incomparable value.

Remember, too, that all who succeed in life get off to a bad start, and pass through many heartbreaking struggles before they "arrive." The turning point in the lives of those who succeed, usually comes at the moment of some crisis, through which they are introduced to their "other selves."

John Bunyan wrote the Pilgrim's Progress, which is among the finest of all English literature, after he had been confined in prison and sorely punished, because of his views on the subject of religion.

O. Henry discovered the genius which slept within his brain, after he had met with great misfortune, and was confined in a prison cell, in Columbus, Ohio. Being *forced*, through misfortune, to become acquainted with his "other self," and to use his *imagination*, he discovered himself to be a great author instead of a miserable criminal and outcast. Strange and varied are the ways of life, and stranger still are the ways of Infinite Intelligence, through which men are sometimes forced to undergo all sorts of punishment before discovering their own brains, and their own capacity to create useful ideas through imagination.

Edison, the world's greatest inventor and scientist, was a "tramp" telegraph operator, he failed innumerable times before he was driven, finally, to the discovery of the genius which slept within his brain.

Charles Dickens began by pasting labels on blacking pots. The tragedy of his first love penetrated the depths of his soul, and converted him into one of the world's truly great authors. That tragedy produced, first, David Copperfield, then a succession of other works that made this a richer and better world for all who read his books. Disappointment over love affairs, generally has the effect of driving men to drink, and women to ruin; and this, because most people never learn the art of transmuting their strongest emotions into dreams of a constructive nature.

Helen Keller became deaf, dumb, and blind shortly after birth. Despite her greatest misfortune, she has written her name indelibly in the pages of the history of the great. Her entire life has served as evidence that no one ever is defeated until defeat has been accepted as a reality.

Robert Burns was an illiterate country lad, he was cursed by poverty, and grew up to be a drunkard in the bargain. The world was made better for his having lived, because he clothed beautiful thoughts in poetry, and thereby plucked a thorn and planted a rose in its place.

Booker T. Washington was born in slavery, handicapped by race and color. Because he was tolerant, had an open mind at all times, on all subjects, and was a dreamer, he left his impress for good on an entire race.

Beethoven was deaf, Milton was blind, but their names will last as long as time endures, because they dreamed and translated their dreams into organized thought.

Before passing to the next chapter, kindle anew in your mind the fire of hope, faith, courage, and tolerance. If you have these states of mind, and a working knowledge of the principles described, all else that you need will come to you, when you are *ready* for it. Let Emerson state the thought in these words, "Every proverb, every book, every byword that belongs to thee for aid and comfort shall surely come home through open or winding passages. Every friend whom not thy fantastic will, but the great and tender soul in thee craveth, shall lock thee in his embrace."

There is a difference between *Wishing* for a thing and being *ready* to receive it. No one is ready for a thing, until he believes he can acquire it. The state of mind must be *belief*, not mere hope or wish. Open-mindedness is essential for belief. Closed minds do not inspire faith, courage, and belief.

Remember, no more effort is required to aim high in life, to demand abundance and prosperity, than is required to accept misery and poverty. A great poet has correctly stated this universal truth through these lines:

"I bargained with Life for a penny,
And Life would pay no more,
However I begged at evening
When I counted my scanty stor . . .

"For Life is a. just employer,
He gives you what you ask,
But once you have set the wages,
Why, you must bear the task.

"I worked for a menial's hire,
Only to learn, dismayed,
That any wage I had asked of Life,
Life would have willingly paid."

Desire Outwits Mother Nature

As a fitting climax to this chapter, I wish to introduce one of the most unusual persons I have ever known. I first saw him twenty-four years ago, a few minutes after he was born. He came into the world without any physical sign of ears, and the doctor admitted, when pressed for an opinion, that the child might be deaf, and mute for life.

I challenged the doctor's opinion. I had the right to do so, I was the child's father. I, too, reached a decision, and rendered an opinion, but I expressed the opinion silently, in the secrecy of my own heart. I decided that my son would hear and speak. Nature could send me a child without ears, but Nature could not induce me to accept the reality of the affliction.

In my own mind I knew that my son would hear and speak. How? I was sure there must be a way, and I knew I would find it. I thought of the words of the immortal Emerson, "The whole course of things goes to teach us faith. We need only obey.

There is guidance for each of us, and by lowly listening, we shall hear the right word."

The right word? *desire*! More than anything else, I *desired* that my son should not be a deaf mute. From that desire I never receded, not for a second.

Many years previously, I had written, "Our only limitations are those we set up in our own minds." For the first time, I wondered if that statement were true. Lying on the bed in front of me was a newly born child, without the natural equipment of hearing. Even though he might hear and speak, he was obviously disfigured for life. Surely, this was a limitation which that child had not set up in his own mind.

What could I do about it? Somehow I would find a way to transplant into that child's mind my own *burning desire* for ways and means of conveying sound to his brain without the aid of ears.

As soon as the child was old enough to cooperate, I would fill his mind so completely with a *burning desire* to hear, that Nature would, by methods of her own, translate it into physical reality.

All this thinking took place in my own mind, but I spoke of it to no one. Every day I renewed the pledge I had made to myself, not to accept a deaf mute for a son.

As he grew older, and began to take notice of things around him, we observed that he had a slight degree of hearing. When he reached the age when children usually begin talking, he made no attempt to speak, but we could tell by his actions that he could hear certain sounds slightly. That was all I wanted to know! I was convinced that if he could hear, even slightly, he might develop still greater hearing capacity. Then something happened which gave me hope. It came from an entirely unexpected source.

We bought a Victrola. When the child heard the music for the first time, he went into ecstasies, and promptly appropriated the machine. He soon showed a preference for certain records, among them, "It's a Long Way to Tipperary." On one occasion, he played that piece over and over, for almost two hours, standing in front of the Victrola, with his teeth clamped on the edge of the case. The significance of this self-formed habit of his did not become clear to us until years afterward, for we had never heard of the principle of "bone conduction" of sound at that time.

Shortly after he appropriated the Victrola, I discovered that he could hear me quite clearly when I spoke with my lips touching his mastoid bone, or at the base of the brain. These discoveries placed in my possession the necessary media by which I began to translate into reality my Burning Desire to help my son develop hearing and speech. By that time he was making stabs at speaking certain words. The outlook was far from encouraging, but *desire backed by faith* knows no such word as impossible.

Having determined that he could hear the sound of my voice plainly, I began, immediately, to transfer to his mind the desire to hear and speak. I soon discovered that the child enjoyed bedtime stories, so I went to work, creating stories designed to develop in him self-reliance, imagination, and a keen desire to hear and to be normal.

There was one story in particular, which I emphasized by giving it some new and dramatic coloring each time it was told. It was designed to plant in his mind the thought that his affliction was not a liability, but an asset of great value. Despite the fact that all the philosophy I had examined clearly indicated that *every adversity brings with it the seed of an equivalent advantage*, I must confess that I had not the slightest idea how this affliction could ever become an asset. However, I continued my practice of wrapping that philosophy in bedtime stories, hoping the time would come when he would find some plan by which his handicap could be made to serve some useful purpose.

Reason told me plainly, that there was no adequate compensation for the lack of ears and natural hearing equipment. *desire* backed by *faith*, pushed reason aside, and inspired me to carry on.

As I analyze the experience in retrospect, I can see now, that my son's faith in me had much to do with the astounding results. He did not question anything I told him. I sold him the idea that he had a distinct advantage over his older brother, and that this advantage would reflect itself in many ways. For example, the teachers in school would observe that he had no ears, and, because of this, they would show him special attention and treat him with extraordinary kindness. They always did. His mother saw to that, by visiting the teachers and arranging with them to give the child the extra attention necessary. I sold him the idea, too, that when he became old enough to sell newspapers, (his older brother had already become a newspaper merchant), he would have a big advantage over his brother, for the reason that people would pay him extra money for his wares, because they could see that he was a bright, industrious boy, despite the fact he had no ears.

We could notice that, gradually, the child's hearing was improving. Moreover, he had not the slightest tendency to be self-conscious, because of his affliction. When he was about seven, he showed the first evidence that our method of servicing his mind was bearing fruit. For several months he begged for the privilege of selling newspapers, but his mother would not give her consent. She was afraid that his deafness made it unsafe for him to go on the street alone.

Finally, he took matters in his own hands. One afternoon, when he was left at home with the servants, he climbed through the kitchen window, shinnied to the ground, and set out on his own.

He borrowed six cents in capital from the neighborhood shoemaker, invested it in papers, sold out, reinvested, and kept repeating until late in the evening. After balancing his accounts, and paying back the six cents he had borrowed from his banker, he had a net profit of forty-two cents. When we got home that night, we found him in bed asleep, with the money tightly clenched in his hand.

His mother opened his hand, removed the coins, and cried. Of all things! Crying over her son's first victory seemed so inappropriate. My reaction was the reverse. I laughed heartily, for I knew that my endeavor to plant in the child's mind an attitude of faith in himself had been successful.

His mother saw, in his first business venture, a little deaf boy who had gone out in the streets and risked his life to earn money. I saw a brave, ambitious, self-reliant little business man whose stock in himself had been increased a hundred percent, because he had gone into business on his own initiative, and had won. The transaction pleased me, because I knew that he had given evidence of a trait of resourcefulness that would go with him all through life. Later events proved this to be true. When his older brother wanted something, he would lie down on the floor, kick his feet in the air, cry for it– and get it. When the "little deaf boy" wanted something, he would plan a way to earn the money, then buy it for himself. He still follows that plan!

Truly, my own son has taught me that handicaps can be converted into stepping stones on which one may climb toward some worthy goal, unless they are accepted as obstacles, and used as alibis.

The little deaf boy went through the grades, high school, and college without being able to hear his teachers, excepting when they shouted loudly, at close range. He did not go to a school for the deaf. *We would not permit him to learn the sign language.* We were determined that he should live a normal life, and associate with normal children, and we stood by that decision, although it cost us many heated debates with school officials.

While he was in high school, he tried an electrical hearing aid, but it was of no value to him; due, we believed, to a condition that was disclosed when the child was six, by Dr. J. Gordon Wilson, of Chicago, when he operated on one side of the boy's head, and discovered that there was no sign of natural hearing equipment.

During his last week in college, (eighteen years after the operation), something happened which marked the most important turning-point of his life. Through what seemed to be mere chance, he came into possession of another electrical hearing device, which was sent to him on trial. He was slow about testing it, due to his disappointment with a similar device. Finally he picked the instrument up, and more or less carelessly, placed it on his head, hooked up the battery, and lo! as if by a stroke of magic, his lifelong *desire for normal hearing became a reality*! For the first time in his life he heard practically as well as any person with normal hearing. "God moves in mysterious ways, His wonders to perform."

Overjoyed because of the Changed World which had been brought to him through his hearing device, he rushed to the telephone, called his mother, and heard her voice perfectly. The next day he plainly heard the voices of his professors in class, for the first time in his life! Previously he could hear them only when they shouted, at short range. He heard the radio. He heard the talking pictures. For the first time in his life, he could converse freely with other people, without the necessity of their having to speak loudly. Truly, he had come into possession of a Changed World.

We had refused to accept Nature's error, and, by *persistent desire*, we had induced Nature to correct that error, through the only practical means available.

desire had commenced to pay dividends, but the victory was not yet complete. The boy still had to find a definite and practical way to convert his handicap into an equivalent asset.

Hardly realizing the significance of what had already been accomplished, but intoxicated with the joy of his newly discovered world of sound, he wrote a letter to the manufacturer of the hearing-aid, enthusiastically describing his experience. Something in his letter; something, perhaps which was not written on the lines, but back of them; caused the company to invite him to New York. When be arrived, he was escorted through the factory, and while talking with the Chief Engineer, telling him about his changed world, a hunch, an idea, or an inspiration— call it what you wish— flashed into his mind. It was this impulse of thought which converted his affliction into an asset, destined to pay dividends in both money and happiness to thousands for all time to come.

The sum and substance of that impulse of thought was this: It occurred to him that he might be of help to the millions of deafened people who go through life without the benefit of hearing devices, if he could find a way to tell them the story of his Changed World. Then and there, he reached a decision to devote the remainder of his life to rendering useful service to the hard of hearing.

For an entire month, he carried on an intensive research, during which he analyzed the entire marketing system of the manufacturer of the hearing device, and created ways and means of communicating with the hard of hearing all over the world for the purpose of sharing with them his newly discovered "Changed World." When this was done, he put in writing a two-year plan, based upon his findings. When he presented the plan to the company, he was instantly given a position, for the purpose of carrying out his ambition.

Little did he dream, when he went to work, that he was destined to bring hope and practical relief to thousands of deafened people who, without his help, would have been doomed forever to deaf mutism.

Shortly after he became associated with the manufacturer of his hearing aid, he invited me to attend a class conducted by his company, for the purpose of teaching deaf mutes to hear, and to speak. I had never heard of such a form of education, therefore I visited the class, skeptical but hopeful that my time would not be entirely wasted. Here I saw a demonstration which gave me a greatly enlarged vision of what I had done to arouse and keep alive in my son's mind the *desire* for normal hearing. I saw deaf mutes actually being taught to hear and to speak, through application of the self-same principle I had used, more than twenty years previously, in saving my son from deaf mutism.

Thus, through some strange turn of the Wheel of Fate, my son, Blair, and I have been destined to aid in correcting deaf mutism for those as yet unborn, because we are the only living human beings, as far as I know, who have established definitely the fact that deaf mutism can be corrected to the extent of restoring to normal life those who suffer with this affliction. It has been done for one; it will be done for others.

There is no doubt in my mind that Blair would have been a deaf mute all his life, if his mother and I had not managed to shape his mind as we did. The doctor who attended at his birth told us, confidentially, the child might never hear or speak. A few weeks ago, Dr. Irving Voorhees, a noted specialist on such cases, examined Blair very thoroughly. He was astounded when he learned how well my son now hears, and speaks, and said his examination indicated that "theoretically, the boy should not be able to hear at all." But the lad does hear, despite the fact that X-ray pictures show there is no opening in the skull, whatsoever, from where his ears should be to the brain.

When I planted in his mind the *desire* to hear and talk, and live as a normal person, there went with that impulse some strange influence which caused Nature to become bridge-builder, and span the gulf of silence between his brain and the outer world, by some means which the keenest medical specialists have not been able to interpret. It would be sacrilege for me to even conjecture as to how Nature performed this miracle. It would be unforgivable if I neglected to tell the world as much as I know of the humble part I assumed in the strange experience. It is my duty, and a privilege to say I believe, and not without reason, that nothing is impossible to the person who backs *desire* with enduring *faith.*

Verily, a *burning desire* has devious ways of transmuting itself into its physical equivalent. Blair *desired* normal hearing; now he has it! He was born with a handicap which might easily have sent one with a less defined *desire* to the street with a bundle of pencils and a tin cup. That handicap now promises to serve as the medium by which he will render useful service to many millions of hard of hearing, also, to give him useful employment at adequate financial compensation the remainder of his life.

The little "white lies" I planted in his mind when he was a child, by leading him to *believe* his affliction would become a great asset, which he could capitalize, has justified itself. Verily, there is nothing, right or wrong, which *belief*, plus *burning desire*, cannot make real. These qualities are free to everyone.

In all my experience in dealing with men and women who had personal problems, I never handled a single case which more definitely demonstrates the power of *desire*. Authors sometimes make the mistake of writing of subjects of which they have but superficial, or very elementary knowledge. It has been my good fortune to have had the privilege of testing the soundness of the *power of desire*, through the affliction of my own son. Perhaps it was providential that the experience came as it did, for surely no one is better prepared than he, to serve as an example of what happens when *desire* is put to the test. If Mother Nature bends to the will of desire, is it logical that mere men can defeat a burning desire?

Strange and imponderable is the power of the human mind! We do not understand the method by which it uses every circumstance, every individual, every physical thing within its reach, as a means of transmuting *desire* into its physical counterpart. Perhaps science will uncover this secret.

I planted in my son's mind the *desire* to hear and to speak as any normal person hears and speaks. That *desire* has now become a reality. I planted in his mind the *desire* to convert his greatest handicap into his greatest asset. That *desire* has been realized. The modus operandi by which this astounding result was achieved is not hard to describe. It consisted of three very definite facts; first, I *mixed faith* with the *desire* for normal hearing, which I passed on to my son. Second, I communicated my desire to him in every conceivable way available, through persistent, continuous effort, over a period of years. Third, *he believed me!*

As this chapter was being completed, news came of the death of Mme. Schuman-Heink. One short paragraph in the news dispatch gives the clue to this unusual woman's stupendous success as a singer. I quote the paragraph, because the clue it contains is none other than *desire*.

Early in her career, Mme. Schuman-Heink visited the director of the Vienna Court Opera, to have him test her voice. But, he did not test it. After taking one look at the awkward and poorly dressed girl, he exclaimed, none too gently, "With such a face, and with no personality at all, how can you ever expect to succeed in opera? My good child, give up the idea. Buy a sewing machine, and go to work. *You can never be a singer.*"

Never is a long time! The director of the Vienna Court Opera knew much about the technique of singing. He knew little about the power of desire, when it assumes the proportion of an obsession. If he had known more of that power, he would not have made the mistake of condemning genius without giving it an opportunity.

Several years ago, one of my business associates became ill. He became worse as time went on, and finally was taken to the hospital for an operation. Just before he was wheeled into the operating room, I took a look at him, and wondered how anyone as thin and emaciated as he, could possibly go through a major operation successfully. The doctor warned me that there was little if any chance of my ever seeing him alive again. But that was the *doctor's opinion*. It was not the opinion of the patient. Just before he was wheeled away, he whispered feebly, "Do not be disturbed, Chief, I will be out of here in a few days." The attending nurse looked at me with pity. But the patient did come through safely. After it was all over, his physician said, "Nothing but his own desire to live saved him. He never would have pulled through if he had not refused to accept the possibility of death."

I believe in the power of *desire* backed by *faith*, because I have seen this power lift men from lowly beginnings to places of power and wealth; I have seen it rob the grave of its victims; I have seen it serve as the medium by which men staged a comeback after having been defeated in a hundred different ways; I have seen it provide my own son with a normal, happy, successful life, despite Nature's having sent him into the world without ears.

How can one harness and use the power of *desire*? This has been answered through this, and the subsequent chapters of this book. This message is going out to the world at the end of the longest, and perhaps, the most devastating depression America has ever known. It is reasonable to presume that the message may come to the attention of many who have been wounded by the depression, those who have lost their fortunes, others who have lost their positions, and great numbers who must reorganize their plans and stage a comeback. To all these I wish to convey the thought that all achievement, no matter what may be its nature, or its purpose, must begin with an intense, *burning desire* for something definite.

Through some strange and powerful principle of "mental chemistry" which she has never divulged, Nature wraps up in the impulse of *strong desire* "that something" which recognizes no such word as impossible, and accepts no such reality as failure.

Chapter Two: Faith

Visualization Of, and Belief in Attainment of Desire: The Second Step toward Riches

Faith is the head chemist of the mind. When *faith* is blended with the vibration of thought, the subconscious mind instantly picks up the vibration, translates it into its spiritual equivalent, and transmits it to Infinite Intelligence, as in the case of prayer.

The emotions of *faith*, *love*, and *Sex* are the most powerful of all the major positive emotions. When the three are blended, they have the effect of "coloring" the vibration of thought in such a way that it instantly reaches the subconscious mind, where it is changed into its spiritual equivalent, the only form that induces a response from Infinite Intelligence.

Love and faith are psychic; related to the spiritual side of man. Sex is purely biological, and related only to the physical. The mixing, or blending, of these three emotions has the effect of opening a direct line of communication between the finite, thinking mind of man, and Infinite Intelligence.

How To Develop Faith

There comes, now, a statement which will give a better understanding of the importance the principle of auto-suggestion assumes in the transmutation of desire into its physical, or monetary equivalent; namely: *faith* is a state of mind which may be induced, or created, by affirmation or repeated instructions to the subconscious mind, through the principle of auto-suggestion.

As an illustration, consider the purpose for which you are, presumably, reading this book. The object is, naturally, to acquire the ability to transmute the intangible thought impulse of *desire* into its physical counterpart, money. By following the instructions laid down in the chapters on auto-suggestion, and the subconscious mind, as summarized in the chapter on auto-suggestion, you may *convince* the subconscious mind that you believe you will receive that for which you ask, and it will act upon that belief, which your subconscious mind passes back to you in the form of "*faith*," followed by definite plans for procuring that which you desire.

The method by which one develops *faith*, where it does not already exist, is extremely difficult to describe, almost as difficult, in fact, as it would be to describe the color of red to a blind man who has never seen color, and has nothing with which to compare what you describe to him. Faith is a state of mind which you may develop at will, after you have mastered the thirteen principles, because it is a state of mind which develops voluntarily, through application and use of these principles.

Repetition of affirmation of orders to your subconscious mind is the only known method of voluntary development of the emotion of faith.

Perhaps the meaning may be made clearer through the following explanation as to the way men sometimes become criminals. Stated in the words of a famous criminologist, "When men first come into contact with crime, they abhor it. If they remain in contact with crime for a time, they become accustomed to it, and endure it. If they remain in contact with it long enough, they finally embrace it, and become influenced by it."

This is the equivalent of saying that any impulse of thought which is repeatedly passed on to the subconscious mind is, finally, accepted and acted upon by the subconscious mind, which proceeds to translate that impulse into its physical equivalent, by the most practical procedure available.

In connection with this, consider again the statement, *all thoughts which have been emotionalized,* (given feeling) *and mixed with faith,* begin immediately to translate themselves into their physical equivalent or counterpart.

The emotions, or the "feeling" portion of thoughts, are the factors which give thoughts vitality, life, and action. The emotions of Faith, Love, and Sex, when mixed with any thought impulse, give it greater action than any of these emotions can do singly.

Not only thought impulses which have been mixed with *faith,* but those which have been mixed with any of the positive emotions, or any of the negative emotions, may reach, and influence the subconscious mind.

From this statement, you will understand that the subconscious mind will translate into its physical equivalent, a thought impulse of a negative or destructive nature, just as readily as it will act upon thought impulses of a positive or constructive nature. This accounts for the strange phenomenon which so many millions of people experience, referred to as "misfortune," or "bad luck."

There are millions of people who *believe* themselves "doomed" to poverty and failure, because of some strange force over which they *believe* they have no control. They are the creators of their own "misfortunes," because of this negative *belief,* which is picked up by the subconscious mind, and translated into its physical equivalent.

This is an appropriate place at which to suggest again that you may benefit, by passing on to your subconscious mind, any *desire* which you wish translated into its physical, or monetary equivalent, in a state of expectancy or *belief* that the transmutation will actually take place. Your *belief*, or *faith*, is the element which determines the action of your subconscious mind. There is nothing to hinder you from "deceiving" your subconscious mind when giving it instructions through autosuggestion, as I deceived my son's subconscious mind.

To make this "deceit" more realistic, conduct yourself just as you would, if you were *already in possession of the material thing which you are demanding*, when you call upon your subconscious mind.

The subconscious mind will transmute into its physical equivalent, by the most direct and practical media available, any order which is given to it in a state of *belief*, or *faith* that the order will be carried out.

Surely, enough has been stated to give a starting point from which one may, through experiment and practice, acquire the ability to mix *faith* with any order given to the subconscious mind. Perfection will come through practice. It cannot come by merely reading instructions.

If it be true that one may become a criminal by association with crime, (and this is a known fact), it is equally true that one may develop faith by voluntarily suggesting to the subconscious mind that one has faith. The mind comes, finally, to take on the nature of the influences which dominate it. Understand this truth, and you will know why it is essential for you to encourage the positive emotions as dominating forces of your mind, and discourage — and eliminate negative emotions.

A mind dominated by positive emotions, becomes a favorable abode for the state of mind known as faith. A mind so dominated may, at will, give the subconscious mind instructions, which it will accept and act upon immediately.

Faith Is a State of Mind Which May Be Induced by Auto-Suggestion

All down the ages, the religionists have admonished struggling humanity to "have faith" in this, that, and the other dogma or creed, but they have failed to tell people HOW to have faith. They have not stated that "faith is a state of mind, and that it may be induced by self-suggestion."

In language which any normal human being can understand, we will describe all that is known about the principle through which *faith* may be developed, where it does not already exist.

Have Faith in yourself; Faith in the Infinite.

Before we begin, you should be reminded again that:

faith is the "eternal elixir" which gives life, power, and action to the impulse of thought!

The foregoing sentence is worth reading a second time, and a third, and a fourth. It is worth reading aloud!

faith is the starting point of all accumulation of riches!

faith is the basis of all "miracles," and all mysteries which cannot be analyzed by the rules of science!

faith is the only known antidote for *failure*!

faith is the element, the "chemical" which, when mixed with prayer, gives one direct communication with Infinite Intelligence.

faith is the element which transforms the ordinary vibration of thought, created by the finite mind of man, into the spiritual equivalent.

faith is the only agency through which the cosmic force of Infinite Intelligence can be harnessed and used by man.

Every one of the foregoing statements is capable of proof!

The proof is simple and easily demonstrated. It is wrapped up in the principle of auto-suggestion. Let us center our attention, therefore, upon the subject of self-suggestion, and find out what it is, and what it is capable of achieving.

I *thoughts which are mixed with any of the feelings of emotions, constitute a "magnetic" force which attracts, from the vibrations of the ether, other similar, or related thoughts* t is a well known fact that one comes, finally, to *believe* whatever one repeats to one's self, whether the statement be true or false. If a man repeats a lie over and over, he will eventually accept the lie as truth. Moreover, he will *believe* it to be the truth.

Every man is what he is, because of the *dominating thoughts* which he permits to occupy his mind. Thoughts which a man deliberately places in his own mind, and encourages with sympathy, and with which he mixes any one or more of the emotions, constitute the motivating forces, which direct and control his every movement, act, and deed!

Comes, now, a very significant statement of truth:

. A thought thus "magnetized" with emotion may be compared to a seed which, when planted in fertile soil, germinates, grows, and multiplies itself over and over again, until that which was originally one small seed, becomes countless millions of seeds of the *same brand!*

The ether is a great cosmic mass of eternal forces of vibration. It is made up of both destructive vibrations and constructive vibrations. It carries, at all times, vibrations of fear, poverty, disease, failure, misery; and vibrations of prosperity, health, success, and happiness, just as surely as it carries the sound of hundreds of orchestrations of music, and hundreds of human voices, all of which maintain their own individuality, and means of identification, through the medium of radio.

From the great storehouse of the ether, the human mind is constantly attracting vibrations which harmonize with that which *dominates* the human mind. Any thought, idea, plan, or purpose which one holds in one's mind attracts, from the vibrations of the ether, a host of its relatives, adds these "relatives" to its own force, and grows until it becomes the dominating, *motivating master* of the individual in whose mind it has been housed.

Now, let us go back to the starting point, and become informed as to how the original seed of an idea, plan, or purpose may be planted in the mind. The information is easily conveyed: any idea, plan, or purpose may be placed in the mind through repetition of thought. This is why you are asked to write out a statement of your major purpose, or Definite Chief Aim, commit it to memory, and repeat it, in audible words, day after day, until these vibrations of sound have reached your subconscious mind.

We are what we are, because of the vibrations of thought which we pick up and register, through the stimuli of our daily environment.

Resolve to throw off the influences of any unfortunate environment, and to build your own life to *order*. Taking inventory of mental assets and liabilities, you will discover that your greatest weakness is lack of self-confidence. This handicap can be surmounted, and timidity translated into courage, through the aid of the principle of autosuggestion. The application of this principle may be made through a simple arrangement of positive thought impulses stated in writing, memorized, and repeated, until they become a part of the working equipment of the subconscious faculty of your mind.

Self-Confidence Formula

First. I know that I have the ability to achieve the object of my Definite Purpose in life, therefore, I demand of myself persistent, continuous action toward its attainment, and I here and now promise to render such action.

Second. I realize the dominating thoughts of my mind will eventually reproduce themselves in outward, physical action, and gradually transform themselves into physical reality, therefore, I will concentrate my thoughts for thirty minutes daily, upon the task of thinking of the person I intend to become, thereby creating in my mind a clear mental picture of that person.

Third. I know through the principle of auto-suggestion, any desire that I persistently hold in my mind will eventually seek expression through some practical means of attaining the object back of it, therefore, I will devote ten minutes daily to demanding of myself the development of *self-confidence.*

Fourth. I have clearly written down a description of my *definite chief aim* in life, and I will never stop trying, until I shall have developed sufficient self-confidence for its attainment.

Fifth. I fully realize that no wealth or position can long endure, unless built upon truth and justice, therefore, I will engage in no transaction which does not benefit all whom it affects. I will succeed by attracting to myself the forces I wish to use, and the cooperation of other people. I will induce others to serve me, because of my willingness to serve others. I will eliminate hatred, envy, jealousy, selfishness, and cynicism, by developing love for all humanity, because I know that a negative attitude toward others can never bring me success. I will cause others to believe in me, because I will believe in them, and in myself.

I will sign my name to this formula, commit it to memory, and repeat it aloud once a day, with full *faith* that it will gradually influence my *thoughts* and *actions* so that I will become a self-reliant, and successful person.

Back of this formula is a law of Nature which no man has yet been able to explain. It has baffled the scientists of all ages. The psychologists have named this law "auto-suggestion," and let it go at that.

The name by which one calls this law is of little importance. The important fact about it is— it works for the glory and success of mankind, *if* it is used constructively. On the other hand, if used destructively, it will destroy just as readily. In this statement may be found a very significant truth, namely; that those who go down in defeat, and end their lives in poverty, misery, and distress, do so because of negative application of the principle of auto-suggestion. The cause may be found in the fact that *all impulses of thought have a tendency to clothe themselves in their physical equivalent.*

The subconscious mind, (the chemical laboratory in which all thought impulses are combined, and made ready for translation into physical reality), makes no distinction between constructive and destructive thought impulses. It works with the material we feed it, through our thought impulses. The subconscious mind will translate into reality a thought driven by *fear* just as readily as it will translate into reality a thought driven by *courage*, or *faith.*

The pages of medical history are rich with illustrations of cases of "suggestive suicide." A man may commit suicide through negative suggestion, just as effectively as by any other means. In a midwestern city, a man by the name of Joseph Grant, a bank official, "borrowed" a large sum of the bank's money, without the consent of the directors. He lost the money through gambling. One afternoon, the Bank Examiner came and began to check the accounts. Grant left the bank, took a room in a local hotel, and when they found him, three days later, he was lying in bed, wailing and moaning, repeating over and over these words, "My God, this will kill me! I cannot stand the disgrace." In a short time he was dead. The doctors pronounced the case one of "mental suicide."

Just as electricity will turn the wheels of industry, and render useful service if used constructively; or snuff out life if wrongly used, so will the law of auto-suggestion lead you to peace and prosperity, or down into the valley of misery, failure, and death, according to your degree of understanding and application of it.

If you fill your mind with *fear*, doubt and unbelief in your ability to connect with, and use the forces of Infinite Intelligence, the law of auto– suggestion will take this spirit of unbelief and use it as a pattern by which your subconscious mind will translate it into its physical equivalent.

This statement is as true as the statement that two and two are four!

Like the wind which carries one ship East, and another West, the law of auto-suggestion will lift you up or pull you down, according to the way you set your sails of *thought*. The law of auto-suggestion, through which any person may rise to altitudes of achievement which stagger the imagination, is well described in the following verse:

"If you think you are beaten, you are,
If you think you dare not, you don't
If you like to win, but you think you can't,
It is almost certain you won't.

"If you think you'll lose, you're lost
For out of the world we find,
Success begins with a fellow's will–
It's all in the state of mind.

"If you think you are outclassed, you are,
You've got to think high to rise,
You've got to be sure of yourself before
You can ever win a prize.

"Life's battles don't always go
To the stronger or faster man,
But soon or late the man who wins
Is the man *who thinks he can*!"

Observe the words which have been emphasized, and you will catch the deep meaning which the poet had in mind.

Somewhere in your make-up (perhaps in the cells of your brain) there lies sleeping, the seed of achievement which, if aroused and put into action, would carry you to heights, such as you may never have hoped to attain.

Just as a master musician may cause the most beautiful strains of music to pour forth from the strings of a violin, so may you arouse the genius which lies asleep in your brain, and cause it to drive you upward to whatever goal you may wish to achieve.

Abraham Lincoln was a failure at everything he tried, until he was well past the age of forty. He was a Mr. Nobody from Nowhere, until a great experience came into his life, aroused the sleeping genius within his heart and brain, and gave the world one of its really great men. That "experience" was mixed with the emotions of sorrow and *love*. It came to him through Anne Rutledge, the only woman whom he ever truly loved.

It is a known fact that the emotion of *love* is closely akin to the state of mind known as *faith*, and this for the reason that Love comes very near to translating one's thought impulses into their spiritual equivalent. During his work of research, the author discovered, from the analysis of the life-work and achievements of hundreds of men of outstanding accomplishment, that there was the influence of a woman's love back of nearly *every one of them*. The emotion of love, in the human heart and brain, creates a favorable field of magnetic attraction, which causes an influx of the higher and finer vibrations which are afloat in the ether.

If you wish evidence of the power of *faith*, study the achievements of men and women who have employed it. At the head of the list comes the Nazarene. Christianity is the greatest single force which influences the minds of men. The basis of Christianity is *faith*, no matter how many people may have perverted, or misinterpreted the meaning of this great force, and no matter how many dogmas and creeds have been created in its name, which do not reflect its tenets.

The sum and substance of the teachings and the achievements of Christ, which may have been interpreted as "miracles," were nothing more nor less than *faith*. If there are any such phenomena as "miracles" they are produced only through the state of mind known as *faith*! Some teachers of religion, and many who call themselves Christians, neither understand nor practice *faith*.

Let us consider the power of *faith*, as it is now being demonstrated, by a man who is well known to all of civilization, Mahatma Gandhi, of India. In this man the world has one of the most astounding examples known to civilization, of the possibilities of *faith*. Gandhi wields more potential power than any man living at this time, and this, despite the fact that he has none of the orthodox tools of power, such as money, battle ships, soldiers, and materials of warfare. Gandhi has no money, he has no home, he does not own a suit of clothes, but *he does have power*. How does he come by that power?

He created it out of his understanding of the principle of faith, and through his ability to transplant that faith into the minds of two hundred million people.

Gandhi has accomplished, through the influence of *faith*, that which the strongest military power on earth could not, and never will accomplish through soldiers and military equipment. He has accomplished the astounding feat of *influencing* two hundred million minds to *coalesce and move in unison, as a single mind.*

What other force on earth, except *faith* could do as much?

There will come a day when employees as well as employers will discover the possibilities of *faith*. That day is dawning. The whole world has had ample opportunity, during the recent business depression, to witness what the *lack of faith* will do to business.

Surely, civilization has produced a sufficient number of intelligent human beings to make use of this great lesson which the depression has taught the world. During this depression, the world had evidence in abundance that widespread *fear* will paralyze the wheels of industry and business. Out of this experience will arise leaders in business and industry who will profit by the example which Gandhi has set for the world, and they will apply to business the same tactics which he has used in building the greatest following known in the history of the world. These leaders will come from the rank and file of the unknown men, who now labor in the steel plants, the coal mines, the automobile factories, and in the small towns and cities of America.

Business is due for a reform, make no mistake about this! The methods of the past, based upon economic combinations of *force* and *fear*, will be supplanted by the better principles of *faith* and cooperation. Men who labor will receive more than daily wages; they will receive dividends from the business, the same as those who supply the capital for business; but, first they must *Give more to their employers*, and stop this bickering and bargaining by force, at the expense of the public. They must earn the right to dividends!

Moreover, and this is the most important thing of all– *they will be led by leaders who will understand and apply the principles employed by Mahatma Gandhi.* Only in this way may leaders get from their followers the spirit of *full* cooperation which constitutes power in its highest and most enduring form.

This stupendous machine age in which we live, and from which we are just emerging, has taken the soul out of men. Its leaders have driven men as though they were pieces of cold machinery; they were forced to do so by the employees who have bargained, at the expense of all concerned, to get and not to give. The watchword of the future will be *human happiness and contentment*, and when this state of mind shall have been attained, the production will take care of itself, more effectively than anything that has ever been accomplished where men did not, and could not mix *faith* and individual interest with their labor.

Because of the need for faith and cooperation in operating business and industry, it will be both interesting and profitable to analyze an event which provides an excellent understanding of the method by which industrialists and business men accumulate great fortunes, by giving before they try to get.

The event chosen for this illustration dates back to 1900, when the United States Steel Corporation was being formed. As you read the story, keep in mind these fundamental facts and you will understand how *ideas* have been converted into huge fortunes.

First, the huge United States Steel Corporation was born in the mind of Charles M. Schwab, in the form of an *idea* he created through his *imagination* Second, he mixed *faith* with his *idea*. Third, he formulated a *plan* for the transformation of his *idea* into physical and financial reality. Fourth, he put his plan into action with his famous speech at the University Club. Fifth, he applied, and followed-through on his *plan* with *persistence*, and backed it with firm *decision* until it had been fully carried out. Sixth, he prepared the way for success by a *Burning desire* for success.

If you are one of those who have often wondered how great fortunes are accumulated, this story of the creation of the United States Steel Corporation will be enlightening. If you have any doubt that men can *Think and Grow Rich* this story should dispel that doubt, because you can plainly see in the story of the United States Steel, the application of a major portion of the thirteen principles described in this book.

This astounding description of the power of an *idea* was dramatically told by John Lowell, in the New York World- Telegram, with whose courtesy it is here reprinted.

"A *pretty after-dinner speech for a billion dollars*

"When, on the evening of December 12, 1900, some eighty of the nation's financial nobility gathered in the banquet hail of the University Club on Fifth Avenue to do honor to a young man from out of the West, not half a dozen of the guests realized they were to witness the most significant episode in American industrial history.

"J. Edward Simmons and Charles Stewart Smith, their hearts full of gratitude for the lavish hospitality bestowed on them by Charles M. Schwab during a recent visit to Pittsburgh, had arranged the dinner to introduce the thirty-eight-year-old steel man to eastern banking society. But they didn't expect him to stampede the convention. They warned him, in fact, that the bosoms within New York's stuffed shirts would not be responsive to oratory, and that, if he didn't want to bore the Stilhnans and Harrimans and Vanderbilts, he had better limit himself to fifteen or twenty minutes of polite vaporings and let it go at that. " Even John Pierpont Morgan, sitting on the right hand of Schwab as became his imperial dignity, intended to grace the banquet table with his presence only briefly. And so far as the press and public were concerned, the whole affair was of so little moment that no mention of it found its way into print the next day.

"So the two hosts and their distinguished guests ate their way through the usual seven or eight courses. There was little conversation and what there was of it was restrained. Few of the bankers and brokers had met Schwab, whose career had flowered along the banks of the Monongahela, and none knew him well. But before the evening was over, they— and with them Money Master Morgan – were to be swept off their feet, and a billion dollar baby, the United States Steel Corporation, was to be conceived. "It is perhaps unfortunate, for the sake of history, that no record of Charlie Schwab's speech at the dinner ever was made. He repeated some parts of it at a later date during a similar meeting of Chicago bankers. And still later, when the Government brought suit to dissolve the Steel Trust, he gave his own version, from the witness stand, of the remarks that stimulated Morgan into a frenzy of financial activity.

"It is probable, however, that it was a 'homely' speech, somewhat ungrammatical (for the niceties of language never bothered Schwab), full of epigram and threaded with wit. But aside from that it had a galvanic force and effect upon the five billions of estimated capital that was represented by the diners. After it was over and the gathering was still under its spell, although Schwab had talked for ninety minutes, Morgan led the orator to a recessed window where, dangling their legs from the high, uncomfortable seat, they talked for an hour more.

"The magic of the Schwab personality had been turned on, full force, but what was more important and lasting was the full-fledged, clear-cut program he laid down for the aggrandizement of Steel. Many other men had tried to interest Morgan in slapping together a steel trust after the pattern of the biscuit, wire and hoop, sugar, rubber, whisky, oil or chewing gum combinations. John W. Gates, the gambler, had urged it, but Morgan distrusted him. The Moore boys, Bill and Jim, Chicago stock jobbers who had glued together a match trust and a cracker corporation, had urged it and failed. Elbert H. Gary, the sanctimonious country lawyer, wanted to foster it, but he wasn't big enough to be impressive. Until Schwab's eloquence took J. P. Morgan to the heights from which he could visualize the solid results of the most daring financial undertaking ever conceived, the project was regarded as a delirious dream of easy-money crackpots.

"The financial magnetism that began, a generation ago, to attract thousands of small and sometimes inefficiently managed companies into large and competition-crushing combinations, had become operative in the steel world through the devices of that jovial business pirate, John W. Gates. Gates already had formed the American Steel and Wire Company out of a chain of small concerns, and together with Morgan had created the Federal Steel Company. The National Tube and American Bridge companies were two more Morgan concerns, and the Moore Brothers had forsaken the match and cookie business to form the 'American' group— Tin Plate, Steel Hoop, Sheet Steel— and the National Steel Company.

"But by the side of Andrew Carnegie's gigantic vertical trust, a trust owned and operated by fifty-three partners, those other combinations were picayune. They might combine to their heart's content but the whole lot of them couldn't make a dent in the Carnegie organization, and Morgan knew it.

"The eccentric old Scot knew it, too. From the magnificent heights of Skibo Castle he had viewed, first with amusement and then with resentment, the attempts of Morgan's smaller companies to cut into his business. When the attempts became too bold, Carnegie's temper was translated into anger and retaliation. He decided to duplicate every mill owned by his rivals. Hitherto, he hadn't been interested in wire, pipe, hoops, or sheet. Instead, he was content to sell such companies the raw steel and let them work it into whatever shape they wanted. Now, with Schwab as his chief and able lieutenant, he planned to drive his enemies to the wall.

"So it was that in the speech of Charles M. Schwab, Morgan saw the answer to his problem of combination. A trust without Carnegie—giant of them all—would be no trust at all, a plum pudding, as one writer said, without the plums.

"Schwab's speech on the night of December 12, 1900, undoubtedly carried the inference, though not the pledge, that the vast Carnegie enterprise could be brought under the Morgan tent. He talked of the world future for steel, of reorganization for efficiency, of specialization, of the scrapping of unsuccessful mills and concentration of effort on the flourishing properties, of economies in the ore traffic, of economies in overhead and administrative departments, of capturing foreign markets.

"More than that, he told the buccaneers among them wherein lay the errors of their customary piracy. Their purposes, he inferred, bad been to create monopolies, raise prices, and pay themselves fat dividends out of privilege. Schwab condemned the system in his heartiest manner. The shortsightedness of such a policy, he told his hearers, lay in the fact that it restricted the market in an era when everything cried for expansion. By cheapening the cost of steel, he argued, an ever-expanding market would be created; more uses for steel would be devised, and a goodly portion of the world trade could be captured. Actually, though he did not know it, Schwab was an apostle of modern mass production.

"So the dinner at the University Club came to an end. Morgan went home, to think about Schwab's rosy predictions. Schwab went back to Pittsburgh to run the steel business for 'Wee Andra Carnegie,' while Gary and the rest went back to their stock tickers, to fiddle around in anticipation of the next move.

"It was not long coming. It took Morgan about one week to digest the feast of reason Schwab had placed before him. When he had assured himself that no financial indigestion was to result, he sent for Schwab—and found that young man rather coy. Mr. Carnegie, Schwab indicated, might not like it if he found his trusted company president had been flirting with the Emperor of Wall Street, the Street upon which Carnegie was resolved never to tread. Then it was suggested by John W. Gates the go-between, that if Schwab 'happened' to be in the Bellevue Hotel in Philadelphia, J. P. Morgan might also 'happen' to be there. When Schwab arrived, however, Morgan was inconveniently ill at his New York home, and so, on the elder man's pressing invitation, Schwab went to New York and presented himself at the door of the financier's library.

"Now certain economic historians have professed the belief that from the beginning to the end of the drama, the stage was set by Andrew Carnegie— that the dinner to Schwab, the famous speech, the Sunday night conference between Schwab and the Money King, were events arranged by the canny Scot. The truth is exactly the opposite. When Schwab was called in to consummate the deal, he didn't even know whether 'the little boss, ' as Andrew was called, would so much as listen to an offer to sell, particularly to a group of men whom Andrew regarded as being endowed with something less than holiness. But Schwab did take into the conference with him, in his own handwriting, six sheets of copper-plate figures, representing to his mind the physical worth and the potential earning capacity of every steel company he regarded as an essential star in the new metal firmament.

"Four men pondered over these figures all night. The chief, of course, was Morgan, steadfast in his belief in the Divine Right of Money. With him was his aristocratic partner, Robert Bacon, a scholar and a gentleman. The third was John W. Gates whom Morgan scorned as a gambler and used as a tool. The fourth was Schwab, who knew more about the processes of making and selling steel than any whole group of men then living. Throughout that conference, the Pittsburgher's figures were never questioned. If he said a company was worth so much, then it was worth that much and no more. He was insistent, too, upon including in the combination only those concerns he nominated. He had conceived a corporation in which there would be no duplication, not even to satisfy the greed of friends who wanted to unload their companies upon the broad Morgan shoulders. Thus he left out, by design, a number of the larger concerns upon which the Walruses and Carpenters of Wall Street had cast hungry eyes.

"When dawn came, Morgan rose and straightened his back. Only one question remained.

"' Do you think you can persuade Andrew Carnegie to sell? ' he asked.

"' I can try, ' said Schwab.

"' If you can get him to sell, I will undertake the matter, ' said Morgan.

"So far so good. But would Carnegie sell? How much would he demand? (Schwab thought about $320,000,000). What would he take payment in? Common or preferred stocks? Bonds? Cash? Nobody could raise a third of a billion dollars in cash.

"There was a golf game in January on the frost-cracking heath of the St. Andrews links in Westchester, with Andrew bundled up in sweaters against the cold, and Charlie talking volubly, as usual, to keep his spirits up. But no word of business was mentioned until the pair sat down in the cozy warmth of the Carnegie cottage hard by. Then, with the same persuasiveness that had hypnotized eighty millionaires at the University Club, Schwab poured out the glittering promises of retirement in comfort, of untold millions to satisfy the old man's social caprices. Carnegie capitulated, wrote a figure on a slip of paper, handed it to Schwab and said, 'all right, that's what we'll sell for.'

"The figure was approximately $400,000,000, and was reached by taking the $320,000,000 mentioned by Schwab as a basic figure, and adding to it $80,000,000 to represent the increased capital value over the previous two years.

"Later, on the deck of a trans-Atlantic liner, the Scotsman said ruefully to Morgan, 'I wish I had asked you for $100,000,000 more.'

"' If you had asked for it, you'd have gotten it, ' Morgan told him cheerfully.

"There was an uproar, of course. A British correspondent cabled that the foreign steel world was 'appalled' by the gigantic combination. President Hadley, of Yale, declared that unless trusts were regulated the country might expect 'an emperor in Washington within the next twenty-five years. ' But that able stock manipulator, Keene, went at his work of shoving the new stock at the public so vigorously that all the excess water— estimated by some at nearly $600,000,000— was absorbed in a twinkling. So Carnegie had his millions, and the Morgan syndicate had $62,000,000 for all its 'trouble,' and all the 'boys,' from Gates to Gary, had their millions.

"The thirty-eight-year-old Schwab had his reward. He was made president of the new corporation and remained in control until 1930."

The dramatic story of "Big Business" which you have just finished, was included in this book, because it is a perfect illustration of the method by which *desire can be transmuted into its physical equivalent!*

I imagine some readers will question the statement that a mere, intangible *desire* can be converted into its physical equivalent. Doubtless some will say, "You cannot convert *nothing* into *something!*" The answer is in the story of United States Steel.

That giant organization was created in the mind of one man. The plan by which the organization was provided with the steel mills that gave it financial stability was created in the mind of the same man. His *faith*, his *desire*, his *imagination*, his *persistence* were the real ingredients that went into United States Steel. The steel mills and mechanical equipment acquired by the corporation, *after it had been brought into legal existence*, were incidental, but careful analysis will disclose the fact that the appraised value of the properties acquired by the corporation increased in value by an estimated *six hundred million dollars*, by the mere transaction which consolidated them under one management.

In other words, Charles M. Schwab's *idea*, plus the *faith* with which he conveyed it to the minds of J. P. Morgan and the others, was marketed for a profit of approximately $600,000,000. Not an insignificant sum for a single *idea!*

What happened to some of the men who took their share of the millions of dollars of profit made by this transaction, is a matter with which we are not now concerned. The important feature of the astounding achievement is that it serves as unquestionable evidence of the soundness of the philosophy described in this book, because this philosophy was the warp and the woof of the entire transaction. Moreover, the practicability of the philosophy has been established by the fact that the United States Steel Corporation prospered, and became one of the richest and most powerful corporations in America, employing thousands of people, developing new uses for steel, and opening new markets; thus proving that the $600,000,000 in profit which the Schwab *idea* produced was earned.

Riches begin in the form of *thought!*

The amount is limited only by the person in whose mind the *thought* is put into motion. *faith* removes limitations! Remember this when you are ready to bargain with Life for whatever it is that you ask as your price for having passed this way.

Remember, also, that the man who created the United States Steel Corporation was practically unknown at the time. He was merely Andrew Carnegie's "Man Friday" until he gave birth to his famous *idea*. After that he quickly rose to a position of power, fame, and riches.

There are no limitations to the mind except those we acknowledge both poverty and riches are the offspring of thought

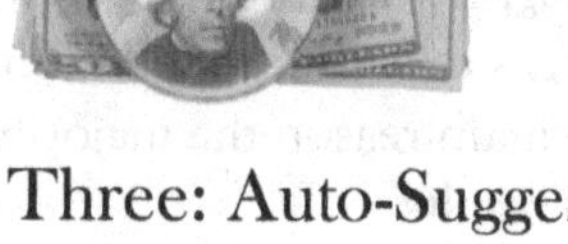

Chapter Three: Auto-Suggestion

The Medium for Influencing the Subconscious Mind: the Third Step Toward Riches

Auto-Suggestion is a term which applies to all suggestions and all self-administered stimuli which reach one's mind through the five senses. Stated in another way, auto-suggestion is self-suggestion. It is the agency of communication between that part of the mind where conscious thought takes place, and that which serves as the seat of action for the subconscious mind.

Through the dominating thoughts which one permits to remain in the conscious mind, (whether these thoughts be negative or positive, is immaterial), the principle of auto-suggestion voluntarily reaches the subconscious mind and influences it with these thoughts.

Auto-Suggestion: No thought, whether it be negative or positive, *can enter the subconscious mind without the aid of the principle of auto-suggestion*, with the exception of thoughts picked up from the ether. Stated differently, all sense impressions which are perceived through the five senses, are stopped by the *conscious* thinking mind, and may be either passed on to the subconscious mind, or rejected, at will. The conscious faculty serves, therefore, as an outer-guard to the approach of the subconscious.

Nature has so built man that he has *absolute control* over the material which reaches his subconscious mind, through his five senses, although this is not meant to be construed as a statement that man always *exercises* this control. In the great majority of instances, he does *not* exercise it, which explains why so many people go through life in poverty.

Recall what has been said about the subconscious mind resembling a fertile garden spot, in which weeds will grow in abundance, if the seeds of more desirable crops are not sown therein. is the agency of control through which an individual may voluntarily feed his subconscious mind on thoughts of a creative nature, or, by neglect, permit thoughts of a destructive nature to find their way into this rich garden of the mind.

You were instructed, in the last of the six steps described in the chapter on Desire, to read *aloud* twice daily the *written* statement of your *desire for money*, and to *see and feel* yourself *already* in possession of the money! By following these instructions, you communicate the object of your *desire* directly to your *subconscious* mind in a spirit of absolute *faith*. Through repetition of this procedure, you voluntarily create thought habits which are favorable to your efforts to transmute desire into its monetary equivalent.

Go back to these six steps described in chapter two, and read them again, very carefully, before you proceed further. Then (when you come to it), read very carefully the four instructions for the organization of your "Master Mind" group, described in the chapter on Organized Planning. By comparing these two sets of instructions with that which has been stated on auto-suggestion, you, of course, will see that the instructions involve the application of the principle of auto-suggestion.

Remember, therefore, when reading aloud the statement of your desire (through which you are endeavoring to develop a "money consciousness"), that the mere reading of the words is of *No consequence– unless* you mix emotion, or feeling with your words. If you repeat a million times the famous Emil Coué formula, "Day by day, in every way, I am getting better and better," without mixing emotion and *faith* with your words, you will experience no desirable results. Your subconscious mind recognizes and acts upon *Only* thoughts which have been well-mixed with emotion or feeling.

This is a fact of such importance as to warrant repetition in practically every chapter, because the lack of understanding of this is the main reason the majority of people who try to apply the principle of auto-suggestion get no desirable results.

Plain, unemotional words do not influence the subconscious mind. You will get no appreciable results until you learn to reach your subconscious mind with thoughts, or spoken words which have been well emotionalized with *belief*.

Do not become discouraged, if you cannot control and direct your emotions the first time you try to do so. Remember, there is no such possibility as *something for nothing*. Ability to reach, and influence your subconscious mind has its price, and you must pay that price. You cannot cheat, even if you desire to do so. The price of ability to influence your subconscious mind is everlasting *persistence* in applying the principles described here. You cannot develop the desired ability for a lower price. You, and *you alone*, must decide whether or not the reward for which you are striving (the "money consciousness"), is worth the price you must pay for it in effort.

Wisdom and "cleverness" alone, will not attract and retain money except in a few very rare instances, where the law of averages favors the attraction of money through these sources. The method of attracting money described here, does not depend upon the law of averages. Moreover, the method plays no favorites. It will work for one person as effectively as it will for another. Where failure is experienced, it is the individual, not the method, which has failed. If you try and fail, make another effort, and still another, until you succeed.

Your ability to use the principle of auto-suggestion will depend, very largely, upon your capacity to *concentrate* upon a given *desire* until that desire becomes a *burning obsession.*

When you begin to carry out the instructions in connection with the six steps described in the second chapter, it will be necessary for you to make use of the principle of *concentration.*

Let us here offer suggestions for the effective use of concentration. When you begin to carry out the first of the six steps, which instructs you to "fix in your own mind the *exact* amount of money you desire," hold your thoughts on that amount of money by *concentration*, or fixation of attention, with your eyes closed, until you can *actually see* the physical appearance of the money. Do this at least once each day. As you go through these exercises, follow the instructions given in the chapter on *faith*, and see yourself actually *in possession of the money!*

Here is a most significant fact— the subconscious mind takes any orders given it in a spirit of absolute *faith*, and acts upon those orders, although the orders often have to be presented over and over again, through repetition, before they are interpreted by the subconscious mind. Following the preceding statement, consider the possibility of playing a perfectly legitimate "trick" on your subconscious mind, by making it believe, because you believe it, that you must have the amount of money you are visualizing, that this money is already awaiting your claim, that the subconscious mind *must* hand over to you practical plans for acquiring the money which is yours.

Hand over the thought suggested in the preceding paragraph to your *imagination*, and see what your imagination can, or will do, to create practical plans for the accumulation of money through transmutation of your desire.

Do not wait for a definite plan, through which you intend to exchange services or merchandise in return for the money you are visualizing, but begin at once to see yourself in possession of the money, *demanding* and *expecting* meanwhile, that your subconscious mind will hand over the plan, or plans you need. Be on the alert for these plans, and when they appear, put them into *action immediately*. When the plans appear, they will probably "flash" into your mind through the sixth sense, in the form of an "inspiration." This inspiration may be considered a direct "telegram," or message from Infinite Intelligence. Treat it with respect, and act upon it as soon as you receive it. Failure to do this will be *fatal* to your success.

In the fourth of the six steps, you were instructed to "Create a definite plan for carrying out your desire, and begin at once to put this plan into action." You should follow this instruction in the manner described in the preceding paragraph. Do not trust to your "reason when creating your plan for accumulating money through the transmutation of desire. Your reason is faulty. Moreover, your reasoning faculty may be lazy, and, if you depend entirely upon it to serve you, it may disappoint you.

When visualizing the money you intend to accumulate, (with closed eyes), see yourself rendering the service, or delivering the merchandise you intend to give in return for this money. This is important!

Summary of Instructions

The fact that you are reading this book is an indication that you earnestly seek knowledge. It is also an indication that you are a student of this subject. If you are only a student, there is a chance that you may learn much that you did not know, but you will learn only by assuming an attitude of humility. If you choose to follow some of the instructions but neglect, or refuse to follow others–you will fail! To get satisfactory results, you must follow *all* instructions in a spirit of *faith.*

The instructions given in connection with the six steps in the second chapter will now be summarized, and blended with the principles covered by this chapter, as follows:

First. Go into some quiet spot (preferably in bed at night) where you will not be disturbed or interrupted, close your eyes, and repeat aloud, (so you may hear your own words) the written statement of the amount of money you intend to accumulate, the time limit for its accumulation, and a description of the service or merchandise you intend to give in return for the money. As you carry out these instructions, *see yourself already in possession of the money.*

For example :– Suppose that you intend to accumulate $50,000 by the first of January, five years hence, that you intend to give personal services in return for the money, in the Capacity of a salesman. Your written statement of your purpose should be similar to the following:

"By the first day of January, 19.., I will have in my possession $50,000, which will come to me in various amounts from time to time during the interim.

"In return for this money I will give the most efficient service of which I am capable, rendering the fullest possible quantity, and the best possible quality of service in the capacity of salesman of (describe the service or merchandise you intend to sell).

"I believe that I will have this money in my possession. My faith is so strong that I can now see this money before my eyes. I can touch it with my hands. It is now awaiting transfer to me at the time, and in the proportion that I deliver the service I intend to render in return for it. I am awaiting a plan by which to accumulate this money, and I will follow that plan, when it is received."

Second. Repeat this program night and morning until you can see, (in your imagination) the money you intend to accumulate.

Third. Place a written copy of your statement where you can see it night and morning, and read it just before retiring, and upon arising until it has been memorized.

Remember, as you carry out these instructions, that you are applying the principle of auto-suggestion, for the purpose of giving orders to your subconscious mind. Remember, also, that your subconscious mind will act *only* upon instructions which are emotionalized, and handed over to it with "feeling." *faith* is the strongest, and most productive of the emotions. Follow the instructions given in the chapter on *faith.*

These instructions may, at first, seem abstract. Do not let this disturb you. Follow the instructions, no matter how abstract or impractical they may, at first, appear to be. The time will soon come, if you do as you have been instructed, in spirit as well as in act, when a whole new universe of power will unfold to you.

Scepticism, in connection with *all* new ideas, is characteristic of all human beings. But if you follow the instructions outlined, your scepticism will soon be replaced by belief, and this, in turn, will soon become crystallized into *absolute faith.* Then you will have arrived at the point where you may truly say, "I am the master of my fate, I am the captain of my soul!"

Many philosophers have made the statement, that man is the master of his own earthly destiny, but most of them have failed to say why he is the master. The reason that man may be the master of his own earthly status, and especially his financial status, is thoroughly explained in this chapter. Man may become the master of himself, and of his environment, because he has the *power to influence his own subconscious mind,* and through it, gain the cooperation of Infinite Intelligence.

You are now reading the chapter which represents the keystone to the arch of this philosophy. The instructions contained in this chapter must be understood and *applied with persistence,* if you succeed in transmuting desire into money.

The actual performance of transmuting *desire* into money, involves the use of auto-suggestion as an agency by which one may reach, and influence, the subconscious mind. The other principles are simply tools with which to apply auto-suggestion. Keep this thought in mind, and you will, at all times, be conscious of the important part the principle of auto-suggestion is to play in your efforts to accumulate money through the methods described in this book.

Carry out these instructions as though you were a small child. Inject into your efforts something of the *faith* of a child. The author has been most careful, to see that no impractical instructions were included, because of his sincere desire to be helpful.

After you have read the entire book, come back to this chapter, and follow in spirit, and in action, this instruction:

Read the entire chapter aloud once every night, until you become thoroughly convinced that the principle of auto-suggestion is sound, that it will accomplish for you all that has been claimed for it. As you read, underscore with a pencil every sentence which impresses you favorably.

Follow the foregoing instruction to the letter, and it will open the way for a complete understanding, and mastery of the principles of success.

Chapter Four: Specialized Knowledge

Personal Experiences or Observations: the Fourth Step Toward Riches

There are two kinds of knowledge. One is general, the other is specialized. General knowledge, no matter how great in quantity or variety it may be, is of but little use in the accumulation of money. The faculties of the great universities possess, in the aggregate, practically every form of general knowledge known to civilization. Most of the professors have but little or no money. They specialize on teaching knowledge, but they do not specialize on the organization, or the use of knowledge.

knowledge will not attract money, unless it is organized, and intelligently directed, through practical *plans of action,* to the *definite end* of accumulation of money. Lack of understanding of this fact has been the source of confusion to millions of people who falsely believe that "knowledge is power." It is nothing of the sort! Knowledge is only potential power. It becomes power only when, and if, it is organized into definite plans of action, and directed to a definite end.

This "missing link" in all systems of education known to civilization today, may be found in the failure of educational institutions to teach their students *how to organize and use knowledge after they acquire it.*

Many people make the mistake of assuming that, because Henry Ford had but little "schooling," he is not a man of "education." Those who make this mistake do not know Henry Ford, nor do they understand the real meaning of the word "educate." That word is derived from the Latin word "educo," meaning to educe, to draw out, to *develop from within.*

An educated man is not, necessarily, one who has an abundance of general or specialized knowledge. An educated man is one who has so developed the faculties of his mind that he may acquire anything he wants, or its equivalent, without violating the rights of others. Henry Ford comes well within the meaning of this definition.

During the world war, a Chicago newspaper published certain editorials in which, among other statements, Henry Ford was called "an ignorant pacifist." Mr. Ford objected to the statements, and brought suit against the paper for libeling him. When the suit was tried in the Courts, the attorneys for the paper pleaded justification, and placed Mr. Ford, himself, on the witness stand, for the purpose of proving to the jury that he was ignorant. The attorneys asked Mr. Ford a great variety of questions, all of them intended to prove, by his own evidence, that, while he might possess considerable specialized knowledge pertaining to the manufacture of automobiles, he was, in the main, ignorant.

Mr. Ford was plied with such questions as the following: "Who was Benedict Arnold?" and "How many soldiers did the British send over to America to put down the Rebellion of 1776?" In answer to the last question, Mr. Ford replied, "I do not know the exact number of soldiers the British sent over, but I have heard that it was a considerably larger number than ever went back."

Finally, Mr. Ford became tired of this line of questioning, and in reply to a particularly offensive question, he leaned over, pointed his finger at the lawyer who had asked the question, and said, "If I should really *want* to answer the foolish question you have just asked, or any of the other questions you have been asking me, let me remind you that I have a row of electric push-buttons on my desk, and by pushing the right button, I can summon to my aid men who can answer *any* question I desire to ask concerning the business to which I am devoting most of my efforts. Now, will you kindly tell me, *why* I should clutter up my mind with general knowledge, for the purpose of being able to answer questions, when I have men around me who can supply any knowledge I require?"

There certainly was good logic to that reply.

That answer floored the lawyer. Every person in the courtroom realized it was the answer, not of an ignorant man, but of a man of *education.* Any man is educated who knows where to get knowledge when he needs it, and how to organize that knowledge into definite plans of action. Through the assistance of his "Master Mind" group, Henry Ford had at his command all the specialized knowledge he needed to enable him to become one of the wealthiest men in America. It was not essential that he have this knowledge in his own mind. Surely no person who has sufficient inclination and intelligence to read a book of this nature can possibly miss the significance of this illustration.

Before you can be sure of your ability to transmute *desire* into its monetary equivalent, you will require *specialized knowledge* of the service, merchandise, or profession which you intend to offer in return for fortune. Perhaps you may need much more specialized knowledge than you have the ability or the inclination to acquire, and if this should be true, you may bridge your weakness through the aid of your "Master Mind" group.

Andrew Carnegie stated that he, personally, knew nothing about the technical end of the steel business; moreover, he did not particularly care to know anything about it. The specialized knowledge which he required for the manufacture and marketing of steel, he found available through the individual units of his *master mind group*.

The accumulation of great fortunes calls for *power*, and power is acquired through highly organized and intelligently directed specialized knowledge, but that knowledge does not, necessarily, have to be in the possession of the man who accumulates the fortune.

The preceding paragraph should give hope and encouragement to the man with ambition to accumulate a fortune, who has not possessed himself of the necessary "education" to supply such specialized knowledge as he may require. Men sometimes go through life suffering from "inferiority complexes," because they are not men of "education." The man who can organize and direct a "Master Mind" group of men who possess knowledge useful in the accumulation of money, is just as much a man of education as any man in the group. *Remember this*, if you suffer from a feeling of inferiority, because your schooling has been limited.

Thomas A. Edison had only three months of "schooling" during his entire life. He did not lack education, neither did he die poor.

Henry Ford had less than a sixth grade "schooling" but he has managed to do pretty well by himself, financially.

Specialized knowledge is among the most plentiful, and the cheapest forms of service which may be had! If you doubt this, consult the payroll of any university.

It Pays to Know How to Purchase Knowledge

First of all, decide the sort of specialized knowledge you require, and the purpose for which it is needed. To a large extent your major purpose in life, the goal toward which you are working, will help determine what knowledge you need. With this question settled, your next move requires that you have accurate information concerning dependable sources of knowledge. The more important of these are:

(a) One's own experience and education

(b) Experience and education available through cooperation of others (Master Mind Alliance)

© Colleges and Universities

(d) Public Libraries (Through books and periodicals in which may be found all the knowledge organized by civilization)

(e) Special Training Courses (Through night schools and home study schools in particular.)

As knowledge is acquired it must be organized and put into use, for a definite purpose, through practical plans. Knowledge has no value except that which can be gained from its application toward some worthy end. This is one reason why college degrees are not valued more highly. They represent nothing but miscellaneous knowledge.

If you contemplate taking additional schooling, first determine the purpose for which you want the knowledge you are seeking, then learn where this particular sort of knowledge can be obtained, from reliable sources.

Successful men, in all callings, never stop acquiring specialized knowledge related to their major purpose, business, or profession. Those who are not successful usually make the mistake of believing that the knowledge acquiring period ends when one finishes school. The truth is that schooling does but little more than to put one in the way of learning how to acquire practical knowledge.

With this Changed World which began at the end of the economic collapse, came also astounding changes in educational requirements. The order of the day is *Specialization*! This truth was emphasized by Robert P. Moore, secretary of appointments of Columbia University.

"*Specialists most sought*

"Particularly sought after by employing companies are candidates who have specialized in some field— business-school graduates with training in accounting and statistics, engineers of all varieties, journalists, architects, chemists, and also outstanding leaders and activity men of the senior class.

"The man who has been active on the campus, whose personality is such that he gets along with all kinds of people and who has done an adequate job with his studies has a most decided edge over the strictly academic student. Some of these, because of their all-around qualifications, have received several offers of positions, a few of them as many as six.

"In departing from the conception that the 'straight A' student was invariably the one to get the choice of the better jobs, Mr. Moore said that most companies look not only to academic records but to activity records and personalities of the students.

"One of the largest industrial companies, the leader in its field, in writing to Mr. Moore concerning prospective seniors at the college, said:

"' We are interested primarily in finding men who can make exceptional progress in management work. For this reason we emphasize qualities of character, intelligence and personality far more than specific educational background.'

"Apprenticeship' Proposed"

Proposing a system of 'apprenticing' students in offices, stores and industrial occupations during the summer vacation, Mr. Moore asserts that after the first two or three years of college, every student should be asked 'to choose a definite future course and to call a halt if he has been merely pleasantly drifting without purpose through an unspecialized academic curriculum.'

"Colleges and universities must face the practical consideration that all professions and occupations now demand specialists," he said, urging that educational institutions accept more direct responsibility for vocational guidance. One of the most reliable and practical sources of knowledge available to those who need specialized schooling, is the night schools operated in most large cities. The correspondence schools give specialized training anywhere the U. S. mails go, on all subjects that can be taught by the extension method. One advantage of home study training is the flexibility of the study programed which permits one to study during spare time. Another stupendous advantage of home study training (if the school is carefully chosen), is the fact that most courses offered by home study schools carry with them generous privileges of consultation which can be of priceless value to those needing specialized knowledge. No matter where you live, you can share the benefits.

Anything acquired without effort, and without cost is generally unappreciated, often discredited; perhaps this is why we get so little from our marvelous opportunity in public schools. The *self-discipline* one receives from a definite programed of specialized study makes up to some extent, for the wasted opportunity when knowledge was available without cost. Correspondence schools are highly organized business institutions. Their tuition fees are so low that they are forced to insist upon prompt payments. Being asked to pay, whether the student makes good grades or poor, has the effect of causing one to follow through with the course when he would otherwise drop it. The correspondence schools have not stressed this point sufficiently, for the truth is that their collection departments constitute the very finest sort of training on *decision, promptness, action and the habit of finishing that which one begins.*

I learned this from experience, more than twenty-five years ago. I enrolled for a home study course in Advertising. After completing eight or ten lessons I stopped studying, but the school did not stop sending me bills. Moreover, it insisted upon payment, whether I kept up my studies or not. I decided that if I had to pay for the course (which I had legally obligated myself to do), I should complete the lessons and get my money's worth. I felt, at the time, that the collection system of the school was somewhat too well organized, but I learned later in life that it was a valuable part of my training for which no charge had been made. Being forced to pay, I went ahead and completed the course. Later in life I discovered that the efficient collection system of that school had been worth much in the form of money earned, because of the training in advertising I had so reluctantly taken.

We have in this country what is said to be the greatest public school system in the world. We have invested fabulous sums for fine buildings, we have provided convenient transportation for children living in the rural districts, so they may attend the best schools, but there is one astounding weakness to this marvelous system– *it is free*! One of the strange things about human beings is that they value only that which has a price. The free schools of America, and the free public libraries, do not impress people because they are free. This is the major reason why so many people find it necessary to acquire additional training after they quit school and go lo work. It is also one of the major reasons why *employers give greater consideration to employees who take home study courses*. They have learned, from experience, that any person who has the ambition to give up a part of his spare time to studying at home has in him those qualities which make for leadership. This recognition is not a charitable gesture, it is sound business judgment upon the part of the employers.

There is one weakness in people for which there is no remedy. It is the universal weakness of *Lack of ambition!* Persons, especially salaried people, who schedule their spare time, to provide for home study, seldom remain at the bottom very long. Their action opens the way for the upward climb, removes many obstacles from their path, and gains the friendly interest of those who have the power to put them in the way of *opportunity*.

The home study method of training is especially suited to the needs of employed people who find, after leaving school, that they must acquire additional specialized knowledge, but cannot spare the time to go back to school.

The changed economic conditions prevailing since the depression have made it necessary for thousands of people to find additional, or new sources of income. For the majority of these, the solution to their problem may be found only by acquiring specialized knowledge. Many will be forced to change their occupations entirely. When a merchant finds that a certain line of merchandise is not selling, he usually supplants it with another that is in demand. The person whose business is that of marketing personal services must also be an efficient merchant. If his services do not bring adequate returns in one occupation, he must change to another, where broader opportunities are available.

Stuart Austin Wier prepared himself as a Construction Engineer and followed this line of work until the depression limited his market to where it did not give him the income he required. He took inventory of himself, decided to change his profession to law, went back to school and took special courses by which he prepared himself as a corporation lawyer. Despite the fact the depression had not ended, he completed his training, passed the Bar Examination, and quickly built a lucrative law practice, in Dallas, Texas; in fact he is turning away clients.

Just to keep the record straight, and to anticipate the alibis of those who will say, "I couldn't go to school because I have a family to support," or "I'm too old," I will add the information that Mr. Wier was past forty, and married when he went back to school. Moreover, by carefully selecting highly specialized courses, in colleges best prepared to teach the subjects chosen, Mr. Wier completed in two years the work for which the majority of law students require four years. *It pays to know how to purchase knowledge!*

The person who stops studying merely because he has finished school is forever hopelessly doomed to mediocrity, no matter what may be his calling. The way of success is the way of continuous pursuit of knowledge.

Let Us Consider a Specific Instance

During the depression a salesman in a grocery store found himself without a position. Having had some bookkeeping experience, he took a special course in accounting, familiarized himself with all the latest bookkeeping and office equipment, and went into business for himself. Starting with the grocer for whom he had formerly worked, he made contracts with more than 100 small merchants to keep their books, at a very nominal monthly fee. His idea was so practical that he soon found it necessary to set up a portable office in a light delivery truck, which he equipped with modern bookkeeping machinery. He now has a fleet of these bookkeeping offices "on wheels" and employs a large staff of assistants, thus providing small merchants with accounting service equal to the best that money can buy, at very nominal cost.

Specialized knowledge, plus imagination, were the ingredients that went into this unique and successful business. Last year the owner of that business paid an income tax of almost ten times as much as was paid by the merchant for whom he worked when the depression forced upon him a temporary adversity which proved to be a blessing in disguise.

The beginning of this successful business was an *idea*!

Inasmuch as I had the privilege of supplying the unemployed salesman with that idea, I now assume the further privilege of suggesting another idea which has within it the possibility of even greater income. Also the possibility of rendering useful service to thousands of people who badly need that service.

The idea was suggested by the salesman who gave up selling and went into the business of keeping books on a wholesale basis. When the plan was suggested as a solution of his unemployment problem, he quickly exclaimed, "I like the idea, but I would not know how to turn it into cash." In other words, he complained he would not know how to market his bookkeeping knowledge after he acquired it.

So, that brought up another problem which had to be solved. With the aid of a young woman typist, clever at hand lettering, and who could put the story together, a very attractive book was prepared, describing the advantages of the new system of book-keeping. The pages were neatly typed and pasted in an ordinary scrapbook, which was used as a silent salesman with which the story of this new business was so effectively told that its owner soon had more accounts than he could handle.

There are thousands of people, all over the country, who need the services of a merchandising specialist capable of preparing an attractive brief for use in marketing personal services. The aggregate annual income from such a service might easily exceed that received by the largest employment agency, and the benefits of the service might be made far greater to the purchaser than any to be obtained from an employment agency.

The *idea* here described was born of necessity, to bridge an emergency which had to be covered, but it did not stop by merely serving one person. The woman who created the idea has a keen *imagination*. She saw in her newly born brain-child the making of a new profession, one that is destined to render valuable service to thousands of people who need practical guidance in marketing personal services.

Spurred to action by the instantaneous success of her first *"prepared plan to market personal services,"* this energetic woman turned next to the solution of a similar problem for her son who had just finished college, but had been totally unable to find a market for his services. The plan she originated for his use was the finest specimen of merchandising of personal services I have ever seen.

When the plan book had been completed, it contained nearly fifty pages of beautifully typed, properly organized information, telling the story of her son's native ability, schooling, personal experiences, and a great variety of other information too extensive for description. The plan book also contained a complete description of the position her son desired, together with a marvelous word picture of the exact plan he would use in filling the position.

The preparation of the plan book required several week's labor, during which time its creator sent her son to the public library almost daily, to procure data needed in selling his services to best advantage. She sent him, also to all the competitors of his prospective employer, and gathered from them vital information concerning their business methods which was of great value in the formation of the plan he intended to use in filling the position he sought. When the plan had been finished, it contained more than half a dozen very fine suggestions for the use and benefit of the prospective employer. (The suggestions were put into use by the company).

One may be inclined to ask, "Why go to all this trouble to secure a job?" The answer is straight to the point, also it is dramatic, because it deals with a subject which assumes the proportion of a tragedy with millions of men and women whose sole source of income is personal services.

The answer is, "*doing a thing well never is trouble! The plan prepared by this woman for the benefit of her son, helped him get the job for which he applied, at the first interview, at a salary fixed by himself.*"

Moreover– and this, too, is important– *The position did not require the young man to start at the bottom. He began as a junior executive, at an executive's salary.*

"Why go to all this trouble?" do you ask?

Well, for one thing, the *planned presentation* of this young man's application for a position clipped off no less than ten years of time he would have required to get to where he began, had he "started at the bottom and worked his way up."

This idea of starting at the bottom and working one's way up may appear to be sound, but the major objection to it is this– too many of those who begin at the bottom never manage to lift their heads high enough to be seen by *opportunity*, so they remain at the bottom. It should be remembered, also, that the outlook from the bottom is not so very bright or encouraging. It has a tendency to kill off ambition. We call it "getting into a rut," which means that we accept our fate because we form the *habit* of daily routine, a habit that finally becomes so strong we cease to try to throw it off. And that is another reason why it pays to start one or two steps above the bottom. By so doing one forms the *habit* of looking around, of observing how others get ahead, of seeing *opportunity*, and of embracing it without hesitation.

Dan Halpin is a splendid example of what I mean. During his college days, he was manager of the famous 1930 National Championship Notre Dame football team, when it was under the direction of the late Knute Rockne.

Perhaps he was inspired by the great football coach to aim high, and *not mistake temporary defeat for failure,* just as Andrew Carnegie, the great industrial leader, inspired his young business lieutenants to set high goals for themselves. At any rate, young Halpin finished college at a mighty unfavorable time, when the depression had made jobs scarce, so, after a fling at investment banking and motion pictures, he took the first opening with a potential future he could find— selling electrical hearing aids on a commission basis. *Anyone could start in that sort of job, and halpin knew it*, but it was enough to open the door of opportunity to him.

For almost two years, he continued in a job not to his liking, and he would never have risen above that job if he had not done something about his dissatisfaction. He aimed, first, at the job of Assistant Sales Manager of his company, and got the job. That one step upward placed him high enough above the crowd to enable him to see still greater opportunity, also, it placed him where *opportunity could see him.*

He made such a fine record selling hearing aids, that A. M. Andrews, Chairman of the Board of the Dictograph Products Company, a business competitor of the company for which Halpin worked, wanted to know something about that man Dan Halpin who was taking big sales away from the long established Dictograph Company. He sent for Halpin. When the interview was over, Halpin was the new Sales Manager, in charge of the Acousticon Division. Then, to test young Halpin's metal, Mr. Andrews went away to Florida for three months, leaving him to sink or swim in his new job. He did not sink! Knute Rockne's spirit of "All the world loves a winner, and has no time for a loser inspired him to put so much into his job that he was recently elected Vice-President of the company, and General Manager of the Acousticon and Silent Radio Division, a job which most men would be proud to earn through ten years of loyal effort. Halpin turned the trick in little more than six months.

It is difficult to say whether Mr. Andrews or Mr. Halpin is more deserving of eulogy, for the reason that both showed evidence of having an abundance of that very rare quality known as *imagination*. Mr. Andrews deserves credit for seeing, in young Halpin, a "go-getter" of the highest order. Halpin deserves credit for *refusing to compromise with life by accepting and keeping a job he did not want*, and that is one of the major points I am trying to emphasize through this entire philosophy— that we rise to high positions or remain at the bottom *because of conditions we can control if we desire to control them.*

I am also trying to emphasize another point, namely, that both success and failure are largely the results of *habit*! I have not the slightest doubt that Dan Halpin's close association with the greatest football coach America ever knew, planted in his mind the same brand of *desire* to excel which made the Notre Dame football team world famous. Truly, there is something to the idea that hero-worship is helpful, provided one worships a *winner*. Halpin tells me that Rockne was one of the world's greatest leaders of men in all history.

My belief in the theory that business associations are vital factors, both in failure and in success, was recently demonstrated, when my son Blair was negotiating with Dan Halpin for a position. Mr. Halpin offered him a beginning salary of about one half what he could have gotten from a rival company. I brought parental pressure to bear, and induced him to accept the place with Mr. Halpin, because *I believe that close association with one who refuses to compromise with circumstances he does not like, is an asset that can never be measured in terms of money.*

The bottom is a monotonous, dreary, unprofitable place for any person. That is why I have taken the time to describe how lowly beginnings may be circumvented by proper planning. Also, that is why so much space has been devoted to a description of this new profession, created by a woman who was inspired to do a fine job of *planning* because she wanted her son to have a favorable "break."

With the changed conditions ushered in by the world economic collapse, came also the need for newer and better ways of marketing *personal services*. It is hard to determine why someone had not previously discovered this stupendous need, in view of the fact that more money changes hands in return for personal services than for any other purpose. The sum paid out monthly, to people who work for wages and salaries, is so huge that it runs into hundreds of millions, and the annual distribution amounts to billions.

Perhaps some will find, in the *idea* here briefly described, the nucleus of the riches they *desire*! Ideas with much less merit have been the seedlings from which great fortunes have grown. Woolworth's Five and Ten Cent Store idea, for example, had far less merit, but it piled up a fortune for its creator.

Those seeing *opportunity* lurking in this suggestion will find valuable aid in the chapter on Organized Planning. Incidentally, an efficient merchandiser of personal services would find a growing demand for his services wherever there are men and women who seek better markets for their services. By applying the Master Mind principle, a few people with suitable talent, could form an alliance, and have a paying business very quickly. One would need to be a fair writer, with a flair for advertising and selling, one handy at typing and hand lettering, and one should be a first class business getter who would let the world know about the service. If one person possessed all these abilities, he might carry on the business alone, until it outgrew him.

The woman who prepared the "Personal Service Sales Plan" for her son now receives requests from all parts of the country for her cooperation in preparing similar plans for others who desire to market their personal services for more money. She has a staff of expert typists, artists, and writers who have the ability to dramatize the case history so effectively that one's personal services can be marketed for much more money than the prevailing wages for similar services. She is so confident of her ability that she accepts, as the major portion of her fee, a percentage of the increased pay she helps her clients to earn.

It must not be supposed that her plan merely consists of clever salesmanship by which she helps men and women to demand and receive more money for he same services they formerly sold for less pay. She looks after the interests of the purchaser as well as the seller of personal services, and so prepares her plans that the employer receives full value for the additional money he pays. The method by which she accomplishes this astonishing result is a professional secret which she discloses to no one excepting her own clients.

If you have the *imagination*, and seek a more profitable outlet for your personal services, this suggestion may be the stimulus for which you have been searching. The *idea* is capable of yielding an income far greater than that of the "average" doctor, lawyer, or engineer whose education required several years in college. The idea is saleable to those seeking new positions, in practically all positions calling for managerial or executive ability, and those desiring re-arrangement of incomes in their present positions.

There is no fixed price for sound *ideas*!

Back of all *ideas* is specialized knowledge. Unfortunately, for those who do not find riches in abundance, specialized knowledge is more abundant and more easily acquired than *ideas*. Because of this very truth, there is a universal demand and an ever-increasing opportunity for the person capable of helping men and women to sell their personal services advantageously. Capability means *imagination*, the one quality needed to combine specialized knowledge with *ideas*, in the form of *organized plans* designed to yield riches.

If you have *imagination* this chapter may present you with an idea sufficient to serve as the beginning of the riches you desire. Remember, the *idea* is the main thing. Specialized knowledge may be found just around the corner–any corner!

Chapter Five: Imagination

The Workshop of the Mind: the Fifth Step Toward Riches

The imagination is literally the workshop wherein are fashioned all plans created by man. The impulse, the *desire*, is given shape, form, and *action* through the aid of the imaginative faculty of the mind.

It has been said that man can create anything which he can imagine.

Of all the ages of civilization, this is the most favorable for the development of the imagination, because it is an age of rapid change. On every hand one may contact stimuli which develop the imagination.

Through the aid of his imaginative faculty, man has discovered, and harnessed, more of Nature's forces during the past fifty years than during the entire history of the human race, previous to that time. He has conquered the air so completely, that the birds are a poor match for him in flying. He has harnessed the ether, and made it serve as a means of instantaneous communication with any part of the world. He has analyzed, and weighed the sun at a distance of millions of miles, and has determined, through the aid of *imagination*, the elements of which it consists. He has discovered that his own brain is both a broadcasting, and a receiving station for the vibration of thought, and he is beginning now to learn how to make practical use of this discovery. He has increased the speed of locomotion, until he may now travel at a speed of more than three hundred miles an hour. The time will soon come when a man may breakfast in New York, and lunch in San Francisco.

Man's only limitation, within reason, *lies in his development and use of his imagination*. He has not yet reached the apex of development in the use of his imaginative faculty. He has merely discovered that he has an imagination, and has commenced to use it in a very elementary way.

Two forms of imagination

The imaginative faculty functions in two forms. One is known as "synthetic imagination," and the other as "creative imagination."

Synthetic imagination:— Through this faculty, one may arrange old concepts, ideas, or plans into new combinations. This faculty creates nothing. It merely works with the material of experience, education, and observation with which it is fed. It is the faculty used most by the inventor, with the exception of the who draws upon the creative imagination, when he cannot solve his problem through synthetic imagination.

Creative imagination:— Through the faculty of creative imagination, the finite mind of man has direct communication with Infinite Intelligence. It is the faculty through which "hunches" and "inspirations" are received. It is by this faculty that all basic, or new ideas are handed over to man.

It is through this faculty that thought vibrations from the minds of others are received. It is through this faculty that one individual may "tune in," or communicate with the subconscious minds of other men.

The creative imagination works automatically, in the manner described in subsequent pages. This faculty functions *only* when the conscious mind is vibrating at an exceedingly rapid rate, as for example, when the conscious mind is stimulated through the emotion of a strong desire.

The creative faculty becomes more alert, more receptive to vibrations from the sources mentioned, in proportion to its development through *Use*. This statement is significant! Ponder over it before passing on.

Keep in mind as you follow these principles, that the entire story of how one may convert *desire* into money cannot be told in one statement. The story will be complete, only when one has *mastered, assimilated,* and *begun to make use* of all the principles.

The great leaders of business, industry, finance, and the great artists, musicians, poets, and writers became great, because they developed the faculty of creative imagination.

Both the synthetic and creative faculties of imagination become more alert with use, just as any muscle or organ of the body develops through use.

Desire is only a thought, an impulse. It is nebulous and ephemeral. It is abstract, and of no value, until it has been transformed into its physical counterpart. While the synthetic imagination is the one which will be used most frequently, in the process of transforming the impulse of *desire* into money, you must keep in mind the fact, that you may face circumstances and situations which demand use of the creative imagination as well.

Your imaginative faculty may have become weak through inaction. It can be revived and made alert through *use*. This faculty does not die, though it may become quiescent through lack of use.

Center your attention, for the time being, on the development of the synthetic imagination, because this is the faculty which you will use more often in the process of converting desire into money.

Transformation of the intangible impulse, of *desire*, into the tangible reality, of *money*, calls for the use of a plan, or plans. These plans must be formed with the aid of the imagination, and mainly, with the synthetic faculty.

Read the entire book through, then come back to this chapter, and begin at once to put your imagination to work on the building of a plan, or plans, for the transformation of your *desire* into money. Detailed instructions for the building of plans have been given in almost every chapter. Carry out the instructions best suited to your needs, reduce your plan to writing, if you have not already done so. The moment you complete this, you will have *definitely* given concrete form to the intangible *desire*. Read the preceding sentence once more. Read it aloud, very slowly, and as you do so, remember that the moment you reduce the statement of your desire, and a plan for its realization, to writing, you have actually *taken the first* of a series of steps, which will enable you to convert the thought into its physical counterpart.

The earth on which you live, you, yourself, and every other material thing are the result of evolutionary change, through which microscopic bits of matter have been organized and arranged in an orderly fashion.

Moreover— and this statement is of stupendous importance— this earth, every one of the billions of individual cells of your body, and every atom of matter, began as an intangible form of energy.

Desire is thought impulse! Thought impulses are forms of energy. When you begin with the thought impulse, *desire*, to accumulate money, you are drafting into your service the same "stuff" that Nature used in creating this earth, and every material form in the universe, including the body and brain in which the thought impulses function.

As far as science has been able to determine, the entire universe consists of but two elements–matter and energy.

Through the combination of energy and matter, has been created everything perceptible to man, from the largest star which floats in the heavens, down to, and including man, himself.

You are now engaged in the task of trying to profit by Nature's method. You are (sincerely and earnestly, we hope), trying to adapt yourself to Nature's laws, by endeavoring to convert *desire* into its physical or monetary equivalent.

You can do it! It has been done before!

You can build a fortune through the aid of laws which are immutable. But, first, you must become familiar with these laws, and learn to *use* them. Through repetition, and by approaching the description of these principles from every conceivable angle, the author hopes to reveal to you the secret through which every great fortune has been accumulated. Strange and paradoxical as it may seem, the "secret" is *not a secret*. Nature, herself, advertises it in the earth on which we live, the stars, the planets suspended within our view, in the elements above and around us, in every blade of grass, and every form of life within our vision.

Nature advertises this "secret" in the terms of biology, in the conversion of a tiny cell, so small that it may be lost on the point of a pin, into the *human being* now reading this line. The conversion of desire into its physical equivalent is, certainly, no more miraculous!

Do not become discouraged if you do not fully comprehend all that has been stated. Unless you have long been a student of the mind, it is not to be expected that you will assimilate all that is in this chapter upon a first reading.

But you will, in time, make good progress.

The principles which follow will open the way for understanding of imagination. Assimilate that which you understand, as you read this philosophy for the first time, then, when you reread and study it, you will discover that something has happened to clarify it, and give you a broader understanding of the whole. Above all, *do not stop*, nor hesitate in your study of these principles until you have read the book at least *three* times, for 95 96 then, you will not want to stop.

How to Make Practical Use of Imagination

Ideas are the beginning points of all fortunes. Ideas are products of the imagination. Let us examine a few well known ideas which have yielded huge fortunes, with the hope that these illustrations will convey definite information concerning the method by which imagination may be used in accumulating riches.

The Enchanted Kettle

Fifty years ago, an old country doctor drove to town, hitched his horse, quietly slipped into a drug store by the back door, and began "dickering" with the young drug clerk.

His mission was destined to yield great wealth to many people. It was destined to bring to the South the most far-flung benefit since the Civil War.

For more than an hour, behind the prescription counter, the old doctor and the clerk talked in low tones. Then the doctor left. He went out to the buggy and brought back a large, old fashioned kettle, a big wooden paddle (used for stirring the contents of the kettle), and deposited them in the back of the store.

The clerk inspected the kettle, reached into his inside pocket, took out a roll of bills, and handed it over to the doctor. The roll contained exactly $500.00—the clerk's entire savings! The doctor handed over a small slip of paper on which was written a secret formula. The words on that small slip of paper were worth a King's ransom! But not to the doctor! Those magic words were needed to start the kettle to boiling, but neither the doctor nor the young clerk knew what fabulous fortunes were destined to flow from that kettle.

The old doctor was glad to sell the outfit for five hundred dollars. The money would pay off his debts, and give him freedom of mind. The clerk was taking a big chance by staking his entire life's savings on a mere scrap of paper and an old kettle! He never dreamed his investment would start a kettle to overflowing with gold that would surpass the miraculous performance of Aladdin's lamp.

What the clerk really purchased was an *idea*! The old kettle and the wooden paddle, and the secret message on a slip of paper were incidental. The strange performance of that kettle began to take place after the new owner mixed with the secret instructions an ingredient of which the doctor knew nothing.

Read this story carefully, give your imagination a test! See if you can discover what it was that the young man added to the secret message, which caused the kettle to overflow with gold. Remember, as you read, that this is not a story from Arabian Nights. Here you have a story of facts, stranger than fiction, facts which began in the form of an *idea*.

Let us take a look at the vast fortunes of gold this idea has produced. It has paid, and still pays huge fortunes to men and women all over the world, who distribute the contents of the kettle to millions of people.

The Old Kettle is now one of the world's largest consumers of sugar, thus providing jobs of a permanent nature to thousands of men and women engaged in growing sugar cane, and in refining and marketing sugar.

The Old Kettle consumes, annually, millions of glass bottles, providing jobs to huge numbers of glass workers.

The Old Kettle gives employment to an army of clerks, stenographers, copy writers, and advertising experts throughout the nation. It has brought fame and fortune to scores of artists who have created magnificent pictures describing the product.

The Old Kettle has converted a small Southern city into the business capital of the South, where it now benefits, directly, or indirectly, every business and practically every resident of the city. The influence of this idea now benefits every civilized country in the world, pouring out a continuous stream of gold to all who touch it.

Gold from the kettle built and maintains one of the most prominent colleges of the South, where thousands of young people receive the training essential for success.

The Old Kettle has done other marvelous things. All through the world depression, when factories, banks and business houses were folding up and quitting by the thousands, the owner of this Enchanted Kettle went marching on, giving continuous employment to an army of men and women all over the world, and paying out extra portions of gold to those who, long ago, had faith in the idea.

If the product of that old brass kettle could talk, it would tell thrilling tales of romance in every language. Romances of love, romances of business, romances of professional men and women who are daily being stimulated by it.

The author is sure of at least one such romance, for he was a part of it, and it all began not far from the very spot on which the drug clerk purchased the old kettle. It was here that the author met his wife, and it was she who first told him of the Enchanted Kettle. It was the product of that Kettle they were drinking when he asked her to accept him "for better or worse."

Now that you know the content of the Enchanted Kettle is a world famous drink, it is fitting that the author confess that the home city of the drink supplied him with a wife, also that the drink itself provides him with stimulation of thought without intoxication, and thereby it serves to give the refreshment of mind which an author must have to do his best work.

Whoever you are, wherever you may live, whatever occupation you may be engaged in, just remember in the future, every time you see the words "Coca-Cola," that its vast empire of wealth and influence grew out of a single *idea*, and that the mysterious ingredient the drug clerk— Asa Candler— mixed with the secret formula was. . . *imagination*

Stop and think of that, for a moment.

Remember, also, that the thirteen steps to riches, described in this book, were the media through which the influence of Coca-Cola has been extended to every city, town, village, and cross-roads of the world, and that ANY *idea* you may create, as sound and meritorious as Coca-Cola, has the possibility of duplicating the stupendous record of this world-wide thirst-killer.

Truly, thoughts are things, and their scope of operation is the world, itself.

What I Would Do If I Had a Million Dollars

This story proves the truth of that old saying, "where there's a will, there's a way." It was told to me by that beloved educator and clergyman, the late Frank W. Gunsaulus, who began his preaching career in the stockyards region of South Chicago.

While Dr. Gunsaulus was going through college, he observed many defects in our educational system, defects which he believed he could correct, if he were the head of a college. His deepest desire was to become the directing head of an educational institution in which young men and women would be taught to "learn by doing."

He made up his mind to organize a new college in which he could carry out his ideas, without being handicapped by orthodox methods of education.

He needed a million dollars to put the project across! Where was he to lay his hands on so large a sum of money? That was the question that absorbed most of this ambitious young preacher's thought.

But he couldn't seem to make any progress.

Every night he took that thought to bed with him. He got up with it in the morning. He took it with him everywhere he went. He turned it over and over in his mind until it became a consuming obsession with him. A million dollars is a lot of money. He recognized that fact, but he also recognized the truth that the only limitation is that which one sets up in one's own mind.

Being a philosopher as well as a preacher, Dr. Gunsaulus recognized, as do all who succeed in life, that *definiteness of purpose* is the starting point from which one must begin. He recognized, too, that definiteness of purpose takes on animation, life, and power when backed by a *burning desire* to translate that purpose into its material equivalent.

He knew all these great truths, yet he did not know where, or how to lay his hands on a million dollars. The natural procedure would have been to give up and quit, by saying, "Ah well, my idea is a good one, but I cannot do anything with it, because I never can procure the necessary million dollars." That is exactly what the majority of people would have said, but it is not what Dr. Gunsaulus said. What he said, and what he did are so important that I now introduce him, and let him speak for himself.

"One Saturday afternoon I sat in my room thinking of ways and means of raising the money to carry out my plans. For nearly two years, I had been thinking, but I had done nothing but think!

"The time had come for *action*!

"I made up my mind, then and there, that I would get the necessary million dollars within a week. How? I was not concerned about that. The main thing of importance was the decision to get the money within a specified time, and I want to tell you that the moment I reached a definite decision to get the money within a specified time, a strange feeling of assurance came over me, such as I had never before experienced. Something inside me seemed to say, 'Why didn't you reach that decision a long time ago? The money was waiting for you all the time!'

"Things began to happen in a hurry. I called the newspapers and announced I would preach a sermon the following morning, entitled, 'What I would do if I had a Million Dollars.'

"I went to work on the sermon immediately, but I must tell you, frankly, the task was not difficult, because I had been preparing that sermon for almost two years. The spirit back of it was a part of me!

"Long before midnight I had finished writing the sermon. I went to bed and slept with a feeling of confidence, for I could see myself already in. possession of the million dollars.

"Next morning I arose early, went into the bathroom, read the sermon, then knelt on my knees and asked that my sermon might come to the attention of someone who would supply the needed money.

"While I was praying I again had that feeling of assurance that the money would be forthcoming. In my excitement, I walked out without my sermon, and did not discover the oversight until I was in my pulpit and about ready to begin delivering it.

"It was too late to go back for my notes, and what a blessing that I couldn't go back! Instead, my own subconscious mind yielded the material I needed. When I arose to begin my sermon, I closed my eyes, and spoke with all my heart and soul of my dreams. I not only talked to my audience, but I fancy I talked also to God. I told what I would do with a million dollars if that amount were placed in my hands. I described the plan I had in mind for organizing a great educational institution, where young people would learn to do practical things, and at the same time develop their minds.

"When I had finished and sat down, a man slowly arose from his seat, about three rows from the rear, and made his way toward the pulpit. I wondered what he was going to do. He came into the pulpit, extended his hand, and said, 'Reverend, I liked your sermon. I believe you can do everything you said you would, if you had a million dollars. To prove that I believe in you and your sermon, if you will come to my office tomorrow morning, I will give you the million dollars. My name is Phillip D. Armour."'

Young Gunsaulus went to Mr. Armour's office and the million dollars was presented to him. With the money, he founded the Armour Institute of Technology.

That is more money than the majority of preachers ever see in an entire lifetime, yet the thought impulse back of the money was created m the young preacher's mind in a fraction of a minute. The necessary million dollars came as a result of an idea. Back of the idea was a *desire* which young Gunsaulus had been nursing in his mind for almost two years.

Observe this important fact... *he got the money within thirty-six hours after he reached a definite decision in his own mind to get it, and decided upon a definite plan for getting it!*

There was nothing new or unique about young Gunsaulus' vague thinking about a million dollars, and weakly hoping for it. Others before him, and many since his time, have had similar thoughts. But there was something very unique and different about the decision he reached on that memorable Saturday, when he put vagueness into the background, and definitely said, "I *will* get that money within a week!"

God seems to throw Himself on the side of the man who knows exactly what he wants, if he is determined to get *just that*!

Moreover, the principle through which Dr. Gunsaulus got his million dollars is still alive! It is available to you! This universal law is as workable today as it was when the young preacher made use of it so successfully. This book describes, step by step, the thirteen elements of this great law, and suggests how they may be put to use.

Observe that Asa Candler and Dr. Frank Gunsaulus had one characteristic in common. Both knew the astounding truth that *ideas can be transmuted into cash through the power of definite purpose, plus definite plans.*

If you are one of those who believe that hard work and honesty, alone, will bring riches, perish the thought! It is not true! Riches, when they come in huge quantities, are never the result of HARD work! Riches come, if they come at all, in response to definite demands, based upon the application of definite principles, and not by chance or luck. Generally speaking, an idea is an impulse of thought that impels action, by an appeal to the imagination. All master salesmen know that ideas can be sold where merchandise cannot. Ordinary salesmen do not know this—that is why they are "ordinary."

A publisher of books, which sell for a nickel, made a discovery that should be worth much to publishers generally. He learned that many people buy titles, and not contents of books. By merely changing the name of one book that was not moving, his sales on that book jumped upward more than a million copies. The inside of the book was not changed in any way. He merely ripped off the cover bearing the title that did not sell, and put on a new cover with a title that had "box-office" value.

That, as simple as it may seem, was an *idea*! It was *imagination.*

There is no standard price on ideas. The creator of ideas makes his own price, and, if he is smart, gets it.

The moving picture industry created a whole flock of millionaires. Most of them were men who couldn't create ideas— *but*— they had the imagination to recognize ideas when they saw them.

The next flock of millionaires will grow out of the radio business, which is new and not overburdened with men of keen imagination. The money will be made by those who discover or create new and more meritorious radio programed and have the imagination to recognize merit, and to give the radio listeners a chance to profit by it.

The sponsor! That unfortunate victim who now pays the cost of all radio "entertainment," soon will become idea conscious, and demand something for his money. The man who beats the sponsor to the draw, and supplies programed that render useful service, is the man who will become rich in this new industry.

Crooners and light chatter artists who now pollute the air with wisecracks and silly giggles, will go the way of all light timbers, and their places will be taken by real artists who interpret carefully planned programed which have been designed to service the minds of men, as well as provide entertainment.

Here is a wide open field of opportunity screaming its protest at the way it is being butchered, because of lack of imagination, and begging for rescue at any price. Above all, the thing that radio needs is new *ideas*!

If this new field of opportunity intrigues you, perhaps you might profit by the suggestion that the successful radio programed of the future will give more attention to creating "buyer" audiences, and less attention to "listener" audiences. Stated more plainly, the builder of radio programed who succeeds in the future, must find practical ways to convert "listeners" into "buyers." Moreover, the successful producer of radio programed in the future must key his features so that he can definitely show its effect upon the audience.

Sponsors are becoming a bit weary of buying glib selling talks, based upon statements grabbed out of thin air. They want, and in the future will demand, indisputable proof that the Whoosit programed not only gives millions of people the silliest giggle ever, but that the silly giggler can sell merchandise!

Another thing that might as well be understood by those who contemplate entering this new field of opportunity, radio advertising is going to be handled by an entirely new group of advertising experts, separate and distinct from the old time newspaper and magazine advertising agency men. The old timers in the advertising game cannot read the modern radio scripts, because they have been schooled to *see* ideas. The new radio technique demands men who can interpret ideas from a written manuscript in terms of *sound*! It cost the author a year of hard labor, and many thousands of dollars to learn this.

Radio, right now, is about where the moving pictures were, when Mary Pickford and her curls first appeared on the screen. There is plenty of room in radio for those who can produce or recognize *ideas*.

If the foregoing comment on the opportunities of radio has not started your idea factory to work, you had better forget it. Your opportunity is in some other field. If the comment intrigued you in the slightest degree, then go further into it, and you may find the one *idea* you need to round out your career.

Never let it discourage you if you have no experience in radio. Andrew Carnegie knew very little about making steel— I have Carnegie's own word for this—but he made practical use of two of the principles described in this book, and made the steel business yield him a fortune.

The story of practically every great fortune starts with the day when a creator of ideas and a seller of ideas got together and worked in harmony. Carnegie surrounded himself with men who could do all that he could not do. Men who created ideas, and men who put ideas into operation, and made himself and the others fabulously rich.

Millions of people go through life hoping for favorable "breaks." Perhaps a favorable break can get one an opportunity, but the safest plan is not to depend upon luck. It was a favorable "break" that gave me the biggest opportunity of my life— but— twenty-five years of determined effort had to be devoted to that opportunity before it became an asset.

The "break" consisted of my good fortune in meeting and gaining the cooperation of Andrew Carnegie. On that occasion Carnegie planted in my mind the idea of organizing the principles of achievement into a philosophy of success. Thousands of people have profited by the discoveries made in the twenty-five years of research, and several fortunes have been accumulated through the application of the philosophy. The beginning was simple. It was an *idea* which anyone might have developed.

The favorable break came through Carnegie, but what about the *Determination, definiteness of purpose*, and the *desire to attain the goal*, and the *persistent effort of twenty-five years*? It was no ordinary *desire* that survived disappointment, discouragement, temporary defeat, criticism, and the constant reminding of "waste of time." It was a *burning desire*! *An obsession*!

When the idea was first planted in my mind by Mr. Carnegie, it was coaxed, nursed, and enticed to remain alive. Gradually, the idea became a giant under its own power, and it coaxed, nursed, and drove me. Ideas are like that. First you give life and action and guidance to ideas, then they take on power of their own and sweep aside all opposition.

Ideas are intangible forces, but they have more power than the physical brains that give birth to them. They have the power to live on, after the brain that creates them has returned to dust. For example, take the power of Christianity. That began with a simple idea, born in the brain of Christ. Its chief tenet was, "do unto others as you would have others do unto you." Christ has gone back to the source from whence He came, but His *idea* goes marching on. Some day, it may grow up, and come into its own, then it will have fulfilled Christ's deepest *desire*. The *idea* has been developing only two thousand years. Give it time!

Success requires no explanations
Failure permits no alibis

Chapter Six: Organized Planning

The Crystallization of Desire into Action: the Sixth Step Toward Riches

You have learned that everything man creates or acquires, begins in the form of *desire*, that desire is taken on the first lap of its journey, from the abstract to the concrete, into the workshop of the *imagination*, where *plans* for its transition are created and organized.

In Chapter two, you were instructed to take six definite, practical steps, as your first move in translating the desire for money into its monetary equivalent. One of these steps is the formation of a *definite*, practical plan, or plans, through which this transformation may be made. You will now be instructed how to build plans which will be practical, viz:—

(a) Ally yourself with a group of as many people as you may need for the creation, and carrying out of your plan, or plans for the accumulation of money— making use of the "Master Mind" principle described in a later chapter. (Compliance with this instruction is absolutely essential. Do not neglect it.)

(b) Before forming your "Master Mind" alliance, decide what advantages, and benefits, you may offer the individual members of your group, in return for their cooperation. No one will work indefinitely without some form of compensation. No intelligent person will either request or expect another to work without adequate compensation, although this may not always be in the form of money.

(c) Arrange to meet with the members of your "Master Mind" group at least twice a week, and more often if possible, until you have jointly perfected the necessary plan, or plans for the accumulation of money.

(d) Maintain *perfect harmony* between yourself and every member of your "Master Mind" group. If you fail to carry out this instruction to the letter, you may expect to meet with failure. The "Master Mind" principle cannot obtain where *perfect harmony* does not prevail.

Keep in mind these facts:—

First. You are engaged in an undertaking of major importance to you. To be sure of success, you must have plans which are faultless.

Second. You must have the advantage of the experience, education, native ability and imagination of other minds. This is in harmony with the methods followed by every person who has accumulated a great fortune.

No individual has sufficient experience, education, native ability, and knowledge to insure the accumulation of a great fortune, without the cooperation of other people. Every plan you adopt, in your endeavor to accumulate wealth, should be the joint creation of yourself and every other member of your "Master Mind" group. You may originate your own plans, either in whole or in part, but *see that those plans are checked, and approved by the members of your "master mind" alliance.*

If the first plan which you adopt does not work successfully, replace it with a new plan, if this new plan fails to work, replace it, in turn with still another, and so on, until you find a plan which DOES WORK. Right here is the point at which the majority of men meet with failure, because of their lack of *persistence* in creating new plans to take the place of those which fail.

The most intelligent man living cannot succeed in accumulating money– nor in any other undertaking– without plans which are practical and workable. Just keep this fact in mind, and remember when your plans fail, that temporary defeat is not permanent failure. It may only mean that your plans have not been sound. Build other plans. Start all over again.

Thomas A. Edison "failed" ten thousand times before he perfected the incandescent electric light bulb. That is– he met with temporary defeat ten thousand times, before his efforts were crowned with success.

Temporary defeat should mean only one thing, the certain knowledge that there is something wrong with your plan. Millions of men go through life in misery and poverty, because they lack a sound plan through which to accumulate a fortune.

Henry Ford accumulated a fortune, not because of his superior mind, but because he adopted and followed a *plan* which proved to be sound. A thousand men could be pointed out, each with a better education than Ford's, yet each of whom lives in poverty, because he does not possess the *right* plan for the accumulation of money.

Your achievement can be no greater than your *plans* are sound. That may seem to be an axiomatic statement, but it is true. Samuel Insull lost his fortune of over one hundred million dollars. The Insull fortune was built on plans which were sound. The business depression forced Mr. Insull to *Change his plans*; and the *change* brought "temporary defeat," because his new plans were *Not sound.* Mr. Insull is now an old man, he may, consequently, accept "failure" instead of "temporary defeat," but if his experience turns out to be *failure*, it will be for the reason that he lacks the fire of *persistence* to rebuild his plans.

No man is ever whipped, until he *quits*– in his own mind.

This fact will be repeated many times, because it is so easy to "take the count" at the first sign of defeat.

James J. Hill met with temporary defeat when he first endeavored to raise the necessary capital to build a railroad from the East to the West, but he, too turned defeat into victory through new plans.

Henry Ford met with temporary defeat, not only at the beginning of his automobile career, but after he had gone far toward the top. He created new plans, and went marching on to financial victory.

We see men who have accumulated great fortunes, but we often recognize only their triumph, overlooking the temporary defeats which they had to surmount before "arriving."

No follower of this philosophy can reasonably expect to accumulate a fortune without experiencing "temporary defeat." When defeat comes, accept it as a signal that your plans are not sound, rebuild those plans, and set sail once more toward your coveted goal. If you give up before your goal has been reached, you are a "quitter."

A quitter never wins–and– a winner never quits.

Lift this sentence out, write it on a piece of paper in letters an inch high, and place it where you will see it every night before you go to sleep, and every morning before you go to work.

When you begin to select members for your "Master Mind" group, endeavor to select those who do not take defeat seriously.

Some people foolishly believe that only *money* can make money. This is not true! *desire*, transmuted into its monetary equivalent, through the principles laid down here, is the agency through which money is "made." Money, of itself, is nothing but inert matter. It cannot move, think, or talk, but it can "hear" when a man who *desires* it, calls it to come!

Planning the Sale of Services

The remainder of this chapter has been given over to a description of ways and means of marketing personal services. The information here conveyed will be of practical help to any person having any form of personal services to market, but it will be of priceless benefit to those who aspire to leadership in their chosen occupations.

Intelligent planning is essential for success in any undertaking designed to accumulate riches. Here will be found detailed instructions to those who must begin the accumulation of riches by selling personal services.

It should be encouraging to know that practically all the great fortunes began in the form of compensation for personal services, or from the sale of *ideas*. What else, except ideas and personal services, would one not possessed of property have to give in return for riches?

Broadly speaking, there are two types of people in the world. One type is known as *leaders*, and the other as *Followers*. Decide at the outset whether you intend to become a leader in your chosen calling, or remain a follower. The difference in compensation is vast. The follower cannot reasonably expect the compensation to which a leader is entitled, although many followers make the mistake of expecting such pay.

It is no disgrace to be a follower. On the other hand, it is no credit to remain a follower. Most great leaders began in the capacity of followers. They became great leaders because they were *intelligent followers*. With few exceptions, the man who cannot follow a leader intelligently, cannot become an efficient leader. The man who can follow a leader most efficiently, is usually the man who develops into leadership most rapidly. An intelligent follower has many advantages, among them the *opportunity to acquire knowledge from his leader.*

The Major Attributes of Leadership: the Following Are Important Factors of Leadership:–

1. *Unwavering courage* based upon knowledge of self, and of one's occupation. No follower wishes to be dominated by a leader who lacks self-confidence and courage. No intelligent follower will be dominated by such a leader very long.

2. *Self-control.* The man who cannot control himself, can never control others. Self-control sets a mighty example for one's followers, which the more intelligent will emulate.

3. A *keen sense of justice.* Without a sense of fairness and justice, no leader can command and retain the respect of his followers.

4. *Definiteness of decision.* The man who wavers in his decisions, shows that he is not sure of himself.

He cannot lead others successfully.

5. *Definiteness of plans.* The successful leader must plan his work, and work his plan. A leader who moves by guesswork, without practical, definite plans, is comparable to a ship without a rudder. Sooner or later he will land on the rocks.

6. *The habit of doing more than paid for.* One of the penalties of leadership is the necessity of willingness, upon the part of the leader, to do more than he requires of his followers.

7. *A pleasing personality.* No slovenly, careless person can become a successful leader. Leadership calls for respect. Followers will not respect a leader who does not grade high on all of the factors of a Pleasing Personality.

8. *Sympathy and understanding.* The successful leader must be in sympathy with his followers. Moreover, he must understand them and their problems.

9. *Mastery of detail.* Successful leadership calls for mastery of details of the leader's position.

10. *Willingness to assume full responsibility.* The successful leader must be willing to assume responsibility for the mistakes and the shortcomings of his followers. If he tries to shift this responsibility, he will not remain the leader. If one of his followers makes a mistake, and shows himself incompetent, the leader must consider that it is he who failed.

11. *Cooperation.* The successful leader must understand, and apply the principle of cooperative effort and be able to induce his followers to do the same. Leadership calls for *power*, and power calls for *cooperation*.

There are two forms of Leadership. The first, and by far the most effective, is *Leadership by consent* of, and with the sympathy of the followers. The second is *leadership by force*, without the consent and sympathy of the followers.

History is filled with evidences that Leadership by Force cannot endure. The downfall and disappearance of "Dictators" and kings is significant. It means that people will not follow forced leadership indefinitely.

The world has just entered a new era of relationship between leaders and followers, which very clearly calls for new leaders, and a new brand of leadership in business and industry. Those who belong to the old school of leadership-by-force, must acquire an understanding of the new brand of leadership (cooperation) or be relegated to the rank and file of the followers. There is no other way out for them.

The relationship of employer and employee, or of leader and follower, in the future, will be one of mutual cooperation, based upon an equitable division of the profits of business. In the future, the relationship of employer and employee will be more like a partnership than it has been in the past.

Napoleon, Kaiser Wilhelm of Germany, the Czar of Russia, and the King of Spain were examples of leadership by force. Their leadership passed. Without much difficulty, one might point to the prototypes of these ex-leaders, among the business, financial, and labor leaders of America who have been dethroned or slated to go. Leadership-by-consent of the followers is the only brand which can endure!

Men may follow the forced leadership temporarily, but they will not do so willingly.

The new brand of *leadership* will embrace the eleven factors of leadership, described in this chapter, as well as some other factors. The man who makes these the basis of his leadership, will find abundant opportunity to lead in any walk of life. The depression was prolonged, largely, because the world lacked *leadership* of the new brand. At the end of the depression, the demand for leaders who are competent to apply the new methods of leadership has greatly exceeded the supply. Some of the old type of leaders will reform and adapt themselves to the new brand of leadership, but generally speaking, the world will have to look for new timber for its leadership. This necessity may be your *opportunity*!

The 10 Major Causes of Failure in Leadership

We come now to the major faults of leaders who fail, because it is just as essential to know *what not to do* as it is to know what to do.

1. *Inability to organize details.* Efficient leadership calls for ability to organize and to master details. No genuine leader is ever "too busy" to do anything which may be required of him in his capacity as leader. When a man, whether he is a leader or follower, admits that he is "too busy" to change his plans, or to give attention to any emergency, he admits his inefficiency. The successful leader must be the master of all details connected with his position. That means, of course, that he must acquire the habit of relegating details to capable lieutenants.

2. *Unwillingness to render humble service.* Truly great leaders are willing, when occasion demands, to perform any sort of labor which they would ask another to perform. "The greatest among ye shall be the servant of all" is a truth which all able leaders observe and respect.

3. *Expectation of pay for what they "know" instead of what they do with that which they know.* The world does not pay men for that which they "know." It pays them for what they *do*, or induce others to do.

4. *Fear of competition from followers.* The leader who fears that one of his followers may take his position is practically sure to realize that fear sooner or later. The able leader trains understudies to whom he may delegate, at will, any of the details of his position. Only in this way may a leader multiply himself and prepare himself to be at many places, and give attention to many things at one time. It is an eternal truth that men receive more pay for their *ability to get others to perform*, than they could possibly earn by their own efforts. An efficient leader may, through his knowledge of his job and the magnetism of his personality, greatly increase the efficiency of others, and induce them to render more service and better service than they could render without his aid.

5. *Lack of imagination.* Without imagination, the leader is incapable of meeting emergencies, and of creating plans by which to guide his followers efficiently.

6. *Selfishness.* The leader who claims all the honor for the work of his followers, is sure to be met by resentment. The really great leader *claims none of the honors.* He is contented to see the honors, when there are any, go to his followers, because he knows that most men will work harder for commendation and recognition than they will for money alone.

7. *Intemperance.* Followers do not respect an intemperate leader. Moreover, intemperance in any of its various forms, destroys the endurance and the vitality of all who indulge in it.

8. *Disloyalty.* Perhaps this should have come at the head of the list. The leader who is not loyal to his trust, and to his associates, those above him, and those below him, cannot long maintain his leadership. Disloyalty marks one as being less than the dust of the earth, and brings down on one's head the contempt he deserves. Lack of loyalty is one of the major causes of failure in every walk of life.

9. *Emphasis of the "authority" of leadership.* The efficient leader leads by encouraging, and not by trying to instil fear in the hearts of his followers. The leader who tries to impress his followers with his "authority" comes within the category of leadership through *force.* If a leader is a real leader, he will have no need to advertise that fact except by his conduct– his sympathy, understanding, fairness, and a demonstration that he knows his job.

10. *Emphasis of title.* The competent leader requires no "title" to give him the respect of his followers. The man who makes too much over his title generally has little else to emphasize. The doors to the office of the real leader are open to all who wish to enter, and his working quarters are free from formality or ostentation.

These are among the more common of the causes of failure in leadership. Any one of these faults is sufficient to induce failure. Study the list carefully if you aspire to leadership, and make sure that you are free of these faults.

Some Fertile Fields in Which "New Leadership" Will Be Required

Before leaving this chapter, your attention is called to a few of the fertile fields in which there has been a decline of leadership, and in which the new type of leader may find an abundance of *opportunity.*

First. In the field of politics there is a most insistent demand for new leaders; a demand which indicates nothing less than an emergency. The majority of politicians have, seemingly, become high-grade, legalized racketeers. They have increased taxes and debauched the machinery of industry and business until the people can no longer stand the burden.

Second. The banking business is undergoing a reform. The leaders in this field have almost entirely lost the confidence of the public. Already the bankers have sensed the need of reform, and they have begun it.

Third. Industry calls for new leaders. The old type of leaders thought and moved in terms of dividends instead of thinking and moving in terms of human equations! The future leader in industry, to endure, must regard himself as a quasi-public official whose duty it is to manage his trust in such a way that it will work hardship on no individual, or group of individuals. Exploitation of working men is a thing of the past. Let the man who aspires to leadership in the field of business, industry, and labor remember this.

Fourth. The religious leader of the future will be forced to give more attention to the temporal needs of his followers, in the solution of their economic and personal problems of the present, and less attention to the dead past, and the yet unborn future.

Fifth. In the professions of law, medicine, and education, a new brand of leadership, and to some extent, new leaders will become a necessity. This is especially true in the field of education. The leader in that field must, in the future, find ways and means of teaching people *how to apply* the knowledge they receive in school. He must deal more with *practice* and less with *theory.*

Sixth. New leaders will be required in the field of Journalism. Newspapers of the future, to be conducted successfully, must be divorced from "special privilege" and relieved from the subsidy of advertising. They must cease to be organs of propaganda for the interests which patronize their advertising columns. The type of newspaper which publishes scandal and lewd pictures will eventually go the way of all forces which debauch the human mind.

These are but a few of the fields in which opportunities for new leaders and a new brand of leadership are now available. The world is undergoing a rapid change. This means that the media through which the changes in human habits are promoted, must be adapted to the changes. The media here described, are the ones which, more than any others, determine the trend of civilization.

When and How to Apply for a Position

The information described here is the net result of many years of experience during which thousands of men and women were helped to market their services effectively. It can, therefore, be relied upon as sound and practical.

Media Through Which Services May Be Marketed

Experience has proved that the following media offer the most direct and effective methods of bringing the buyer and seller of personal services together.

1. *Employment bureaus.* Care must be taken to select only reputable bureaus, the management of which can show adequate records of achievement of satisfactory results. There are comparatively few such bureaus.

2. *Advertising* in newspapers, trade journals, magazines, and radio. Classified advertising may usually be relied upon to produce satisfactory results in the case of those who apply for clerical or ordinary salaried positions. Display advertising is more desirable in the case of those who seek executive connections, the copy to appear in the section of the paper which is most apt to come to the attention of the class of employer being sought. The copy should be prepared by an expert, who understands how to inject sufficient selling qualities to produce replies.

3. *Personal letters of application,* directed to particular firms or individuals most apt to need such services as are being offered. Letters should be neatly typed, *always,* and signed by hand. With the letter, should be sent a complete "brief" or outline of the applicant's qualifications. Both the letter of application and the brief of experience or qualifications should be prepared by an expert. (See instructions as to information to be supplied).

4. *Application through personal acquaintances.* When possible, the applicant should endeavor to approach prospective employers through some mutual acquaintance. This method of approach is particularly advantageous in the case of those who seek executive connections and do not wish to appear to be "peddling" themselves.

5. *Application in person.* In some instances, it may be more effective if the applicant offers personally, his services to prospective employers, in which event a complete written statement of qualifications for the position should be presented, for the reason that prospective employers often wish to discuss with associates, one's record.

Information to Be Supplied in a Written "Brief"

This brief should be prepared as carefully as a lawyer would prepare the brief of a case to be tried m court. Unless the applicant is experienced in the preparation of such briefs, an expert should be consulted, and his services enlisted for this purpose. Successful merchants employ men and women who understand the art and the psychology of advertising to present the merits of their merchandise. One who has personal services for sale should do the same. The following information should appear in the brief:

1. Education. State briefly, but definitely, what schooling you have had, and in what subjects you specialized in school, giving the reasons for that specialization.

2. Experience. If you have had experience in connection with positions similar to the one you seek, describe it fully, state names and addresses of former employers. Be sure to bring out clearly any special experience you may have had which would equip you to fill the position you seek.

3. References. Practically every business firm desires to know all about the previous records, antecedents, etc., of prospective employees who seek positions of responsibility. Attach to your brief photostatic copies of letters from:

a. Former employers
b. Teachers under whom you studied
c. Prominent people whose judgement may be relied upon.

4. Photograph of self. Attach to your brief a recent, unmounted photograph of yourself.

5. Apply for a specific position. Avoid application for a position without describing *exactly* what particular position you seek. Never apply for "just a position." That indicates you lack specialized qualifications.

6. State your qualifications for the particular position for which you apply. Give full details as to the reason you believe you are qualified for the particular position you seek. This is *the application*. It will determine, more than anything else, what consideration you receive.

7. Offer to go to work on probation. In the majority of instances if you are determined to have the position for which you apply, it will be most effective if you offer to work for a week, or a month, or for a sufficient length of time to enable your prospective employer to judge your value *without pay*. This may appear to be a radical suggestion, but experience has proved that it seldom fails to win at least a trial. If you are *sure of your qualifications*, a trial is all you need. Incidentally, such an offer indicates that you have confidence in your ability to fill the position you seek. It is most convincing. If your offer is accepted, and you make good, more than likely you will be paid for your "probation" period. Make clear the fact that your offer is based upon:

a. Your confidence in your ability to fill the position.
b. Your confidence in your prospective employer's decision to employ you after trial.
c. Your *determination* to have the position you seek.

8. Knowledge of your prospective employer's business. Before applying for a position, do sufficient research in connection with the business to familiarize yourself thoroughly with that business, and indicate in your brief the knowledge you have acquired in this field. This will be impressive, as it will indicate that you have imagination, and a real interest in the position you seek.

Remember that it is not the lawyer who knows the most law, but the one who best prepares his case, who wins. If your "case" is properly prepared and presented, your victory will have been more than half won at the outset.

Do not be afraid of making your brief too long. Employers are just as much interested in purchasing the services of well-qualified applicants as you are in securing employment. In fact, the success of most successful employers is due, in the main, to their ability to select well-qualified lieutenants. They want all the information available.

Remember another thing; neatness in the preparation of your brief will indicate that you are a painstaking person. I have helped to prepare briefs for clients which were so striking and out of the ordinary that they resulted in the employment of the applicant without a personal interview.

When your brief has been completed, have it neatly bound by an experienced binder, and lettered by an artist, or printer similar to the following:

brief of the qualifications of Robert K. Smith applying for the position of Private Secretary to The President of the Blank Company, Inc. Change names each time brief is shown.

This personal touch is sure to command attention. Have your brief neatly typed or mimeographed on the finest paper you can obtain, and bound with a heavy paper of the book-cover variety, the binder to be changed, and the proper firm name to be inserted if it is to be shown to more than one company. Your photograph should be pasted on one of the pages of your brief. Follow these instructions to the letter, improving upon them wherever your imagination suggests.

Successful salesmen groom themselves with care. They understand that first impressions are lasting. Your brief is your salesman. Give it a good suit of clothes, so it will stand out in bold contrast to anything your prospective employer ever saw, in the way of an application for a position. If the position you seek is worth having, it is worth going after with care. Moreover, if you sell yourself to an employer in a manner that impresses him with your individuality, you probably will receive more money for your services from the very start, than you would if you applied for employment in the usual conventional way.

If you seek employment through an advertising agency, or an employment agency, have the agent use copies of your brief in marketing your services. This will help to gain preference for you, both with the agent, and the prospective employers.

How to Get the Exact Position You Desire

Everyone enjoys doing the kind of work for which he is best suited. An artist loves to work with paints, a craftsman with his hands, a writer loves to write. Those with less definite talents have their preferences for certain fields of business and industry. If America does anything well, it offers a full range of occupations, tilling the soil, manufacturing, marketing, and the professions.

First. Decide *exactly* what kind of a job you want. If the job doesn't already exist, perhaps you can create it.

Second. Choose the company, or individual for whom you wish to work.

Third. Study your prospective employer, as to policies, personnel, and chances of advancement.

Fourth. By analysis of yourself, your talents and capabilities, figure *what you can offer*, and plan ways and means of giving advantages, services, developments, ideas that you believe you can successfully deliver.

Fifth. Forget about "a job." Forget whether or not there is an opening. Forget the usual routine of "have you got a job for me?" Concentrate on what you can give.

Sixth. Once you have your plan in mind, arrange with an experienced writer to put it on paper in neat form, and in full detail.

Seventh. Present it to the proper person with authority and he will do the rest. Every company is looking for men who can give something of value, whether it be ideas, services, or "connections." Every company has room for the man who has a definite plan of action which is to the advantage of that company.

This line of procedure may take a few days or weeks of extra time, but the difference in income, in advancement, and in gaining recognition will save years of hard work at small pay. It has many advantages, the main one being that it will often save from one to five years of time in reaching a chosen goal.

Every person who starts, or "gets in" half way up the ladder, does so by deliberate and careful planning, (excepting, of course, the Boss' son).

The New Way of Marketing Services "Jobs" Are Now "Partnerships"

Men and women who market their services to best advantage in the future, must recognize the stupendous change which has taken place in connection with the relationship between employer and employee.

In the future, the "Golden Rule," and not the "Rule of Gold" will be the dominating factor in the marketing of merchandise as well as personal services. The future relationship between employers and their employees will be more in the nature of a partnership consisting of:

a. The employer

b. The employee

c. The public they serve

This new way of marketing personal services is called new for many reasons, first, both the employer and the employee of the future will be considered as fellow-employees whose business it will be to *serve the public efficiently*. In times past, employers, and employees have bartered among themselves, driving the best bargains they could with one another, not considering that in the final analysis they were, in reality, *bargaining at the expense of the third party, the public they served.*

The depression served as a mighty protest from an injured public, whose rights had been trampled upon in every direction by those who were clamoring for individual advantages and profits. When the debris of the depression shall have been cleared away, and business shall have been once again restored to balance, both employers and employees will recognize that they are *no longer privileged to drive bargains at the expense of those whom they serve.* The real employer of the future will be the public. This should be kept uppermost in mind by every person seeking to market personal services effectively.

Nearly every railroad in America is in financial difficulty. Who does not remember the day when, if a citizen enquired at the ticket office, the time of departure of a train, he was abruptly referred to the bulletin board instead of being politely given the information?

The street car companies have experienced a "change of times" also. There was a time not so very long ago when street car conductors took pride in giving argument to passengers. Many of the street car tracks have been removed and passengers ride on a bus, whose driver is "the last word in politeness."

All over the country street car tracks are rusting from abandonment, or have been taken up. Where ever street cars are still in operation, passengers may now ride without argument, and one may even hail the car in the middle of the block, and the motorman will *obligingly* pick him up.

How times have changed! That is just the point I am trying to emphasize. *Times have changed!* Moreover, the change is reflected not merely in railroad offices and on street cars, but in other walks of life as well. The "public-be-damned" policy is now passé. It has been supplanted by the "we-are-obligingly-at-your-service, sir," policy.

The bankers have learned a thing or two during this rapid change which has taken place during the past few years. Impoliteness on the part of a bank official, or bank employee today is as rare as it was conspicuous a dozen years ago. In the years past, some bankers (not all of them, of course), carried an atmosphere of austerity which gave every would-be borrower a chill when he even thought of approaching his banker for a loan.

The thousands of bank failures during the depression had the effect of removing the mahogany doors behind which bankers formerly barricaded themselves. They now sit at desks in the open, where they may be seen and approached at will by any depositor, or by anyone who wishes to see them, and the whole atmosphere of the bank is one of courtesy and understanding.

It used to be customary for customers to have to stand and wait at the corner grocery until the clerks were through passing the time of day with friends, and the proprietor had finished making up his bank deposit, before being waited upon. Chain stores, managed by *courteous men* who do everything in the way of service, short of shining the customer's shoes, have *pushed the old-time merchants into the background. Time marches on!*

"Courtesy" and "Service" are the watch-words of merchandising today, and apply to the person who is marketing personal services even more directly than to the employer whom he serves, because, in the final analysis, both the employer and his employee are *Employed by the public they serve.* If they fail to serve well, they pay by the loss of their privilege of serving.

We can all remember the time when the gas-meter reader pounded on the door hard enough to break the panels. When the door was opened, he pushed his way in, uninvited, with a scowl on his face which plainly said, "what-the-hell-did-you-keep-me-waiting- for?" All that has undergone a change. The meter-man now conducts himself as a gentleman who is "delighted-to-be-at-your-service- sir." Before the gas companies learned that their scowling meter-men were accumulating liabilities never to be cleared away, the polite salesmen of oil burners came along and did a land office business.

During the depression, I spent several months in the anthracite coal region of Pennsylvania, studying conditions which all but destroyed the coal industry. Among several very significant discoveries, was the fact that greed on the part of operators and their employees was the chief cause of the loss of business for the operators, and loss of jobs for the miners.

Through the pressure of a group of overzealous labor leaders, representing the employees, and the greed for profits on the part of the operators, the anthracite business suddenly dwindled. The coal operators and their employees drove sharp bargains with one another, adding the cost of the "bargaining" to the price of the coal, until, finally, they discovered they had *built up a wonderful business for the manufacturers of oil burning outfits and the producers of crude oil.*

"The wages of sin is death!" Many have read this in the Bible, but few have discovered its meaning. Now, and for several years, the entire world has been listening *by force*, to a sermon which might well be called "*whatsoever a man soweth, that shall he also reap.*"

Nothing as widespread and effective as the depression could possibly be "just a coincidence." Behind the depression was a *cause.* Nothing ever happens without a *cause.* In the main, the cause of the depression is traceable directly to the worldwide habit of trying to *reap* without *sowing.*

This should not be mistaken to mean that the depression represents a crop which the world is being *forced* to reap without having *sown.* The trouble is that the world sowed the wrong sort of seed. Any farmer knows he cannot sow the seed of thistles, and reap a harvest of grain. Beginning at the outbreak of the world war, the people of the world began to sow the seed of service inadequate in both quality and quantity. Nearly everyone was engaged in the pastime of trying to *get without giving.*

These illustrations are brought to the attention of those who have personal services to market, to show that we are where we are, and what we are, because of our own conduct! If there is a principle of cause and effect, which controls business, finance, and transportation, this same principle controls individuals and determines their economic status.

What Is Your "QQS" Rating?

The causes of success in marketing services *effectively* and permanently, have been clearly described. Unless those causes are studied, analyzed, understood and *applied*, no man can market his services effectively and permanently. Every person must be his own salesman of personal services. The *quality* and the *quantity* of service rendered, and the *soirit* in which it is rendered, determine to a large extent, the price, and the duration of employment. To market Personal services effectively, (which means a permanent market, at a satisfactory price, under pleasant conditions), one must adopt and follow the "QQS" formula which means that *quality*, plus *quantity*, plus the proper *spirit* of cooperation, equals perfect salesmanship of service. Remember the "QQS" formula, but do more–*apply it as a habit!*

Let us analyze the formula to make sure we understand exactly what it means.

1. *quality* of service shall be construed to mean the performance of every detail, in connection with your position, in the most efficient manner possible, with the object of greater efficiency always in mind.

2. *quantity* of service shall be understood to mean the *habit* of rendering all the service of which you are capable, at all times, with the purpose of increasing the amount of service rendered as greater skill is developed through practice and experience. Emphasis is again placed on the word *habit*.

3. *spirit* of service shall be construed to mean the *habit* of agreeable, harmonious conduct which will induce cooperation from associates and fellow employees.

Adequacy of *quality* and *quantity* of service is not sufficient to maintain a permanent market for your services. The conduct, or the *spirit* in which you deliver service, is a strong determining factor in connection with both the price you receive, and the duration of employment.

Andrew Carnegie stressed this point more than others in connection with his description of the factors which lead to success in the marketing of personal services. He emphasized again, and again, the necessity for *harmonious conduct*. He stressed the fact that he would not retain any man, no matter how great a *quantity*, or how efficient the *quality* of his work, unless he worked in a spirit of *harmony*. Mr. Carnegie insisted upon men being *agreeable*.

To prove that he placed a high value upon this quality, he permitted many men who conformed to his standards to become very wealthy. Those who did not conform, had to make room for others.

The importance of a pleasing personality has been stressed, because it is a factor which enables one to render service in the proper *spirit*. If one has a personality which *pleases*, and renders service in a spirit of *harmony*, these assets often make up for deficiencies in both the *quality*, and the *quantity* of service one renders. Nothing, however, can be *successfully substituted for pleasing conduct*.

The Capital Value of Your Services

The person whose income is derived entirely from the sale of personal services is no less a merchant than the man who sells commodities, and it might well be added, such a person is subject to *exactly the same rules* of conduct as the merchant who sells merchandise.

This has been emphasized, because the majority of people who live by the sale of personal services make the mistake of considering themselves free from the rules of conduct, and the responsibilities attached to those who are engaged in marketing commodities.

The new way of marketing services has practically forced both employer and. employee into partnership alliances, through which both take into consideration the rights of the third party, *The public they serve.*

The day of the "go-getter" has passed. He has been supplanted by the "go-giver." High-pressure methods in business finally blew the lid off. There will never be the need to put the lid back on, because, in the future, business will be conducted by methods that will require no pressure.

The actual capital value of your brains may be determined by the amount of income you can produce (by marketing your services). A fair estimate of the capital value of your services may be made by multiplying your annual income by sixteen and two-thirds, as it is reasonable to estimate that your annual income represents six percent of your capital value. Money rents for 6% per annum. Money is worth no more than brains. It is often worth much less.

Competent "brains," if effectively marketed, represent a much more desirable form of capital than that which is required to conduct a business dealing in commodities, because "brains" are a form of capital which cannot be permanently depreciated through depressions, nor can this form of capital be stolen or spent. Moreover, the money which is essential for the conduct of business is as worthless as a sand dune, until it has been mixed with efficient "brains."

The Thirty Major Causes of Failure: How Many of These Are Holding You Back?

Life's greatest tragedy consists of men and women who earnestly try, and fail! The tragedy lies in the overwhelmingly large majority of people who fail, as compared to the few who succeed.

I have had the privilege of analyzing several thousand men and women, 98% of whom were classed as "failures." There is something radically wrong with a civilization, and a system of education, which permit 98% of the people to go through life as failures. But I did not write this book for the purpose of moralizing on the rights and wrongs of the world; that would require a book a hundred times the size of this one.

My analysis work proved that there are thirty major reasons for failure, and thirteen major principles through which people accumulate fortunes. In this chapter, a description of the thirty major causes of failure will be given. As you go over the list, check yourself by it, point by point, for the purpose of discovering how many of these causes-of-failure stand between you and success.

1. *Unfavorable hereditary background.* There is but little, if anything, which can be done for people who are born with a deficiency in brain power. This philosophy offers but one method of bridging this weakness— through the aid of the Master Mind. Observe with profit, however, that this is the *only* one of the thirty causes of failure which may not be easily corrected by any individual.

2. *Lack of a well-defined purpose in life.* There is no hope of success for the person who does not have a central purpose, or definite goal at which to aim. Ninety-eight out of every hundred of those whom I have analyzed, had no such aim. Perhaps this was the

3. *Lack of ambition to aim above mediocrity.* We offer no hope for the person who is so indifferent as not to want to get ahead in life, and who is not willing to pay the price.

4. *Insufficient education.* This is a handicap which may be overcome with comparative ease. Experience has proven that the best-educated people are often those who are known as "self-made," or self-educated. It takes more than a college degree to make one a person of education. Any person who is educated is one who has learned to get whatever he wants in life without violating the rights of others. Education consists, not so much of knowledge, but of knowledge effectively and persistently *applied.* Men are paid, not merely for what they know, but more particularly for *what they do with that which they know.*

5. *Lack of self-discipline.* Discipline comes through self-control. This means that one must control all negative qualities. Before you can control conditions, you must first control yourself. Self-mastery is the hardest job you will ever tackle. If you do not conquer self, you will be conquered by self. You may see at one and the same time both your best friend and your greatest enemy, by stepping in front of a mirror.

6. *Ill health.* No person may enjoy outstanding success without good health. Many of the causes of ill health are subject to mastery and control. These, in the main are:

a. Overeating of foods not conducive to health

b. Wrong habits of thought; giving expression to negatives.

c. Wrong use of, and over indulgence in sex. d. Lack of proper physical exercise e. An inadequate supply of fresh air, due to improper breathing.

7. *Unfavorable environmental influences during childhood.* "As the twig is bent, so shall the tree grow." Most people who have criminal tendencies acquire them as the result of bad environment, and improper associates during childhood.

8. *Procrastination.* This is one of the most common causes of failure. "Old Man Procrastination" stands within the shadow of every human being, waiting his opportunity to spoil one's chances of success. Most of us go through life as failures, because we are waiting for the "time to be right" to start doing something worthwhile. Do not wait. The time will never be "just right." Start where you stand, and work with whatever tools you may have at your command, and better tools will be found as you go along.

9. *Lack of persistence.* Most of us are good "starters" but poor "finishers" of everything we begin. Moreover, people are prone to give up at the first signs of defeat. There is no substitute for *persistence.* The person who makes *persistence* his watch-word, discovers that "Old Man Failure" finally becomes tired, and makes his departure. Failure cannot cope with *persistence.*

10. *Negative personality.* There is no hope of success for the person who repels people through a negative personality. Success comes through the application of *power,* and power is attained through the cooperative efforts of other people. A negative personality will not induce cooperation.

11. *Lack of controlled sexual urge.* Sex energy is the most powerful of all the stimuli which move people into *action.* Because it is the most powerful of the emotions, it must be controlled, through transmutation, and converted into other channels.

12. *Uncontrolled desire for "something for nothing."* The gambling instinct drives millions of people to failure. Evidence of this may be found in a study of the Wall Street crash of '29, during which millions of people tried to make money by gambling on stock margins.

13. *Lack of a well defined power of decision.* Men who succeed reach decisions promptly, and change them, if at all, very slowly. Men who fail, reach decisions, if at all, very slowly, and change them frequently, and quickly. Indecision and procrastination are twin brothers. Where one is found, the other may usually be found also. Kill off this pair before they completely "hog-tie" you to the treadmill of *failure.*

14. *One or more of the six basic fears.* These fears have been analyzed for you in a later chapter. They must be mastered before you can market your services effectively.

15. *Wrong selection of a mate in marriage.* This a most common cause of failure. The relationship of marriage brings people intimately into contact. Unless this relationship is harmonious, failure is likely to follow. Moreover, it will be a form of failure that is marked by misery and unhappiness, destroying all signs of *ambition.*

16. *Over-caution.* The person who takes no chances, generally has to take whatever is left when others are through choosing. Over-caution is as bad as under-caution. Both are extremes to be guarded against. Life itself is filled with the element of chance.

17. *Wrong selection of associates in business.* This is one of the most common causes of failure in business. In marketing personal services, one should use great care to select an employer who will be an inspiration, and who is, himself, intelligent and successful. We emulate those with whom we associate most closely. Pick an employer who is worth emulating.

18. *Superstition and prejudice.* Superstition is a form of fear. It is also a sign of ignorance. Men who succeed keep open minds and are afraid of nothing.

19. *Wrong selection of a vocation.* No man can succeed in a line of endeavor which he does not like. The most essential step in the marketing of personal services is that of selecting an occupation into which you can throw yourself wholeheartedly.

20. *Lack of concentration of effort.* The "jack-of-all-trades" seldom is good at any. Concentrate all of your efforts on one *definite chief aim.*

21. *The habit of indiscriminate spending.* The spend-thrift cannot succeed, mainly because he stands eternally in *fear of poverty.* Form the habit of systematic saving by putting aside a definite percentage of your income. Money in the bank gives one a very safe foundation of *courage* when bar-gaining for the sale of personal services. Without money, one must take what one is offered, and be glad to get it.

22. *Lack of enthusiasm.* Without enthusiasm one cannot be convincing. Moreover, enthusiasm is contagious, and the person who has it, under control, is generally welcome in any group of people.

23. *Intolerance.* The person with a "closed" mind on any subject seldom gets ahead. Intolerance means that one has stopped acquiring knowledge. The most damaging forms of intolerance are those connected with religious, racial, and political differences of opinion.

24. *Intemperance.* The most damaging forms of intemperance are connected with eating, strong drink, and sexual activities. Overindulgence in any of these is fatal to success.

25. *Inability to cooperate with others.* More people lose their positions and their big opportunities in life, because of this fault, than for all other reasons combined. It is a fault which no well-informed business man, or leader will tolerate.

26. *Possession of power that was not acquired through self effort.* (Sons and daughters of wealthy men, and others who inherit money which they did not earn). Power in the hands of one who did not acquire it gradually, is often fatal to success. *Quick riches* are more dangerous than poverty.

27. *Intentional dishonesty.* There is no substitute for honesty. One may be temporarily dishonest by force of circumstances over which one has no control, without permanent damage. But, there is no hope for the person who is dishonest by choice. Sooner or later, his deeds will catch up with him, and he will pay by loss of reputation, and perhaps even loss of liberty.

28. *Egotism and vanity.* These qualities serve as red lights which warn others to keep away. *They are fatal to success.*

29. *Guessing instead of thinking.* Most people are too indifferent or lazy to acquire facts with which to *think accurately.* They prefer to act on "opinions" created by guesswork or snap-judgments.

30. *Lack of capital.* This is a common cause of failure among those who start out in business for the first time, without sufficient reserve of capital to absorb the shock of their mistakes, and to carry them over until they have established a *reputation.*

31. Under this, name any particular cause of failure from which you have suffered that has not been included in the foregoing list.

In these thirty major causes of failure is found a description of the tragedy of life, which obtains for practically every person who tries and fails. It will be helpful if you can induce someone who knows you well to go over this list with you, and help to analyze you by the thirty causes of failure. It may be beneficial if you try this alone. Most people cannot see themselves as others see them. You may be one who cannot.

The oldest of admonitions is "Man, know thyself!" If you market merchandise successfully, you must know the merchandise. The same is true in marketing personal services. You should know all of your weaknesses in order that you may either bridge them or eliminate them entirely. You should know your strength in order that you may call attention to it when selling your services. You can know yourself only through accurate analysis.

The folly of ignorance in connection with self was displayed by a young man who applied to the manager of a well known business for a position. He made a very good impression until the manager asked him what salary he expected. He replied that he had no fixed sum in mind (lack of a definite aim). The manager then said, "We will pay you all you are worth, after we try you out for a week."

"I will not accept it," the applicant replied, "because *I am getting more than that where I am now employed.*"

Before you even start to negotiate for a readjustment of your salary in your present position, or to seek employment elsewhere, *Be sure that you are worth more than you now receive.*

It is one thing to *want* money– everyone wants more–but it is something entirely different to be *worth more*! Many people mistake their *wants* for their *just dues.* Your financial requirements or wants have nothing whatever to do with your *worth.* Your value is established entirely by your ability to render useful service or your capacity to induce others to render such service.

Take Inventory of Yourself: 28 Questions You Should Answer

Annual self-analysis is an essential in the effective marketing of personal services, as is annual inventory in merchandising. Moreover, the yearly analysis should disclose a *Decrease in faults*, and an increase in *virtues*. One goes ahead, stands still, or goes backward in life. One's object should be, of course, to go ahead. Annual self-analysis will disclose whether advancement has been, made, and if so, how much. It will also disclose any backward steps one may have made. The effective marketing of personal services requires one to move forward even if the progress is slow.

Your annual self-analysis should be made at the end of each year, so you can include in your New Year's Resolutions any improvements which the analysis indicates should be made. Take this inventory by asking yourself the following questions, and by checking your answers with the aid of someone who will not permit you to deceive yourself as to their accuracy.

Self-analysis Questionnaire for Personal Inventory

1. Have I attained the goal which I established as my objective for this year? (You should work with a definite yearly objective to be attained as a part of your major life objective).

2. Have I delivered service of the best possible *quality* of which I was capable, or could I have improved any part of this service?

3. Have I delivered service in the greatest possible *quantity* of which I was capable?

4. Has the spirit of my conduct been harmonious, and cooperative at all times?

5. Have I permitted the habit of *procrastination* to decrease my efficiency, and if so, to what extent?

6. Have I improved my *personality*, and if so, in what ways?

7. Have I been *persistent* in following my plans through to completion?

8. Have I reached *decisions promptly and definitely* on all occasions?

9. Have I permitted any one or more of the six basic fears to decrease my efficiency?

10. Have I been either "over-cautious," or "under-cautious?"

11. Has my relationship with my associates in work been pleasant, or unpleasant? If it has been

unpleasant, has the fault been partly, or wholly mine?

12. Have I dissipated any of my energy through lack of *concentration* of effort?
13. Have I been open minded and tolerant in connection with all subjects?
14. In what way have I improved my ability to render service?
15. Have I been intemperate in any of my habits?
16. Have I expressed, either openly or secretly, any form of *egotism?*
17. Has my conduct toward my associates been such that it has induced them to *respect* me?
18. Have my opinions and *decisions* been based upon guesswork, or accuracy of analysis and *thought?*
19. Have I followed the habit of budgeting my time, my expenses, and my income, and have I been conservative in these budgets?
20. How much time have I devoted to *unprofitable* effort which I might have used to better advantage?
21. How may I *re-budget* my time, and change my habits so I will be more efficient during the coming year?
22. Have I been guilty of any conduct which was not approved by my conscience?
23. In what ways have I rendered *more service and better service* than I was paid to render?
24. Have I been unfair to anyone, and if so, in what way?
25. If I had been the purchaser of my own services for the year, would I be satisfied with my purchase?
26. Am I in the right vocation, and if not, why not?
27. Has the purchaser of my services been satisfied with the service I have rendered, and if not, why not?
28. What is my present rating on the fundamental principles of success? (Make this rating fairly, and frankly, and have it checked by someone who is courageous enough to do it accurately).

Having read and assimilated the information conveyed through this chapter, you are now ready to create a practical plan for marketing your personal services. In this chapter will be found an adequate description of every principle essential in planning the sale of personal services, including the major attributes of leadership; the most common causes of failure in leadership; a description of the fields of opportunity for leadership; the main causes of failure in all walks of life, and the important questions which should be used in self-analysis. This extensive and detailed presentation of accurate information has been included, because it will be needed by all who must begin the accumulation of riches by marketing personal services. Those who have lost their fortunes, and those who are just beginning to earn money, have nothing but personal services to offer in return for riches, therefore it is essential that they have available the practical information needed to market services to best advantage.

The information contained in this chapter will be of great value to all who aspire to attain leadership in any calling. It will be particularly helpful to those aiming to market their services as business or industrial executives.

Complete assimilation and understanding of the information here conveyed will be helpful in marketing one's own services, and it will also help one to become more analytical and capable of judging people. The information will be priceless to personnel directors, employment managers, and other executives charged with the selection of employees, and the maintenance of efficient organizations. If you doubt this statement, test its soundness by answering in writing the twenty-eight self-analysis questions. That might be both interesting and profitable, even though you do not doubt the soundness of the statement.

Where and How One May Find Opportunities to Accumulate Riches

Now that we have analyzed the principles by which riches may be accumulated, we naturally ask, "where may one find favorable opportunities to apply these principles?" Very well, let us take inventory and see what the United States of America offer the person seeking riches, great or small.

To begin with, let us remember, all of us, that we live in a country where every law-abiding citizen enjoys freedom of thought and freedom of deed unequaled anywhere in the world. Most of us have never taken inventory of the advantages of this freedom. We have never compared our unlimited freedom with the curtailed freedom in other countries.

Here we have freedom of thought, freedom in the choice and enjoyment of education, freedom in religion, freedom in politics, freedom in the choice of a business, profession or occupation, freedom to accumulate and own without molestation, *all the property we can accumulate*, freedom to choose our place of residence, freedom in marriage, freedom through equal opportunity to all races, freedom of travel from one state to another, freedom in our choice of foods, and freedom to *aim for any station in life for which we have prepared ourselves*, even for the presidency of the United States.

We have other forms of freedom, but this list will give a bird's eye view of the most important, which constitute *opportunity* of the highest order. This advantage of freedom is all the more conspicuous because the United States is the only country guaranteeing to every citizen, whether native born or naturalized, so broad and varied a list of freedom.

Next, let us recount some of the blessings which our widespread freedom has placed within our hands. Take the average American family for example (meaning, the family of average income) and sum up the benefits available to every member of the family, in this land of *opportunity* and plenty!

a. *Food.* Next to freedom of thought and deed comes *food, clothing,* and *shelter*, the three basic necessities of life.

Because of our universal freedom the average American family has available, at its very door, the choicest selection of food to be found anywhere in the world, and at prices within its financial range.

A family of two, living in the heart of Times Square district of New York City, far removed from the source of production of foods, took careful inventory of the cost of a simple breakfast, with this astonishing result:

Articles of food;	Cost at the breakfast table:
Grape Fruit Juice(From Florida)	02
Rippled Wheat Breakfast food (Kansas Farm).	02
Tea (From China).	02
Bananas (From South America)	02½
Toasted Bread (From Kansas Farm)	01
Fresh Country Eggs (From Utah).	07
Sugar (From Cuba, or Utah)	00½
Butter and Cream (From New England).	03
Grand total	20

It is not very difficult to obtain *food* in a country where two people can have breakfast consisting of all they want or need for a dime apiece! Observe that this simple breakfast was gathered, by some strange form of magic (?) from China, South America, Utah, Kansas and the New England States, and delivered on the breakfast table, ready for consumption, in the very heart of the most crowded city in America, at a cost well within the means of the most humble laborer.

The cost included all federal, state and city taxes! (Here is a fact the politicians did not mention when they were crying out to the voters to throw their opponents out of office because the people were being taxed to death).

b. *shelter*. This family lives in a comfortable apartment, heated by steam, lighted with electricity, with gas for cooking, all for $65.00 a month. In a smaller city, or a more sparsely settled part of New York city, the same apartment could be had for as low as $20.00 a month.

The toast they had for breakfast in the food estimate was toasted on an electric toaster, which cost but a few dollars, the apartment is cleaned with a vacuum sweeper that is run by electricity. Hot and cold water is available, at all times, in the kitchen and the bathroom. The food is kept cool in a refrigerator that is run by electricity. The wife curls her hair, washes her clothes and irons them with easily operated electrical equipment, on power obtained by sticking a plug in the wall. The husband shaves with an electric shaver, and they receive entertainment from all over the world, twenty four hours a day, if they want it, without cost, by merely turning the dial of their radio.

There are other conveniences in this apartment, but the foregoing list will give a fair idea of some of the concrete evidences of the freedom we, of America, enjoy. (And this is neither political nor economic propaganda).

c. *clothing*. Anywhere in the United States, the woman of average clothing requirements can dress very comfortably and neatly for less than $200.00 a year, and the average man can dress for the same, or less.

Only the three basic necessities of food, clothing, and shelter have been mentioned. The average American citizen has other privileges and advantages available in return for modest effort, not exceeding eight hours per day of labor. Among these is the privilege of automobile transportation, with which one can go and come at will, at very small cost.

The average American has security of property rights not found in any other country in the world. He can place his surplus money in a bank with the assurance that his government will protect it, and make good to him if the bank fails. If an American citizen wants to travel from one state to another he needs no passport, no one's permission. He may go when he pleases, and return at will. Moreover, he may travel by train, private automobile, bus, airplane, or ship, as his pocketbook permits. In Germany, Russia, Italy, and most of the other European and Oriental countries, the people cannot travel with so much freedom, and at so little cost.

The "Miracle" That Has Provided These Blessings

We often hear politicians proclaiming the freedom of America, when they solicit votes, but seldom do they take the time or devote sufficient effort to the analysis of the source or nature of this "freedom." Having no axe to grind, no grudge to express, no ulterior motives to be carried out, I have the privilege of going into a frank analysis of that mysterious, abstract, greatly misunderstood "*something*" which gives to every citizen of America more blessings, more opportunities to accumulate wealth, more freedom of every nature, than may be found in any other country.

I have the right to analyze the source and nature of this *unseen power*, because I know, and have known for more than a quarter of a century, many of the men who organized that power, and many who are now responsible for its maintenance.

The name of this mysterious benefactor of mankind is *capital!*

Capital consists not alone of money, but more particularly of highly organized, intelligent groups of men who plan ways and means of using money efficiently for the good of the public, and profitably to themselves.

These groups consist of scientists, educators, chemists, inventors, business analysts, publicity men, transportation experts, accountants, lawyers, doctors, and both men and women who have highly specialized knowledge in all fields of industry and business. They pioneer, experiment, and blaze trails in new fields of endeavor. They support colleges, hospitals, public schools, build good roads, publish newspapers, pay most of the cost of government, and take care of the multitudinous detail essential to human progress. Stated briefly, the capitalists are the brains of civilization, because they supply the entire fabric of which all education, enlightenment and human progress consists.

Money, without brains, always is dangerous. Properly used, it is the most important essential of civilization. The simple breakfast here described could not have been delivered to the New York family at a dime each, or at any other price, if organized capital had not provided the machinery, the ships, the railroads, and the huge armies of trained men to operate them.

Some slight idea of the importance of *organized capital* may be had by trying to imagine yourself burdened with the responsibility of collecting, without the aid of capital, and delivering to the New York City family, the simple breakfast described.

To supply the tea, you would have to make a trip to China or India, both a very long way from America. Unless you are an excellent swimmer, you would become rather tired before making the round trip. Then, too, another problem would confront you. What would you use for money, even if you had the physical endurance to swim the ocean?

To supply the sugar, you would have to take another long swim to Cuba, or a long walk to the sugar beet section of Utah. But even then, you might come back without the sugar, because organized effort and money are necessary to produce sugar, to say nothing of what is required to refine, transport, and deliver it to the breakfast table anywhere in the United States.

The eggs, you could deliver easily enough from the barn yards near New York City, but you would have a very long walk to Florida and return, before you could serve the two glasses of grapefruit juice.

You would have another long walk, to Kansas, or one of the other wheat growing states, when you went after the four slices of wheat bread.

The Rippled Wheat Biscuits would have to be omitted from the menu, because they would not be available except through the labor of a trained organization of men and suitable machinery, *all of which call for capital.*

While resting, you could take off for another little swim down to South America, where you would pick up a couple of bananas, and on your return, you could take a short walk to the nearest farm having a dairy and pick up some butter and cream. Then your New York City family would be ready to sit down and enjoy breakfast, and you could collect your two dimes for your labor!

Seems absurd, doesn't it? Well, the procedure described would be the only possible way these simple items of food could be delivered to the heart of New York City, if we had no capitalistic system.

The sum of money required for the building and maintenance of the railroads and steam ships used in the delivery of that simple breakfast is so huge that it staggers one's imagination. It runs into hundreds of millions of dollars, not to mention the armies of trained employees required to man the ships and trains. But, transportation is only a part of the requirements of modern civilization in capitalistic America. Before there can be anything to haul, something must be grown from the ground, or manufactured and prepared for market. This calls for more millions of dollars for equipment, machinery, boxing, marketing, and for the wages of millions of men and women.

Steam ships and railroads do not spring up from the earth and function automatically. They come in response to the call of civilization, through the labor and ingenuity and organizing ability of men who have *imagination, faith, enthusiasm, decision, persistence*! These men are known as capitalists. They are motivated by the desire to build, construct, achieve, render useful service, earn profits and accumulate riches. And, because they *render service without which there would be no civilization*, they put themselves in the way of great riches.

Just to keep the record simple and understandable, I will add that these capitalists are the self-same men of whom most of us have heard soap-box orators speak. They are the same men to whom radicals, racketeers, dishonest politicians and grafting labor leaders refer as "the predatory interests," or "Wall Street."

I am not attempting to present a brief for or against any group of men or any system of economics. I am not attempting to condemn collective bargaining when I refer to "grafting labor leaders," nor do I aim to give a clean bill of health to all individuals known as capitalists.

The purpose of this book–A purpose to which I have faithfully devoted over a quarter of a century–is to present to all who want the knowledge, the most dependable philosophy through which individuals may accumulate riches in whatever amounts they desire.

I have here analyzed the economic advantages of the capitalistic system for the two-fold purpose of showing:

1. that all who seek riches must recognize and adapt themselves to the system that controls all approaches to fortunes, large or small, and

2. to present the side of the picture opposite to that being shown by politicians and demagogues who deliberately becloud the issues they bring up, by referring to organized capital as if it were something poisonous.

This is a capitalistic country, it was developed through the use of capital, and we who claim the right to partake of the blessings of freedom and opportunity, we who seek to accumulate riches here, may as well know that neither riches nor opportunity would be available to us if *organized capital* had not provided these benefits.

For more than twenty years it has been a somewhat popular and growing pastime for radicals, self-seeking politicians, racketeers, crooked labor leaders, and on occasion religious leaders, to take pot-shots at "*Wall Street, the money changers*, and *big business*."

The practice became so general that we witnessed during the business depression, the unbelievable sight of high government officials lining up with the cheap politicians, and labor leaders, with the openly avowed purpose of throttling the system which has made Industrial America the richest country on earth. The line-up was so general and so well organized that it prolonged the worst depression America has ever known. It cost millions of men their jobs, because those jobs were inseparably a part of the industrial and capitalistic system which form the very backbone of the nation.

During this unusual alliance of government officials and self-seeking individuals who were endeavoring to profit by declaring "open season" on the American system of industry, a certain type of labor leader joined forces with the politicians and offered to deliver voters in return for legislation designed to permit men to *take riches away from industry by organized force of numbers, instead of the better method of giving a fair day's work for a fair day's pay.*

Millions of men and women throughout the nation are still engaged in this popular pastime of trying to *get* without *giving*. Some of them are lined up with labor unions, where they demand *shorter hours and more pay*! Others do not take the trouble to work at all. *They demand government relief and are getting it.* Their idea of their rights of freedom was demonstrated in New York City, where violent complaint was registered with the Postmaster, by a group of "relief beneficiaries," because the Postmen awakened them at 7: 30 A. M. to deliver Government relief checks. They *demanded* that the time of delivery be set up to 10: 00 o'clock.

If you are one of those who believe that riches can be accumulated by the mere act of men who organize themselves into groups and demand *more pay for less service*, if you are one of those who *demand* Government relief without early morning disturbance when the money is delivered to you, if you are one of those who believe in trading their votes to politicians in return for the passing of laws which permit the raiding of the public treasury, you may rest securely on your belief, with certain knowledge that no one will disturb you, because *this is a free country where every man may think as he pleases*, where nearly everybody can live with but little effort, where many may live well without doing any work whatsoever.

However, you should know the full truth concerning this freedom of which so many people boast, and so few understand. As great as it is, as far as it reaches, as many privileges as it provides, It was not a pretty sight! It did not increase our respect for mob psychology through which men cast reason to the winds and start trying to *get* without giving.

We who went through those six discouraging years, when fear was in the saddle, and faith was on the ground, cannot forget how ruthlessly the *law of economics* exacted its toll from both rich and poor, weak and strong, old and young. We shall not wish to go through another such experience.

These observations are not founded upon short-time experience. They are the result of twenty-five years of careful analysis of the methods of both the most successful and the most unsuccessful men America has known.

Chapter Seven: Decision

The Mastery of Procrastination: the Seventh Step Toward Riches

Accurate analysis of over 25,000 men and women who had experienced failure, disclosed the fact that *lack of decision* was near the head of the list of the 30 major causes of *failure*. This is no mere statement of a theory– it is a fact.

Procrastination, the opposite of *decision*, is a common enemy which practically every man must conquer.

You will have an opportunity to test your capacity to reach quick and definite *decisions* when you finish reading this book, and are ready to begin putting into *action* the principles which it describes.

Analysis of several hundred people who had accumulated fortunes well beyond the million dollar mark, disclosed the fact that every one of them had the habit of *reaching decisions promptly*, and of changing these decisions *slowly*, if, and when they were changed. People who fail to accumulate money, without exception, have the habit of reaching decisions, *if at all*, very slowly, and of changing these decisions quickly and often.

One of Henry Ford's most outstanding qualities is his habit of reaching decisions quickly and definitely, and changing them slowly. This quality is so pronounced in Mr. Ford, that it has given him the reputation of being obstinate. It was this quality which prompted Mr. Ford to continue to manufacture his famous Model "T" (the world's ugliest car), when all of his advisors, and many of the purchasers of the car, were urging him to change it.

Perhaps, Mr. Ford delayed too long in making the change, but the other side of the story is, that Mr. Ford's firmness of decision yielded a huge fortune, before the change in model became necessary. There is but little doubt that Mr. Ford's habit of definiteness of decision assumes the proportion of obstinacy, but this quality is preferable to slowness in reaching decisions and quickness in changing them.

The majority of people who fail to accumulate money sufficient for their needs, are, generally, easily influenced by the "opinions" of others. They permit the newspapers and the "gossiping" neighbors to do their "thinking" for them. "Opinions are the cheapest commodities on earth. Everyone has a flock of opinions ready to be wished upon anyone who will accept them. If you are influenced by "opinions" when you reach *decisions*, you will not succeed in any undertaking, much less in that of transmuting *Your own desire* into money.

If you are influenced by the opinions of others, you will have no *desire* of your own.

Keep your own counsel, when you begin to put into practice the principles described here, by reaching your own decisions and following them. Take no one into your confidence, *except* the members of your "Master Mind" group, and be very sure in your selection of this group, that you choose *only* those who will be in *complete sympathy and harmony with your purpose.*

Close friends and relatives, while not meaning to do so, often handicap one through "opinions" and sometimes through ridicule, which is meant to be humorous. Thousands of men and women carry inferiority complexes with them all through life, because some well-meaning, but ignorant person destroyed their confidence through "opinions" or ridicule.

You have a brain and mind of your own. *Use it*, and reach your own decisions. If you need facts or information from other people, to enable you to reach decisions, as you probably will in many instances; acquire these facts or secure the information you need quietly, without disclosing your purpose.

It is characteristic of people who have but a smattering or a veneer of knowledge to try to give the impression that they have much knowledge. Such people generally do *too much* talking, and *too little* listening. Keep your eyes and ears wide open— and your mouth *closed*, if you wish to acquire the habit of prompt *decision*. Those who talk too much do little else. If you talk more than you listen, you not only deprive yourself of many opportunities to accumulate useful knowledge, but you also disclose your *plans* and *purposes* to people who will take great delight in defeating you, because they envy you.

Remember, also, that every time you open your mouth in the presence of a person who has an abundance of knowledge, you display to that person, your exact stock of knowledge, or your *lack* of it! Genuine wisdom is usually conspicuous through modesty and silence.

Keep in mind the fact that every person with whom you associate is, like yourself, seeking the opportunity to accumulate money. If you talk about your plans too freely, you may be surprised when you learn that some other person has beaten you to your goal by *Putting into action ahead of you*, the plans of which you talked unwisely.

Let one of your first decisions be to *keep a closed mouth and open ears and eyes.*

As a reminder to yourself to follow this advice, it will be helpful if you copy the following epigram in large letters and place it where you will see it daily.

"Tell the world what you intend to do, but first show it."

This is the equivalent of saying that "deeds, and not words, are what count most."

Freedom or Death on a Decision

The value of decisions depends upon the courage required to render them. The great decisions, which served as the foundation of civilization, were reached by assuming great risks, which often meant the possibility of death.

Lincoln's decision to issue his famous Proclamation of Emancipation, which gave freedom to the colored people of America, was rendered with full understanding that his act would turn thousands of friends and political supporters against him. He knew, too, that the carrying out of that proclamation would mean death to thousands of men on the battlefield. In the end, it cost Lincoln his life. That required courage.

Socrates' decision to drink the cup of poison, rather than compromise in his personal belief, was a decision of courage. It turned Time ahead a thousand years, and gave to people then unborn, the right to freedom of thought and of speech.

The decision of Gen. Robert E. Lee, when he came to the parting of the way with the Union, and took up the cause of the South, was a decision of courage, for he well knew that it might cost him his own life, that it would surely cost the lives of others.

But, the greatest decision of all time, as far as any American citizen is concerned, was reached in Philadelphia, July 4, 1776, when fifty-six men signed their names to a document, which they well knew would bring freedom to all Americans, or leave every one of the fifty-six hanging from a gallows!

You have heard of this famous document, but you may not have drawn from it the great lesson in personal achievement it so plainly taught.

We all remember the date of this momentous decision, but few of us realize what courage that decision required. We remember our history, as it was taught; we remember dates, and the names of the men who fought; we remember Valley Forge, and Yorktown; we remember George Washington, and Lord Cornwall is. But we know little of the real forces back of these names, dates, and places. We know still less of that intangible *power*, which insured us freedom long before Washington's armies reached Yorktown.

We read the history of the Revolution, and falsely imagine that George Washington was the Father of our Country, that it was he who won our freedom, while the truth is—Washington was only an accessory after the fact, because victory for his armies had been insured long before Lord Cornwall is surrendered. This is not intended to rob Washington of any of the glory he so richly merited. Its purpose, rather, is to give greater attention to the astounding *power* that was the real cause of his victory.

It is nothing short of tragedy that the writers of history have missed, entirely, even the slightest reference to the irresistible *power*, which gave birth and freedom to the nation destined to set up new standards of independence for all the peoples of the earth. I say it is a tragedy, because it is the self-same *power* which must be used by every individual who surmounts the difficulties of Life, and forces Life to pay the price asked.

Let us briefly review the events which gave birth to this *power*. The story begins with an incident in Boston, March 5, 1770. British soldiers were patrolling the streets, by their presence, openly threatening the citizens. The colonists resented armed men marching in their midst. They began to express their resentment openly, hurling stones as well as epithets, at the marching soldiers, until the commanding officer gave orders, "Fix bayonets. . . . Charge!"

The battle was on. It resulted in the death and injury of many. The incident aroused such resentment that the Provincial Assembly, (made up of prominent colonists), called a meeting for the purpose of taking definite action. Two of the members of that Assembly were, John Hancock, and Samuel Adams—*long live their names*! They spoke up courageously, and declared that a move must be made to eject all British soldiers from Boston.

Remember this—a *decision*, in the minds of two men, might properly be called the beginning of the freedom which we, of the United States now enjoy. Remember, too, that the *decision* of these two men called for *faith*, and *courage*, because it was dangerous.

Before the Assembly adjourned, Samuel Adams was appointed to call on the Governor of the Province, Hutchinson, and demand the withdrawal of the British troops.

The request was granted, the troops were removed from Boston, but the incident was not closed. It had caused a situation destined to change the entire trend of civilization. Strange, is it not, how the great changes, such as the American Revolution, and the World War, often have their beginnings in circumstances which seem unimportant? It is interesting, also, to observe that these important changes usually begin in the form of a *definite decision* in the minds of a relatively small number of people. Few of us know the history of our country well enough to realize that John Hancock, Samuel Adams, and Richard Henry Lee (of the Province of Virginia) were the real Fathers of our Country.

Richard Henry Lee became an important factor in this story by reason of the fact that he and Samuel Adams communicated frequently (by correspondence), sharing freely their fears and their hopes concerning the welfare of the people of their Provinces. From this practice, Adams conceived the idea that a mutual exchange of letters between the thirteen Colonies might help to bring about the coordination of effort so badly needed in connection with the solution of their problems. Two years after the clash with the soldiers in Boston (March '72), Adams presented this idea to the Assembly, in the form of a motion that a Correspondence Committee be established among the Colonies, with definitely appointed correspondents in each Colony, "for the purpose of friendly cooperation for the betterment of the Colonies of British America."

Mark well this incident! It was the beginning of the organization of the far-flung *power* destined to give freedom to you, and to me. The Master Mind had already been organized. It consisted of Adams, Lee, and Hancock. "I tell you further, that if two of you agree upon the earth concerning anything for which you ask, it will come to you from My Father, who is in Heaven."

The Committee of Correspondence was organized. Observe that this move provided the way for increasing the power of the Master Mind by adding to it men from all the Colonies. Take notice that this procedure constituted the first *organized planning* of the disgruntled Colonists.

In union there is strength! The citizens of the Colonies had been waging disorganized warfare against the British soldiers, through incidents similar to the Boston riot, but nothing of benefit had been accomplished. Their individual grievances had not been consolidated under one Master Mind. No group of individuals had put their hearts, minds, souls, and bodies together in one definite *decision* to settle their difficulty with the British once and for all, until Adams, Hancock, and Lee got together.

Meanwhile, the British were not idle. They, too, were doing some *planning* and "Master-Minding" on their own account, with the advantage of having back of them money, and organized soldiery.

The Crown appointed Gage to supplant Hutchinson as the Governor of Massachusetts. One of the new Governor's first acts was to send a messenger to call on Samuel Adams, for the purpose of endeavoring to stop his opposition— by *fear*.

We can best understand the spirit of what happened by quoting the conversation between Col. Fenton, (the messenger sent by Gage), and Adams.

Col. Fenton: "I have been authorized by Governor Gage, to assure you, Mr. Adams, that the Governor has been empowered to confer upon you such benefits as would be satisfactory, [endeavor to win Adams by promise of bribes], upon the condition that you engage to cease in your opposition to the measures of the government. It is the Governor's advice to you, Sir, not to incur the further displeasure of his majesty. Your conduct has been such as makes you liable to penalties of an Mt of Henry VIII, by which persons can be sent to England for trial for treason, or misprision of treason, at the discretion of a governor of a province. But, *by changing your political course*, you will not only receive great personal advantages, but you will make your peace with the King."

Samuel Adams had the choice of two *decisions*. He could cease his opposition, and receive personal bribes, or he could *continue, and run the risk of being hanged!*

Clearly, the time had come when Adams was forced to reach instantly, a *decision* which could have cost his life. The majority of men would have found it difficult to reach such a decision. The majority would have sent back an evasive reply, but not Adams! He insisted upon Col. Fenton's word of honor, that the Colonel would deliver to the Governor the answer exactly as Adams would give it to him.

Adams' answer, "Then you may tell Governor Gage that I trust I have long since made my peace with the King of Kings. No personal consideration shall induce me to abandon the righteous cause of my Country. And, *tell governor gage it is the advice of Samuel Adams to him*, no longer to insult the feelings of an exasperated people."

Comment as to the character of this man seems unnecessary. It must be obvious to all who read this astounding message that its sender possessed loyalty of the highest order. This is important. (Racketeers and dishonest politicians have prostituted the honor for which such men as Adams died).

When Governor Gage received Adams' caustic reply, he flew into a rage, and issued a proclamation which read, "I do, hereby, in his majesty's name, offer and promise his most gracious pardon to all persons who shall forthwith lay down their arms, and return to the duties of peaceable subjects, excepting only from the benefit of such pardon, *Samuel Adams* and *John Hancock*, whose offences are of too flagitious a nature to admit of any other consideration but that of condign punishment."

As one might say, in modern slang, Adams and Hancock were "on the spot!" The threat of the irate Governor forced the two men to reach another *decision*, equally as dangerous. They hurriedly called a secret meeting of their staunchest followers. (Here the Master Mind began to take on momentum). After the meeting had been called to order, Adams locked the door, placed the key in his pocket, and informed all present that it was imperative that a Congress of the Colonists be organized, and that *no man should leave the room until the decision for such a congress had been reached.*

Great excitement followed. Some weighed the possible consequences of such radicalism. (Old Man Fear). Some expressed grave doubt as to the wisdom of so definite a decision in defiance of the Crown. Locked in that room were *two men* immune to Fear, blind to the possibility of Failure. Hancock and Adams. Through the influence of their minds, the others were induced to agree that, through the

Correspondence Committee, arrangements should be made for a meeting of the First Continental Congress, to be held in Philadelphia, September 5, 1774.

Remember this date. It is more important than July 4, 1776. If there had been no *decision* to hold a Continental Congress, there could have been no signing of the Declaration of Independence.

Before the first meeting of the new Congress, another leader, in a different section of the country was deep in the throes of publishing a "Summary View of the Rights of British America." He was Thomas Jefferson, of the Province of Virginia, whose relationship to Lord Dunmarra, (representative of the Crown in Virginia), was as strained as that of Hancock and Adams with their Governor.

Shortly after his famous Summary of Rights was published, Jefferson was informed that he was subject to prosecution for high treason against his majesty's government. Inspired by the threat, one of Jefferson's colleagues, Patrick Henry, boldly spoke his mind, concluding his remarks with a sentence which shall remain forever a classic, "If this be treason, then make the most of it."

It was such men as these who, without power, without authority, without military strength, without money, sat in solemn consideration of the destiny of the colonies, beginning at the opening of the First Continental Congress, and continuing at intervals for two years– until on June 7, 1776, Richard Henry Lee arose, addressed the Chair, and to the startled Assembly made this motion:

"Gentlemen, I make the motion that these United Colonies are, and of right ought to be free and independent states, that they be absolved from all allegiance to the British Crown, and that all political connection between them and the state of Great Britain is, and ought to be totally dissolved."

Lee's astounding motion was discussed fervently, and at such length that he began to lose patience. Finally, after days of argument, he again took the floor, and declared, in a clear, firm voice, "Mr. President, we have discussed this issue for days. It is the only course for us to follow. Why, then Sir, do we longer delay? Why still deliberate? Let this happy day give birth to an American Republic. Let her arise, not to devastate and to conquer, but to re-establish the reign of peace, and of law. The eyes of Europe are fixed upon us. She demands of us a living example of freedom, that may exhibit a contrast, in the felicity of the citizen, to the ever increasing tyranny."

Before his motion was finally voted upon, Lee was called back to Virginia, because of serious family illness, but before leaving, he placed his cause in the hands of his friend, Thomas Jefferson, who promised to fight until favorable action was taken. Shortly thereafter the President of the Congress (Hancock), appointed Jefferson as Chairman of a Committee to draw up a Declaration of Independence.

Long and hard the Committee labored, on a document which would mean, when accepted by the Congress, that *every man who signed it, would be signing his own death warrant*, should the Colonies lose in the fight with Great Britain, which was sure to follow.

The document was drawn, and on June 28, the original draft was read before the Congress. For several days it was discussed, altered, and made ready. On July 4, 1776, Thomas Jefferson stood before the Assembly, and fearlessly read the most mementos *decision* ever placed upon paper.

"When in the course of human events it is necessary for one people to dissolve the political bands which have connected them with another, and to assume, among the powers of the earth, the separate and equal station to which the laws of Nature, and of Nature's God entitle them, a decent respect to the opinions of mankind requires that they should declare the causes which impel them to the separation. . . "

When Jefferson finished, the document was voted upon, accepted, and signed by the fifty-six men, every one staking his own life upon his *decision* to write his name. By that *decision* came into existence a nation destined to bring to mankind forever, the privilege of making *decisions*.

By decisions made in a similar spirit of Faith, and only by such decisions, can men solve their personal problems, and win for themselves high estates of material and spiritual wealth. Let us not forget this!

Analyze the events which led to the Declaration of Independence, and be convinced that this nation, which now holds a position of commanding respect and power among all nations of the world, was born of a *decision* created by a Master Mind, consisting of fifty-six men. Note well, the fact that it was their *decision* which insured the success of Washington's armies, because the spirit of that decision was in the heart of every soldier who fought with him, and served as a spiritual power which recognizes no such thing as *failure*.

Note, also, (with great personal benefit), that the *power* which gave this nation its freedom, is the self-same power that must be used by every individual who becomes self-determining. This *power* is made up of the principles described in this book. It will not be difficult to detect, in the story of the Declaration of Independence, at least six of these principles; *desire*, *decision*, *faith*, *persistence*, *the master mind*, and *organized planning*.

Throughout this philosophy will be found the suggestion that thought, backed by strong *desire*, has a tendency to transmute itself into its physical equivalent. Before passing on, I wish to leave with you the suggestion that one may find in this story, and in the story of the organization of the United States Steel Corporation, a perfect description of the method by which thought makes this astounding transformation.

In your search for the secret of the method, do not look for a miracle, because you will not find it. You will find only the eternal laws of Nature. These laws are available to every person who has the *faith* and the *courage* to use them. They may be used to bring freedom to a nation, or to accumulate riches. There is no charge save the time necessary to understand and appropriate them.

Those who reach *decisions* promptly and definitely, know what they want, and generally get it. The leaders in every walk of life *decide* quickly, and firmly. That is the major reason why they are leaders. The world has the habit of making room for the man whose words and actions show that he knows where he is going.

Indecision is a habit which usually begins in youth. The habit takes on permanency as the youth goes through graded school, high school, and even through college, without *definiteness of purpose*. The major weakness of all educational systems is that they neither teach nor encourage the habit of *definite decision*.

It would be beneficial if no college would permit the enrollment of any student, unless and until the student declared his major purpose in matriculating. It would be of still greater benefit, if every student who enters the graded schools were compelled to accept training in the *habit* OF *decision*, and forced to pass a satisfactory examination on this subject before being permitted to advance in the grades.

The habit of *decisions* acquired because of the deficiencies of our school systems, goes with the student into the occupation he chooses . . . *If* . . in fact, he chooses his occupation. Generally, the youth just out of school seeks any job that can be found. He takes the first place he finds, because he has fallen into the habit of *decisions*. Ninety-eight out of every hundred people working for wages today, are in the positions they hold, because they lacked the *definiteness of decision* to *Plan a definite position*, and the knowledge of how to choose an employer.

Definiteness of decision always requires courage, sometimes very great courage. The fifty-six men who signed the Declaration of Independence staked their lives on the *decision* to affix their signatures to that document. The person who reaches a *definite decision* to procure the particular job, and make life pay the price he asks, does not stake his life on that decision; he stakes his *economic freedom*. Financial independence, riches, desirable business and professional positions are not within reach of the person who neglects or refuses to *expect*, *plan*, and *demand* these things. The person who desires riches in the same spirit that Samuel Adams desired freedom for the Colonies, is sure to accumulate wealth.

In the chapter on Organized Planning, you will find complete instructions for marketing every type of personal services. You will find also detailed information on how to choose the employer you prefer, and the particular job you desire. These instructions will be of no value to you *unless you definitely decide* to organize them into a plan of action.

Chapter Eight: Persistence

The Sustained Effort Necessary to Induce Faith: the Eighth Step Toward Riches

Persistence is an essential factor in the procedure of transmuting *desire* into its monetary equivalent.

The basis of persistence is the *power of will*.

Will-power and desire, when properly combined, make an irresistible pair. Men who accumulate great fortunes are generally known as cold-blooded, and sometimes ruthless. Often they are misunderstood. What they have is will-power, which they mix with persistence, and place back of their desires to insure the attainment of their objectives.

Henry Ford has been generally misunderstood to be ruthless and cold-blooded. This misconception grew out of Ford's habit of following through in all of his plans with *persistence*.

The majority of people are ready to throw their aims and purposes overboard, and give up at the first sign of opposition or misfortune. A few carry on *despite* all opposition, until they attain their goal. These few are the Fords, Carnegies, Rockefellers, and Edisons.

There may be no heroic connotation to the word "persistence," but the quality is to the character of man what carbon is to steel.

The building of a fortune, generally, involves the application of the entire thirteen factors of this philosophy. These principles must be understood, they must be applied with *persistence* by all who accumulate money.

If you are following this book with the intention of applying the knowledge it conveys, your first test as to your *persistence* will come when you begin to follow the six steps described in the second chapter. Unless you are one of the two out of every hundred who already have a Definite goal at which you are aiming, and a definite plan for its attainment, you may read the instructions, and then pass on with your daily routine, and never comply with those instructions.

The author is checking you up at this point, because lack of persistence is one of the major causes of failure. Moreover, experience with thousands of people has proved that lack of persistence is a weakness common to the majority of men. It is a weakness which may be overcome by effort. The ease with which lack of persistence may be conquered will depend entirely upon the *intensity of one's desire.*

The starting point of all achievement is *desire.* Keep this constantly in mind. Weak desires bring weak results, just as a small amount of fire makes a small amount of heat. If you find yourself lacking in persistence, this weakness may be remedied by building a stronger fire under your desires.

Continue to read through to the end, then go back to Chapter two, and start immediately to carry out the instructions given in connection with the six steps. The eagerness with which you follow these instructions will indicate clearly, how much, or how little you really *desire* to accumulate money. If you find that you are indifferent, you may be sure that you have not yet acquired the "money consciousness" which you must possess, before you can be sure of accumulating a fortune.

Fortunes gravitate to men whose minds have been prepared to "attract" them, just as surely as water gravitates to the ocean. In this book may be found all the stimuli necessary to "attune" any normal mind to the vibrations which will attract the object of one's desires.

If you find you are weak in *persistence,* center your attention upon the instructions contained in the chapter on "Power"; surround yourself with a "*master mind*" group, and through the cooperative efforts of the members of this group, you can develop persistence. You will find additional instructions for the development of persistence in the chapters on auto-suggestion, and the subconscious mind. Follow the instructions outlined in these chapters until your habit nature hands over to your subconscious mind, a clear picture of the object of your *desire.* From that point on, you will not be handicapped by lack of persistence.

Your subconscious mind works continuously, while you are awake, and while you are asleep.

Spasmodic, or occasional effort to apply the rules will be of no value to you. To get *results,* you must apply all of the rules until their application becomes a fixed habit with you. In no other way can you develop the necessary "money consciousness."

Poverty is attracted to the one whose mind is favorable to it, as money is attracted to him whose mind has been deliberately prepared to attract it, and through the same laws. *Poverty consciousness will voluntarily seize the mind which is not occupied with the money consciousness.* A poverty consciousness develops without conscious application of habits favorable to it. The money consciousness must be created to order, unless one is born with such a consciousness.

Catch the full significance of the statements in the preceding paragraph, and you will understand the importance of *persistence* in the accumulation of a fortune. Without *persistence,* you will be defeated, even before you start. With *persistence* you will win.

If you have ever experienced a nightmare, you will realize the value of persistence. You are lying in bed, half awake, with a feeling that you are about to smother. You are unable to turn over, or to move a muscle. You realize that you *must begin* to regain control over your muscles. Through persistent effort of will-power, you finally manage to move the fingers of one hand. By continuing to move your fingers, you extend your control to the muscles of one arm, until you can lift it. Then you gain control of the other arm in the same manner. You finally gain control over the muscles of one leg, and then extend it to the other leg. *Then– with one supreme effort of will–* you regain complete control over your muscular system, and "snap" out of your nightmare. The trick has been turned step by step.

You may find it necessary to "snap" out of your mental inertia, through a similar procedure, moving slowly at first, then increasing your speed, until you gain complete control over your will. Be *persistent* no matter how slowly you may, at first, have to move. *With persistence will come success.*

If you select your "Master Mind" group with care, you will have in it, at least one person who will aid you in the development of *persistence.* Some men who have accumulated great fortunes, did so because of necessity. They developed the habit of *persistence,* because they were so closely driven by circumstances, that they had to become persistent.

There is no substitute for persistence! It cannot be supplanted by any other quality! Remember this, and it will hearten you, in the beginning, when the going may seem difficult and slow.

Those who have cultivated the *habit* of persistence seem to enjoy insurance against failure. No matter how many times they are defeated, they finally arrive up toward the top of the ladder. Sometimes it appears that there is a hidden Guide whose duty is to test men through all sorts of discouraging experiences. Those who pick themselves up after defeat and keep on trying, arrive; and the world cries, "Bravo! I knew you could do it!" The hidden Guide lets no one enjoy great achievement without passing the *persistence test.* Those who can't take it, simply do not make the grade.

Those who can "take it" are bountifully rewarded for their *persistence.* They receive, as their compensation, whatever goal they are pursuing. That is not all! They receive something infinitely more important than material compensation— the knowledge that *"every failure brings with it the seed of an equivalent advantage."*

There are exceptions to this rule; a few people know from experience the soundness of persistence. They are the ones who have not accepted defeat as being anything more than temporary. They are the ones whose *desires* are so *persistently applied* that defeat is finally changed into victory. We who stand on the side-lines of Life see the overwhelmingly large number who go down in defeat, never to rise again. We see the few who take the punishment of defeat as an urge to greater effort. These, fortunately, never learn to accept Life's reverse gear. But what we *do not see,* what most of us never suspect of existing, is the silent but irresistible *power* which comes to the rescue of those who fight on in the face of discouragement. If we speak of this power at all we call it *persistence,* and let it go at that. One thing we all know, if one does not possess *persistence,* one does not achieve noteworthy success in any calling.

As these lines are being written, I look up from my work, and see before me, less than a block away, the great mysterious "Broadway," the "Graveyard of Dead Hopes," and the "Front Porch of Opportunity." From all over the world people have come to Broadway, seeking fame, fortune, power, love, or whatever it is that human beings call success. Once in a great while someone steps out from the long procession of seekers, and the world hears that another person has mastered Broadway. But Broadway is not easily nor quickly conquered. She acknowledges talent, recognizes genius, pays off in money, only after one has refused to *quit.*

Then we know he has discovered the secret of how to conquer Broadway. The secret is always inseparably attached to one word, *persistence!*

The secret is told in the struggle of Fannie Hurst, whose *persistence* conquered the Great White Way. She came to New York in 1915, to convert writing into riches. The conversion did not come quickly, *but it came.* For four years Miss Hurst learned about "The Sidewalks of New York" from first hand experience. She spent her days laboring, and her nights *hoping.* When hope grew dim, she did not say, "Alright Broadway, you win!" She said, "Very well, Broadway, you may whip some, but not me. I'm going to force you to give up."

One publisher (The Saturday Evening Post) sent her thirty six rejection slips, before she "broke the ice and got a story across. The average writer, like the "average" in other walks of life, would have given up the job when the first rejection slip came. She pounded the pavements for four years to the tune of the publisher's "*no*," because she was determined to win.

Then came the "payoff." The spell had been broken, the unseen Guide had tested Fannie Hurst, and she could take it. From that time on publishers made a beaten path to her door. Money came so fast she hardly had time to count it. Then the moving picture men discovered her, and money came not in small change, but in floods. The moving picture rights to her latest novel, "Great Laughter," brought $100,000.00, said to be the highest price ever paid for a story before publication. Her royalties from the sale of the book probably will run much more.

Briefly, you have a description of what *persistence* is capable of achieving. Fannie Hurst is no exception. Wherever men and women accumulate great riches, you may be sure they first acquired *persistence*. Broadway will give any beggar a cup of coffee and a sandwich, but it demands *persistence* of those who go after the big stakes.

Kate Smith will say "amen" when she reads this. For years she sang, without money, and without price, before any microphone she could reach. Broadway said to her, "Come and get it, if you can take it." She did take it until one happy day Broadway got tired and said, "Aw, what's the use? You don't know when you're whipped, so name your price, and go to work in earnest." Miss Smith named her price! It was plenty. Away up in figures so high that one week's salary is far more than most people make in a whole year.

Verily it pays to be *persistent*!

And here is an encouraging statement which carries with it a suggestion of great significance—*thousands of singers who excel Kate Smith are walking up and down Broadway looking for a "break"– without success.* Countless others have come and gone, many of them sang well enough, but they failed to make the grade because they lacked the courage to keep on keeping on, until Broadway became tired of turning them away. Persistence is a state of mind, therefore it can be cultivated. Like all states of mind, persistence is based upon definite causes, among them these:—

a. *Definiteness of purpose.* Knowing what one wants is the first and, perhaps, the most important step toward the development of persistence. A strong motive forces one to surmount many difficulties.

b. *Desire.* It is comparatively easy to acquire and to maintain persistence in pursuing the object of intense desire.

c. *Self-reliance.* Belief in one's ability to carry out a plan encourages one to follow the plan through with persistence. (Self-reliance can be developed through the principle described in the chapter on auto-suggestion).

d. *Definiteness of plans.* Organized plans, even though they may be weak and entirely impractical, encourage persistence.

e. *Accurate knowledge.* Knowing that one's plans are sound, based upon experience or observation, encourages persistence; "guessing" instead of "knowing" destroys persistence.

f. *Co-operation.* Sympathy, understanding, and harmonious cooperation with others tend to develop persistence.

g. *Will-Power.* The habit of concentrating one's thoughts upon the building of plans for the attainment of a definite purpose, leads to persistence.

h. *Habit.* Persistence is the direct result of habit. The mind absorbs and becomes a part of the daily experiences upon which it feeds. Fear, the worst of all enemies, can be effectively cured by forced repetition of acts of courage. Everyone who has seen active service in war knows this.

Before leaving the subject of *persistence*, take inventory of yourself, and determine in what particular, if any, you are lacking in this essential quality. Measure yourself courageously, point by point, and see how many of the eight factors of persistence you lack. The analysis may lead to discoveries that will give you a new grip on yourself.

Symptoms of Lack of Persistence

Here you will find the real enemies which stand between you and noteworthy achievement. Here you will find not only the "symptoms" indicating weakness of *persistence*, but also the deeply seated subconscious causes of this weakness. Study the list carefully, and face yourself squarely *if you really wish to know who you are, and what you are capable of doing.* These are the weaknesses which must be mastered by all who accumulate riches.

1. Failure to recognize and to clearly define exactly what one wants.
2. Procrastination, with or without cause. (Usually backed up with a formidable array of alibis and excuses).
3. Lack of interest in acquiring specialized knowledge.
4. Indecision, the habit of "passing the buck" on all occasions, instead of facing issues squarely. (Also backed by alibis).
5. The habit of relying upon alibis instead of creating definite plans for the solution of problems.
6. Self-satisfaction. There is but little remedy for this affliction, and no hope for those who suffer from it.
7. Indifference, usually reflected in one's readiness to compromise on all occasions, rather than meet opposition and fight it.
8. The habit of blaming others for one's mistakes, and accepting unfavorable circumstances as being unavoidable.
9. *Weakness of desire*, due to neglect in the choice of *motives* that impel action.
10. Willingness, even eagerness, to quit at the first sign of defeat. (Based upon one or more of the 6 basic fears).
11. Lack of *organized plans*, placed in writing where they may be analyzed.
12. The habit of neglecting to move on ideas, or to grasp opportunity when it presents itself.
13. *Wishing* instead of *willing*.
14. The habit of compromising with *poverty* instead of aiming at riches. General absence of ambition to be, to do, and to own.
15. Searching for all the shortcuts to riches, trying to *get* without *giving* a fair equivalent, usually reflected in the habit of gambling, endeavoring to drive "sharp" bargains.
16. *Fear of criticism,* failure to create plans and to put them into action, because of what other people will think, do, or say. This enemy belongs at the head of the list, because it generally exists in one's subconscious mind, where its presence is not recognized. (See the Six Basic Fears in a later chapter).

Let us examine some of the symptoms of the Fear of Criticism. The majority of people permit relatives, friends, and the public at large to so influence them that they cannot live their own lives, because they fear criticism.

Huge numbers of people make mistakes in marriage, stand by the bargain, and go through life miserable and unhappy, because they fear criticism which may follow if they correct the mistake. (Anyone who has submitted to this form of fear knows the irreparable damage it does, by destroying ambition, self-reliance, and the desire to achieve).

Millions of people neglect to acquire belated educations, after having left school, because they fear criticism.

Countless numbers of men and women, both young and old, permit relatives to wreck their lives in the name of *duty*, because they fear criticism. (Duty does not require any person to submit to the destruction of his personal ambitions and the right to live his own life in his own way).

People refuse to take chances in business, because they fear the criticism which may follow if they fail. The fear of criticism, in such cases is stronger than the *desire* for success.

Too many people refuse to set high goals for themselves, or even neglect selecting a career, because they fear the criticism of relatives and "friends" who may say "Don't aim so high, people will think you are crazy.

When Andrew Carnegie suggested that I devote twenty years to the organization of a philosophy of individual achievement my first impulse of thought was fear of what people might say. The suggestion set up a goal for me, far out of proportion to any I had ever conceived. As quick as a flash, my mind began to create alibis and excuses, all of them traceable to the inherent *fear of criticism*. Something inside of me said, "You can't do it– the job is too big, and requires too much time– what will your relatives think of you ?– how will you earn a living?– no one has ever organized a philosophy of success, what right have you to believe you can do it?– who are you, anyway, to aim so high?– remember your humble birth– what do you know about philosophy– people will think you are crazy–(and they did)– why hasn't some other person done this before now?"

These, and many other questions flashed into my mind, and demanded attention. It seemed as if the whole world had suddenly turned its attention to me with the purpose of ridiculing me into giving up all desire to carry out Mr. Carnegie's suggestion.

I had a fine opportunity, then and there, to kill off ambition before it gained control of me. Later in life, after having analyzed thousands of people, I discovered that *most ideas are still-born, and need the breath of life injected into them through definite plans of immediate action*. The time to nurse an idea is at the time of its birth. Every minute it lives, gives it a better chance of surviving. The *fear of criticism* is at the bottom of the destruction of most ideas which never reach the *planning* and *action* stage.

Many people believe that material success is the result of favorable "breaks." There is an element of ground for the belief, but those depending entirely upon luck, are nearly always disappointed, because they overlook another important factor which must be present before one can be sure of success. It is the knowledge with which favorable "breaks" can be made to order.

During the depression, W. C. Fields, the comedian, lost all his money, and found himself without income, without a job, and his means of earning a living (vaudeville) no longer existed. Moreover, he was past sixty, when many men consider themselves "old." He was so eager to stage a comeback that he offered to work without pay, in a new field (movies). In addition to his other troubles, he fell and injured his neck. To many that would have been the place to give up and *quit*. But Fields was *persistent*. He knew that if he carried on he would get the "breaks" sooner or later, and he did get them, but not by chance.

Marie Dressler found herself down and out, with her money gone, with no job, when she was about sixty. She, too, went after the "breaks," and got them. Her *persistence* brought an astounding triumph late in life, long beyond the age when most men and women are done with ambition to achieve.

Eddie Cantor lost his money in the 1929 stock crash, but he still had his *persistence* and his courage. With these, plus two prominent eyes, he exploited himself back into an income of $10,000 a week! Verily, if one has *persistence*, one can get along very well without many other qualities.

The only "break" anyone can afford to rely upon is a self-made "break." These come through the application of *persistence*. The starting point is *definiteness of purpose*.

Examine the first hundred people you meet, ask them what they want most in life, and ninety eight of them will not be able to tell you. If you press them for an answer, some will say– security, many will say– *money*, a few will say– happiness, others will say– *fame and power*, and still others will say– social recognition, ease in living, ability to sing, dance, or *write*, but none of them will be able to define these terms, or give the slightest indication of a *plan* by which they hope to attain these vaguely expressed wishes. Riches do not respond to wishes. They respond only to definite plans, backed by definite desires, through constant *persistence*.

How to Develop Persistence

There are four simple steps which lead to the habit of *persistence*. They call for no great amount of intelligence, no particular amount of education, and but little time or effort. The necessary steps are:–

1. A *definite purpose backed by burning desire for its fulfillment.*
2. A *definite plan, expressed in continuous action.*
3. A *mind closed tightly against all negative and discouraging influences*, including negative suggestions of relatives, friends and acquaintances.
4. A *friendly alliance with one or more persons who will encourage one to follow through with both plan and purpose.*

These four steps are essential for success in all walks of life. The entire purpose of the thirteen principles of this philosophy is to enable one to take these four steps as a matter of habit.

These are the steps by which one may control one's economic destiny.

They are the steps that lead to freedom and independence of thought.

They are the steps that lead to riches, in small or great quantities.

They lead the way to power, fame, and worldly recognition.

They are the four steps which guarantee favorable "breaks."

They are the steps that convert dreams into physical realities.

They lead, also, to the mastery of *fear, discouragement, indifference.*

There is a magnificent reward for all who learn to take these four steps. It is the privilege of writing one's own ticket, and of making Life yield whatever price is asked.

I have no way of knowing the facts, but I venture to conjecture that Mrs. Wallis Simpson's great love for a man was not accidental, nor the result of favorable "breaks" alone. There was a burning desire, and careful searching at every step of the way. Her first duty was to love. What is the greatest thing on earth? The Master called it love–not man made rules, criticism, bitterness, slander, or political "marriages," but love.

She knew what she wanted, not after she met the Prince of Wales, but long before that. Twice when she had failed to find it, she had the courage to continue her search. "To thine own self be true, and it must follow, as the night the day, thou canst not then be false to any man."

Her rise from obscurity was of the slow, progressive, *persistent* order, but it was *sure*! She triumphed over unbelievably long odds; and, no matter who you are, or what you may think of Wallis Simpson, or the king who gave up his Crown for her love, she is an astounding example of applied *persistence*, an instructor on the rules of self-determination, from whom the entire world might profitably take lessons.

When you think of Wallis Simpson, think of one who knew what she wanted, and shook the greatest empire on earth to get it. Women who complain that this is a man's world, that women do not have an equal chance to win, owe it to themselves to study carefully the life of this unusual woman, who, at an age which most women consider "old," captured the affections of the most desirable bachelor in the entire world.

And what of King Edward? What lesson may we learn from his part in the world's greatest drama of recent times? Did he pay too high a price for the affections of the woman of his choice?

Surely no one but he can give the correct answer. The rest of us can only conjecture. This much we know, the king came into the world without his own consent. He was born to great riches, without requesting them. He was persistently sought in marriage; politicians and statesmen throughout Europe tossed dowagers and princesses at his feet. Because he was the first born of his parents, he inherited a crown, which he did not seek, and perhaps did not desire. For more than forty years he was not a free agent, could not live his life in his own way, had but little privacy, and finally assumed duties inflicted upon him when he ascended the throne.

Some will say, "With all these blessings, King Edward should have found peace of mind, contentment, and joy of living."

The truth is that back of all the privileges of a crown, all the money, the fame, and the power inherited by King Edward, there was an emptiness which could be filled only by love.

His greatest *desire* was for love. Long before he met Wallis Simpson, he doubtless felt this great universal emotion tugging at the strings of his heart, beating upon the door of his soul, and crying out for expression.

And when he met a kindred spirit, crying out for this same Holy privilege of expression, he recognized it, and without fear or apology, opened his heart and bade it enter. All the scandal-mongers in the world cannot destroy the beauty of this international drama, through which two people found love, and had the courage to face open criticism, renounce *all else* to give it holy expression.

King Edward's *decision* to give up the crown of the world's most powerful empire, for the privilege of going the remainder of the way through life with the woman of his choice, was a decision that required courage. The decision also had a price, but who has the right to say the price was too great? Surely not He who said, "He among you who is without sin, let him cast the first stone."

As a suggestion to any evil-minded person who chooses to find fault with the Duke of Windsor, because his *desire* was for *love*, and for openly declaring his love for Wallis Simpson, and giving up his throne for her, let it be remembered that the *open declaration* was not essential. He could have followed the custom of clandestine liaison which has prevailed in Europe for centuries, without giving up either his throne, or the woman of his choice, and there would have been *no complaint from either church or laity*. But this unusual man was built of sterner stuff. His love was clean. It was deep and sincere. It represented the one thing which, above *all else* he truly *desired*, therefore, he took what he wanted, and paid the price demanded.

If Europe had been blessed with more rulers with the human heart and the traits of honesty of ex-king Edward, for the past century, that unfortunate hemisphere now seething with greed, hate, lust, political connivance, and threats of war, would have a *different and a better story to tell.* A story in which Love and not Hate would rule.

In the words of Stuart Austin Wier we raise our cup and drink this toast to ex-king Edward and Wallis Simpson:

"Blessed is the man who has come to know that our muted thoughts are our sweetest thoughts.

"Blessed is the man who, from the blackest depths, can see the luminous figure of *love*, and seeing, sing; and singing, say: 'Sweeter far than uttered lays are the thoughts I have of you.'"

In these words would we pay tribute to the two people who, more than all others of modern times, have been the victims of criticism and the recipients of abuse, because they found Life's greatest treasure, and claimed it. Mrs. Simpson read and approved this analysis.

Most of the world will applaud the Duke of Windsor and Wallis Simpson, because of their *persistence* in searching until they found life's greatest reward. *All of us can profit* by following their example in our own search for that which we demand of life.

What mystical power gives to men of *persistence* the capacity to master difficulties? Does the quality of *persistence* set up in one's mind some form of spiritual, mental or chemical activity which gives one access to supernatural forces? Does Infinite Intelligence throw itself on the side of the person who still fights on, after the battle has been lost, with the whole world on the opposing side?

These and many other similar questions have arisen in my mind as I have observed men like Henry Ford, who started at scratch, and built an Industrial Empire of huge proportions, with little else in the way of a beginning but *persistence*. Or, Thomas A. Edison, who, with less than three months of schooling, became the world's leading inventor and converted *persistence* into the talking machine, the moving picture machine, and the incandescent light, to say nothing of half a hundred other useful inventions.

I had the happy privilege of analyzing both Mr. Edison and Mr. Ford, year by year, over a long period of years, and therefore, the opportunity to study them at close range, so I speak from actual knowledge when I say that I found no quality save *persistence*, in either of them, that even remotely suggested the major source of their stupendous achievements.

As one makes an impartial study of the prophets, philosophers, "miracle" men, and religious leaders of the past, one is drawn to the inevitable conclusion that *persistence*, concentration of effort, and *definiteness of purpose*, were the major sources of their achievements.

Consider, for example, the strange and fascinating story of Mohammed; analyze his life, compare him with men of achievement in this modern age of industry and finance, and observe how they have one outstanding trait in common, *persistence*!

If you are keenly interested in studying the strange power which gives potency to *persistence*, read a biography of Mohammed, especially the one by Essad Bey. This brief review of that book, by Thomas Sugrue, in the Herald-Tribune, will provide a preview of the rare treat in store for those who take the time to read the entire story of one of the most astounding examples of the power of *persistence* known to civilization.

The Last Great Prophet: Reviewed by Thomas Sugrue

"Mohammed was a prophet, but he never performed a miracle. He was not a mystic; he had no formal schooling; he did not begin his mission until he was forty. When he announced that he was the Messenger of God, bringing word of the true religion, he was ridiculed and labeled a lunatic.

Children tripped him and women threw filth upon him. He was banished from his native city, Mecca, and his followers were stripped of their worldly goods and sent into the desert after him. When he had been preaching ten years he had nothing to show for it but banishment, poverty and ridicule. Yet before another ten years had passed, he was dictator of all Arabia, ruler of Mecca, and the head of a New World religion which was to sweep to the Danube and the Pyrenees before exhausting the impetus he gave it. That impetus was three-fold: the power of words, the efficacy of prayer and man's kinship with God.

"His career never made sense. Mohammed was born to impoverished members of a leading family of Mecca. Because Mecca, the crossroads of the world, home of the magic stone called the Caaba, great city of trade and the center of trade routes, was unsanitary, its children were sent to be raised in the desert by Bedouins. Mohammed was thus nurtured, drawing strength and health from the milk of nomad, vicarious mothers. He tended sheep and soon hired out to a rich widow as leader of her caravans. He traveled to all parts of the Eastern World, talked with many men of diverse beliefs and observed the decline of Christianity into warring sects. When he was twenty-eight, Khadija, the widow, looked upon him with favor, and married him. Her father would have objected to such a marriage, so she got him drunk and held him up while he gave the paternal blessing. For the next twelve years Mohammed lived as a rich and respected and very shrewd trader. Then he took to wandering in the desert, and one day he returned with the first verse of the Koran and told Khadija that the archangel Gabriel had appeared to him and said that he was to be the Messenger of God.

"The Koran, the revealed word of God, was the closest thing to a miracle in Mohammed's life. He had not been a poet; he had no gift of words. Yet the verses of the Koran, as he received them and recited them to the faithful, were better than any verses which the professional poets of the tribes could produce. This, to the Arabs, was a miracle. To them the gift of words was the greatest gift, the poet was all-powerful. In addition the Koran said that all men were equal before God, that the world should be a democratic state– Islam. It was this political heresy, plus Mohammed's desire to destroy all the 360 idols in the courtyard of the Caaba, which brought about his banishment. The idols brought the desert tribes to Mecca, and that meant trade. So the business men of Mecca, the capitalists, of which he had been one, set upon Mohammed. Then he retreated to the desert and demanded sovereignty over the world.

"The rise of Islam began. Out of the desert came a flame which would not be extinguished– a democratic army fighting as a unit and prepared to die without wincing. Mohammed had invited the Jews and Christians to join him; for he was not building a new religion. He was calling all who believed in one God to join in a single faith. If the Jews and Christians had accepted his invitation Islam would have conquered the world. They didn't. They would not even accept Mohammed's innovation of humane warfare. When the armies of the prophet entered Jerusalem not a single person was killed because of his faith. When the crusaders entered the city, centuries later, not a Moslem man, woman, or child was spared. But the Christians did accept one Moslem idea– the place of learning, the university."

Chapter Nine: Power of the Master Mind

The Driving Force: the Ninth Step Toward Riches

Power is essential for success in the accumulation of money.

Plans are inert and useless, without sufficient *power* to translate them into *action*. This chapter will describe the method by which an individual may attain and apply *power.*

power may be defined as "organized and intelligently directed *knowledge.*" Power, as the term is here used, refers to *organized* effort, sufficient to enable an individual to transmute *desire* into its monetary equivalent. *organized* effort is produced through the coordination of effort of two or more people, who work toward a *definite* end, in a spirit of harmony.

Power is required for the accumulation of money! Power is necessary for the retention of money after it has been accumulated!

Let us ascertain how power may be acquired. If power is "organized knowledge," let us examine the sources of knowledge:

a. *Infinite intelligence.* This source of knowledge may be contacted through the procedure described in another chapter, with the aid of Creative Imagination.

b. *Accumulated experience.* The accumulated experience of man, (or that portion of it which has been organized and recorded), may be found in any well-equipped public library. An important part of this accumulated experience is taught in public schools and colleges, where it has been classified and organized.

c. *Experiment and research.* In the field of science, and in practically every other walk of life, men are gathering, classifying, and organizing new facts daily. This is the source to which one must turn when knowledge is not available through "accumulated experience." Here, too, the Creative Imagination must often be used.

Knowledge may be acquired from any of the foregoing sources. It may be converted into *power* by organizing it into definite *plans* and by expressing those plans in terms of *action.*

Examination of the three major sources of knowledge will readily disclose the difficulty an individual would have, if he depended upon his efforts alone, in assembling knowledge and expressing it through definite plans in terms of *action.* If his plans are comprehensive, and if they contemplate large proportions, he must, generally, induce others to cooperate with him, before he can inject into them the necessary element of *power.*

Gaining Power Through the "Master Mind"

The "Master Mind" may be defined as: "Coordination of knowledge and effort, in a spirit of harmony, between two or more people, for the attainment of a definite purpose."

No individual may have great power without availing himself of the "Master Mind." In a preceding chapter, instructions were given for the creation of *plans* for the purpose of translating *desire* into its monetary equivalent. If you carry out these instructions with *persistence* and intelligence, and use discrimination in the selection of your "Master Mind" group, your objective will have been half-way reached, even before you begin to recognize it.

So you may better understand the "intangible" potentialities of power available to you, through a properly chosen "Master Mind" group, we will here explain the two characteristics of the Master Mind principle, one of which is economic in nature, and the other psychic. The economic feature is obvious. Economic advantages may be created by any person who surrounds himself with the advice, counsel, and personal cooperation of a group of men who are willing to lend him wholehearted aid, in a spirit of *perfect harmony.* This form of cooperative alliance has been the basis of nearly every great fortune. Your understanding of this great truth may definitely determine your financial status.

The psychic phase of the Master Mind principle is much more abstract, much more difficult to comprehend, because it has reference to the spiritual forces with which the human race, as a whole, is not well acquainted. You may catch a significant suggestion from this statement: "No two minds ever come together without, thereby, creating a third, invisible, intangible force which may be likened to a third mind."

Keep in mind the fact that there are only two known elements in the whole universe, energy and matter. It is a well known fact that matter may be broken down into units of molecules, atoms, and electrons. There are units of matter which may be isolated, separated, and analyzed.

Likewise, there are units of energy.

The human mind is a form of energy, a part of it being spiritual in nature. When the minds of two people are coordinated in a *spirit of harmony*, the spiritual units of energy of each mind form an affinity, which constitutes the "psychic" phase of the Master Mind.

The Master Mind principle, or rather the economic feature of it, was first called to my attention by Andrew Carnegie, over twenty-five years ago. Discovery of this principle was responsible for the choice of my life's work.

Mr. Carnegie's Master Mind group consisted of a staff of approximately fifty men, with whom he surrounded himself, for the *definite purpose* of manufacturing and marketing steel. He attributed his entire fortune to the *power* he accumulated through this "Master Mind."

Analyze the record of any man who has accumulated a great fortune, and many of those who have accumulated modest fortunes, and you will find that they have either consciously, or unconsciously employed the "Master Mind" principle.

Great power can be accumulated through no other principle!

Energy is Nature's universal set of building blocks, out of which she constructs every material thing in the universe, including man, and every form of animal and vegetable life. Through a process which only Nature completely understands, she translates energy into matter.

Nature's building blocks are available to man, in the energy involved in *thinking*! Man's brain may be compared to an electric battery. It absorbs energy from the ether, which permeates every atom of matter, and fills the entire universe.

It is a well known fact that a group of electric batteries will provide more energy than a single battery. It is also a well known fact that an individual battery will provide energy in proportion to the number and capacity of the cells it contains.

The brain functions in a similar fashion. This accounts for the fact that some brains are more efficient than others, and leads to this significant statement—a group of brains coordinated (or connected) in a spirit of harmony, will provide more thought-energy than a single brain, just as a group of electric batteries will provide more energy than a single battery.

Through this metaphor it becomes immediately obvious that the Master Mind principle holds the secret of the *power* wielded by men who surround themselves with other men of brains.

There follows, now, another statement which will lead still nearer to an understanding of the psychic phase of the Master Mind principle: When a group of individual brains are coordinated and function in Harmony, the increased energy created through that alliance, becomes available to every individual brain in the group.

It is a well known fact that Henry Ford began his business career under the handicap of poverty, illiteracy, and ignorance. It is an equally well known fact that, within the inconceivably short period of ten years, Mr. Ford mastered these three handicaps, and that within twenty-five years he made himself one of the richest men in America. Connect with this fact, the additional knowledge that Mr.

Ford's most rapid strides became noticeable, from the time he became a personal friend of Thomas A. Edison, and you will begin to understand what the influence of one mind upon another can accomplish. Go a step farther, and consider the fact that Mr. Ford's most outstanding achievements began from the time that he formed the acquaintances of Harvey Firestone, John Burroughs, and Luther Burbank, (each a man of great brain capacity), and you will have further evidence that *power* may be produced through friendly alliance of minds.

There is little if any doubt that Henry Ford is one of the best informed men in the business and industrial world. The question of his wealth needs no discussion. Analyze Mr. Ford's intimate personal friends, some of whom have already been mentioned, and you will be prepared to understand the following statement:– "Men take on the nature and the habits and the *power of thought* of those with whom they associate in a spirit of sympathy and harmony."

Henry Ford whipped poverty, illiteracy, and ignorance by allying himself with great minds, whose vibrations of thought he absorbed into his own mind. Through his association with Edison, Burbank, Burroughs, and Firestone, Mr. Ford added to his own brain power, the sum and substance of the intelligence, experience, knowledge, and spiritual forces of these four men. Moreover, he appropriated, and made use of the Master Mind principle through the methods of procedure described in this book.

This principle is available to you!

We have already mentioned Mahatma Gandhi. Perhaps the majority of those who have heard of Gandhi, look upon him as merely an eccentric little man, who goes around without formal wearing apparel, and makes trouble for the British Government. In reality, Gandhi is not eccentric, but *he is the most powerful man now living.* (Estimated by the number of his followers and their faith in their leader.) Moreover, he is probably the most powerful man who has ever lived. His power is passive, but it is real.

Let us study the method by which he attained his stupendous *power.* It may be explained in a few words. He came by *power* through inducing over two hundred million people to coordinate, with mind and body, in a spirit of *harmony*, for a *definite purpose.*

In brief, Gandhi has accomplished a *miracle*, for it is a miracle when two hundred million people can be induced– not forced– to cooperate in a spirit of *harmony*, for a limitless time. If you doubt that this is a miracle, try to induce *any two people* to cooperate in a spirit of harmony for any length of time.

Every man who manages a business knows what a difficult matter it is to get employees to work together in a spirit even remotely resembling *harmony*.

The list of the chief sources from which *power* may be attained is, as you have seen, headed by *infinite intelligence.* When two or more people coordinate in a spirit of *harmony*, and work toward a definite objective, they place themselves in position, through that alliance, to absorb power directly from the great universal storehouse of Infinite Intelligence. This is the greatest of all sources of *power.* It is the source to which the genius turns. It is the source to which every great leader turns, (whether he may be conscious of the fact or not).

The other two major sources from which the knowledge, necessary for the accumulation of *power*, may be obtained are no more reliable than the five senses of man. The senses are not always reliable. Infinite Intelligence does not err.

In subsequent chapters, the methods by which Infinite Intelligence may be most readily contacted will be adequately described. This is not a course on religion. No fundamental principle described in this book should be interpreted as being intended to interfere either directly, or indirectly, with any man's religious habits. This book has been confined, exclusively, to instructing the reader how to transmute the *definite purpose of desire for money,* into its monetary equivalent.

Read, *think*, and meditate as you read. Soon, the entire subject will unfold, and you will see it in perspective. You are now seeing the detail of the individual chapters.

Money is as shy and elusive as the "old time" maiden. It must be wooed and won by methods not unlike those used by a determined lover, in pursuit of the girl of his choice. And, coincidental as it is, the *power* used in the "wooing" of money is not greatly different from that used in wooing a maiden. That power, when successfully used in the pursuit of money must be mixed with *faith.* It must be mixed with *desire.* It must be mixed with *persistence.* It must be applied through a plan, and that plan must be set into *action.*

When money comes in quantities known as "the big money," it flows to the one who accumulates it, as easily as water flows down hill. There exists a great unseen stream of *power*, which may be compared to a river; except that one side flows in one direction, carrying all who get into that side of the stream, onward and upward to *wealth*– and the other side flows in the opposite direction, carrying all who are unfortunate enough to get into it (and not able to extricate themselves from it), downward to misery and *poverty.*

Every man who has accumulated a great fortune, has recognized the existence of this stream of life. It consists of one's *thinking process.* The positive emotions of thought form the side of the stream which carries one to fortune. The negative emotions form the side which carries one down to poverty.

This carries a thought of stupendous importance to the person who is following this book with the object of accumulating a fortune.

If you are in the side of the stream of *power* which leads to poverty, this may serve as an oar, by which you may propel yourself over into the other side of the stream. It can serve you *only* through application and use. Merely reading, and passing judgment on it, either one way or another, will in no way benefit you.

Some people undergo the experience of alternating between the positive and negative sides of the stream, being at times on the positive side, and at times on the negative side. The Wall Street crash of '29 swept millions of people from the positive to the negative side of the stream. These millions are struggling, some of them in desperation and fear, to get back to the positive side of the stream. This book was written especially for those millions.

Poverty and riches often change places. The Crash taught the world this truth, although the world will not long remember the lesson. Poverty may, and generally does, voluntarily take the place of riches. When riches take the place of poverty, the change is usually brought about through well conceived and carefully executed *plans.* Poverty needs no plan. It needs no one to aid it, because it is bold and ruthless. Riches are shy and timid. They have to be "attracted."

Anybody can *wish*
for riches, and most
people do, but only a few
know that a definite plan,
plus a *burning desire*
for wealth, are the only
dependable means of

accumulating wealth.

Chapter Ten: The Mystery of Sex

Transmutation: the Tenth Step Toward Riches

The meaning of the word "transmute" is, in simple language, "the changing, or transferring of one element, or form of energy, into another."

The emotion of sex brings into being a state of mind.

Because of ignorance on the subject, this state of mind is generally associated with the physical, and because of improper influences, to which most people have been subjected, in acquiring knowledge of sex, things essentially physical have highly biased the mind.

The emotion of sex has back of it the possibility of three constructive potentialities, they are:—

1. The perpetuation of mankind.
2. The maintenance of health, (as a therapeutic agency, it has no equal).
3. The transformation of mediocrity into genius through transmutation.

Sex transmutation is simple and easily explained. It means the switching of the mind from thoughts of physical expression, to thoughts of some other nature.

Sex desire is the most powerful of human desires. When driven by this desire, men develop keenness of imagination, courage, will-power, persistence, and creative ability unknown to them at other times. So strong and impelling is the desire for sexual contact that men freely run the risk of life and reputation to indulge it. When harnessed, and redirected along other lines, this motivating force maintains all of its attributes of keenness of imagination, courage, etc., which may be used as powerful creative forces in literature, art, or in any other profession or calling, including, of course, the accumulation of riches.

The transmutation of sex energy calls for the exercise of will-power, to be sure, but the reward is worth the effort. The desire for sexual expression is inborn and natural. The desire cannot, and should not be submerged or eliminated. But it should be given an outlet through forms of expression which enrich the body, mind, and spirit of man. If not given this form of outlet, through transmutation, it will seek outlets through purely physical channels.

A river may be dammed, and its water controlled for a time, but eventually, it will force an outlet. The same is true of the emotion of sex. It may be submerged and controlled for a time, but its very nature causes it to be ever seeking means of expression. If it is not transmuted into some creative effort it will find a less worthy outlet.

Fortunate, indeed, is the person who has discovered how to give sex emotion an outlet through some form of creative effort, for he has, by that discovery, lifted himself to the status of a genius.

Scientific research has disclosed these significant facts:

1. The men of greatest achievement are men with highly developed sex natures; men who have learned the art of sex transmutation.

2. The men who have accumulated great fortunes and achieved outstanding recognition in literature, art, industry, architecture, and the professions, were motivated by the influence of a woman.

The research from which these astounding discoveries were made, went back through the pages of biography and history for more than two thousand years. Wherever there was evidence available in connection with the lives of men and women of great achievement, it indicated most convincingly that they possessed highly developed sex natures.

The emotion of sex is an "irresistible force," against which there can be no such opposition as an "immovable body." When driven by this emotion, men become gifted with a super power for action. Understand this truth, and you will catch the significance of the statement that sex transmutation will lift one to the status of a genius.

The emotion of sex contains the secret of creative ability. Destroy the sex glands, whether in man or beast, and you have removed the major source of action. For proof of this, observe what happens to any animal after it has been castrated. A bull becomes as docile as a cow after it has been altered sexually. Sex alteration takes out of the male, whether man or beast, all the fight that was in him. Sex alteration of the female has the same effect.

The Ten Mind Stimuli

The human mind responds to stimuli, through which it may be "keyed up" to high rates of vibration, known as enthusiasm, creative imagination, intense desire, etc. The stimuli to which the mind responds most freely are:–

1. The desire for sex expression
2. Love
3. A burning desire for fame, power, or financial gain, *money*
4. Music
5. Friendship between either those of the same sex, or those of the opposite sex.
6. A Master Mind alliance based upon the harmony of two or more people who ally themselves for spiritual or temporal advancement.
7. Mutual suffering, such as that experienced by people who are persecuted.
8. Auto-suggestion
9. Fear
10. Narcotics and alcohol.

The desire for sex expression comes at the head of the list of stimuli, which most effectively "step up" the vibrations of the mind and start the "wheels" of physical action. Eight of these stimuli are natural and constructive. Two are destructive. The list is here presented for the purpose of enabling you to make a comparative study of the major sources of mind stimulation.

From this study, it will be readily seen that the emotion of sex is, by great odds, the most intense and powerful of all mind stimuli. This comparison is necessary as a foundation for proof of the statement that transmutation of sex energy may lift one to the status of a genius. Let us find out what constitutes a genius.

Some wiseacre has said that a genius is a man who "wears long hair, eats queer food, lives alone, and serves as a target for the joke makers." A better definition of a genius is, "a man who has discovered how to increase the vibrations of thought to the point where he can freely communicate with sources of knowledge not available through the ordinary rate of vibration of thought."

The person who thinks will want to ask some questions concerning this definition of genius. The first question will be, "How may one communicate with sources of knowledge which are not available through the *ordinary* rate of vibration of thought?"

The next question will be, "Are there known sources of knowledge which are available only to genii, and if so, *what are these sources*, and exactly how may they be reached?"

We shall offer proof of the soundness of some of the more important statements made in this book– or at least we shall offer evidence through which you may secure your own proof through experimentation, and in doing so, we shall answer both of these questions.

"Genius" Is Developed Through the Sixth Sense

The reality of a "sixth sense" has been fairly well established. This sixth sense is "Creative Imagination." The faculty of creative imagination is one which the majority of people never use during an entire lifetime, and if used at all, it usually happens by mere accident. A relatively small number of people use, *with deliberation and purpose aforethought*, the faculty of creative imagination. Those who use this faculty voluntarily, and with understanding of its functions, are *genii*.

The faculty of creative imagination is the direct link between the finite mind of man and Infinite Intelligence. All so-called revelations, referred to in the realm of religion, and all discoveries of basic or new principles in the field of invention, take place through the faculty of creative imagination.

When ideas or concepts flash into one's mind, through what is popularly called a "hunch," they come from one or more of the following sources:—

1. Infinite Intelligence
2. One's subconscious mind, wherein is stored every sense impression and thought impulse which ever reached the brain through any of the five senses
3. From the mind of some other person who has just released the thought, or picture of the idea or concept, through conscious thought, or
4. From the other person's subconscious storehouse.

There are no other *known* sources from which "inspired" ideas or "hunches" may be received.

The creative imagination functions best when the mind is vibrating (due to some form of mind stimulation) at an exceedingly high rate. That is, when the mind is functioning at a rate of vibration higher than that of ordinary, normal thought.

When brain action has been stimulated, through one or more of the ten mind stimulants, it has the effect of lifting the individual far above the horizon of ordinary thought, and permits him to envision distance, scope, and quality of *thoughts* not available on the lower plane, such as that occupied while one is engaged in the solution of the problems of business and professional routine.

When lifted to this higher level of thought, through any form of mind stimulation, an individual occupies, relatively, the same position as one who has ascended in an airplane to a height from which he may see over and beyond the horizon line which limits his vision, while on the ground. Moreover, while on this higher level of thought, the individual is not hampered or bound by any of the stimuli which circumscribe and limit his vision while wrestling with the problems of gaining the three basic necessities of food, clothing, and shelter. He is in a world of thought in which the *ordinary*, work-a-day thoughts have been as effectively removed as are the hills and valleys and other limitations of physical vision, when he rises in an airplane.

While on this exalted plane of *thought*, the creative faculty of the mind is given freedom for action. The way has been cleared for the sixth sense to function, it becomes receptive to ideas which could not reach the individual under any other circumstances. The "sixth sense" is the faculty which marks the difference between a genius and an ordinary individual.

The creative faculty becomes more alert and receptive to vibrations, originating outside the individual's subconscious mind, the more this faculty is used, and the more the individual relies upon it, and makes demands upon it for thought impulses. This faculty can be cultivated and developed only through use.

That which is known as ones conscience operates entirely through the faculty of the sixth sense.

The great artists, writers, musicians, and poets become great, because they acquire the habit of relying upon the "still small voice" which speaks from within, through the faculty of creative imagination. It is a fact well known to people who have "keen" imaginations that their best ideas come through so-called "hunches."

There is a great orator who does not attain to greatness, until he closes his eyes and begins to rely entirely upon the faculty of Creative Imagination. When asked why he closed his eyes just before the climaxes of his oratory, he replied, "I do it, because, then I speak through ideas which come to me from within."

One of America's most successful and best known financiers followed the habit of closing his eyes for two or three minutes before making a decision.

When asked why he did this, he replied, "With my eyes closed, I am able to draw upon a source of superior intelligence."

The late Dr. Elmer R. Gates, of Chevy Chase, Maryland, created more than 200 useful patents, many of them basic, through the process of cultivating and using the creative faculty. His method is both significant and interesting to one interested in attaining to the status of genius, in which category Dr. Gates, unquestionably belonged. Dr. Gates was one of the really great, though less publicized scientists of the world.

In his laboratory, he had what he called his "personal communication room." It was practically sound proof, and so arranged that all light could be shut out. It was equipped with a small table, on which he kept a pad of writing paper. In front of the table, on the wall, was an electric pushbutton, which controlled the lights. When Dr. Gates desired to draw upon the forces available to him through his Creative Imagination, he would go into this room, seat himself at the table, shut off the lights, and *concentrate* upon the *known* factors of the invention on which he was working, remaining in that position until ideas began to "flash" into his mind in connection with the *unknown* factors of the invention.

On one occasion, ideas came through so fast that he was forced to write for almost three hours. When the thoughts stopped flowing, and he examined his notes, he found they contained a minute description of principles which bad not a parallel among the known data of the scientific world.

Moreover, the answer to his problem was intelligently presented in those notes. In this manner Dr. Gates completed over 200 patents, which had been begun, but not completed, by "half-baked" brains. Evidence of the truth of this statement is in the United States Patent Office.

Dr. Gates earned his living by "sitting for ideas" for individuals and corporations. Some of the largest corporations in America paid him substantial fees, by the hour, for "sitting for ideas."

The reasoning faculty is often faulty, because it is largely guided by one's accumulated experience. Not all knowledge, which one accumulates through "experience," is accurate. Ideas received through the creative faculty are much more reliable, for the reason that they come from sources more reliable than any which are available to the reasoning faculty of the mind.

The major difference between the genius and the ordinary "crank" inventor, may be found in the fact that the genius works through his faculty of creative imagination, while the "crank" knows nothing of this faculty. The scientific inventor (such as Mr. Edison, and Dr. Gates), makes use of both the synthetic and the creative faculties of imagination.

For example, the scientific inventor, or "genius, begins an invention by organizing and combining the known ideas, or principles accumulated through experience, through the synthetic faculty (the reasoning faculty). If he finds this accumulated knowledge to be insufficient for the completion of his invention, he then draws upon the sources of knowledge available to him through his creative faculty. The method by which he does this varies with the individual, but this is the sum and substance of his procedure:

1. *He stimulates his mind so that it vibrates on a higher-than-average plane*, using one or more of the ten mind stimulants or some other stimulant of his choice.

2. *He concentrates* upon the known factors (the finished part) of his invention, and creates in his mind a perfect picture of unknown factors (the unfinished part), of his invention. He holds this picture in mind until it has been taken over by the subconscious mind, then relaxes by clearing his mind of *all* thought, and waits for his answer to "flash" into his mind.

Sometimes the results are both definite and immediate. At other times, the results are negative, depending upon the state of development of the "sixth sense," or creative faculty.

Mr. Edison tried out more than 10,000 different combinations of ideas through the synthetic faculty of his imagination before he "tuned in" through the creative faculty, and got the answer which perfected the incandescent light. His experience was similar when he produced the talking machine.

There is plenty of reliable evidence that the faculty of creative imagination exists. This evidence is available through accurate analysis of men who have become leaders in their respective callings, without having had extensive educations. Lincoln was a notable example of a great leader who achieved greatness, through the discovery, and use of his faculty of creative imagination. He discovered, and began to use this faculty as the result of the stimulation of love which he experienced after he met Anne Rutledge, a statement of the highest significance, in connection with the study of the source of genius.

The pages of history are filled with the records of great leaders whose achievements may be traced directly to the influence of women who aroused the creative faculties of their minds, through the stimulation of sex desire. Napoleon Bonaparte was one of these. When inspired by his first wife, Josephine, he was irresistible and invincible. When his "better judgment" or reasoning faculty prompted him to put Josephine aside, he began to decline. His defeat and St. Helena were not far distant.

If good taste would permit, we might easily mention scores of men, well known to the American people, who climbed to great heights of achievement under the stimulating influence of their wives, only to drop back to destruction *after* money and power went to their heads, and they put aside the old wife for a new one. Napoleon was not the only man to discover that sex influence, from the right source, is more powerful than any substitute of expediency, which may be created by mere reason.

The human mind responds to stimulation!

Among the greatest, and most powerful of these stimuli is the urge of sex. When harnessed and transmuted, this driving force is capable of lifting men into that higher sphere of thought which enables them to master the sources of worry and petty annoyance which beset their pathway on the lower plane.

Unfortunately, only the genii have made the discovery. Others have accepted the experience of sex urge, without discovering one of its major potentialities– a fact which accounts for the great number of "others" as compared to the limited number of genii.

For the purpose of refreshing the memory, in connection with the facts available from the biographies of certain men, we here present the names of a few men of outstanding achievement, each of whom was known to have been of a highly sexed nature. The genius which was their's, undoubtedly found its source of power in transmuted sex energy:

George Washington
Napoleon Bonaparte
William Shakespeare
Abraham Lincoln
Ralph Waldo Emerson
Robert Burns
Thomas Jefferson
Elbert Hubbard
Elbert H. Gary
Oscar Wilde
Woodrow Wilson
John H. Patterson
Andrew Jackson
Enrico Caruso

Your own knowledge of biography will enable you to add to this list. Find, if you can, a single man, in all history of civilization, who achieved outstanding success in any calling, who was not driven by a well developed sex nature.

If you do not wish to rely upon biographies of men not now living, take inventory of those whom you know to be men of great achievement, and see if you can find one among them who is not highly sexed.

Sex energy is the creative energy of all genii. There never has been, and never will be a great leader, builder, or artist lacking in this driving force of sex. Surely no one will misunderstand these statements to mean that *all* who are highly sexed are genii! Man attains to the status of a genius *only* when, and *if*, he stimulates his mind so that it draws upon the forces available, through the creative faculty of the imagination. Chief among the stimuli with which this "stepping up" of the vibrations may be produced is sex energy. The mere possession of this energy is not sufficient to produce a genius. The energy must be transmuted from desire for physical contact, into some other form of desire and action, before it will lift one to the status of a genius.

Far from becoming genii, because of great sex desires, the majority of men lower themselves, through misunderstanding and misuse of this great force, to the status of the lower animals.

Why Men Seldom Succeed Before Forty

I discovered, from the analysis of over 25,000 people, that men who succeed in an outstanding way, seldom do so before the age of forty, and more often they do not strike their real pace until they are well beyond the age of fifty. This fact was so astounding that it prompted me to go into the study of its cause most carefully, carrying the investigation over a period of more than twelve years.

This study disclosed the fact that the major reason why the majority of men who succeed do not begin to do so before the age of forty to fifty, is their tendency to *dissipate* their energies through over indulgence in physical expression of the emotion of sex. The majority of men never learn that the urge of sex has other possibilities, which far transcend in importance, that of mere physical expression. The majority of those who make this discovery, do so after having wasted many years at a period when the sex energy is at its height, prior to the age of forty-five to fifty. This usually is followed by noteworthy achievement.

The lives of many men up to, and sometimes well past the age of forty, reflect a continued dissipation of energies, which could have been more profitably turned into better channels. Their finer and more powerful emotions are sown wildly to the four winds. Out of this habit of the male, grew the term, "sowing his wild oats."

The desire for sexual expression is by far the strongest and most impelling of all the human emotions, and for this very reason this desire, when harnessed and transmuted into action, other than that of physical expression, may raise one to the status of a genius.

One of America's most able business men frankly admitted that his attractive secretary was responsible for most of the plans he created. He admitted that her presence lifted him to heights of creative imagination, such as he could experience under no other stimulus.

One of the most successful men in America owes most of his success to the influence of a very charming young woman, who has served as his source of inspiration for more than twelve years. Everyone knows the man to whom this reference is made, but not everyone knows the *real source* of his achievements.

History is not lacking in examples of men who attained to the status of genii, as the result of the use of artificial mind stimulants in the form of alcohol and narcotics. Edgar Allen Poe wrote the "Raven" while under the influence of liquor, "dreaming dreams that mortal never dared to dream before." James Whitcomb Riley did his best writing while under the influence of alcohol. Perhaps it was thus he saw "the ordered intermingling of the real and the dream, the mill above the river, and the mist above the stream." Robert Burns wrote best when intoxicated, "For Auld Lang Syne, my dear, we'll take a cup of kindness yet, for Auld Lang Syne."

But let it be remembered that many such men have destroyed themselves in the end. Nature has prepared her own potions with which men may safely stimulate their minds so they vibrate on a plane that enables them to tune in to fine and rare thoughts which come from— no man knows where! No satisfactory substitute for Nature's stimulants has ever been found.

It is a fact well known to psychologists that there is a very close relationship between sex desires and spiritual urges— a fact which accounts for the peculiar behavior of people who participate in the orgies known as religious "revivals," common among the primitive types.

The world is ruled, and the destiny of civilization is established, by the human emotions. People are influenced in their actions, not by reason so much as by "feelings." The creative faculty of the mind is set into action entirely by emotions, and not by cold reason. The most powerful of all human emotions is that of sex. There are other mind stimulants, some of which have been listed, but no one of them, nor all of them combined, can equal the driving power of sex.

A mind stimulant is any influence which will either temporarily, or permanently, increase the vibrations of thought. The ten major stimulants, described, are those most commonly resorted to. Through these sources one may commune with Infinite Intelligence, or enter, at will, the storehouse of the subconscious mind, either one's own, or that of another person, a procedure which is all there is of genius.

A teacher, who has trained and directed the efforts of more than 30,000 sales people, made the astounding discovery that highly sexed men are the most efficient salesmen. The explanation is, that the factor of personality known as "personal magnetism" is nothing more nor less than sex energy. Highly sexed people always have a plentiful supply of magnetism. Through cultivation and understanding, this vital force may be drawn upon and used to great advantage in the relationships between people. This energy may be communicated to others through the following media:

1. The hand-shake. The touch of the hand indicates, instantly, the presence of magnetism, or the lack of it.
2. The tone of voice. Magnetism, or sex energy, is the factor with which the voice may be colored, or made musical and charming.
3. Posture and carriage of the body. Highly sexed people move briskly, and with grace and ease.
4. The vibrations of thought. Highly sexed people mix the emotion of sex with their thoughts, or may do so at will, and in that way, may influence those around them.
5. Body adornment. People who are highly sexed are usually very careful about their personal appearance. They usually select clothing of a style becoming to their personality, physique, complexion, etc.

When employing salesmen, the more capable sales manager looks for the quality of personal magnetism as the first requirement of a salesman. People who lack sex energy will never become enthusiastic nor inspire others with enthusiasm, and enthusiasm is one of the most important requisites in salesmanship, no matter what one is selling.

The public speaker, orator, preacher, lawyer, or salesman who is lacking in sex energy is a "flop," as far as being able to influence others is concerned. Couple with this the fact, that most people can be influenced only through an appeal to their emotions, and you will understand the importance of sex energy as a part of the salesman's native ability. Master salesmen attain the status of mastery in selling, because they, either consciously, or unconsciously, transmute the energy of sex into *sales enthusiasm!* In this statement may be found a very practical suggestion as to the actual meaning of sex transmutation.

The salesman who knows how to take his mind off the subject of sex, and direct it in sales effort with as much enthusiasm and determination as he would apply to its original purpose, has acquired the art of sex transmutation, whether he knows it or not. The majority of salesmen who transmute their sex energy do so without being in the least aware of what they are doing, or how they are doing it.

Transmutation of sex energy calls for more will power than the average person cares to use for this purpose. Those who find it difficult to summon will-power sufficient for transmutation, may gradually acquire this ability. Though this requires will-power, the reward for the practice is more than worth the effort.

The entire subject of sex is one with which the majority of people appear to be unpardonably ignorant. The urge of sex has been grossly misunderstood, slandered, and burlesqued by the ignorant and the evil minded, for so long that the very word sex is seldom used in polite society. Men and women who are known to be blessed— yes, *blessed*—with highly sexed natures, are usually looked upon as being people who will bear watching. Instead of being called blessed, they are usually called cursed.

Millions of people, even in this age of enlightenment, have inferiority complexes which they developed because of this false belief that a highly sexed nature is a curse. These statements, of the virtue of sex energy, should not be construed as justification for the libertine. The emotion of sex is a virtue *only* when used intelligently, and with discrimination. It may be misused, and often is, to such an extent that it debases, instead of enriches, both body and mind. The better use of this power is the burden of this chapter.

It seemed quite significant to the author, when he made the discovery that practically every great leader, whom he had the privilege of analyzing, was a man whose achievements were largely inspired by a woman. In many instances, the "woman in the case" was a modest, self-denying wife, of whom the public had heard but little or nothing. In a few instances, the source of inspiration has been traced to the "other woman." Perhaps such cases may not be entirely unknown to you.

Intemperance in sex habits is just as detrimental as intemperance in habits of drinking and eating. In this age in which we live, an age which began with the world war, intemperance in habits of sex is common. This orgy of indulgence may account for the shortage of great leaders. No man can avail himself of the forces of his creative imagination, while dissipating them. Man is the only creature on earth which violates Nature's purpose in this connection. Every other animal indulges its sex nature in moderation, and with purpose which harmonizes with the laws of nature. Every other animal responds to the call of sex only in "season." Man's inclination is to declare "open season."

Every intelligent person knows that stimulation in excess, through alcoholic drink and narcotics, is a form of intemperance which destroys the vital organs of the body, including the brain. Not every person knows, however, that over indulgence in sex expression may become a habit as destructive and as detrimental to creative effort as narcotics or liquor.

A sex-mad man is not essentially different than a dope-mad man! Both have lost control over their faculties of reason and will-power. Sexual overindulgence may not only destroy reason and will-power, but it may also lead to either temporary, or permanent insanity. Many cases of hypochondria (imaginary illness) grow out of habits developed in ignorance of the true function of sex.

From these brief references to the subject, it may be readily seen that ignorance on the subject of sex transmutation, forces stupendous penalties upon the ignorant on the one hand, and withholds from them equally stupendous benefits, on the other.

Widespread ignorance on the subject of sex is due to the fact that the subject has been surrounded with mystery and beclouded by dark silence. The conspiracy of mystery and silence has had the same effect upon the minds of young people that the psychology of prohibition had. The result has been increased curiosity, and desire to acquire more knowledge on this "verboten" subject; and to the shame of all lawmakers, and most physicians— by training best qualified to educate youth on that subject-information has not been easily available.

Seldom does an individual enter upon highly creative effort in any field of endeavor before the age of forty. The average man reaches the period of his greatest capacity to create between forty and sixty. These statements are based upon analysis of thousands of men and women who have been carefully observed. They should be encouraging to those who fail to arrive before the age of forty, and to those who become frightened at the approach of "old age," around the forty-year mark. The years between forty and fifty are, as a rule, the most fruitful. Man should approach this age, not with fear and trembling, but with hope and eager anticipation.

If you want evidence that most men do not begin to do their best work before the age of forty, study the records of the most successful men known to the American people, and you will find it. Henry Ford had not "hit his pace" of achievement until he had passed the age of forty. Andrew Carnegie was well past forty before he began to reap the reward of his efforts. James J. Hill was still running a telegraph key at the age of forty. His stupendous achievements took place after that age. Biographies of American industrialists and financiers are filled with evidence that the period from forty to sixty is the most productive age of man.

Between the ages of thirty and forty, man begins to learn (if he ever learns), the art of sex transmutation. This discovery is generally accidental, and more often than otherwise, the man who makes it is totally unconscious of his discovery. He may observe that his powers of achievement have increased around the age of thirty-five to forty, but in most cases, he is not familiar with the cause of this change; that Nature begins to harmonize the emotions of love and sex in the individual, between the ages of thirty and forty, so that he may draw upon these great forces, and apply them jointly as stimuli to action.

Sex, alone, is a mighty urge to action, but its forces are like a cyclone–they are often uncontrollable. When the emotion of love begins to mix itself with the emotion of sex, the result is calmness of purpose, poise, accuracy of judgment, and balance. What person, who has attained to the age of forty, is so unfortunate as to be unable to analyze these statements, and to corroborate them by his own experience?

When driven by his desire to please a woman, based solely upon the emotion of sex, a man may be, and usually is, capable of great achievement, but his actions may be disorganized, distorted, and totally destructive. When driven by his desire to please a woman, based upon the motive of sex alone, a man may steal, cheat, and even commit murder. But when the emotion of *love* is mixed with the emotion of sex, that same man will guide his actions with more sanity, balance, and reason.

Criminologists have discovered that the most hardened criminals can be reformed through the influence of a woman's love. There is no record of a criminal having been reformed solely through the sex influence. These facts are well known, but their cause is not. Reformation comes, if at all, through the heart, or the emotional side of man, not through his head, or reasoning side. Reformation means, "a change of heart." It does not mean a "change of head." A man may, because of reason, make certain changes in his personal conduct to avoid the consequences of undesirable effects, but *genuine reformation* comes only through a change of heart–through a *desire* to change.

Love, Romance, and Sex are all emotions capable of driving men to heights of super achievement. Love is the emotion which serves as a safety valve, and insures balance, poise, and constructive effort. When combined, these three emotions may lift one to an altitude of a genius. There are genii, however, who know but little of the emotion of love. Most of them may be found engaged in some form of action which is destructive, or at least, not based upon justice and fairness toward others. If good taste would permit, a dozen genii could be named in the field of industry and finance, who ride ruthlessly over the rights of their fellow men. They seem totally lacking in conscience. The reader can easily supply his own list of such men.

The emotions are states of mind. Nature has provided man with a "chemistry of the mind" which operates in a manner similar to the principles of chemistry of matter. It is a well known fact that, through the aid of chemistry of matter, a chemist may create a deadly poison by mixing certain elements, none of which are– in themselves– harmful in the right proportions. The emotions may, likewise, be combined so as to create a deadly poison. The emotions of sex and jealousy, when mixed, may turn a person into an insane beast.

The presence of any one or more of the destructive emotions in the human mind, through the chemistry of the mind, sets up a poison which may destroy one's sense of justice and fairness. In extreme cases, the presence of any combination of these emotions in the mind may destroy one's reason.

The road to genius consists of the development, control, and use of sex, love, and romance. Briefly, the process may be stated as follows:

Encourage the presence of these emotions as the dominating thoughts in one's mind, and discourage the presence of all the destructive emotions. The mind is a creature of habit. It thrives upon the dominating thoughts fed it. Through the faculty of will-power, one may discourage the presence of any emotion, and encourage the presence of any other. Control of the mind, through the power of will, is not difficult. Control comes from persistence, and habit. The secret of control lies in understanding the process of transmutation. When any negative emotion presents itself in one's mind, it can be transmuted into a positive, or constructive emotion, by the simple procedure of changing one's thoughts.

There is no other road to genius than through voluntary self effort! A man may attain to great heights of financial or business achievement, solely by the driving force of sex energy, but history is filled with evidence that he may, and usually does, carry with him certain traits of character which rob him of the ability to either hold, or enjoy his fortune. This is worthy of analysis, thought, and meditation, for it states a truth, the knowledge of which may be helpful to women as well as men. Ignorance of this has cost thousands of people their privilege of *happiness*, even though they possessed riches.

The emotions of love and sex leave their unmistakable marks upon the features. Moreover, these signs are so visible, that all who wish may read them. The man who is driven by the storm of passion, based upon sex desires alone, plainly advertises that fact to the entire world, by the expression of his eyes, and the lines of his face. The emotion of love, when mixed with the emotion of sex, softens, modifies, and beautifies the facial expression. No character analyst is needed to tell you this—you may observe it for yourself.

The emotion of love brings out, and develops, the artistic and the aesthetic nature of man. It leaves its impress upon one's very soul, even after the fire has been subdued by time and circumstance.

Memories of love never pass. They linger, guide, and influence long after the source of stimulation has faded. There is nothing new in this. Every person, who has been moved by *genuine love*, knows that it leaves enduring traces upon the human heart. The effect of love endures, because love is spiritual in nature. The man who cannot be stimulated to great heights of achievement by love, is hopeless—he is dead, though he may seem to live.

Even the memories of love are sufficient to lift one to a higher plane of creative effort. The major force of love may spend itself and pass away, like a fire which has burned itself out, but it leaves behind indelible marks as evidence that it passed that way. Its departure often prepares the human heart for a still greater love.

Go back into your yesterdays, at times, and bathe your mind in the beautiful memories of past love. It will soften the influence of the present worries and annoyances. It will give you a source of escape from the unpleasant realities of life, and maybe—who knows?—your mind will yield to you, during this temporary retreat into the world of fantasy, ideas, or plans which may change the entire financial or spiritual status of your life.

If you believe yourself unfortunate, because you have "loved and lost," perish the thought. One who has loved truly, can never lose entirely. Love is whimsical and temperamental. Its nature is ephemeral, and transitory. It comes when it pleases, and goes away without warning. Accept and enjoy it while it remains, but spend no time worrying about its departure. Worry will never bring it back.

Dismiss, also, the thought that love never comes but once. Love may come and go, times without number, but there are no two love experiences which affect one in just the same way. There may be, and there usually is, one love experience which leaves a deeper imprint on the heart than all the others, but all love experiences are beneficial, except to the person who becomes resentful and cynical when love makes its departure.

There should be no disappointment over love, and there would be none if people understood the difference between the emotions of love and sex. The major difference is that love is spiritual, while sex is biological. No experience, which touches the human heart with a spiritual force, can possibly be harmful, except through ignorance, or jealousy.

Love is, without question, life's greatest experience. It brings one into communion with Infinite Intelligence. When mixed with the emotions of romance and sex, it may lead one far up the ladder of creative effort. The emotions of love, sex, and romance, are sides of the eternal triangle of achievement-building genius. Nature creates genii through no other force.

Love is an emotion with many sides, shades, and colors. The love which one feels for parents, or children is quite different from that which one feels for one's sweetheart. The one is mixed with the emotion of sex, while the other is not.

The love which one feels in true friendship is not the same as that felt for one's sweetheart, parents, or children, but it, too, is a form of love.

Then, there is the emotion of love for things inanimate, such as the love of Nature's handiwork. But the most intense and burning of all these various kinds of love, is that experienced in the blending of the emotions of love and sex. Marriages, not blessed with the eternal affinity of love, properly balanced and proportioned, with sex, cannot be happy ones—and seldom endure. Love, alone, will not bring happiness in marriage, nor will sex alone. When these two beautiful emotions are blended, marriage may bring about a state of mind, closest to the spiritual that one may ever know on this earthly plane.

When the emotion of romance is added to those of love and sex, the obstructions between the finite mind of man and Infinite Intelligence are removed.

Then a genius has been born!

What a different story is this, than those usually associated with the emotion of sex. Here is an interpretation of the emotion which lifts it out of the commonplace, and makes of it potter's clay in the hands of God, from which He fashions all that is beautiful and inspiring. It is an interpretation which would, when properly understood, bring harmony out of the chaos which exists in too many marriages. The disharmonies often expressed in the form of nagging, may usually be traced to lack of knowledge on the subject of sex. Where love, romance and the proper understanding of the emotion and function of sex abide, there is no disharmony between married people.

Fortunate is the husband whose wife understands the true relationship between the emotions of love, sex, and romance. When motivated by this holy triumvirate, no form of labor is burdensome, because even the most lowly form of effort takes on the nature of a labor of love.

It is a very old saying that "a man's wife may either make him or break him," but the reason is not always understood. The "making" and "breaking" is the result of the wife's understanding, or lack of understanding of the emotions of love, sex, and romance.

Despite the fact that men are polygamous, by the very nature of their biological inheritance, it is true that no woman has as great an influence on a man as his wife, unless he is married to a woman totally unsuited to his nature. If a woman permits her husband to lose interest in her, and become more interested in other women, it is usually because of her ignorance, or indifference toward the subjects of sex, love, and romance. This statement presupposes, of course, that genuine love once existed between a man and his wife. The facts are equally applicable to a man who permits his wife's interest in him to die.

Married people often bicker over a multitude of trivialities. If these are analyzed accurately, the real cause of the trouble will often be found to be indifference, or ignorance on these subjects.

Man's greatest motivating force is his desire to please woman! The hunter who excelled during prehistoric days, before the dawn of civilization, did so, because of his desire to appear great in the eyes of woman. Man's nature has not changed in this respect. The "hunter" of today brings home no skins of wild animals, but he indicates his desire for her favor by supplying fine clothes, motor cars, and wealth. Man has the same desire to please woman that he had before the dawn of civilization. The only thing that has changed, is his method of pleasing. Men who accumulate large fortunes, and attain to great heights of power and fame, do so, mainly, to satisfy their desire to please women.

Take women out of their lives, and great wealth would be useless to most men. It is this inherent desire of man to please woman, which gives woman the power to make or break a man.

The woman who understands man's nature and tactfully caters to it, need have no fear of competition from other women. Men may be "giants" with indomitable will-power when dealing with other men, but they are easily managed by the women of their choice.

Most men will not admit that they are easily influenced by the women they prefer, because it is in the nature of the male to want to be recognized as the stronger of the species. Moreover, the intelligent woman recognizes this "manly trait" and very wisely makes no issue of it.

Some men know that they are being influenced by the women of their choice— their wives, sweethearts, mothers or sisters— but they tactfully refrain from rebelling against the influence because they are intelligent enough to know that *no man is happy or complete without the modifying influence of the right woman.* The man who does not recognize this important truth deprives himself of the power which has done more to help men achieve success than all other forces combined.

Chapter Eleven: The Subconscious Mind

The Connecting Link: the Eleventh Step Toward Riches

The subconscious mind consists of a field of consciousness, in which every impulse of thought that reaches the objective mind through any of the five senses, is classified and recorded, and from which thoughts may be recalled or withdrawn as letters may be taken from a filing cabinet.

It receives, and files, sense impressions or thoughts, regardless of their nature. You may *voluntarily* plant in your subconscious mind any plan, thought, or purpose which you desire to translate into its physical or monetary equivalent. The subconscious acts first on the dominating desires which have been mixed with emotional feeling, such as faith.

Consider this in connection with the instructions given in the chapter on *desire*, for taking the six steps there outlined, and the instructions given in the chapter on the building and execution of plans, and you will understand the importance of the thought conveyed.

The subconscious mind works day and night. Through a method of procedure, unknown to man, the subconscious mind draws upon the forces of Infinite Intelligence for the power with which it voluntarily transmutes one's desires into their physical equivalent, making use, always of the most practical media by which this end may be accomplished.

You cannot entirely control your subconscious mind, but you can voluntarily hand over to it any plan, desire, or purpose which you wish transformed into concrete form. Read, again, instructions for using the subconscious mind, in the chapter on autosuggestion.

There is plenty of evidence to support the belief that the subconscious mind is the connecting link between the finite mind of man and Infinite Intelligence. It is the intermediary through which one may draw upon the forces of Infinite Intelligence at will. It, alone, contains the secret process by which mental impulses are modified and changed into their spiritual equivalent. It, alone, is the medium through which prayer may be transmitted to the source capable of answering prayer.

The possibilities of creative effort connected with the subconscious mind are stupendous and imponderable. They inspire one with awe.

I never approach the discussion of the subconscious mind without a feeling of littleness and inferiority due, perhaps, to the fact that man's entire stock of knowledge on this subject is so pitifully limited. The very fact that the subconscious mind is the medium of communication between the thinking mind of man and Infinite Intelligence is, of itself, a thought which almost paralyzes one's reason.

After you have accepted, as a reality, the existence of the subconscious mind, and understand its possibilities, as a medium for transmuting your *desires* into their physical or monetary equivalent, you will comprehend the full significance of the instructions given in the chapter on *desire*. You will also understand why you have been repeatedly admonished to *make your desires clear, and to reduce them to writing*. You will also understand the necessity of *persistence* in carrying out instructions.

The thirteen principles are the stimuli with which you acquire the ability to reach, and to influence your subconscious mind. Do not become discouraged, if you cannot do this upon the first attempt. Remember that the subconscious mind may be voluntarily directed only through habit, under the directions given in the chapter on *faith*. You have not yet had time to master faith. Be patient. Be persistent.

A good many statements in the chapters on faith and auto-suggestion will be repeated here, for the benefit of *your* subconscious mind. Remember, your subconscious mind functions voluntarily, whether you make any effort to influence it or not. This, naturally, suggests to you that thoughts of fear and poverty, and all negative thoughts serve as stimuli to your subconscious mind, unless, you master these impulses and give it more desirable food upon which it may feed.

The subconscious mind will not remain idle! If you fail to plant *desires* in your subconscious mind, it will feed upon the thoughts which reach it as the result of your neglect. We have already explained that thought impulses, both negative and positive are reaching the subconscious mind continuously, from the four sources which were mentioned in the chapter on Sex Transmutation.

For the present, it is sufficient if you remember that you are living daily, in the midst of all manner of thought impulses which are reaching your subconscious mind, without your knowledge. Some of these impulses are negative, some are positive. You are now engaged in trying to help shut off the flow of negative impulses, and to aid in voluntarily influencing your subconscious mind, through positive impulses of *desire*.

When you achieve this, you will possess the key which unlocks the door to your subconscious mind. Moreover, you will control that door so completely, that no undesirable thought may influence your subconscious mind.

Everything which man creates, *begins* in the form of a thought impulse. Man can create nothing which he does not first conceive in *thought*. Through the aid of the imagination, thought impulses may be assembled into plans. The imagination, when under control, may be used for the creation of plans or purposes that lead to success in one's chosen occupation.

All thought impulses, intended for transmutation into their physical equivalent, voluntarily planted in the subconscious mind, must pass through the imagination, and be mixed with faith. The "mixing" of faith with a plan, or purpose, intended for submission to the subconscious mind, may be done *only* through the imagination.

From these statements, you will readily observe that voluntary use of the subconscious mind calls for coordination and application of all the principles.

Ella Wheeler Wilcox gave evidence of her understanding of the power of the subconscious mind when she wrote:

"You never can tell what a thought will do
In bringing you hate or love–
For thoughts are things, and their airy wings
Are swifter than carrier doves.
They follow the law of the universe–
Each thing creates its kind,
And they speed O'er the track to bring you back
Whatever went out from your mind."

Mrs. Wilcox understood the truth, that thoughts which go out from one's mind, also embed themselves deeply in one's subconscious mind, where they serve as a magnet, pattern, or blueprint by which the subconscious mind is influenced while translating them into their physical equivalent. Thoughts are truly things, for the reason that every material thing begins in the form of thought-energy.

The subconscious mind is more susceptible to influence by impulses of thought mixed with "feeling" or emotion, than by those originating solely in the reasoning portion of the mind. In fact, there is much evidence to support the theory, that *only* emotionalized thoughts have any *action* influence upon the subconscious mind. It is a well known fact that emotion or feeling, rules the majority of people. If it is true that the subconscious mind responds more quickly to, and is influenced more readily by thought impulses which are well mixed with emotion, it is essential to become familiar with the more important of the emotions. There are seven major positive emotions, and seven major negative emotions. The negatives voluntarily inject themselves into the thought impulses, which insure passage into the subconscious mind. The positives must be injected, through the principle of auto-suggestion, into the thought impulses which an individual wishes to pass on to his subconscious mind. (Instructions have been given in the chapter on auto-suggestion.)

These emotions, or feeling impulses, may be likened to yeast in a loaf of bread, because they constitute the *action* element, which transforms thought impulses from the passive to the active state. Thus may one understand why thought impulses, which have been well mixed with emotion, are acted upon more readily than thought impulses originating in "cold reason."

You are preparing yourself to influence and control the "inner audience" of your subconscious mind, in order to hand over to it the *desire* for money, which you wish transmuted into its monetary equivalent. It is essential, therefore, that you understand the method of approach to this "inner audience." You must speak its language, or it will not heed your call. It understands best the language of emotion or feeling. Let us, therefore describe here the seven major positive emotions, and the seven major negative motions, so that you may draw upon the positives, and avoid the negatives, when giving instructions to your subconscious mind.

The Seven Major Positive Emotions

The emotion of *desire*
The emotion of *faith*
The emotion of *love*
The emotion of *sex*
The emotion of *enthusiasm*
The emotion of *romance*
The emotion of *hope*

There are other positive emotions, but these are the seven most powerful, and the ones most commonly used in creative effort. Master these seven emotions (they can be mastered only by *use*), and the other positive emotions will be at your command when you need them. Remember, in this connection, that you are studying a book which is intended to help you develop a "money consciousness" by filling your mind with positive emotions. One does not become money conscious by filling one's mind with negative emotions.

The Seven Major Negative Emotions (To Be Avoided)

The emotion of *fear*
The emotion of *jealousy*
The emotion of *hatred*
The emotion of *revenge*
The emotion of *greed*
The emotion of *superstition*
The emotion of anger

Positive and negative emotions cannot occupy the mind at the same time. One or the other must dominate. It is your responsibility to make sure that positive emotions constitute the dominating influence of your mind. Here the law of *habit* will come to your aid. Form the habit of applying and using the positive emotions! Eventually, they will dominate your mind so completely, that the negatives cannot enter it.

Only by following these instructions literally, and continuously, can you gain control over your subconscious mind. The presence of a single negative in your conscious mind is sufficient to destroy all chances of constructive aid from your subconscious mind.

If you are an observing person, you must have noticed that most people resort to prayer *only* after everything else has *failed*! Or else they pray by a ritual of meaningless words. And, because it is a fact that most people who pray, do so *only after everything else has failed*, they go to prayer with their minds filled with *fear* and *doubt*, which are the emotions the subconscious mind acts upon, and passes on to Infinite Intelligence. Likewise, that is the emotion which Infinite Intelligence receives, and *acts upon*.

If you pray for a thing, but have fear as you pray, that you may not receive it, or that your prayer will not be acted upon by Infinite Intelligence, your prayer will have been in vain.

Prayer does, sometimes, result in the realization of that for which one prays. If you have ever had the experience of receiving that for which *you* prayed, go back in your memory, and recall your actual *state of mind*, while you were praying, and you will know, for sure, that the theory here described is more than a theory.

The time will come when the schools and educational institutions of the country will teach the "science of prayer." Moreover, then prayer may be, and will be reduced to a science. When that time comes, (it will come as soon as mankind is ready for it, and demands it), no one will approach the Universal Mind in a state of fear, for the very good reason that there will be no such emotion as fear. Ignorance, superstition, and false teaching will have disappeared, and man will have attained his true status as a child of Infinite Intelligence. A few have already attained this blessing.

If you believe this prophesy is far-fetched, take a look at the human race in retrospect. Less than a hundred years ago, men believed the lightning to be evidence of the wrath of God, and feared it. Now, thanks to the power of *faith*, men have harnessed the lightning and made it turn the wheels of industry. Much less than a hundred years ago, men believed the space between the planets to be nothing but a great void, a stretch of dead nothingness. Now, thanks to this same power of *faith*, men know that far from being either dead or a void, the space between the planets is very much alive, that it is the highest form of vibration known, excepting, perhaps, the vibration of *thought*. Moreover, men know that this living, pulsating, vibratory energy which permeates every atom of matter, and fills every niche of space, connects every human brain with every other human brain.

What reason have men to believe that this same energy does not connect every human brain with Infinite Intelligence? There are no toll-gates between the finite mind of man and Infinite Intelligence.

The communication costs nothing except Patience, Faith, Persistence, Understanding, and a *sincere desire* to communicate. Moreover, the approach can be made only by the individual himself. Paid prayers are worthless. Infinite Intelligence does no business by proxy. You either go direct, or you do not communicate.

You may buy prayer books and repeat them until the day of your doom, without avail. Thoughts which you wish to communicate to Infinite Intelligence, must undergo transformation, such as can be given only through your own subconscious mind.

The method by which you may communicate with Infinite Intelligence is very similar to that through which the vibration of sound is communicated by radio. If you understand the working principle of radio, you of course, know that sound cannot be communicated through the ether until it has been "stepped up," or changed into a rate of vibration which the human ear cannot detect. The radio sending station picks up the sound of the human voice, and "scrambles," or modifies it by stepping up the vibration millions of times. Only in this way, can the vibration of sound be communicated through the ether. After this transformation has taken place, the ether "picks up" the energy (which originally was in the form of vibrations of sound), carries that energy to radio receiving stations, and these receiving sets "step" that energy back down to its original rate of vibration so it is recognized as sound.

The subconscious mind is the intermediary, which translates one's prayers into terms which Infinite Intelligence can recognize, presents the message, and brings back the answer in the form of a definite plan or idea for procuring the object of the prayer. Understand this principle, and you will know why mere words read from a prayer book cannot, and will never serve as an agency of communication between the mind of man and Infinite Intelligence.

Before your prayer will reach Infinite Intelligence (a statement of the author's theory only), it probably is transformed from its original thought vibration into terms of spiritual vibration. Faith is the only known agency which will give your thoughts a spiritual nature. *faith* and *fear* make poor bedfellows. Where one is found, the other cannot exist.

Chapter Twelve: The Brain

A Broadcasting and Receiving Station for Thought: the Twelfth Step Toward Riches

More than twenty years ago, the author, working in conjunction with the late Dr. Alexander Graham Bell, and Dr. Elmer R. Gates, observed that every human brain is both a broadcasting and receiving station for the vibration of thought.

Through the medium of the ether, in a fashion similar to that employed by the radio broadcasting principle, every human brain is capable of picking up vibrations of thought which are being released by other brains.

In connection with the statement in the preceding paragraph, compare, and consider the description of the Creative Imagination, as outlined in the chapter on Imagination. The Creative Imagination is the "receiving set" of the brain, which receives thoughts, released by the brains of others. It is the agency of communication between one's conscious, or reasoning mind, and the four sources from which one may receive thought stimuli.

When stimulated, or "stepped up" to a high rate of vibration, the mind becomes more receptive to the vibration of thought which reaches it through the ether from outside sources. This "stepping up" process takes place through the positive emotions, or the negative emotions. Through the emotions, the vibrations of thought may be increased.

Vibrations of an exceedingly high rate are the only vibrations picked up and carried, by the ether, from one brain to another. Thought is energy traveling at an exceedingly high rate of vibration. Thought, which has been modified or "stepped up" by any of the major emotions, vibrates at a much higher rate than ordinary thought, and it is this type of thought which passes from one brain to another, through the broadcasting machinery of the human brain.

The emotion of sex stands at the head of the list of human emotions, as far as intensity and driving force are concerned. The brain which has been stimulated by the emotion of sex, vibrates at a much more rapid rate than it does when that emotion is quiescent or absent.

The result of sex transmutation, is the increase of the rate of vibration of thoughts to such a pitch that the Creative Imagination becomes highly receptive to ideas, which it picks up from the ether. On the other hand, when the brain is vibrating at a rapid rate, it not only attracts thoughts and ideas released by other brains through the medium of the ether, but it gives to one's own thoughts that "feeling" which is essential before those thoughts will be picked up and acted upon by one's subconscious mind.

Thus, you will see that the broadcasting principle is the factor through which you mix feeling, or emotion with your thoughts and pass them on to your subconscious mind.

The subconscious mind is the "sending station" of the brain, through which vibrations of thought are broadcast. The Creative Imagination is the "receiving set," through which the vibrations of thought are picked up from the ether.

Along with the important factors of the subconscious mind, and the faculty of the Creative Imagination, which constitute the sending and receiving sets of your mental broadcasting machinery, consider now the principle of auto-suggestion, which is the medium by which you may put into operation your "broadcasting" station.

Through the instructions described in the chapter on auto-suggestion, you were definitely informed of the method by which *desire* may be transmuted into its monetary equivalent.

Operation of your mental "broadcasting" station is a comparatively simple procedure. You have but three principles to bear in mind, and to apply, when you wish to use your broadcasting station—the *subconscious mind, creative imagination, and auto-suggestion*. The stimuli through which you put these three principles into action have been described— the procedure begins with *desire*.

The Greatest Forces Are "Intangible"

The depression brought the world to the very border-line of understanding of the forces which are intangible and unseen. Through the ages which have passed, man has depended too much upon his physical senses, and has limited his knowledge to physical things, which he could see, touch, weigh, and measure.

We are now entering the most marvelous of all ages—an age which will teach us something of the intangible forces of the world about us. Perhaps we shall learn, as we pass through this age, that the "other self" is more powerful than the physical self we see when we look into a mirror.

Sometimes men speak lightly of the intangibles— the things which they cannot perceive through any of their five senses, and when we hear them, it should remind us that all of us are controlled by forces which are unseen and intangible.

The whole of mankind has not the power to cope with, nor to control the intangible force wrapped up in the rolling waves of the oceans. Man has not the capacity to understand the intangible force of gravity, which keeps this little earth suspended in mid-air, and keeps man from falling from it, much less the power to control that force. Man is entirely subservient to the intangible force which comes with a thunder storm, and he is just as helpless in the presence of the intangible force of electricity— nay, he does not even know what electricity is, where it comes from, or what is its purpose!

Nor is this by any means the end of man's ignorance in connection with things unseen and intangible. He does not understand the intangible force (and intelligence) wrapped up in the soil of the earth— the force which provides him with every morsel of food he eats, every article of clothing he wears, every dollar he carries in his pockets.

The Dramatic Story of the Brain

Last, but not least, man, with all of his boasted culture and education, understands little or nothing of the intangible force (the greatest of all the intangibles) of thought. He knows but little concerning the physical brain, and its vast network of intricate machinery through which the power of thought is translated into its material equivalent, but he is now entering an age which shall yield enlightenment on the subject. Already men of science have begun to turn their attention to the study of this stupendous thing called a brain, and, while they are still in the kindergarten stage of their studies, they have uncovered enough knowledge to know that the central switchboard of the human brain, the number of lines which connect the brain cells one with another, equal the figure one, followed by fifteen million ciphers.

"The figure is so stupendous," said Dr. C. Judson Herrick, of the University of Chicago, "that astronomical figures dealing with hundreds of millions of light years, become insignificant by comparison.

It has been determined that there are from 10,000,000,000 to 14,000,000,000 nerve cells in the human cerebral cortex, and we know that these are arranged in definite patterns. These arrangements are not haphazard. They are orderly. Recently developed methods of electro-physiology draw off action currents from very precisely located cells, or fibers with micro-electrodes, amplify them with radio tubes, and record potential differences to a millionth of a volt."

It is inconceivable that such a network of intricate machinery should be in existence for the sole purpose of carrying on the physical functions incidental to growth and maintenance of the physical body. Is it not likely that the same system, which gives billions of brain cells the media for communication one with another, provides, also the means of communication with other intangible forces?

After this book had been written, just before the manuscript went to the publisher, there appeared in the New York Times, an editorial showing that at least one great University, and one intelligent investigator in the field of mental phenomena, are carrying on an organized research through which conclusions have been reached that parallel many of those described in this and the following chapter. The editorial briefly analyzed the work carried on by Dr. Rhine, and his associates at Duke University, viz:—"What is 'Telepathy'?

"A month ago we cited on this page some of the remarkable results achieved by Professor Rhine and his associates in Duke University from more than a hundred thousand tests to determine the existence of 'telepathy' and 'clairvoyance.' These results were summarized in the first two articles in Harpers Magazine. In the second which has now appeared, the author, E. H. Wright, attempts to summarize what has been learned, or what it seems reasonable to infer, regarding the exact nature of these 'extrasensory' modes of perception.

"The actual existence of telepathy and clairvoyance now seems to some scientists enormously probable as the result of Rhine's experiments. Various percipients were asked to name as many cards in a special pack as they could without looking at them and without other sensory access to them. About a score of men and women were discovered who could regularly name so many of the cards correctly that 'there was not one chance in many a million of their having done their feats by luck or accident.'

"But how did they do them? These powers, assuming that they exist, do not seem to be sensory. There is no known organ for them. The experiments worked just as well at distances of several hundred miles as they did in the same room. These facts also dispose, in Mr. Wright's opinion, of the attempt to explain telepathy or clairvoyance through any physical theory of radiation. All known forms of radiant energy decline inversely as the square of the distance traversed. Telepathy and clairvoyance do not. But they do vary through physical causes as our other mental powers do. Contrary to widespread opinion, they do not improve when the percipient is asleep or half-asleep, but, on the contrary, when he is most wide-awake and alert. Rhine discovered that a narcotic will invariably lower a percipient's score, while a stimulant will always send it higher. The most reliable performer apparently cannot make a good score unless he tries to do his best.

"One conclusion that Wright draws with some confidence is that telepathy and clairvoyance are really one and the same gift. That is, the faculty that 'sees' a card face down on a table seems to be exactly the same one that 'reads' a thought residing only in another mind. There are several grounds for believing this. So far, for example, the two gifts have been found in every person who enjoys either of them. In every one so far the two have been of equal vigor, almost exactly. Screens, walls, distances, have no effect at all on either. Wright advances from this conclusion to express what he puts forward as no more than the mere 'hunch' that other extra-sensory experiences, prophetic dreams, premonitions of disaster, and the like, may also prove to be part of the same faculty. The reader is not asked to accept any of these conclusions unless he finds it necessary, but the evidence that Rhine has piled up must remain impressive."

In view of Dr. Rhine's announcement in connection with the conditions under which the mind responds to what he terms extra–sensory modes of perception, I now feel privileged to add to his testimony by stating that my associates and I have discovered what we believe to be the ideal conditions under which the mind can be stimulated so that the sixth sense described in the next chapter, can be made to function in a practical way.

The conditions to which I refer consist of a close working alliance between myself and two members of my staff. Through experimentation and practice, we have discovered how to stimulate our minds (by applying the principle used in connection with the "Invisible Counselors" described in the next chapter) so that we can, by a process of blending our three minds into one, find the solution to a great variety of personal problems which are submitted by my clients.

The procedure is very simple. We sit down at a conference table, clearly state the nature of the problem we have under consideration, then begin discussing it. Each contributes whatever thoughts that may occur. The strange thing about this method of mind stimulation is that it places each participant in communication with unknown sources of knowledge definitely outside his own experience.

If you understand the principle described in the chapter on the Master Mind, you of course recognize the round-table procedure here described as being a practical application of the Master Mind.

This method of mind stimulation, through harmonious discussion of definite subjects, between three people, illustrates the simplest and most practical use of the Master Mind.

By adopting and following a similar plan any student of this philosophy may come into possession of the famous Carnegie formula briefly described in the introduction. If it means nothing to you at this time, mark this page and read it again after you have finished the last chapter.

The "depression" was a blessing in disguise.

It reduced the whole world to a new starting- point that gives every one a new opportunity.

Chapter Thirteen: The Sixth Sense

The Door to the Temple of Wisdom: the Thirteenth Step Toward Riches

The "thirteenth" principle is known as the *sixth sense*, through which Infinite Intelligence may, and will communicate voluntarily, without any effort from, or demands by, the individual. This principle is the apex of the philosophy. It can be assimilated, understood, and applied *only* by first mastering the other twelve principles.

The *Sixth Sense* is that portion of the subconscious mind which has been referred to as the Creative Imagination. It has also been referred to as the "receiving set" through which ideas, plans, and thoughts flash into the mind. The "flashes" are sometimes called "hunches" or "inspirations."

The sixth sense defies description! It cannot be described to a person who has not mastered the other principles of this philosophy, because such a person has no knowledge, and no experience with which the sixth sense may be compared. Understanding of the sixth sense comes only by meditation through mind development from within. The sixth sense probably is the medium of contact between the finite mind of man and Infinite Intelligence, and for this reason, it is a mixture of both the mental and the spiritual. It is believed to be the point at which the mind of man contacts the Universal Mind.

After you have mastered the principles described in this book, you will be prepared to accept as truth a statement which may, otherwise, be incredible to you, namely:

Through the aid of the sixth sense, you will be warned of impending dangers in time to avoid them, and notified of opportunities in time to embrace them.

There comes to your aid, and to do your bidding, with the development of the sixth sense, a "guardian angel" who will open to you at all times the door to the Temple of Wisdom.

Whether or not this is a statement of truth, you will never know, except by following the instructions described in the pages of this book, or some similar method of procedure.

The author is not a believer in, nor an advocate of "miracles," for the reason that he has enough knowledge of Nature to understand that Nature never deviates from her established laws. Some of her laws are so incomprehensible that they produce what appear to be "miracles." The sixth sense comes as near to being a miracle as anything I have ever experienced, and it appears so, only because I do not understand the method by which this principle is operated.

This much the author does know— that there is a power, or a First Cause, or an Intelligence, which permeates every atom of matter, and embraces every unit of energy perceptible to man— that this Infinite Intelligence converts acorns into oak trees, causes water to flow down hill in response to the law of gravity, follows night with day, and winter with summer, each maintaining its proper place and relationship to the other. This Intelligence may, through the principles of this philosophy, be induced to aid in transmuting *desires* into concrete, or material form. The author has this knowledge, because he has experimented with it— and has *experienced it.*

Step by step, through the preceding chapters, you have been led to this, the last principle. If you have mastered each of the preceding principles, you are now prepared to accept, without being skeptical, the stupendous claims made here. If you have not mastered the other principles, you must do so before you may determine, definitely, whether or not the claims made in this chapter are fact or fiction.

While I was passing through the age of "hero-worship" I found myself trying to imitate those whom I most admired. Moreover, I discovered that the element of *faith*, with which I endeavored to imitate my idols, gave me great capacity to do so quite successfully.

I have never entirely divested myself of this habit of hero-worship, although I have passed the age commonly given over to such. My experience has taught me that the next best thing to being truly great, is to emulate the great, by feeling and action, as nearly as possible.

Long before I had ever written a line for publication, or endeavored to deliver a speech in public, I followed the habit of reshaping my own character, by trying to imitate the nine men whose lives and life-works had been most impressive to me. These nine men were, Emerson, Paine, Edison, Darwin, Lincoln, Burbank, Napoleon, Ford, and Carnegie.

Every night, over a long period of years, I held an imaginary Council meeting with this group whom I called my "Invisible Counselors."

The procedure was this. Just before going to sleep at night, I would shut my eyes, and see, in my imagination, this group of men seated with me around my Council Table. Here I had not only an opportunity to sit among those whom I considered to be great, but I actually dominated the group, by serving as the Chairman.

I had a very *definite purpose* in indulging my imagination through these nightly meetings. My purpose was to rebuild my own character so it would represent a composite of the characters of my imaginary counselors. Realizing, as I did, early in life, that I had to overcome the handicap of birth in an environment of ignorance and superstition, I deliberately assigned myself the task of voluntary rebirth through the method here described.

Building Character Through Auto-suggestion

Being an earnest student of psychology, I knew, of course, that all men have become what they are, because of their *dominating thoughts and desires.* I knew that every deeply seated desire has the effect of causing one to seek outward expression through which that desire may be transmuted into reality. I knew that self-suggestion is a powerful factor in building character, that it is, in fact, the sole principle through which character is built.

With this knowledge of the principles of mind operation, I was fairly well armed with the equipment needed in rebuilding my character. In these imaginary Council meetings I called on my Cabinet members for the knowledge I wished each to contribute, addressing myself to each member in audible words, as follows:

"Mr. Emerson, I desire to acquire from you the marvelous understanding of Nature which distinguished your life. I ask that you make an impress upon my subconscious mind, of whatever qualities you possessed, which enabled you to understand and adapt yourself to the laws of Nature. I ask that you assist me in reaching and drawing upon whatever sources of knowledge are available to this end.

"Mr. Burbank, I request that you pass on to me the knowledge which enabled you to so harmonize the laws of Nature that you caused the cactus to shed its thorns, and become an edible food. Give me access to the knowledge which enabled you to make two blades of grass grow where but one grew before, and helped you to blend the coloring of the flowers with more splendor and harmony, for you, alone, have successfully gilded the lily.

"Napoleon, I desire to acquire from you, by emulation, the marvelous ability you possessed to inspire men, and to arouse them to greater and more determined spirit of action. Also to acquire the spirit of enduring *faith,* which enabled you to turn defeat into victory, and to surmount staggering obstacles. Emperor of Fate, King of Chance, Man of Destiny, I salute you!

"Mr. Paine, I desire to acquire from you the freedom of thought and the courage and clarity with which to express convictions, which so distinguished you!

"Mr. Darwin, I wish to acquire from you the marvelous patience, and ability to study cause and effect, without bias or prejudice, so exemplified by you in the field of natural science.

"Mr. Lincoln, I desire to build into my own character the keen sense of justice, the untiring spirit of patience, the sense of humor, the human understanding, and the tolerance, which were your distinguishing characteristics.

"Mr. Carnegie, I am already indebted to you for my choice of a life-work, which has brought me great happiness and peace of mind. I wish to acquire a thorough understanding of the principles of organized effort, which you used so effectively in the building of a great industrial enterprise.

"Mr. Ford, you have been among the most helpful of the men who have supplied much of the material essential to my work. I wish to acquire your spirit of persistence, the determination, poise, and self-confidence which have enabled you to master poverty, organize, unify, and simplify human effort, so I may help others to follow in your footsteps.

"Mr. Edison, I have seated you nearest to me, at my right, because of the personal cooperation you have given me, during my research into the causes of success and failure. I wish to acquire from you the marvelous spirit of *faith,* with which you have uncovered so many of Nature's secrets, the spirit of unremitting toil with which you have so often wrested victory from defeat."

My method of addressing the members of the imaginary Cabinet would vary, according to the traits of character in which I was, for the moment, most interested in acquiring. I studied the records of their lives with painstaking care. After some months of this nightly procedure, I was astounded by the discovery that these imaginary figures became, apparently real.

Each of these nine men developed individual characteristics, which surprised me. For example, Lincoln developed the habit of always being late, then walking around in solemn parade. When he came, he walked very slowly, with his hands clasped behind him, and once in a while, he would stop as he passed, and rest his hand, momentarily, upon my shoulder. He always wore an expression of seriousness upon his face. Rarely did I see him smile. The cares of a sundered nation made him grave.

That was not true of the others. Burbank and Paine often indulged in witty repartee which seemed, at times, to shock the other members of the cabinet. One night Paine suggested that I prepare a lecture on "The Age of Reason," and deliver it from the pulpit of a church which I formerly attended. Many around the table laughed heartily at the suggestion. Not Napoleon! He drew his mouth down at the corners and groaned so loudly that all turned and looked at him with amazement. To him the church was but a pawn of the State, not to be reformed, but to be used, as a convenient inciter to mass activity by the people.

On one occasion Burbank was late. When he came, he was excited with enthusiasm, and explained that he had been late, because of an experiment he was making, through which he hoped to be able to grow apples on any sort of tree. Paine chided him by reminding him that it was an apple which started all the trouble between man and woman. Darwin chuckled heartily as he suggested that Paine should watch out for little serpents, when he went into the forest to gather apples, as they had the habit of growing into big snakes. Emerson observed—" No serpents, no apples," and Napoleon remarked, "No apples, no state!"

Lincoln developed the habit of always being the last one to leave the table after each meeting. On one occasion, he leaned across the end of the table, his arms folded, and remained in that position for many minutes. I made no attempt to disturb him. Finally, he lifted his head slowly, got up and walked to the door, then turned around, came back, and laid his hand on my shoulder and said, "My boy, you will need much courage if you remain steadfast in carrying out your purpose in life. But remember, when difficulties overtake you, the common people have common sense. Adversity will develop it."

One evening Edison arrived ahead of all the others. He walked over and seated himself at my left, where Emerson was accustomed to sit, and said, "You are destined to witness the discovery of the secret of life. When the time comes, you will observe that life consists of great swarms of energy, or entities, each as intelligent as human beings think themselves to be. These units of life group together like hives of bees, and remain together until they disintegrate, through lack of harmony.

These units have differences of opinion, the same as human beings, and often fight among themselves. These meetings which you are conducting will be very helpful to you. They will bring to your rescue some of the same units of life which served the members of your Cabinet, during their lives. These units are eternal. *They never die*! Your own thoughts and *desires* serve as the magnet which attracts units of life, from the great ocean of life out there. Only the friendly units are attracted—the ones which harmonize with the nature of your *desires*."

The other members of the Cabinet began to enter the room. Edison got up, and slowly walked around to his own seat. Edison was still living when this happened. It impressed me so greatly that I went to see him, and told him about the experience. He smiled broadly, and said, "Your dream was more a reality than you may imagine it to have been." He added no further explanation to his statement.

These meetings became so realistic that I became fearful of their consequences, and discontinued them for several months. The experiences were so uncanny, I was afraid if I continued them I would lose sight of the fact that the meetings were purely experiences of my imagination.

Some six months after I had discontinued the practice I was awakened one night, or thought I was, when I saw Lincoln standing at my bedside. He said, "The world will soon need your services. It is about to undergo a period of chaos which will cause men and women to lose faith, and become panic stricken. Go ahead with your work and complete your philosophy. That is your mission in life. If you neglect it, for any cause whatsoever, you will be reduced to a primal state, and be compelled to retrace the cycles through which you have passed during thousands of years.

"I was unable to tell, the following morning, whether I had dreamed this, or had actually been awake, and I have never since found out which it was, but I do know that the dream, if it were a dream, was so vivid in my mind the next day that I resumed my meetings the following night.

At our next meeting, the members of my Cabinet all filed into the room together, and stood at their accustomed places at the Council Table, while Lincoln raised a glass and said, "Gentlemen, let us drink a toast to a friend who has returned to the fold."

After that, I began to add new members to my Cabinet, until now it consists of more than fifty, among them Christ, St. Paul, Galileo, Copernicus, Aristotle, Plato, Socrates, Homer, Voltaire, Bruno, Spinoza, Drummond, Kant, Schopenhauer, Newton, Confucius, Elbert Hubbard, Brann, Ingersol, Wilson, and William James.

This is the first time that I have had the courage to mention this. Heretofore, I have remained quiet on the subject, because I knew, from my own attitude in connection with such matters, that I would be misunderstood if I described my unusual experience. I have been emboldened now to reduce my experience to the printed page, because I am now less concerned about what "they say" than I was in the years that have passed. One of the blessings of maturity is that it sometimes brings one greater courage to be truthful, regardless of what those who do not understand, may think or say.

Lest I be misunderstood, I wish here to state most emphatically, that I still regard my Cabinet meetings as being purely imaginary, but I feel entitled to suggest that, while the members of my Cabinet may be purely fictional, and the meetings existent only in my own imagination, they have led me into glorious paths of adventure, rekindled an appreciation of true greatness, encouraged creative endeavor, and emboldened the expression of honest thought.

Somewhere in the cell-structure of the brain, is located an organ which receives vibrations of thought ordinarily called "hunches." So far, science has not discovered where this organ of the sixth sense is located, but this is not important. The fact remains that human beings do receive accurate knowledge, through sources other than the physical senses. Such knowledge, generally, is received when the mind is under the influence of extraordinary stimulation. Any emergency which arouses the emotions, and causes the heart to beat more rapidly than normal may, and generally does, bring the sixth sense into action. Anyone who has experienced a near accident while driving, knows that on such occasions, the sixth sense often comes to one's rescue, and aids, by split seconds, in avoiding the accident.

These facts are mentioned preliminary to a statement of fact which I shall now make, namely, that during my meetings with the "Invisible Counselors" I find my mind most receptive to ideas, thoughts, and knowledge which reach me through the sixth sense. I can truthfully say that I owe entirely to my "Invisible Counselors" full credit for such ideas, facts, or knowledge as I received through "inspiration."

On scores of occasions, when I have faced emergencies, some of them so grave that my life was in jeopardy, I have been miraculously guided past these difficulties through the influence of my "Invisible Counselors."

My original purpose in conducting Council meetings with imaginary beings, was solely that of impressing my own subconscious mind, through the principle of auto-suggestion, with certain characteristics which I desired to acquire. In more recent years, my experimentation has taken on an entirely different trend. I now go to my imaginary counselors with every difficult problem which confronts me and my clients. The results are often astonishing, although I do not depend entirely on this form of Counsel.

You, of course, have recognized that this chapter covers a subject with which a majority of people are not familiar. The Sixth Sense is a subject that will be of great interest and benefit to the person whose aim is to accumulate vast wealth, but it need not claim the attention of those whose desires are more modest.

Henry Ford, undoubtedly understands and makes practical use of the sixth sense. His vast business and financial operations make it necessary for him to understand and use this principle. The late Thomas A. Edison understood and used the sixth sense in connection with the development of inventions, especially those involving basic patents, in connection with which he had no human experience and no accumulated knowledge to guide him, as was the case while he was working on the talking machine, and the moving picture machine.

Nearly all great leaders, such as Napoleon, Bismark, Joan of Arc, Christ, Buddha, Confucius, and Mohammed, understood, and probably made use of the sixth sense almost continuously. The major portion of their greatness consisted of their knowledge of this principle.

The sixth sense is not something that one can take off and put on at will. Ability to use this great power comes slowly, through application of the other principles outlined in this book. Seldom does any individual come into workable knowledge of the sixth sense before the age of forty. More often the knowledge is not available until one is well past fifty, and this, for the reason that the spiritual forces, with which the sixth sense is so closely related, do not mature and become usable except through years of meditation, self-examination, and serious thought.

No matter who you are, or what may have been your purpose in reading this book, you can profit by it without understanding the principle described in this chapter. This is especially true if your major purpose is that of accumulation of money or other material things.

The chapter on the sixth sense was included, because the book is designed for the purpose of presenting a complete philosophy by which individuals may unerringly guide themselves in attaining whatever they ask of life. The starting point of all achievement is *desire*. The finishing point is that brand of *knowledge* which leads to understanding– understanding of self, understanding of others, understanding of the laws of Nature, recognition and understanding of *happiness*.

This sort of understanding comes in its fullness only through familiarity with, and use of the principle of the sixth sense, hence that principle had to be included as a part of this philosophy, for the benefit of those who demand more than money.

Having read the chapter, you must have observed that while reading it, you were lifted to a high level of mental stimulation. Splendid! Come back to this again a month from now, read it once more, and observe that your mind will soar to a still higher level of stimulation. Repeat this experience from time to time, giving no concern as to how much or how little you learn at the time, and eventually you will find yourself in possession of a power that will enable you to throw off discouragement, master fear, overcome procrastination, and draw freely upon your imagination. Then you will have felt the touch of that unknown "something" which has been the moving spirit of every truly great thinker leader, artist, musician, writer, statesman. Then you will be in position to transmute your *desires* into their physical or financial counterpart as easily as you may lie down and quit at the first sign of opposition.

Faith Vs. Fear!

Previous chapters have described how to develop *faith*, through Auto-suggestion, Desire and the Subconscious. The next chapter presents detailed instructions for the mastery of *fear*.

Here will be found a full description of the six fears which are the cause of all discouragement, timidity, procrastination, indifference, indecision, and the lack of ambition, self-reliance, initiative, self-control, and enthusiasm.

Search yourself carefully as you study these six enemies, as they may exist only in your subconscious mind, where their presence will be hard to detect.

Remember, too, as you analyze the "Six Ghosts of Fear," that they are nothing but ghosts because they exist only in one's mind.

Remember, also, that ghosts– creations of uncontrolled imagination– have caused most of the damage people have done to their own minds, therefore, ghosts can be as dangerous as if they lived and walked on the earth in physical bodies.

The Ghost of the Fear of Poverty, which seized the minds of millions of people in 1929, was so real that it caused the worst business depression this country has ever known. Moreover, this particular ghost still frightens some of us out of our wits.

Chapter Fourteen: How to Outwit the Six Ghosts of Fear

Take Inventory of Yourself, as You Read this Closing Chapter, and Find out How Many of the "Ghosts" Are Standing in Your Way

Before you can put any portion of this philosophy into successful use, your mind must be prepared to receive it. The preparation is not difficult. It begins with study, analysis, and understanding of three enemies which you shall have to clear out. These are *decisions*, *doubt*, and *fear*!

The Sixth Sense will never function while these three negatives, or any of them remain in your mind. The members of this unholy trio are closely related; where one is found, the other two are close at hand.

decisions is the seedling of *fear*! Remember this, as you read. Indecision crystalizes into *doubt*, the two blend and become *fear*! The "blending" process often is slow. This is one reason why these three enemies are so dangerous. They germinate and grow without their presence being observed.

The remainder of this chapter describes an end which must be attained before the philosophy, as a whole, can be put into practical use. It also analyzes a condition which has, but lately, reduced huge numbers of people to poverty, and it states a truth which must be understood by all who accumulate riches, whether measured in terms of money or a state of mind of far greater value than money. The purpose of this chapter is to turn the spotlight of attention upon the cause and the cure of the six basic fears. Before we can master an enemy, we must know its name, its habits, and its place of abode. As you read, analyze yourself carefully, and determine which, if any, of the six common fears have attached themselves to you.

Do not be deceived by the habits of these subtle enemies. Sometimes they remain hidden in the subconscious mind, where they are difficult to locate, and still more difficult to eliminate.

The Six Basic Fears

There are six basic fears, with some combination of which every human suffers at one tune or another. Most people are fortunate if they do not suffer from the entire six. Named in the order of their most common appearance, they are:—

The fear of *poverty*
The fear of *criticism*
The fear of *ill health*
The fear of *loss of love of someone*
The fear of *old age*
The fear of *death*

All other fears are of minor importance, they can be grouped under these six headings.

The prevalence of these fears, as a curse to the world, runs in cycles. For almost six years, while the depression was on, we floundered in the cycle of *fear of poverty.* During the world-war, we were in the cycle of *fear of death.* Just following the war, we were in the cycle of *fear of ill health,* as evidenced by the epidemic of disease which spread itself all over the world.

Fears are nothing more than states of mind. One's state of mind is subject to control and direction. Physicians, as everyone knows, are less subject to attack by disease than ordinary laymen, for the reason that physicians *do not fear disease.* Physicians, without fear or hesitation, have been known to physically contact hundreds of people, daily, who were suffering from such contagious diseases as small-pox, without becoming infected. Their immunity against the disease consisted, largely, if not solely, in their absolute lack of *fear.*

Man can create nothing which he does not first conceive in the form of an impulse of thought. Following this statement, comes another of still greater importance, namely, *man's thought impulses begin immediately to translate themselves into their physical equivalent, whether those thoughts are voluntary or involuntary.* Thought impulses which are picked up through the ether, by mere chance (thoughts which have been released by other minds) may determine one's financial, business, professional, or social destiny just as surely as do the thought impulses which one creates by intent and design.

We are here laying the foundation for the presentation of a fact of great importance to the person who does not understand why some people appear to be "lucky" while others of equal or greater ability, training, experience, and brain capacity, seem destined to ride with misfortune. This fact may be explained by the statement that every human being has the ability to completely control his own mind, and with this control, obviously, every person may open his mind to the tramp thought impulses which are being released by other brains, or close the doors tightly and admit only thought impulses of his own choice.

Nature has endowed man with absolute control over but one thing, and that is *thought.* This fact, coupled with the additional fact that everything which man creates, begins in the form of a thought, leads one very near to the principle by which *fear* may be mastered.

If it is true that *all thought has a tendency to clothe itself in its physical equivalent* (and this is true, beyond any reasonable room for doubt), it is equally true that thought impulses of fear and poverty cannot be translated into terms of courage and financial gain.

The people of America began to think of poverty, following the Wall Street crash of 1929. Slowly, but surely that mass thought was crystalized into its physical equivalent, which was known as a "depression." This had to happen, it is in conformity with the laws of Nature.

The Fear of Poverty

There can be no compromise between *poverty* and *riches*! The two roads that lead to poverty and riches travel in opposite directions. If you want riches, you must refuse to accept any circumstance that leads toward poverty. (The word "riches" is here used in its broadest sense, meaning financial, spiritual, mental and material estates). The starting point of the path that leads to riches is *desire*. In chapter one, you received full instructions for the proper use of *desire*. In this chapter, on *fear*, you have complete instructions for preparing your mind to make practical use of *desire*.

Here, then, is the place to give yourself a challenge which will definitely determine how much of this philosophy you have absorbed. Here is the point at which you can turn prophet and foretell, accurately, what the future holds in store for you. If, after reading this chapter, you are willing to accept poverty, you may as well make up your mind to receive poverty. This is one decision you cannot avoid.

If you demand riches, determine what form, and how much will be required to satisfy you. You know the road that leads to riches. You have been given a road map which, if followed, will keep you on that road. If you neglect to make the start, or stop before you arrive, no one will be to blame, but *you*. This responsibility is yours. No alibi will save you from accepting the responsibility if you now fail or refuse to demand riches of Life, because the acceptance calls for but one thing— incidentally, the only thing you can control—and that is a *state of mind*. A state of mind is something that one assumes. It cannot be purchased, it must be created.

Fear of poverty is a state of mind, nothing else! But it is sufficient to destroy one's chances of achievement in any undertaking, a truth which became painfully evident during the depression.

This fear paralyzes the faculty of reason, destroys the faculty of imagination, kills off self-reliance, undermines enthusiasm, discourages initiative, leads to uncertainty of purpose, encourages procrastination, wipes out enthusiasm and makes self-control an impossibility. It takes the charm from one's personality, destroys the possibility of accurate thinking, diverts concentration of effort, it masters persistence, turns the will-power into nothingness, destroys ambition, beclouds the memory and invites failure in every conceivable form; it kills love and assassinates the finer emotions of the heart, discourages friendship and invites disaster in a hundred forms, leads to sleeplessness, misery and unhappiness— and all this despite the obvious truth that we live in a world of over-abundance of everything the heart could desire, with nothing standing between us and our desires, excepting lack of a definite purpose.

The Fear of Poverty is, without doubt, the most destructive of the six basic fears. It has been placed at the head of the list, because it is the most difficult to master. Considerable courage is required to state the truth about the origin of this fear, and still greater courage to accept the truth after it has been stated. The fear of poverty grew out of man's inherited tendency to *prey upon his fellow man economically*. Nearly all animals lower than man are motivated by instinct, but their capacity to "think" is limited, therefore, they prey upon one another physically. Man, with his superior sense of intuition, with the capacity to think and to reason, does not eat his fellow man bodily, he gets more satisfaction out of "eating" him *financially*. Man is so avaricious that every conceivable law has been passed to safeguard him from his fellow man.

Of all the ages of the world, of which we know anything, the age in which we live seems to be one that is outstanding because of man's money-madness. A man is considered less than the dust of the earth, unless he can display a fat bank account; but if he has money— *never mind how he acquired it*— he is a "king" or a "big shot"; he is above the law, he rules in politics, he dominates in business, and the whole world about him bows in respect when he passes.

Nothing brings man so much suffering and humility as *poverty*! Only those who have experienced poverty understand the full meaning of this.

It is no wonder that man fears poverty. Through a long line of inherited experiences man has learned, for sure, that some men cannot be trusted, where matters of money and earthly possessions are concerned. This is a rather stinging indictment, the worst part of it being that it is true.

The majority of marriages are motivated by the wealth possessed by one, or both of the contracting parties. It is no wonder, therefore, that the divorce courts are busy.

So eager is man to possess wealth that he will acquire it in whatever manner he can— through legal methods if possible— through other methods if necessary or expedient.

Self-analysis may disclose weaknesses which one does not like to acknowledge. This form of examination is essential to all who demand of Life more than mediocrity and poverty. Remember, as you check yourself point by point, that you are both the court and the jury, the prosecuting attorney and the attorney for the defense, and that you are the plaintiff and the defendant, also, that you are on trial. Face the facts squarely. Ask yourself definite questions and demand direct replies. When the examination is over, you will know more about yourself. If you do not feel that you can be an impartial judge in this self-examination, call upon someone who knows you well to serve as judge while you cross-examine yourself. You are after the truth. Get it, no matter at what cost even though it may temporarily embarrass you!

The majority of people, if asked what they fear most, would reply, "I fear nothing." The reply would be inaccurate, because few people realize that they are bound, handicapped, whipped spiritually and physically through some form of fear. So subtle and deeply seated is the emotion of fear that one may go through life burdened with it, never recognizing its presence. Only a courageous analysis will disclose the presence of this universal enemy. When you begin such an analysis, search deeply into your character. Here is a list of the symptoms for which you should look:

Symptoms of the Fear of Poverty

Indifference. Commonly expressed through lack of ambition; willingness to tolerate poverty; acceptance of whatever compensation life may offer without protest; mental and physical laziness; lack of initiative, imagination, enthusiasm and self-control

Indecision. The habit of permitting others to do one's thinking. Staying "on the fence."

Doubt. Generally expressed through alibis and excuses designed to cover up, explain away, or apologize for one's failures, sometimes expressed in the form of envy of those who are successful, or by criticizing them.

Worry. Usually expressed by finding fault with others, a tendency to spend beyond one's income, neglect of personal appearance, scowling and frowning; intemperance in the use of alcoholic drink, sometimes through the use of narcotics; nervousness, lack of poise, self-consciousness and lack of self-reliance.

Over-caution. The habit of looking for the negative side of every circumstance, thinking and talking of possible failure instead of concentrating upon the means of succeeding. Knowing all the roads to disaster, but never searching for the plans to avoid failure. Waiting for "the right time" to begin putting ideas and plans into action, until the waiting becomes a permanent habit. Remembering those who have failed, and forgetting those who have succeeded. Seeing the hole in the doughnut, but overlooking the doughnut. Pessimism, leading to indigestion, poor elimination, auto-intoxication, bad breath and bad disposition.

Procrastination. The habit of putting off until tomorrow that which should have been done last year. Spending enough time in creating alibis and excuses to have done the job. This symptom is closely related to over-caution, doubt and worry. Refusal to accept responsibility when it can be avoided. Willingness to compromise rather than put up a stiff fight. Compromising with difficulties instead of harnessing and using them as stepping stones to advancement. Bargaining with Life for a penny, instead of demanding prosperity, opulence, riches, contentment and happiness. Planning what to do *if and when overtaken by failure, instead of burning all bridges and making retreat impossible.* Weakness of, and often total lack of self-confidence, definiteness of purpose, self-control, initiative, enthusiasm, ambition, thrift and sound reasoning ability. *Expecting poverty instead of demanding riches.* Association with those who accept poverty instead of seeking the company of those who demand and receive riches.

Money Talks!

Some will ask, "why did you write a book about money? Why measure riches in dollars, alone?" Some will believe, and rightly so, that there are other forms of riches more desirable than money. Yes, there are riches which cannot be measured in terms of dollars, but there are millions of people who will say, "Give me all the money I need, and I will find everything else I want."

The major reason why I wrote this book on how to get money is the fact that the world has but lately passed through an experience that left millions of men and women paralyzed with the *fear of poverty.* What this sort of fear does to one was well described by Westbrook Pegler, in the New York World-Telegram, viz:

"Money is only clam shells or metal discs or scraps of paper, and there are treasures of the heart and soul which money cannot buy, but most people, being broke, are unable to keep this in mind and sustain their spirits. When a man is down and out and on the street, unable to get any job at all, something happens to his spirit which can be observed in the droop of his shoulders, the set of his hat, his walk and his gaze. He cannot escape a feeling of inferiority among people with regular employment, even though he knows they are definitely not his equals in character, intelligence or ability.

"These people—even his friends—feel, on the other hand, a sense of superiority and regard him, perhaps unconsciously, as a casualty. He may borrow for a time, but not enough to carry on in his accustomed way, and he cannot continue to borrow very long. But borrowing in itself, when a man is borrowing merely to live, is a depressing experience, and the money lacks the power of earned money to revive his spirits. Of course, none of this applies to bums or habitual ne'er-do-wells, but only to men of normal ambitions and self-respect.

Women Conceal Despair

"Women in the same predicament must be different. We somehow do not think of women at all in considering the down-and-outers. They are scarce in the breadlines, they rarely are seen begging on the streets, and they are not recognizable in crowds by the same plain signs which identify busted men. Of course, I do not mean the shuffling hags of the city streets who are the opposite number of the confirmed male bums. I mean reasonably young, decent and intelligent women. There must be many of them, but their despair is not apparent. Maybe they kill themselves.

"When a man is down and out he has time on his hands for brooding. He may travel miles to see a man about a job and discover that the job is filled or that it is one of those jobs with no base pay but only a commission on the sale of some useless knick-knack which nobody would buy, except out of pity. Turning that down, he finds himself back on the street with nowhere to go but just anywhere. So he walks and walks. He gazes into store windows at luxuries which are not for him, and feels inferior and gives way to people who stop to look with an active interest. He wanders into the railroad station or puts himself down in the library to ease his legs and soak up a little heat, but that isn't looking for a job, so he gets going again. He may not know it, but his aimlessness would give him away even if the very lines of his figure did not. He may be well dressed in the clothes left over from the days when he had a steady job, but the clothes cannot disguise the droop.

Money Makes Difference

"He sees thousands of other people, bookkeepers or clerks or chemists or wagon hands, busy at their work and envies them from the bottom of his soul. They have their independence, their self-respect and manhood, and he simply cannot convince himself that he is a good man, too, though he argue it out and arrive at a favorable verdict hour after hour.

"It is just money which makes this difference in him. With a little money he would be himself again.

"Some employers take the most shocking advantage of people who are down and out. The agencies hang out little colored cards offering miserable wages to busted men—$ 12 a week, $15 a week. An $18 a week job is a plum, and anyone with $25 a week to offer does not hang the job in front of an agency on a colored card. I have a want ad clipped from a local paper demanding a clerk, a good, clean penman, to take telephone orders for a sandwich shop from 11 A. M. to 2 P. M. for $8 a month— not $8 a week but $8 a month. The ad says also, 'State religion. ' Can you imagine the brutal effrontery of anyone who demands a good, clean penman for 11 cents an hour inquiring into the victim's religion? But that is what busted people are offered."

The Fear of Criticism

Just how man originally came by this fear, no one can state definitely, but one thing is certain— he has it in a highly developed form. Some believe that this fear made its appearance about the time that politics became a "profession." Others believe it can be traced to the age when women first began to concern themselves with "styles" in wearing apparel.

This author, being neither a humorist nor a prophet, is inclined to attribute the basic fear of criticism to that part of man's inherited nature which prompts him not only to take away his fellow man's goods and wares, but to justify his action by *criticism* of his fellow man's character. It is a well known fact that a thief will criticize the man from whom he steals—that politicians seek office, not by displaying their own virtues and qualifications, but by attempting to besmirch their opponents.

The fear of criticism takes on many forms, the majority of which are petty and trivial. Bald-headed men, for example, are bald for no other reason than their fear of criticism. Heads become bald because of the tight fitting bands of hats which cut off the circulation from the roots of the hair. Men wear hats, not because they actually need them, but mainly because "everyone is doing it." The individual falls into line and does likewise, lest some other individual *criticize* him. Women seldom have bald heads, or even thin hair, because they wear hats which fit their heads loosely, the only purpose of the hats being adornment.

But, it must not be supposed that women are free from the fear of criticism. If any woman claims to be superior to man with reference to this fear, ask her to walk down the street wearing a hat of the vintage of 1890.

The astute manufacturers of clothing have not been slow to capitalize this basic fear of criticism, with which all mankind has been cursed. Every season the styles in many articles of wearing apparel change. Who establishes the styles? Certainly not the purchaser of clothing, but the manufacturer. Why does he change the styles so often? The answer is obvious. He changes the styles so he can sell more clothes.

For the same reason the manufacturers of automobiles (with a few rare and very sensible exceptions) change styles of models every season. No man wants to drive an automobile which is not of the latest style, although the older model may actually be the better car.

We have been describing the manner in which people behave under the influence of fear of criticism as applied to the small and petty things of life. Let us now examine human behavior when this fear affects people in connection with the more important events of human relationship. Take for example practically any person who has reached the age of "mental maturity" (from 35 to 40 years of age, as a general average), and if you could read the secret thoughts of his mind, you would find a very decided disbelief in most of the fables taught by the majority of the dogmatists and theologians a few decades back.

Not often, however, will you find a person who has the courage to openly state his belief on this subject. Most people will, if pressed far enough, tell a lie rather than admit that they do not believe the stories associated with that form of religion which held people in bondage prior to the age of scientific discovery and education.

Why does the average person, even in this day of enlightenment, shy away from denying his belief in the fables which were the basis of most of the religions a few decades ago? The answer is, "because of the fear of criticism." Men and women have been burned at the stake for daring to express disbelief in ghosts. It is no wonder we have inherited a consciousness which makes us fear criticism. The time was, and not so far in the past, when criticism carried severe punishments—it still does in some countries.

The fear of criticism robs man of his initiative, destroys his power of imagination, limits his individuality, takes away his self-reliance, and does him damage in a hundred other ways. Parents often do their children irreparable injury by criticizing them. The mother of one of my boyhood chums used to punish him with a switch almost daily, always completing the job with the statement, "You'll land in the penitentiary before you are twenty." He was sent to a Reformatory at the age of seventeen.

Criticism is the one form of service, of which everyone has too much. Everyone has a stock of it which is handed out, gratis, whether called for or not. One's nearest relatives often are the worst offenders. It should be recognized as a crime (in reality it is a crime of the worst nature), for any parent to build inferiority complexes in the mind of a child, through unnecessary criticism. Employers who understand human nature, get the best there is in men, not by criticism, but by constructive suggestion. Parents may accomplish the same results with their children. Criticism will plant *fear* in the human heart, or resentment, but it will not build love or affection.

Symptoms of the Fear of Criticism

This fear is almost as universal as the fear of poverty, and its effects are just as fatal to personal achievement, mainly because this fear destroys initiative, and discourages the use of imagination. The major symptoms of the fear are:

Self-consciousness. Generally expressed through nervousness, timidity in conversation and in meeting strangers, awkward movement of the hands and limbs, shifting of the eyes.

Lack of poise. Expressed through lack of voice control, nervousness in the presence of others, poor posture of body, poor memory.

Personality. Lacking in firmness of decision, personal charm, and ability to express opinions definitely. The habit of side-stepping issues instead of meeting them squarely. Agreeing with others without careful examination of their opinions.

Inferiority complex. The habit of expressing self-approval by word of mouth and by actions, as a means of covering up a feeling of inferiority. Using "big words" to impress others, (often without knowing the real meaning of the words). Imitating others in dress, speech and manners. Boasting of imaginary achievements. This sometimes gives a surface appearance of a feeling of superiority.

Extravagance. The habit of trying to "keep up with the Joneses," spending beyond one's income.

Lack of initiative. Failure to embrace opportunities for self-advancement, fear to express opinions, lack of confidence in one's own ideas, giving evasive answers to questions asked by superiors, hesitancy of manner and speech, deceit in both words and deeds.

Lack of Ambition. Mental and physical laziness, lack of self-assertion, slowness in reaching decisions, easily influenced by others, the habit of criticizing others behind their backs and flattering them to their faces, the habit of accepting defeat without protest, quitting an undertaking when opposed by others, suspicious of other people without cause, lacking in tactfulness of manner and speech, unwillingness to accept the blame for mistakes.

The Fear of Ill Health

This fear may be traced to both physical and social heredity. It is closely associated, as to its origin, with the causes of fear of Old Age and the fear of Death, because it leads one closely to the border of "terrible worlds" of which man knows not, but concerning which he has been taught some discomforting stories. The opinion is somewhat general, also, that certain unethical people engaged in the business of "selling health" have had not a little to do with keeping alive the fear of ill health.

In the main, man fears ill health because of the terrible pictures which have been planted in his mind of what may happen if death should overtake him. He also fears it because of the economic toll which it may claim.

A reputable physician estimated that 75% of all people who visit physicians for professional service are suffering with hypochondria (imaginary illness). It has been shown most convincingly that the fear of disease, even where there is not the slightest cause for fear, often produces the physical symptoms of the disease feared.

Powerful and mighty is the human mind! It builds or it destroys.

Playing upon this common weakness of fear of ill health, dispensers of patent medicines have reaped fortunes. This form of imposition upon credulous humanity became so prevalent some twenty years ago that Colliers' Weekly Magazine conducted a bitter campaign against some of the worst offenders in the patent medicine business.

During the "flu" epidemic which broke out during the world war, the mayor of New York City took drastic steps to check the damage which people were doing themselves through their inherent fear of ill health. He called in the newspaper men and said to them, "Gentlemen, I feel it necessary to ask you not to publish any scare headlines concerning the 'flu' epidemic. Unless you cooperate with me, we will have a situation which we cannot control." The newspapers quit publishing stories about the "flu," and within one month the epidemic had been successfully checked.

Through a series of experiments conducted some years ago, it was proved that people may be made ill by suggestion. We conducted this experiment by causing three acquaintances to visit the "victims," each of whom asked the question, "What ails you? You look terribly ill." The first questioner usually provoked a grin, and a nonchalant "Oh, nothing, I'm alright," from the victim. The second questioner usually was answered with the statement, "I don't know exactly, but I do feel badly." The third questioner was usually met with the frank admission that the victim was actually feeling ill.

Try this on an acquaintance if you doubt that it will make him uncomfortable, but do not carry the experiment too far. There is a certain religious sect whose members take vengeance upon their enemies by the "hexing" method. They call it "placing a spell" on the victim.

There is overwhelming evidence that disease sometimes begins in the form of negative thought impulse. Such an impulse may be passed from one mind to another, by suggestion, or created by an individual in his own mind.

A man who was blessed with more wisdom than this incident might indicate, once said "When anyone asks me how I feel, I always want to answer by knocking him down."

Doctors send patients into new climates for their health, because a change of "mental attitude" is necessary. The seed of fear of ill health lives in every human mind. Worry, fear, discouragement, disappointment in love and business affairs, cause this seed to germinate and grow. The recent business depression kept the doctors on the run, because every form of negative thinking may cause ill health.

Disappointments in business and in love stand at the head of the list of causes of fear of ill health. A young man suffered a disappointment in love which sent him to a hospital. For months he hovered between life and death. A specialist in suggestive therapeutics was called in. The specialist changed nurses, placing him in charge of a very charming young woman who began (by pre-arrangement with the doctor) to make love to him the first day of her arrival on the job. Within three weeks the patient was discharged from the hospital, still suffering, but with an entirely different malady. *He was in love again.* The remedy was a hoax, but the patient and the nurse were later married. Both are in good health at the time of this writing.

Symptoms of the Fear of Ill Health

The symptoms of this almost universal fear are:

Auto-Suggestion. The habit of negative use of self-suggestion by looking for, and expecting to find the symptoms of all kinds of disease. "Enjoying" imaginary illness and speaking of it as being real. The habit of trying all "fads" and "isms" recommended by others as having therapeutic value. Talking to others of operations, accidents and other forms of illness. Experimenting with diets, physical exercises, reducing systems, without professional guidance. Trying home remedies, patent medicines and "quack" remedies.

Hypochondria. The habit of talking of illness, concentrating the mind upon disease, and expecting its appearance until a nervous break occurs. Nothing that comes in bottles can cure this condition. It is brought on by negative thinking and nothing but positive thought can affect a cure. Hypochondria, (a medical term for imaginary disease) is said to do as much damage on occasion, as the disease one fears might do. Most so-called cases of "nerves" come from imaginary illness.

Exercise. Fear of ill health often interferes with proper physical exercise, and results in over-weight, by causing one to avoid outdoor life.

Susceptibility. Fear of ill health breaks down Nature's body resistance, and creates a favorable condition for any form of disease one may contact.

The fear of ill health often is related to the fear of Poverty, especially in the case of the hypochondriac, who constantly worries about the possibility of having to pay doctor's bills, hospital bills, etc. This type of person spends much time preparing for sickness, talking about death, saving money for cemetery lots, and burial expenses, etc.

Self-coddling. The habit of making a bid for sympathy, using imaginary illness as the lure. (People often resort to this trick to avoid work). The habit of feigning illness to cover plain laziness, or to serve as an alibi for lack of ambition.

Intemperance. The habit of using alcohol or narcotics to destroy pains such as headaches, neuralgia, etc., instead of eliminating the cause.

The habit of reading about illness and worrying over the possibility of being stricken by it. The habit of reading patent medicine advertisements.

The Fear of Loss of Love

The original source of this inherent fear needs but little description, because it obviously grew out of man's polygamous habit of stealing his fellow-man's mate, and his habit of taking liberties with her whenever he could.

Jealousy, and other similar forms of dementia praecox grow out of man's inherited fear of the loss of love of someone. This fear is the most painful of all the six basic fears. It probably plays more havoc with the body and mind than any of the other basic fears, as it often leads to permanent insanity.

The fear of the loss of love probably dates back to the stone age, when men stole women by brute force. They continue to steal females, but their technique has changed. Instead of force, they now use persuasion, the promise of pretty clothes, motor cars, and other "bait" much more effective than physical force. Man's habits are the same as they were at the dawn of civilization, but he expresses them differently.

Careful analysis has shown that women are more susceptible to this fear than men. This fact is easily explained. Women have learned, from experience, that men are polygamous by nature, that they are not to be trusted in the hands of rivals.

Symptoms of the Fear of Loss of Love

The distinguishing symptoms of this fear are:—

Jealousy. The habit of being suspicious of friends and loved ones without any reasonable evidence of sufficient grounds. (Jealousy is a form of dementia praecox which sometimes becomes violent without the slightest cause). The habit of accusing wife or husband of infidelity without grounds. General suspicion of everyone, absolute faith in no one.

Fault finding. The habit of finding fault with friends, relatives, business associates and loved ones upon the slightest provocation, or without any cause whatsoever.

Gambling. The habit of gambling, stealing, cheating, and otherwise taking hazardous chances to provide money for loved ones, with the belief that love can be bought. The habit of spending beyond one's means, or incurring debts, to provide gifts for loved ones, with the object of making a favorable showing. Insomnia, nervousness, lack of persistence, weakness of will, lack of self-control, lack of self-reliance, bad temper.

The Fear of Old Age

In the main, this fear grows out of two sources. First, the thought that old age may bring with it *poverty*. Secondly, and by far the most common source of origin, from false and cruel teachings of the past which have been too well mixed with "fire and brimstone," and other bogies cunningly designed to enslave man through fear.

In the basic fear of old age, man has two very sound reasons for his apprehension— one growing out of his distrust of his fellow man, who may seize whatever worldly goods he may possess, and the other arising from the terrible pictures of the world beyond, which were planted in his mind, through social heredity before he came into full possession of his mind.

The possibility of ill health, which is more common as people grow older, is also a contributing cause of this common fear of old age. Eroticism also enters into the cause of the fear of old age, as no man cherishes the thought of diminishing sex attraction.

The most common cause of fear of old age is associated with the possibility of poverty. "Poorhouse" is not a pretty word. It throws a chill into the mind of every person who faces the possibility of having to spend his declining years on a poor farm.

Another contributing cause of the fear of old age, is the possibility of loss of freedom and independence, as old age may bring with it the loss of both physical and economic freedom.

Symptoms of the Fear of Old Age

The commonest symptoms of this fear are:

The tendency to slow down and develop an inferiority complex at the age of mental maturity, around the age of forty, falsely believing one's self to be "slipping" because of age. (The truth is that man's most useful years, mentally and spiritually, are those between forty and sixty).

The habit of speaking apologetically of one's self as "being old" merely because one has reached the age of forty, or fifty, instead of reversing the rule and expressing gratitude for having reached the age of wisdom and understanding.

The habit of killing off initiative, imagination, and self-reliance by falsely believing one's self too old to exercise these qualities. The habit of the man or woman of forty dressing with the aim of trying to appear much younger, and affecting mannerisms of youth; thereby inspiring ridicule by both friends and strangers.

The Fear of Death

To some this is the cruelest of all the basic fears. The reason is obvious. The terrible pangs of fear associated with the thought of death, in the majority of cases, may be charged directly to religious fanaticism. So-called "heathen" are less afraid of death than the more "civilized." For hundreds of millions of years man has been asking the still unanswered questions, "whence" and "whither." Where did I come from, and where am I going?

During the darker ages of the past, the more cunning and crafty were not slow to offer the answer to these questions, *for a price*. Witness, now, the major source of origin of the *fear of death*.

"Come into my tent, embrace my faith, accept my dogmas, and I will give you a ticket that will admit you straightaway into heaven when you die," cries a leader of sectarianism. "Remain out of my tent," says the same leader, "and may the devil take you and burn you throughout eternity."

Eternity is a long time. *Fire* is a terrible thing. The thought of eternal punishment, with fire, not only causes man to fear death, it often causes him to lose his reason. It destroys interest in life and makes happiness impossible.

During my research, I reviewed a book entitled "A Catalogue of the Gods," in which were listed the 30,000 gods which man has worshiped. Think of it! Thirty thousand of them, represented by everything from a crawfish to a man. It is little wonder that men have become frightened at the approach of death.

While the religious leader may not be able to provide safe conduct into heaven, nor, by lack of such provision, allow the unfortunate to descend into hell, the possibility of the latter seems so terrible that the very thought of it lays hold of the imagination in such a realistic way that it paralyzes reason, and sets up the fear of death.

In truth, *no man knows*, and no man has ever known, what heaven or hell is like, nor does any man know if either place actually exists. This very lack of positive knowledge opens the door of the human mind to the charlatan so he may enter and control that mind with his stock of legerdemain and various brands of pious fraud and trickery.

The fear of *death* is not as common now as it was during the age when there were no great colleges and universities. Men of science have turned the spotlight of truth upon the world, and this truth is rapidly freeing men and women from this terrible fear of *death*. The young men and young women who attend the colleges and universities are not easily impressed by "fire" and "brimstone." Through the aid of biology, astronomy, geology, and other related sciences, the fears of the dark ages which gripped the minds of men and destroyed their reason have been dispelled.

Insane asylums are filled with men and women who have gone mad, because of the *fear of death*.

This fear is useless. Death will come, no matter what anyone may think about it. Accept it as a necessity, and pass the thought out of your mind. It must be a, necessity, or it would not come to all. Perhaps it is not as bad as it has been pictured.

The entire world is made up of only two things, *energy* and *matter*. In elementary physics we learn that neither matter nor energy (the only two realities known to man) can be created nor destroyed. Both matter and energy can be transformed, but neither can be destroyed.

Life is energy, if it is anything. If neither energy nor matter can be destroyed, of course life cannot be destroyed. Life, like other forms of energy, may be passed through various processes of transition, or change, but it cannot be destroyed. Death is mere transition.

If death is not mere change, or transition, then nothing comes after death except a long, eternal, peaceful sleep, and sleep is nothing to be feared. Thus you may wipe out, forever, the fear of Death.

Symptoms of the Fear of Death

The general symptoms of this fear are:—

The habit of *thinking* about dying instead of making the most of *life*, due, generally, to lack of purpose, or lack of a suitable occupation. This fear is more prevalent among the aged, but sometimes the more youthful are victims of it. The greatest of all remedies for the fear of death is a *Burning desire for achievement*, backed by useful service to others. A busy person seldom has time to think about dying. He finds life too thrilling to worry about death. Sometimes the fear of death is closely associated with the Fear of Poverty, where one's death would leave loved ones poverty-stricken. In other cases, the fear of death is caused by illness and the consequent breaking down of physical body resistance. The commonest causes of the fear of death are: ill-health, poverty, lack of appropriate occupation, disappointment over love, insanity, religious fanaticism.

Old Man Worry

Worry is a state of mind based upon fear. It works slowly, but persistently. It is insidious and subtle. Step by step it "digs itself in" until it paralyzes one's reasoning faculty, destroys self-confidence and initiative. Worry is a form of sustained fear caused by indecision therefore it is a state of mind which can be controlled.

An unsettled mind is helpless. Indecision makes an unsettled mind. Most individuals lack the willpower to reach decisions promptly, and to stand by them after they have been made, even during normal business conditions. During periods of economic unrest (such as the world recently experienced), the individual is handicapped, not alone by his inherent nature to be slow at reaching decisions, but he is influenced by the indecision of others around him who have created a state of "mass indecision."

During the depression the whole atmosphere, all over the world, was filled with "Fearenza" and "Worryitis," the two mental disease germs which began to spread themselves after the Wall Street frenzy in 1929. There is only one known antidote for these germs; it is the habit of prompt and firm *decision*. Moreover, it is an antidote which every individual must apply for himself.

We do not worry over conditions, once we have reached a decision to follow a definite line of action.

I once interviewed a man who was to be electrocuted two hours later. The condemned man was the calmest of some eight men who were in the death-cell with him. His calmness prompted me to ask him how it felt to know that he was going into eternity in a short while. With a smile of confidence on his face, he said, "It feels fine. Just think, brother, my troubles will soon be over. I have had nothing but trouble all my life. It has been a hardship to get food and clothing. Soon I will not need these things. I have felt fine ever since I learned *for certain* that I must die. I made up my mind then, to accept my fate in good spirit."

As he spoke he devoured a dinner of proportions sufficient for three men, eating every mouthful of the food brought to him, and apparently enjoying it as much as if no disaster awaited him. *decision* gave this man resignation to his fate! Decision can also prevent one's acceptance of undesired circumstances.

The six basic fears become translated into a state of worry, through indecision. Relieve yourself, forever of the fear of death, by reaching a decision to accept death as an inescapable event. Whip the fear of poverty by reaching a decision to get along with whatever wealth you can accumulate *without worry*. Put your foot upon the neck of the fear of criticism by reaching a decision *not to worry* about what other people think, do, or say. Eliminate the fear of old age by reaching a decision to accept it, not as a handicap, but as a great blessing which carries with it wisdom, self-control, and understanding not known to youth.

Acquit yourself of the fear of ill health by the decision to forget symptoms. Master the fear of loss of love by reaching a decision to get along without love, if that is necessary.

Kill the habit of worry, in all its forms, by reaching a general, blanket decision that nothing which life has to offer is worth the price of worry. With this decision will come poise, peace of mind, and calmness of thought which will bring happiness.

A man whose mind is filled with fear not only destroys his own chances of intelligent action, but, he transmits these destructive vibrations to the minds of all who come into contact with him, and destroys, also their chances.

Even a dog or a horse knows when its master lacks courage; moreover, a dog or a horse will pick up the vibrations of fear thrown off by its master, and behave accordingly. Lower down the line of intelligence in the animal kingdom, one finds this same capacity to pick up the vibrations of fear. A honey-bee immediately senses fear in the mind of a person—for reasons unknown, a bee will sting the person whose mind is releasing vibrations of fear, much more readily than it will molest the person whose mind registers no fear.

The vibrations of fear pass from one mind to another just as quickly and as surely as the sound of the human voice passes from the broadcasting station to the receiving set of a radio—and *By the self-same medium.*

Mental telepathy is a reality. Thoughts pass from one mind to another, voluntarily, whether or not this fact is recognized by either the person releasing the thoughts, or the persons who pick up those thoughts.

The person who gives expression, by word of mouth, to negative or destructive thoughts is practically certain to experience the results of those words in the form of a destructive "kick-back." The release of destructive thought impulses, alone, without the aid of words, produces also a "kickback" in more ways than one. First of all, and perhaps most important to be remembered, the person who releases thoughts of a destructive nature, must suffer damage through the breaking down of the faculty of creative imagination. Secondly, the presence in the mind of any destructive emotion develops a negative personality which repels people, and often converts them into antagonists. The third source of damage to the person who entertains or releases negative thoughts, lies in this significant fact— these thought-impulses are not only damaging to others, but they *embed themselves in the subconscious mind of the person releasing them,* and there become a part of his character.

One is never through with a thought, merely by releasing it. When a thought is released, it spreads in every direction, through the medium of the ether, but it also plants itself permanently in the subconscious mind of the person releasing it.

Your business in life is, presumably to achieve success. To be successful, you must find peace of mind, acquire the material needs of life, and above all, attain *happiness.* All of these evidences of success begin in the form of thought impulses.

You may control your own mind, you have the power to feed it whatever thought impulses you choose. With this privilege goes also the responsibility of using it constructively. You are the master of your own earthly destiny just as surely as you have the power to control your own thoughts. You may influence, direct, and eventually control your own environment, making your life what you want it to be— or, you may neglect to exercise the privilege which is yours, to make your life to order, thus casting yourself upon the broad sea of "Circumstance" where you will be tossed hither and yon, like a chip on the waves of the ocean.

The Devil's Workshop: the Seventh Basic Evil

In addition to the Six Basic Fears, there is another evil by which people suffer. It constitutes a rich soil in which the seeds of failure grow abundantly. It is so subtle that its presence often is not detected. This affliction cannot properly be classed as a fear. *It is more deeply seated and more often fatal than all of the six fears.* For want of a better name, let us call this evil *susceptibility to negative influences.*

Men who accumulate great riches always protect themselves against this evil! The poverty stricken never do! Those who succeed in any calling must prepare their minds to resist the evil. If you are reading this philosophy for the purpose of accumulating riches, you should examine yourself very carefully, to determine whether you are susceptible to negative influences. If you neglect this self-analysis, you will forfeit your right to attain the object of your desires.

Make the analysis searching. After you read the questions prepared for this self-analysis, hold yourself to a strict accounting in your answers. Go at the task as carefully as you would search for any other enemy you knew to be awaiting you in ambush and deal with your own faults as you would with a more tangible enemy.

You can easily protect yourself against highway robbers, because the law provides organized cooperation for your benefit, but the "seventh basic evil" is more difficult to master, because it strikes when you are not aware of its presence, when you are asleep, and while you are awake. Moreover, its weapon is intangible, because it consists of merely— a *state of mind.* This evil is also dangerous because it strikes in as many different forms as there are human experiences. Sometimes it enters the mind through the well-meant words of one's own relatives. At other times, it bores from within, through one's own mental attitude. Always it is as deadly as poison, even though it may not kill as quickly.

How to Protect Yourself Against Negative Influences

To protect yourself against negative influences, whether of your own making, or the result of the activities of negative people around you, recognize that you have a *will-power*, and put it into constant use, until it builds a wall of immunity against negative influences in your own mind.

Recognize the fact that you, and every other human being, are, by nature, lazy, indifferent, and susceptible to all suggestions which harmonize with your weaknesses.

Recognize that you are, by nature, susceptible to all the six basic fears, and set up. habits for the purpose of counteracting all these fears.

Recognize that negative influences often work on you through your subconscious mind, therefore they are difficult to detect, and keep your mind closed against all people who depress or discourage you in any way.

Clean out your medicine chest, throw away all pill bottles, and stop pandering to colds, aches, pains and imaginary illness.

Deliberately seek the company of people who influence you to *think and act for yourself.*

Do not *expect* troubles as they have a tendency not to disappoint.

Without doubt, the most common weakness of all human beings is the habit of leaving their minds open to the negative influence of other people. This weakness is all the more damaging, because most people do not recognize that they are cursed by it, and many who acknowledge it, neglect or refuse to correct the evil until it becomes an uncontrollable part of their daily habits.

To aid those who wish to see themselves as they really are, the following list of questions has been prepared. Read the questions and state your answers aloud, so you can hear your own voice. This will make it easier for you to be truthful with yourself.

Self-analysis Test Questions

Do you complain often of "feeling bad," and if so, what is the cause?

Do you find fault with other people at the slightest provocation?

Do you frequently make mistakes in your work, and if so, why?
Are you sarcastic and offensive in your conversation?
Do you deliberately avoid the association of anyone, and if so, why?
Do you suffer frequently with indigestion? If so, what is the cause?
Does life seem futile and the future hopeless to you? If so, why?
Do you like your occupation? If not, why?
Do you often feel self-pity, and if so why?
Are you envious of those who excel you?
To which do you devote most time, thinking of *success*, or of *failure*?
Are you gaining or losing self-confidence as you grow older?
Do you learn something of value from all mistakes?
Are you permitting some relative or acquaintance to worry you? If so, why?
Are you sometimes "in the clouds" and at other times in the depths of despondency?
Who has the most inspiring influence upon you? What is the cause?
Do you tolerate negative or discouraging influences which you can avoid?
Are you careless of your personal appearance? If so, when and why?
Have you learned how to "drown your troubles" by being too busy to be annoyed by them?
Would you call yourself a "spineless weakling" if you permitted others to do your thinking for you?
Do you neglect internal bathing until auto-intoxication makes you ill-tempered and irritable?
How many preventable disturbances annoy you, and why do you tolerate them?
Do you resort to liquor, narcotics, or cigarettes to "quiet your nerves"? If so, why do you not try will-power instead?
Does anyone "nag" you, and if so, for what reason?
Do you have a *definite major purpose*, and if so, what is it, and what plan have you for achieving it?
Do you suffer from any of the Six Basic Fears? If so, which ones?
Have you a method by which you can shield yourself against the negative influence of others?
Do you make deliberate use of auto-suggestion to make your mind positive?
Which do you value most, your material possessions, or your privilege of controlling your own thoughts?
Are you easily influenced by others, against your own judgment?
Has today added anything of value to your stock of knowledge or state of mind?
Do you face squarely the circumstances which make you unhappy, or sidestep the responsibility?
Do you analyze all mistakes and failures and try to profit by them or, do you take the attitude that this is not your duty?
Can you name three of your most damaging weaknesses? What are you doing to correct them?
Do you encourage other people to bring their worries to you for sympathy?
Do you choose, from your daily experiences, lessons or influences which aid in your personal advancement?
Does your presence have a negative influence on other people as a rule?
What habits of other people annoy you most?
Do you form your own opinions or permit yourself to be influenced by other people?
Have you learned how to create a mental state of mind with which you can shield yourself against all discouraging influences?
Does your occupation inspire you with faith and hope?

Are you conscious of possessing spiritual forces of sufficient power to enable you to keep your mind free from all forms of *fear*?

Does your religion help you to keep your own mind positive?

Do you feel it your duty to share other people's worries? If so, why?

If you believe that "birds of a feather flock together" what have you learned about yourself by studying the friends whom you attract?

What connection, if any, do you see between the people with whom you associate most closely, and any unhappiness you may experience?

Could it be possible that some person whom you consider to be a friend is, in reality, your worst enemy, because of his negative influence on your mind?

By what rules do you judge who is helpful and who is damaging to you?

Are your intimate associates mentally superior or inferior to you?

How much time out of every 24 hours do you devote to:

a. your occupation

b. sleep

c. play and relaxation

d. acquiring useful knowledge e. plain waste

Who among your acquaintances,

a. encourages you most

b. cautions you most

c. discourages you most

d. helps you most in other ways

What is your greatest worry? Why do you tolerate it?

When others offer you free, unsolicited advice, do you accept it without question, or analyze their motive?

What, above all else, do you most *desire*? Do you intend to acquire it? Are you willing to subordinate all other desires for this one? How much time daily do you devote to acquiring it?

Do you change your mind often? If so, why?

Do you usually finish everything you begin?

Are you easily impressed by other people's business or professional titles, college degrees, or wealth?

Are you easily influenced by what other people think or say of you?

Do you cater to people because of their social or financial status?

Whom do you believe to be the greatest person living?

In what respect is this person superior to yourself?

How much time have you devoted to studying and answering these questions? (At least one day is necessary for the analysis and the answering of the entire list.)

If you have answered all these questions truthfully, you know more about yourself than the majority of people. Study the questions carefully, come back to them once each week for several months, and be astounded at the amount of additional knowledge of great value to yourself, you will have gained by the simple method of answering the questions truthfully. If you are not certain concerning the answers to some of the questions, seek the counsel of those who know you well, especially those who have no motive in flattering you, and see yourself through their eyes. The experience will be astonishing.

You have *absolute control* over but one thing, and that is your thoughts. This is the most significant and inspiring of all facts known to man! It reflects man's Divine nature. This Divine prerogative is the sole means by which you may control your own destiny. If you fail to control your own mind, you may be sure you will control nothing else.

If you must be careless with your possessions, let it be in connection with material things. Your mind is your spiritual estate! Protect and use it with the care to which Divine Royalty is entitled. You were given a *will-power* for this purpose.

Unfortunately, there is no legal protection against those who, either by design or ignorance, poison the minds of others by negative suggestion. This form of destruction should be punishable by heavy legal penalties, because it may and often does destroy one's chances of acquiring material things which are protected by law.

Men with negative minds tried to convince Thomas A. Edison that he could not build a machine that would record and reproduce the human voice, "because" they said, "no one else had ever produced such a machine." Edison did not believe them. He knew that the mind could produce *anything the mind could conceive and believe,* and that knowledge was the thing that lifted the great Edison above the common herd.

Men with negative minds told F. W. Woolworth, he would go "broke" trying to run a store on five and ten cent sales. He did not believe them. He knew that he could do anything, within reason, if he backed his plans with faith. Exercising his right to keep other men's negative suggestions out of his mind, he piled up a fortune of more than a hundred million dollars.

Men with negative minds told George Washington he could not hope to win against the vastly superior forces of the British, but he exercised his Divine right to *believe,* therefore this book was published under the protection of the Stars and Stripes, while the name of Lord Cornwallis has been all but forgotten.

Doubting Thomases scoffed scornfully when Henry Ford tried out his first crudely built automobile on the streets of Detroit. Some said the thing never would become practical. Others said no one would pay money for such a contraption.

Ford said, "I'll belt the earth with dependable motor cars," and he did!

His decision to trust his own judgment has already piled up a fortune far greater than the next five generations of his decedents can squander. For the benefit of those seeking vast riches, let it be remembered that practically the sole difference between Henry Ford and a majority of the more than one hundred thousand men who work for him, is *this–ford has a mind and controls it, the others have minds which they do not try to control.*

Henry Ford has been repeatedly mentioned, because he is an astounding example of what a man with a mind of his own, and a will to control it, can accomplish. His record knocks the foundation from under that time-worn alibi, "I never had a chance." Ford never had a chance, either, but he *created an opportunity and backed it with persistence until it made him richer than Croesus.*

Mind control is the result of self-discipline and habit. You either control your mind or it controls you. There is no hall-way compromise. The most practical of all methods for controlling the mind is the habit of keeping it busy with a definite purpose, backed by a definite plan. Study the record of any man who achieves noteworthy success, and you will observe that he has control over his own mind, moreover, that he exercises that control and directs it toward the attainment of definite objectives. Without this control, success is not possible.

Fifty-seven Famous Alibis: by Old Man If

People who do not succeed have one distinguishing trait in common. They know all the reasons for failure, and have what they believe to be air-tight alibis to explain away their own lack of achievement.

Some of these alibis are clever, and a few of them are justifiable by the facts. But alibis cannot be used for money. The world wants to know only one thing—*have you achieved success?*

A character analyst compiled a list of the most commonly used alibis. As you read the list, examine yourself carefully, and determine how many of these alibis, if any, are your own property. Remember, too, the philosophy presented in this book makes every one of these alibis obsolete.

If I didn't have a wife and family . . .

If I had enough "pull" . . .

If I had money . . .

If I had a good education . . .

If I could get a job . . .

If I had good health . . .

If I only had time . . .

If times were better . . .

If other people understood me . . .

If conditions around me were only different . . .

If I could live my life over again . . .

If I did not fear what "*they*" would say . . .

If I had been given a chance . . .

If I now had a chance . . .

If other people didn't "have it in for me" . . .

If nothing happens to stop me . . .

If I were only younger . . .

If I could only do what I want . . .

If I had been born rich . . .

If I could meet "the right people" . . .

If I had the talent that some people have . . .

If I dared assert myself . . .

If I only had embraced past opportunities . . .

If people didn't get on my nerves . . .

If I didn't have to keep house and look after the children . . .

If I could save some money . . .

If the boss only appreciated me . . .

If I only had somebody to help me . . .

If my family understood me . . .

If I lived in a big city . . .

If I could just get started . . .

If I were only free . . .

If I had the personality of some people . . .

If I were not so fat . . .

If my talents were known . . .
If I could just get a "break" . . .
If I could only get out of debt . . .
If I hadn't failed . . .
If I only knew how . . .
If everybody didn't oppose me . . .
If I didn't have so many worries . . .
If I could marry the right person . . .
If people weren't so dumb . . .
If my family were not so extravagant . . .
If I were sure of myself . . .
If luck were not against me . . .
If I had not been born under the wrong star . . .
If it were not true that "what is to be will be" . . .
If I did not have to work so hard . . .
If I hadn't lost my money . . .
If I lived in a different neighborhood . . .
If I didn't have a "past" . . .
If I only had a business of my own . . .
If other people would only listen to me . . .

If (and this is the greatest of them all) I had the courage to see myself as I really am, I would find out what is wrong with me, and correct it, then I might have a chance to profit by my mistakes and learn something from the experience of others, for I know that there is something *wrong* with me, or I would now be where I *would have been if* I had spent more time analyzing my weaknesses, and less time building alibis to cover them.

Building alibis with which to explain away failure is a national pastime. The habit is as old as the human race, and is fatal to success! Why do people cling to their pet alibis? The answer is obvious. They defend their alibis because *they create* them! A man's alibi is the child of his own imagination. It is human nature to defend one's own brain-child.

Building alibis is a deeply rooted habit. Habits are difficult to break, especially when they provide justification for something we do. Plato had this truth in mind when he said, "The first and best victory is to conquer self. To be conquered by self is, of all things, the most shameful and vile."

Another philosopher had the same thought in mind when he said, "It was a great surprise to me when I discovered that most of the ugliness I saw in others, was but a reflection of my own nature." "It has always been a mystery to me," said Elbert Hubbard, "why people spend so much time deliberately fooling themselves by creating alibis to cover their weaknesses. If used differently, this same time would be sufficient to cure the weakness, then no alibis would be needed.

"In parting, I would remind you that "Life is a checkerboard, and the player opposite you is *time*. If you hesitate before moving, or neglect to move promptly, your men will be wiped off the board by *time*. You are playing against a partner who will not tolerate *decisions*!"

Previously you may have had a logical excuse for not having forced Life to come through with whatever you asked, but that alibi is now obsolete, because you are in possession of the Master Key that unlocks the door to Life's bountiful riches.

The Master Key is intangible, but it is powerful! It is the privilege of creating, in your own mind, a *burning desire* for a definite form of riches. There is no penalty for the use of the Key, but there is a price you must pay if you do not use it. The price is *failure*. There is a reward of stupendous proportions if you put the Key to use. It is the satisfaction that comes to all who conquer self and force Life to pay whatever is asked.

The reward is worthy of your effort. Will you make the start and be convinced?

"If we are related," said the immortal Emerson, "we shall meet." In closing, may I borrow his thought, and say, "If we are related, we have, through these pages, met."

The Law of Success

In Sixteen Lessons

Table of Contents

A Personal Statement by the Author

Some thirty years ago a young clergyman by the name of Gunsaulus announced in the newspapers of Chicago that he would preach a sermon the following Sunday morning entitled:

"WHAT I WOULD DO IF I HAD A MILLION DOLLARS!"

The announcement caught the eye of Philip D. Armour, the wealthy packing-house king, who decided to hear the sermon.

In his sermon Dr. Gunsaulus pictured a great school of technology where young men and young women could be taught how to succeed in life by developing the ability to THINK in practical rather than in theoretical terms; where they would be taught to "learn by doing." "If I had a million dollars," said the young preacher, "I would start such a school."

After the sermon was over Mr. Armour walked down the aisle to the pulpit, introduced himself, and said, "Young man, I believe you could do all you said you could, and if you will come down to my office tomorrow morning I will give you the million dollars you need."

There is always plenty of capital for those who can create practical plans for using it. That was the beginning of the Armour Institute of Technology, one of the very practical schools of the country. The school was born in the "imagination" of a young man who never would have been heard of outside of the community in which he preached had it not been for the "imagination," plus the capital, of Philip D. Armour. Every great railroad, and every outstanding financial institution and every mammoth business enterprise, and every great invention, began in the imagination of some one person.

F. W. Woolworth created the Five and Ten Cent Store Plan in his "imagination" before it became a reality and made him a multi-millionaire. Thomas A. Edison created the talking machine and the moving picture machine and the incandescent electric light bulb and scores of other useful inventions, in his own "imagination," before they became a reality. During the Chicago fire scores of merchants whose stores went up in smoke stood near the smoldering embers of their former places of business, grieving over their loss. Many of them decided to go away into other cities and start over again. In the group was Marshall Field, who saw, in his own "imagination," the world's greatest retail store, standing on the selfsame spot where his former store had stood, which was then but a ruined mass of smoking timbers. That store became a reality.

Fortunate is the young man or young woman who learns, early in life, to use imagination, and doubly so in this age of greater opportunity.

Imagination is a faculty of the mind which can be cultivated, developed, extended and broadened by use. If this were not true, this course on the Fifteen Laws of Success never would have been created, because it was first conceived in the author's "imagination," from the mere seed of an idea which was sown by a chance remark of the late Andrew Carnegie. Wherever you are, whoever you are, whatever you may be following as an occupation, there is room for you to make yourself more useful, and in that manner more productive, by developing and using your "imagination." Success in this world is always a matter of individual effort, yet you will only be deceiving yourself if you believe that you can succeed without the cooperation of other people.

Success is a matter of individual effort only to the extent that each person must decide, in his or her own mind, what is wanted. This involves the use of "imagination." From this point on, achieving success is a matter of skillfully and tactfully inducing others to co-operate. Before you can secure co-operation from others; nay, before you have the right to ask for or expect co-operation from other people, you must first show a willingness to co-operate with them. For this reason the eighth lesson of this course, THE HABIT OF DOING MORE THAN PAID FOR, is one which should have your serious and thoughtful attention.

The law upon which this lesson is based, would, of itself, practically insure success to all who practice it in all they do.

In the back pages of this Introduction you will observe a Personal Analysis Chart in which ten well-known men have been analyzed for your study and comparison. Observe this chart carefully and note the "danger points" which mean failure to those who do not observe these signals. Of the ten men analyzed, eight are known to be successful, while two may be considered failures.

Study, carefully, the reason why these two men failed. Then, study yourself. In the two columns which have been left blank for that purpose, give yourself a rating on each of the Fifteen Laws of Success at the beginning of this course; at the end of the course rate yourself again and observe the improvements you have made.

The purpose of the Law of Success course is to enable you to find out how you may become more capable in your chosen field of work. To this end you will be analyzed and all of your qualities classified so you may organize them and make the best possible use of them.

You may not like the work in which you are now engaged.

There are two ways of getting out of that work. One way is to take but little interest in what you are doing, aiming merely to do enough with which to "get by." Very soon you will find a way out, because the demand for your services will cease.

The other and better way is by making yourself so useful and efficient in what you are now doing that you will attract the favorable attention of those who have the power to promote you into more responsible work that is more to your liking.

It is your privilege to take your choice as to which way you will proceed.

Again you are reminded of the importance of Lesson Nine of this course, through the aid of which you may avail yourself of this "better way" of promoting yourself.

Thousands of people walked over the great Calumet Copper Mine without discovering it. Just one lone man used his "imagination," dug down into the earth a few feet, investigated, and discovered the richest copper deposit on earth.

You and every other person walk, at one time or another, over your "Calumet Mine."

Discovery is a matter of investigation and use of "imagination."

This course on the Fifteen Laws of Success may lead the way to your "Calumet," and you may be surprised when you discover that you were standing right over this rich mine, in the work in which you are now engaged.

In his lecture on "Acres of Diamonds," Russell Conwell tells us that we need not seek opportunity in the distance; that we may find it right where we stand! THIS IS A

TRUTH WELL WORTH REMEMBERING!

NAPOLEON HILL,
Author of The Law of Success

The Author's Acknowledgment of Help
Rendered Him in the Writing of This Course

This course is the result of careful analysis of the life-work of over one hundred men and women who have achieved unusual success in their respective callings. The author of the course has been more than twenty years in gathering, classifying, testing and organizing the Fifteen Laws upon which the course is based. In his labor he has received valuable assistance either in person or by studying the life-work of the following men:

Henry Ford
Thomas A. Edison
Harvey S. Firestone
John D. Rockefeller
Charles M. Schwab
Woodrow Wilson
Darwin P. Kingsley
Wm. Wrigley, Jr.
A. D. Lasker
E. A. Filene
James J. Hill
Captain George
Dr. E. W. Strickler
Edwin C. Barnes
Robert L. Taylor
Fiddling Bob
George Eastman
Edward Bok
Cyrus H. K. Curtis
George W. Perkins
Henry L. Doherty
George S. Parker
Dr. C. O. Henry
General Rufus A. Ayers
Judge Elbert H. Gary
William Howard Taft
Dr. Elmer Gates
John W. Davis
M. Alex-Samuel Insulander
Elbert Hubbard
Luther Burbank
O. H. Harriman
John Burroughs
E. H. Harriman

E. M. Statler
Andrew Carnegie
John Wanamaker
Marshall Field
Charles P. Steinmetz
Frank Vanderlip
Theodore Roosevelt
Wm. H. French
Dr. Alexander Graham Bell **(To whom the author owes credit for most of Lesson One.)**

Of the men named, perhaps Henry Ford and Andrew Carnegie should be acknowledged as having contributed most toward the building of this course, for the reason that it was Andrew Carnegie who first suggested the writing of the course and Henry Ford whose life-work supplied much of the material out of which the course was developed.

Some of these men are now deceased, but to those who are still living the author wishes to make here grateful acknowledgment of the service they have rendered, without which this course never could have been written.

The author has studied the majority of these men at close range, in person. With many of them he enjoys, or did enjoy before their death, the privilege of close personal friendship which enabled him to gather from their philosophy facts that would not have been available under other conditions.

The author is grateful for having enjoyed the privilege of enlisting the services of the most powerful men on earth, in the building of the Law of Success course. That privilege has been remuneration enough for the work done, if nothing more were ever received for it.

These men have been the backbone and the foundation and the skeleton of American business, finance, industry and statesmanship.

The Law of Success course epitomizes the philosophy and the rules of procedure which made each of these men a great power in his chosen field of endeavor. It has been the author's intention to present the course in the plainest and most simple terms available, so it could be mastered by very young men and young women, of the high-school age.

With the exception of the psychological law referred to in Lesson One as the "Master Mind," the author lays no claim to having created anything basically new in this course. What he has done, however, has been to organize old truths and known laws into PRACTICAL, USABLE FORM, where they may be properly interpreted and applied by the workaday man whose needs call for a philosophy of simplicity.

In passing upon the merits of the Law of Success Judge Elbert H. Gary said: "Two outstanding features connected with the philosophy impress me most. One is the simplicity with which it has been presented, and the other is the fact that its soundness is so obvious to all that it will be immediately accepted." The student of this course is warned against passing judgment upon it before having read the entire sixteen lessons. This especially applies to this Introduction, in which it has been necessary to include brief reference to subjects of a more or less technical and scientific nature. The reason for this will be obvious after the student has read the entire sixteen lessons.

The student who takes up this course with an open mind, and sees to it that his or her mind remains "open" until the last lesson shall have been read, will be richly rewarded with a broader and more accurate view of life as a whole.

Lesson One: THE MASTER MIND

This is a course on the fundamentals of Success.

Success is very largely a matter of adjusting one's self to the ever-varying and changing environments of life, in a spirit of harmony and poise. Harmony is based upon understanding of the forces constituting one's environment; therefore, this course is in reality a blueprint that may be followed straight to success, because it helps the student to interpret, understand and make the most of these environmental forces of life.

Before you begin reading the Law of Success lessons you should know something of the history of the course. You should know exactly what the course promises to those who follow it until they have assimilated the laws and principles upon which it is based. You should know its limitations as well as its possibilities as an aid in your fight for a place in the world.

From the viewpoint of entertainment the Law of Success course would be a poor second for most any of the monthly periodicals of the "Snappy Story" variety which may be found upon the news stands of today.

The course has been created for the serious-minded person who devotes at least a portion of his or her time to the business of succeeding in life. The author of the Law of Success course has not intended to compete with those who write purely for the purpose of entertaining.

The author's aim, in preparing this course, has been of a two-fold nature, namely, first–to help the earnest student find out what are his or her weaknesses, and, secondly–to help create a DEFINITE PLAN for bridging those weaknesses.

The most successful men and women on earth have had to correct certain weak spots intheir personalities before they began to succeed. The most outstanding of these weaknesses which stand between men and women and success are INTOLERANCE, CUPIDITY, GREED, JEALOUSY, SUSPICION, REVENGE, EGOTISM, CONCEIT, THE TENDENCY TO REAP WHERE THEY HAVE NOT SOWN, and the HABIT OF SPENDING MORE THAN THEY EARN.

All of these common enemies of mankind, and many more not here mentioned, are covered by the Law of Success course in such a manner that any person of reasonable intelligence may master them with but little effort or inconvenience.

You should know, at the very outset, that the Law of Success course has long since passed through the experimental state; that it already has to its credit a record of achievement that is worthy of serious thought and analysis. You should know, also, that the Law of Success course has been examined and endorsed by some of the most practical minds of this generation.

The Law of Success course was first used as a lecture, and was delivered by its author in practically every city and in many of the smaller localities, throughout the United States, over a period of more than seven years. Perhaps you were one of the many hundreds of thousands of people who heard this lecture.

During these lectures the author had assistants located in the audiences for the purpose of interpreting the reaction of those who heard the lecture, and in this manner he learned exactly what effect it had upon people. As a result of this study and analysis many changes were made.

The first big victory was gained for the Law of Success philosophy when it was used by the author as the basis of a course with which 3,000 men and women were trained as a sales army.

The majority of these people were without previous experience, of any sort, in the field of selling. Through this training they were enabled to earn more than One Million Dollars ($1,000,000.00) for themselves and paid the author $30,000.00 for his services, covering a period of approximately six months.

The individuals and small groups of salespeople who have found success through the aid of this course are too numerous to be mentioned in this Introduction, but the number is large and the benefits they derived from the course were definite. The Law of Success philosophy was brought to the attention of the late Don R. Mellett, former publisher of the Canton (Ohio) Daily News, who formed a partnership with the author of the course and was preparing to resign as publisher of the Canton Daily News and take up the business management of the author's affairs when he was assassinated on July 16,1926.

Prior to his death Mr. Mellett had made arrangements with Judge Elbert H. Gary, who was then Chairman of the Board of the United States Steel Corporation, to present the Law of Success course to every employee of the Steel Corporation, at a total cost of something like $150,000.00. This plan was halted because of Judge Gary's death, but it proves that the author of the Law of Success has produced an educational plan of an enduring nature.

Judge Gary was eminently prepared to judge the value of such a course, and the fact that he analyzed the Law of Success philosophy and was preparing to invest the huge sum of $150,000.00 in it is proof of the soundness of all that is said in behalf of the course.

You will observe, in this General Introduction to the course, a few technical terms which may not be plain to you. Do not allow this to bother you. Make no attempt at first reading to understand these terms. They will be plain to you after you read the remainder of the course. This entire Introduction is intended only as a background for the other fifteen lessons of the course, and you should read it as such. You will not be examined on this Introduction, but you should read it many times, as you will get from it at each reading a thought or an idea which you did not get on previous readings.

In this Introduction you will find a description of a newly discovered law of psychology which is the very foundation stone of all outstanding personal achievements. This law has been referred to by the author as the "Master Mind," meaning a mind that is developed through the harmonious co-operation of two or more people who ally themselves for the purpose of accomplishing any given task.

If you are engaged in the business of selling you may profitably experiment with this law of the "Master Mind" in your daily work. It has been found that a group of six or seven salespeople may use the law so effectively that their sales may be increased to unbelievable proportions.

Life Insurance is supposed to be the hardest thing on earth to sell. This ought not to be true, with an established necessity such as life insurance, but it is. Despite this fact, a small group of men working for the Prudential Life Insurance Company, whose sales are mostly small policies, formed a little friendly group for the purpose of experimenting with the law of the "Master Mind," with the result that every man in the group wrote more insurance during the first three months of the experiment than he had ever written in an entire year before.

What may be accomplished through the aid of this principle, by any small group of intelligent life insurance salesmen who have learned how to apply the law of the "Master Mind", will stagger the imagination of the most highly optimistic and imaginative person.

The same may be said of other groups of salespeople who are engaged in selling merchandise and other more tangible forms of service than life insurance. Bear this in mind as you read this Introduction to the Law of Success course and it is not unreasonable to expect that this Introduction, alone, may give you sufficient understanding of the law to change the entire course of your life.

It is the personalities back of a business which determine the measure of success the business will enjoy. Modify those personalities so they are more pleasing and more attractive to the patrons of the business and the business will thrive. In any of the great cities of the United States one may purchase merchandise of similar nature and price in scores of stores, yet you will find there is always one outstanding store which does more business than any of the others, and the reason for this is that back of that store is a man, or men, who has attended to the personalities of those who come in contact with the public. People buy personalities as much as merchandise, and it is a question if they are not influenced more by the personalities with which they come in contact than they are by the merchandise.

Life insurance has been reduced to such a scientific basis that the cost of insurance does not vary to any great extent, regardless of the company from which one purchases it, yet out of the hundreds of life insurance companies doing business less than a dozen companies do the bulk of the business of the United States.

Why? Personalities! Ninety-nine people out of every hundred who purchase life insurance policies do not know what is in their policies and, what seems more startling, do not seem to care. What they really purchase is the pleasing personality of some man or woman who knows the value of cultivating such a personality.

Your business in life, or at least the most important part of it, is to achieve success. Success, within the meaning of that term as covered by this course on the Fifteen Laws of Success, is "the attainment of your Definite Chief Aim without violating the rights of other people." Regardless of what your major aim in life may be, you will attain it with much less difficulty after you learn how to cultivate a pleasing personality and after you have learned the delicate art of allying yourself with others in a given undertaking without friction or envy.

One of the greatest problems of life, if not, in fact, the greatest, is that of learning the art of harmonious negotiation with others. This course was created for the purpose of teaching people how to negotiate their way through life with harmony and poise, free from the destructive effects of disagreement and friction which bring millions of people to misery, want and failure every year.

With this statement of the purpose of the course you should be able to approach the lessons with the feeling that a complete transformation is about to take place in your personality. You cannot enjoy outstanding success in life without power, and you can never enjoy power without sufficient personality to influence other people to cooperate with you in a spirit of harmony. This course shows you step-by-step how to develop such a personality.

Lesson by lesson, the following is a statement of that which you may expect to receive from the Fifteen Laws of Success:

I. A DEFINITE CHIEF AIM will teach you how to save the wasted effort which the majority of people expend in trying to find their lifework. This lesson will show you how to do away forever with aimlessness and fix your heart and hand upon some definite, well-conceived purpose as a life-work.

II. SELF-CONFIDENCE will help you master the six basic fears with which every person is cursed–the fear of Poverty, the fear of Ill Health, the fear of Old Age, the fear of Criticism, the fear of Loss of Love of Someone and the fear of Death. It will teach you the difference between egotism and real self-confidence which is based upon definite, usable knowledge.

III. HABIT OF SAVING will teach you how to distribute your income systematically so that a definite percentage of it will steadily accumulate, thus forming one of the greatest known sources of personal power. No one may succeed in life without saving money. There is no exception to this rule, and no one may escape it.

IV. INITIATIVE AND LEADERSHIP will show you how to become a leader instead of a follower in your chosen field of endeavor. It will develop in you the instinct for leadership which will cause you gradually to gravitate to the top in all undertakings in which you participate.

V. IMAGINATION will stimulate your mind so that you will conceive new ideas and develop new plans which will help you in attaining the object of your Definite Chief Aim. This lesson will teach you how to "build new houses out of old stones," so to speak. It will show you how to create new ideas out of old, well-known concepts, and how to put old ideas to new uses. This one lesson, alone, is the equivalent of a very practical course in salesmanship, and it is sure to prove a veritable gold mine of knowledge to the person who is in earnest.

VI. ENTHUSIASM will enable you to "saturate" all with whom you come in contact with interest in you and in your ideas. Enthusiasm is the foundation of a Pleasing Personality, and you must have such a personality in order to influence others to cooperate with you.

VII. SELF-CONTROL is the "balance wheel" with which you control your enthusiasm and direct it where you wish it to carry you. This lesson will teach you, in a most practical manner, to become "the master of your fate, the Captain of your Soul."

VIII. THE HABIT OF DOING MORE THAN PAID FOR is one of the most important lessons of the Law of Success course. It will teach you how to take advantage of the Law of Increasing Returns, which will eventually insure you a return in money far out of proportion to the service you render. No one may become a real leader in any walk of life without practicing the habit of doing more work and better work than that for which he is paid.

IX. PLEASING PERSONALITY is the "fulcrum" on which you must place the "crow-bar" of your efforts, and when so placed, with intelligence, it will enable you to remove mountains of obstacles. This one lesson, alone, has made scores of Master Salesmen. It has developed leaders over night. It will teach you how to transform your personality so that you may adapt yourself to any environment, or to any other personality, in such a manner that you may easily dominate.

X. ACCURATE THINKING is one of the important foundation stones of all enduring success. This lesson teaches you how to separate "facts" from mere "information." It teaches you how to organize known facts into two classes: the "important" and the "unimportant." It teaches you how to determine what is an "important" fact. It teaches you how to build definite working plans, in the pursuit of any calling, out of FACTS.

XI. CONCENTRATION teaches you how to focus your attention upon one subject at a time until you have worked out practical plans for mastering that subject. It will teach you how to ally yourself with others in such a manner that you may have the use of their entire knowledge to back you up in your own plans and purposes. It will give you a practical working knowledge of the forces around you, and show you how to harness and use these.

XII. CO-OPERATION will teach you the value of teamwork in all you do. In this lesson you will be taught how to apply the law of the "Master Mind" described in this Introduction and in Lesson Two of this course. This lesson will show you how to coordinate your own efforts with those of others, in such a manner that friction, jealousy, strife, envy and cupidity will be eliminated. You will learn how to make use of all that other people have learned about the work in which you are engaged.

XIII. PROFITING BY FAILURE will teach you how to make stepping stones out of all of your past and future mistakes and failures. It will teach you the difference between "failure" and "temporary defeat," a difference which is very great and very important. It will teach you how to profit by your own failures and by the failures of other people.

XIV. TOLERANCE will teach you how to avoid the disastrous effects of racial and religious prejudices which mean defeat for millions of people who permit themselves to become entangled in foolish argument over these subjects, thereby poisoning their own minds and closing the door to reason and investigation. This lesson is the twin sister of the one on **ACCURATE THOUGHT,** for the reason that no one may become an Accurate Thinker without practicing tolerance.

Intolerance closes the book of Knowledge and writes on the cover, "Finis! I have learned it all!" Intolerance makes enemies of those who should be friends. It destroys opportunity and fills the mind with doubt, mistrust and prejudice.

XV. PRACTICING THE GOLDEN RULE will teach you how to make use of this great universal law of human conduct in such a manner that you may easily get harmonious co-operation from any individual or group of individuals. Lack of understanding of the law upon which the Golden Rule philosophy is based is one of the major causes of failure of millions of people who remain in misery, poverty and want all their lives. This lesson has nothing whatsoever to do with religion in any form, nor with sectarianism, nor have any of the other lessons of this course on the Law of Success. When you have mastered these Fifteen Laws and made them your own, as you may do within a period of from fifteen to thirty weeks, you will be ready to develop sufficient personal power to insure the attainment of your Definite Chief Aim. The purpose of these Fifteen Laws is to develop or help you organize all the knowledge you have, and all you acquire in the future, so you may turn this knowledge into **POWER**.

You should read the Law of Success course with a notebook by your side, for you will observe that ideas will begin to "flash" into your mind as you read, as to ways and means of using these laws in advancing your own interests.

You should also begin teaching these laws to those in whom you are most interested, as it is a well-known fact that the more one tries to teach a subject the more he learns about that subject. A man who has a family of young boys and girls may so indelibly fix these Fifteen Laws of Success in their minds that this teaching will change the entire course of their lives. The man with a family should interest his wife in studying this course with him, for reasons which will be plain before you complete reading this Introduction.

POWER is one of the three basic objects of human endeavor.

POWER is of two classes–that which is developed through coordination of natural physical laws, and that which is developed by organizing and classifying **KNOWLEDGE.**

POWER growing out of organized knowledge is the more important because it places in man's possession a tool with which he may transform, redirect and to some extent harness and use the other form of power.

The object of this reading course is to mark the route by which the student may safely travel in gathering such facts as he may wish to weave into his fabric of **KNOWLEDGE.**

There are two major methods of gathering knowledge, namely, by studying, classifying and assimilating facts which have been organized by other people, and through one's own process of gathering, organizing and classifying facts, generally called "personal experience."

This lesson deals mainly with the ways and means of studying the facts and data gathered and classified by other people.

The state of advancement known as "civilization" is but the measure of knowledge which the race has accumulated. This knowledge is of two classes–mental and physical.

Among the useful knowledge organized by man, he has discovered and cataloged the eighty-odd physical elements of which all material forms in the universe consist.

By study and analysis and accurate measurements man has discovered the "bigness" of the material side of the universe as represented by planets, suns and stars, some of which are known to be over ten million times as large as the little earth on which he lives.

On the other hand, man has discovered the "littleness" of the physical forms which constitute the universe by reducing the eighty-odd physical elements to molecules, atoms, and, finally, to the smallest particle, the electron. An electron cannot be seen; it is but a center of force consisting of a positive or a negative. The electron is the beginning of everything of a physical nature.

MOLECULES, ATOMS AND ELECTRONS:

To understand both the detail and the perspective of the process through which knowledge is gathered, organized and classified, it seems essential for the student to begin with the smallest and simplest particles of physical matter, because these are the A B C's with which Nature has constructed the entire framework of the physical portion of the universe.

The molecule consists of atoms, which are said to be little invisible particles of matter revolving continuously with the speed of lightning, on exactly the same principle that the earth revolves around the sun.

These little particles of matter known as atoms, which revolve in one continuous circuit, in the molecule, are said to be made up of electrons, the smallest particles of physical matter. As already stated, the electron is nothing but two forms of force. The electron is uniform, of but one class, size and nature; thus in a grain of sand or a drop of water the entire principle upon which the whole universe operates is duplicated.

How marvelous! How stupendous! You may gather some slight idea of the magnitude of it all the next time you eat a meal, by remembering that every article of food you eat, the plate on which you eat it, the tableware and the table itself are, in final analysis, but a collection of ELECTRONS.

In the world of physical matter, whether one is looking at the largest star that floats through the heavens or the smallest grain of sand to be found on earth, the object under observation is but an organized collection of molecules, atoms and electrons revolving around one another at inconceivable speed.

Every particle of physical matter is in a continuous state of highly agitated motion. Nothing is ever still, although nearly all physical matter may appear, to the physical eye, to be motionless.

There is no "solid" physical matter. The hardest piece of steel is but an organized mass of revolving molecules, atoms and electrons. Moreover, the electrons in a piece of steel are of the same nature, and move at the same rate of speed as the electrons in gold, silver, brass or pewter.

The eighty-odd forms of physical matter appear to be different from one another, and they are different, because they are made up of different combinations of atoms (although the electrons in these atoms are always the same, except that some electrons are positive and some are negative, meaning that some carry a positive charge of electrification while others carry a negative charge).

Through the science of chemistry, matter may be broken up into atoms which are, within themselves, unchangeable. The eighty-odd elements are created through and by reason of combining and changing of the positions of the atoms. To illustrate the modus operandi of chemistry through which this change of atomic position is wrought, in terms of modern science:

"Add four electrons (two positive and two negative) to the hydrogen atom, and you have the element lithium; knock out of the lithium atom (composed of three positive and three negative electrons) one positive and one negative electron, and you have one atom of helium (composed of two positive and two negative electrons).

Thus it may be seen that the eighty-odd physical elements of the universe differ from one another only in the number of electrons composing their atoms, and the number and arrangement of those atoms in the molecules of each element.

As an illustration, an atom of mercury contains eighty positive charges (electrons) in its nucleus, and eighty negative outlying charges (electrons). If the chemist were to expel two of its positive electrons it would instantly become the metal known as platinum. If the chemist could then go a step further and take from it a negative ("planetary") electron, the mercury atom would then have lost two positive electrons and one negative; that is, one positive charge on the whole; hence it would retain seventy-nine positive charges in the nucleus and seventy-nine outlying negative electrons, thereby becoming GOLD !

The formula through which this electronic change might be produced has been the object of diligent search by the alchemists all down the ages, and by the modern chemists of today.

It is a fact known to every chemist that literally tens of thousands of synthetic substances may be composed out of only four kinds of atoms, viz.: hydrogen, oxygen, nitrogen and carbon.

"Differences in the number of electrons in atoms confer upon them qualitative (chemical) differences, though all atoms of any one element are chemically alike. Differences in the number and spatial arrangement of these atoms (in groups of molecules) constitute both physical and chemical differences in substances, i.e., in compounds. Quite different substances are produced by combinations of precisely the same kinds of atoms, but in different proportions.

"Take from a molecule of certain substances one single atom, and they may be changed from a compound necessary to life and growth into a deadly poison. Phosphorus is an element, and thus contains but one kind of atoms; but some phosphorus is yellow and some is red, varying with the spatial distribution of the atoms in the molecules composing the phosphorus."

It may be stated as a literal truth that the atom is the universal particle with which Nature builds all material forms, from a grain of sand to the largest star that floats through space.

The atom is Nature's"building block" out of which she erects an oak tree or a pine, a rock of sandstone or granite, a mouse or an elephant.

Some of the ablest thinkers have reasoned that the earth on which we live, and every material particle on the earth, began with two atoms which attached themselves to each other, and through hundreds of millions of years of flight through space, kept contacting and accumulating other atoms until, step by step, the earth was formed. This, they point out, would account for the various and differing strata of the earth's substances, such as the coal beds, the iron ore deposits, the gold and silver deposits, the copper deposits, etc.

They reason that, as the earth whirled through space, it contacted groups of various kinds of nebulae, or atoms, which it promptly appropriated, through the law of magnetic attraction.

There is much to be seen, in the earth's surface composition, to support this theory, although there may be no positive evidence of its soundness.

These facts concerning the smallest analyzable particles of matter have been briefly referred to as a starting point from which we shall undertake to ascertain how to develop and apply the law of POWER.

It has been noticed that all matter is in a constant state of vibration or motion; that the molecule is made up of rapidly moving particles called atoms, which, in turn, are made up of rapidly moving particles called electrons.

THE VIBRATING FLUID OF MATTER: In every particle of matter there is an invisible "fluid" or force which causes the atoms to circle around one another at an inconceivable rate of speed.

This "fluid" is a form of energy which has never been analyzed. Thus far it has baffled the entire scientific world. By many scientists it is believed to be the same energy as that which we call electricity. Others prefer to call it vibration. It is believed by some investigators that the rate of speed with which this force (call it whatever you will) moves determines to a large extent the nature of the outward visible appearance of the physical objects of the universe.

One rate of vibration of this "fluid energy" causes what is known as sound. The human ear can detect only the sound which is produced through from 32,000 to 38,000 vibrations per second.

As the rate of vibrations per second increases above that which we call sound they begin to manifest themselves in the form of heat. Heat begins with about 1,500,000 vibrations per second.

Still higher up the scale vibrations begin to register in the form of light. 3,000,000 vibrations per second create violet light.

Above this number vibration sheds ultra-violet rays (which are invisible to the naked eye) and other invisible radiations. And, still higher up the scale–just how high no one at present seems to know–vibrations create the power with which man THINKS.

It is the belief of the author that the "fluid" portion of all vibration, out of which grow all known forms of energy, is universal in nature; that the "fluid" portion of sound is the same as the "fluid" portion of light, the difference in effect between sound and light being only a difference in rate of vibration, also that the "fluid" portion of thought is exactly the same as that in sound, heat and light, excepting the number of vibrations per second.

Just as there is but one form of physical matter, of which the earth and all the other planets, suns and stars are composed–the electron, so is there but one form of "fluid" energy, which causes all matter to remain in a constant state of rapid motion.

AIR AND ETHER: The vast space between the suns, moons, stars and other planets of the universe is filled with a form of energy known as ether. It is this author's belief that the "fluid" energy which keeps all particles of matter in motion is the same as the universal "fluid" known as ether which fills all the space of the universe. Within a certain distance of the earth's surface, estimated by some to be about fifty miles, there exists what is called air, which is a gaseous substance composed of oxygen and nitrogen. Air is a conductor of sound vibrations, but a nonconductor of light and the higher vibrations, which are carried by the ether. The ether is a conductor of all vibrations from sound to thought.

Air is a localized substance which performs, in the main, the service of feeding all animal and plant life with oxygen and nitrogen, without which neither could exist. Nitrogen is one of the chief necessities of plant life and oxygen one of the mainstays of animal life. Near the top of very high mountains the air becomes very light, because it contains but little nitrogen, which is the reason why plant life cannot exist there. On the other hand, the "light" air found in high altitudes consists largely of oxygen, which is the chief reason why tubercular patients are sent to high altitudes.

Even this brief statement concerning molecules, atoms, electrons, air, ether and the like, may be heavy reading to the student, but, as will be seen shortly, this introduction plays an essential part as the foundation of this lesson.

Do not become discouraged if the description of this foundation appears to have none of the thrilling effects of a modern tale of fiction. You are seriously engaged in finding out what are your available powers and how to organize and apply these powers. To complete this discovery successfully you must combine determination, persistency and a well-defined DESIRE to gather and organize knowledge.

The late Dr. Alexander Graham Bell, inventor of the long distance telephone and one of the accepted authorities on the subject of vibration, is here introduced in support of this author's theories concerning the subject of vibration:

> "Suppose you have the power to make an iron rod vibrate with any desired frequency in a dark room. At first, when vibrating slowly, its movement will be indicated by only one sense, that of touch. As soon as the vibrations increase, a low sound will emanate from it and it will appeal to two senses.
>
> "At about 32,000 vibrations to the second the sound will be loud and shrill, but at 40,000 vibrations it will be silent and the movements of the rod will not be perceived by touch. Its movements will be perceived by no ordinary human sense.
>
> "From this point up to about 1,500,000 vibrations per second, we have no sense that can appreciate any effect of the intervening vibrations. After that stage is reached, movement is indicated first by the sense of temperature and then, when the rod becomes red hot, by the sense of sight. At 3,000,000 it sheds violet light. Above that it sheds ultra-violet rays and other invisible radiations, some of which can be perceived by instruments and employed by us.
>
> "Now it has occurred to me that there must be a great deal to be learned about the effect of those vibrations in the great gap where the ordinary human senses are unable to hear, see or feel the movement. The power to send wireless messages by ether vibrations lies in that gap, but the gap is so great that it seems there must be much more. You must make machines practically to supply new senses, as the wireless instruments do.
>
> "Can it be said, when you think of that great gap, that there are not many forms of vibrations that may give us results as wonderful as, or even more wonderful than, the wireless waves? It seems to me that in this gap lie the vibrations which we have assumed to be given off by our brains and nerve cells when we think. But then, again, they may be higher up, in the scale beyond the vibrations that produce the

ultra-violet rays. [AUTHOR'S NOTE: The last sentence suggests the theory held by this author.]

"Do we need a wire to carry these vibrations? Will they not pass through the ether without a wire, just as the wireless waves do? How will they be perceived by the recipient? Will he hear a series of signals or will he find that another man's thoughts have entered into his brain?

"We may indulge in some speculations based on what we know of the wireless waves, which, as I have said, are all we can recognize of a vast series of vibrations which theoretically must exist. If the thought waves are similar to the wireless waves, they must pass from the brain and flow endlessly around the world and the universe. The body and the skull and other solid obstacles would form no obstruction to their passage, as they pass through the ether which surrounds the molecules of every substance, no matter how solid and dense.

"You ask if there would not be constant interference and confusion if other people's thoughts were flowing through our brains and setting up thoughts in them that did not originate with ourselves?

"How do you know that other men's thoughts are not interfering with yours now? I have noticed a good many phenomena of mind disturbances that I have never been able to explain. For instance, there is the inspiration or the discouragement that a speaker feels in addressing an audience. I have experienced this many times in my life and have never been able to define exactly the physical causes of it.

"Many recent scientific discoveries, in my opinion, point to a day not far distant perhaps, when men will read one another's thoughts, when thoughts will be conveyed directly from brain to brain without intervention of speech, writing or any of the present known methods of communication.

"It is not unreasonable to look forward to a time when we shall see without eyes, hear without ears and talk without tongues.

"Briefly, the hypothesis that mind can communicate directly with mind rests on the theory that thought or vital force is a form of electrical disturbance, that it can be taken up by induction and transmitted to a distance either through a wire or simply through the all-pervading ether, as in the case of wireless telegraph waves.

"There are many analogies which suggest that thought is of the nature of an electrical disturbance. A nerve, which is of the same substance as the brain, is an excellent conductor of the electric current. When we first passed an electrical current through the nerves of a dead man we were shocked and amazed to see him sit up and move. The electrified nerves produced contraction of the muscles very much as in life.

"The nerves appear to act upon the muscles very much as the electric current acts upon an electromagnet. The current magnetizes a bar of iron placed at right angles to it, and the nerves produce, through the intangible current of vital force that flows through them, contraction of the muscular fibers that are arranged at right angles to them.

"It would be possible to cite many reasons why thought and vital force may be regarded as of the same nature as electricity. The electric current is held to be a wave motion of the ether, the hypothetical substance that fills all space and pervades all substances. We believe that there must be ether because without it the electric current could not pass through a vacuum, or sunlight through space. It is reasonable to believe that only a wave motion of a similar character can produce the phenomena of thought and vital force. We may assume that the brain cells act as a battery and that the current produced flows along the nerves.

"But does it end there? Does it not pass out of the body in waves which flow around the world unperceived by our senses, just as the wireless waves passed unperceived before Hertz and others discovered their existence?"

EVERY MIND BOTH A BROADCASTING AND A RECEIVING STATION:

This author has proved, times too numerous to enumerate, to his own satisfaction at least, that every human brain is both a broadcasting and a receiving station for vibrations of thought frequency.

If this theory should turn out to be a fact, and methods of reasonable control should be established, imagine the part it would play in the gathering, classifying and organizing of knowledge. The possibility, much less the probability, of such a reality, staggers the mind of man!

Thomas Paine was one of the great minds of the American Revolutionary Period. To him more, perhaps, than to any other one person, we owe both the beginning and the happy ending of the Revolution, for it was his keen mind that both helped in drawing up the Declaration of Independence and in persuading the signers of that document to translate it into terms of reality.

In speaking of the source of his great storehouse of knowledge, Paine thus described it: "Any person, who has made observations on the state of progress of the human mind, by observing his own, cannot but have observed that there are two distinct classes of what are called Thoughts: those that we produce in ourselves by reflection and the act of thinking, and those that bolt into the mind of their own accord. I have always made it a rule to treat these voluntary visitors with civility, taking care to examine, as well as I was able, if they were worth entertaining; and it is from them I have acquired almost all the knowledge that I have. As to the learning that any person gains from school education, it serves only like a small capital, to put him in the way of beginning learning for himself afterwards. Every person of learning is finally his own teacher, the reason for which is, that principles cannot be impressed upon the memory; their place of mental residence is the understanding, and they are never so lasting as when they begin by conception."

In the foregoing words Paine, the great American patriot and philosopher, described an experience which at one time or another is the experience of every person. Who is there so unfortunate as not to have received positive evidence that thoughts and even complete ideas will "pop" into the mind from outside sources?

What means of conveyance is there for such visitors except the ether? Ether fills the boundless space of the universe. It is the medium of conveyance for all known forms of vibration such as sound, light and heat. Why should it not be, also, the medium of

conveyance of the vibration of Thought?

Every mind, or brain, is directly connected with every other brain by means of the ether. Every thought released by any brain may be instantly picked up and interpreted by all other brains that are "en rapport" with the sending brain. This author is as sure of this fact as he is that the chemical formula H_2O will produce water. Imagine, if you can, what a part this principle plays in every walk of life.

Nor is the probability of ether being a conveyor of thought from mind to mind the most astounding of its performances. It is the belief of this author that every thought vibration released by any brain is picked up by the ether and kept in motion in circuitous wave lengths corresponding in length to the intensity of the energy used in their release; that these vibrations remain in motion forever; that they are one of the two sources from which thoughts which "pop" into one's mind emanate, the other source being direct and, immediate contact through the ether with the brain releasing the thought vibration.

Thus it will be seen that if this theory is a fact the boundless space of the whole universe is now and will continue to become literally a mental library wherein may be found all the thoughts released by mankind.

The author is here laying the foundation for one of the most important hypotheses enumerated in the lesson Self-confidence, a fact which the student should keep in mind as he approaches that lesson.

This is a lesson on Organized Knowledge. Most of the useful knowledge to which the human race has become heir has been preserved and accurately recorded in Nature's Bible. By turning back the pages of this unalterable Bible man has read the story of the terrific struggle through and out of which the present civilization has grown. The pages of this Bible are made up of the physical elements of which this earth and the other planets consist, and of the ether which fills all space.

By turning back the pages written on stone and covered near the surface of this earth on which he lives, man has uncovered the bones, skeletons, footprints and other unmistakable evidence of the history of animal life on this earth, planted there for his enlightenment and guidance by the hand of Mother Nature throughout unbelievable periods of time. The evidence is plain and unmistakable. The great stone pages of Nature's Bible found on this earth and the endless pages of that Bible represented by the ether wherein all past human thought has been recorded, constitute an authentic source of communication between the Creator and man. This Bible was begun before man had reached the thinking stage; indeed, before man had reached the amoeba (one-cell animal) stage of development.

This Bible is above and beyond the power of man to alter.

Moreover, it tells its story not in the ancient dead languages or hieroglyphics of half savage races, but in universal language which all who have eyes may read. Nature's Bible, from which we have derived all the knowledge that is worth knowing, is one that no man may alter or in any manner tamper with.

The most marvelous discovery yet made by man is that of the recently discovered radio principle, which operates through the aid of ether, an important portion of Nature's Bible. Imagine the ether picking up the ordinary vibration of sound, and transforming that vibration from audio-frequency into radio-frequency, carrying it to a properly attuned receiving station and there transforming it back into its original form of audio frequency, all in the flash of a second. It should surprise no one that such a force could gather up the vibration of thought and keep that vibration in motion forever. The established and known fact of instantaneous transmission of sound, through the agency of the ether, by means of the modern radio apparatus, removes the theory of transmission of thought vibration from mind to mind from the possible to the probable.

THE MASTER MIND:

We come, now, to the next step in the description of the ways and means by which one may gather, classify and organize useful knowledge, through harmonious alliance of two or more minds, out of which grows a Master Mind.

The term **"Master Mind"** is abstract, and has no counterpart in the field of known facts, except to a small number of people who have made a careful study of the effect of one mind upon other minds.

This author has searched in vain through all the textbooks and essays available on the subject of the human mind, but nowhere has been found even the slightest reference to the principle here described as the "Master Mind." The term first came to the attention of the author through an interview with Andrew Carnegie, in the manner described in Lesson Two.

CHEMISTRY OF THE MIND:

It is this author's belief that the mind is made up of the same universal "fluid" energy as that which constitutes the ether which fills the universe. It is a fact as well known to the layman as to the man of scientific investigation, that some minds clash the moment they come in contact with each other, while other minds show a natural affinity for each other. Between the two extremes of natural antagonism and natural affinity growing out of the meeting or contacting of minds there is a wide range of possibility for varying reactions of mind upon mind. Some minds are so naturally adapted to each other that **"love at first sight"** is the inevitable outcome of the contact.

Who has not known of such an experience? In other cases minds are so antagonistic that violent mutual dislike shows itself at first meeting. These results occur without a word being spoken, and without the slightest signs of any of the usual causes for love and hate acting as a stimulus.

It is quite probable that the **"mind"** is made up of a fluid or substance or energy, call it what you will, similar to (if not in fact the same substance as) the ether. When two minds come close enough to each other to form a contact, the mixing of the units of this "mind stuff" (let us call it the electrons of the ether) sets up a chemical reaction and starts vibrations which affect the two individuals pleasantly or unpleasantly. The effect of the meeting of two minds is obvious to even the most casual observer. Every effect must have a cause! What could be more reasonable than to suspect that the cause of the change in mental attitude between two minds which have just come in close contact is none other than the disturbance of the electrons or units of each mind in the process of rearranging themselves in the new field created by the contact? For the purpose of establishing this lesson upon a sound foundation we have gone a long way toward success by admitting that the meeting or coming in close contact of two minds sets up in each of those minds a certain noticeable "effect" or state of mind quite different from the one existing immediately prior to the contact. While it is desirable it is not essential to know what is the "cause" of this reaction of mind upon mind. That the reaction takes place, in every instance, is a known fact which gives us a starting point from which we may show what is meant by the term **"Master Mind."**

A Master Mind may be created through the bringing together or blending, in a spirit of perfect harmony, of two or more minds. Out of this harmonious blending the chemistry of the mind creates a third mind which may be appropriated and used by one or all of the individual minds. This Master Mind will remain available as long as the friendly, harmonious alliance between the individual minds exists. It will disintegrate and all evidence of its former existence will disappear the moment the friendly alliance is broken.

This principle of mind chemistry is the basis and cause for practically all the so-called **"soul-mate"** and "eternal triangle" cases, so many of which unfortunately find their way into the divorce courts and meet with popular ridicule from ignorant and uneducated people who manufacture vulgarity and scandal out of one of the greatest of Nature's laws.

The entire civilized world knows that the first two or three years of association after marriage are often marked by much disagreement, of a more or less petty nature. These are the years of "adjustment." If the marriage survives them it is more than apt to become a permanent alliance. These facts no experienced married person will deny. Again we see the "effect" without understanding the "cause."

While there are other contributing causes, yet, in the main, lack of harmony during these early years of marriage is due to the slowness of the chemistry of the minds in blending harmoniously.

Stated differently, the electrons or units of the energy called the mind are often neither extremely friendly nor antagonistic upon first contact; but, through constant association they gradually adapt themselves in harmony, except in rare cases where association has the opposite effect of leading, eventually, to open hostility between these units.

It is a well-known fact that after a man and a woman have lived together for ten to fifteen years they become practically indispensable to each other, even though there may not be the slightest evidence of the state of mind called love. Moreover, this association and relationship sexually not only develops a natural, affinity between the two minds, but it actually causes the two people to take on a similar facial expression and to resemble each other closely in many other marked ways. Any competent analyst of human nature can easily go into a crowd of strange people and pick out the wife after having been introduced to her husband. The expression of the eyes, the contour of the faces and the tone of the voices of people who have long been associated in marriage, become similar to a marked degree.

So marked is the effect of the chemistry of the human mind that any experienced public speaker may quickly interpret the manner in which his statements are accepted by his audience.

Antagonism in the mind of but one person in an audience of one thousand may be readily detected by the speaker who has learned how to "feel" and register the effects of antagonism. Moreover, the public speaker can make these interpretations without observing or in any manner being influenced by the expression on the faces of those in his audience. On account of this fact an audience may cause a speaker to rise to great heights of oratory, or heckle him into failure, without making a sound or denoting a single expression of satisfaction or dissatisfaction through the features of the face.

All **"Master Salesmen"** know the moment the "psychological time for closing" has arrived; not by what the prospective buyer says, but from the effect of the chemistry of his mind as interpreted or "felt" by the salesman. Words often belie the intentions of those speaking them but a correct interpretation of the chemistry of the mind leaves no loophole for such a possibility. Every able salesman knows that the majority of buyers have the habit of affecting a negative attitude almost to the very climax of a sale. Every able lawyer has developed a sixth sense whereby he is enabled to **"feel"** his way through the most artfully selected words of the clever witness who is lying, and correctly interpret that which is in the witness's mind, through the chemistry of the mind.

Many lawyers have developed this ability without knowing the real source of it; they possess the technique without the scientific understanding upon which it is based. Many salesmen have done the same thing.

One who is gifted in the art of correctly the chemistry of the minds of others may, figuratively speaking, walk in at the front door of the mansion of a given mind and leisurely explore the entire building, noting all its details, walking out again with a complete picture of the interior of the building, without the owner of the building so much as knowing that he has entertained a visitor. It will be observed, in the lesson Accurate Thinking, that this principle may be put to a very practical use (having reference to the principle of the chemistry of the mind). The principle is referred to merely as an approach to the major principles of this lesson.

Enough has already been stated to introduce the principle of mind chemistry, and to prove, with the aid of the student's own everyday experiences and casual observations that the moment two minds come within close range of each other a noticeable mental change takes place in both, sometimes registering in the nature of antagonism and at other times registering in the nature of friendliness. Every mind has what might be termed an electric field. The nature of this field varies, depending upon the "mood" of the individual mind back of it, and upon the nature of the chemistry of the mind creating the "field."

It is believed by this author that the normal or natural condition of the chemistry of any individual mind is the result of his physical heredity plus the nature of thoughts which have dominated that mind; that every mind is continuously changing to the extent that the individual's philosophy and general habits of thought change the chemistry of his or her mind. These principles the author BELIEVES to be true. That any individual may voluntarily change the chemistry of his or her mind so that it will either attract or repel all with whom it comes in contact is a KNOWN FACT! Stated in another manner, any person may assume a mental attitude which will attract and please others or repel and antagonize them, and this without the aid of words or facial expression or other form of bodily movement or demeanor.

Go back, now, to the definition of a **"Master Mind"** -a mind which grows out of the blending and coordination of two or more minds, **IN A SPIRIT OF PERFECT HARMONY,** and you will catch the full significance of the word "harmony" as it is here used. Two minds will not blend nor can they be co-ordinated unless the element of perfect harmony is present, wherein lies the secret of success or failure of practically all business and social partnerships.

Every sales manager and every military commander and every leader in any other walk of life understands the necessity of an "esprit de corps"-a spirit of common understanding and cooperation-in the attainment of success. This mass spirit of harmony of purpose is obtained through discipline, voluntary or forced, of such a nature that the individual minds become blended into a **"Master Mind,"** by which is meant that the chemistry of the individual minds is modified in such a manner that these minds blend and function as one.

The methods through which this blending process takes place are as numerous as the individuals engaged in the various forms of leadership. Every leader has his or her own method of coordinating the minds of the followers. One will use force. Another uses persuasion. One will play upon the fear of penalties while another plays upon rewards, in order to reduce the individual minds of a given group of people to where they may be blended into a mass mind. The student will not have to search deeply into history of statesmanship, politics, business or finance, to discover the technique employed by the leaders in these fields in the process of blending the minds of individuals into a mass mind.

The really great leaders of the world, however, have been provided by Nature with a combination of mind chemistry favorable as a nucleus of attraction for other minds. Napoleon was a notable example of a man possessing the magnetic type of mind which had a very decided tendency to attract all minds with which it came in contact. Soldiers followed Napoleon to certain death without flinching, because of the impelling or attracting nature of his personality, and that personality was nothing more nor less than the chemistry of his mind.

No group of minds can be blended into a Master Mind if one of the individuals of that group possesses one of these extremely negative, repellent minds. The negative and positive minds will not blend in the sense here described as a Master Mind. Lack of knowledge of this fact has brought many an otherwise able leader to defeat. Any able leader who understands this principle of mind chemistry may temporarily blend the minds of practically any group of people, so that it will represent a mass mind, but the composition will disintegrate almost the very moment the leader's presence is removed from the group. The most successful life insurance sales organizations and other sales forces meet once a week, or more often, for the purpose of–OF WHAT?

FOR THE PURPOSE OF MERGING THE INDIVIDUAL MINDS INTO A MASTER MIND WHICH WILL, FOR A LIMITED NUMBER OF DAYS, SERVE AS A STIMULUS TO THE INDIVIDUAL MINDS!

It may be, and generally is, true that the leaders of these groups do not understand what actually takes place in these meetings, which are usually called "pep meetings." The routine of such meetings is usually given over to talks by the leader and other members of the group, and occasionally from someone outside of the group, meanwhile the minds of the individuals are contacting and recharging one another.

The brain of a human being may be compared to an electric battery in that it will become exhausted or run down, causing the owner of it to feel despondent, discouraged and lacking in "pep."

Who is so fortunate as never to have had such a feeling? The human brain, when in this depleted condition, must be recharged, and the manner in which this is done is through contact with a more vital mind or minds. The great leaders understand the necessity of this "recharging" process, and, moreover, they understand how to accomplish this result.

THIS KNOWLEDGE IS THE MAIN FEATURE WHICH DISTINGUISHES A LEADER FROM A FOLLOWER!

Fortunate is the person who understands this principle sufficiently well to keep his or her brain vitalized or "recharged" by periodically contacting it with a more vital mind. Sexual contact is one of the most effective of the stimuli through which a mind may be recharged, providing the contact is intelligently made, between man and woman who have genuine affection for each other.

Any other sort of sexual relationship is a devitalizer of the mind. Any competent practitioner of Psycho-therapeutics can "recharge" a brain within a few minutes.

Before passing away from the brief reference made to sexual contact as a means of revitalizing a depleted mind it seems appropriate to call attention to the fact that all of the great leaders, in whatever walks of life they have arisen, have been and are people of highly sexed natures. (The word "sex" is not an indecent word. You'll find it in all the dictionaries.)

There is a growing tendency upon the part of the best informed physicians and other health practitioners, to accept the theory that all diseases begin when the brain of the individual is in a depleted or devitalized state. Stated in another way, it is a known fact that a person who has a perfectly vitalized brain is practically, if not entirely, immune from all manner of disease.

Every intelligent health practitioner, of whatever school or type, knows that "Nature" or the mind cures disease in every instance where a cure is effected. Medicines, faith, laying on of hands, chiropractic, osteopathy and all other forms of outside stimulant are nothing more than artificial aids to NATURE, or, to state it correctly, mere methods of setting the chemistry of the mind into motion to the end that it readjusts the cells and tissues of the body, revitalizes the brain and otherwise causes the human machine to function normally.

The most orthodox practitioner will admit the truth, of this statement.

What, then, may be the possibilities of the future developments in the field of mind chemistry?

Through the principle of harmonious blending of minds perfect health may be enjoyed.

Through the aid of this same principle sufficient power may be developed to solve the problem of economic pressure which constantly presses upon every individual.

We may judge the future possibilities of mind chemistry by taking inventory of its past achievements, keeping in mind the fact that these achievements have been largely the result of accidental discovery and of chance groupings of minds. We are approaching the time when the professorate of the universities will teach mind chemistry the same as other subjects are now taught. Meanwhile, study and experimentation in connection with this subject open vistas of possibility for the individual student.

MIND CHEMISTRY AND ECONOMIC POWER:

That mind chemistry may be appropriately applied to the workaday affairs of the economic and commercial world is a demonstrable fact.

Through the blending of two or more minds, in a spirit of **PERFECT HARMONY,** the principle of mind chemistry may be made to develop sufficient power to enable the individuals whose minds have been thus blended to perform seemingly superhuman feats. Power is the force with which man achieves success in any undertaking. Power, in unlimited quantities, may, be enjoyed by any group of men, or men and women, who possess the wisdom with which to submerge their own personalities and their own immediate individual interests, through the blending of their minds in a spirit of perfect harmony.

Observe, profitably, the frequency with which the word "harmony" appears throughout this Introduction! There can be no development of a "Master Mind" where this element of **PERFECT** HARMONY does not exist. The individual units of the mind will not blend with the individual units of another mind **UNTIL THE TWO MINDS HAVE BEEN AROUSED AND WARMED, AS IT WERE, WITH A SPIRIT OF PERFECT HARMONY OF PURPOSE.** The moment two minds begin to take divergent roads of interest the individual units of each mind separate, and the third element, known as a **"MASTER MIND,"** which grew out of the friendly or harmonious alliance, will disintegrate.

We come, now, to the study of some well-known men who have accumulated great power (also great fortunes) through the application of mind chemistry.

Let us begin our study with three men who are known to be men of great achievement in their respective fields of economic, business and professional endeavor.

Their names are Henry Ford, Thomas A. Edison and Harvey S. Firestone.

Of the three Henry Ford is, by far, the most POWERFUL, having reference to economic and financial power. Mr. Ford is the most powerful man now living on earth. Many who have studied Mr. Ford believe him to be the most powerful man who ever lived.

As far as is known Mr. Ford is the only man now living, or who ever lived, with sufficient power to outwit the money trust of the United States. Mr. Ford gathers millions of dollars with as great ease as a child fills its bucket with sand when playing on the beach.

It has been said, by those who were in position to know, that Mr. Ford, if he needed it, could send out the call for money and gather in a billion dollars (a thousand million dollars) and have it available for use within one week. No one who knows of Ford's achievements doubts this. Those who know him well know that he could do it with no more effort than the average man expends in raising the money with which to pay a month's house rent. He could get this money, if he needed it, through the intelligent application of the principles on which this course is based.

While Mr. Ford's new automobile was in the process of perfection, in 1927, it is said that he received advance orders, with cash payments, for more than 375,000 cars. At an estimated price of $600.00 per car this would amount to $225,000,000.00 which he received before a single car was delivered. Such is the power of confidence in Ford's ability.

Mr. Edison, as everyone knows, is a philosopher, scientist and inventor. He is, perhaps, the keenest Bible student on earth; a student of Nature's Bible, however, and not of the myriads of man made Bibles. Mr. Edison has such a keen insight into Mother Nature's Bible that he has harnessed and combined, for the good of mankind, more of Nature's laws than any other person now living or who ever lived. It was he who brought together the point of a needle and a piece of revolving wax, in such a way that the vibration of the human voice may be recorded and reproduced through the modern talking machine. (And it may be Edison who will eventually enable man to pick up and correctly interpret the vibrations of thought which are now recorded in the boundless universe of ether, just as he has enabled man to record and reproduce the spoken word.)

It was Edison who first harnessed the lightning and made it serve as a light for man's use, through the aid of the incandescent electric light bulb.

It was Edison who gave the world the modern moving picture.

These are but a few of his outstanding achievements. These modern "miracles" which he has performed (not by trickery, under the sham pretense of superhuman power, but in the very midst of the bright light of science) transcend all of the so-called "miracles" described in the man-made books of fiction.

Mr. Firestone is the moving spirit in the great Firestone Tire industry, in Akron, Ohio. His industrial achievements are so well known wherever automobiles are used that no special comment on them seems necessary.

All three of these men began their careers, business and professional, without capital and with but little schooling of that type usually referred to as "education."

All three men are now well educated. All three are wealthy.

All three are powerful. Now let us inquire into the source of their wealth and power.

Thus far we have been dealing only with effect; the true philosopher wishes to understand the cause of a given effect.

It is a matter of general knowledge that Mr. Ford, Mr. Edison and Mr. Firestone are close personal friends, and have been so for many years; that in former years they were in the habit of going away to the woods once a year for a period of rest, meditation and recuperation.

But it is not generally known–it is a grave doubt if these three men themselves know it –that there exists between the three men a bond of harmony which has caused their minds to become blended into a **"Master Mind"** which is the real source of the power of each. This mass mind, growing out of the co-ordination of the individual minds of Ford, Edison and Firestone, has enabled these men to "tune in" on forces (and sources of knowledge) with which most men are to no extent familiar.

If the student doubts either the principle or the effects here described, let him remember that more than half the theory here set forth is a known fact. For example, it is known that these three men have great power. It is known that they are wealthy. It is known that they began without capital and with but little schooling. It is known that they form periodic mind contacts. It is known that they are harmonious and friendly. It is known that their achievements are so outstanding as to make it impossible to compare these achievements with those of other men in their respective fields of activity.

All these **"effects"** are known to practically every schoolboy in the civilized world, therefore there can be no dispute as far as effects are concerned.

Of one fact connected with the cause of the achievements of Edison, Ford and Firestone we may be sure, namely, that these achievements were in no way based upon trickery, deceit, the "supernatural" or so-called "revelations" or any other form of unnatural law. These men do not possess a stock of legerdemain.

They work with natural laws; laws which, for the most part, are well known to all economists and leaders in the field of science, with the possible exception of the law upon which chemistry of the mind is based. As yet chemistry of the mind is not sufficiently developed to be classed, by scientific men, in their catalogue of known laws.

A **"Master Mind"** may be created by any group of people who will co-ordinate their minds, in a spirit of perfect harmony.

The group may consist of any number from two upward. Best results appear available from the blending of six or seven minds.

When two or more people harmonize their minds and produce the effect known as a **"Master Mind,"** each person in the group becomes vested with the power to contact with and gather knowledge through the "subconscious" minds of all the other members of the group. This power becomes immediately noticeable, having the effect of stimulating the mind to a higher rate of vibration, and otherwise evidencing itself in the form of a more vivid imagination and the consciousness of what appears to be a sxth sense. It is through this sixth sense that new ideas will "flash" into the mind. These ideas take on the nature and form of the subject dominating the mind of the individual. If the entire group has met for the purpose of discussing a given subject, ideas concerning that subject will come pouring into the minds of all present, as if an outside influence were dictating them. The minds of those participating in the **"Master Mind"** become as magnets, attracting ideas and thought stimuli of the most highly organized and practical nature, from no one knows where!

The process of mind-blending here described as a "Master Mind" may be likened to the act of one who connects many electric batteries to a single transmission wire, thereby "stepping up" the power flowing over that line. Each battery added increases the power passing over that line by the amount of energy the battery carries. Just so in the case of blending individual minds into a "Master Mind." Each mind, through the principle of mind chemistry, stimulates all the other minds in the group, until the mind energy thus becomes so great that it penetrates to and connects with the universal energy known as ether, which, in turn, touches every atom of the entire universe.

The modern radio apparatus substantiates, to a considerable extent, the theory here expounded. Powerful sending or broadcasting stations must be erected through which the vibration of sound is "stepped up" before it can be picked up by the much higher vibrating energy of the ether and carried in all directions. A "Master Mind" made up of many individual minds, so blended that they produce a strong vibrating energy, constitutes almost an exact counterpart of the radio broadcasting station.

Every public speaker has felt the influence of mind chemistry, for it is a well-known fact that as soon as the individual minds of an audience become "en rapport" (attuned to the rate of vibration of the mind of the speaker) with the speaker, there is a noticeable increase of enthusiasm in the speaker's mind, and he often rises to heights of oratory which surprise all, including himself.

The first five to ten minutes of the average speech are devoted to what is known as "warming up." By this is meant the process through which the minds of the speaker and his audience are becoming blended in a spirit of PERFECT HARMONY.

Every speaker knows what happens when this state of "perfect harmony" fails to materialize upon part of his audience.

The seemingly supernatural phenomena occurring in spiritualistic meetings are the result of the reaction, upon one another, of the minds in the group. These phenomena seldom begin to manifest themselves under ten to twenty minutes after the group is formed, for the reason that this is about the time required for the minds in the group to become harmonized or blended.

The "messages" received by members of a spiritualistic group probably come from one of two sources, or from both, namely:

First: From the vast storehouse of the subconscious mind of some member of the group; or Second: From the universal storehouse of the ether, in which, it is more than probable, all thought vibration is preserved.

Neither any known natural law nor human reason supports the theory of communication with individuals who have died.

It is a known fact that any individual may explore the store of knowledge in another's mind, through this principle of mind chemistry, and it seems reasonable to suppose that this power may be extended to include contact with whatever vibrations are available in the ether, if there are any.

The theory that all the higher and more refined vibrations, such as those growing out of thought, are preserved in the ether grows out of the known fact that neither matter nor energy (the two known elements of the universe) may be either created or destroyed. It is reasonable to suppose that all vibrations which have been "stepped up" sufficiently to be picked up and absorbed in the ether, will go on forever. The lower vibrations, which do not blend with or otherwise contact the ether, probably live a natural life and die out.

All the so-called geniuses probably gained their reputations because, by mere chance or otherwise, they formed alliances with other minds which enabled them to "step up" their own mind vibrations to where they were enabled to contact the vast Temple of Knowledge recorded and filed in the ether of the universe. All of the great geniuses, as far as this author has been enabled to gather the facts, were highly sexed people. The fact that sexual contact is the greatest known mind stimulant lends color to the theory herein described.

Inquiring further into the source of economic power, as manifested by the achievements of men in the field of business, let us study the case of the Chicago group known as the "Big Six," consisting of Wm. Wrigley, Jr., who owns the chewing gum business bearing his name, and whose individual income is said to be more than Fifteen Million Dollars a year; John R. Thompson, who operates the chain of lunch rooms bearing his name; Mr. Lasker, who owns the Lord & Thomas Advertising Agency; Mr. McCullough, who owns the Parmalee Express Company, the largest transfer business in America; and Mr. Ritchie and Mr. Hertz, who own the Yellow Taxicab business.

A reliable financial reporting company has estimated the yearly income of these six men at upwards of Twenty-five Million Dollars ($25,000,000.00), or an average of more than Four Million Dollars a year per man.

Analysis of the entire group of six men discloses the fact that not one of them had any special educational advantages; that all began without capital or extensive credit; that their financial achievement has been due to their own individual plans, and not to any fortunate turn of the wheel of chance.

Many years ago these six men formed a friendly alliance, meeting at stated periods for the purpose of assisting one another with ideas and suggestions in their various and sundry lines of business endeavor.

With the exception of Hertz and Ritchie none of the six men were in any manner associated in a legal Partnership. These meetings were strictly for the purpose of cooperating on the give and take basis of assisting one another with ideas and suggestions, and occasionally by endorsing notes and other securities to assist some member of the group who had met with an emergency making such help necessary.

It is said that each of the individuals belonging to this Big Six group is a millionaire many times over. As a rule there is nothing worthy of special comment on behalf of a man who does nothing more than accumulate a few million dollars. However, there is something connected with the financial success of this particular group of men that is well worth comment, study, analysis and even emulation, and that "something" is the fact that they have learned how to coordinate their individual minds by blending them in a spirit of perfect harmony, thereby creating a "Master Mind" that unlocks, to each individual of the group, doors which are closed to most of the human race.

The United States Steel Corporation is one of the strongest and most powerful industrial organizations in the world. The Idea out of which this great industrial giant grew was born in the mind of Elbert H. Gary, a more or less commonplace small-town lawyer who was born and reared in a small Illinois town near Chicago.

Mr. Gary surrounded himself with a group of men whose minds he successfully blended in a spirit of perfect harmony, thereby creating the "Master Mind" which is the moving spirit of the great United States Steel Corporation.

Search where you will, wherever you find an outstanding success in business, finance, industry or in any of the professions, you may be sure that back of the success is some individual who has applied the principle of mind chemistry, out of which a "Master Mind" has been created. These outstanding successes often appear to be the handiwork of but one person, but search closely and the other individuals whose minds have been coordinated with his own may be found. Remember that two or more persons may operate the principle of mind chemistry so as to create a "Master Mind". POWER (Man-power) IS ORGANIZED KNOWLEDGE, EXPRESSED THROUGH INTELLIGENT EFFORTS!

No effort can be said to be ORGANIZED unless the individuals engaged in the effort co-ordinate their knowledge and energy in a spirit of perfect harmony. Lack of such harmonious coordination of effort is the main cause of practically every business failure.

An interesting experiment was conducted by this author, in collaboration with the students of a well-known college. Each student was requested to write an essay on "How and Why Henry Ford Became Wealthy."

Each student was required to describe, as a part of his or her essay, what was believed to be the nature of Ford's real assets, of what these assets consisted in detail.

The majority of the students gathered financial statements and inventories of the Ford assets and used these as the basis of their estimates of Ford's wealth. Included in these "sources of Ford's wealth" were such as cash in banks, raw and finished materials in stock, real estate and buildings, good-will, estimated at from ten to twenty-five per cent of the value of the material assets.

One student out of the entire group of several hundred answered as follows:

"Henry Ford's assets consist, in the main, of two items, viz.:

(l)Working capital and raw and finished materials; (2)The knowledge, gained from experience, of Henry Ford, himself, and the co-operation of a well trained

> organization which understands how to apply this knowledge to best advantage from the Ford viewpoint. It is impossible to estimate, with anything approximating correctness, the actual dollars and cents value of either of these two groups of assets, but it is my opinion that their relative values are:
>
> "The organized knowledge of the Ford Organization ... 75%
>
> The value of cash and physical assets of every nature, including raw and finished materials ...25%"

This author is of the opinion that this statement was not compiled by the young man whose name was signed to it, without the assistance of some very analytical and experienced mind or minds.

Unquestionably the biggest asset that Henry Ford has is his own brain. Next to this would come the brains of his immediate circle of associates, for it has been through coordination of these that the physical assets which he controls were accumulated. Destroy every plant the Ford Motor Company owns: every piece of machinery, every atom of raw or finished material, every finished automobile, and every dollar on deposit in any bank, and Ford would still be the most powerful man, economically, on earth. The brains which have built the Ford business could duplicate it again in short order. Capital is always available, in unlimited quantities, to such brains as Ford's.

Ford is the most powerful man on earth (economically) because he has the keenest and most practical conception of the principle of ORGANIZED KNOWLEDGE of any man on earth, as far as this author has the means of knowing.

Despite Ford's great power and financial success, it may be that he has blundered often in the application of the principles through which he accumulated this power. There is but little doubt that Ford's methods of mind co-ordination have often been crude; they must needs have been in the earlier days of this experience, before he gained the wisdom of application that would naturally go with maturity of years.

Neither can there be much doubt that Ford's application of the principle of mind chemistry was, at least at the start, the result of a chance alliance with other minds, particularly the mind of Edison. It is more than probable that Mr. Ford's remarkable insight into the laws of nature was first begun as the result of his friendly alliance with his own wife long before he ever met either Mr. Edison or Mr. Firestone. Many a man who never knows the real source of his success is made by his wife, through application of the "Master Mind" principle. Mrs. Ford is a most remarkably intelligent woman, and this author has reason to believe that it was her mind, blended with Mr. Ford's, which gave him his first real start toward power.

It may be mentioned, without in any way depriving Ford of any honor or glory, that in his earlier days of experience he had to combat the powerful enemies of illiteracy and ignorance to a greater extent than did either Edison or Firestone, both of whom were gifted by natural heredity with a most fortunate aptitude for acquiring and applying knowledge. Ford had to hew this talent out of the rough, raw timbers of his hereditary estate.

Within an inconceivably short period of time Ford has mastered three of the most stubborn enemies of mankind and transformed them into assets constituting the very foundation of his success. These enemies are: Ignorance, illiteracy and poverty!

Any man who can stay the hand of these three savage forces, much less harness and use them to good account, is well worth close study by the less fortunate individuals.

This is an age of INDUSTRIAL POWER in which we are living!

The source of all this POWER is ORGANIZED EFFORT.

Not only has the management of industrial enterprises efficiently organized individual workers, but, in many instances, mergers of industry have been effected in such a manner and to the end that these combinations (as in the case of the United States Steel Corporation, for example) have accumulated practically unlimited power.

One may hardly glance at the news of a day's events without seeing a report of some business, industrial or financial merger, bringing under one management enormous resources and thus creating great power.

One day it is a group of banks; another day it is a chain of railroads; the next day it is a combination of steel plants, all merging for the purpose of developing power through highly organized and co-ordinated effort.

Knowledge, general in nature and unorganized, is not POWER; it is only potential power–the material out of which real power may be developed. Any modern library contains an unorganized record of all the knowledge of value to which the present stage of civilization is heir, but this knowledge is not power because it is not organized.

Every form of energy and every species of animal or plant life, to survive, must be organized. The oversized animals whose bones have filled Nature's boneyard through extinction have left mute but certain evidence that non-organization means annihilation.

From the electron–the smallest particle of matter–to the largest star in the universe: these and every material thing in between these two extremes offer proof positive that one of Nature's first laws is that of ORGANIZATION. Fortunate is the individual who recognizes the importance of this law and makes it his business to familiarize himself with the various ways in which the law may be applied to advantage.

The astute businessman has not only recognized the importance of the law of organized effort, but he has made this law the warp and the woof of his POWER.

Without any knowledge, whatsoever, of the principle of mind chemistry, or that such a principle exists, many men have accumulated great power by merely organizing the knowledge they possessed.

The majority of all who have discovered the principle of mind chemistry and developed that principle into a "MASTER MIND" have stumbled upon this knowledge by the merest of accident; often failing to recognize the real nature of their discovery or to understand the source of their power.

This author is of the opinion that all living persons who at the present time are consciously making use of the principle of mind chemistry in developing power Lesson One THE MASTER MIND through the blending of minds, may be counted on the fingers of the two hands, with, perhaps, several fingers left to spare.

If this estimate is even approximately true the student will readily see that there is but slight danger of the field of mind chemistry practice becoming overcrowded.

It is a well-known fact that one of the most difficult tasks that any business man must perform is that of inducing those who are associated with him to coordinate their efforts in a spirit of harmony. To induce continuous co-operation between a group of workers, in any undertaking, is next to impossible. Only the most efficient leaders can accomplish this highly desired object, but once in a great while such a leader will rise above the horizon in the field of industry, business or finance, and then the world hears of a Henry Ford, Thomas A. Edison, John D. Rockefeller, Sr., E. H. Harriman or James J. Hill.

Power and Success are Practically Synonymous Terms!

One grows out of the other; therefore, any person who has the knowledge and the ability to develop power, through the principle of harmonious co-ordination of effort between individual minds, or in any other manner, may be successful in any reasonable undertaking that is possible of successful termination.

It must not be assumed that a "Master Mind" will immediately spring, mushroom fashion, out of every group of minds which make pretense of co-ordination in a spirit of HARMONY!

Harmony, in the real sense of meaning of the word.

Harmony is the nucleus around which the state of mind known as "Master Mind" must be developed. Without this element of harmony there can be no "Master Mind," a truth which cannot be repeated too often.

Woodrow Wilson had in mind the development of a "Master Mind," to be composed of groups of minds representing the civilized nations of the world, in his proposal for establishing the League of Nations. Wilson's conception was the most far- reaching humanitarian idea ever created in the mind of man, because it dealt with a principle which embraces sufficient power to establish a real Brotherhood of Man on earth. The League of Nations, or some similar blending of international minds, in a spirit of harmony, is sure to become a reality.

The time when such unity of minds will take place will be measured largely by the time required for the great universities and NON-SECTARIAN institutions of learning to supplant ignorance and superstition with understanding and wisdom. This time is rapidly approaching.

THE PSYCHOLOGY OF THE REVIVAL MEETING:

The old religious orgy known as the "revival" offers a favorable opportunity to study the principle of mind chemistry known as "Master Mind."

It will be observed that music plays no small part in bringing about the harmony essential to the blending of a group of minds in a revival meeting. Without music the revival meeting would be a tame affair.

During revival services the leader of the meeting has no difficulty in creating harmony in the minds of his devotees, but it is a well-known fact that this state of harmony lasts no longer than the presence of the leader, after which the "Master Mind" he has temporarily created disintegrates.

By arousing the emotional nature of his followers the revivalist has no difficulty, under the proper stage setting and with the embellishment of the right sort of music, in creating a "Master Mind" which becomes noticeable to all who come in contact with it. The very air becomes charged with a positive, pleasing influence which changes the entire chemistry of all minds present.

This author, through experiments conducted with a group of scientific investigators and laymen (who were unaware of the nature of the experiment), has created the same state of mind and the same positive atmosphere. On many occasions this author has witnessed the creation of the same positive atmosphere in a group of men and women engaged in the business of salesmanship.

The author helped conduct a school of salesmanship for Harrison Parker, founder of the Co-operative Society, of Chicago, who transformed the nature of a group of 3,000 men and women (all of whom were without former sales experience) who sold more than $10,000,000.00 worth of securities in less than nine months, and earned more than $1,000,000 for themselves.

It was found that the average person who joined this school would reach the zenith of his or her selling power within one week, after which it was necessary to revitalize the individual's brain through a group sales meeting. These sales meetings were conducted on very much the same order as are the modern revival meetings of the religionist, with much the same stage equipment, including music and "high-powered" speakers who exhorted the salespeople in very much the same manner as does the modern religious revivalist.

Call it religion, psychology, mind chemistry or anything you please (they are all based upon the same principle), but there is nothing more certain than the fact that wherever a group of minds are brought into contact, in a spirit of PERFECT HARMONY, each mind in the group becomes immediately supplemented and reinforced by a noticeable energy called a "Master Mind."

For all this writer professes to know this uncharted energy may be the Spirit of the Lord, but it operates just as favorably when called by any other name.

The human brain and nervous system constitute a piece of intricate machinery which but few, if any, understand. When controlled and properly directed this piece of machinery can be made to perform wonders of achievement and if not controlled it will perform wonders fantastic and phantom-like in nature, as may be seen by examining the inmates of any insane asylum.

The human brain has direct connection with a continuous influx of energy from which man derives his power to think. The brain receives this energy, mixes it with the energy created by the food taken into the body, and distributes it to every portion of the body, through the aid of the blood and the nervous system. It thus becomes what we call life.

From what source this outside energy comes no one seems to know; all we know about it is that we must have it or die. It seems reasonable to suppose that this energy is none other than that which we call ether, and that it flows into the body along with the oxygen from the air, as we breathe.

Every normal human body possesses a first-class chemical laboratory and a stock of chemicals sufficient to carry on the business of breaking up, assimilating and properly mixing and compounding the food we take into the body, preparatory to distributing it to wherever it is needed as a body builder.

Ample tests have been made, both with man and beast, to prove that the energy known as the mind plays an important part in this chemical operation of compounding and transforming food into the required substances to build and keep the body in repair.

It is known that worry, excitement or fear will interfere with the digestive process, and in extreme cases stop this process altogether, resulting in illness or death. It is obvious, then, that the mind enters into the chemistry of food digestion and distribution.

It is believed by many eminent authorities, although it may never have been scientifically proved, that the energy known as mind or thought may become contaminated with negative or "unsociable" units to such an extent that the whole nervous system is thrown out of working order, digestion is interfered with and various and sundry forms of disease will manifest themselves. Financial difficulties and unrequited love affairs head the list of causes of such mind disturbances.

A negative environment such as that existing where some member of the family is constantly "nagging," will interfere with the chemistry of the mind to such an extent that the individual will lose ambition and gradually sink into oblivion. It is because of this fact that the old saying that a man's wife may either "make" or "break" him is literally true. In a subsequent lesson a whole chapter on this subject is addressed to the wives of men.

Any high-school student knows that certain food combinations will, if taken into the stomach, result in indigestion, violent pain and even death. Good health depends, in part at least, upon a food combination that "harmonizes." But harmony of food combinations is not sufficient to insure good health; there must be harmony, also, between the units of energy known as the mind.

"Harmony" seems to be one of Nature's laws, without which there can be no such thing as

ORGANIZED ENERGY, or life in any form whatsoever. The health of the body as well as the mind is literally built around, out of and upon the principle of HARMONY! The energy known as life begins to disintegrate and death approaches when the organs of the body stop working in harmony.

The moment harmony ceases at the source of any form of organized energy (power) the units of that energy are thrown into a chaotic state of disorder and the power is rendered neutral or passive.

Harmony is also the nucleus around which the principle of mind chemistry known as a "Master Mind" develops power.

Destroy this harmony and you destroy the power growing out of the co-ordinated effort of a group of individual minds.

This truth has been stated, restated and presented in every manner which the author could conceive, with unending repetition, for the reason that unless the student grasps this principle and learns to apply it this lesson is useless.

Success in life, no matter what one may call success, is very largely a matter of adaptation to environment in such a manner that there is harmony between the individual and his environment. The palace of a king becomes as a hovel of a peasant if harmony does not abound within its walls. Conversely stated, the hut of a peasant may be made to yield more happiness than that of the mansion of the rich man, if harmony obtains in the former and not in the latter.

Without perfect harmony the science of astronomy would be useless because the stars and planets would clash with one another, and all would be in a state of chaos and disorder.

Without the law of harmony an acorn might grow into a heterogeneous tree consisting of the wood of the oak, poplar, maple and what not.

Without the law of harmony the blood might deposit the food which grows fingernails on the scalp where hair is supposed to grow, and thus create a horny growth which might easily be mistaken, by the superstitious, to signify man's relationship to a certain imaginary gentleman with horns, often referred to by the more primitive type.

Without the law of harmony there can be no organization of knowledge, for what, may one ask, is organized knowledge except the harmony of facts and truths and natural laws?

The moment discord begins to creep in at the front door harmony edges out at the back door, so to speak, whether the application is made to a business partnership or the orderly movement of the planets of the heavens.

If the student gathers the impression that the author is laying undue stress upon the importance of HARMONY, let it be remembered that lack of harmony is the first, and often the last and only, cause of FAILURE!

There can be no poetry nor music nor oratory worthy of notice without the presence of harmony.

Good architecture is largely a matter of harmony. Without harmony a house is nothing but a mass of building material, more or less a monstrosity.

Sound business management plants the very sinews of its existence in harmony.

Every well-dressed man or woman is a living picture and a moving example of harmony.

With all these workaday illustrations of the important part which harmony plays in the affairs of the world–nay, in the operation of the entire universe–how could any intelligent person leave harmony out of his "Definite Aim" in life? As well have no "definite aim" as to omit harmony as the chief stone of its foundation.

The human body is a complex organization of organs, glands, blood vessels, nerves, brain cells, muscles, etc. The mind energy which stimulates to action and co-ordinates the efforts of the component parts of the body is also a plurality of ever-varying and changing energies. From birth until death there is continuous struggle, often assuming the nature of open combat, between the forces of the mind. For example, the lifelong struggle between the motivating forces and desires of the human mind, which takes place between the impulses of right and wrong, is well known to everyone.

Every human being possesses at least two distinct mind powers or personalities, and as many as six distinct personalities have been discovered in one person. One of man's most delicate tasks is that of harmonizing these mind forces so that they may be organized and directed toward the orderly attainment of a given objective. Without this element of harmony no individual can become an accurate thinker.

It is no wonder that leaders in business and industrial enterprises, as well as those in politics and other fields of endeavor, find it so difficult to organize groups of people so they will function in the attainment of a given objective, without friction. Each individual human being possesses forces, within himself, which are hard to harmonize, even when he is placed in the environment most favorable to harmony. If the chemistry of the individual's mind is such that the units of his mind cannot be easily harmonized, think how much more difficult it must be to harmonize a group of minds so they will function as one, in an orderly manner, through what is known as a "Master Mind."

The leader who successfully develops and directs the energies of a "Master Mind" must possess tact, patience, persistence, self-confidence, intimate knowledge of mind chemistry and the ability to adapt himself (in a state of perfect poise and harmony) to quickly changing circumstances, without showing the least sign of annoyance.

How many are there who can measure up to this requirement?

The successful leader must possess the ability to change the color of his mind, chameleon-like, to fit every circumstance that arises in connection with the object of his leadership. Moreover, he must possess the ability to change from one mood to another without showing the slightest signs of anger or lack of self-control. The successful leader must understand the Fifteen Laws of Success and be able to put into practice any combination of these Fifteen Laws whenever occasion demands. Without this ability no leader can be powerful, and without power no leader can long endure.

THE MEANING OF EDUCATION:

There has long been a general misconception of the meaning of the word "educate." The dictionaries have not aided in the elimination of this misunderstanding, because they have defined the word "educate" as an act of imparting knowledge.

The word educate has its roots in the Latin word *educo,* which means to develop FROM WITHIN; to educe; to draw out; to grow through the law of USE.

Nature hates idleness in all its forms. She gives continuous life only to those elements which are in use. Tie up an arm, or any other portion of the body, taking it out of use, and the idle part will soon atrophy and become lifeless. Reverse the order, give an arm more than normal use, such as that engaged in by the blacksmith who wields a heavy hammer all day long, and that arm (developed from within) grows strong.

Power grows out of ORGANIZED KNOWLEDGE, but, mind you, it "grows out of it" through application and use!

A man may become a walking encyclopaedia of knowledge without possessing any power of value. This knowledge becomes power only to the extent that it is organized, classified and put into action. Some of the best educated men the world has known possessed much less general knowledge than some who have been known as fools, the difference between the two being that the former put what knowledge they possessed into use while the latter made no such application.

An "educated" person is one who knows how to acquire everything he needs in the attainment of his main Purpose in life, without violating the rights of his fellow men.

It might be a surprise to many so-called men of "learning" to know that they come nowhere near qualification as men of "education." It might also be a great surprise to many who believe they suffer from lack of "learning" to know that they are well "educated."

The successful lawyer is not necessarily the one who memorizes the greatest number of principles of law. On the contrary, the successful lawyer is the one who knows where to find a principle of law, plus a variety of opinions supporting that principle which fit the immediate needs of a given case. In other words, the successful lawyer is he who knows where to find the law he wants when he needs it.

This principle applies, with equal force, to the affairs of industry and business. Henry Ford had but little elementary schooling, yet he is one of the best "educated" men in the world because he has acquired the ability so to combine natural and economic laws, to say nothing of the minds of men, that he has the power to get anything of a material nature he wants.

Some years ago during the world war Mr. Ford brought suit against the Chicago Tribune, charging that newspaper with libelous publication of statements concerning him, one of which was the statement that Ford was an "ignoramus," an ignorant pacifist, etc.

When the suit came up for trial the attorneys for the Tribune undertook to prove, by Ford himself, that their statement was true; that he was ignorant, and with this object in view they catechized and cross-examined him on all manner of subjects. One question they asked was:

"How many soldiers did the British send over to subdue the rebellion in the Colonies in 1776?"

With a dry grin on his face Ford nonchalantly replied:

"I do not know just how many, but I have heard that it was a lot more than ever went back."

Loud laughter from Court, jury, court-room spectators, and even from the frustrated lawyer who had asked the question.

This line of interrogation was continued for an hour or more, Ford keeping perfectly calm the meanwhile. Finally, however, he had permitted the "smart aleck" lawyers to play with him until he was tired of it, and in reply to a question which was particularly obnoxious and insulting, Ford straightened himself up, pointed his finger at the questioning lawyer and replied:

"If I should really wish to answer the foolish question you have just asked, or any of the others you have been asking, let me remind you that I have a row of electric pushbuttons hanging over my desk and by placing my finger on the right button I could call in men who could give me the correct answer to all the questions you have asked and to many that you have not the intelligence either to ask or answer. Now, will you kindly tell me why I should bother about filling my mind with a lot of useless details in order to answer every fool question that anyone may ask, when I have able men all about me who can supply me with all the facts I want when I call for them?"

This answer is quoted from memory, but it substantially relates Ford's answer.

There was silence in the court-room. The questioning attorney's under jaw dropped down, his eyes opened widely; the judge leaned forward from the bench and gazed in Mr. Ford's direction; many of the jury awoke and looked around as if they had heard an explosion (which they actually had).

In the vernacular of the day, Ford's reply knocked the questioner cold. Up to the time of that reply the lawyer had been enjoying considerable fun at what he believed to be Ford's expense, by adroitly displaying his (the lawyer's) sample case of general knowledge and comparing it with what he inferred to be Ford's ignorance as to many events and subjects. But that answer spoiled the lawyer's fun.

It also proved once more (to all who had the intelligence to accept the proof) that true education means mind development; not merely the gathering and classifying of knowledge.

Ford could not, in all probability, have named the capitals of all the States of the United States, but he could have and in fact had gathered the "capital" with which to "turn many wheels" within every State in the Union.

Education–let us not forget this–consists of the power with which to get everything one needs when he needs it, without violating the rights of his fellow men. Ford comes well within that definition, and for the reason which the author has here tried to make plain, by relating the foregoing incident connected with the simple Ford philosophy. There are many men of "learning" who could easily entangle Ford, theoretically, with a maze of questions none of which he, personally, could answer. But Ford could turn right around and wage a battle in industry, or finance that would exterminate those same men, with all of their knowledge and all of their wisdom.

Ford could not go into his chemical laboratory and separate water into its component atoms of hydrogen and oxygen and then recombine these atoms in their former order, but he knows how to surround himself with chemists who can do this for him if he wants it done. The man who can intelligently use the knowledge possessed by another is as much or more a man of education as the person who merely has the knowledge but does not know what to do with it.

The president of a well-known college inherited a large tract of very poor land. This land had no timber of commercial value, no minerals or other valuable appurtenances, therefore it was nothing but a source of expense to him, for he had to pay taxes on it. The State built a highway through the land. An "uneducated" man who was riving his automobile over this road observed that this poor land was on top of a muntain which commanded a wonderful view for many miles in all directions. He (the ignorant one) also observed that the land was covered with a growth of small pines and other saplings. He bought fifty acres of the land for $10.00 an acre. Near the public highway he built a unique log house to which he attached a large dining room. Near the house he put in a gasoline filling station. He built a dozen single-room log houses along the road, these he rented out to tourists at $3.00 a night, each. The dining room, gasoline filling station and log houses brought him a net income of $15,000.00 the first year.

The next year he extended his plan by adding fifty more log houses, of three rooms each, which he now rents out as summer country homes to people in a near-by city, at a rental of $150.00 each for the season.

The building material cost him nothing, for it grew on his land in abundance (that same land which the college president believed to be worthless).

Moreover, the unique and unusual appearance of the log bungalows served as an advertisement of the plan, whereas many would have considered it a real calamity had they been compelled to build out of such crude materials.

Less than five miles from the location of these log houses this same man purchased an old worked-out farm of 150 acres, for $25.00 an acre, a price which the seller believed to be extremely high.

By building a dam, one hundred feet in length, the purchaser of this old farm turned a stream of water into a lake that covered fifteen acres of the land, stocked the lake with fish, then sold the farm off in building lots to people who wanted summering places around the lake. The total profit realized from this simple transaction was more than $25,000.00, and the time required for its consummation was one summer.

Yet this man of vision and imagination was not "educated" in the orthodox meaning of that term.

Let us keep in mind the fact that it is through these simple illustrations of the use of organized knowledge that one may become educated and powerful. In speaking of the transaction here related, the college president who sold the fifty acres of worthless land for $500.00 said:

"Just think of it! That man, whom most of us might call ignorant, mixed his ignorance with fifty acres of worthless land and made the combination yield more yearly than I earn from five years of application of so-called education."

There is an opportunity, if not scores of them, in every State in America, to make use of the idea here described. From now on make it your business to study the lay of all land you see that is similar to that described in this lesson, and you may find a suitable place for developing a similar money-making enterprise. The idea is particularly adaptable in localities where bathing beaches are few, as people naturally like such conveniences.

The automobile has caused a great system of public highways to be built throughout the United States. On practically every one of these highways there is a suitable spot for a "Cabin City" for tourists which can be turned into a regular moneymaking mint by the man with the IMAGINATION and SELF-CONFIDENCE to do it.

There are opportunities to make money all around you.

This course was designed to help you "see" these opportunities, and to inform you how to make the most of them after you discover them.

WHO CAN PROFIT MOST BY THE LAW OF SUCCESS PHILOSOPHY?

RAILROAD OFFICIALS who want a better spirit of co-operation between their trainmen and the public they serve.

SALARIED PEOPLE who wish to increase their earning power and market their services to better advantage.

SALESPEOPLE who wish to become masters in their chosen field. The Law of Success philosophy covers every known law of selling, and includes many features not included in any other course.

INDUSTRIAL PLANT MANAGERS who understand the value of greater harmony among their employees.

RAILROAD EMPLOYEES who wish to establish records of efficiency which will lead to more responsible positions, with greater pay.

MERCHANTS who wish to extend their business by adding new customers. The Law of Success philosophy will help any merchant increase his business by teaching him how to make a walking advertisement of every customer who comes into his store.

AUTOMOBILE AGENTS who wish to increase the selling power of their salesmen. A large part of the Law of Success course was developed from the lifework and experience of the greatest automobile salesman living, and it is therefore of unusual help to the Sales Manager who is directing the efforts of Automobile Salesmen.

LIFE INSURANCE AGENTS who wish to add new policy-holders and increase the insurance on present policy-holders. One Life Insurance Salesman, in Ohio, sold a Fifty Thousand Dollar policy to one of the officials of the Central Steel Company, as the result of but one reading of the lesson on "Profiting by Failures." This same salesman has become one of the star men of the New York Life Insurance Company's staff, as the result of his training in the Fifteen Laws of Success.

SCHOOL TEACHERS who wish to advance to the top in their present occupation, or who are looking for an opportunity to enter the more profitable field of business as a life-work.

STUDENTS, both College and High School, who are undecided as to what field of endeavor they wish to enter as a life-work. The Law of Success course covers a complete Personal Analysis service which helps the student of the philosophy to determine the work for which he or she is best fitted.

BANKERS who wish to extend their business through better and more courteous methods of serving their clients.

BANK CLERKS who are ambitious to prepare themselves for executive positions in the field of banking, or in some commercial or industrial field.

PHYSICIANS and DENTISTS who wish to extend their practice without violating the ethics of their profession by direct advertising. A prominent physician has said that the Law of Success course is worth $1,000.00 to any professional man or woman whose professional ethics prevent direct advertising.

PROMOTERS who wish to develop new and heretofore unworked combinations in business or industry.

The principle described in this Introductory Lesson is said to have made a small fortune for a man who used it as the basis of a real estate promotion.

REAL ESTATE MEN who wish new methods for promoting sales.

This Introductory Lesson contains a description of an entirely new real-estate promotion plan which is sure to make fortunes for many who will put it to use. This plan may be put into operation in practically every State. Moreover, it may be employed by men who never promoted an enterprise.

FARMERS who wish to discover new methods of marketing their products so as to give them greater net returns, and those who own lands suitable for subdivision promotion under the plan referred to at the end of this Introductory Lesson. Thousands of farmers have "gold mines" in the land they own which is not suitable for cultivation, which could be used for recreation and resort purposes, on a highly profitable basis.

STENOGRAPHERS and BOOKKEEPERS who are looking for a practical plan to promote themselves into higher and better paying positions. The Law of Success course is said to be the best course ever written on the subject of marketing personal services.

PRINTERS who want a larger volume of business and more efficient production as the result of better cooperation among their own employees.

DAY LABORERS who have the ambition to advance into more responsible positions, in work that has greater responsibilities and consequently offers more pay.

LAWYERS who wish to extend their clientele through dignified, ethical methods which will bring them to the attention, in a favorable way, of a greater number of people who need legal services.

BUSINESS EXECUTIVES who wish to expand their present business, or who wish to handle their present volume with less expense, as the result of greater co-operation between their employees.

LAUNDRY OWNERS who wish to extend their business by teaching their drivers how to serve more courteously and efficiently.

LIFE INSURANCE GENERAL AGENTS who wish bigger and more efficient sales organizations.

CHAIN STORE MANAGERS who want a greater volume of business as the result of more efficient individual sales efforts.

MARRIED PEOPLE who are unhappy, and therefore unsuccessful, because of lack of harmony and cooperation in the home.

To all described in the foregoing classification the Law of Success philosophy offers both DEFINITE and SPEEDY aid.

SUMMARY OF Lesson One THE MASTER MIND

The purpose of this summary is to aid the student in mastering the central idea around which the lesson has been developed. This idea is represented by the term "Master Mind" which has been described in great detail throughout the lesson.

All new ideas, and especially those of an abstract nature, find lodgment in the human mind only after much repetition, a well known truth which accounts for the restatement, in this summary, of the principle known as the "Master Mind."

A "Master Mind" may be developed by a friendly alliance, in a spirit of harmony of purpose, between two or more minds. This is an appropriate place at which to explain that out of every alliance of minds, whether in a spirit of harmony or not, there is developed another mind which affects all participating in the alliance. No two or more minds ever met without creating, out of the contact, another mind, but not always is this invisible creation a "Master Mind."

There may be, and altogether too often there is, developed out of the meeting of two or more minds a negative power which is just the opposite to a "Master Mind." There are certain minds which, as has already been stated throughout this lesson, cannot be made to blend in a spirit of harmony. This principle has its comparable analogy in chemistry, reference to which may enable the student to grasp more clearly the principle here referred to.

For example, the chemical formula H_2O (meaning the combining of two atoms of hydrogen with one atom of oxygen) changes these two elements into water. One atom of hydrogen and one atom of oxygen will not produce water; moreover, they cannot be made to associate themselves in harmony!

There are many known elements which, when combined, are immediately transformed from harmless into deadly poisonous substances. Stated differently, many well known poisonous elements are neutralized and rendered harmless when combined with certain other elements.

Just as the combining of certain elements changes their entire nature, the combining of certain minds changes the nature of those minds, producing either a certain degree of what has been called a "Master Mind," or its opposite, which is highly destructive.

Any man who has found his mother-in-law to be incompatible has experienced the negative application of the principle known as a "Master Mind." For some reason as yet unknown to investigators in the field of mind behavior, the majority of mothers-in-law appear to affect their daughters' husbands in a highly negative manner, the meeting of their minds with those of their sons-in-law creating a highly antagonistic influence instead of a "Master Mind."

This fact is too well-known as a truth to make extended comment necessary. Some minds will not be harmonized and cannot be blended into a "Master Mind," a fact which all leaders of men will do well to remember. It is the leader's responsibility so to group his men that those who have been placed at the most strategic points in his organization are made up of individuals whose minds CAN and WILL BE blended in a spirit of friendliness and harmony.

Ability so to group men is the chief outstanding quality of leadership. In Lesson Two of this course the student will discover that this ability was the main source of both the power and fortune accumulated by the late Andrew Carnegie.

Knowing nothing whatsoever of the technical end of the steel business, Carnegie so combined and grouped the men of which his "Master Mind" was composed that he built the most successful steel industry known to the world during his life-time. Henry Ford's gigantic success may be traced to the successful application of this selfsame principle. With all the self-reliance a man could have, Ford, nevertheless, did not depend upon himself for the knowledge necessary in the successful development of his industries. Like Carnegie, he surrounded himself with men who supplied the knowledge which he, himself, did not and could not possess. Moreover, Ford picked men who could and did harmonize in group effort.

The most effective alliances, which have resulted in the creation of the principle known as the "Master Mind," have been those developed out of the blending of the minds of men and women. The reason for this is the fact that the minds of male and female will more readily blend in harmony than will the minds of males. Also, the added stimulus of sexual contact often enters into the development of a "Master Mind" between a man and a woman.

It is a well-known fact that the male of the species is keener and more alert for "the chase," let the goal or object of the chase be what it may, when inspired and urged on by a female. This human trait begins to manifest itself in the male at the age of puberty, and continues throughout his life. The first evidence of it may be observed in athletics, where boys are playing before an audience made up of females.

Remove the women from the audience and the game known as football would soon become a very tame affair. A boy will throw himself into a football game with almost superhuman effort when he knows that the girl of his choice is observing him from the grandstand.

And that same boy will throw himself into the game of accumulating money with the same enthusiasm when inspired and urged on by the woman of his choice; especially if that woman knows how to stimulate his mind with her own, through the law of the "Master Mind."

On the other hand, that same woman may, through a negative application of the law of the "Master Mind" (nagging, jealousy, selfishness, greed, vanity), drag this man down to sure defeat!

The late Elbert Hubbard understood the principle here described so well that when he discovered that the incompatibility between himself and his first wife was dragging him down to sure defeat he ran the gamut of public opinion by divorcing her and marrying the woman who is said to have been the main source of his inspiration. Not every man would have had the courage to defy public opinion, as Hubbard did, but who is wise enough to say that his action was not for the best interest of all concerned?

A man's chief business in life is to succeed!

The road to success may be, and generally is, obstructed by many influences which must be removed before the goal can be reached. One of the most detrimental of these obstacles is that of unfortunate alliance with minds which do not harmonize. In such cases the alliance must be broken or the end is sure to be defeat and failure. The man who has mastered the six basic fears, one of which is the Fear of Criticism, will have no hesitancy in taking what may seem to the more convention-bound type of mind to be drastic action when he finds himself circumscribed and bound down by antagonistic alliances, no matter of what nature or with whom they may be. It is a million times better to meet and face criticism than to be dragged down to failure and oblivion on account of alliances which are not harmonious, whether the alliances be of a business or social nature.

To be perfectly frank, the author is here justifying divorce, when the conditions surrounding marriage are such that harmony cannot prevail. This is not intended to convey the belief that lack of harmony may not be removed through other methods than that of divorce; for there are instances where the cause of antagonism may be removed and harmony established without taking the extreme step of divorce. While it is true that some minds will not blend in a spirit of harmony, and cannot be forced or induced to do so, because of the chemical nature of the individuals' brains, **DO NOT BE TOO READY TO CHARGE THE OTHER PARTY TO YOUR ALLIANCE WITH ALL THE RESPONSIBILITY OF LACK OF HARMONY–REMEMBER, THE TROUBLE MAY BE WITH YOUR OWN BRAIN!**

Remember, also, that a mind which cannot and will not harmonize with one person or persons may harmonize perfectly with other types of minds. Discovery of this truth has resulted in radical changes in methods of employing men. It is no longer customary to discharge a man because he does not fit in the position for which he was originally hired. The discriminating leader endeavors to place such a man in some other position, where, it has been proved more than once, misfits may become valuable men.

The student of this course should be sure that the principle described as the "Master Mind" is thoroughly understood before proceeding with the remaining lessons of the course. The reason for this is the fact that practically the entire course is closely associated with this law of mind operation.

If you are not sure that you understand this law, communicate with the author of the course and secure further explanation by asking such questions as you may wish concerning points in connection with which you believe you need further information. You cannot spend too much time in seriou thought and contemplation in connection with the law of the "Master Mind," for the reason that when you have mastered this law and have learned how to apply it new worlds of opportunity will open to you.

This Introductory Lesson, while not really intended as a separate lesson of the Law of Success course, contains sufficient data to enable the student who has an aptitude for selling to become a Master Salesman.

Any sales organization may make effective use of the law of the "Master Mind" by grouping the salesmen in groups of two or more people who will ally themselves in a spirit of friendly cooperation and apply this law as suggested in this lesson.

An agent for a well-known make of automobile, who employs twelve salesmen, has grouped his organization in six groups of two men each, with the object of applying the law of the "Master Mind," with the result that all the salesmen have established new high sales records. This same organization has created what it calls the "One-A-Week Club," meaning that each man belonging to the Club has averaged the sale of one car a week since the Club was organized. **The results of this effort have been surprising to all!**

Each man belonging to the Club was provided with a list of 100 prospective purchasers of automobiles. Each salesman sends one postal card a week to each of his 100 prospective purchasers, and makes personal calls on at least ten of these each day.

Each postal card is confined to the description of but one advantage of the automobile the salesman is selling, and asks for a personal interview. Interviews have increased rapidly, as have, also, sales!

The agent who employs these salesmen has offered an extra cash bonus to each salesman who earns the right to membership in the "One-A-Week Club" by averaging one car a week.

The plan has injected new vitality into the entire organization. Moreover, the results of the plan are showing in the weekly sales record of each salesman.

A similar plan could be adopted very effectively by Life Insurance Agencies. Any enterprising General Agent might easily double or even triple the volume of his business, with the same number of salesmen, through the use of this plan.

Practically no changes whatsoever would need to be made in the method of use of the plan. The Club might be called the "Policy-A-Week Club," meaning that each member pledged himself to sell at least one policy, of an agreed minimum amount, each week.

The student of this course who has mastered the second lesson, and understands how to apply the fundamentals of that lesson (A Definite Chief Aim) will be able to make much more effective use of the plan here described.

It is not suggested or intended that any student shall undertake to apply the principles of this lesson, which is merely an Introductory Lesson, until he has mastered at least the next five lessons of the Law of Success course.

The main purpose of this Introductory Lesson is to state some of the principles upon which the course is founded. These principles are more accurately described, and the student is taught in a very definite manner how to apply them, in the individual lessons of the course.

The automobile sales organization referred to in this summary meets at luncheon once a week. One hour and a half is devoted to luncheon and to the discussion of ways and means of applying the principles of this course. This gives each man an opportunity to profit by the ideas of all the other members of the organization.

Two tables are set for the luncheon.

At one table all who have earned the right to membership in the One-A-Week Club are seated. At the other table, which is serviced with tinware instead of china, all who did not earn the right to membership in the Club are seated. These, needless to say, become the object of considerable good-natured chiding from the more fortunate members seated at the other table.

It is possible to make an almost endless variety of adaptations of this plan, both in the field of automobile salesmanship and in other fields of selling. The justification for its use is that it pays!

It pays not only the leader or manager of the organization, but every member of the sales force as well.

This plan has been briefly described for the purpose of showing the student of this course how to make practical application of the principles outlined in this course. The final acid test of any theory or rule or principle is that it will ACTUALLY WORK!

The law of the "Master Mind" has been proved sound because it WORKS. If you understand this law you are now ready to proceed with Lesson Two, in which you will be further and much more deeply initiated in the application of the principles described in this Introductory Lesson.

YOUR SIX MOST DANGEROUS ENEMIES–
An After-the-Lesson Visit With Author

The Six Specters are: Fear of Poverty, Fear of Death, Fear of Ill-Health, Fear of the Loss of Love, Fear of Old Age, Fear of Criticism. Every person on earth is afraid of something. Most fears are inherited. In this essay you may study the six basic fears which do the most damage. Your fears must be mastered before you can win in any worthwhile undertaking in life. Find out how many of the six fears are bothering you, but more important than this, determine, also how to conquer these fears.

Here You have the opportunity to study our six worst enemies. These enemies are not beautiful. As you read about these ugly characters analyze yourself and find out which of them does YOU the most damage!

The purpose of this essay is to help the readers of this course throw off these deadly enemies.

Observe that the six characters are at your back, where you cannot conveniently see them.

Every human being on this earth is bound down to some extent by one or more of these unseen FEARS. The first step to be taken in killing off these enemies is to find out where and how you acquired them.

They got their grip upon you through two forms of heredity.

One is known as physical heredity, to which Darwin devoted so much study. The other is known as social heredity, through which the fears, superstitions and beliefs of men who lived during the dark ages have been passed on from one generation to another. Let us study, first, the part that physical heredity has played in creating these six BASIC FEARS. Starting at the beginning, we find that Nature has been a cruel builder. From the lowest form of life to the highest, Nature has permitted the stronger to prey upon the weaker forms of animal life.

The fish prey upon the worms and insects, eating them bodily. Birds prey upon the fish. Higher forms of animal life prey upon the birds, and upon one another, all the way up the line to man. And, man preys upon all the other lower forms of animal life, and upon MAN!

The whole story of evolution is one unbroken chain of evidence of cruelty and destruction of the weaker by the stronger.

No wonder the weaker forms of animal life have learned to FEAR the stronger. The Fear consciousness is born in every living animal.

So much for the FEAR instinct that came to us through physical heredity. Now let us examine social heredity, and find out what part it has played in our make-up. The term "social heredity" has reference to everything that we are taught, everything we learn or gather from observation and experience with other living beings.

Lay aside any prejudices and fixed opinions you may have formed, at least temporarily, and you may know the truth about your Six Worst Enemies, starting with:

THE FEAR OF POVERTY:

It requires courage to tell the truth about the history of this enemy of mankind, and still greater courage to hear the truth after it has been told.

The Fear of Poverty grows out of man's habit of preying upon his fellow men, economically. The animals which have instinct, but no power to THINK, prey upon one another physically. Man, with his superior sense of intuition, and his more powerful weapon of THOUGHT, does not eat his fellow man bodily; he gets more pleasure from eating him FINANCIALLY.

So great an offender is man, in this respect, that nearly every state and nation has been obliged to pass laws, scores of laws, to protect the weak from the strong. Every blue-sky law is indisputable evidence of man's nature to prey upon his weaker brother economically.

The second of the Six Basic Fears with which man is bound down is:

THE FEAR OF OLD AGE:

This Fear grows out of two major causes. First, the thought that Old Age may bring with it POVERTY. Secondly, from false and cruel sectarian teachings which have been so well mixed with fire and brimstone that every human being learned to Fear Old Age because it meant the approach of another and, perhaps, a more horrible world than this.

The third of the Six Basic Fears is:

THE FEAR OF ILL HEALTH:

This Fear is born of both physical and social heredity. From birth until death there is eternal warfare within every physical body; warfare between groups of cells, one group being known as the friendly builders of the body, and the other as the destroyers, or "disease germs." The seed of Fear is born in the physical body, to begin with, as the result of Nature's cruel plan of permitting the stronger forms of cell life to prey upon the weaker. Social heredity has played its part through lack of cleanliness and knowledge of sanitation. Also, through the law of suggestion cleverly manipulated by those who profited by ILL HEALTH.

The fourth of the Six Basic Fears is:

THE FEAR OF LOSS OF LOVE OF SOMEONE:

This Fear fills the asylums with the insanely jealous, for jealousy is nothing but a form of insanity. It also fills the divorce courts and causes murders and other forms of cruel punishment. It is a holdover, handed down through social heredity, from the stone age when man preyed upon his fellow man by stealing his mate by physical force. The method, but not the practice, has now changed to some extent. Instead of physical force man now steals his fellow man's mate with pretty colorful ribbons and fast motor cars and bootleg whisky, and sparkling rocks and stately mansions.

Man is improving. He now "entices" where once he "drove."

The fifth of the Six Basic Fears is:

THE FEAR OF CRITICISM:

Just how and where man got this Fear is difficult to determine, but it is certain that he has it.

But for this Fear men would not become bald-headed. Bald heads come from tightly fitting hat-bands, which cut off the circulation from the roots of the hair. Women seldom are bald because they wear loose fitting hats. But for Fear of Criticism man would lay aside his hat and keep his hair.

The makers of clothing have not been slow to capitalize this Basic Fear of mankind. Every season the styles change, because the clothes makers know that few people have the courage to wear a garment that is one season out of step with what "They are all wearing." If you doubt this (you gentlemen) start down the street with last year's narrow-brimmed straw hat on, when this year's style calls for the broad brim. Or (you ladies), take a walk down the street on Easter morning with last year's hat on. Observe how uncomfortable you are, thanks to your unseen enemy, the FEAR OF CRITICISM.

The sixth, and last of the Six Basic Fears is the most dreaded of them all. It is called:

THE FEAR OF DEATH:

For tens of thousands of years man has been asking the still unanswered questions– "WHENCE?" and "WHITHER?" The more crafty of the race have not been slow to offer the answer to this eternal question, "Where did I come from and where am I going after Death?" "Come into my tent," says one leader, "and you may go to Heaven after Death." Heaven was then pictured as a wonderful city whose streets were lined with gold and studded with precious stones. "Remain out of my tent and you may go straight to hell." Hell was then pictured as a blazing furnace where the poor victim might have the misery of burning forever in brimstone. *No wonder mankind FEARS DEATH!*

Take another look at the picture at the beginning of this essay and determine, if you can, which of the Six Basic Fears is doing you the greatest damage. An enemy discovered is an enemy half whipped.

Thanks to the schools and colleges man is slowly discovering these Six Enemies. The most effective tool with which to fight them is ORGANIZED KNOWLEDGE. Ignorance and Fear are twin sisters. They are generally found together.

But for IGNORANCE and SUPERSTITION the Six Basic Fears would disappear from man's nature in one generation. In every public library may be found the remedy for these six enemies of mankind, providing you know what books to read. Begin by reading The Science of Power, by Benjamin Kidd, and you will have broken the strangle hold of most of your Six Basic Fears. Follow this by reading Emerson's essay on Compensation. Then select some good book on auto-suggestion (self-suggestion) and inform yourself on the principle through which your beliefs of today become the realities of tomorrow. Mind In the Making, by Robinson, will give you a good start toward understanding your own mind.

Through the principle of social heredity the IGNORANCE and SUPERSTITION of the dark ages have been passed on to you. But, you are living in a modern age. On every hand you may see evidence that every EFFECT has a natural CAUSE. Begin, now, to study effects by their causes and soon you will emancipate your mind from the burden of the Six Basic Fears.

Begin by studying men who have accumulated great wealth, and find out the CAUSE of their achievements. Henry Ford is a good subject to start with. Within the short period of twenty-five years he has whipped POVERTY and made himself the most powerful man on earth. There was no luck or chance or accident back of his achievement. It grew out of his careful observation of certain principles which are as available to you as they were to him.

Henry Ford is not bound down by the Six Basic Fears; make no mistake about this. If you feel that you are too far away from Ford to study him accurately, then begin by selecting two people whom you know close at hand; one representing your idea of FAILURE and the other corresponding to your idea of SUCCESS. Find out what made one a failure and the other a success. Get the real FACTS. In the process of gathering these facts you will have taught yourself a great lesson on CAUSE and EFFECT.

Nothing ever just "happens." Everything, from the lowest animal form that creeps on the earth or swims in the seas, on up to man, is the EFFECT of Nature's evolutionary process. Evolution is orderly change." No "miracles" are connected with this orderly change.

Not only do the physical shapes and colors of animals undergo slow, orderly change from one generation to another, but the mind of man is also undergoing constant change. Herein lies your hope for improvement. You have the power to force your mind through a process of rather quick change. In a single month of properly directed self-suggestion you may place your foot upon the neck of every one of your Six Basic Fears. In twelve months of persistent effort you may drive the entire herd into the corner where it will never again do you any serious injury.

You will resemble, tomorrow, the DOMINATING THOUGHTS that you keep alive in your mind today! Plant in your mind the seed of DETERMINATION to whip your Six Basic Fears and the battle will have been half won then and there. Keep this intention in your mind and it will slowly push your Six Worst Enemies out of sight, as they exist nowhere except in your own mind.

The man who is powerful FEARS nothing; not even God. The POWERFUL man loves God, but FEARS Him never!

Enduring power never grows out of FEAR. Any power that is built upon FEAR is bound to crumble and disintegrate. Understand this great truth and you will never be so unfortunate as to try to raise yourself to power through the FEARS of other people who may owe you temporary allegiance.

Man is of soul and body formed for deeds
Of high resolve; on fancy's boldest wing
To soar unwearied, fearlessly to turn
The keenest pangs to peacefulness, and taste
The joys which mingled sense and spirit yield;
Or he is formed for abjectness and woe,
To grovel on the dunghill of his fears,
To shrink at every sound, to quench the flame
Of natural love in sensualism, to know
That hour as blest when on his worthless days
The frozen hand of death shall set its seal,
Yet fear the cure, though hating the disease.
The one is man that shall hereafter be,
The other, man as vice has made him now.

Lesson Two: A DEFINITE CHIEF AIM

You are at the beginning of a course of philosophy which, for the first time in the history of the world, has been organized from the known factors which have been used and must always be used by successful people.

Literary style has been completely subordinated for the sake of stating the principles and laws included in this course in such a manner that they may be quickly and easily assimilated by people in every walk of life.

Some of the principles described in the course are familiar to all who will read the course. Others are here stated for the first time. It should be kept in mind, from the first lesson to the last, that the value of the philosophy lies entirely in the thought stimuli it will produce in the mind of the student, and not merely in the lessons themselves.

Stated in another way, this course is intended as a mind stimulant that will cause the student to organize and direct to a DEFINITE end the forces of his or her mind, thus harnessing the stupendous power which most people waste in spasmodic, purposeless thought.

Singleness of purpose is essential for success, no matter what may be one's idea of the definition of success. Yet singleness of purpose is a quality which may, and generally does, call for thought on many allied subjects.

This author traveled a long distance to watch Jack Dempsey train for an oncoming battle. It was observed that he did not rely entirely upon one form of exercise, but resorted to many forms. The punching bag helped him develop one set of muscles, and also trained his eye to be quick. The dumbbells trained still another set of muscles.

Running developed the muscles of his legs and hips. A well-balanced food ration supplied the materials needed for building muscle without fat. Proper sleep, relaxation and rest habits provided still other qualities which he must have in order to win.

The student of this course is, or should be, engaged in the business of training for success in the battle of life. To win there are many factors which must have attention. A well-organized, alert and energetic mind is produced by various and sundry stimuli, all of which are plainly described in these lessons.

It should be remembered, however, that the mind requires, for its development, a variety of exercise, just as the physical body, to be properly developed, calls for many forms of systematic exercise.

Horses are trained to certain gaits by trainers who hurdle-jump them over handicaps which cause them to develop the desired steps, through habit and repetition. The human mind must be trained in a similar manner, by a variety of thought-inspiring stimuli.

You will observe, before you have gone very far into this philosophy, that the reading of these lessons will superinduce a flow of thoughts covering a wide range of subjects. For this reason the student should read the course with a notebook and pencil at hand, and follow the practice of recording these thoughts or "ideas" as they come into the mind.

By following this suggestion the student will have a collection of ideas, by the time the course has been read two or three times, sufficient to transform his or her entire life-plan.

By following this practice it will be noticed, very soon, that the mind has become like a magnet in that it will attract useful ideas right out of the "thin air," to use the words of a noted scientist who has experimented with this principle for a great number of years. You will do yourself a great injustice if you undertake this course with even a remote feeling that you do not stand in need of more knowledge than you now possess. In truth, no man knows enough about any worthwhile subject to entitle him to feel that he has the last word on that subject.

In the long, hard task of trying to wipe out some of my own ignorance and make way for some of the useful truths of life, I have often seen, in my imagination, the Great Marker who stands at the gateway entrance of life and writes "Poor Fool" on the brow of those who believe they are wise, and "Poor Sinner" on the brow of those who believe they are saints.

Which, translated into workaday language, means that none of us know very much, and by the very nature of our being can never know as much as we need to know in order to live sanely and enjoy life while we live.

Humility is a forerunner of success!

Until we become humble in our own hearts we are not apt to profit greatly by the experiences and thoughts of others.

Sounds like a preachment on morality? Well, what if it does?

Even "preachments," as dry and lacking in interest as they generally are, may be beneficial if they serve to reflect the shadow of our real selves so we may get an approximate idea of our smallness and superficiality. Success in life is largely predicated upon our knowing men!

The best place to study the man-animal is in your own mind, by taking as accurate an inventory as possible of YOURSELF. When you know yourself thoroughly (if you ever do) you will also know much about others.

To know others, not as they seem to be, but as they really are, study them through:

1-The posture of the body, and the way they walk.

2-The tone of the voice, its quality, pitch, volume.

3-The eyes, whether shifty or direct.

4-The use of words, their trend, nature and quality. Through these open windows you may literally "walk right into a man's soul" and take a look at the REAL MAN!

Going a step further, if you would know men study them:

When angry

When in love

When money is involved
When eating (alone, and unobserved, as they believe)
When writing
When in trouble
When joyful and triumphant
When downcast and defeated
When facing catastrophe of a hazardous nature
When trying to make a "good impression" on others
When informed of another's misfortune
When informed of another's good fortune
When losing in any sort of a game of sport
When winning at sport
When alone, in a meditative mood.

Before you can know any man, as he really is, you must observe him in all the foregoing moods, and perhaps more, which is practically the equivalent of saying that you have no right to judge others at sight. Appearances count, there can be no doubt of that, but appearances are often deceiving.

This course has been so designed that the student who masters it may take inventory of himself and of others by other than "snap-judgment" methods. The student who masters this philosophy will be able to look through the outer crust of personal adornment, clothes, so-called culture and the like, and down deep into the heart of all about him.

This is a very broad promise!

It would not have been made if the author of this philosophy had not known, from years of experimentation and analysis, that the promise can be met. Some who have examined the manuscripts of this course have asked why it was not called a course in Master Salesmanship. The answer is that the word "salesmanship" is commonly associated with the marketing of goods or services, and it would, therefore, narrow down and circumscribe the real nature of the course. It is true that this is a course in Master Salesmanship, providing one takes a deeper-than-the-average view of the meaning of salesmanship.

This philosophy is intended to enable those who master it to "sell" their way through life successfully, with the minimum amount of resistance and friction. Such a course, therefore, must help the student organize and make use of much truth which is overlooked by the majority of people who go through life as mediocres.

Not all people are so constituted that they wish to know the truth about all matters vitally affecting life. One of the great surprises the author of this course has met with, in connection with his research activities, is that so few people are willing to hear the truth when it shows up their own weaknesses.

We prefer illusions to realities!

New truths, if accepted at all, are taken with the proverbial grain of salt. Some of us demand more than a mere pinch of salt; we demand enough to pickle new ideas so they become useless.

For these reasons the Introductory Lesson of this course, and this lesson as well, cover subjects intended to pave the way for new ideas so those ideas will not be too severe a shock to the mind of the student.

The thought the author wishes to "get across" has been quite plainly stated by the editor of the American Magazine, in an editorial which appeared in a recent issue, in the following words:

"On a recent rainy night, Carl Lomen, the reindeer king of Alaska, told me a true story. It has stuck in my crop ever since. And now I am going to pass it along.

"'A certain Greenland Eskimo,' said Lomen, 'was taken on one of the American North Polar expeditions a number of years ago. Later, as a reward for faithful service, he was brought to New York City for a short visit. At all the miracles of sight and sound he as filled with a most amazed wonder. When he returned to his native village he told stories of buildings that rose into the very face of the sky; of streetcars, which he described as houses that moved along the trail, with people living in them as they moved; of mammoth bridges, artificial lights, and all the other dazzling concomitants of the metropolis.

"'His people looked at him coldly and walked away. And forthwith throughout the whole village he was dubbed "Sagdluk," meaning "the Liar," and this name he carried in shame to his grave. Long before his death his original name was entirely forgotten.

"'When Knud Rasmussen made his trip from Greenland to Alaska he was accompanied by a Greenland Eskimo named Mitek (Eider Duck). Mitek visited Copenhagen and New York, where he saw many things for the first time and was greatly impressed. Later, upon his return to Greenland, he recalled the tragedy of Sagdluk, and decided that it would not be wise to tell the truth. Instead, he would narrate stories that his people could grasp, and thus save his reputation.

"'So he told them how he and Doctor Rasmussen maintained a kayak on the banks of a great river, the Hudson, and how, each morning, they paddled out for their hunting. Ducks, geese and seals were to be had a-plenty, and they enjoyed the visit immensely.

"'Mitek, in the eyes of his countrymen, is a very honest man. His neighbors treat him with rare respect.'

"The road of the truth-teller has always been rocky. Socrates sipping the hemlock, Stephen stoned, Bruno burned at the stake, Galileo terrified into retraction of his starry truths–forever could one follow that bloody trail through the pages of history.

"Something in human nature makes us resent the impact of new ideas."

We hate to be disturbed in the beliefs and prejudices that have been handed down with the family furniture. At maturity too many of us go into hibernation, and live off the fat of ancient fetishes. If a new idea invades our, den we rise up snarling from our winter sleep.

The Eskimos, at least, had some excuse. They were unable to visualize the startling pictures drawn by Sagdluk. Their simple lives had been too long circumscribed by the brooding arctic night.

But there is no adequate reason why the average man should ever close his mind to fresh "slants" on life. He does, just the same. Nothing is more tragic–or more common –than mental inertia. For every ten men who are physically lazy there are ten thousand with stagnant minds. And stagnant minds are the breeding places of fear.

An old farmer up in Vermont always used to wind up his prayers with this plea: "Oh, God, give me an open mind!" If more people followed his example they might escape being hamstrung by prejudices. And what a pleasant place to live in the world would be.

Every person should make it his business to gather new ideas from sources other than the environment in which he daily lives and works.

The mind becomes withered, stagnant, narrow and closed unless it searches for new ideas. The farmer should come to the city quite often, and walk among the strange faces and the tall buildings. He will go back to his farm, his mind refreshed, with more courage and greater enthusiasm.

The city man should take a trip to the country every so often and freshen his mind with sights new and different from those associated with his daily labors. Everyone needs a change of mental environment at regular periods, the same as a change and variety of food are essential. The mind becomes more alert, more elastic and more ready to work with speed and accuracy after it has been bathed in new ideas, outside of one's own field of daily labor.

As a student of this course you will temporarily lay aside the set of ideas with which you perform your daily labors, and enter a field of entirely new (and in some instances, heretofore unheard of) ideas.

Splendid! You will come out, at the other end of this course, with a new stock of ideas which will make you more efficient, more enthusiastic and more courageous, no matter in what sort of work you may be engaged.

Do not be afraid of new ideas! They may mean to you the difference between success and failure.

Some of the ideas introduced in this course will require no further explanation or proof of their soundness because they are familiar to practically everyone. Other ideas here introduced are new, and for that very reason many students of this philosophy may hesitate to accept them as sound.

Every principle described in this course has been thoroughly tested by the author, and the majority of the principles covered have been tested by scores of scientists and others who were quite capable of distinguishing between the merely theoretic and the practical.

For these reasons all principles here covered are known to be workable in the exact manner claimed for them. However, no student of this course is asked to accept any statement made in these lessons without having first satisfied himself or herself, by tests, experiments and analysis, that the statement is sound.

The major evil the student is requested to avoid is that of forming opinions without definite FACTS as the basis, which brings to mind Herbert Spencer's famous admonition, in these words

"There is a principle which is a bar against all information; which is proof against all argument; and which cannot fail to keep a man in everlasting ignorance. This principle is contempt prior to examination."

It may be well to bear this principle in mind when you come to study the Law of the Master Mind de scribed in these lessons. This law embodies an entirely new principle of mind operation, and, for this reason alone, it will be difficult for many students to accept it as sound until after they have experimented with it.

When the fact is considered, however, that the Law of the Master Mind is believed to be the real basis of most of the achievements of those who are considered geniuses, this Law takes on an aspect which calls for more than "snap-judgment" opinions.

It is believed by many scientific men whose opinions on the subject have been given the author of this philosophy, that the Law of the Master Mind is the basis of practically all of the more important achievements resulting from group or co-operative effort.

The late Dr. Alexander Graham Bell said he believed the Law of the Master Mind, as it has been described in this philosophy, was not only sound, but that all the higher institutions of learning would soon be teaching that Law as a part of their courses in psychology.

Charles P. Steinmetz said he had experimented with the Law and had arrived at the same conclusion as that stated in these lessons, long before he talked to the author of the Law of Success philosophy about the subject.

Luther Burbank and John Burroughs made similar statements.

Edison was never interrogated on the subject, but other statements of his indicate that he would endorse the Law as being a possibility, if not in fact a reality.

Dr. Elmer Gates endorsed the Law, in a conversation with this author more than fifteen years ago. Dr. Gates is a scientist of the highest order, ranking along with Steinmetz, Edison and Bell.

The author of this philosophy has talked to scores of intelligent business men who, while they were not scientists, admitted they believed in the soundness of the Law of the Master Mind. It is hardly excusable, therefore, for men of less ability to judge such matters, to form opinions as to this Law, without serious, systematic investigation.

Let me lay before you a brief outline of what this lesson is and what it is intended to do for you!

Having prepared myself for the practice of law I will offer this introduction as a "statement of my case." The evidence with which to back up my case will be presented in the sixteen lessons of which the course is composed.

The facts out of which this course has been prepared have been gathered through more than twenty-five years of business and professional experience, and my only explanation of the rather free use of the personal pronoun throughout the course is that I am writing from first-hand experience.

Before this Reading Course on the Law of Success was published the manuscripts were submitted to two prominent universities with the request that they be read by competent professors with the object of eliminating or correcting any statements that appeared to be unsound, from an economic viewpoint.

This request was complied with and the manuscripts were carefully examined, with the result that not a single change was made with the exception of one or two slight changes in wording.

One of the professors who examined the manuscripts expressed himself, in part, as follows: "It is a tragedy that every boy and girl who enters high school is not efficiently drilled on the fifteen major parts of your Reading Course on the Law of Success. It is regrettable that the great university with which I am connected, and every other university, does not include your course as a part of its curriculum."

Inasmuch as this Reading Course is intended as a map or blueprint that will guide you in the attainment of that coveted goal called "Success," may it not be well here to define success?

Success is the development of the power with which to get whatever one wants in life without interfering with the rights of others.

I would lay particular stress upon the word "power" because it is inseparably related to success. We are living in a world and during an age of intense competition, and the law of the survival of the fittest is everywhere in evidence. Because of these facts all who would enjoy enduring success must go about its attainment through the use of power.

And what is power?

Power is organized energy or effort. This course is properly called the Law of Success for the reason that it teaches how one may organize facts and knowledge and the faculties of one's mind into a unit of power.

This course brings you a definite promise, namely:

That through its mastery and application you can get whatever you want, with but two qualifying words - "within reason."

This qualification takes into consideration your education, your wisdom or your lack of it, your physical endurance, your temperament, and all of the other qualities mentioned in the sixteen lessons of this course as being the factors most essential in the attainment of success.

Without a single exception those who have attained unusual success have done so, either consciously or unconsciously, through the aid of all or a portion of the fifteen major factors of which this course is compiled. If you doubt this statement, then master these sixteen lessons so you can go about the analysis with reasonable accuracy and analyze such men as Carnegie, Rockefeller, Hill, Harriman, Ford and others of this type who have accumulated great fortunes of material wealth, and you will see that they understood and applied the principle of organized effort which runs, like a golden cord of indisputable evidence, throughout this course.

Nearly twenty years ago I interviewed Mr. Carnegie for the purpose of writing a story about him. During the interview I asked him to what he attributed his success. With a merry little twinkle in his eyes he said:

"Young man, before I answer your question will you please define your term 'success'?"

After waiting until he saw that I was somewhat embarrassed by his request he continued: "By success you have reference to my money, have you not?" I assured him that money was the term by which most people measured success, and he then said:

"Oh, well-if you wish to know how I got my money-if that is what you call success-I will answer your question by saying that we have a master mind here in our business, and that mind is made up of more than a score of men who constitute my personal staff of superintendents and managers and accountants and chemists and other necessary types. No one person in this group is the master mind of which I speak, but the sum total of the minds in the group, co-ordinated, organized and directed to a definite end in a spirit of harmonious co-operation is the power that got my money for me. No two minds in the group are exactly alike, but each man in the group does the thing that he is supposed to do and he does it better than any other person in the world could do it."

Then and there the seed out of which this course has been developed was sown in my mind, but that seed did not take root or germinate until later. This interview marked the beginning of years of research which led, finally, to the discovery of the principle of psychology described in the Introductory Lesson as the "Master Mind."

I heard all that Mr. Carnegie said, but it took the knowledge gained from many years of subsequent contact with the business world to enable me to assimilate that which he said and clearly grasp and understand the principle back of it, which was nothing more nor less than the principle of organized effort upon which this course on the Law of Success is founded.

Carnegie's group of men constituted a "Master Mind" and that mind was so well-organized, so well co-ordinated, so powerful, that it could have accumulated millions of dollars for Mr. Carnegie in practically any sort of endeavor of a commercial or industrial nature. The steel business in which that mind was engaged was but an incident in connection with the accumulation of the Carnegie wealth. The same wealth could have been accumulated had the "Master Mind" been directed in the coal business or the banking business or the grocery business, for the reason that back of the mind was power -that sort of power which you may have when you shall have organized the faculties of your own mind and allied yourself with other well organized minds for the attainment of a definite chief aim in life.

A careful check-up with several of Mr. Carnegie's former business associates, which was made after this course was begun, proves conclusively not only that there is such a law as that which has been called the "Master Mind," but that this law was the chief source of Mr. Carnegie's success.

Perhaps no man was ever associated with Mr. Carnegie who knew him better than did Mr. C. M. Schwab. In the following words Mr. Schwab has very accurately described that "subtle something" in Mr. Carnegie's personality which enabled him to rise to such stupendous heights.

"I never knew a man with so much imagination, lively intelligence and instinctive comprehension. You sensed that he probed your thoughts and took stock of everything

that you had ever done or might do. He seemed to catch at your next word before it was spoken. The play of his mind was dazzling and his habit of close observation gave him a store of knowledge about innumerable matters.

"But his outstanding quality, from so rich an endowment, was the power of inspiring other men. Confidence radiated from him. You might be doubtful about something and discuss the matter with Mr. Carnegie. In a flash he would make you see that it was right and then absolutely believe it; or he might settle your doubts by pointing out its weakness. This quality of attracting others, then spurring them on, arose from his own strength.

"The results of his leadership were remarkable. Never before inn history of industry, I imagine, was there a man who, without understanding his business in its working details, making no pretense of technical knowledge concerning steel or engineering, was yet able to build up such an enterprise.

"Mr. Carnegie's ability to inspire men rested on something deeper than any faculty of judgment."

In the last sentence Mr. Schwab has conveyed a thought which corroborates the theory of the "Master Mind" to which the author of this course has attributed the chief source of Mr. Carnegie's power.

Mr. Schwab has also confirmed the statement that Mr. Carnegie could have succeeded as well in any other business as he did in the steel business. It is obvious that his success was due to his understanding of his own mind and the minds of other men, and not to mere knowledge of the steel business itself.

This thought is most consoling to those who have not yet attained outstanding success, for it shows that success is solely a matter of correctly applying laws and principles which are available to all; and these laws, let us not forget, are fully described in the Sixteen Lessons of this course.

Mr. Carnegie learned how to apply the law of the "Master Mind." This enabled him to organize the faculties of his own mind and the faculties of other men's minds, and coordinate the whole behind a DEFINITE CHIEF AIM.

Every strategist, whether in business or war or industry or other callings, understands the value of organized, co-ordinated effort. Every military strategist understands the value of sowing seeds of dissension in the ranks of the opposing forces, because this breaks up the power of co-ordination back of the opposition. During the late world war much was heard about the effects of propaganda, and it seems not an exaggeration to say that the disorganizing forces of propaganda were much more destructive than were all the guns and explosives used in the war.

One of the most important turning-points of the world war came when the allied armies were placed under the direction of the French General, Foch. There are well-informed military men who claim that this was the move which spelled doom for the opposing armies.

Any modern railroad bridge is an excellent example of the value of organized effort, because it demonstrates quite simply and clearly how thousands of tons of weight may be borne by a comparatively small group of steel bars and beams so arranged that the weight is spread over the entire group.

There was a man who had seven sons who were always quarreling among themselves. One day he called them together and informed them that he wished to demonstrate just what their lack of co-operative effort meant. He had prepared a bundle of seven sticks which he had carefully tied together. One by one he asked his sons to take the bundle and break it. Each son tried, but in vain. Then he cut the strings and handed one of the sticks to each of his sons and asked him to break it over his knee. After the sticks had all been broken, with ease, he said:

"When you boys work together in a spirit of harmony you resemble the bundle of sticks, and no one can defeat you; but when you quarrel among yourselves anyone can defeat you one at a time."

There is a worthwhile lesson in this story of the man and his seven quarrelsome sons, and it may be applied to the people of a community, the employees and employers in a given place of employment, or to the state and nation in which we live.

Organized effort may be made a power, but it may also be a dangerous power unless guided with intelligence, which is the chief reason why the sixteenth lesson of this course is devoted largely to describing how to direct the power of organized effort so that it will lead to success; that sort of success which is founded upon truth and justice and fairness that lead to ultimate happiness.

One of the outstanding tragedies of this age of struggle and money-madness is the fact that so few people are engaged in the effort which they like best. One of the objects of this course is to help each student find his or her particular niche in the world's work, where both material prosperity and happiness in abundance may be found. For this purpose a Character Analysis Chart accompanies the sixteenth lesson. This chart is designed to help the student take inventory of himself and find out what latent ability and hidden forces lie sleeping within him.

This entire course is intended as a stimulus with which to enable you to see yourself and your hidden forces as they are, and to awaken in you the ambition and the vision and the determination to cause you to go forth and claim that which is rightfully yours.

Less than thirty years ago a man was working in the same shop with Henry Ford, doing practically the same sort of work that he was doing. It has been said that this man was really a more competent workman, in that particular sort of work, than Ford. Today this man is still engaged in the same sort of work, at wages of less than a hundred dollars a week, while Mr. Ford is the world's richest man.

What outstanding difference is there between these two men which has so widely separated them in terms of material wealth? Just this–Ford understood and applied the principle of organized effort while the other man did not.

That you may gain a still more concrete vision of just how this principle of organized effort can be made powerful, stop for a moment and allow your imagination to draw a picture of what would likely be the result if every newspaper and every Rotary Club and every Kiwanis Club and every Advertising Club and every Woman's Club and every other civic organization of a similar nature, in your city, or in any other city in the United States, should form an alliance for the purpose of pooling their power and using it for the benefit of all members of these organizations.

Power is organized effort, as has already been stated! Success is based upon power!

That you may have a clear conception of what is meant by the term "organized effort" I have made use of the foregoing illustrations, and for the sake of further emphasis I am going to repeat the statement that the accumulation of great wealth and the attainment of any high station in life such as constitute what we ordinarily call success, are based upon the vision to comprehend and the ability to assimilate and apply the major principles of the sixteen lessons of this course.

This course is in complete harmony with the principles of economics and the principles of Applied Psychology. You will observe that those lessons, which depend, for their practical application, upon knowledge of psychology, have been supplemented with sufficient explanation of the psychological principles involved to render the lessons easily understood.

Before the manuscripts for this course went to the publisher they were submitted to some of the foremost bankers and business men of America, that they might be examined, analyzed and criticized by the most practical type of mind. One of the best known bankers in New York City returned the manuscripts with the following comment:

"I hold a master's degree from Yale, but I would willingly exchange all that this degree has brought me in return for what your course on the Law of Success would have brought me had I been afforded the privilege of making it a part of my training while I was studying at Yale.

"My wife and daughter have also read the manuscripts, and my wife has named your course 'the master key-board of life' because she believes that all who understand how to apply it may play a perfect symphony in their respective callings, just as a pianist may play any tune when once the keyboard of the piano and the fundamentals of music have been mastered."

No two people on earth are exactly alike, and for this reason no two people would be expected to attain from this course the same viewpoint. Each student should read the course, understand it and then appropriate from its contents whatever he or she needs to develop a well-rounded personality.

Before this appropriation can be properly made it will be necessary for the student to analyze himself, through the use of the questionnaire that comes with the sixteenth lesson of the course, for the purpose of finding out what his deficiencies may be. This questionnaire should not be filled out until the student thoroughly masters the contents of the entire course, for he will then be in position to answer the questions with more accuracy and understanding of himself. Through the aid of this questionnaire an experienced character analyst can take inventory of one's faculties as easily and as accurately as a merchant can inventory the goods on his shelves.

This course has been compiled for the purpose of helping the student find out what are his or her natural talents, and for the purpose of helping organize, coordinate and put into use the knowledge gained from experience. For more than twenty years I have been gathering, classifying and organizing the material that has gone into the course. During the past fourteen years I have analyzed more than 16,000 men and women, and all of the vital facts gathered from these analyses have been carefully organized and woven into this course. These analyses brought out many interesting facts which have helped to make this course practical and usable. For example, it was discovered that ninety-five per cent of all who were analyzed were failures, and but five per cent were successes. (By the term "failure" is meant that they had failed to find happiness and the ordinary necessities of life without struggle that was almost unbearable.) Perhaps this is about the proportion of successes and failures that might be found if all the people of the world were accurately analyzed. The struggle for a mere existence is terrific among people who have not learned how to organize and direct their natural talents, while the attainment of those necessities, as well as the acquiring of many of the luxuries, is comparatively simple among those who have mastered the principle of organized effort.

One of the most startling facts brought to light by those 16,000 analyses was the discovery that the ninety-five per cent who were classed as failures were in that class because they had no definite chief aim in life, while the five per cent constituting the successful ones not only had purposes that were definite, but they had, also, definite plans for the attainment of their purposes.

Another important fact disclosed by these analyses was that the ninety-five per cent constituting the failures were engaged in work which they did not like, while the five per cent constituting the successful ones were doing that which they liked best. It is doubtful whether a person could be a failure while engaged in work which he liked best. Another vital fact learned from the analyses was that all of the five per cent who were succeeding had formed the habit of systematic saving of money, while the ninety-five per cent who were failures saved nothing. This is worthy of serious thought. One of the chief objects of this course is to aid the student in performing his or her chosen work in such a manner that it will yield the greatest returns in both money and happiness.

Definite Chief Aim

The key-note of this entire lesson may be found in the word "definite."

It is most appalling to know that ninety-five per cent of the people of the world are drifting aimlessly through life, without the slightest conception of the work for which they are best fitted, and with no conception whatsoever of even the need of such a thing as a definite objective toward which to strive.

There is a psychological as well as an economic reason for the selection of a definite chief aim in life. Let us devote our attention to the psychological side of the question first. It is a well-established principle of psychology that a person's acts are always in harmony with the dominating thoughts of his or her mind.

Any definite chief aim that is deliberately fixed in the mind and held there, with the determination to realize it, finally saturates the entire subconscious mind until it automatically influences the physical action of the body toward the attainment of that purpose.

Your definite chief aim in life should be selected with deliberate care, and after it has been selected it should be written out and placed where you will see it at least once a day, the psychological effect of which is to impress this purpose upon your subconscious mind so strongly that it accepts that purpose as a pattern or blueprint that will eventually dominate your activities in life and lead you, step by step, toward the attainment of the object back of that purpose.

The principle of psychology through which you can impress your definite chief aim upon your subconscious mind is called Auto-suggestion, or suggestion which you repeatedly make to yourself. It is a degree of self-hypnotism, but do not be afraid of it on that account, for it was this same principle through the aid of which Napoleon lifted himself from the lowly station of poverty-stricken Corsican to the dictatorship of France. It was through the aid of this same principle that Thomas A. Edison has risen from the lowly beginning of a news butcher to where he is accepted as the leading inventor of the world. It was through the aid of this same principle that Lincoln bridged the mighty chasm between his lowly birth, in a log cabin in the mountains of Kentucky, and the presidency of the greatest nation on earth. It was through the aid of this same principle that Theodore Roosevelt became one of the most aggressive leaders that ever reached the presidency of the United States.

You need have no fear of the principle of Auto-suggestion as long as you are sure that the objective for which you are striving is one that will bring you happiness of an enduring nature. Be sure that your definite purpose is constructive; that its attainment will bring hardship and misery to no one; that it will bring you peace and prosperity, then apply, to the limit of your understanding, the principle of self-suggestion for the speedy attainment of this purpose.

On the street corner, just opposite the room in which I am writing, I see a man who stands there all day long and sells peanuts. He is busy every minute. When not actually engaged in making a sale he is roasting and packing the peanuts in little bags. He is one of that great army constituting the ninety-five per cent who have no definite purpose in life. He is selling peanuts, not because he likes that work better than anything else he might do, but because he never sat down and thought out a definite purpose that would bring him greater returns for his labor. He is selling peanuts because he is a drifter on the sea of life, and one of the tragedies of his work is the fact that the same amount of effort that he puts into it, if directed along other lines, would bring him much greater returns.

Another one of the tragedies of this man's work is the fact that he is unconsciously making use of the principle of self-suggestion, but he is doing it to his own disadvantage. No doubt, if a picture could be made of his thoughts, there would be nothing in that picture except a peanut roaster, some little paper bags and a crowd of people buying peanuts. This man could get out of the peanut business if he had the vision and the ambition first to imagine himself in a more profitable calling, and the perseverance to hold that picture before his mind until it influenced him to take the necessary steps to enter a more profitable calling. He puts sufficient labor into his work to bring him a substantial return if that labor were directed toward the attainment of a definite purpose that offered bigger returns.

One of my closest personal friends is one of the best known writers and public speakers of this country. About ten years ago he caught sight of the possibilities of this principle of self-suggestion and began, immediately, to harness it and put it to work. He worked out a plan for its application that proved to be very effective. At that time he was neither a writer nor a speaker.

Each night, just before going to sleep, he would shut his eyes and see, in his imagination, a long council table at which he placed (in his imagination) certain well-known men whose characteristics he wished to absorb into his own personality. At the end of the table he placed Lincoln, and on either side of the table he placed Napoleon, Washington, Emerson and Elbert Hubbard. He then proceeded to talk to these imaginary figures that he had seated at his imaginary council table, something after this manner:

Mr. Lincoln: I desire to build in my own character those qualities of patience and fairness toward all mankind and the keen sense of humor which were your outstanding characteristics. I need these qualities and I shall not be contented until I have developed them.

Mr. Washington: I desire to build in my own character those qualities of patriotism and self-sacrifice and leadership which were your outstanding characteristics.

Mr. Emerson: I desire to build in my own character those qualities of vision and the ability to interpret the laws of Nature as written in the rocks of prison walls and growing trees and flowing brooks and growing flowers and the faces of little children, which were your outstanding characteristics.

Napoleon: I desire to build in my own character those qualities of self-reliance and the strategic ability to master obstacles and profit by mistakes and develop strength out of defeat, which were your outstanding characteristics.

Mr. Hubbard: I desire to develop the ability to equal and even to excel the ability that you possessed with which to express yourself in clear, concise and forceful language.

Night after night, for many months, this man saw these men seated around that imaginary council table until finally he had imprinted their outstanding characteristics upon his own subconscious mind so clearly that he began to develop a personality which was a composite of their personalities.

The subconscious mind may be likened to a magnet, and when it has been vitalized and thoroughly saturated with any definite purpose it has a decided tendency to attract all that is necessary for the fulfillment of that purpose. Like attracts like, and you may see evidence of this law in every blade of grass and every growing tree. The acorn attracts from the soil and the air the necessary materials out of which to grow an oak tree. It never grows a tree that is part oak and part poplar. Every grain of wheat that is planted in the soil attracts the materials out of which to grow a stalk of wheat.

It never makes a mistake and grows both oats and wheat on the same stalk.

And men are subject, also, to this same Law of Attraction. Go into any cheap boarding house district in any city and there you will find people of the same general trend of mind associated together. On the other hand, go into any prosperous community and there you will find people of the same general tendencies associated together. Men who are successful always seek the company of others who are successful, while men who are on the ragged side of life always seek the company of those who are in similar circumstances. "Misery loves company."

Water seeks its level with no finer certainty than man seeks the company of those who occupy his own general status financially and mentally. A professor of Yale University and an illiterate hobo have nothing in common. They would be miserable if thrown together for any great length of time. Oil and water will mix as readily as will men who have nothing in common.

All of which leads up to this statement:

That you will attract to you people who harmonize with your own philosophy of life, whether you wish it or not. This being true, can you not see the importance of vitalizing your mind with a definite chief aim that will attract to you people who will be of help to you and not a hindrance? Suppose your definite chief aim is far above your present station in life. What of it? It is your privilege–nay, your DUTY, to aim high in life. You owe it to yourself and to the community in which you live to set a high standard for yourself.

There is much evidence to justify the belief that nothing within reason is beyond the possibility of attainment by the man whose definite chief aim has been well developed.

Some years ago Louis Victor Eytinge was given a life sentence in the Arizona penitentiary. At the time of his imprisonment he was an all-around "bad man," according to his own admissions. In addition to this it was believed that he would die of tuberculosis within a year.

Eytinge had reason to feel discouraged, if anyone ever had. Public feeling against him was intense and he did not have a single friend in the world who came forth and offered him encouragement or help. Then something happened in his own mind that gave him back his health, put the dreaded "white plague" to rout and finally unlocked the prison gates and gave him his freedom.

What was that "something"?

Just this: He made up his mind to whip the white plague and regain his health. That was a very definite chief aim. In less than a year from the time the decision was made he had won. Then he extended that definite chief aim by making up his mind to gain his freedom. Soon the prison walls melted from around him.

No undesirable environment is strong enough to hold the man or woman who understands how to apply the principle of Auto-suggestion in the creation of a definite chief aim. Such a person can throw off the shackles of poverty; destroy the most deadly disease germs; rise from a lowly station in life to power and plenty.

All great leaders base their leadership upon a definite chief aim. Followers are willing followers when they know that their leader is a person with a definite chief aim who has the courage to back up that purpose with action. Even a balky horse knows when a driver with a definite chief aim takes hold of the reins; and yields to that driver. When a man with a definite chief aim starts through a crowd everybody stands aside and makes a way for him, but let a man hesitate and show by his actions that he is not sure which way he wants to go and the crowd will step all over his toes and refuse to budge an inch out of his way.

Nowhere is the lack of a definite chief aim more noticeable or more detrimental than it is in the relationship between parent and child. Children sense very quickly the wavering attitude of their parents and take advantage of that attitude quite freely. It is the same all through life–men with a definite chief aim command respect and attention at all times.

So much for the psychological viewpoint of a definite purpose. Let us now turn to the economic side of the question.

If a steamship lost its rudder, in mid-ocean, and began circling around, it would soon exhaust its fuel supply without reaching shore, despite the fact that it would use up enough energy to carry it to shore and back several times.

The man who labors without a definite purpose that is backed up by a definite plan for its attainment, resembles the ship that has lost its rudder. Hard labor and good intentions are not sufficient to carry a man through to success,.for how may a man be sure that he has attained success unless he has established in his mind some definite object that he wishes?

Every well-built house started in the form of a definite purpose plus a definite plan in the nature of a set of blueprints. Imagine what would happen if one tried to build a house by the haphazard method, without plans. Workmen would be in each other's way, building material would be piled all over the lot before the foundation was completed, and everybody on the job would have a different notion as to how the house ought to be built. Result, chaos and misunderstandings and cost that would be prohibitive.

Yet had you ever stopped to think that most people finish school, take up employment or enter a trade or profession without the slightest conception of anything that even remotely resembles a definite purpose or a definite plan? In view of the fact that science has provided reasonably accurate ways and means of analyzing character and determining the life-work for which people are best fitted, does it not seem a modern tragedy that ninety-five per cent of the adult population of the world is made up of men and women who are failures because they have not found their proper niches in the world's work?

If success depends upon power, and if power is organized effort, and if the first step in the direction of organization is a definite purpose, then one may easily see why such a purpose is essential.

Until a man selects a definite purpose in life he dissipates his energies and spreads his thoughts over so many subjects and in so many different directions that they lead not to power, but to indecision and weakness.

With the aid of a small reading glass you can teach yourself a great lesson on the value of organized effort. Through the use of such a glass you can focus the sun-rays on a definite spot so strongly that they will bum a hole through a plank. Remove the glass (which represents the definite purpose) and the same rays of sun may shine on that same plank for a million years without burning it.

A thousand electric dry batteries, when properly organized and connected together with wires, will produce enough power to run a good sized piece of machinery for several hours, but take those same cells singly, disconnected, and not one of them would exert enough energy to turn the machinery over once. The faculties of your mind might properly be likened to those dry cells. When you organize your faculties, according to the plan laid down in the sixteen lessons of this Reading Course on the Law of Success, and direct them toward the attainment of a definite purpose in life, you then take advantage of the co-operative or accumulative principle out of which power is developed, which is called Organized Effort.

Andrew Carnegie's advice was this: "Place all your eggs in one basket and then watch the basket to see that no one kicks it over." By that advice he meant, of course, that we should not dissipate any of our energies by engaging in side lines. Carnegie was a sound economist and he knew that most men would do well if they so harnessed and directed their energies that some one thing would be done well.

When the plan back of this Reading Course was first born I remember taking the first manuscript to a professor of the University of Texas, and in a spirit of enthusiasm I suggested to him that I had discovered a principle that would be of aid to me in every public speech I delivered thereafter, because I would be better prepared to organize and marshal my thoughts.

He looked at the outline of the fifteen points for a few minutes, then turned to me and said:

"Yes, your discovery is going to help you make better speeches, but that is not all it will do. It will help you become a more effective writer, for I have noticed in your previous writings a tendency to scatter your thoughts. For instance, if you started to describe a beautiful mountain yonder in the distance you would be apt to sidetrack your description by calling attention to a beautiful bed of wild flowers, or a running brook, or a singing bird, detouring here and there, zigzag fashion, before finally arriving at the proper point from which to view the mountain. In the future you are going to find it much less difficult to describe an object, whether you are speaking or writing, because your fifteen points represent the very foundation of organization." A man who had no legs once met a man who was blind. To prove conclusively that the lame man was a man of vision he proposed to the blind man that they form an alliance that would be of great benefit to both. "You let me climb upon your back," said he to the blind man, "then I will use your legs and you may use my eyes. Between the two of us we will get along more rapidly."

Out of allied effort comes greater power. This is a point that is worthy of much repetition, because it forms one of the most important parts of the foundation of this Reading Course. The great fortunes of the world have been accumulated through the use of this principle of allied effort. That which one man can accomplish single handed, during an entire life-time, is but meagre at best, no matter how well organized that man may be, but that which one man may accomplish through the principle of alliance with other men is practically without limitation.

That "master mind" to which Carnegie referred during MY interview with him was made up of more than a score of minds. In that group were men of practically every temperament and inclination. Each man was there to play a certain part and he did nothing else. There was perfect understanding and teamwork between these men. It was Carnegie's business to keep harmony among them.

And he did it wonderfully well.

If you are familiar with the game of football you know, of course, that the winning team is the one that best co-ordinates the efforts of its players. Team-work is the thing that wins. It is the same in the great game of life.

In your struggle for success you should keep constantly in mind the necessity of knowing what it is that you want–of knowing precisely what is your definite purpose– and the value of the principle of organized effort in the attainment of that which constitutes your definite purpose.

In a vague sort of way nearly everyone has a definite purpose–namely, the desire for money! But this is not a definite purpose within the meaning of the term as it is used in this lesson. Before your purpose could be considered definite, even though that purpose were the accumulation of money, you would have to reach a decision as to the precise method through which you intend to accumulate that money. It would be insufficient for you to say that you would make money by going into some sort of business. You would have to decide just what line of business. You would also have to decide just where you would locate. You would also have to decide the business policies under which you would conduct your business.

In answering the question, "What Is Your Definite Purpose In Life?" that appears in the questionnaire which I have used for the analysis of more than 16,000 people, many answered as follows:

"My definite purpose in life is to be of as much service to the world as possible and earn a good living."

That answer is about as definite as a frog's conception of the size of the universe is accurate!

The object of this lesson is not to inform you as to what your life-work should be, for indeed this could be done with accuracy only after you had been completely analyzed, but it is intended as a means of impressing upon your mind a clear conception of the value of a definite purpose of some nature, and of the value of understanding the principle of organized effort as a means of attaining the necessary power with which to materialize your definite purpose.

Careful observation of the business philosophy of more than one hundred men and women who have attained outstanding success in their respective callings, disclosed the fact that each was a person of prompt and definite decision.

The habit of working with a definite chief aim will breed in you the habit of prompt decision, and this habit will come to your aid in all that you do.

Moreover, the habit of working with a definite chief aim will help you to concentrate all your attention on any given task until you have mastered it.

Concentration of effort and the habit of working with a definite chief aim are two of the essential factors in success which are always found together. One leads to the other. The best known successful business men were all men of prompt decision who worked always with one main, outstanding purpose as their chief aim.

Some Notable Examples Are as Follows:

Woolworth chose, as his definite chief aim, the belting of America with a chain of Five and Ten Cent Stores, and concentrated his mind upon this one task until he "made it and it made him."

Wrigley concentrated his mind on the production and sale of a five-cent package of chewing gum and turned this one idea into millions of dollars.

Edison concentrated upon the work of harmonizing natural laws and made his efforts uncover more useful inventions than any other man who ever lived.

Henry L. Doherty concentrated upon the building and operation of public utility plants and made himself a multimillionaire.

Ingersoll concentrated on a dollar watch and girdled the earth with "tickers" and made this one idea yield him a fortune.

Statler concentrated on "homelike hotel-service" and made himself wealthy as well as useful to millions of people who use his service.

Edwin C. Barnes concentrated on the sale of Edison Dictating Machines, and retired, while still a young man, with more money than he needs.

Woodrow Wilson concentrated his mind on the White House for twenty-five years, and became its chief tenant, thanks to his knowledge of the value of sticking to a definite chief aim.

Lincoln concentrated his mind on freeing the slaves and became our greatest American President while doing it.

Martin W. Littleton heard a speech which filled him with the desire to become a great lawyer, concentrated his mind on that one aim, and is now said to be the most successful lawyer in America, whose fees for a single case seldom fall below $50,000.00.

Rockefeller concentrated on oil and became the richest man of his generation.

Ford concentrated on "flivvers" and made himself the richest and most powerful man who ever lived.

Carnegie concentrated on steel and made his efforts build a great fortune and plastered his name on public libraries throughout America.

Gillette concentrated on a safety razor, gave the entire world a "close shave" and made himself a multimillionaire.

George Eastman concentrated on the kodak and made the idea yield him a fortune while bringing much pleasure to millions of people.

Russell Conwell concentrated on one simple lecture, "Acres of Diamonds," and made the idea yield more than $6,000,000.

Hearst concentrated on sensational newspapers and made the idea worth millions of dollars.

Helen Keller concentrated on learning to speak, and, despite the fact that she was deaf, dumb and blind, realized her definite chief aim.

John H. Patterson concentrated on cash registers and made himself rich and others "careful."

The late Kaiser of Germany concentrated on war and got a big dose of it, let us not forget the fact!

Fleischmann concentrated on the humble little cake of yeast and made things hump themselves all over the world.

Marshall Field concentrated on the world's greatest retail store and lo! It rose before him, a reality.

Philip Armour concentrated on the butchering business and established a great industry, as well as a big fortune.

Millions of people are concentrating, daily, on POVERTY and FAILURE and getting both in overabundance.

Wright Brothers concentrated on the airplane and mastered the air.

Pullman concentrated on the sleeping car and the idea made him rich and millions of people comfortable in travel.

The Anti-Saloon League concentrated on the Prohibition Amendment and (whether for better or worse) made it a reality.

Thus it will be seen that all who succeed work with some definite, outstanding aim as the object of their labors.

There is some one thing that you can do better than anyone else in the world could do it. Search until you find out what this particular line of endeavor is, make it the object of your definite chief aim and then organize all of your forces and attack it with the belief that you are going to win. In your search for the work for which you are best fitted, it will be well if you bear in mind the fact that you will most likely attain the greatest success by finding out what work you like best, for it is a well known fact that a man generally best succeeds in the particular line of endeavor into which he can throw his whole heart and soul.

Let us go back, for the sake of clarity and emphasis, to the psychological principles upon which this lesson is founded, because it will mean a loss that you can ill afford if you fail to grasp the real reason for establishing a definite chief aim in your mind.

These principles are as follows:

First: Every voluntary movement of the human body is caused, controlled and directed by thought, through the operation of the mind.

Second: The presence of any thought or idea in your consciousness tends to produce an associated feeling and to urge you to transform that feeling into appropriate muscular action that is in perfect harmony with the nature of the thought.

For example, if you think of winking your eyelid and there are no counter influences or thoughts in your mind at the time to arrest action, the motor nerve will carry your thought from the seat of government, in your brain, and appropriate or corresponding muscular action takes place immediately.

Stating this principle from another angle: You choose, for example, a definite purpose as your lifework and make up your mind that you will carry out that purpose. From the very moment that you make this choice, this purpose becomes the dominating thought in your consciousness, and you are constantly on the alert for facts, information and knowledge with which to achieve that purpose. From the time that you plant a definite purpose in your mind, your mind begins, both consciously and unconsciously, to gather and store away the material with which you are to accomplish that purpose.

Desire is the factor which determines what your definite purpose in life shall be. No one can select your dominating desire for you, but once you select it yourself it becomes your definite chief aim and occupies the spotlight of your mind until it is satisfied by transformation into reality, unless you permit it to be pushed aside by conflicting desires.

To emphasize the principle that I am here trying to make clear, I believe it not unreasonable to suggest that to be sure of successful achievement, one's definite chief aim in life should be backed up with a burning desire for its achievement. I have noticed that boys and girls who enter college and pay their way through by working seem to get more out of their schooling than do those whose expenses are paid for them. The secret of this may be found in the fact that those who are willing to work their way through are blessed with a burning desire for education, and such a desire, if the object of the desire is within reason, is practically sure of realization.

Science has established, beyond the slightest room for doubt, that through the principle of Auto-suggestion any deeply rooted desire saturates the entire body and mind with the nature of the desire and literally transforms the mind into a powerful magnet that will attract the object of the desire, if it be within reason. For the enlightenment of those who might not properly interpret the meaning of this statement I will endeavor to state this principle in another way. For example, merely desiring an automobile will not cause that automobile to come rolling in, but, if there is a burning desire for an automobile, that desire will lead to the appropriate action through which an automobile may be paid for.

Merely desiring freedom would never release a man who was confined in prison if it were not sufficiently strong to cause him to do something to entitle himself to freedom. These are the steps leading from desire to fulfillment: First the burning desire, then the crystallization of that desire into a definite purpose, then sufficient appropriate action to achieve that purpose. Remember that these three steps are always necessary to insure success.

I once knew a very poor girl who had a burning desire for a wealthy husband, and she finally got him, but not without having transformed that desire into the development of a very attractive personality which, in turn, attracted the desired husband. I once had a burning desire to be able to analyze character accurately and that desire was so persistent and so deeply seated that it practically drove me into ten years of research and study of men and women.

George S. Parker makes one of the best fountain pens in the world, and despite the fact that his business is conducted from the little city of Janesville, Wisconsin, he has spread his product all the way around the globe and he has his pen on sale in every civilized country in the world. More than twenty years ago, Mr. Parker's definite purpose was established in his mind, and that purpose was to produce the best fountain pen that money could buy. He backed that purpose with a burning desire for its realization and if you carry a fountain pen the chances are that you have evidence in your own possession that it has brought him abundant success.

You are a contractor and builder, and, like men who build houses out of mere wood and brick and steel, you must draw up a set of plans after which to shape your success building. You are living in a wonderful age, when the materials that go into success are plentiful and cheap. You have at your disposal, in the archives of the public libraries, the carefully compiled results of two thousand years of research covering practically every possible line of endeavor in which one would wish to engage. If you would become a preacher you have at hand the entire history of what has been learned by men who have preceded you in this field. If you would become a mechanic you have at hand the entire history of the inventions of machines and the discovery and usages of metals and things metallic in nature. If you would become a lawyer you have at your disposal the entire history of law procedure. Through the Department of Agriculture, at Washington, you have at your disposal all that has been learned about farming and agriculture, where you may use it should you wish to find your life-work in this field.

The world was never so resplendent with opportunity as it is today. On every hand there is an ever-increasing demand for the services of the man or the woman who makes a better mouse-trap or performs better stenographic service or preaches a better sermon or digs a better ditch or runs a more accommodating bank.

This lesson will not be completed until you shall have made your choice as to what your definite chief aim in life is to be and then recorded a description of that purpose in writing and placed it where you may see it every morning when you arise and every night when you retire.

Procrastination is–but why preach about it? You know that you are the hewer of your own wood and the drawer of your own water and the shaper of your own definite chief aim in life; therefore, why dwell upon that which you already know?

A definite purpose is something that you must create for yourself. No one else will create it for you and it will not create itself. What are you going to do about it? and when? and how?

Start now to analyze your desires and find out what it is that you wish, then make up your mind to get it. Lesson Three will point out to you the next step and show you how to proceed. Nothing is left to chance, in this Reading Course. Every step is marked plainly. Your part is to follow the directions until you arrive at your destination, which is represented by your definite chief aim. Make that aim clear and back it up with persistence which does not recognize the word "impossible."

When you come to select your definite chief aim just keep in mind the fact that you cannot aim too high.

Also keep in mind the never-varying truth that you'll get nowhere if you start nowhere. If your aim in life is vague your achievements will also be vague, and it might well be added, very meager. Know what you want, when you want it, why you want it and HOW you intend to get it. This is known to teachers and students of psychology as the WWWH formula- "what, when, why and how."

Read this lesson four times, at intervals of one week apart.

You will see much in the lesson the fourth time you read it that you did not see the first time.

Your success in mastering this course and in making it bring you success will depend very largely, if not entirely, upon how well you follow ALL the instructions it contains.

Do not set up your own rules of study. Follow those laid down in the Course, as they are the result of years of thought and experimentation. If you wish to experiment wait until you master this course in the manner suggested by its author. You will then be in position to experiment more safely. For the present content yourself by being the student. You will, let us hope, become the teacher as well as the student after you have followed the Course until you have mastered it.

If you follow the instructions laid down in this Course for the guidance of its students, you can no more fail than water can run uphill above the level of its source.

INSTRUCTIONS FOR APPLYING THE PRINCIPLES OF THIS LESSON

Through the Introductory Lesson of this course you became familiar with the principle of psychology known as the "Master Mind."

You are now ready to begin use of this principle as a means of transforming your definite chief aim into reality. It must have occurred to you that one might as well have no definite chief aim unless one has, also, a very definite and practical plan for making that aim become a reality.

Your first step is to decide what your major aim in life shall be. Your next step is to write out a clear, concise statement of this aim. This should be followed by a statement, in writing, of the plan or plans through which you intend to attain the object of your aim.

Your next and final step will be the forming of an alliance with some person or persons who will cooperate with you in carrying out these plans and transforming your definite chief aim into reality.

The purpose of this friendly alliance is to employ the law of the "Master Mind" in support of your plans. The alliance should be made between yourself and those who have your highest and best interests at heart. If you are a married man your wife should be one of the members of this alliance, providing there exists between you a normal state of confidence and sympathy. Other members of this alliance may be your mother, father, brothers or sisters, or some close friend or friends.

If you are a single person your sweetheart, if you have one, should become a member of your alliance. This is no joke-you are now studying one of the most powerful laws of the human mind, and you will serve your own best interests by seriously and earnestly following the rules laid down in this lesson, even though you may not be sure where they will lead you.

Those who join with you in the formation of a friendly alliance for the purpose of aiding you in the creation of a "Master Mind" should sign, with you, your statement of the object of your definite chief aim. Every member of your alliance must be fully acquainted with the nature of your object in forming the alliance. Moreover, every member must be in hearty accord with this object, and in full sympathy with you. Each member of your alliance must be supplied with a written copy of your statement of your definite chief aim. With this exception, however, you are explicitly instructed to keep the object of your chief aim to yourself. The world is full of "Doubting Thomases" and it will do your cause no good to have these rattle-brained people scoffing at you and your ambitions. Remember, what you need is friendly encouragement and help, not derision and doubt.

If you believe in prayer you are instructed to make your definite chief aim the object of your prayer at, least once every twenty-four hours, and more often if convenient. If you believe there is a God who can and will aid those who are earnestly striving to be of constructive service in the world, surely you feel that you have a right to petition Him for aid in the attainment of what should be the most important thing in life to you.

If those who have been invited to join your friendly alliance believe in prayer, ask them, also, to include the object of this alliance as a part of their daily prayer.

Comes, now, one of the most essential rules which you must follow. Arrange with one or all of the members of your friendly alliance to state to you, in the most positive and definite terms at their command, that THEY KNOW YOU CAN AND WILL REALIZE THE OBJECT OF YOUR DEFINITE CHIEF AIM. This affirmation or statement should be made to you at least once a day; more often if possible.

These steps must be followed persistently, with full faith that they will lead you where you wish to go! It will not suffice to carry out these plans for a few days or a few weeks and then discontinue them. YOU MUST FOLLOW THE DESCRIBED PROCEDURE. UNTIL YOU ATTAIN THE OBJECT OF YOUR DEFINITE CHIEF AIM, REGARDLESS OF THE TIME REQUIRED.

From time to time it may become necessary to change the plans you have adopted for the achievement of the object of your definite chief aim. Make these changes without hesitation. No human being has sufficient foresight to build plans which need no alteration or change.

If any member of your friendly alliance loses faith in the law known as the "Master Mind," immediately remove that member and replace him or her with some other person.

Andrew Carnegie stated to the author of this course that he had found it necessary to replace some of the members of his "Master Mind." In fact he stated that practically every member of whom his alliance was originally composed had, in time, been removed and replaced with some other person who could adapt himself more loyally and enthusiastically to the spirit and object of the alliance.

You cannot succeed when surrounded by disloyal and unfriendly associates, no matter what may be the object of your definite chief aim. Success is built upon loyalty, faith, sincerity, co-operation and the other positive forces with which one must surcharge his environment.

Many of the students of this course will want to form friendly alliances with those with whom they are associated professionally or in business, with the object of achieving success in their business or profession. In such cases the same rules of procedure which have been here described should be followed. The object of your definite chief aim may be one that will benefit you individually, or it may be one that will benefit the business or profession with which you are connected. The law of the "Master Mind" will work the same in either case. If you fail, either temporarily or permanently, in the application of this law it will be for the reason that some member of your alliance did not enter into the spirit of the alliance with faith, loyalty and sincerity of purpose.

The last sentence is worthy of a second reading!

The object of your definite chief aim should become your "hobby." You should ride this "hobby" continuously; you should sleep with it, eat with it, play with it, work with it, live with it and THINK with it.

Whatever you want you may get if you want it with sufficient intensity, and keep on wanting it, providing the object wanted is one within reason, and you ACTUALLY BELIEVE YOU WILL GET IT. There is a difference, however, between merely "wishing" for something and ACTUALLY BELIEVING you will get it. Lack of understanding of this difference has meant failure to millions of people. The "doers" are the "believers" in all walks of life. Those who BELIEVE they can achieve the object of their definite chief aim do not recognize the word impossible. Neither do they acknowledge temporary defeat. They KNOW they are going to succeed, and if one plan fails they quickly replace it with another plan.

Every noteworthy achievement met with some sort of temporary setback before success came. Edison made more than ten thousand experiments before he succeeded in making the first talking machine record the words, "Mary had a little lamb."

If there is one word which should stand out in your mind in connection with this lesson, it is the word PERSISTENCE!

You now have within your possession the pass-key to achievement. You have but to unlock the door to the Temple of Knowledge and walk in. But you must go to the Temple; it will not come to you. If these laws are new to you the "going" will not be easy at first. You will stumble many times, but keep moving. Very soon you will come to the brow of the mountain you have been climbing, and you will behold, in the valleys below, the rich estate of KNOWLEDGE which shall be your reward for your faith and efforts.

Everything has a price. There is no such possibility as "something for nothing." In your experiments with the Law of the Master Mind you are jockeying with Nature, in her highest and noblest form. Nature cannot be tricked or cheated. She will give up to you the object of your struggles only after you have paid her price, which is CONTINUOUS, UNYIELDING, PERSISTENT EFFORT! What more could be said on this subject?

You have been shown what to do, when to do it, how to do it and why you should do it. If you will master the next lesson, on Self-confidence, you will then have the faith in yourself to enable you to carry out the instructions laid down for your guidance in this lesson.

Master of human destinies am I!
Fame, love, and fortune on my footsteps wait.
Cities and fields I walk; I penetrate
Deserts and seas remote, and passing by
Hovel and mart and palace–soon or late
I knock, unbidden, once at every gate!
If sleeping, wake–if feasting, rise before
I turn away. It is the hour of fate,
And they who follow me reach every state
Mortals desire, and conquer every foe
Save death; but those who doubt or hesitate,
Condemned to failure, penury, and woe,
Seek me in vain and uselessly implore.
I answer not, and I return no more! – **INGALLS.**

Lesson Three: SELF-CONFIDENCE

Before approaching the fundamental principles upon which this lesson is founded it will be of benefit to you to keep in mind the fact that it is practical; that it brings you the discoveries of more than twenty-five years of research; that it has the approval of the leading scientific men and women of the world who have tested every principle involved.

Skepticism is the deadly enemy of progress and self-development. You might as well lay this book aside and stop right here as to approach this lesson with the feeling that it was written by some long-haired theorist who had never tested the principles upon which the lesson is based.

Surely this is no age for the skeptic, because it is an age in which we have seen more of Nature's laws uncovered and harnessed than had been discovered in all past history of the human race. Within three decades we have witnessed the mastery of the air; we have explored the ocean; we have all but annihilated distances on the earth; we have harnessed the lightning and made it turn the wheels of industry; we have made seven blades of grass grow where but one grew before; we have instantaneous communication between the nations of the world. Truly, this is an age of illumination and unfoldment, but we have as yet barely scratched the surface of knowledge. However, when we shall have unlocked the gate that leads to the secret power which is stored up within us it will bring us knowledge that will make all past discoveries pale into oblivion by comparison.

Thought is the most highly organized form of energy known to man, and this is an age of experimentation and research that is sure to bring us into greater understanding of that mysterious force called thought, which reposes within us. We have already found out enough about the human mind to know that a man may throw off the accumulated effects of a thousand generations of fear, through the aid of the principle of Autosuggestion. We have already discovered the fact that fear is the chief reason for poverty and failure and misery that takes on a thousand different forms. We have already discovered the fact that the man who masters fear may march on to successful achievement in practically any undertaking, despite all efforts to defeat him. The development of self-confidence starts with the elimination of this demon called fear, which sits upon a man's shoulder and whispers into his ear, "You can't do it–you are afraid to try–you are afraid of public opinion–you are afraid that you will fail–you are afraid you have not the ability."

This fear demon is getting into close quarters. Science has found a deadly weapon with which to put it to flight, and this lesson on self-confidence has brought you this weapon for use in your battle with the world-old enemy of progress, fear. THE SIX BASIC FEARS OF MANKIND: Every person falls heir to the influence of six basic fears. Under these six fears may be listed the lesser fears. The six basic or major fears are here enumerated and the sources from which they are believed to have grown are described.

The six basic fears are:

- a) The fear of Poverty
- b) The fear of Old Age
- c) The fear of Criticism
- d) The fear of Loss of Love of Someone.
- e) The fear of Ill Health
- f) The fear of Death.

Study the list, then take inventory of your own fears and ascertain under which of the six headings you can classify them.

Every human being who has reached the age of understanding is bound down, to some extent, by one or more of these six basic fears. As the first step in the elimination of these six evils let us examine the sources from whence we inherited them.

PHYSICAL AND SOCIAL HEREDITY

All that man is, both physically and mentally, he came by through two forms of heredity. One is known as physical heredity and the other is called social heredity. Through the law of physical heredity man has slowly evolved from the amoeba (a single-cell animal form), through stages of development corresponding to all the known animal forms now on this earth, including those which are known to have existed but which are now extinct.

Every generation through which man has passed has added to his nature something of the traits, habits and physical appearance of that generation. Man's physical inheritance, therefore, is a heterogeneous collection of many habits and physical forms. There seems little, if any, doubt that while the six basic fears of man could not have been inherited through physical heredity (these six basic fears being mental states of mind and therefore not capable of transmission through physical heredity), it is obvious that through physical heredity a most favorable lodging place for these six fears has been provided.

For example, it is a well-known fact that the whole process of physical evolution is based upon death, destruction, pain and cruelty; that the elements of the soil of the earth find transportation, in their upward climb through evolution, based upon the death of one form of life in order that another and higher form may subsist. All vegetation lives by "eating" the elements of the soil and the elements of the air. All forms of animal life live by "eating" some other and weaker form, or some form of vegetation.

The cells of all vegetation have a very high order of intelligence. The cells of all animal life likewise have a very high order of intelligence.

Undoubtedly the animal cells of a fish have learned, out of bitter experience, that the group of animal cells known as a fish hawk are to be greatly feared. By reason of the fact that many animal forms (including that of most men) live by eating the smaller and weaker animals, the "cell intelligence" of these animals which enter into and become a part of man brings with it the FEAR growing out of their experience in having been eaten alive.

This theory may seem to be far-fetched, and in fact it may not be true, but it is at least a logical theory if it is nothing more. The author makes no particular point of this theory, nor does he insist that it accounts for any of the six basic fears. There is another, and a much better explanation of the source of these fears, which we will proceed to examine, beginning with a description of social heredity.

By far the most important part of man's make-up comes to him through the law of social heredity, this term having reference to the methods by which one generation imposes upon the minds of the generation under its immediate control the superstitions, beliefs, legends and ideas which it, in turn, inherited from the generation preceding. The term "social heredity" should be understood to mean any and all sources through which a person acquires knowledge, such as schooling of religious and all other natures; reading, word of mouth conversation, story-telling and all manner of thought inspiration coming from what is generally accepted as one's "personal experiences." Through the operation of the law of social heredity anyone having control of the mind of a child may, through intense teaching, plant in that child's mind any idea, whether false or true, in such a manner that the child accepts it as true and it becomes as much a part of the child's personality as any cell or organ of its physical body (and just as hard to change in its nature) .

It is through the law of social heredity that the religionist plants in the child mind dogmas and creeds and religious ceremonies too numerous to describe, holding those ideas before that mind until the mind accepts them and forever seals them as a part of its irrevocable belief.

The mind of a child which has not come into the age of general understanding, during an average period covering, let us say, the first two years of its life, is plastic, open, clean and free. Any idea planted in such a mind by one in whom the child has confidence takes root and grows, so to speak, in such a manner that it never can be eradicated or wiped out, no matter how opposed to logic or reason that idea may be.

Many religionists claim that they can so deeply implant the tenets of their religion in the mind of a child that there never can be room in that mind for any other religion, either in whole or in part. The claims are not greatly overdrawn.

With this explanation of the manner in which the law of social heredity operates the student will be ready to examine the sources from which man inherits the six basic fears. Moreover, any student (except those who have not yet grown big enough to examine truth that steps upon the "pet corns" of their own superstitions) may check the soundness of the principle of social heredity as it is here applied to the six basic fears, without going outside of his or her own personal experiences.

Fortunately, practically the entire mass of evidence submitted in this lesson is of such a nature that all who sincerely seek the truth may ascertain, for themselves, whether the evidence is sound or not.

For the moment at least, lay aside your prejudices and preconceived ideas (you may always go back and pick them up again, you know) while we study the origin and nature of man's Six Worst Enemies, the six basic fears, beginning with:

THE FEAR OF POVERTY: It requires courage to tell the truth about the origin of this fear, and still greater courage, perhaps, to accept the truth after it has been told. The fear of poverty grew out of man's inherited tendency to prey upon his fellow man economically. Nearly all forms of lower animals have instinct but appear not to have the power to reason and think; therefore, they prey upon one another physically. Man, with his superior sense of intuition, thought and reason, does not eat his fellow men bodily; he gets more satisfaction out of eating them FINANCIALLY!

Of all the ages of the world of which we know anything, the age in which we live seems to be the age of money worship. A man is considered less than the dust of the earth unless he can display a fat bank account. Nothing brings man so much suffering and humiliation as does POVERTY. No wonder man FEARS poverty. Through a long line of inherited experiences with the man-animal man has learned, for certain, that this animal cannot always be trusted where matters of money and other evidences of earthly possessions are concerned.

Many marriages have their beginning (and oftentimes their ending) solely on the basis of the wealth possessed by one or both of the contracting parties.

It is no wonder that the divorce courts are busy!

"Society" could quite properly be spelled "$ociety," because it is inseparably associated with the dollar mark. So eager is man to possess wealth that he will acquire it in whatever manner he can; through legal methods, if possible, through other methods if necessary.

The fear of poverty is a terrible thing!

A man may commit murder, engage in robbery, rape and all other manner of violation of the rights of others and still regain a high station in the minds of his fellow men, PROVIDING always that he does not lose his wealth. Poverty, therefore, is a crime–an unforgivable sin, as it were.

No wonder man fears it!

Every statute book in the world bears evidence that the fear of poverty is one of the six basic fears of mankind, for in every such book of laws may be found various and sundry laws intended to protect the weak from the strong. To spend time trying to prove either that the fear of poverty is one of man's inherited fears, or that this fear has its origin in man's nature to cheat his fellow man, would be similar to trying to prove that three times two are six. Obviously no man would ever fear poverty if he had any grounds for trusting his fellow men, for there is food and shelter and raiment and luxury of every nature sufficient for the needs of every person on earth, and all these blessings would be enjoyed by every person except for the swinish habit that man has of trying to push all the other "swine" out of the trough, even after he has all and more than he needs.

The second of the six basic fears with which man is bound is:

THE FEAR OF OLD AGE: In the main this fear grows out of two sources. First, the thought that Old Age may bring with it POVERTY. Secondly, and by far the most common source of origin, from false and cruel sectarian teachings which have been so well mixed with "fire and brimstone" and with "purgatories" and other bogies that human beings have learned to fear Old Age because it meant the approach of another, and possibly a much more HORRIBLE, world than this one which is known to be bad enough.

In the basic fear of Old Age man has two very sound reasons for his apprehension: the one growing out of distrust of his fellow men who may seize whatever worldly goods he may possess, and the other arising from the terrible pictures of the world to come which were deeply planted in his mind, through the law of social heredity, long before he came into possession of that mind. Is it any wonder that man fears the approach of Old Age?

The third of the six basic fears is:

THE FEAR OF CRITICISM: Just how man acquired this basic fear it would be hard, if not impossible, definitely to determine, but one thing is certain, he has it in well-developed form.

Some believe that this fear made its appearance in the mind of man about the time that politics came into existence. Others believe its source can be traced no further than the first meeting of an organization of females known as a "Woman's Club." Still another school of humorists charges the origin to the contents of the Holy Bible, whose pages abound with some very vitriolic and violent forms of criticism. If the latter claim is correct, and those who believe literally all they find in the Bible are not mistaken, then God is responsible for man's inherent fear of Criticism, because God caused the Bible to be written.

This author, being neither a humorist nor a "prophet," but just an ordinary workaday type of person, is inclined to attribute the basic fear of Criticism to that part of man's inherited nature which prompts him not only to take away his fellow man's goods and wares, but to justify his action by CRITICISM of his fellow man's character.

The fear of Criticism takes on many different forms, the majority of which are petty and trivial in nature, even to the extent of being childish in the extreme.

Bald-headed men, for example, are bald for no other reason than their fear of Criticism.

Heads become bald because of the protection of hats with tight fitting bands which cut off the circulation at the roots of the hair. Men wear hats, not because they actually need them for the sake of comfort, but mainly because "everybody's doing it," and the individual falls in line and does it also, lest some other individual CRITICIZE him.

Women seldom have bald heads, or even thin hair, because they wear hats that are loose, the only purpose of which is to make an appearance.

But it must not be imagined that women are free from the fear of Criticism associated with hats. If any woman claims to be superior to man with reference to this fear, ask her to walk down the street wearing a hat that is one or two seasons out of style!

The makers of all manner of clothing have not been slow to capitalize this basic fear of Criticism with which all mankind is cursed. Every season, it will be observed, the "styles" in many articles of wearing apparel change. Who establishes the "styles"? Certainly not the purchaser of clothes, but the manufacturer of clothes. Why does he change the styles so often? Obviously this change is made so that the manufacturer can sell more clothes.

For the same reason the manufacturers of automobiles (with a few rare and very sensible exceptions) change styles every season.

The manufacturer of clothing knows how the man-animal fears to wear a garment which is one season out of step with "that which they are all wearing now."

Is this not true? Does not your own experience back it up?

We have been describing the manner in which people behave under the influence of the fear of Criticism as applied to the small and petty things of life. Let us now examine human behavior under this fear when it affects people in connection with the more important matters connected with human intercourse. Take, for example, practically any person who has reached the age of "mental maturity" (from thirty-five to forty-five years of age, as a general average), and if you could read his or her mind you would find in that mind a very decided disbelief of and rebellion against most of the fables taught by the majority of the religionists.

Powerful and mighty is the fear of CRITICISM!

The time was, and not so very long ago at that, when the word "infidel" meant ruin to whomsoever it was applied. It is seen, therefore, that man's fear of CRITICISM is not without ample cause for its existence.

The fourth basic fear is that of:

THE FEAR OF LOSS OF LOVE OF SOMEONE: The source from which this fear originated needs but little description, for it is obvious that it grew out of man's nature to steal his fellow man's mate; or at least to take liberties with her, unknown to her rightful "lord" and master. By nature all men are polygamous, the statement of a truth which will, of course, bring denials from those who are either too old to function in a normal way sexually, or have, from some other cause, lost the contents of certain glands which are responsible for man's tendency toward the plurality of the opposite sex.

There can be but little doubt that jealousy and all other similar forms of more or less mild dementia praecox (insanity) grew out of man's inherited fear of the Loss of Love of Someone.

Of all the "sane fools" studied by this author, that represented by a man who has become jealous of some woman, or that of a woman who has become jealous of some man, is the oddest and strangest. The author, fortunately, never had but one case of personal experience with this form of insanity, but from that experience he learned enough to justify him in stating that the fear of the Loss of Love of Someone is one of the most painful, if not in fact the most painful, of all the six basic fears. And it seems reasonable to add that this fear plays more havoc with the human mind than do any of the other six basic fears, often leading to the more violent forms of permanent insanity.

The fifth basic fear is that of:

THE FEAR OF ILL HEALTH: This fear has its origin, to considerable extent also, in the same sources from which the fears of Poverty and Old Age are derived.

The fear of Ill Health must needs be closely associated with both Poverty and Old Age, because it also leads toward the border line of "terrible worlds" of which man knows not, but of which he has heard some discomforting stories.

The author strongly suspects that those engaged in the business of selling good health methods have had considerable to do with keeping the fear of Ill Health alive in the human mind.

For longer than the record of the human race can be relied upon, the world has known of various and sundry forms of therapy and health purveyors. If a man gains his living from keeping people in good health it seems but natural that he would use every means at his command for persuading people that they needed his services. Thus, in time, it might be that people would inherit a fear of Ill Health.

The sixth and last of the six basic fears is that of:

THE FEAR OF DEATH: To many this is the worst of all the six basic fears, and the reason why it is so regarded becomes obvious to even the casual student of psychology.

The terrible pangs of fear associated with DEATH may be charged directly to religious fanaticism, the source which is more responsible for it than are all other sources combined.

So-called "heathen" are not as much afraid of DEATH as are the "civilized," especially that portion of the civilized population which has come under the influence of theology.

For hundreds of millions of years man has been asking the still unanswered (and, it may be, the unanswerable) questions, "WHENCE?" and "WHITHER?" "Where did I come from and where am I going after death?"

The more cunning and crafty, as well as the honest but credulous, of the race have not been slow to offer the answer to these questions. In fact the answering of these questions has become one of the so-called "learned" professions, despite the fact that but little learning is required to enter this profession.

Witness, now, the major source of origin of the fear of DEATH!

"Come into my tent, embrace my faith, accept my dogmas (and pay my salary) and I will give you a ticket that will admit you straightway into heaven when you die," says the leader of one form of sectarianism. "Remain out of my tent," says this same leader, "and you will go direct to hell, where you will burn throughout eternity."

While, in fact, the self-appointed leader may not be able to provide safe-conduct into heaven nor, by lack of such provision, allow the unfortunate seeker after truth to descend into hell, the possibility of the latter seems so terrible that it lays hold of the mind and creates that fear of fears, the fear of DEATH!

In truth no man knows, and no man has ever known, what heaven or hell is like, or if such places exist, and this very lack of definite knowledge opens the door of the human mind to the charlatan to enter and control that mind with his stock of legerdemain and various brands of trickery, deceit and fraud.

The truth is this–nothing less and nothing more–That NO MAN KNOWS NOR HAS ANY MAN EVER KNOWN WHERE WE COME FROM AT BIRTH OR WHERE WE GO AT DEATH. Any person claiming otherwise is either deceiving himself or he is a conscious impostor who makes it a business to live without rendering service of value, through play upon the credulity of humanity.

Be it said, in their behalf, however, the majority of those engaged in "selling tickets into heaven" actually believe not only that they know where heaven exists, but that their creeds and formulas will give safe passage to all who embrace them.

This belief may be summed up in one word-CREDULITY!

It is hardly sufficient to state that social heredity is the method through which man gathers all knowledge that reaches him through the five senses. It is more to the point to state HOW social heredity works, in as many different applications as will give the student a comprehensive understanding of that law.

Let us begin with some of the lower forms of animal life and examine the manner in which they are affected by the law of social heredity.

Shortly after this author began to examine the major sources from which men gather the knowledge which makes them what they are, some thirty-odd years ago, he discovered the nest of a ruffed grouse. The nest was so located that the mother bird could be seen from a considerable distance when she was on the nest. With the aid of a pair of field glasses the bird was closely watched until the young birds were hatched out. It happened that the regular daily observation was made but a few hours after the young birds came out of the shell. Desiring to know what would happen, the author approached the nest. The mother bird remained near by until the intruder was within ten or twelve feet of her, then she disarranged her feathers, stretched one wing over her leg and went hobbling away, making a pretense of being crippled. Being somewhat familiar with the tricks of mother birds, the author did not follow, but, instead, went to the nest to take a look at the little ones. Without the slightest signs of fear they turned their eyes toward him, moving their heads first one way and then another. He reached down and picked one of them up. With no signs of fear it stood in the palm of his hand. He laid the bird back in the nest and went away to a safe distance to give the mother bird a chance to return.

The wait was short. Very soon she began cautiously to edge her way back toward the nest until she was within a few feet of it, when she spread her wings and ran as fast as she could, uttering, meanwhile, a series of sounds similar to those of a hen when she has found some morsel of food and wishes to call her brood to partake of it. She gathered the little birds around and continued to quiver in a highly excited manner, shaking her wings and ruffling her feathers. One could almost hear her words as she gave the little birds their first lesson in self-defense, through the law of SOCIAL HEREDITY:

"You silly little creatures! Do you not know that men are your enemies? Shame on you for allowing that man to pick you up in his hands. It's a wonder he didn't carry you off and eat you alive! The next time you see a man approaching make yourselves scarce. Lie down on the ground, run under leaves, go anywhere to get out of sight, and remain out of sight until the enemy is well on his way."

The little birds stood around and listened to the lecture with intense interest. After the mother bird had quieted down the author again started to approach the nest. When within twenty feet or so of the guarded household the mother bird again started to lead him in the other direction by crumpling up her wing and hobbling along as if she were crippled. He looked at the nest, but the glance was in vain. The little birds were nowhere to be found! They had learned rapidly to avoid their natural enemy, thanks to their natural instinct.

Again the author retreated, awaited until the mother bird had reassembled her household, then came out to visit them, but with similar results. When he approached the spot where he last saw the mother bird not the slightest signs of the little fellows were to be found.

When a small boy the author captured a young crow and made a pet of it. The bird became quite well satisfied with its domestic surroundings and learned to perform many tricks requiring considerable intelligence. After the bird was big enough to fly it was permitted to go wherever it pleased. Sometimes it would be gone for many hours, but it always returned home before dark.

One day some wild crows became involved in a fight with an owl in a field near the house where the pet crow lived. As soon as the pet heard the "caw, caw, caw" of its wild relatives it flew up on top of the house, and with signs of great agitation, walked from one end of the house to the other. Finally it took wing and flew in the direction of the "battle." The author followed to see what would happen. In a few minutes he came up with the pet. It was sitting on the lower branches of a tree and two wild crows were sitting on a limb just above, chattering and walking back and forth, acting very much in the same fashion that angry parents behave toward their offspring when chastising them.

As the author approached, the two wild crows flew away, one of them circling around the tree a few times, meanwhile letting out a terrible flow of most abusive language, which, no doubt, was directed at its foolish relative who hadn't enough sense to fly while the flying was good.

The pet was called, but it paid no attention. That evening it returned home, but would not come near the house. It sat on a high limb of an apple tree and talked in crow language for about ten minutes, saying, no doubt, that it had decided to go back to the wild life of its fellows, then flew away and did not return until two days later, when it came back and did some more talking in crow language, keeping at a safe distance meanwhile. It then went away and never returned.

Social heredity had robbed the author of a fine pet!

The only consolation he got from the loss of his crow was the thought that it had shown fine sportsmanship by coming back and giving notice of its intention to depart. Many farm hands had left the farm without going to the trouble of this formality.

It is a well-known fact that a fox will prey upon all manner of fowl and small animals with the exception of the skunk. No reason need be stated as to why Mr. Skunk enjoys immunity. A fox may tackle a skunk once, but never twice! For this reason a skunkhide, when nailed to a chicken roost, will keep all but the very young and inexperienced foxes at a safe distance.

The odor of a skunk, once experienced, is never to be forgotten. No other smell even remotely resembles it. It is nowhere recorded that any mother fox ever taught her young how to detect and keep away from the familiar smell of a skunk, but all who are informed on "fox lore" know that foxes and skunks never seek lodgment in the same cave.

But one lesson is sufficient to teach the fox all it cares to know about skunks. Through the law of social heredity, operating via the sense of smell, one lesson serves for an entire life-time.

A bullfrog can be caught on a fish-hook by attaching a small piece of red cloth or any other small red object to the hook and dangling it in front of the frog's nose. That is, Mr. Frog may be caught in this manner, provided he is hooked the first time he snaps at the bait, but if he is poorly hooked and makes a get-away, or if he feels the point of the hook when he bites at the bait but is not caught, he will never make the same mistake again. The author spent many hours in stealthy attempt to hook a particularly desirable specimen which had snapped and missed, before learning that but one lesson in social heredity is enough to teach even a humble "croaker" that bits of red flannel are things to be let alone.

The author once owned a very fine male Airedale dog which caused no end of annoyance by his habit of coming home with a young chicken in his mouth. Each time the chicken was taken away from the dog and he was soundly switched, but to no avail; he continued in his liking for fowl.

For the purpose of saving the dog, if possible, and as an experiment with social heredity, this dog was taken to the farm of a neighbor who had a hen and some newly hatched chickens. The hen was placed in the barn and the dog was turned in with her. As soon as everyone was out of sight the dog slowly edged up toward the hen, sniffed the air in her direction a time or two (to make sure she was the kind of meat for which he was looking), then made a dive toward her. Meanwhile Mrs. Hen had been doing some "surveying" on her own account, for she met Mr. Dog more than halfway; moreover, she met him with such a surprise of wings and claws as he had never before experienced. The first round was clearly the hen's. But a nice fat bird, reckoned the dog, was not to slip between his paws so easily; therefore he backed away a short distance, then charged again. This time Mrs. Hen lit upon his back, drove her claws into his skin and made effective use of her sharp bill! Mr. Dog retreated to his comer, looking for all the world as if he were listening for someone to ring the bell and call the fight off until he got his bearings. But Mrs. Hen craved no time for deliberation; she had her adversary on the ran and showed that she knew the value of the offensive by keeping him on the run.

One could almost understand her words as she flogged the poor Airedale from one corner to another, keeping up a series of rapid-fire sounds which for all the world resembled the remonstrations of an angry mother who had been called upon to defend her offspring from an attack by older boys.

The Airedale was a poor soldier! After running around the barn from corner to corner for about two minutes he spread himself on the ground as flat as he could and did his best to protect his eyes with his paws. Mrs. Hen seemed to be making a special attempt to peck out his eyes.

The owner of the hen then stepped in and retrieved her–or, more accurately stating it, he retrieved the dog–which in no way appeared to meet with the dog's disapproval. The next day a chicken was placed in the cellar where the dog slept. As soon as he saw the bird he tucked his tail between his legs and ran for a corner! He never again attempted to catch a chicken. One lesson in social heredity, via the sense of "touch," was sufficient to teach him that while chicken-chasing may offer some enjoyment, it is also fraught with much hazard.

All these illustrations, with the exception of the first, describe the process of gathering knowledge through direct experience. Observe the marked difference between knowledge gathered by direct experience and that which is gathered through the training of the young by the old, as in the case of the ruffed grouse and her young. The most impressive lessons are those learned by the young from the old, through highly colored or emotionalized methods of teaching. When the mother grouse spread her wings, stood her feathers on end, shook herself like a man suffering with the palsy and chattered to her young in a highly excited manner, she planted the fear of man in their hearts in a manner which they were never to forget.

The term "social heredity," as used in connection with this lesson, has particular reference to all methods through which a child is taught any idea, dogma, creed, religion or system of ethical conduct, by its parents or those who may have authority over it, before reaching the age at which it may reason and reflect upon such teaching in its own way; estimating the age of such reasoning power at, let us say, seven to twelve years.

There are myriads of forms of fear, but none are more deadly than the fear of poverty and old age. We drive our bodies as if they were slaves because we are so afraid of poverty that we wish to hoard money for–what–old age! This common form of fear drives us so hard that we overwork our bodies and bring on the very thing we are struggling to avoid.

What a tragedy to watch a man drive himself when he begins to arrive along about the forty-year mile post of life–the age at which he is just beginning to mature mentally. At forty a man is just entering the age in which he is able to see and understand and assimilate the handwriting of Nature, as it appears in the forests and flowing brooks and faces of men and little children, yet this devil fear drives him so hard that he becomes blinded and lost in the entanglement of a maze of conflicting desires.

The principle of organized effort is lost sight of, and instead of laying hold of Nature's forces which are in evidence all around him, and permitting those forces to carry him to the heights of great achievement, he defies them and they become forces of destruction.

Perhaps none of these great forces of Nature are more available for man's unfoldment than is the principle of Auto-suggestion, but ignorance of this force is leading the majority of the human race to apply it so that it acts as a hindrance and not as a help.

Let us here enumerate the facts which show just how this misapplication of a great force of Nature takes place:

Here is a man who meets with some disappointment; a friend proves false, or a neighbor seems indifferent. Forthwith he decides (through self-suggestion) all men are untrustworthy and all neighbors unappreciative. These thoughts so deeply embed themselves in his subconscious mind that they color his whole attitude toward others.

Go back, now, to what was said in Lesson Two, about the dominating thoughts of a man's mind attracting people whose thoughts are similar.

Apply the Law of Attraction and you will soon see and understand why the unbeliever attracts other unbelievers.

Reverse the Principle:

Here is a man who sees nothing but the best there is in all whom he meets. If his

neighbors seem indifferent he takes no notice of that fact, for he makes it his business to fill his mind with dominating thoughts of optimism and good cheer and faith in others. If people speak to him harshly he speaks back in tones of softness. Through the operation of this same eternal Law of Attraction he draws to himself the attention of people whose attitude toward life and whose dominating thoughts harmonize with his own.

Tracing the principle a step further:

Here is a man who has been well schooled and has the ability to render the world some needed service. Somewhere, sometime, he has heard it said that modesty is a great virtue and that to push himself to the front of the stage in the game of life savors of egotism. He quietly slips in at the back door and takes a seat at the rear while other players in the game of life boldly step to the front. He remains in the back row because he fears "what they will say."

Public opinion, or that which he believes to be public opinion, has him pushed to the rear and the world hears but little of him. His schooling counts for naught because he is afraid to let the world know that he has had it. He is constantly suggesting to himself (thus using the great force of Auto-suggestion to his own detriment) that he should remain in the background lest he be criticized, as if criticism would do him any damage or defeat his purpose.

Here is another man who was born of poor parents. Since the first day that he can remember he has seen evidence of poverty. He has heard talk of poverty. He has felt the icy hand of poverty on his shoulders and it has so impressed him that he fixes it in his mind as a curse to which he must submit. Quite unconsciously he permits himself to fall victim of the belief "once poor always poor" until that belief becomes the dominating thought of his mind. He resembles a horse that has been harnessed and broken until it forgets that it has the potential power with which to throw off that harness. Auto-suggestion is rapidly relegating him to the back of the stage of life.

Finally he becomes a quitter. Ambition is gone. Opportunity comes his way no longer, or if it does he has not the vision to see it. He has accepted his FATE! It is a well-established fact that the faculties of the mind, like the limbs of the body, atrophy and wither away if not used. Self-confidence is no exception. It develops when used but disappears if not used.

One of the chief disadvantages of inherited wealth is the fact that it too often leads to inaction and loss of Self-confidence. Some years ago a baby boy was born to Mrs. E. B. McLean, in the city of Washington. His inheritance was said to be around a hundred million dollars. When this baby was taken for an airing in its carriage it was surrounded by nurses and assistant nurses and detectives and other servants whose duty was to see that no harm befell it. As the years passed by this same vigilance was kept up. This child did not have to dress himself; he had servants who did that. Servants watched over him while he slept and while he was at play. He was not permitted to do anything that a servant could do for him. He had grown to the age of ten years. One day he was playing in the yard and noticed that the back gate had been left open. In all of his life he had never been outside of that gate alone, and naturally that was just the thing that he wished to do. During a moment when the servants were not looking he dashed out at the gate, and was run down and killed by an automobile before he reached the middle of the street.

He had used his servants' eyes until his own no longer served him as they might have done had he learned to rely upon them.

Twenty years ago the man whom I served as secretary sent his two sons away to school. One of them went to the University of Virginia and the other to a college in New York. Each month it was a part of my task to make out a check for $100.00 for each of these boys. This was their "pin money," to be spent as they wished. How profitably I remember the way I envied those boys as I made out those checks each month. I often wondered why the hand of fate bore me into the world in poverty. I could look ahead and see how these boys would rise to the high stations in life while I remained a humble clerk.

In due time the boys returned home with their "sheep-skins." Their father was a wealthy man who owned banks and railroads and coal mines and other property of great value. Good positions were waiting for the boys in their father's employ. But, twenty years of time can play cruel tricks on those who have never had to struggle. Perhaps a better way to state this truth would be that time gives those who have never had to struggle a chance to play cruel tricks on themselves! At any rate, these two boys brought home from school other things besides their sheep-skins. They came back with well developed capacities for strong drink–capacities which they developed because the hundred dollars which each of them received each month made it unnecessary for them to struggle.

Theirs is a long and sad story, the details of which will not interest you, but you will be interested in their "finis". As this lesson is being written I have on my desk a copy of the newspaper published in the town where these boys lived. Their father has been bankrupted and his costly mansion, where the boys were born, has been placed on the block for sale. One of the boys died of delirium tremens and the other one is in an insane asylum.

Not all rich men's sons turn out so unfortunately, but the fact remains, nevertheless, that inaction leads to atrophy and this, in turn, leads to loss of ambition and self-confidence, and without these essential qualities a man will be carried through life on the wings of uncertainty, just as a dry leaf may be carried here and there on the bosom of the stray winds.

Far from being a disadvantage, struggle is a decided advantage, because it develops those qualities which would forever lie dormant without it. Many a man has found his place in the world because of having been forced to struggle for existence early in life. Lack of knowledge of the advantages accruing from struggle has prompted many a parent to say, "I had to work hard when I was young, but I shall see to it that my children have an easy time!" Poor foolish creatures. An "easy" time usually turns out to be a greater handicap than the average young man or woman can survive. There are worse things in this world than being forced to work in early life. Forced idleness is far worse than forced labor. Being forced to work, and forced to do your best, will breed in you temperance and self-control and strength of will and content and a hundred other virtues which the idle will never know.

Not only does lack of the necessity for struggle lead to weakness of ambition and willpower, but, what is more dangerous still, it sets up in a person's mind a state of lethargy that leads to the loss of Self-confidence. The person who has quit struggling because effort is no longer necessary is literally applying the principle of Auto-suggestion in undermining his own power of Self-confidence. Such a person will finally drift into a frame of mind in which he will actually look with more or less contempt upon the person who is forced to carry on.

The human mind, if you will pardon repetition, may be likened to an electric battery. It may be positive or it may be negative. Self-confidence is the quality with which the mind is recharged and made positive.

Let us apply this line of reasoning to salesmanship and see what part Self-confidence plays in this great field of endeavor. One of the greatest salesmen this country has ever seen was once a clerk in a newspaper office.

It will be worth your while to analyze the method through which he gained his title as "the world's leading salesman."

He was a timid young man with a more or less retiring sort of nature. He was one of those who believe it best to slip in by the back door and take a seat at the rear of the stage of life. One evening he heard a lecture on the subject of this lesson, Self-confidence, and that lecture so impressed him that he left the lecture hall with a firm determination to pull himself out of the rut into which he had drifted. He went to the Business Manager of the paper and asked for a position as solicitor of advertising and was put to work on a commission basis. Everyone in the office expected to see him fail, as this sort of salesmanship calls for the most positive type of sales ability.

He went to his room and made out a list of a certain type of merchants on whom he intended to call. One would think that he would naturally have made up his list of the names of those whom he believed he could sell with the least effort, but he did nothing of the sort. He placed on his list only the names of the merchants on whom other advertising solicitors had called without making a sale. His list consisted of only twelve names. Before he made a single call he went out to the city park, took out his list of twelve names, read it over a hundred times, saying to himself as he did so, "You will purchase advertising space from me before the end of the month."

Then he began to make his calls. The first day he closed sales with three of the twelve "impossibilities." During the remainder of the week he made sales to two others. By the end of the month he had opened advertising accounts with all but one of the merchants that he had on the list. For the ensuing month he made no sales, for the reason that he made no calls except on this one obstinate merchant. Every morning when the store opened he was on hand to interview this merchant and every morning the merchant said "No." The merchant knew he was not going to buy advertising space, but this young man didn't know it. When the merchant said No the young man did not hear it, but kept right on coming. On the last day of the month, after having told this persistent young man No for thirty consecutive times, the merchant said:

"Look here, young man, you have wasted a whole month trying to sell me; now, what I would like to know is this–why have you wasted your time?"

"Wasted my time nothing," he retorted; "I have been going to school and you have been my teacher.

Now I know all the arguments that a merchant can bring up for not buying, and besides that I have been drilling myself in Self-confidence."

Then the merchant said: "I will make a little confession of my own. I, too, have been going to school, and you have been my teacher. You have taught me a lesson in persistence that is worth money to me, and to show you my appreciation I am going to pay my tuition fee by giving you an order for advertising space."

And that was the way in which the Philadelphia North American's best advertising account was brought in. Likewise, it marked the beginning of a reputation that has made that same young man a millionaire.

He succeeded because he deliberately charged his own mind with sufficient Self-confidence to make that mind an irresistible force. When he sat down to make up that list of twelve names he did something that ninety-nine people out of a hundred would not have done–he selected the names of those whom he believed it would be hard to sell, because he understood that out of the resistance he would meet with in trying to sell them would come strength and Self-confidence. He was one of the very few people who understand that all rivers and some men are crooked because of following the line of least resistance.

I am going to digress and here break the line of thought for a moment while recording a word of advice to the wives of men. Remember, these lines are intended only for wives, and husbands are not expected to read that which is here set down.

From having analyzed more than 16,000 people, the majority of whom were married men, I have learned something that may be of value to wives. Let me state my thought in these words:

You have it within your power to send your husband away to his work or his business or his profession each day with a feeling of Self-confidence that will carry him successfully over the rough spots of the day and bring him home again, at night, smiling and happy. One of my acquaintances of former years married a woman who had a set of false teeth. One day his wife dropped her teeth and broke the plate. The husband picked up the pieces and began examining them. He showed such interest in them that his wife said:

"You could make a set of teeth like those if you made up your mind to do it."

This man was a farmer whose ambitions had never carried him beyond the bounds of his little farm until his wife made that remark. She walked over and laid her hand on his shoulder and encouraged him to try his hand at dentistry. She finally coaxed him to make the start, and today he is one of the most prominent and successful dentists in the state of Virginia. I know him well, for he is my father!

No one can foretell the possibilities of achievement available to the man whose wife stands at his back and urges him on to bigger and better endeavor, for it is a well-known fact that a woman can arouse a man so that he will perform almost superhuman feats. It is your right and your duty to encourage your husband and urge him on in worthy undertakings until he shall have found his place in the world. You can induce him to put forth greater effort than can any other person in the world. Make him believe that nothing within reason is beyond his power of achievement and you will have rendered him a service that will go a long way toward helping him win in the battle of life.

One of the most successful men in his line in America gives entire credit for his success to his wife. When they were first married she wrote a creed which he signed and placed over his desk. This is a copy of the creed:

I believe in myself. I believe in those who work with me. I believe in my employer. I believe in my friends. I believe in my family. I believe that God will lend me everything I need with which to succeed if I do my best to earn it through faithful and honest service. I believe in prayer and I will never close my eyes in sleep without praying for divine guidance to the end that I will be patient with other people and tolerant with those who do not believe as I do. I believe that success is the result of intelligent effort and does not depend upon luck or sharp practices or double-crossing friends, fellow men or my employer. I believe I will get out of life exactly what I put into it, therefore I will be careful to conduct myself toward others as I would want them to act toward me. I will not slander those whom I do not like. I will not slight my work no matter what I may see others doing. I will render the best service of which I am capable because I have pledged myself to succeed in life and I know that success is always the result of conscientious and efficient effort. Finally, I will forgive those who offend me because I realize that I shall sometimes offend others and I will need their forgiveness.

Signed ....

The woman who wrote this creed was a practical psychologist of the first order. With the influence and guidance of such a woman as a helpmate any man could achieve noteworthy success.

Analyze this creed and you will notice how freely the personal pronoun is used. It starts off with the affirmation of Self-confidence, which is perfectly proper. No man could make this creed his own without developing the positive attitude that would attract to him people who would aid him in his struggle for success.

This would be a splendid creed for every salesman to adopt. It might not hurt your chances for success if you adopted it. Mere adoption, however, is not enough. You must practice it! Read it over and over until you know it by heart. Then repeat it at least once a day until you have literally transformed it into your mental make-up. Keep a copy of it before you as a daily reminder of your pledge to practice it. By doing so you will be making efficient use of the principle of Auto-suggestion as a means of developing Self-confidence. Never mind what anyone may say about your procedure. Just remember that it is your business to succeed, and this creed, if mastered and applied, will go a long way toward helping you.

You learned in Lesson Two that any idea you firmly fix in your subconscious mind, by repeated affirmation, automatically becomes a plan or blueprint which an unseen power uses in directing your efforts toward the attainment of the objective named in the plan.

You have also learned that the principle through which you may fix any idea you choose in your mind is called Auto-suggestion, which simply means a suggestion that you give to your own mind. It was this principle of Auto-suggestion that Emerson had in mind when he wrote:

"Nothing can bring you peace but yourself!"

You might well remember that Nothing can bring you success but yourself. Of course you will need the co-operation of others if you aim to attain success of a far-reaching nature, but you will never get that cooperation unless you vitalize your mind with the positive attitude of Self-confidence.

Perhaps you have wondered why a few men advance to highly paid positions while others all around them, who have as much training and who seemingly perform as much work, do not get ahead. Select any two people of these two types that you choose, and study them, and the reason why one advances and the other stands still will be quite obvious to you. You will find that the one who advances believes in himself.

You will find that he backs this belief with such dynamic, aggressive action that he lets others know that he believes in himself. You will also notice that this Self-confidence is contagious; it is impelling;

it is persuasive; it attracts others.

You will also find that the one who does not advance shows clearly, by the look on his face, by the posture of his body, by the lack of briskness in his step, by the uncertainty with which he speaks, that he lacks Self-confidence. No one is going to pay much attention to the person who has no confidence in himself.

He does not attract others because his mind is a negative force that repels rather than attracts.

In no other field of endeavor does Self-confidence or the lack of it play such an important part as in the field of salesmanship, and you do not need to be a character analyst to determine, the moment you meet him, whether a salesman possesses this quality of Self-confidence. If he has it the signs of its influence are written all over him. He inspires you with confidence in him and in the goods he is selling the moment he speaks.

We come, now, to the point at, which you are ready to take hold of the principle of Auto-suggestion and make direct use of it in developing yourself into a positive and dynamic and self-reliant person. You are instructed to copy the following formula, sign it and commit it to memory:

SELF-CONFIDENCE FORMULA

First: I know that I have the ability to achieve the object of my definite purpose, therefore I demand of myself persistent, aggressive and continuous action toward its attainment.

Second: I realize that the dominating thoughts of my mind eventually reproduce themselves in outward, bodily action, and gradually transform themselves into physical reality, therefore I will concentrate My mind for thirty minutes daily upon the task of thinking of the person I intend to be, by creating a mental picture of this person and then transforming that picture into reality through practical service.

Third: I know that through the principle of Auto-suggestion, any desire that I persistently hold in my mind will eventually seek expression through some practical means of realizing it, therefore I shall devote ten minutes daily to demanding of myself the development of the factors named in the sixteen lessons of this Reading Course on the Law of Success.

Fourth: I have clearly mapped out and written down a description of my definite purpose in life, for the coming five years. I have set a price on my services for each of these five years; a price that I intend to earn and receive, through strict application of the principle of efficient, satisfactory service which I will render in advance.

Fifth: I fully realize that no wealth or position can long endure unless built upon truth and justice, therefore I will engage in no transaction which does not benefit all whom it affects. I will succeed by attracting to me the forces I wish to use, and the co-operation of other people. I will induce others to serve me because I will first serve them. I will eliminate hatred, envy, jealousy, selfishness and cynicism by developing love for all humanity, because I know that a negative attitude toward others can never bring me success. I will cause others to believe in me because I will believe in them and in myself.

I will sign my name to this formula, commit it to memory and repeat it aloud once a day with full faith that it will gradually influence my entire life so that I will become a successful and happy worker in my chosen field of endeavor.

Signed..

Before you sign your name to this formula make sure that you intend to carry out its instructions.

Back of this formula lies a law that no man can explain. The psychologists refer to this law as Auto-suggestion and let it go at that, but you should bear in mind one point about which there is no uncertainty, and that is the fact that whatever this law is it actually works!

Another point to be kept in mind is the fact that, just as electricity will turn the wheels of industry and serve mankind in a million other ways, or snuff out life if wrongly applied, so will this principle of Auto-suggestion lead you up the mountain-side of peace and prosperity, or down into the valley of misery and poverty, according to the application you make of it. If you fill your mind with doubt and unbelief in your ability to achieve, then the principle of Auto-suggestion takes this spirit of unbelief and sets it up in your subconscious mind as your dominating thought and slowly but surely draws you into the whirlpool of failure. But, if you fill your mind with radiant Self-confidence, the principle of Auto-suggestion takes this belief and sets it up as your dominating thought and helps you master the obstacles that fall in your way until you reach the mountain-top of success.

THE POWER OF HABIT

Having, myself, experienced all the difficulties that stand in the road of those who lack the understanding to make practical application of this great principle of Autosuggestion, let me take you a short way into the principle of habit, through the aid of which you may easily apply the principle of Auto-suggestion in any direction and for any purpose whatsoever.

Habit grows out of environment; out of doing the same thing or thinking the same thoughts or repeating the same words over and over again. Habit may be likened to the groove on a phonograph record, while the human mind may be likened to the needle that fits into that groove. When any habit has been well formed, through repetition of thought or action, the mind has a tendency to attach itself to and follow the course of that habit as closely as the phonograph needle follows the groove in the wax record.

Habit is created by repeatedly directing one or more of the five senses of seeing, hearing, smelling, tasting and feeling, in a given direction. It is through this repetition principle that the injurious drug habit is formed. It is through this same principle that the desire for intoxicating drink is formed into a habit.

After habit has been well-established it will automatically control and direct our bodily activity, wherein may be found a thought that can be transformed into a powerful factor in the development of Self-confidence. The thought is this: Voluntarily, and by force if necessary, direct your efforts and your thoughts along a desired line until you have formed the habit that will lay hold of you and continue,voluntarily, to direct your efforts along the same line.

The object in writing out and repeating the Self-confidence formula is to form the habit of making belief in yourself the dominating thought of your mind until that thought has been thoroughly imbedded in your subconscious mind, through the principle of habit. You learned to write by repeatedly directing the muscles of your arm and hand over certain outlines known as letters, until finally you formed the habit of tracing these outlines. Now you write with ease and rapidity, without tracing each letter slowly. Writing has become a habit with you.

The principle of habit will lay hold of the faculties of your mind just the same as it will influence the physical muscles of your body, as you can easily prove by mastering and applying this lesson on Self-confidence. Any statement that you repeatedly make to yourself, or any desire that you deeply plant in your mind through repeated statement, will eventually seek expression through your physical, outward bodily efforts. The principle of habit is the very foundation upon which this lesson on Self-confidence is built, and if you will understand and follow the directions laid down in this lesson you will soon know more about the law of habit, from first-hand knowledge, than could be taught you by a thousand such lessons as this.

You have but little conception of the possibilities which lie sleeping within you, awaiting but the awakening hand of vision to arouse you, and you will never have a better conception of those possibilities unless you develop sufficient Self-confidence to lift you above the commonplace influences of your present environment. The human mind is a marvelous, mysterious piece of machinery, a fact of which I was reminded a few months ago when I picked up Emerson's Essays and re-read his essay on Spiritual Laws. A strange thing happened. I saw in that essay, which I had read scores of times previously, much that I had never noticed before. I saw more in this essay than I had seen during previous readings because the unfoldment of my mind since the last reading had prepared me to interpret more.

The human mind is constantly unfolding, like the petals of a flower, until it reaches the maximum of development. What this maximum is, where it ends, or whether it ends at all or not, are unanswerable questions, but the degree of unfoldment seems to vary according to the nature of the individual and the degree to which he keeps his mind at work. A mind that is forced or coaxed into analytical thought every day seems to keep on unfolding and developing greater powers of interpretation.

Down in Louisville, Kentucky, lives Mr. Lee Cook, a man who has practically no legs and has to wheel himself around on a cart. In spite of the fact that Mr. Cook has been without legs since birth, he is the owner of a great industry and a millionaire through his own efforts. He has proved that a man can get along very well without legs if he has a well developed Self-confidence.

In the city of New York one may see a strong able-bodied and able-headed young man, without legs, rolling himself down Fifth Avenue every afternoon,with cap in hand, begging for a living. His head is perhaps as sound and as able to think as the average.

This young man could duplicate anything that Mr. Cook, of Louisville, has done, if he thought of himself as Mr. Cook thinks of himself.

Henry Ford owns more millions of dollars than he will ever need or use. Not so many years ago, he was working as a laborer in a machine shop, with but little schooling and without capital. Scores of other men, some of them with better organized brains than his, worked near him. Ford threw off the poverty consciousness, developed confidence in himself, thought of success and attained it. Those who worked around him could have done as well had they thought as he did.

Milo C. Jones, of Wisconsin, was stricken down with paralysis a few years ago. So bad was the stroke that he could not turn himself in bed or move a muscle of his body. His physical body was useless, but there was nothing wrong with his brain, so it began to function in earnest, probably for the first time in its existence. Lying flat on his back in bed, Mr. Jones made that brain create a definite purpose. That purpose was prosaic and humble enough in nature, but it was definite and it was a purpose, something that he had never known before.

His definite purpose was to make pork sausage. Calling his family around him he told of his plans and began directing them in carrying the plans into action. With nothing to aid him except a sound mind and plenty of Self-confidence, Milo C. Jones spread the name and reputation of "Little Pig Sausage" all over the United States, and accumulated a fortune besides.

All this was accomplished after paralysis had made it impossible for him to work with his hands. Where thought prevails power may be found!

Henry Ford has made millions of dollars and is still making millions of dollars each year because he believed in Henry Ford and transformed that belief into a definite purpose and backed that purpose with a definite plan. The other machinists who worked along with Ford, during the early days of his career, visioned nothing but a weekly pay envelope and that was all they ever got. They demanded nothing out of the ordinary of themselves. If you want to get more be sure to demand more of yourself.

Notice that this demand is to be made on yourself!

There comes to mind a well known poem whose author expressed a great psychological truth:

If you think you are beaten, you are;
If you think you dare not, you don't;
If you like to win, but you think you can't,
It is almost certain you won't.

If you think you'll lose you've lost,
For out of the world we find
Success begins with a fellow's will-
It's all in the state of mind.
If you think you are outclassed, you are-
You've got to think high to rise.
You've got to be sure of yourself before
You can ever win a prize.
Life's battles don't always go
To the stronger or faster man; But soon or late the man who wins
Is the man who thinks he can.

It can do no harm if you commit this poem to memory and use it as a part of your working equipment in the development of Self-confidence.

Somewhere in your make-up there is a "subtle something" which, if it were aroused by the proper outside influence, would carry you to heights of achievement such as you have never before anticipated. Just as a master player can take hold of a violin and cause that instrument to pour forth the most beautiful and entrancing strains of music, so is there some outside influence that can lay hold of your mind and cause you to go forth into the field of your chosen endeavor and play a glorious symphony of success. No man knows what hidden forces lie dormant within you. You, yourself, do not know your capacity for achievement, and you never will know until you come in contact with that particular stimulus which arouses you to greater action and extends your vision, develops your Self-confidence and moves you with a deeper desire to achieve.

It is not unreasonable to expect that some statement, some idea or some stimulating word of this Reading Course on the Law of Success will serve as the needed stimulus that will re-shape your destiny and re-direct your thoughts and energies along a pathway that will lead you, finally, to your coveted goal of life. It is strange, but true, that the most important turning-points of life often come at the most unexpected times and in the most unexpected ways. I have in mind a typical example of how some of the seemingly unimportant experiences of life often turn out to be the most important of all, and I am relating this ease because it shows, also, what a man can accomplish when he awakens to a full understanding of the value of Self-confidence. The incident to which I refer happened in the city of Chicago, while I was engaged in the work of character analysis. One day a tramp presented himself at my office and asked for an interview. As I looked up from my work and greeted him he said, "I have come to see the man who wrote this little book," as he removed from his pocket a copy of a book entitled Self-confidence, which I had written many years previously. "It must have been the hand of fate," he continued, "that slipped this book into my pocket yesterday afternoon, because I was about ready to go out there and punch a hole in Lake Michigan. I had about come to the conclusion that everything and everybody, including God, had it in for me until I read this book, and it gave me a new viewpoint and brought me the courage and the hope that sustained me through the night. I made up my mind that if I could see the man who wrote this book he could help me get on my feet again. Now, I am here and I would like to know what you can do for a man like me."

While he was speaking I had been studying him from head to foot, and I am frank to admit that down deep in my heart I did not believe there was anything I could do for him, but I did not wish to tell him so. The glassy stare in his eyes, the lines of discouragement in his face, the posture of his body, the ten days' growth of beard on his face, the nervous manner about this man all conveyed to me the impression that he was hopeless, but I did not have the heart to tell him so, therefore I asked him to sit down and tell me his whole story. I asked him to be perfectly frank and tell me, as nearly as possible, just what had brought him down to the ragged edge of life. I promised him that after I had heard his entire story I would then tell him whether or not I could be of service to him. He related his story, in lengthy detail, the sum and substance of which was this: He had invested his entire fortune in a small manufacturing business. When the world war began in 1914, it was impossible for him to get the raw materials necessary in the operation of his factory, and he therefore failed. The loss of his money broke his heart and so disturbed his mind that he left his wife and children and became a tramp. He had actually brooded over his loss until he had reached the point at which he was contemplating suicide.

After he had finished his story, I said to him: "I have listened to you with a great deal of interest, and I wish that there was something which I could do to help you, but there is absolutely nothing."

He became as pale as he will be when he is laid away in a coffin, and settled back in his chair and dropped his chin on his chest as much as to say, "That settles it." I waited for a few seconds, then said:

"While there is nothing that I can do for you, there is a man in this building to whom I will introduce you, if you wish, who can help you regain your lost fortune and put you back on your feet again." These words had barely fallen from my lips when he jumped up, grabbed me by the hands and said, "For God's sake lead me to this man."

It was encouraging to note that he had asked this "for God's sake." This indicated that there was still a spark of hope within his breast, so I took him by the arm and led him out into the laboratory where my psychological tests in character analysis were conducted, and stood with him in front of what looked to be a curtain over a door. I pulled the curtain aside and uncovered a tall looking-glass in which he saw himself from head to foot. Pointing my finger at the glass I said:

"There stands the man to whom I promised to introduce you. There is the only man in this world who can put you back on your feet again, and unless you sit down and become acquainted with that man, as you never became acquainted with him before, you might just as well go on over and 'punch a hole' in Lake Michigan, because you will be of no value to yourself or to the world until you know this man better."

He stepped over to the glass, rubbed his hands over his bearded face, studied himself from head to foot for a few moments, then stepped back, dropped his head and began to weep. I knew that the lesson had been driven home, so I led him back to the elevator and sent him away. I never expected to see him again, and I doubted that the lesson would be sufficient to help him regain his place in the world, because he seemed to be too far gone for redemption. He seemed to be not only down, but almost out.

A few days later I met this man on the street. His transformation had been so complete that I hardly recognized him. He was walking briskly, with his head tilted back. That old, shifting, nervous posture of his body was gone. He was dressed in new clothes from head to foot. He looked prosperous and he felt prosperous. He stopped me and related what had happened to bring about his rapid transformation from a state of abject failure to one of hope and promise.

"I was just on my way to your office," he explained, "to bring you the good news. I went out the very day that I was in your office, a down-and-out tramp, and despite my appearance I sold myself at a salary of $3,000.00 a year. Think of it, man, three thousand dollars a year! And my employer advanced me money enough with which to buy some new clothes, as you can see for yourself. He also advanced me some money to send home to my family, and I am once more on the road to success. It seems like a dream when I think that only a few days ago I had lost hope and faith and courage, and was actually contemplating suicide.

"I was coming to tell you that one of these days, when you are least expecting me, I will pay you another visit, and when I do. I will be a successful man. I will bring with me a check, signed in blank and made payable to you, and you may fill in the amount because you have saved me from myself by introducing me to myself–that self which I never knew until you stood me in front of that looking-glass and pointed out the real me."

As that man turned and departed in the crowded streets of Chicago I saw, for the first time in my life,what strength and power and possibility lie hidden in the mind of the man who has never discovered the value of Self-reliance. Then and there I made up my mind that I, too, would stand in front of that same looking-glass and point an accusing finger at myself for not having discovered the lesson which I had helped another to learn. I did stand before that same looking-glass, and as I did so I then and there fixed in my mind, as my definite purpose in life, the determination to help men and women discover the forces that lie sleeping within them. The book you hold in your hands is evidence that my definite purpose is being carried out.

The man whose story I have related is now the president of one of the largest and most successful concerns of its kind in America, with a business that extends from coast to coast and from Canada to Mexico.

A short while after the incident just related, a woman came to my office for personal analysis. She was then a teacher in the Chicago public schools. I gave her an analysis chart and asked her to fill it out. She had been at work on the chart but a few minutes when she came back to my desk, handed back the chart and said, "I do not believe I will fill this out." I asked her why she had decided not to fill out the chart and she replied: "To be perfectly frank with you, one of the questions in this chart put me to thinking and I now know what is wrong with me, therefore I feel it unnecessary to pay you a fee to analyze me." With that the woman went away and I did not hear from her for two years. She went to New York City, became a writer of advertising copy for one of the largest agencies in the country and her income at the time she wrote me was $10,000.00 a year.

This woman sent me a check to cover the cost of my analysis fee, because she felt that the fee had been earned, even though I did not render her the service that I usually render my clients. It is impossible for anyone to foretell what seemingly insignificant incident may lead to an important turning-point in one's career, but there is no denying the fact that these "turning-points" may be more readily recognized by those who have well-rounded-out confidence in themselves.

One of the irreparable losses to the human race lies in the lack of knowledge that there is a definite method through which Self-confidence can be developed in any person of average intelligence. What an immeasurable loss to civilization that young men and women are not taught this known method of developing Self-confidence before they complete their schooling, for no one who lacks faith in himself is really educated in the proper sense of the term.

Oh, what glory and satisfaction would be the happy heritage of the man or woman who could pull aside the curtain of fear that hangs over the human race and shuts out the sunlight of understanding that Self-confidence brings, wherever it is in evidence. Where fear controls, noteworthy achievement becomes an impossibility, a fact which rings to mind the definition of fear, as stated by a great philosopher: "Fear is the dungeon of the mind into which it runs and hides and seeks seclusion. Fear brings on superstition and superstition is the dagger with which hypocrisy assassinates the soul."

In front of the typewriter on which I am writing the manuscripts for this Reading Course hangs a sign with the following wording, in big letters: "Day by day in every way I am becoming more successful."

A skeptic who read that sign asked if I really believed "that stuff and I replied, "Of course not. All it ever did for me was to help me get out of the coal mines, where I started as a laborer, and find a place in the world in which I am serving upwards of 100,000 people, in whose minds I am planting the same positive thought that this sign brings out; therefore, why should I believe in it?"

As this man started to leave he said: "Well, perhaps there is something to this sort of philosophy, after all, for I have always been afraid that I would be a failure, and so far my fears have been thoroughly realized."

You are condemning yourself to poverty, misery and failure, or you are driving yourself on toward the heights of great achievement, solely by the thoughts you think. If you demand success of yourself and back up this demand with intelligent action you are sure to win. Bear in mind, though, that there is a difference between demanding success and just merely wishing for it. You should find out what this difference is, and take advantage of it.

Go at the task of developing Self-confidence with faith. Never mind "what they will say" because you might as well know that "they" will be of little aid to you in your climb up the mountain-side of life toward the object of your definite purpose. You have within you all the power you need with which to get whatever you want or need in this world, and about the best way to avail yourself of this power is to believe in yourself.

"Know thyself, man; know thyself."

This has been the advice of the philosophers all down the ages. When you really know yourself you will know that there is nothing foolish about hanging a sign in front of you that reads like this: "Day by day in every way I am becoming more successful," with due apologies to the Frenchman who made this motto popular. I am not afraid to place this sort of suggestion in front of my desk, and, what is more to the point, I am not afraid to believe that it will influence me so that I will become a more positive and aggressive human being.

More than twenty-five years ago I learned my first lesson in Self-confidence building. One night I was sitting before an open fire-place, listening to a conversation between some older men, on the subject of Capital and Labor. Without invitation I joined in the conversation and said something about employers and employees settling their differences on the Golden Rule basis. My remarks attracted the attention of one of the men, who turned to me, with a look of surprise on his face and said:

"Why, you are a bright boy, and if you would go out and get a schooling you would make your mark in the world."

Those remarks fell on "fertile" ears, even though that was the first time anyone had ever told me that I was bright, or that I might accomplish anything worthwhile in life.

The remark put me to thinking, and the more I allowed my mind to dwell upon that thought the more certain I became that the remark had back of it a possibility.

It might be truthfully stated that whatever service I am rendering the world and whatever good I accomplish, should be credited to that off-hand remark.

Suggestions such as this are often powerful, and none the less so when they are deliberate and self-expressed. Go back, now, to the Self-confidence formula and master it, for it will lead you into the "power-house" of your own mind, where you will tap a force that can be made to carry you to the very top of the Ladder of Success.

Others will believe in you only when you believe in yourself. They will "tune in" on your thoughts and feel toward you just as you feel toward yourself. The law of mental telepathy takes care of this. You are continuously broadcasting what you think of yourself, and if you have no faith in yourself others will pick up the vibrations of your thoughts and mistake them for their own. Once understand the law of mental telepathy and you will know why Self-confidence is the second of the Fifteen Laws of Success.

You should be cautioned, however, to learn the difference between Self-confidence, which is based upon sound knowledge of what you know and what you can do, and egotism, which is only based upon what you wish you knew or could do. Learn the difference between these two terms or you will make yourself boresome, ridiculous and annoying to people of culture and understanding. Self-confidence is something which should never be proclaimed or announced except through intelligent performance of constructive deeds.

If you have Self-confidence those around you will discover this fact. Let them make the discovery. They will feel proud of their alertness in having made the discovery, and you will be free from the suspicion of egotism. Opportunity never stalks the person with a highly developed state of egotism, but brick bats and ugly remarks do. Opportunity forms affinities much more easily and quickly with Self-confidence than it does with egotism. Self-praise is never a proper measure of self-reliance. Bear this in mind and let your Self-confidence speak only through the tongue of constructive service rendered without fuss or flurry.

Self-confidence is the product of knowledge. Know yourself, know how much you know (and how little), why you know it, and how you are going to use it. "Four-flushers" come to grief, therefore, do not pretend to know more than you actually do know. There's no use of pretense, because any educated person will measure you quite accurately after hearing you speak for three minutes. What you really are will speak so loudly that what you "claim" you are will not be heard.

If you heed this warning the last four pages of this one lesson may mark one of the most important turning-points of your life.

Believe in yourself, but do not tell the world what you can do–SHOW IT!

You are now ready for Lesson Four, which will take you the next step up the Ladder of Success.

Lesson Three SELF-CONFIDENCE

DISCONTENTMENT–An After-the-Lesson Visit With the Author

The supreme mystery of the universe is life! We come here without our consent, from whence we know not! We go away without our consent, whither, we know not!

We are eternally trying to solve this great riddle of "LIFE," and, for what purpose and to what end?

That we are placed on this earth for a definite reason there can be no doubt by any thinker. May it not be possible that the power which placed us here will know what to do with us when we pass on beyond the Great Divide?

Would it not be a good plan to give the Creator who placed us here on earth, credit for having enough intelligence to know what to do with us after we pass on; or, should we assume the intelligence and the ability to control the future life in our own way? May it not be possible that we can co-operate with the Creator very intelligently by assuming to control our conduct on this earth to the end that we may be decent to one another and do all the good we can in all the ways we can during this life, leaving the hereafter to one who probably knows, better than we, what is best for us?

From birth until death the mind is always reaching out for that which it does not possess.

The little child, playing with its toys on the floor, sees another child with a different sort of toy and immediately tries to lay hands on that toy.

The female child (grown tall) believes the other woman's clothes more becoming than her own and sets out to duplicate them.

The male child (grown tall) sees another man with a bigger collection of railroads or banks or merchandise and says to himself: "How fortunate! How fortunate! How can I separate him from his belongings?"

F. W. Woolworth, the Five and Ten Cent Store king, stood on Fifth Avenue in New York City and gazed upward at the tall Metropolitan Building and said: "How wonderful! I will build one much taller." The crowning achievement of his life was measured by the Woolworth Building. That building stands as a temporary symbol of man's nature to excel the handiwork of other men. A MONUMENT TO THE VANITY OF MAN, WITH BUT LITTLE ELSE TO JUSTIFY ITS EXISTENCE!

The little ragged newsboy on the street stands, with wide-open mouth, and envies the business man as he alights from his automobile at the curb and starts into his office.

"How happy I would be," the newsboy says to himself, "if I owned a Lizzie." And, the business man seated at his desk inside, thinks how happy he would be if he could add another million dollars to his already over swollen bank roll.

The grass is always sweeter on the other side of the fence, says the jackass, as he stretches his neck in the attempt to get to it.

Turn a crowd of boys into an apple orchard and they will pass by the nice mellow apples on the ground. The red, juicy ones hanging dangerously high in the top of the tree look much more tempting, and up the tree they will go.

The married man takes a sheepish glance at the daintily dressed ladies on the street and thinks how fortunate he would be if his wife were as pretty as they. Perhaps she is much prettier, but he misses that beauty because–well, because "the grass is always greener on the other side of the fence." Most divorce cases grow out of man's tendency to climb the fence into the other fellow's pastures.

Happiness is always just around the bend; always in sight but just out of reach. Life is never complete, no matter what we have or how much of it we possess. One thing calls for something else to go with it.

Milady buys a pretty hat. She must have a gown to match it. That calls for new shoes and hose and gloves, and other accessories that run into a big bill far beyond her husband's means.

Man longs for a home–just a plain little house setting off in the edge of the woods. He builds it, but it is not complete; he must have shrubbery and flowers and landscaping to go with it. Still it is not complete; he must have a beautiful fence around it, with a graveled driveway.

That calls for a motor car and a garage in which to house it.

All these little touches have been added, but to no avail! The place is now too small.

He must have a house with more rooms. The Ford Coupe must be replaced by a Cadillac sedan, so there will be room for company in the cross country tours. On and on the story goes, ad inflnitum!

The young man receives a salary sufficient to keep him and his family fairly comfortable. Then comes a promotion and an advance in salary of a thousand dollars a year. Does he lay the extra thousand dollars away in the savings account and continue living as before? He does nothing of the sort. Immediately he must trade the old car in for a new one. A porch must be added to the house. The wife needs a new wardrobe. The table must be set with better food and more of it. (Pity his poor, groaning stomach.) At the end of the year is he better off with the increase? He is nothing of the sort! The more he gets the more he wants, and the rule applies to the man with millions the same as to the man with but a few thousands.

The young man selects the girl of his choice, believing he cannot live without her. After he gets her he is not sure that he can live with her. If a man remains a bachelor he wonders why he is so stupid as to deprive himself of the joys of married life. If he marries he wonders how she happened to catch him off guard long enough to "harpoon" him.

And the god of Destiny cries out "O fool, O fool! You are damned if you DO and you are damned if you DON'T."

At every crossroad of Life the imps of Discontentment stand in the shadows of the back-ground, with a grin of mockery on their faces, crying out "Take the road of your own choice! We will get you in the end!"

At last man becomes disillusioned and begins to learn that Happiness and Contentment are not of this world. Then begins the search for the pass-word that will open the door to him in some world of which he knows not. Surely there must be Happiness on the other side of the Great Divide. In desperation his tired, care-worn heart turns to religion for hope and encouragement.

But, his troubles are not over; they are just starting!

"Come into our tent and accept our creed," says one sect, "and you may go straight to heaven after death." Poor man hesitates, looks and listens. Then he hears the call of another brand of religion whose leader says:

"Stay out of the other camp or you'll go straight to hell! They only sprinkle water on your head, but we push you all the way under, thereby insuring you safe passage into the Land of Promise."

In the midst of sectarian claims and counter-claims Poor man becomes undecided. Not knowing whether to turn this way or that, he wonders which brand of religion offers the safest passage-way, until Hope vanishes.

"Myself when young did eagerly frequent Doctor and Saint and heard great argument

About it and about; but evermore Came out by the same door where in I went."

Always seeking but never finding–thus might be described man's struggle for Happiness and Contentment. His mind becomes an eternal question mark, searching hither and yon for an answer to the questions– "Whence and Whither?"

"The worldly hope men set their Hearts upon
Turns Ashes–or it prospers; and anon,
Like Snow upon the Desert's
Dusty Face
Lighting a little Hour or two is gone."

Life is an everlasting question-mark!

That which we want most is always in the embryonic distance of the future. Our power to acquire is always a decade or so behind our power to DESIRE!

And, if we catch up with the thing we want we no longer want it!

Fortunate is the young woman who learns this great truth and keeps her lover always guessing, always on the defensive lest he may lose her.

Our favorite author is a hero and a genius until we meet him in person and learn the sad truth that, after all, he is only a man. "How often must we learn this lesson? Men cease to interest us when we find their limitations. The only sin is limitation. As soon as you once come up with a man's limitations, it is all over with him."–EMERSON.

How beautiful the mountain yonder in the distance; but, the moment we draw near it we find it to be nothing but a wretched collection of rocks and dirt and trees.

Out of this truth grew the oft-repeated adage "Familiarity breeds contempt."

Beauty and Happiness and Contentment are states of mind. They can never be enjoyed except through vision of the afar. The most beautiful painting of Rembrandt becomes a mere smudge of daubed paint if we come too near it.

Destroy the Hope of unfinished dreams in man's heart and he is finished.

The moment a man ceases to cherish the vision of future achievement he is through. Nature has built man so that his greatest and only lasting Happiness is that which he feels in the pursuit of some yet unattained object. Anticipation is sweeter than realization. That which is at hand does not satisfy. The only enduring satisfaction is that which comes to the Person who keeps alive in his heart the HOPE of future achievement. When that hope dies write FINIS across the human heart.

Life's greatest inconsistency is the fact that most of that which we believe is not true. Russel Conwell wrote the most popular lecture ever delivered in the English language. He called it "Acres of Diamonds." The central idea of the lecture was the statement that one need not seek opportunity in the distance; that opportunity may be found in the vicinity of one's birth. Perhaps! But, how many believe it?

Opportunity may be found wherever one really looks for it, and nowhere else! To most men the picking looks better on the other side of the fence. How futile to urge one to try out one's luck in the little home-town when it is man's nature to look for opportunity in some other locality.

Do not worry because the grass looks sweeter on the other side of the fence. Nature intended it so. Thus does she allure us and groom us for the life-long task of GROWTH THROUGH STRUGGLE.

Lesson Four: THE HABIT OF SAVING

"Man is a combination of flesh, bone, blood, hair and brain cells. These are the building materials out of which he shapes, through the Law of Habit, his own personality."

To advise one to save money without describing how to save would be somewhat like drawing the picture of a horse and writing under it, "This is a horse." It is obvious to all that the saving of money is one of the essentials for success, but the big question uppermost in the minds of the majority of those who do not save is:

"How can I do it?"

The saving of money is solely a matter of habit. For this reason this lesson begins with a brief analysis of the Law of Habit.

It is literally true that man, through the Law of Habit, shapes his own personality.

Through repetition, any act indulged in a few times becomes a habit, and the mind appears to be nothing more than a mass of motivating forces growing out of our daily habits.

When once fixed in the mind a habit voluntarily impels one to action. For example, follow a given route to your daily work, or to some other place that you frequently visit, and very soon the habit has been formed and your mind will lead you over that route without thought on your part. Moreover, if you start out with the intention of traveling in another direction, without keeping the thought of the change in routes constantly in mind, you will find yourself following the old route.

Public speakers have found that the telling over and over again of a story, which may be based upon pure fiction, brings into play the Law of Habit, and very soon they forget whether the story is true or not.

WALLS OF LIMITATION BUILT THROUGH HABIT

Millions of people go through life in poverty and want because they have made destructive use of the Law of Habit. Not understanding either the Law of Habit or the Law of Attraction through which "like attracts like," those who remain in poverty seldom realize that they are where they are as the result of their own acts.

Fix in your mind the thought that your ability is limited to a given earning capacity and you will never earn more than that, because the law of habit will set up a definite limitation of the amount you can earn, your subconscious mind will accept this limitation, and very soon you will feel yourself "slipping" until finally you will become so hedged in by FEAR OF POVERTY (one of the six basic fears) that opportunity will no longer knock at your door; your doom will be sealed; your fate fixed.

Formation of the Habit of Saving does not mean that you shall limit your earning capacity; it means just the opposite–that you shall apply this law so that it not only conserves that which you earn, in a systematic manner, but it also places you in the way of greater opportunity and gives you the vision, the self-confidence, the imagination, the enthusiasm, the initiative and leadership actually to increase your earning capacity.

Stating this great law in another way, when you thoroughly understand the Law of Habit you may insure yourself success in the great game of moneymaking by "playing both ends of that game against the middle."

You proceed in this manner:

First, through the law of Definite Chief Aim you set up, in your mind, an accurate, definite description of that which you want, including the amount of money you intend to earn. Your subconscious mind takes over this picture which you have created and uses it as a blueprint, chart or map by which to mold your thoughts and actions into practical plans for attaining the object of your Chief Aim, or purpose. Through the Law of Habit you keep the object of your Definite Chief Aim fixed in your mind (in the manner described in Lesson Two until it becomes firmly and permanently implanted there). This practice will destroy the poverty consciousness and set up, in its place, a prosperity consciousness. You will actually begin to DEMAND prosperity, you will begin to expect it, you will begin to prepare yourself to receive it and to use it wisely, thus paving the way or setting the stage for the development of the Habit of Saving.

Second, having in this manner increased your earning power you will make further use of the Law of Habit by provision, in your written statement of your Definite Chief Aim, for saving a definite proportion of all the money you earn.

Therefore, as your earnings increase, your savings will, likewise, increase in proportion.

By ever urging yourself on and demanding of your self increased earning power, on the one hand, and by systematically laying aside a definite amount of all your earnings, on the other hand, you will soon reach the point at which you have removed all imaginary limitations from your own mind and you will then be well started on the road toward financial independence.

Nothing could be more practical or more easily accomplished than this!

Reverse the operation of the Law of Habit, by setting up in your mind the Fear of Poverty, and very soon this fear will reduce your earning capacity until you will be barely able to earn sufficient money to take care of your actual necessities.

The publishers of newspapers could create a panic in a week's time by filling their columns with news items concerning the actual business failures of the country, despite the fact that but few businesses compared to the total number in existence, actually fail. The so-called "crime waves" are very largely the products of sensational journalism. A single murder case, when exploited by the newspapers of the country, through scare headlines, is sufficient to start a regular "wave" of similar crimes in various localities. Following the repetition in the daily papers of the Hickman murder story, similar cases began to be reported from other parts of the country.

We are the victims of our habits, no matter who we are or what may be our life-calling. Any idea that is deliberately fixed in the mind, or any idea that is permitted to set itself up in the mind, as the result of suggestion, environment, the influence of associates, etc., is sure to cause us to indulge in acts which conform to the nature of the idea.

Form the habit of thinking and talking of prosperity and abundance, and very soon material evidence of these will begin to manifest itself in the nature of wider opportunity and new and unexpected opportunity.

Like attracts like! If you are in business and have formed the habit of talking and thinking about "business being bad" business will be bad. One pessimist, providing he is permitted to continue his destructive influence long enough, can destroy the work of half a dozen competent men, and he will do it by setting adrift in the minds of his associates the thought of poverty and failure.

Don't be this type of man or woman.

One of the most successful bankers in the state of Illinois has this sign hanging in his private office: "WE TALK AND THINK ONLY OF ABUNDANCE HERE. IF YOU HAVE A TALE OF WOE PLEASE KEEP IT, AS WE DO NOT WANT IT."

No business firm wants the services of a pessimist, and those who understand the Law of Attraction and the Law of Habit will no more tolerate the pessimist than they would permit a burglar to roam around their place of business, for the reason that one such person will destroy the usefulness of those around him.

In tens of thousands of homes the general topic of conversation is poverty and want, and that is just what they are getting. They think of poverty, they talk of poverty, they accept poverty as their lot in life.

They reason that because their ancestors were poor before them they, also, must remain poor.

The poverty consciousness is formed as the result of the habit of thinking of and fearing poverty. "Lo! The thing I had feared has come upon me."

THE SLAVERY OF DEBT

Debt is a merciless master, a fatal enemy of the savings habit.

Poverty, alone, is sufficient to kill off ambition, destroy self-confidence and destroy hope, but add to it the burden of debt and all who are victims of these two cruel taskmasters are practically doomed to failure.

No man can do his best work, no man can express himself in terms that command respect, no man can either create or carry out a definite purpose in life, with heavy debt hanging over his head. The man who is bound in the slavery of debt is just as helpless as the slave who is bound by ignorance, or by actual chains.

The author has a very close friend whose income is $1,000 a month. His wife loves "society" and tries to make a $20,000 showing on a $12,000 income, with the result that this poor fellow is usually about $8,000 in debt. Every member of his family has the "spending habit," having acquired this from the mother. The children, two girls and one boy, are now of the age when they are thinking of going to college, but this is impossible because of the father's debts. The result is dissension between the father and his children which makes the entire family unhappy and miserable.

It is a terrible thing even to think of going through life like a prisoner in chains, bound down and owned by somebody else on account of debts. The accumulation of debts is a habit. It starts in a small way and grows to enormous proportions slowly, step by step, until finally it takes charge of one's very soul.

Thousands of young men start their married lives with unnecessary debts hanging over their heads and never manage to get out from under the load. After the novelty of marriage begins to wear off (as it usually does) the married couple begin to feel the embarrassment of want, and this feeling grows until it leads, oftentimes, to open dissatisfaction with one another, and eventually to the divorce court.

A man who is bound by the slavery of debt has no time or inclination to set up or work out ideals, with the result that he drifts downward with time until he eventually begins to set up limitations in his own mind, and by these he hedges himself behind prison walls of FEAR and doubt from which he never escapes.

No sacrifice is too great to avoid the misery of debt!

"Think of what you owe yourself and those who are dependent upon you and resolve to be no man's debtor," is the advice of one very successful man whose early chances were destroyed by debt. This man came to himself soon enough to throw off the habit of buying that which he did not need and eventually worked his way out of slavery. Most men who develop the habit of debt will not be so fortunate as to come to their senses in time to save themselves, because debt is something like quicksand in that it has a tendency to draw its victim deeper and deeper into the mire.

The Fear of Poverty is one of the most destructive of the six basic fears described in Lesson Three. The man who becomes hopelessly in debt is seized with this poverty fear, his ambition and self-confidence become paralyzed, and he sinks gradually into oblivion.

There are two classes of debts, and these are so different in nature that they deserve to be here described, as follows:

1. There are debts incurred for luxuries which become a dead loss.

2. There are debts incurred in the course of professional or business trading which represent service or merchandise that can be converted back into assets.

The first class of debts is the one to be avoided. The second class may be indulged in, providing the one incurring the debts uses judgment and does not go beyond the bounds of reasonable limitation. The moment one buys beyond his limitations he enters the realm of speculation, and speculation swallows more of its victims than it enriches. Practically all people who live beyond their means are tempted to speculate with the hope that they may recoup, at a single turn of the wheel of fortune, so to speak, their entire indebtedness. The wheel generally stops at the wrong place and, far from finding themselves out of debt, such people as indulge in speculation are bound more closely as slaves of debt.

The Fear of Poverty breaks down the will-power of its victims, and they then find themselves unable to restore their lost fortunes, and, what is still more sad, they lose all ambition to extricate themselves from the slavery of debt.

Hardly a day passes that one may not see an account in the newspapers of at least one suicide as the result of worry over debts. The slavery of debt causes more suicides every year than all other causes combined, which is a slight indication of the cruelty of the poverty fear.

During the war millions of men faced the front-line trenches without flinching, knowing that death might overtake them any moment. Those same men, when facing the Fear of Poverty, often cringe and out of sheer desperation, which paralyzes their reason, sometimes commit suicide.

The person who is free from debt may whip poverty and achieve outstanding financial success, but, if he is bound by debt, such achievement is but a remote possibility, and never a probability.

Fear of Poverty is a negative, destructive state of mind. Moreover, one negative state of mind has a tendency to attract other similar states of mind. For example, the Fear of Poverty may attract the fear of Ill Health, and these two may attract the Fear of Old Age, so that the victim finds himself poverty-stricken, in ill health and actually growing old long before the time when he should begin to show the signs of old age. Millions of untimely, nameless graves have been filled by this cruel state of mind known as the Fear of Poverty!

Less than a dozen years ago a young man held a responsible position with the City National Bank, of New York City. Through living beyond his income he contracted a large amount of debts which caused him to worry until this destructive habit began to show up in his work and he was dismissed from the bank's service.

He secured another position, at less money, but his creditors embarrassed him so that he decided to resign and go away into another city, where he hoped to escape them until he had accumulated enough money to pay off his indebtedness. Creditors have a way of tracing debtors, so very soon they were close on the heels of this young man, whose employer found out about his indebtedness and dismissed him from his position. He then searched in vain for employment for two months. One cold night he went to the top of one of the tall buildings on Broadway and jumped off. Debt had claimed another victim.

HOW TO MASTER THE FEAR OF POVERTY

To whip the Fear of Poverty one must take two very definite steps, providing one is in debt. First, quit the habit of buying on credit, and follow this by gradually paying off the debts that you have already incurred.

Being free from the worry of indebtedness you are ready to revamp the habits of your mind and redirect your course toward prosperity. Adopt, as a part of your Definite Chief Aim, the habit of saving a regular proportion of your income, even if this be no more than a penny a day. Very soon this habit will begin to lay hold of your mind and you will actually get joy out of saving.

Any habit may be discontinued by building in its place some other and more desirable habit. The "spending" habit must be replaced by the "saving" habit by all who attain financial independence.

Merely to discontinue an undesirable habit is not enough, as such habits have a tendency to reappear unless the place they formerly occupied in the mind is filled by some other habit of a different nature.

The discontinuance of a habit leaves a "hole" in the mind, and this hole must be filled up with some other form of habit or the old one will return and claim its place.

Throughout this course many psychological formulas, which the student has been requested to memorize and practice, have been described. You will find such a formula in Lesson Three, the object of which is to develop Self-confidence.

These formulas may be assimilated so they become a part of your mental machinery, through the Law of Habit, if you will follow the instructions for their use which accompany each of them.

It is assumed that you are striving to attain financial independence. The accumulation of money is not difficult after you have once mastered the Fear of Poverty and developed in its place the Habit of Saving.

The author of this course would be greatly disappointed to know that any student of the course got the impression from anything in this or any of the other lessons that Success is measured by dollars alone.

However, money does represent an important factor in success, and it must be given its proper value in any philosophy intended to help people in becoming useful, happy and prosperous.

The cold, cruel, relentless truth is that in this age, of materialism a man is no more than so many grains of sand, which may be blown helter-skelter by every stray wind of circumstance, unless he is entrenched behind the power of money!

Genius may offer many rewards to those who possess it, but the fact still remains that genius without money with which to give it expression is but an empty, skeleton-like honor.

The man without money is at the mercy of the man who has it!

And this goes, regardless of the amount of ability he may possess, the training he has had or the native genius with which he was gifted by nature.

There is no escape from the fact that people will weigh you very largely in the light of bank balances,no matter who you are or what you can do. The first question that arises, in the minds of most people, when they meet a stranger, is, "How much money has he?" If he has money he is welcomed into homes and business opportunities are thrown his way. All sorts of attention are lavished upon him. He is a prince, and as such is entitled to the best of the land.

But if his shoes are run down at the heels, his clothes are not pressed, his collar is dirty, and he shows plainly the signs of impoverished finances, woe be his lot, for the passing crowd will step on his toes and blow the smoke of disrespect in his face.

These are not pretty statements, but they have one virtue–THEY ARE TRUE!

This tendency to judge people by the money they have, or their power to control money, is not confined to any one class of people. We all have a touch of it, whether we recognize the fact or not.

Thomas A. Edison is one of the best known and most respected inventors in the world, yet it is no misstatement of facts to say that he would have remained a practically unknown, obscure personage had he not followed the habit of conserving his resources and shown his ability to save money.

Henry Ford never would have got to first base with his "horseless carriage" had he not developed, quite early in life, the habit of saving. Moreover, had Mr. Ford not conserved his resources and hedged himself behind their power he would have been "swallowed up" by his competitors or those who covetously desired to take his business away from him, long, long years ago.

Many a man has gone a very long way toward success, only to stumble and fall, never again to rise, because of lack of money in times of emergency. The mortality rate in business each year, due to lack of reserve capital for emergencies, is stupendous. To this one cause are due more of the business failures than to all other causes combined!

Reserve Funds are essential in the successful operation of business!

Likewise, Savings Accounts are essential to success on the part of individuals. Without a savings fund the individual suffers in two ways: first, by inability to seize opportunities that come only to the person with some ready cash, and, second, by embarrassment due to some unexpected emergency calling for cash.

It might be said, also, that the individual suffers in still a third respect by not developing the Habit of Saving, through lack of certain other qualities essential for success which grow out of the practice of the Habit of Saving.

The nickels, dimes and pennies which the average person allows to slip through his fingers would, if systematically saved and properly put to work, eventually bring financial independence.

Through the courtesy of a prominent Building and Loan Association the following table has been compiled, showing what a monthly saving of $5.00, $10.00, $25.00 or $50.00 will amount to at the end of ten years. These figures are startling when one comes to consider the fact that the average person spends from $5.00 to $50.00 a month for useless merchandise or so-called "entertainment."

The making and saving of money is a science.

The rules by which money is accumulated are so simple that anyone may follow them. The main prerequisite is a willingness to subordinate the present to the future, by eliminating unnecessary expenditures for luxuries.

A young man, who was earning only $20.00 a week as chauffeur for a prominent New York banker, was induced by his employer to keep an accurate account of every cent he spent for one week. The following is an itemized list of his expenses:

Cigarettes	.75
Chewing gum	.30
Soda fountain	1.80
Cigars for associates	1.50
Moving picture show	1.00
Shaves, including tips	1.60
Newspaper, daily and Sunday	.22
Shoe shines	.30
	7.47
Board and room	12.00
Money on hand	.53
	$20.00

These figures tell a tragic story which might as well apply to thousands of other people as to the young man who kept this account. His actual savings out of $20.00 were only 53 cents. He spent $7.47 for items, every one of which could have been greatly reduced, and most of which could have been eliminated entirely. In fact, by shaving himself and shining his own shoes, he could have saved every cent of the $7.47.

Now turn to the table made up by the Building and Loan Association and observe what the saving of $7.47 a week would amount to. Suppose the amount this young man actually saved had been only $25.00 a month; the saving would have increased to the snug sum of $5,000.00 by the end of the first ten years.

The young man in question was twenty-one years old at the time he kept this expense account. By the time he reached the age of thirty-one years he could have had a substantial amount in the bank, had he saved $25.00 a month, and this saving would have brought him many opportunities that would have led directly to financial independence.

Some who are short-sighted, pseudo-philosophers, are fond of pointing to the fact that no one can become rich merely by saving a few dollars a week. This may be true enough, as far as the reasoning goes (which is not very far) but the other side of the story is that the saving of even a small sum of money places one in position where, oftentimes, this small sum may enable one to take advantage of business opportunities which lead directly and quite rapidly to financial independence.

The foregoing table, showing what a saving of $5.00 a month will amount to at the end of ten years, should be copied and pasted on your mirror, where it will stare you in the face every morning when you get up and every night as you retire, providing you have not already acquired the habit of systematic saving of money. This table should be reproduced, in letters and figures an inch tall, and placed on the walls of every public school throughout the land, where it might serve as a constant reminder to all school children of the value of the savings habit.

Some years ago, before giving serious thought to the value of the savings habit, this author made up an account of the money which had slipped through his fingers. The amount was so alarming that it resulted in the writing of this lesson, and adding the Habit of Saving as one of the Fifteen Laws of Success. Following is an itemized statement of this account:

$ 4,000.00	inherited, invested in automobile supply business with a friend who lost the entire amount in one year.
$3,600.00	extra money earned from sundry writing for magazines and newspapers, all spent uselessly.
$30,000.00	earned from training 3,000 salesmen, with the aid of the Law of Success philosophy, invested in a magazine which was not a success because there was no reserve capital back of it.
$3,400.00	extra money earned from public addresses, lectures, etc., all of which was spent as it came in.
$6,000.00	estimated amount that could have been saved during a period of ten years, out of regular earnings, at the rate of only $50 a month.

$47,000.00

This amount, had it been saved and invested as received, in Building and Loan Associations, or in some other manner that would have earned compound interest, would have grown into the sum of $94,000.00 at the time this lesson is being written. The author is not a victim of any of the usual habits of dissipation, such as gambling, drinking and excessive entertaining. It is almost unbelievable that a man whose habits of living are reasonably moderate could spend $47,000.00 within a little over ten years without having anything to show for the money, but it can be done!

A capital reserve of $94,000.00, working at compound interest, is sufficient to give any man all the financial freedom he needs.

I recall one occasion when the president of a large corporation sent me a check for $500.00 for an address I delivered at a banquet given to the employees, and I distinctly recall what went through my mind when I opened the letter and saw the check. I had wanted a new automobile and this check was exactly the amount required for the first payment. I had it spent before it had been in my hands thirty seconds.

Perhaps this is the experience of the majority of people. They think more of how they are going to SPEND what they have than they do about ways and means of SAVING. The idea of saving, and the self-control and self-sacrifice which must accompany it, is always accompanied by thoughts of an unpleasant nature, but oh, how it does thrill one to think of SPENDING.

There is a reason for this, and that reason is the fact that most of us have developed the habit of spending while neglecting the Habit of Saving, and any idea that frequents the human mind but seldom is not as welcome as that which frequents it often. In truth, the Habit of Saving can be made as fascinating as the habit of spending, but not until it has become a regular, well grounded, systematic habit. We like to do that which is often repeated, which is but another way of stating what the scientists have discovered, that we are victims of our habits.

The habit of saving money requires more force of character than most people have developed, for the reason that saving means self-denial and sacrifice of amusements and pleasures in scores of different ways.

For this very reason one who develops the savings habit acquires, at the same time, many of the other needed habits which lead to success: especially Self-control, Self-confidence, Courage, Poise and Freedom from Fear.

HOW MUCH SHOULD ONE SAVE?

The first question that will arise is, "How Much Should One Save?" The answer cannot be given in a few words, for the amount one should save depends upon many conditions, some of which may be within one's control and some of which may not be. Generally speaking, a man who works for a salary should apportion his income about as follows:

Savings Account..........................	20%
Living-Clothes, Food and Shelter..	50%
Education..................................	10%
Recreation................................	10%
Life Insurance...........................	10%
	100%

The following, however, indicates the approximate distribution which the average man actually makes of his income:

Savings Account......................	NOTHING
Living–Clothes, Food and Shelter..	60%
Education.................................	0%
Recreation................................	35%
Life Insurance............................	5%
	100%

Under the item of "recreation" is included, of course, many expenditures that do not really "recreate," such as money spent for alcoholic drinks, dinner parties and other similar items which may actually serve to undermine one's health and destroy character.

An experienced analyst of men has stated that he could tell very accurately, by examining a man's monthly budget, what sort of a life the man is living; moreover, that he will get most of his information from the one item of "recreation." This, then, is an item to be watched as carefully as the greenhouse keeper watches the thermometer which controls the life and death of his plants.

Those who keep budget accounts often include an item called "entertainment," which, in a majority of cases, turns out to be an evil because it depletes the income heavily and when carried to excess depletes, also, the health.

We are living, right now, in an age when the item of "entertainment" is altogether too high in most budget allowances. Tens of thousands of people who earn not more than $50.00 a week are spending as much as one third of their incomes for what they call "entertainment," which comes in a bottle, with a questionable label on it, at anywhere from $6.00 to $12.00 a quart. Not only are these unwise people wasting the money that should go into a savings fund, but, of far greater danger, they are destroying both character and health.

Nothing in this lesson is intended as a preachment on morality, or on any other subject.

We are here dealing with cold facts which, to a large extent, constitute the building materials out of which SUCCESS may be created.

However, this is an appropriate place to state some FACTS which have such a direct bearing on the subject of achieving success that they cannot be omitted without weakening this entire course in general and this lesson in particular.

The author of this course is NOT a reformer! Neither is he a preacher on morals, as this field of useful endeavor is quite well covered by others who, are able workers. What is here stated, therefore, is intended as a necessary part of a course of philosophy whose purpose is to mark a safe road over which one may travel to honorable achievement.

During the year 1926 the author was in partnership with the late Don R. Mellett, who was, at that time, the publisher of the Canton (Ohio) Daily News. Mr. Mellett became interested in the Law of Success philosophy because it offered, as he believed, sound counsel to young men and young women who really wish to get ahead in life. Through the pages of the Daily News Mr. Mellett was conducting a fierce battle against the underworld forces of Canton. With the aid of detectives and investigators, some of whom were supplied by the Governor of Ohio, Mr. Mellett and the author gathered accurate data concerning the way most of the people in Canton were living.

In July, 1926, Mr. Mellett was assassinated from ambush, and four men, one of them a former member of the Canton police force, are now serving life sentences in the Ohio State Penitentiary for the crime.

During the investigation into crime conditions in Canton all reports came to the author's office, and the data here described are, therefore, known to be absolutely accurate.

One of the officials of a large industrial plant whose salary was $6,000.00 a year paid a Canton bootlegger an average of $300.00 a month for the liquor (if "stuff can be called liquor) which he used for "entertaining." His wife participated in these "entertainments" which took place in his own home.

A paying teller in a bank, whose salary was $150.00 a month, was spending an average of $75.00 a month for liquor, and in addition to this unpardonable waste of money, out of a salary which was none too great at most, he was traveling at a pace and with a crowd which meant ruin for him later on.

The superintendent of a large manufacturing plant, whose salary was $5,000.00 a year, and who should have been saving at least $125.00 a month, was actually saving nothing. His bootlegger's bill averaged $150.00 a month.

A policeman whose income was $160.00 a month was spending over $400.00 a month on dinner parties, at a near-by roadhouse. Where he got the difference between his legitimate income and his actual expenditures is a question that reflects no particular credit on the policeman.

A bank official whose income, as near as it could be estimated from his previous years' income tax reports, was about $8,000.00 a year, had a monthly bootlegger's bill of more than $500.00 during the three months that his activities were checked by the Mellett investigators.

A young man who worked in a department store, at a salary of $20.00 a week, was spending an average of $35.00 a week with one bootlegger. The assumption was that he was stealing the difference from his employer. Old Man Trouble awaited this young man, just around the corner, although it is not known by the author whether or not the two have come together as yet.

A salesman for a life insurance company, whose income was not known because he worked on a commission basis, was spending an average of $200.00 a month with one bootlegger. No record of any savings account was found, and the assumption is that he had none. This assumption was later confirmed when the company for which the young man worked had him arrested for embezzlement of its funds. No doubt he was spending the money which he should have turned in to the company. He is now serving a long sentence in the Ohio State Penitentiary.

A young lad who was attending high school was spending large sums for liquor. The actual amount was not obtainable for the reason that he paid cash as he got the liquor, and the bootlegger's records did not, therefore, disclose the actual amount. Later this boy's parents had him locked up "to save him from himself."It was found that he was stealing money from a savings fund kept by his mother, somewhere about the house. He had stolen and spent more than $300.00 of this money when discovered.

This author conducted a Lecture Bureau in forty-one high schools, where he lectured once a month during the entire school season. The principals of these high schools stated that less than two per cent of the students showed any tendency toward saving money, and an examination through the aid of a questionnaire prepared for that purpose disclosed the fact that only five per cent of the students, out of a total of 11,000, of the high-school age, believed that the savings habit was one of the essentials for success.

It is no wonder the rich are becoming richer and the poor are becoming poorer!

Call this a socialistic statement, if you please, but the facts bear out its accuracy. It is not difficult for any man to become rich, in a country of spendthrifts such as this, where millions of people spend every cent that comes into their possession.

Many years ago, before the present wave of mania for spending spread over the country, F. W. Woolworth devised a very simple method of catching the nickels and dimes that millions of people throw away for trash, and his system netted him over ONE HUNDRED MILLION DOLLLARS in a few years' time. Woolworth has died, but his system of saving nickels and dimes continues, and his estate is growing bigger and bigger.

Five and Ten Cent Stores are usually painted with a bright red front. That is an appropriate color, for red denotes danger. Every Five and Ten Cent Store is a striking monument that proves, to a nicety, that one of the cardinal faults of this generation is the SPENDING HABIT.

We are all victims of HABIT!

Unfortunately for most of us, we are reared by parents who have no conception whatsoever of the psychology of habit, and, without being aware of their fault, most parents aid and abet their offspring in the development of the spending habit by overindulgence with spending money, and by lack of training in the Habit of Saving.

The habits of early childhood cling to us all through life.

Fortunate, indeed, is the child whose parents have the foresight and the understanding of the value, as a character builder, of the Habit of Saving, to inculcate this habit in the minds of their children.

It is a training that yields rich rewards.

Give the average man $100.00 that he did not contemplate receiving, and what will he do with it? Why, he will begin to cogitate in his own mind on how he can SPEND the money. Dozens of things that he needs, or THINKS he needs, will flash into his mind, but it is a rather safe bet that it will never occur to him (unless he has acquired the savings habit) to make this $100.00 the beginning of a savings account. Before night comes he will have the $100.00 spent, or at least he will have decided in his mind how he is going to SPEND IT, thus adding more fuel to the already too bright flame of Habit of Spending.

We are ruled by our habits!

It requires force of character, determination and power of firm DECISION to open a savings account and then add to it a regular, if small, portion of all subsequent income.

There is one rule by which any man may determine, well in advance, whether or not he will ever enjoy the financial freedom and independence which is so universally desired by all men, and this rule has absolutely nothing to do with the amount of one's income.

The rule is that if a man follows the systematic habit of saving a definite proportion of all money he earns or receives in other ways, he is practically sure to place himself in a position of financial independence. If he saves nothing, he IS ABSOLUTELY SURE NEVER TO BE FINANCIALLY INDEPENDENT, no matter how much his income may be.

The one and only exception to this rule is that a man who does not save might possibly inherit such a large sum of money that he could not spend it, or he might inherit it under a trust which would protect it for him, but these eventualities are rather remote; so much so, in fact, that YOU cannot rely upon such a miracle happening to you.

This author enjoys a rather close acquaintance with many hundreds of people throughout the United States and in some foreign countries. For nearly twenty-five years he has been watching many of these acquaintances, and knows, therefore, from actual experience, how they live, why some of them have failed while others have succeeded, and the REASONS FOR BOTH FAILURE AND SUCCESS.

This list of acquaintances covers men who control hundreds of millions of dollars, and actually own many millions which they have acquired. Also men who have had millions of dollars, all of which passed through their fingers and they are now penniless.

For the purpose of showing the student of this philosophy just how the law of habit becomes a sort of pivotal point on which success or failure turns, and exactly why no man can become financially independent without developing the habit of SYSTEMATIC SAVING, the living habits of some of these many acquaintances will be described.

We will begin with a complete history, in his own words, of a man who has made a million dollars in the field of advertising, but who now has nothing to show for his efforts. This story first appeared in the American Magazine, and it is here reprinted through the courtesy of the publishers of that publication.

The story is true, in every respect, and it has been included as a part of this lesson because the author of the story, Mr. W. C. Freeman, is willing to have his mistakes made public with the hope that others may avoid them.

"I HAVE MADE A MILLION DOLLLARS BUT I HAVEN'T GOT A CENT"

While it is embarrassing, yes, humiliating, publicly to confess to an outstanding fault that has made a good deal of a mess of my life today, nevertheless I have decided to

make this confession for the good it may do.

I am going to make a clean breast of how I let slip through my fingers all the money I have earned thus far in my life-time, which approximates one million dollars. This amount I made through my working the field of advertising, except a few thousand dollars I earned up to twenty-five years of age by teaching in country schools and by writing newsletters to some country weeklies and daily newspapers.

Maybe one lone million does not seem a lot of money in these days of many millions and even billions; but it is a big sum of money, just the same. If there are any who think to the contrary, let them count a million. I tried to figure out the other night how long it would take to do so. I found I could count an average of one hundred a minute.

On this basis it would take me twenty days of eight hours each, plus six hours and forty minutes on the twenty-first day to do the stunt. I doubt very much if you or I were given an assignment to count one million one-dollar bills, upon the promise that all of them would be ours at the end of that time, that we could complete it. It would probably drive us mad–and a lot of use the money would be to us then, wouldn't it?

Let me say at the outset of my story that I do not regret, not for one minute, that I spent ninety per cent of the money I made. To wish any of this ninety per cent back at this time would make me feel that I would have denied much happiness to my family and to many others.

My only regret is that I spent all of my money, and more besides. If I had today the ten per cent I could have saved easily, I would have one hundred thousand dollars safely invested, and no debts. If I had this money I would feel really and truly that I was rich; and I mean just this, for I have never had a desire to accumulate money for money's sake.

Those school-teaching and newspaper-correspondence days of mine brought some cares and responsibilities, but they were met optimistically.

I married at the age of twenty-one, with the full approval of parents on both sides, who believed thoroughly in the doctrine preached by Henry Ward Beecher, that "early marriages are virtuous marriages."

Just one month and one day after I was married my father met a tragic death. He was suffocated by coal gas. Having been an educator all his life–and one of the best–he had not accumulated any money.

When he passed out of our family circle it was up to all of us to pull together and get along somehow, which we did.

Apart from the void left in our home by my father's death (my wife and I and my mother and only sister lived together), we had a joyful life, despite the fact that it was a tight squeeze to make ends meet.

My mother, who was exceptionally talented and resourceful (she had taught school with my father until I was born), decided to open our home to a married couple, old friends of the family. They came to live with us and their board helped to pay expenses. My mother was known far and wide for the wonderful meals she served. Later on, two well-to-do women friends of the family were taken into our home; thus increasing our revenue.

My sister helped very substantially by teaching a kindergarten class, which met in the big living-room of our home; my wife contributed her share to the household by taking charge of the sewing and mending.

Those were very happy days. Nobody in the household was extravagant or had any extravagant tendencies except perhaps myself, for I was always inclined to be free with money. I liked to make gifts to the family and to entertain friends.

When the first baby came into our home–a boy–we all thought heaven had opened its doors to us. My wife's parents, who took the keenest and deepest interest in our affairs, and who were always ready to lend a helping hand, were equally happy over the coming of their first grandchild. My brother-in-law, much older than my wife, and a bachelor, could not understand at first the joy we all felt; but even he began to strut around like a proud peacock after a while. What a difference a baby makes in a home!

I am injecting these details into my story merely to emphasize how the early days of my life were lived. I had no opportunity to spend much money, and yet I had as much happiness in those days as I have ever had since.

The strange thing about it all is that the experience of those days did not teach me the value of money. If anybody ever had a practical lesson to guide him in his future, I certainly had it.

But let me tell you how this early experience affected me. The birth of my son inspired me to do something that would make more money than I was getting at teaching school and in writing for newspapers. I did not want my wife, mother and sister to feel that they would have to continue indefinitely to do their part in sustaining the household. Why should a fellow, big and strong and healthy as I have always been, and with a reasonable amount of ability, be content to remain a spoke in the wheel? Why shouldn't I be the whole wheel, as far as providing for the family was concerned?

Following my desire to make more money, I took on the selling of books in addition to teaching and writing for newspapers. This earned for me quite a little extra money. Finally, I gave up teaching and concentrated on selling books, and writing for newspapers.

My book-selling took me to Bridgeton, New Jersey. It was here that I got my first real start in making money. I had to be away from home a great deal to do this work, but the sacrifice was worth while. I earned enough money in a few weeks to send more money home than I had contributed to the household in any year from my school-teaching and newspaper correspondence. After combing the territory in the Bridgeton zone, I became interested in a newspaper in that city, the Morning Star. It seemed to me that the editor and publisher of this paper needed a helper I called on him and told him so. He said, "Heavens young man, how can I hire you? I am not earning enough money to pay for my own living!"

"That's just it," said I. "I believe together we can make the Star a success. I'll tell you what I'll do: I'll work for you for one week for one dollar a day. At the end of the week, if I have made good, I'll expect you to pay me three dollars a day for the second week; and then, if I continue to do well, I'll expect you to pay me six dollars a day for the third week and will continue from then on until the paper makes enough money to pay me fifty dollars a week."

The owner agreed to my proposition. At the end of two months, I was being paid fifty dollars a week which in those days was considered a big salary. I began to feel that I was well on my way toward making money–but all I wanted it for was to make my family more comfortable. Fifty dollars a week was just four times as much as I had made teaching school.

My job on the Star embraced editorial writing (not very brilliant), reporting (just ordinary), the writing and selling of advertisements (fairly successful), proof reading, bill collecting, and so forth. It kept me humping six days a week; but I could stand it, for I was strong and healthy, and, besides, the work was very interesting. I also contributed correspondence to the New York Sun, Philadelphia Record, and the Trenton (N. J.) Times, which brought me in an average of one hundred and fifty dollars a month, for this was a good news territory.

I learned a lesson on the Star which eventually shaped the course of my life. I found out that there is a great deal more money to be earned by selling advertising for newspapers than in writing for them. Advertising brings grist to the mill.

I put over one advertising stunt on the Star–a write-up of the south Jersey oyster industry, paid for by the oyster men– that brought in three thousand dollars cash, which the publisher divided with me fifty-fifty. I had never seen so much money at one time in all my life. Think of it! Fifteen hundred dollars–twenty-five per cent more than I had made in two years of school-teaching and odd tasks.

Did I save this money or any part of it? I did not. What was the use? I could do so much with it to make my wife, boy, mother and sister happy that I let it go far easier than I had made it.

But would it not have been a fine thing if I had put this money away for a rainy day? My work in Bridegton attracted the attention of Sam Hudson, New Jersey correspondent of the Philadelphia Record, who was a shining example of that type of newspaper men whose greatest pleasure in life is doing things for others.

Sam told me that it was time for me to get located in a big city. He thought I had it in me to make good. He said he would get me a job in Philadelphia. He did, and I moved with my wife and baby to Germantown. I was given charge of the advertising department of the Germantown (Philadelphia) Gazette, a weekly newspaper.

At the start I did not make as much money as I had earned in Bridegton, because I had to give up my newspaper correspondence. The news for this section was covered by other correspondents. But very soon I was making twenty-five per cent more money. The Gazette increased its size three times to accommodate its advertising, and each time I received a very substantial increase in salary.

In addition to this, I was given a job to gather social news for the Sunday edition of the Philadelphia Press. Bradford Merrill, managing editor of that newspaper, now a very important New York newspaper executive, assigned me a big territory to cover. This kept me busy every night in the week except Saturdays. I was paid five dollars a column; but I averaged seven columns every Sunday; which made me thirty-five dollars a week extra.

It was more money for me to spend, and I spent it. I did not know anything about budgeting my expenses. I just let it go as it came. I did not have time, or thought I hadn't, to watch my step in spending.

A year later I was invited to join the advertising staff of the Philadelphia Press, a big opportunity for a young man, for I got wonderful training under the management of William L. McLean, now the owner of the Philadelphia Evening Bulletin. I still retained my job as gatherer of social news–so my income was just about the same as I had been making in Germantown.

But before long my work attracted the attention of James Elverson, Sr., publisher of the old Saturday Night and Golden Days, who had just purchased the Philadelphia Inquirer. I was offered and accepted the advertising management of this newspaper. This meant a big increase in my income. And soon afterward there came a happy increase in my family, the birth of a daughter. Then I was able to do what I had longed to do since the birth of my son. I got the family together again under one roof–my wife and two babies, my mother and sister. At last I was able to relieve my mother of any cares or responsibilities, and never again did she have either as long as she lived. She died in her eighty-first year, twenty-five years after my father's death. I shall never forget her last words to me: "Will, you have never caused me a moment's worry since you were born, and I could not have had more than you have given me had I been the Queen of England."

I was making at this time four times more money than my father had made as superintendent of public schools in my home town of Phillipsburg, New Jersey.

All the money, however, passed out of my pockets as easily as water flows through a sieve. Expenses increased with every increase in my income, which is the habit, I suppose, with most people. There was no sane reason, though, for letting my expenses go beyond my income, which I did. I found myself piling up debts, and from this time on I was never out of debt. I did not worry about my debts, though, for I thought I could pay them off at any time. It never occurred to me–not until fully twenty-five years later–that debt eventually would bring upon me not only great anxiety and unhappiness, but that I would lose friends and credit as well.

But I must pat myself on the back for one thing: I was giving full rein to my big fault–spending money as fast as I made it, often faster; but I never shirked my work. I was always trying to find more things to do, and I always found them. I spent very little time with my family. I would go home to dinner every night and romp with the babies until their bedtime, then I would return to the office and often work.

So the years went by. Another daughter arrived. Presently I wanted my daughters to have a pony and cart, and I wanted my son to have a riding horse. Then I thought I needed a team to take me around with the family, driving them to a closed coupe or an open trap. I got them all. Instead of one horse and a carry-all, or perhaps a team, which would have been sufficient for our needs and something we could have afforded, I had to have a stable, with all that goes with it. This outfit cost me nearly one fourth of my annual income.

Then I took up golf. This was in my forty-first year. I went at my play the same as I went at my work–put my whole heart in it. I learned to play pretty well. My son and elder daughter played with me, and they learned to play well, too.

It was necessary that my younger daughter should spend the winter in the South and summers in the Adirondacks; but instead of her mother going with her alone, I felt it would be fine if the son and other daughter went along with them. This arrangement was carried out. They went to Pinehurst, North Carolina, every winter and to expensive resorts in the Adirondacks or in New Hampshire in the summer.

All this took a great deal of money. My son and elder daughter were keen about golf and spent a lot of money on it. I also disbursed quite a little on golf courses around New York. Between the three of us we won 80 prizes, most of which are now in storage. I sat down one day and calculated what these prizes had cost me. I discovered that each trophy had cost $250.00 or a total of $45,000.00 over a period of fifteen years, an average of $3,000.00 a year. Ridiculous, wasn't it?

I entertained lavishly at my home. Montclair folks thought I was a millionaire. I frequently invited groups of business men to have a day of golf at the club, and then to have dinner with me in the eve They would have been satisfied with a plain home dinner, but, no, I must serve them an elaborate affair staged by a famous caterer. These dinners never cost less than ten dollars a plate, which did not include to money spent for music while they were dining. I had a negro quartet come to the house. Our dining-room comfortably seated twenty people, and it was filled to capacity many times.

It was all very lovely, and I was glad to be their host. In fact, I was very happy over it. I never stopped to think how rapidly I was piling up debts. The day came when they began to bother me a lot. I had entertained so many guests at the golf club one month, paying for luncheons, cigars, and greens fees, that my bill was four hundred and fifty dollars. This attracted the attention of the directors of the club, who were all good friends of mine and very much interested in my welfare. They made it their business to tell me that I was spending entirely too much money, and they wished for my sake that I could check my expenses.

This gave me a bit of a jolt. It made me think seriously long enough to get rid of my horses and traps–at a big sacrifice, of course. I gave up our home and moved back to the city; but I did not leave any unpaid bills in Montclair. I borrowed the money to pay them. It was always easy for me to get all the money I wanted, despite my well-known financial shortcomings.

Here are two sidelights on my experience during my "flaring forties."

Besides spending money foolishly and perhaps recklessly, I loaned it with equal abandon. In cleaning out my desk at home before moving to the city I looked over a package of due bills, the total of which was over forty thousand dollars. That was money handed out to just anybody who came along. I tore them all up; but I realized that if I had that money in hand I wouldn't owe a dollar.

One of the prosperous business men I had entertained many times and who in turn had entertained me, said to me: "Billy, I've got to stop going on outings with you. You spend entirely too much money for me. I can't keep up with you." Think of that coming from a man who was making more money than I was! It should have struck home, but it didn't. I went on spending just the same, and foolishly thinking that I was having a good time, and with no thought of the future. This man is now one of the vice presidents of one of New York's greatest financial institutions, and is reported to be worth many millions of dollars.

I should have taken his advice.

In the fall of 1908, after my disastrous experience of six months in another line of business following my resignation from the Hearst organization, I resumed newspaper work as advertising manager of the New York Evening Mail. I had known Henry L. Stoddard, editor and owner, back in the Philadelphia days, when he was political correspondent for the Press.

Despite the fact that I was bothered by debts, I did the best work of my life on the Evening Mail, and made more money during the five years I was associated with it than I had ever made before. Moreover, Mr. Stoddard gave me the privilege of syndicating advertising talks, which ran in his paper for one thousand consecutive publication days, and earned for me more than fifty-five thousand dollars Mr. Stoddard was very generous in many other ways, and frequently paid me special sums of money for doing what he considered unusual things in the way of developing business. During this period, I was so deeply in debt that, in order to keep things moving as smoothly as possible, but without retrenching in the slightest way in my expenses, I borrowed money from Peter to pay Paul and from Paul to pay Peter. That item of fifty-five thousand dollars earned from syndicating advertising talks would have more than paid all my debts and left a nice nest egg besides. But all of it was spent as easily as though I hadn't a care in the world.

In 1915 I went on my own in the advertising business. From that time until the spring of 1922 my fees ran into very big figures. I was still making more money than I ever did, and was spending it just as fast as I made it, until finally my friends got tired of making me loans.

If I had shown the slightest inclination to curb my expenses to the extent of only ten per cent, these wonderful men would have been willing to divide fifty-fifty with me, letting me pay them five per cent of it and saving five per cent. They did not care so much about the return of the money they had loaned me, as that they wanted to see me pull myself together.

The crash in my affairs came five years ago. Two friends who had stood by me loyally became impatient, and told me frankly that I needed a drastic lesson. They gave it to me all right. I was forced into bankruptcy, which nearly broke my heart. I felt that every person I knew was pointing the finger of scorn at me. This was very foolish. While there was comment, it was not at all unfriendly. It was expressive of keen regret that a man who had attained so much prestige in his profession, and had earned so much money, should have allowed himself to get into financial difficulties.

Proud and sensitive to the core I felt the disgrace of bankruptcy so keenly that I decided to go to Florida, where I had once done a special piece of work for a client. It seemed to me to be the coming El Dorado. I figured that maybe I could make sufficient money in a few years so that I could return to New York, not only with a competency but with enough to pay all my debts in full. For a time it looked as though I would realize this ambition; but I was caught in the big real estate collapse. So here I am back in the old town where I once had big earning power and hundreds of friends and well-wishers.

It has been a strange experience.

One thing is certain: I have learned my lesson at last. I feel sure that opportunities will come my way to redeem myself, and that my earning power will be restored to me. And when that time comes I know that I shall be able to live as well as I ever did, on forty per cent of my income. Then I shall divide the remaining sixty per cent into two parts, setting aside thirty per cent to pay my creditors and thirty per cent for insurance and savings.

If I allowed myself to feel depressed over my past, or filled my mind with worries, I would not be capable of carrying on the fight to redeem myself.

Besides, I would be ungrateful to my Maker for having endowed me with wonderful health all my life. Is there any greater blessing?

I would be ungrateful to the memory of my parents, whose splendid training has kept me anchored pretty safely to moral standards. Slipping from moral moorings is infinitely more serious, in the end, than slipping from the thrift standard.

I would lack appreciation of the encouragement and support I have had in generous measure from hundreds of business men and to many good friends who helped me build a fine reputation in my profession.

These memories are the sunshine of my life. And I shall use them to pave the way to my future achievement.

With abundance of health, unfaltering faith, unflagging energy, unceasing optimism, and unbounded confidence that a man can win his fight, even though he commences late in life to realize the kind of fight he must make–is there anything but death to stop him?

Mr. Freeman's story is the same as that which might be told by thousands of other men who save nothing, with the exception that the amounts of their incomes would vary. The manner of living, the way the money was spent, and why, as told in Mr. Freeman's narrative, show the way the spender's mind works.

Compilation of statistics covering family incomes and expenditures of over 16,000 families of men who have been analyzed by the author disclosed some facts that will be of help to the person who wishes to budget his income and disbursements on a practical working basis that is sound and economical.

The average income runs all the way from $100.00 to $300.00 per month. The budget allowance covering incomes within these two amounts should be about as follows: A family consisting of two persons, whose income is $100.00 a month, should manage to set aside at least $10 or $12a month for the savings account. The cost of shelter, or rent, should not exceed $25 or $30 a month. Food costs should average about $25 to $30. Clothing should be kept within an expenditure of $15 to $20 a month. Recreation and incidentals should be kept down to about $8 to $10 a month.

A family whose income is $100.00 a month, should that income be increased to $125.00, ought to save at least $20 of the amount.

A family of two persons, whose income is $150.00 a month, should budget their funds about as follows: Savings $25. Shelter or rent $35 to $40. Food $35 to $40. Clothes, $20 to $30. Recreation $10 to $15.

On a salary of $200 a month the budget should be: Savings $50. Shelter or rent $40 to $50. Food $35 to $45. Clothes $30 to $35. Recreation $15 to $20.

A family of two, on a salary or income of $300.00 a month, should apportion the income about thus: Savings $55 to $65. Shelter or rent $45 to $60. Food $45 to $60.

Clothes $35 to $45. Recreation and education $50 to $75.

Some might argue that a family of two, making a wry of $300.00 a month, might live just as cheaply as one making but $100 or $125. However, this is not quite correct, because one who has the ability to earn$300.00 a month must as a rule associate with people who make better appearances and more entertainment necessary.

A single man, earning $100.00, $150.00 or $300.00 a month, should save considerably more than a man with a family could save on the same amounts. As a rule, a single man, who has no dependents, and who is not in debt, should live on a budget of $50 a month for room and food, and not to exceed $30 a month for clothes and perhaps $10 for recreation. These amounts might be slightly increased by one who earned from $150.00 to $300.00 a month.

A boy who lives away from home, and whose weekly income is only $20.00 should save $5 of the amount. The remainder should cover cost of food, room and clothes.

A girl, living away from home, on the same income, would require a slightly larger allowance for clothes, as women's wearing apparel is more costly than men's, and it is generally imperative that women watch, more closely than men, their personal appearance.

A family of three will be able to save considerably less than the amounts which can be saved by a family of two. With rare exceptions, however, such as cases where the family is involved in debt which must be absorbed out of the monthly income, any family can save at least five per cent of the gross income.

It is a common practice today for families to purchase automobiles on monthly payments which involve too great an expenditure compared to their income. A man with a Ford income has no business purchasing a Studebaker car. He should curb his desires and content himself with a Ford. Many single men spend their entire incomes, and often go into debt besides, because they maintain automobiles out of keeping with their incomes. This common practice is fatal to success as far as financial independence may be considered a part of success, in thousands of instances.

The installment plan of buying has become so common, and it is so easy to purchase practically anything one desires, that the tendency to spend out of proportion to one's income is rapidly increasing. This tendency must be curbed by the person who has made up his mind to gain financial independence.

It can be done by anyone who is willing to try.

Another evil, which is both an evil and a blessing, is the fact that this country is so very prosperous that money comes easily, and if not watched it goes still more easily. Since the beginning of the World War there has been a steady demand for practically everything manufactured in the United States, and this condition of prosperity has caused people to lapse into a state of careless, unjustified spending.

There is no virtue in "keeping up with the pace set by neighbors" when this means sacrifice of the habit of saving a regular part of one's income. It is far better, in the long run, to be considered a bit behind the times than it is to go along through youth, into the days of maturity, and finally into old age, without having formed the habit of systematic saving.

It is better to sacrifice during the age of youthfulness, than it is to be compelled to do so during the age of maturity, as all who have not developed the habit of saving generally have to do.

There is nothing quite so humiliating, that carries such great agony and suffering, as poverty in old age, when personal services are no longer marketable, and one mutt turn to relatives or to charitable institutions for existence.

A budget system should be maintained by every person, both the married and the single, but no budget system will work out if the person trying to keep it lacks the courage to cut expenses on such items as those of entertainment and recreation. If you feel so weak in will-power that you think it necessary to "keep up with the Smiths" with whom you associate socially, and whose income is greater than your own, or who spend all of their income foolishly, then no budget system can be of service to you.

Forming the savings habit means that, to some extent at least, you must seclude yourself from all except a well-selected group of friends who enjoy you without elaborate entertaining on your part.

To admit that you lack the courage to trim down your expenditures so that you can save money, even if only a small amount, is the equivalent of admitting at the same time a lack of the sort of character which leads to success.

It has been proved times too numerous to be mentioned, that people who have formed the habit of saving money are always given preference in positions of responsibility; therefore, the saving of money not only adds advantages in the nature of preferred employment and a larger bank account, but it also increases the actual earning capacity. Any business man will prefer to employ a person who saves money regularly, not because of the mere fact that such person saves money, but because of the characteristics possessed by such a person which make him or her more efficient. Many firms will not employ a man or a woman who does not save money.

It should be a common practice for all business houses to require all employees to save money. This would be a blessing to thousands of people who would not otherwise have the will-power to form the savings habit.

Henry Ford has gone a very long way, perhaps as far as is expedient, to induce his employees not only to save their money, but to spend what they do spend wisely, and to live sanely and economically. The man who induces his employees to form the habit of saving is a practical philanthropist.

OPPORTUNITIES THAT COME TO THOSE WHO HAVE SAVED MONEY

A few years ago a young man came to Philadelphia, from the farming district of Pennsylvania, and went to work in a printing plant. One of his fellow workmen owned some shares in a Building and Loan Company, and had formed the habit of saving $5.00 a week, through this Association. This young man was influenced by his associate to open an account with the Building and Loan Company. At the end of three years he had saved $900.00. The printing plant for which he worked got into financial difficulty and was about to fail. He came to the rescue with his $900.00 which he had saved in small amounts, and in return was given a half interest in the business.

By inaugurating a system of close economy he helped the business to pay off its indebtedness, and today he is drawing out of it, as his half of the profits, a little better than $25,000.00 a year.

This opportunity never would have come, or, if it had, he would not have been prepared to embrace it, had he not formed the habit of saving money.

When the Ford automobile was perfected, during the early days of its existence, Henry Ford needed capital to promote the manufacture and sale of his product. He turned to a few friends who had saved up a few thousand dollars, one of whom was Senator Couzens. These friends came to his rescue, put in a few thousand dollars with him, and later drew out millions of dollars in profits. When Woolworth first started his Five and Ten Cent Store Plan he had no capital, but he turned to a few friends who had saved, by the closest sort of economy and great sacrifice, a few thousand dollars. These friends staked him and later they were paid back hundreds of thousands of dollars in profits.

Van Heusen (of soft-collar fame) conceived the idea of producing a semi-soft collar for men. His idea was sound, but he had not a cent to promote it. He turned to a few friends who had only a few hundred dollars, who gave him a start, and the collar made each of them wealthy.

The men who started the El Producto Cigar business had but little capital, and what they did have was money they had saved from their small earnings as cigar makers. They had a good idea, and knew how to make a good cigar, but the idea would have died "a-bornin'" had they not saved a little money. With their meager savings they launched the cigar, and a few years later they sold out their business to the American Tobacco Company for $8,000,000.00.

Back of practically every great fortune one may find, as its beginning, a well developed habit of saving money.

John D. Rockefeller was an ordinary bookkeeper. He conceived the idea of developing the oil business, which was then not even considered a business. He needed capital, and because he had developed the habit of saving, and had thereby proved that he could conserve the funds of other people, he had no difficulty in borrowing what money he needed.

It may be truthfully stated that the real basis of the Rockefeller fortune is the habit of saving money which Mr. Rockefeller developed, while working as a bookkeeper at a salary of $40.00 a month.

James J. Hill was a poor young man, working as a telegrapher, at a salary of $30.00 a month. He conceived the idea of the Great Northern Railway System, but his idea was out of proportion to his ability to finance. However, he had formed the habit of saving money, and on the meager salary of

$30.00 a month had saved enough to enable him to pay his expenses on a trip to Chicago, where he interested capitalists in financing his plan. The fact that he, himself, had saved money on a small salary was considered good evidence that he would be a safe man to trust with other people's money.

Most business men will not trust another man with their money unless he has demonstrated his ability to take care of his own and use it wisely. The test, while it is often embarrassing to those who have not formed the Habit of Saving, is a very practical one.

A young man who worked in a printing plant in the city of Chicago wanted to open a small print shop and go into business for himself. He went to a printing supply house manager and made known his wants, saying he desired credit for a printing press and some type and other small equipment.

The first question asked by the manager was "Have you saved any money of your own?"

He had! Out of his salary of $30.00 a week he had saved $15.00 a week regularly for nearly four years. He got the credit he wanted. Later on he got more credit, until today he has built up one of the most successful printing plants in the city of Chicago. His name is George B. Williams, and he is well known, as are also the facts here stated, to the author of this course.

Many years after this incident, the author of this course became acquainted with Mr. Williams, and at the end of the war, in 1918, the author went to Mr. Williams and asked for credit amounting to many thousands of dollars, for the purpose of publishing the Golden Rule Magazine. The first question asked was: "Have you formed the habit of saving money?" Despite the fact that all the money I had saved was lost in the war, the mere fact that I had actually formed the savings habit was the real basis on which I got credit for upward of $30,000.00.

There are opportunities on every corner, but they exist only for those who have ready money, or who can command money because they have formed the Habit of Saving, and developed the other characteristics which go with the formation of the savings habit known by the general term of "character."

The late J. P. Morgan once said he would rather loan a million dollars to a man of sound character, who had formed the habit of saving money, than he would a thousand dollars to a man without character, who was a spendthrift.

Generally speaking, this is the attitude which the world takes toward all men who save money.

It often happens that a small savings account of no more than two or three hundred dollars is sufficient to start one on the highway to financial independence. A few years ago a young inventor invented a household article which was unique and practical. He was handicapped, as inventors so often are, because he did not have the money to market his invention. Moreover, not having formed the savings habit he found it impossible to borrow money through banking sources.

His roommate was a young machinist who had saved $200.00. He came to the inventor's aid with this small sum of money, and had enough of the articles manufactured to give them a start. They went out and sold, from house to house, the first supply, then came back and had another supply made up, and so on, until they had accumulated (thanks to the thrift and savings ability of the roommate) a capital of $1,000.00. With this, plus some credit they secured, they bought the tools for manufacturing their own product.

The young machinist sold his half interest in the business, six years later, for $250,000.00. He never would have handled this much money, during his entire life, had he not formed the habit of saving, which enabled him to come to the rescue of his inventor friend.

This case might be multiplied a thousand times, with but slight variation as to details, as it is fairly descriptive of the beginning of many great fortunes that have been made and are now in the making, in the United States.

It may seem like a sad, cruel fact, but it is a FACT none the less, that if you have no money, and have not developed the habit of saving, you are "out of luck" as far as availing yourself of the opportunity to make money is concerned.

It can do no harm to repeat–in fact it should be repeated over and over again–that the real start of nearly all fortunes, whether great or small, is the formation of the habit of saving money!

Get this basic principle firmly founded in your mind and you will be well on the road toward financial in dependence.

It is a sad sight to see a man, well along in years, who has sentenced himself to the wearisome treadmill of hard labor all the days of his life because he has neglected forming the habit of saving money, yet there are millions of such men living, in the United States alone, today.

The greatest thing in life is FREEDOM!

There can be no real freedom without a reasonable degree of financial independence. It is a terrible thing to be compelled to be at a certain place, at a certain task (perhaps a task which one does not like) for a certain number of hours every working day of the week, for a whole life-time. In some ways this is the same as being in prison, since one's choice of action is always limited. It is really no better than being in prison with the privilege of a "trusty," and in some ways it is even worse because the man who is imprisoned has escaped the responsibility of providing a place to sleep, something to eat and clothes to wear.

The only hope of escape from this life-long toil which curtails freedom is to form the habit of saving money, and then live up to that habit, no matter how much sacrifice it may require. There is no other way out for millions of people, and unless you are one of the rare exceptions this lesson and all these statements of fact are meant for YOU, and apply to you!

> Neither a borrower, nor a lender be:
> For loan oft loses both itself and friend,
> And borrowing dulls the edge of husbandry.
> This above all: to thine own self be true,
> And it must follow, as the night the day,
> Thou canst not then be false to any man.-SHAKESPEARE

Lesson Five: INITIATIVE AND LEADERSHIP

Before you proceed to the mastery of this lesson your attention is directed to the fact that there is perfect co-ordination of thought running throughout this course.

You will observe that the entire sixteen lessons harmonize and blend with each other so that they constitute a perfect chain that has been built, link by link, out of the factors that enter into the development of power through organized effort.

You will observe, also, that the same fundamental principles of Applied Psychology form the foundation of each of these sixteen lessons, although different application is made of these principles in each of the lessons.

This lesson, on Initiative and Leadership, follows the lesson on Self-confidence for the reason that no one could become an efficient leader or take the initiative in any great undertaking without belief in himself.

Initiative and Leadership are associated terms in this lesson for the reason that Leadership is essential for the attainment of Success, and Initiative is the very foundation upon which this necessary quality of Leadership is built. Initiative is as essential to success as a hub is essential to a wagon wheel.

And what is Initiative?

It is that exceedingly rare quality that prompts–nay, impels–a person to do that which ought to be done without being told to do it. Elbert Hubbard expressed himself on the subject of Initiative in the words:

"The world bestows its big prizes, both in money and honors, for one thing, and that is Initiative.

"What is initiative? I'll tell you: It is doing the right thing without being told.

"But next to doing the right thing without being told is to do it when you are told once. That is say, 'Carry the message to Garcia.' Those who can carry a message get high honors, but their pay is not always in proportion.

"Next, there are those who do the right thing when necessity kicks them from behind, and these get indifference instead of honors, and a pittance for pay.

"This kind spend most of the time polishing a bench with a hard luck story.

"Then, still lower down in the scale than this we have the fellow who will not do the right thing even when someone goes along to show him how and stays to see that he does it; he is always out of a job, a receives the contempt he deserves, unless he has a rich pa, in which case destiny patiently waits around the comer with a stuffed club.

"To which class do you belong?"

Inasmuch as you will be expected to take inventory of yourself and determine which of the fifteen factors of this course you need most, after you have completed the sixteenth lesson, it may be well if you begin to get ready for this analysis by answering the question that Elbert Hubbard has asked

To which class do you belong?

One of the peculiarities of Leadership is the fact that it is never found in those who have not acquired the habit of taking the initiative. Leadership is something that you must invite yourself into; it will never thrust itself upon you. If you will carefully analyze all leaders whom you know you will see that they not only exercised Initiative, but they went about their work with a definite purpose in mind. You will also see that they possessed that quality described in the third lesson of this course, Self-confidence. These facts are mentioned in this lesson for the reason that it will profit you to observe that successful people make use of all the factors covered by the sixteen lessons of the course; and, for the more important reason that it will profit you to understand thoroughly the principle of organized effort which this Reading Course is intended to establish in your mind.

This seems an appropriate place to state that this course is not intended as a shortcut to success, nor is it intended as a mechanical formula that you may use in noteworthy achievement without effort on your part. The real value of the course lies in the use that you will make of it, and not in the course itself. The chief purpose of the course is to help you develop in yourself the fifteen qualities covered by the sixteen lessons of the course, and one of the most important of these qualities is Initiative, the subject of this lesson.

We will now proceed to apply the principle upon which this lesson is founded by describing, in detail, just how it served successfully to complete a business transaction which most people would call difficult.

In 1916 I needed $25,000.00 with which to create an educational institution, but I had neither this sum nor sufficient collateral with which to borrow it through the usual banking sources. Did I bemoan my fate or think of what I might accomplish if some rich relative or Good Samaritan would come to my rescue by loaning me the necessary capital?

I did nothing of the sort!

I did just what you will be advised, throughout this course, to do. First of all, I made the securing of this capital my definite chief aim. Second, I laid out a complete plan through which to transform this aim into reality. Backed by sufficient Self-confidence and spurred on by Initiative, I proceeded to put my plan into action. But, before the "action" stage of the plan had been reached, more than six weeks of constant, persistent study and effort and thought were embodied in it. If a plan is to be sound it must be built of carefully chosen material.

You will here observe the application of the principle of organized effort, through the operation of which it is possible for one to ally or associate several interests in such a way that each of these interests is greatly strengthened and each supports all the others, just as one link in a chain supports all the other links.

I wanted this $25,000.00 in capital for the purpose of creating a school of Advertising and Salesmanship. Two things were necessary for the organization of such a school. One was the $25,000.00 capital, which I did not have, and the other was the proper course of instruction, which I did have. My problem was to ally myself with some group of men who needed that which I had, and who would supply the $25,000.00. This alliance had to be made through a plan that would benefit all concerned.

After my plan had been completed, and I was satisfied that it was equitable and sound, I laid it before the owner of a well-known and reputable business college which just then was finding competition quite keen and was badly in need of a plan for meeting this competition.

My plan was presented in about these words:

Whereas, you have one of the most reputable business colleges in the city; and,

Whereas, you need some plan with which to meet the stiff competition in your field;

and, Whereas, your good reputation has provided you with all the credit you need; and, Whereas, I have the plan that will help you meet this competition successfully.

Be it resolved, that we ally ourselves through a plan that will give you that which you need and at the same time supply me with something which I need.

Then I proceeded to unfold my plan, further, in these words:

I have written a very practical course on Advertising and Salesmanship. Having built this course out of my actual experience in training and directing salesmen and my experience in planning and Directing many successful advertising campaigns, I have back of it plenty of evidence of its soundness.

If you will use your credit in helping market this course I will place it in your business college, as one of the regular departments of your curriculum and take entire charge of this newly created department. No other business college in the city will be able to meet your competition, for the reason that no other college has such a course as this.

The advertising that you do in marketing this course will serve, also, to stimulate the demand for your regular business course. You may charge the entire amount that you spend for this advertising, to my department, and the advertising bill will be paid out of that department, leaving you the accumulative advantage that will accrue to your other departments without cost to you.

Now, I suppose you will want to know where I profit by this transaction, and I will tell you. I want you to enter into a contract with me in which it will be agreed that when the cash receipts from my department equal the amount that you have paid out or contracted to pay out for advertising, my department and my course in Advertising and Salesmanship become my own and I may have the privilege of separating this department from your school and running it under my own name.

The plan was agreeable and the contract was closed.

(Please keep in mind that my definite purpose was to secure the use of $25,000.00 for which I had no security to offer.)

In a little less than a year the Business College had paid out slightly more than $25,000.00 for advertising and marketing my course and the other expenses incidental to the operation of this newly organized department, while the department had collected and, turned back to the College, in tuition fees, a sum equaling the amount the College had spent, and I took the department over, as a going and self-sustaining business, according to the terms of my contract.

As a matter of fact this newly created department not only served to attract students for the other departments of the College, but at the same time the tuition fees collected through this new department were sufficient to place it on a self-sustaining basis before the end of the first year.

Now you can see that while the College did not loan me one penny of actual capital, it nevertheless supplied me with credit which served exactly the same purpose.

I said that my plan was founded upon equity; that it contemplated a benefit to all parties concerned. The benefit accruing to me was the use of the $25,000.00, which resulted in an established and self-sustaining business by the end of the first year. The benefit accruing to the college was the students secured cured for its regular commercial and business course as a result of the money spent in advertising my department, all advertising having been done under the name of the College.

Today that business college is one of the most successful schools of its kind, and it stands as a monument of sound evidence with which to demonstrate the value of allied effort.

This incident has been related, not alone because it shows the value of initiative and leadership, but for the reason that it leads up to the subject covered by the next lesson of this Reading Course on the Law of Success, which is imagination.

There are generally many plans through the operation of which a desired object may be achieved, and it often happens to be true that the obvious and usual methods employed are not the best. The usual method of procedure, in the case related, would have been that of borrowing from a bank. You can see that this method was impractical, in this case, for the reason that no collateral was available.

A great philosopher once said: "Initiative is the pass-key that opens the door to opportunity."

I do not recall who this philosopher was, but I know that he was great because of the soundness of his statement.

We will now proceed to outline the exact procedure that you must follow if you are to become a person of initiative and leadership.

First: You must master the habit of procrastination and eliminate it from your make-up. This habit of putting off until tomorrow that which you should have done last week or last year or a score of years ago is gnawing at the very vitals of your being, and you can accomplish nothing until you throw it off.

The method through which you eliminate procrastination is based upon a well-known and scientifically tested principle of psychology which has been referred to in the two preceding lessons of this course as Auto-suggestion.

Copy the following formula and place it conspicuously in your room where you will see it as you retire at night and as you arise in the morning:

INITIATIVE AND LEADERSHIP

Having chosen a definite chief aim as my life-work I now understand it to be my duty to transform this purpose into reality.

Therefore, I will form the habit of taking some definite action each day that will carry me one step nearer the attainment of my definite chief aim.

I know that procrastination is a deadly enemy of all who would become leaders in any undertaking, and I will eliminate this habit from my make-up by:

(a) Doing some one definite thing each day, that ought to be done, without anyone telling me to do it.

(b) Looking around until I find at least one thing that I can do each day, that I have not been in the habit of doing, and that will be of value to others, without expectation of pay.

(c) Telling at least one other person, each day, of the value of practicing this habit of doing something that ought to be done without being told to do it.

I can see that the muscles of the body become strong in proportion to the extent to which they are used, therefore I understand that the habit of initiative also becomes fixed in proportion to the extent that it is practiced.

I realize that the place to begin developing the habit of initiative is in the small, commonplace things connected with my daily work, therefore I will go at my work each day as if I were doing it solely for the purpose of developing this necessary habit of initiative.

I understand that by practicing this habit of taking the initiative in connection with my daily work I will be not only developing that habit, but I will also be attracting the attention of those who will place greater value on my services as a result of this practice.

Signed...

Regardless of what you are now doing, every day brings you face to face with a chance to render some service, outside of the course of your regular duties, that will be of value to others. In rendering this additional service, of your own accord, you of course understand that you are not doing so with the object of receiving monetary pay. You are rendering this service because it provides you with ways and means of exercising, developing and making stronger the aggressive spirit of initiative which you must possess before you can ever become an outstanding figure in the affairs of your chosen field of life-work.

Those who work for money alone, and who receive for their pay nothing but money, are always underpaid, no matter how much they receive. Money is necessary, but the big prizes of life cannot be measured in dollars and cents.

No amount of money could possibly be made to take the place of the happiness and joy and pride that belong to the person who digs a better ditch, or builds a better chicken coop, or sweeps a cleaner floor, or cooks a better meal. Every normal person loves to create something that is better than the average. The joy of creating a work of art is a joy that cannot be replaced by money or any other form of material possession.

I have in my employ a young lady who opens, assorts and answers much of my personal mail. She began in my employ more than three years ago. Then her duties were to take dictation when she was asked to do so. Her salary was about the same as that which others receive for similar service. One day I dictated the following motto which I asked her to typewrite for me:

Remember that your only limitation is the one that you set up in your own mind.

As she handed the typewritten page back to me she said, "Your motto has given me an idea that is going to be of value to both you and me."

I told her I was glad to have been of service to her. The incident made no particular impression on my mind, but from that day on I could see that it had made a tremendous impression on her mind. She began to come back to the office after supper and performed service that she was neither paid for nor expected to perform. Without anyone telling her to do it she began to bring to my desk letters that she had answered for me. She had studied my style and these letters were attended to as well as I could have done it; in some instances much better. She kept up this habit until my personal secretary resigned. When I began to look for someone to take his place, what was more natural than to turn to this young woman to fill the place. Before I had time to give her the position she took it on her initiative. My personal mail began to come to my desk with a new secretary's name attached, and she was that secretary. On her own time, after hours, without additional pay, she had prepared herself for the best position on my staff.

But that is not all. This young lady became so noticeably efficient that she began to attract the attention of others who offered her attractive positions. I have increased her salary many times and she now receives a salary more than four times as large as the amount she received when she first went to work for me as an ordinary stenographer, and, to tell you the truth, I am helpless in the matter, because she has made herself so valuable to me that I cannot get along without her.

That is initiative transformed into practical, understandable terms. I would be remiss in my duties if I failed to direct your attention to an advantage, other than a greatly increased salary, that this young lady's initiative has brought her. It has developed in her a spirit of cheerfulness that brings her happiness which most stenographers never know. Her work is not work–it is a great interesting game at which she is playing.

Even though she arrives at the office ahead of the regular stenographers and remains there long after they have watched the clock tick off five o'clock and quitting time, her hours are shorter by far than are those of the other workers. Hours of labor do not drag on the hands of those who are happy at their work.

This brings us to the next step in our description of the exact procedure that you must follow in developing initiative and leadership.

Second: You of course understand that the only way to get happiness is by giving it away, to others. The same applies to the development of initiative. You can best develop this essential quality in yourself by making it your business to interest those around you in doing the same. It is a well known fact that a man learns best that which he endeavors to teach others. If a man embraces a certain creed or religious faith, the first thing he does is to go out and try to "sell" it to others. And in exact proportion to the extent to which he impresses others does he impress himself.

In the field of salesmanship it is a well-known fact that no salesman is successful in selling others until he has first made a good job of selling himself. Stated conversely, no salesman can do his best to sell others without sooner or later selling himself that which he is trying to sell to others.

Any statement that a person repeats over and over again for the purpose of inducing others to believe it, he, also, will come to believe, and this holds good whether the statement is false or true.

You can now see the advantage of making it your business to talk initiative, think initiative, eat initiative, sleep initiative and practice initiative. By so doing you are becoming a person of initiative and leadership, for it is a well-known fact that people will readily, willingly and voluntarily follow the person who shows by his actions that he is a person of initiative.

In the place where you work or the community in which you live you come in contact with other people. Make it your business to interest every one of them who will listen to you, in the development of initiative. It will not be necessary for you to give your reasons for doing this, nor will it be necessary for you to announce the fact that you are doing it. Just go ahead and do it. In your own mind you will understand, of course, that you are doing it because this practice will help you and will, at least, do those whom you influence in the same practice no harm.

If you wish to try an experiment that will prove both interesting and profitable to you, pick out some person of your acquaintance whom you know to be a person who never does anything that he is not expected to do, and begin selling him your idea of initiative. Do not stop by merely discussing the subject once; keep it up every time you have a convenient opportunity. Approach the subject from a different angle each time.

If you go at this experiment in a tactful and forceful manner you will soon observe a change in the person on whom you are trying the experiment.

And, you will observe something else of more importance still: You will observe a change in yourself!

Do not fail to try this experiment.

You cannot talk initiative to others without developing a desire to practice it yourself. Through the operation of the principle of Auto-suggestion every statement that you make to others leaves its imprint on your own subconscious mind, and this holds good whether your statements are false or true.

You have often heard the saying: "He who lives by the sword will die by the sword."

Properly interpreted, this simply means that we are constantly attracting to ourselves and weaving into our own characters and personalities those qualities which our influence is helping to create in others. If we help others develop the habit of initiative, we, in turn, develop this same habit. If we sow the seeds of hatred and envy and discouragement in others, we, in turn, develop these qualities in ourselves. This principle through which a man comes to resemble in his own nature those whom he most admires is fully brought out in Hawthorne's story, The Great Stone Face, a story that every parent should have his offspring read.

We come, now, to the next step in our description of the exact procedure that you must follow in developing initiative and leadership.

Third: Before we go further let it be understood what is meant by the term "Leadership," as it is used in connection with this Reading Course on the Law of Success. There are two brands of leadership, and one of them is as deadly and destructive as the other is helpful and constructive. The deadly brand, which leads not to success, but to absolute failure, is the brand adopted by pseudo-leaders who force their leadership on unwilling followers. It will not be necessary here to describe this brand or to point out the fields of endeavor in which it is practiced, with the exception of the field of war, and in this field we will mention but one notable example, that of Napoleon.

Napoleon was a leader; there can be no doubt about this, but he led his followers and himself to destruction. The details are recorded in the history of France and the French people, where you may study them if you choose.

It is not Napoleon's brand of leadership that is recommended in this course, although I will admit that Napoleon possessed all the necessary fundamentals for great leadership, excepting one–he lacked the spirit of helpfulness to others as an objective. His desire for the power that comes through leadership was based solely upon self-aggrandizement. His desire for leadership was built upon personal ambition and not upon the desire to lift the French people to a higher and nobler station in the affairs of nations.

The brand of leadership that is recommended through this course of instruction is the brand which leads to self-determination and freedom and self-development and enlightenment and justice. This is the brand that endures. For example, and as a contrast with the brand of leadership through which Napoleon raised himself into prominence, consider our own American commoner, Lincoln. The object of his leadership was to bring truth and justice and understanding to the people of the United States. Even though he died a martyr to his belief in this brand of leadership, his name has been engraved upon the heart of the world in terms of loving kindliness that will never bring aught but good to the world.

Both Lincoln and Napoleon led armies in warfare, but the objects of their leadership were as different as night is different from day. If it would give you a better understanding of the principles upon which this Reading Course is based, you could easily be cited to leadership of today which resembles both the brand that Napoleon employed and that which Lincoln made the foundation of his life-work, but this is not essential; your own ability to look around and analyze men who take the leading parts in all lines of endeavor is sufficient to enable you to pick out the Lincoln as well as the Napoleon types. Your own judgment will help you decide which type you prefer to emulate.

There can be no doubt in your mind as to the brand of leadership that is recommended in this Reading Course, and there should be no question in your mind as to which of the two brands described you will adopt as your brand. We make no recommendations on this subject, however, for the reason that this Reading Course has been prepared as a means of laying before its students the fundamental principles upon which power is developed, and not as a preachment on ethical conduct. We present both the constructive and the destructive possibilities of the principles outlined in this course, that you may become familiar with both, but we leave entirely to your own discretion the choice and application of these principles, believing that your own intelligence will guide you to make a wise selection.

THE PENALTY OF LEADERSHIP

In every field of human endeavor, he that is first must perpetually live in the white light of publicity. Whether the leadership be vested in a man or in a manufactured product, emulation and envy are ever at work.

In art, in literature, in music, in industry, the reward and the punishment are always the same. The reward is widespread recognition; the punishments fierce denial and detraction.

When a man's work becomes a standard for the whole world, it also becomes a target for the shafts of the envious few. If his work be merely mediocre, he will be left severely alone–if he achieve a masterpiece, it will set a million tongues a-wagging.

Jealousy does not protrude its forked tongue at the artist who produces a commonplace painting.

Whatsoever you write, or paint, or play, or sing or build, no one will strive to surpass or slander you, unless your work be stamped with the seal of a genius.

Long, long after a great work or a good work has been done, those who are disappointed or envious continue to cry out that it cannot be done.

Mean voices were raised against the author of the Law of Success before the ink was dry on the first textbooks. Poisoned pens were released against both the author and the philosophy the moment the first edition of the course was printed.

Spiteful little voices in the domain of art were raised against our own Whistler as a mountebank, long after the big world acclaimed him its greatest artistic genius.

Multitudes flocked to Bayreuth to worship at the musical shrine of Wagner, while the little group of those whom he had dethroned and displaced argued angrily that he was no musician at all.

The little world continued to protest that Fulton could never build a steamboat, while the big world flocked to the river banks to see his boat steam by.

Small, narrow voices cried out that Henry Ford would not last another year, but above and beyond the din of their childish prattle Ford went silently about his business and made himself the richest and most powerful man on earth.

The leader is assailed because he is a leader, and the effort to equal him is merely added proof of his leadership.

Failing to equal or to excel, the follower seeks to depreciate and to destroy–but only confirms the superiority of that which he strives to supplant.

There is nothing new in this.

It is as old as the world and as old as the human passions–envy, fear, greed, ambition and the desire to surpass.

And it all avails nothing.

If the leader truly leads, he remains the LEADER!

Master-poet, master-painter, master-workman, each in his turn is assailed, and each holds his laurels through the ages.

That which is good or great makes itself known, no matter how loud the clamor of denial.

A real leader cannot be slandered or damaged by lies of the envious, because all such attempts serve only to turn the spot-light on his ability, and real ability always finds a generous following.

Attempts to destroy real Leadership is love's labor lost, because that which deserves to live, lives!

We come back, now, to the discussion of the third step of the procedure that you must follow in developing initiative and leadership. This third step takes us back for a review of the principle of organized effort, as described in the preceding lessons of this course.

You have already learned that no man can accomplish enduring results of a far-reaching nature without the aid and co-operation of others. You have already learned that when two or more persons ally themselves in any undertaking, in a spirit of harmony and understanding, each person in the alliance thereby multiplies his own powers of achievement. Nowhere is this principle more evidenced than it is in an industry or business in which there is perfect teamwork between the employer and the employees. Wherever you find this teamwork you find prosperity and goodwill on both sides.

Co-operation is said to be the most important word in the English language. It plays an important part in the affairs of the home, in the relationship of man and wife, parents and children. It plays an important part in the affairs of state. So important is this principle of co-operation that no leader can become powerful or last long who does not understand and apply it in his leadership.

Lack of Co-operation has destroyed more business enterprises than have all other causes combined. In my twenty-five years of active business experience and observation I have witnessed the destruction of all manner of business enterprises because of dissension and lack of application of this principle of Co-operation. In the practice of law I have observed the destruction of homes and divorce cases without end as a result of the lack of Co-operation between man and wife. In the study of the histories of nations it becomes alarmingly obvious that lack of Co-operative effort has been a curse to the human race all back down the ages. Turn back the pages of these histories and study them and you will learn a lesson in Co-operation, that will impress itself indelibly upon your mind.

You are paying, and your children and your children's children will continue to pay, for the cost of the most expensive and destructive war the world has ever known, because nations have not yet learned that a part of the world cannot suffer without damage and suffering to the whole world.

This same rule applies, with telling effect, in the conduct of modern business and industry. When an industry becomes disorganized and torn asunder by strikes and other forms of disagreement, both the employers and employees suffer irreparable loss. But, the damage does not stop here; this loss becomes a burden to the public and takes on the form of higher prices and scarcity of the necessities of life.

The people of the United States who rent their homes are feeling the burden, at this very moment, of lack of co-operation between contractors and builders and the workers. So uncertain has the relationship between the contractors and their employees become that the contractors will not undertake a building without adding to the cost an arbitrary sum sufficient to protect them in the event of labor troubles. This additional cost increases rents and places unnecessary burdens upon the backs of millions of people. In this instance the lack of co-operation between a few men places heavy and almost unbearable burdens upon millions of people.

The same evil exists in the operation of our railroads. Lack of harmony and cooperation between the railroad management and the workers has made it necessary for the railroads to increase their freight and passenger rates, and this, in turn, has increased the cost of life's necessities to almost unbearable proportions. Here, again, lack of co-operation between a few leads to hardship for millions of people.

These facts are cited without effort or desire to place the responsibility for this lack of co-operation, since the object of this Reading Course is to help its students get at facts. It may be truthfully stated that the high cost of living that everywhere manifests itself today has grown out of lack of application of the principle of co-operative leadership. Those who wish to decry present systems of government and industrial management may do so, but in the final analysis it becomes obvious to all except those who are not seeking the truth that the evils of government and of industry have grown out of lack of co-operation.

That you may more fully grasp the fundamental principle of co-operative effort you are urged to go to the public library and read The Science of Power, by Benjamin Kidd. Out of scores of volumes by some of the soundest thinkers of the world that I have read during the past fifteen years, no single volume has given me such a full understanding of the possibilities of co-operative effort as has this book. In recommending that you read this book it is not my purpose to endorse the book in its entirety, for it offers some theories with which I am not in accord. If you read it, do so with an open mind and take from it only that which you feel you can use to advantage in achieving the object of your definite chief aim. The book will stimulate thought, which is the greatest service that any book can render. As a matter of fact the chief object of this Reading Course on the Law of Success is to stimulate deliberate thought: particularly that brand of thought that is free from bias and prejudice and is seeking truth no matter where or how or when it may be found.

During the World War I was fortunate enough to listen to a great soldier's analysis of how to be a leader. This analysis was given to the student-officers of the Second Training Camp at Fort Sheridan, by Major C. A. Bach, a quiet, unassuming army officer acting as an instructor. I have preserved a copy of this address because I believe it to be one of the finest lessons on leadership ever recorded.

The wisdom of Major Bach's address is so vital to the business man aspiring to leadership, or to the section boss, or to the stenographer, or to the foreman of the shop, or to the president of the works, that I have preserved it as a part of this Reading Course. It is my earnest hope that through the agency of this course this remarkable dissertation on leadership will find its way into the hands of every employer and every worker and every ambitious person who aspires to leadership in any walk of life. The principles upon which the address is based are as applicable to leadership in business and industry and finance as they are in the successful conduct of warfare. Major Bach spoke as follows:

In a short time each of you men will control the lives of a certain number of other men. You will have in your charge loyal but untrained citizens, who look to you for instruction and guidance. Your word will be their law. Your most casual remark will be remembered. Your mannerisms will be aped. Your clothing, your carriage, your vocabulary, your manner of command will be imitated.

When you join your organization you will find there a willing body of men who ask from you nothing more than the qualities that will command their respect, their loyalty and their obedience.

They are perfectly ready and eager to follow you so long as you can convince them that you have these qualities. When the time comes that they are satisfied you do not possess them you might as well kiss yourself good-bye. Your usefulness in that organization is at an end.

[How remarkably true this is in all manner of leadership.]

From the standpoint of society, the world may be divided into leaders and followers. The professions have their leaders, the financial world has its leaders. In all this leadership it is difficult, if not impossible, to separate from the element of pure leadership that selfish element of personal gain or advantage to the individual, without which any leadership would lose its value.

It is in military service only, where men freely sacrifice their lives for a faith, where men are willing to suffer and die for the right or the prevention of a wrong, that we can hope to realize leadership in its most exalted and disinterested sense. Therefore, when I say leadership, I mean military leadership.

In a few days the great mass of you men will receive commissions as officers. These commissions will not make you leaders; they will merely make you officers. They will place you in a position where you can become leaders if you possess the proper attributes. But you must make good, not so much with the men over you as with the men under you.

Men must and will follow into battle officers who are not leaders, but the driving power behind these men is not enthusiasm but discipline. They go with doubt and trembling that prompts the unspoken question, "What will he do next?" Such men obey the letter of their orders but no more. Of devotion to their commander, of exalted enthusiasm which scorns personal risk, of self-sacrifice to insure his personal safety, they know nothing. Their legs carry them forward because their brain and their training tell them they must go. Their spirit does not go with them.

Great results are not achieved by cold, passive, unresponsive soldiers. They don't go very far and they stop as soon as they can. Leadership not only demands but receives the willing, unhesitating, unfaltering obedience and loyalty of other men; and a devotion that will cause them, when the time comes, to follow their uncrowned king to hell and back again, if necessary.

You will ask yourselves: "Of just what, then, does leadership consist? What must I do to become a leader? What are the attributes of leadership, and how can I cultivate them?"

Leadership is a composite of a number of qualities. [Just as success is a composite of the fifteen factors out of which this Reading Course was built.] Among the most important I would list Self-confidence, Moral Ascendency, Self-Sacrifice, Paternalism, Fairness, Initiative, Decision, Dignity, Courage.

Self-confidence results, first, from exact knowledge; second, the ability to impart that knowledge; and third, the feeling of superiority over others that naturally follows. All these give the officer poise. To lead, you must know! You may bluff all of your men some of the time, but you can't do it all the time.

Men will not have confidence in an officer unless he knows his business, and he must know it from the ground up.

The officer should know more about paper work than his first sergeant and company clerk put together; he should know more about messing than his mess sergeant; more about diseases of the horse than his troop farrier. He should be at least as good a shot as any man in his company.

If the officer does not know, and demonstrates the fact that he does not know, it is entirely human for the soldier to say to himself, "To hell with him. He doesn't know as much about this as I do," and calmly disregard the instructions received.

There is no substitute for accurate knowledge!

Become so well informed that men will hunt you up to ask questions; that your brother officers will say to one another, "Ask Smith–he knows."

And not only should each officer know thoroughly the duties of his own grade, but he should study those of the two grades next above him. A two-fold benefit attaches to this. He prepares himself for duties which may fall to his lot any time during battle; he further gains a broader viewpoint which enables him to appreciate the necessity for the issuance of orders and join more intelligently in their execution.

Not only must the officer know but he must be able to put what he knows into grammatical, interesting, forceful English. He must learn to stand on his feet and speak without embarrassment.

I am told that in British training camps student-officers are required to deliver ten minute talks on any subject they choose. That is excellent practice. For to speak clearly one must think clearly, and clear, logical thinking expresses itself in definite, positive orders.

While self-confidence is the result of knowing more than your men, Moral Ascendency over them is based upon your belief that you are the better man. To gain and maintain this ascendency you must have self-control, physical vitality and endurance and moral force. You must have yourself so well in hand that, even though in battle you be scared stiff, you will never show fear. For if by so much as a hurried movement or a trembling of the hands, or a change of expression, or a hasty order hastily revoked, you indicate your mental condition it will be reflected in your men in a far greater degree.

In garrison or camp many instances will arise to try your temper and wreck the sweetness of your disposition. If at such times you "fly off the handle" you have no business to be in charge of men. For men in anger say and do things that they almost invariably regret afterward.

An officer should never apologize to his men; also an officer should never be guilty of an act for which his sense of justice tells him he should apologize.

Another element in gaining Moral Ascendency lies in the possession of enough physical vitality and endurance to withstand the hardships to which you and your men are subjected, and a dauntless spirit that enables you not only to accept them cheerfully but to minimize their magnitude.

Make light of your troubles, belittle your trials and you will help vitally to build up within your organization an esprit whose value in time of stress cannot be measured. Moral force is the third element in gaining Moral Ascendency. To exert moral force you must live clean; you must have sufficient brain power to see the right and the will to do right.

Be an example to your men!

An officer can be a power for good or a power for evil. Don't preach to them–that will be worse than useless. Live the kind of life you would have them lead, and you will be surprised to see the number that will imitate you.

A loud-mouthed, profane captain who is careless of his personal appearance will have a loud-mouthed, profane, dirty company. Remember what I tell you. Your company will be the reflection of yourself! If you have a rotten company it will be because you are a rotten captain.

Self-sacrifice is essential to leadership. You will give, give, all the time. You will give of yourself physically, for the longest hours, the hardest work and the greatest responsibility are the lot of the captain. He is the first man up in the morning and the last man in at night. He works while others sleep.

You will give of yourself mentally, in sympathy and appreciation for the troubles of men in your charge. This one's mother has died, and that one has lost all his savings in a bank failure. They may desire help, but more than anything else they desire sympathy. Don't make the mistake of turning such men down with the statement that you have troubles of your own, for every time you do that you knock a stone out of the foundation of your house.

Your men are your foundation, and your house of leadership will tumble about your ears unless it rests securely upon them. Finally, you will give of your own slender financial resources. You will frequently spend your own money to conserve the health and well-being of your men or to assist them when in trouble. Generally you get your money back. Very frequently you must charge it off to profit and loss. Even so, it is worth the cost.

When I say that paternalism is essential to leadership I use the term in its better sense. I do not now refer to that form of paternalism which robs men of initiative, self-reliance and self-respect. I refer to the paternalism that manifests itself in a watchful care for the comfort and welfare of those in your charge. Soldiers are much like children. You must see that they have shelter, food and clothing, the best that your utmost efforts can provide. You must see that they have food to eat before you think of your own; that they have each as good a bed as can be provided before you consider where you will sleep. You must be far more solicitous of their comfort than of your own. You must look after their health. You must conserve their strength by not demanding needless exertion or useless labor.

And by doing all these things you are breathing life into what would be otherwise a mere machine. You are creating a soul in your organization that will make the mass respond to you as though it were one man. And that is esprit.

And when your organization has this esprit you will wake up some morning and discover that the tables have been turned; that instead of your constantly looking out for them they have, without even a hint from you, taken up the task of looking out for you. You will find that a detail is always there to see that your tent, if you have one, is promptly pitched; that the most and the cleanest bedding is brought to your tent; that from some mysterious source two eggs have been added to your supper when no one else has any; that an extra man is helping your men give your horse a super grooming; that your wishes are anticipated; that every man is "Johnny-on-the-spot." And then you have arrived!

You cannot treat all men alike! A punishment that would be dismissed by one man with a shrug of the shoulders is mental anguish for another. A company commander who, for a given offense, has a standard punishment that applies to all is either too indolent or too stupid to study the personality of his men. In his case justice is certainly blind.

Study your men as carefully as a surgeon studies a difficult case. And when you are sure of your diagnosis apply the remedy. And remember that you apply the remedy to effect a cure, not merely to see the victim squirm. It may be necessary to cut deep, but when you are satisfied as to your diagnosis don't be diverted from your purpose by any false sympathy for the patient.

Hand in hand with fairness in awarding punishment walks fairness in giving credit. Everybody hates a human hog. When one of your men has accomplished an especially creditable piece of work see that he gets the proper reward. Turn heaven and earth upside down to get it for him. Don't try to take it away from him and hog it for yourself. You may do this and get away with it, but you have lost the respect and loyalty of your men. Sooner or later your brother officers will hear of it and shun you like a leper. In war there is glory enough for all. Give the man under you his due. The man who always takes and never gives is not a leader. He is a parasite.

There is another kind of fairness–that which will prevent an officer from abusing the privileges of his rank. When you exact respect from soldiers be sure you treat them with equal respect. Build up their manhood and self-respect. Don't try to pull it down.

For an officer to be overbearing and insulting in the treatment of enlisted men is the act of a coward. He ties the man to a tree with the ropes of discipline and then strikes him in the face knowing full well that the man cannot strike back.

Consideration, courtesy and respect from officers toward enlisted men are not incompatible with discipline. They are parts of our discipline. Without initiative and decision no man can expect to lead.

In maneuvers you will frequently see, when an emergency arises, certain men calmly give instant orders which later, on analysis, prove to be, if not exactly the right thing, very nearly the right thing to have done. You will see other men in emergency become badly rattled; their brains refuse to work, or they give a hasty order, revoke it; give another, revoke that; in short, show every indication of being in a blue funk.

Regarding the first man you may say: "That man is a genius. He hasn't had time to reason this thing out. He acts intuitively." Forget it! Genius is merely the capacity for taking infinite pains. The man who was ready is the man who has prepared himself. He has studied beforehand the possible situations that might arise; he has made tentative plans covering such situations. When he is confronted by the emergency he is ready to meet it. He must have sufficient mental alertness to appreciate the problem that confronts him and the power of quick reasoning to determine what changes are necessary in his already formulated plan. He must also have the decision to order the execution and stick to his orders.

Any reasonable order in an emergency is better than no order. The situation is there. Meet it. It is better to do something and do the wrong thing than to hesitate, hunt around for the right thing to do and wind up by doing nothing at all. And, having decided on a line of action, stick to it. Don't vacillate. Men have no confidence in an officer who doesn't know his own mind.

Occasionally you will be called upon to meet a situation which no reasonable human being could anticipate. If you have prepared yourself to meet other emergencies which you could anticipate, the mental training you have thereby gained will enable you to act promptly and with calmness.

You must frequently act without orders from higher authority. Time will not permit you to wait for them. Here again enters the importance of studying the work of officers above you. If you have a comprehensive grasp of the entire situation and conform an idea of the general plan of your superiors, that and your previous emergency training will enable you to determine that the responsibility is yours and to issue the necessary orders without delay.

The element of personal dignity is important in military leadership. Be the friend of your men, but do not become their intimate. Your men should stand in awe of you–not fear! If your men presume to become familiar it is your fault, and not theirs. Your actions have encouraged them to do so. And, above all things, don't cheapen yourself by courting their friendship or currying their favor. They will despise you for it. If you are worthy of their loyalty and respect and devotion they will surely give all these without asking. If you are not, nothing that you can do will win them.

It is exceedingly difficult for an officer to be dignified while wearing a dirty, spotted uniform and a three days' stubble of whiskers on his face. Such a man lacks self-respect, and self-respect is an essential of dignity.

There may be occasions when your work entails dirty clothes and an unshaved face. Your men all look that way. At such times there is ample reason for your appearance. In fact, it would be a mistake to look too clean–they would think that you were not doing your share. But as soon as this unusual occasion has passed set an example for personal neatness.

And then I would mention courage. Moral courage you need as well as mental courage–that kind of moral courage which enables you to adhere without faltering to a determined course of action, which your judgment has indicated is the one best suited to secure the desired results.

You will find many times, especially in action, that, after having issued your orders to do a certain thing, you will be beset by misgivings and doubts; you will see, or think you see, other and better means for accomplishing the object sought. You will be strongly tempted to change your orders. Don't do it until it is clearly manifested that your first orders were radically wrong. For, if you do, you will be again worried by doubts as to the efficacy of your second orders.

Every time you change your orders without obvious reason you weaken your authority and impair the confidence of your men. Have the moral courage to stand by your order and see it through.

Moral courage further demands that you assume the responsibility for your own acts. If your subordinates have loyally carried out your orders and the movement you directed is a failure the failure is yours, not theirs. Yours would have been the honor had it been successful. Take the blame if it results in disaster. Don't try to shift it to a subordinate and make him the goat. That is a cowardly act. Furthermore, you will need moral courage to determine the fate of those under you. You will frequently be called upon for recommendations for promotion or demotion of officers and non-commissioned officers in your immediate command.

Keep clearly in mind your personal integrity and the duty you owe your country. Do not let yourself be deflected from a strict sense of justice by feelings of personal friendship. If your own brother is your second lieutenant, and you find him unfit to hold his commission, eliminate him. If you don't your lack of moral courage may result in the loss of valuable lives.

If, on the other hand, you are called upon for a recommendation concerning a man whom, for personal reasons, you thoroughly dislike, do not fail to do him full justice. Remember that your aim is the general good, not the satisfaction of an individual grudge.

I am taking it for granted that you have physical courage. I need not tell you how necessary that is. Courage is more than bravery. Bravery is fearlessness–the absence of fear. The merest dolt may be brave, because he lacks the mentality to appreciate his danger; he doesn't know enough to be afraid.

Courage, however, is that firmness of spirit, that moral backbone which, while fully appreciating the danger involved, nevertheless goes on with the undertaking. Bravery is physical; courage is mental and moral. You may be cold all over; your hands may tremble; your legs may quake; your knees be ready to give way–that is fear. If, nevertheless, you go forward; if, in spite of this physical defection you continue to lead your men against the enemy, you have courage. The physical manifestations of fear will pass away. You may never experience them but once. They are the "buck fever" of the hunter who tries to shoot his first deer. You must not give way to them.

A number of years ago, while taking a course in demolitions, the class of which I was a member was handling dynamite. The instructor said, regarding its manipulation: "I must caution you gentlemen to be careful in the use of these explosives. One man has but one accident." And so I would caution you. If you give way to fear that will doubtless beset you in your first action; if you show the white feather, if you let your men go forward while you hunt a shell crater, you will never again have the opportunity of leading those men.

Use judgment in calling on your men for displays of physical courage or bravery. Don't ask any man to go where you would not go yourself. If your common sense tells you that the place is too dangerous for you to venture into, then it is too dangerous for him. You know his life is as valuable to him as yours is to you.

Occasionally some of your men must be exposed to danger which you cannot share. A message must be taken across a fire-swept zone. You call for volunteers. If your men know you and know that you are "right" you will never lack volunteers, for they will know your heart is in your work, that you are giving your country the best you have, that you would willingly carry the message yourself if you could. Your example and enthusiasm will have inspired them.

And, lastly, if you aspire to leadership, I would urge you to study men. Get under their skins and find out what is inside. Some men are quite different from what they appear to be on the surface. Determine the workings of their mind. Much of General Robert E. Lee's success as a leader may be ascribed to his ability as a psychologist. He knew most of his opponents from West Point days; knew the workings of their minds; and he believed that they would do certain things under certain circumstances. In nearly every case he was able to anticipate their movements and block the execution.

You cannot know your opponent in this war in the same way. But you can know your own men. You can study each to determine wherein lies his strength and his weakness; which man can be relied upon to the last gasp and which cannot.

Know your men, know your business, know yourself!

In all literature you will not find a better description of leadership than this. Apply it to yourself, or to your business, or to your profession, or to the place where you are employed, and you will observe how well it serves as your guide.

Major Bach's address is one that might well be delivered to every boy and girl who graduates in high school. It might well be delivered to every college graduate. It might well become the book of rules for every man who is placed in a position of leadership over other men, no matter in what calling, business or profession.

In Lesson Two you learned the value of a definite chief aim. Let it be here emphasized that your aim must be active and not passive. A definite aim will never be anything else but a mere wish unless you become a person of initiative and aggressively and persistently pursue that aim until it has been fulfilled.

You can get nowhere without persistence, a fact which cannot be too often repeated.

The difference between persistence and lack of it is the same as the difference between wishing for a thing and positively determining to get it.

To become a person of initiative you must form the habit of aggressively and persistently following the object of your definite chief aim until you acquire it, whether this requires one year or twenty years. You might as well have no definite chief aim as to have such an aim without continuous effort to achieve it.

You are not making the most of this course if you do not take some step each day that brings you nearer realization of your definite chief aim. Do not fool yourself, or permit yourself to be misled to believe that the object of your definite chief aim will matter–alive if you only wait. The materialization will come through your own determination, backed by your own carefully laid plans and your own initiative in putting those plans into action, or it will not come at all.

One of the major requisites for Leadership is the power of quick and firm DECISION!

Analysis of more than 16,000 people disclosed the fact that Leaders are always men of ready decision, even in matters of small importance, while the follower is NEVER a person of quick decision.

This is worth remembering!

The follower, in whatever walk of life you find him, is a man who seldom knows what he wants. He vacillates, procrastinates, and actually refuses to reach a decision, even in matters of the smallest importance, unless a Leader induces him to do so. To know that the majority of people cannot and will not reach decisions quickly, if at all, is of great help to the Leader who knows what he wants and has a plan for getting it.

Here it will be observed how closely allied are the two laws covered by Lesson Two and this lesson. The Leader not only works with A DEFINITE CHIEF AIM, but he has a very definite plan for attaining the object of that aim. It will be seen, also, that the Law of Self-confidence becomes an important part of the working equipment of the Leader.

The chief reason why the follower does not reach decisions is that he lacks the Self-confidence to do so. Every Leader makes use of the Law of a Definite Purpose, the Law of Self-confidence and the Law of Initiative and Leadership. And if he is an outstanding, successful Leader he makes use, also, of the Laws of Imagination, Enthusiasm, Self-Control, Pleasing Personality, Accurate Thinking, Concentration and Tolerance. Without the combined use of all these Laws no one may become a really great Leader. Omission of a single one of these Laws lessens the power of the Leader proportionately.

A salesman for the La Salle Extension University called on a real estate dealer, in a small western town, for the purpose of trying to sell the real estate man a course in Salesmanship and Business Management.

When the salesman arrived at the prospective student's office he found the gentleman pecking out a letter by the two-finger method, on an antiquated typewriter. The salesman introduced himself, then proceeded to state his business and describe the course he had come to sell.

The real estate man listened with apparent interest.

After the sales talk had been completed the salesman hesitated, waiting for some signs of "yes" or "no" from his prospective client. Thinking that perhaps he had not made the sales talk quite strong enough, he briefly went over the merits of the course he was selling, a second time. Still there was no response from the prospective student. The salesman then asked the direct question, "You want this course, do you not?"

In a slow, drawling tone of voice, the real estate man replied:

"Well, I hardly know whether I do or not."

No doubt he was telling the truth, because he was one of the millions of men who find it hard to reach decisions.

Being an able judge of human nature the salesman then arose, put on his hat, placed his literature back in his brief case and made ready to leave. Then he resorted to tactics which were somewhat drastic, and took the real estate man by surprise with this startling statement:

"I am going to take it upon myself to say something to you that you will not like, but it may be of help to you.

"Take a look at this office in which you work. The floor is dirty; the walls are dusty; the typewriter you are using looks as if it might be the one Mr. Noah used in the Ark during the big flood; your pants are bagged at the knees; your collar is dirty; your face is unshaved, and you have a look in your eyes that tells me you are defeated.

"Please go ahead and get mad–that's just what I want you to do, because it may shock you into doing some thinking that will be helpful to you and to those who are dependent upon you.

"I can see, in my imagination, the home in which you live. Several little children, none too well dressed, and perhaps none too well fed; a mother whose dress is three seasons out of style, whose eyes carry the same look of defeat that yours do. This little woman whom you married has stuck by you but you have not made good in life as she had hoped, when you were first married, that you would.

"Please remember that I am not now talking to a prospective student, because I would not sell you this course at THIS PARTICULAR MOMENT if you offered to pay cash in advance, because if I did you would not have the initiative to complete it, and we want no failures on our student list.

"The talk I am now giving you will make it impossible, perhaps, for me ever to sell you anything, but it is going to do something for you that has never been done before, providing it makes you think.

"Now, I will tell you in a very few words exactly why you are defeated; why you are pecking out letters on an old typewriter, in an old dirty office, in a little town: IT IS BECAUSE YOU DO NOT HAVE THE POWER TO REACH A DECISION!

"All your life you have been forming the habit of dodging the responsibility of reaching decisions, until you have come, now, to where it is well-nigh impossible for you to do so.

"If you had told me that you wanted the course, or that you did not want it, I could have sympathized with you, because I would have known that lack of funds was what caused you to hesitate, but what did you say? Why, you admitted you did not know whether you wanted it or not.

"If you will think over what I have said I am sure you will acknowledge that it has become a habit with you to dodge the responsibility of reaching clear-cut decisions on practically all matters that affect you."

The real estate man sat glued in his chair, with his under jaw dropped, his eyes bulged in astonishment, but he made no attempt to answer the biting indictment.

The salesman said good-bye and started for the door.

After he had closed the door behind him he again opened it, walked back in, with a smile on his face, took his seat in front of the astonished real estate man, and explained his conduct in this way:

"I do not blame you at all if you feel hurt at my remarks. In fact I sort of hope that you have been offended, but now let me say this, man to man, that I think you have intelligence and I am sure you have ability, but you have fallen into a habit that has whipped you. No man is ever down and out until he is under the sod. You may be temporarily down, but you can get up again, and I am just sportsman enough to give you my hand and offer you a lift, if you will accept my apologies for what I have said.

"You do not belong in this town. You would starve to death in the real estate business in this place, even if you were a Leader in your field. Get yourself a new suit of clothes, even if you have to borrow the money with which to do it, then go over to St. Louis with me and I will introduce you to a real estate man who will give you a chance to earn some money and at the same time teach you some of the important things about this line of work that you can capitalize later on.

"If you haven't enough credit to get the clothes you need I will stand good for you at a store in St. Louis where I have a charge account. I am in earnest and my offer to help you is based upon the highest motive that can actuate a human being. I am successful in my own field, but I have not always been so. I went through just what you are now going through, but, the important thing is that I WENT THROUGH IT, and got it over with, JUST AS YOU ARE GOING TO DO IF YOU WILL FOLLOW MY ADVICE. Will you come with me?"

The real estate man started to arise, but his legs wobbled and he sank back into his chair. Despite the fact that he was a great big fellow, with rather pronounced manly qualities, known as the "he-man" type, his emotions got the better of him and he actually wept.

He made a second attempt and got on his feet, shook hands with the salesman, thanked him for his kindness, and said he was going to follow the advice, but he would do so in his own way.

Calling for an application blank he signed for the course on Salesmanship and Business Management, made the first payment in nickels and dimes, and told the salesman he would hear from him again.

Three years later this real estate man had an organization of sixty salesmen, and one of the most successful real estate businesses in the city of St. Louis. The author of this course (who was advertising manager of the La Salle Extension University at the time this incident happened) has been in this real estate man's office many times and has observed him over a period of more than fifteen years. He is an entirely different man from the person interviewed by the La Salle salesman over fifteen years ago, and the thing that made him different is the same that will make YOU different: it is the power of DECISION which is so essential to Leadership.

This real estate man is now a Leader in the real estate field. He is directing the efforts of other salesmen and helping them to become more efficient. This one change in his philosophy has turned temporary defeat into success. Every new salesman who goes to work for this man is called into his private office, before he is employed, and told the story of his own transformation, word for word just as it occurred when the La Salle salesman first met him in his shabby little real estate office.

Some eighteen years ago the author of this course made his first trip to the little town of Lumberport, W. Va. At that time the only means of transportation leading from Clarksburg, the largest near-by center, to Lumberport, was the Baltimore & Ohio Railroad and an interurban electric line which ran within three miles of the town; one could walk the three miles if he chose.

Upon arrival at Clarksburg I found that the only train going to Lumberport in the forenoon had already gone, and not wishing to wait for the later afternoon train I made the trip by trolley, with the intention of walking the three miles. On the way down the rain began to pour, and those three miles had to be navigated on foot, through deep yellow mud. When I arrived at Lumberport my shoes and pants were muddy, and my disposition was none the better for the experience.

The first person I met was V. L. Hornor, who was then cashier of the Lumberport Bank. In a rather loud tone of voice I asked of him, "Why do you not get that trolley line extended from the junction over to Lumberport so your friends can get in and out of town without drowning in mud?"

"Did you see a river with high banks, at the edge of the town, as you came in?" he asked. I replied that I had seen it. "Well," he continued, "that's the reason we have no street cars running into town. The cost of a bridge would be about $100,000.00, and that is more than the company owning the trolley line is willing to invest. We have been trying for ten years to get them to build a line into town."

"Trying!" I exploded. "How hard have you tried?"

"We have offered them every inducement we could afford, such as free right of way from the junction into the town, and free use of the streets, but that bridge is the stumbling block. They simply will not stand the expense. Claim they cannot afford such an expense for the small amount of revenue they would receive from the three mile extension."

Then the Law of Success philosophy began to come to my rescue!

I asked Mr. Hornor if he would take a walk over to the river with me, that we might look at the spot that was causing so much inconvenience. He said he would be glad to do so.

When we got to the river I began to take inventory of everything in sight. I observed that the Baltimore & Ohio Railroad tracks ran up and down the river banks, on both sides of the river; that the county road crossed the river on a rickety wooden bridge, both approaches to which were over several strands of railroad track, as the railroad company had its switching yards at that point.

While we were standing there a freight train blocked the crossing and several teams stopped on both sides of the train, waiting for an opportunity to get through. The train kept the road blocked for about twenty-five minutes.

With this combination of circumstances in mind it required but little imagination to see that THREE DIFFERENT PARTIES were or could be interested in the building of the bridge such as would be needed to carry the weight of a streetcar.

It was obvious that the Baltimore & Ohio Railroad Company would be interested in such a bridge, because that would remove the county road from their switching tracks, and save them a possible accident on the crossing, to say nothing of much loss of time and expense in cutting trains to allow teams to pass.

It was also obvious that the County Commissioners would be interested in the bridge, because it would raise the county road to a better level and make it more serviceable to the public. And, of course the street railway company was interested in the bridge, but IT DID NOT WISH TO PAY THE ENTIRE COST.

All these facts passed through my mind as I stood there and watched the freight train being cut for the traffic to pass through.

A DEFINITE CHIEF AIM took place in my mind. Also, a definite plan for its attainment. The next day I got together a committee of townspeople, consisting of the mayor, councilmen and some leading citizens, and called on the Division Superintendent of the Baltimore & Ohio Railroad Company, at Grafton. We convinced him that it was worth one third of the cost of the bridge to get the county road off his company's tracks. Next we went to the County Commissioners and found them to be quite enthusiastic over the possibility of getting a new bridge by paying for only one third of it. They promised to pay their one third providing we could arrange for the other two thirds.

We then went to the president of the Traction Company that owned the trolley line, at Fairmont, and laid before him an offer to donate all the rights of way and pay for two thirds of the cost of the bridge providing he would begin building the line into town promptly. We found him receptive, also. Three weeks later a contract had been signed between the Baltimore & Ohio Railroad Company, the Monongahela Valley Traction Company and the County Commissioners of Harrison County, providing for the construction of the bridge, one third of its cost to be paid by each.

Two months later the right of way was being graded and the bridge was under way, and three months after that street cars were running into Lumberport on regular schedule.

This incident meant much to the town of Lumberport, because it provided transportation that enabled people to get in and out of the town without undue effort.

It also meant a great deal to me, because it served to introduce me as one who "got things done." Two very definite advantages resulted from this transaction. The Chief Counsel for the Traction Company gave me a position as his assistant, and later on it was the means of an introduction which led to my appointment as the advertising manager of the La Salle Extension University.

Lumberport, W. Va., was then, and still is a small town, and Chicago was a large city and located a considerable distance away, but news of Initiative and Leadership has a way of taking on wings and traveling.

Four of the Fifteen Laws of Success were combined in the transaction described, namely: A DEFINITE CHIEF AIM, SELF-CONFIDENCE, IMAGINATION and INITIATIVE and LEADERSHIP. The Law of DOING MORE THAN PAID FOR also entered, somewhat, into the transaction, because I was not offered anything and in fact did not expect pay for what I did.

To be perfectly frank I appointed myself to the job of getting the bridge built more as a sort of challenge to those who said it could not be done than I did with the expectation of getting paid for it. By my attitude I rather intimated to Mr. Hornor that I could get the job done, and he was not slow to snap me up and put me to the test.

It may be helpful to call attention here to the part which IMAGINATION played in this transaction. For ten years the townspeople of Lumberport had been trying to get a streetcar line built into town. It must not be concluded that the town was without men of ability, because that would be inaccurate. In fact there were many men of ability in the town, but they had been making the mistake which is so commonly made by us all, of trying to solve their problem through one single source, whereas there were actually THREE SOURCES of solution available to them.

$100,000.00 was too much for one company to assume, for the construction of a bridge, but when the cost was distributed between three interested parties the amount to be borne by each was more reasonable.

The question might be asked: "Why did not some of the local townsmen think of this three-way solution?"

In the first place they were so close to their problem that they failed to take a perspective, bird's-eye view of it, which would have suggested the solution. This, also, is a common mistake, and one that is always avoided by great Leaders. In the second place these townspeople had never before co-ordinated their efforts or worked as an organized group with the sole purpose in mind of finding a way to get a street car line built into town. This, also, is another common error made by men in all walks of life–that of failure to work in unison, in a thorough spirit of cooperation.

I, being an outsider, had less difficulty in getting co-operative action than one of their own group might have had. Too often there is a spirit of selfishness in small communities which prompts each individual to think that his ideas should prevail. It is an important part of the Leader's responsibility to induce people to subordinate their own ideas and interests for the good of the whole, and this applies to matters of a civic, business, social, political, financial or industrial nature.

Success, no matter what may be one's conception of that term, is nearly always a question of one's ability to get others to subordinate their own individualities and follow a Leader. The Leader who has the Personality and the Imagination to induce his followers to accept his plans and carry them out faithfully is always an able Leader.

The next lesson, on IMAGINATION, will take you still further into the art of tactful Leadership. In fact Leadership and Imagination are so closely allied and so essential for success that one cannot be successfully applied without the other. Initiative is the moving force that pushes the Leader ahead, but Imagination is the guiding spirit that tells him which way to go.

Imagination enabled the author of this course to analyze the Lumberport bridge problem, break it up into its three component parts, and assemble these parts in a practical working plan. Nearly every problem may be so broken up into parts which are more easily managed, as parts, than they are when assembled as a whole. Perhaps one of the most important advantages of Imagination is that it enables one to separate all problems into their component parts and to reassemble them in more favorable combinations.

It has been said that all battles in warfare are won or lost, not on the firing line, after the battle begins, but back of the lines, through the sound strategy, or the lack of it, used by the generals who plan the battles.

What is true of warfare is equally true in business, and in most other problems which confront us throughout life. We win or lose according to the nature of the plans we build and carry out, a fact which serves to emphasize the value of the Laws of Initiative and Leadership, Imagination, Self-confidence and a Definite Chief Aim. With the intelligent use of these four laws one may build plans, for any purpose whatsoever, which cannot be defeated by any person or group of persons who do not employ or understand these laws.

There is no escape from the truth here stated!

ORGANIZED EFFORT is effort which is directed according to a plan that was conceived with the aid of Imagination, guided by a Definite Chief Aim, and given momentum with Initiative and Self-confidence. These four laws blend into one and become a power in the hands of a Leader. Without their aid effective leadership is impossible.

You are now ready for the lesson on Imagination. Read that lesson with the thought in mind of all that has been here stated and it will take on a deeper meaning.

INTOLERANCE–An After-the-Lesson Visit With the Author

If you must give expression to prejudice and hatred and intolerance, do not speak it, but write it; write it in the sands, near the water's edge.

When the dawn of Intelligence shall spread over the eastern horizon of human progress, and Ignorance and Superstition shall have left their last footprints on the sands of time, it will be recorded in the last chapter of the book of man's crimes that his most grievous sin was that of Intolerance.

The bitterest intolerance grows out of religious, racial and economic prejudices and differences of opinion. How long, O God, until we poor mortals will understand the folly of trying to destroy one another because we are of different religious beliefs and racial tendencies?

Our allotted time on this earth is but a fleeting moment. Like a candle, we are lighted, shine for a moment, and flicker out. Why can we not learn to so live during this brief earthly visit that when the great Caravan called Death draws up and announces this visit completed we will be ready to fold our tents and silently follow out into the great unknown without fear and trembling?

I am hoping that I will find no Jews or Gentiles, Catholics or Protestants, Germans, Englishmen or Frenchmen when I shall have crossed the bar to the other side. I am hoping that I will find there only human Souls, Brothers and Sisters all, unmarked by race, creed or color, for I shall want to be done with intolerance so I may rest in peace throughout eternity.

YOU will see at the beginning of this section a picture which describes the futility of combat.

The two male deer have engaged in a fight to the finish, each believing that he will be the winner. Off at the side the female awaits the victor, little dreaming that tomorrow the bones of both combatants will be bleaching in the sun.

"Poor foolish animals," someone will say. Perhaps, but not very different from the man family. Man engages his brothers in mortal combat because of competition. The three major forms of competition are sex, economic and religious in nature.

Twenty years ago a great educational institution was doing a thriving business and rendering a worthy service to thousands of students. The two owners of the school married two beautiful and talented young women, who were especially accomplished in the art of piano playing. The two wives became involved in an argument as to which one was the more accomplished in this art. The disagreement was taken up by each of the husbands. They became bitter enemies. Now the bones of that once prosperous school "lie bleaching in the sun."

The two bucks shown in the picture above locked horns over the attention of the doe. The two "man bucks" locked horns over the selfsame impulse.

In one of the great industrial plants two young foremen "locked horns" because one received a promotion which the other believed he should have had. For more than five years the silent undertow of hatred and intolerance showed itself. The men under each of the foremen became inoculated with the spirit of dislike which they saw cropping out in their superiors. Slowly the spirit of retaliation began to spread over the entire plant. The men became divided into little cliques. Production began to fall off. Then came financial difficulty and finally bankruptcy for the company. Now the bones of a once prosperous business "lie bleaching in the sun," and the two foremen and several thousand others were compelled to start all over again, in another field.

Down in the mountains of West Virginia lived two peaceful families of mountain-folk–the Hatfields and the McCoys. They had been friendly neighbors for three generations. A razor-back pig belonging to the McCoy family crawled through the fence into the Hatfield family's corn field. The Hatfields turned their hound loose on the pig. The McCoys retaliated by killing the dog. Then began a feud that has lasted for three generations and cost many lives of the Hatfields and McCoys.

In a fashionable suburb of Philadelphia certain gentlemen of wealth have built their homes. In front of each house the word "INTOLERANCE" is written. One man builds a high steel fence in front of his house. The neighbor next to him, not to be outdone, builds a fence twice as high. Another buys a new motor car and the man next door goes him one better by purchasing two new cars. One remodels his house adding a colonial style porch. The man next door adds a new porch and a Spanish style garage for good measure. The big mansion on top of the hill gives a reception which brings a long line of motor cars filled with people who have nothing in particular in common with the host. Then follows a series of "receptions" all down the "gold-coast" line, each trying to outshine all the others.

The "Mister" (but they don't call him that in fashionable neighborhoods) goes to business in the back seat of a Rolls Royce that is managed by a chauffeur and a footman. Why does he go to business? To make money, of course! Why does he want more money when he already has millions of dollars? So he can keep on out-doing his wealthy neighbors.

Poverty has some advantages–it never drives those who are poverty-stricken to "lock horns" in the attempt to out-poverty their neighbors.

Wherever you see men with their "horns locked" in conflict you may trace the cause of the combat to one of the three causes of intolerance–religious difference of opinion, economic competition or sex competition.

The next time you observe two men engaged in any sort of hostility toward each other, just close your eyes and THINK for a moment and you may see them, in their transformed nature, very much resembling the male deer shown in the picture above. Off at one side you may see the object of the combat–a pile of gold, a religious emblem or a female (or females).

Remember, the purpose of this essay is to tell some of the TRUTH about human nature, with the object of causing its readers to THINK. Its writer seeks no glory or praise, and likely he will receive neither in connection with this particular subject.

Andrew Carnegie and Henry C. Frick did more than any other two men to establish the steel industry. Both made millions of dollars for themselves. Came the day when economic intolerance sprang up between them. To show his contempt for Frick, Carnegie built a tall sky-scraper and named it the "Carnegie Building." Frick retaliated by erecting a much taller building, alongside of the Carnegie Building, naming it the "Frick Building."

These two gentlemen "locked horns" in a fight to the finish, Carnegie lost his mind, and perhaps more, for all we of this world know. What Frick lost is known only to himself and the keeper of the Great Records. In memory their "bones lie bleaching in the sun" of posterity.

The steel men of today are managing things differently. Instead of locking horns they now "interlock directorates," with the result that each is Practically a solidified, strong unit of the whole industry. The steel men of today understand the difference between the meaning of the words COMPETITION and CO-OPERATION; a difference which the remainder of us would do well to understand, also.

In England the men who own the mines and those who run the labor unions "locked horns." Had not the cooler heads unlocked those horns the bones of the British empire (including both the owners of industry and the labor unions) should soon have lain "bleaching in the sun." One year of open combat between the unions and the owners of industry, in Great Britain, would have meant annihilation of the British empire. The other nations of the world would have grabbed all the economic machinery now controlled by Britain.

Let the leaders of American industry and unionism not forget!

Fifteen factors enter into the attainment of SUCCESS. One of these is TOLERANCE.

The other fourteen are mentioned many times in this series of lessons.

Intolerance binds man's legs with the shackles of IGNORANCE and covers his eyes with the scales of FEAR AND SUPERSTITION. Intolerance closes the book of knowledge and writes on the cover "Open not this book again. The last word has been herein written."

It is not your DUTY to be tolerant; it is your PRIVILEGE!

Remember, as you read this article, that sowing the seed of INTOLERANCE is the sole and exclusive business of some men. All wars and all strikes and all other forms of human suffering bring profit to SOME. If this were not true there would be no wars or strikes or other similar forms of hostility.

In the United States today there is a well organized system of propaganda, the object of which is to stir up strife and hostility between the owners of industries and those who work in those industries. Take another look at the picture at the beginning of this article and you may see what will happen to all who lock horns in labor disagreements, and remember that it is always the bones of the workers (and not those of the leaders of either the unions or the industries) that "lie bleaching in the sun" after the fight is over.

When you feel yourself preparing to "lock horns" with someone remember that it will be more profitable if you LOCK HANDS instead! A warm, hearty hand-shake leaves no bones bleaching in the sun.

> "LOVE is the only bow on life's dark cloud. It is the Morning and the Evening Star. It shines upon the cradle of the babe, and sheds its radiance upon the quiet tomb. It is the mother of Art, inspirer of poet, patriot and philosopher. It is the air and light of every heart, builder of every home, kindler of every fire on every hearth. It was the first to dream of immortality. It fills the world with melody, for Music is the voice of Love. Love is the magician, the enchanter, that changes worthless things to joy, and makes right royal kings and queens of common clay. It is the perfume of the

> wondrous flower–the heart–and without that sacred passion, that divine swoon, we are less than beasts; but with it, earth is heaven and we are gods"–INGERSOLL.

Cultivate LOVE for your fellow man and you will no longer want to lock horns with him in futile combat. Love makes every man his brother's keeper.

> Love, indeed, is light from heaven;
> A spark of that immortal fire
> With angels shared, by Allah given,
> To lift from earth our low desire.
> Devotion wafts the mind above,
> But heaven itself descends in love;
> A feeling from the Godhead caught,
> To wean from self each sordid thought;
> A ray of Him who form'd the whole;
> A glory circling round the soul:–BYRON.

Lesson Six: IMAGINATION

IMAGINATION is the workshop of the human mind wherein old ideas and established facts may be reassembled into new combinations and put to new uses. The modern dictionary defines imagination as follows:

"The act of constructive intellect in grouping the materials of knowledge or thought into new, original and rational systems; the constructive or creative faculty; embracing poetic, artistic, philosophic, scientific and ethical imagination.

"The picturing power of the mind; the formation of mental images, pictures, or mental representation of objects or ideas, particularly of objects of sense perception and of mathematical reasoning; also the reproduction and combination, usually with more or less irrational or abnormal modification, of the images or ideas of memory or recalled facts of experience."

Imagination has been called the creative power of the soul, but this is somewhat abstract and goes more deeply into the meaning than is necessary from the viewpoint of a student of this course who wishes to use the course only as a means of attaining material or monetary advantages in life.

If you have mastered and thoroughly understood the preceding lessons of this Reading Course you know that the materials out of which you built your definite chief aim were assembled and combined in your imagination. You also know that self-confidence and initiative and leadership must be created in your imagination before they can become a reality, for it is in the workshop of your imagination that you will put the principle of Auto-suggestion into operation in creating these necessary qualities.

This lesson on imagination might be called the "hub" of this Reading Course, because every lesson of the course leads to this lesson and makes use of the principle upon which it is based, just as all the telephone wires lead to the exchange office for their source of power. You will never have a definite purpose in life, you will never have self-confidence, you will never have initiative and leadership unless you first create these qualities in your imagination and see yourself in possession of them.

Just as the oak tree develops from the germ that lies in the acorn, and the bird develops from the germ that lies asleep in the egg, so will your material achievements grow out of the organized plans that you create in your imagination. First comes the thought; then, organization of that thought into ideas and plans; then transformation of those plans into reality. The beginning, as you will observe, is in your imagination.

The imagination is both interpretative and creative in nature. It can examine facts, concepts and ideas, and it can create new combinations and plans out of these.

Through its interpretative capacity the imagination has one power not generally attributed to it; namely, the power to register vibrations and thought waves that are put into motion from outside sources, just as the radio-receiving apparatus picks up the vibrations of sound. The principle through which this interpretative capacity of the imagination functions is called telepathy; the communication of thought from one mind to another, at long or short distances, without the aid of physical or mechanical appliances, in the manner explained in the Introductory Lesson of this course.

Telepathy is an important factor to a student who is preparing to make effective use of imagination, for the reason that this telepathic capacity of the imagination is constantly picking up thought waves and vibrations of every description. So-called "snap-judgment" and "hunches," which prompt one to form an opinion or decide upon a course of action that is not in harmony with logic and reason, are usually the result of stray thought waves that have registered in the imagination.

The recently developed radio apparatus has enabled us to understand that the elements of the ether are so sensitive and alive that all manner of sound waves are constantly flying here and there with lightning-like speed. You have only to understand the modern radio outfit to understand, also, the principle of telepathy. So well has this principle been established, through psychological research, that we have abundance of proof that two minds which are properly attuned and in harmony with each other may send and receive thought at long distances without the aid of mechanical apparatus of any sort. Rarely have two minds become so well attuned that unbroken chains of thought could be registered in this manner, but there is evidence sufficient to establish the fact that parts of organized thought have been picked up.

That you may understand how closely interwoven are the fifteen factors upon which this Reading Course is based, consider, for example, what happens when a salesman who lacks confidence in himself, and in his goods, walks in to see a prospective buyer. Whether the prospective buyer is conscious of it or not, his imagination immediately "senses" that lack of confidence in the salesman's mind. The salesman's own thoughts are actually undermining his efforts. This will explain, from another angle, why self-confidence is one of the most important factors entering into the great struggle for success.

The principle of telepathy and the law of attraction, through which like attracts like, explain many a failure. If the mind has a tendency to attract from the ether those thought vibrations which harmonize with the dominating thoughts of a given mind, you can easily understand why a negative mind that dwells upon failure and lacks the vitalizing force of self-confidence would not attract a positive mind that is dominated by thoughts of success.

Perhaps these explanations are somewhat abstract to the student who has not made any particular study of the functioning processes of the mind, but it seems necessary to inject them into this lesson as a means of enabling the student to understand and make practical use of the subject of this lesson. The imagination is too often regarded merely as an indefinite, untraceable, indescribable something that does nothing but create fiction. It is this popular disregard of the powers of the imagination that has made necessary these more or less abstract references to one of the most important subjects of this course. Not only is the subject of imagination an important factor in this course; but, it is one of the most interesting subjects, as you will observe when you begin to see how it affects all that you do toward the achievement of your definite chief aim.

You will see how important is the subject of imagination when you stop to realize that it is the only thing in the world over which you have absolute control. Others may deprive you of your material wealth and cheat you in a thousand ways, but no man can deprive you of the control and use of your imagination. Men may deal with you unfairly, as men often do; they may deprive you of your liberty, but they cannot take from you the privilege of using your imagination as you wish.

The most inspiring poem in all literature was written by Leigh Hunt, while he was a poverty-stricken prisoner in an English prison, where he had been unjustly confined because of his advanced views on politics. This poem is entitled Abou Ben Adhem, and it is here reprinted as a reminder that one of the great things a man may do, in his own imagination, is to forgive those who have dealt unjustly with him:

Abou Ben Adhem (may his tribe increase)
Awoke one night from a deep dream of peace,
And saw within the moonlight of his room,
Making it rich and like a lily in bloom,
An angel writing in a book of gold,
Exceeding peace had made Ben Adhem bold,
And to the presence in the room he said:
"What writest thou?"–the vision raised its head,
And, with a look made of all sweet accord,
Answered, "The names of those who love the Lord."
"And is mine one?" said Abou. "Nay, not so,"
Replied the angel, –Abou spoke more low,
But cheerily still; and said, "I pray thee, then,
Write me as one that loves his fellow men."
The angel wrote, and vanished. The next night
It came again, with a great wakening light,
And showed the names whom love of God had blessed,
And, lo! Ben Adhem's name led all the rest!

Civilization, itself, owes its existence to such men as Leigh Hunt, in whose fertile imaginations have been pictured the higher and nobler standards of human relationship. Abou Ben Adhem is a poem that will never die, thanks to this man who pictured in his imagination the hope of an ideal that is constructive.

The major trouble with this world today lies in our lack of understanding of the power of imagination, for if we understood this great power we could use it as a weapon with which to wipe out poverty and misery and injustice and persecution, and this could be done in a single generation. This is a rather broad statement, and no one understands better than the author of this course how useless such a statement would be if the principle upon which it is founded were not explained in terms of the most practical, workaday nature; therefore, let us proceed to describe what is meant.

To make this description understandable we must accept as a reality the principle of telepathy, through the operation of which every thought we release is registering itself in the minds of other people. We need devote no time to proving that telepathy is a reality, for the reason that this lesson on imagination cannot be of the slightest value to the student who has not sufficiently informed himself to understand and accept telepathy as an established principle. We will take it for granted that you are one who accepts and understands this principle.

You have often heard of "mob psychology," which is nothing more nor less than some strong, dominating idea that has been created in the mind of one or more persons and registers itself in the minds of other persons, through the principle of telepathy. So strong is the power of mob psychology that two men fighting in the street will often start a "free-for-all" fight in which by-standers will engage each other in battle without even knowing what they are fighting about, or with whom they are fighting.

On Armistice Day, 1918, we had evidence in abundance to prove the reality of the principle of telepathy, on a scale such as the world had never before witnessed. I remember, distinctly, the impression made on my mind on that eventful day. So strong was this impression that it awakened me at about 3:00 o'clock in the morning, just as effectively as if someone had aroused me by physical force. As I sat up in bed I knew that something out of the ordinary had happened, and so strange and impelling was the effect of this experience that I got up, dressed myself and went out in the streets of Chicago, where I was met by thousands of others who had felt the touch of the same influence. Everyone was asking: "What has happened?"

What had happened was this:

Millions of men had received instructions to cease fighting, and their combined joy set into motion a thought wave that swept the entire world and made itself felt in every normal mind that was capable of registering this thought wave. Perhaps never in the history of the world had so many millions of people thought of the same thing, in the same manner, at the same time. For once in the history of the world everybody felt something in common, and the effect of this harmonized thought was the world-wide "mob psychology" that we witnessed on Armistice Day. In connection with this statement it will be helpful if you recall what was said about the method of creating a "Master Mind," through the harmony of thought of two or more persons, in the Introductory Lesson of this course.

We will bring the application of this principle a little nearer home by showing how it may be made to make or break the harmonious working relationship of a business or industry. You may not have satisfied yourself that it was the harmony of thought of millions of soldiers that registered in the minds of the people of the world and caused the "mob" psychological condition that was everywhere in evidence on Armistice Day, but you will need no proof that a disgruntled person always disturbs everyone with whom he comes in contact. It is a well-established fact that one such person in a place of employment will disrupt the entire organization. The time is almost at hand when neither the workers nor the employers will tolerate the typical "grouch" inside of a place of employment, for the reason that his state of mind registers itself in the minds of those about him, resulting in distrust, suspicion and lack of harmony. The time is near at hand when the workers in a place of employment will no more tolerate one of their own rank and file who is a typical "grouch" than they would a poisonous snake.

Apply the principle in another way: Place among a group of workers one person whose personality is of the positive, optimistic type, and who makes it his business to sow the seeds of harmony around the place where he works, and his influence will reflect itself in every person who works with him.

If every business is "the extended shadow of one man" as Emerson stated, then it behooves that one man to reflect a shadow of confidence and good cheer and optimism and harmony, that these qualities may, in turn, reflect themselves in all who are connected with he business.

In passing to the next step in our application of the power of imagination in the attainment of success we will cite some of the most recent and modern examples of its
use in the accumulation of material wealth and the perfection of some of the leading inventions of the world.

In approaching this next step it should be borne ill mind that "there is nothing new under the sun." Lift, on this earth may be likened to a great kaleidoscope before which the scenes and facts and material substances are ever shifting and changing, and all any man can do is to take these facts and substances and rearrange them in new combinations.

The process through which this is done is called imagination.

We have stated that the imagination is both interpretative and creative in its nature. It can receive impressions or ideas and out of these it can form new combinations.

As our first illustration of the power of imagination in modern business achievement, we will take the case of Clarence Saunders, who organized the Piggly-Wiggly system of self-help grocery stores.

Saunders was a grocery clerk in a small southern retail store. One day he was standing in a line, with a tin tray in his hands, waiting his turn to secure food in a cafeteria. He had never earned more than $20.00 a week before that time, and no one had ever noticed anything about him that indicated unusual ability, but something took place in his mind, as he stood in that line of waiting people, that put his imagination to work. With the aid of his imagination he lifted that "self-help" idea out of the cafeteria in which he found it (not creating anything new, merely shifting an old idea into a new use) and set it down in a grocery store. In an instant the Piggly-Wiggly chain-store grocery plan had been created and Clarence Saunders the twenty-dollar-a-week grocery clerk rapidly became the million-dollar chain-store grocery man of America.

Where, in that transaction, do you see the slightest indication of a performance that you could not duplicate?

Analyze this transaction and measure it by the previous lessons of this course and you will see that Clarence Saunders created a very definite purpose. He supported this purpose with sufficient self-confidence to cause him to take the initiative to transform it into reality. His imagination was the workshop in which these three factors, definite purpose, self-confidence and initiative were brought together and made to supply the momentum for the first step in the organization of the Piggly-Wiggly plan.

Thus are great ideas changed into realities.

When Thomas A. Edison invented the incandescent electric light bulb he merely brought together two old, well known principles and associated them in a new combination. Mr. Edison and practically all others who were informed on the subject of electricity, knew that a light could be produced by heating a small wire with electricity, but the difficult problem was to do this without burning the wire in two. In his experimental research Mr. Edison tried out every conceivable sort of wire, hoping to find some substance that would withstand the tremendous heat to which it had to be subjected before a light could be produced.

His invention was half completed, but it was of no practical value until he could find the missing link that would supply the other half. After thousands of tests and much combining of old ideas in his imagination, Edison finally found this missing link. In his study of physics he had learned, as all other students of this subject learn, that there can be no combustion without the presence of oxygen. He of course knew that the difficulty with his electric light apparatus was the lack of a method through which to control the heat. When it occurred to him that there could be no combustion where there was no oxygen he placed the little wire of his electric light apparatus inside of a glass globe, shut out all the oxygen, and lo! The mighty incandescent light was a reality.

When the sun goes down tonight you step to the wall, press a button and bring it back again, a performance that would have mystified the people of a few generations ago, and yet there is no mystery back of your act. Thanks to the use of Edison's imagination, you have simply brought together two principles both of which were in existence since the beginning of time.

No one who knew him intimately ever accredited Andrew Carnegie with unusual ability, or the power of genius, except in one respect, and that was his ability to select men who could and would co-operate in a spirit of harmony, in carrying out his wishes. But what additional ability did he need in the accumulation of his millions of dollars? Any man who understands the principle of organized effort, as Carnegie understood it, and knows enough about men to be able to select just those types that are needed in the performance of a given task, could duplicate all that Carnegie accomplished.

Carnegie was a man of imagination. He first created a definite purpose and then surrounded himself with men who had the training and the vision and the capacity necessary for the transformation of that purpose into reality. Carnegie did not always create his own plans for the attainment of his definite purpose. He made it his business to know what he wanted, then found the men who could create plans through which to procure it. And that was not only imagination, it was genius of the highest order.

But it should be made clear that men of Mr. Carnegie's type are not the only ones who can make profitable use of imagination. This great power is as available to the beginner in business as it is to the man who has "arrived."

One morning Charles M. Schwab's private car was backed on the side-track at his Bethlehem Steel plant. As he alighted from his car he was met by a young man stenographer who announced that he had come to make sure that any letters or telegrams Mr. Schwab might wish to write would be taken care of promptly. No one told this young man to be on hand, but he had enough imagination to see that his being there would not hurt his chances of advancement. From that day on, this young man was "marked" for promotion. Mr. Schwab singled him out for promotion because he had done that which any of the dozen or so other stenographers in the employ of the Bethlehem Steel Company might have done, but didn't. Today this same man is the president of one of the largest drug concerns in the world and has all of this world's goods and wares that he wants and much more than he needs.

A few years ago I received a letter from a young man who had just finished Business College, and who wanted to secure employment in my office. With his letter he sent a crisp ten-dollar bill that had never been folded. The letter read as follows:

"I have just finished a commercial course in a first-class business college and I want a position in your office because I realize how much it would be worth to a young man, just starting out on his business career, to have the privilege of working under the direction of a man like you.

"If the enclosed ten-dollar bill is sufficient to pay for the time you would spend in giving me my first week's instructions I want you to accept it. I will work the first month without pay and you may set my wages after that at whatever I prove to be worth.

"I want this job more than I ever wanted anything in my life and I am willing to make any reasonable sacrifice to get it. Very cordially,"

This young man got his chance in my office. His imagination gained for him the opportunity that he wanted, and before his first month had expired the president of a life insurance company who heard of this incident offered the young man a private secretary-ship at a substantial salary. He is today an official of one of the largest life insurance companies in the world.

Some years ago a young man wrote to Thomas A. Edison for a position. For some reason Mr. Edison did not reply. By no means discouraged on this account the young man made up his mind that he would not only get a reply from Mr. Edison, but what was more important still, he would actually secure the position he sought. He lived a long distance from West Orange, New Jersey, where the Edison industries are located, and he did not have the money with which to pay his railroad fare. But he did have imagination. He went to West Orange in a freight car, got his interview, told his story in person and got the job he sought.

Today this same man lives in Bradentown,Florida. He has retired from active business, having made all the money he needs. His name, in case you wish to confirm my statements, is Edwin C. Barnes.

By using his imagination, Mr. Barnes saw the advantage of close association with a man like Thomas A. Edison. He saw that such an association would give him the opportunity to study Mr. Edison, and at the same time it would bring him in contact with Mr. Edison's friends, who are among the most influential people of the world.

These are but a few cases in connection with which I have personally observed how men have climbed to high places in the world and accumulated wealth in abundance by making practical use of their imagination.

Theodore Roosevelt engraved his name on the tablets of time by one single act during his tenure of office as President of the United States, and after all else that he did while in that office will have been forgotten this one transaction will record him in history as a man of imagination.

He started the steam shovels to work on the Panama Canal.

Every President, from Washington on up to Roosevelt, could have started the canal and it would have been completed, but it seemed such a colossal undertaking that it required not only imagination but daring courage as well. Roosevelt had both, and the people of the United States have the canal.

At the age of forty–the age at which the average man begins to think he is too old to start anything new–James J. Hill was still sitting at the telegraph key, at a salary of $30.00 per month. He had no capital.

He had no influential friends with capital, but he did have that which is more powerful than either–imagination.

In his mind's eye he saw a great railway system that would penetrate the undeveloped Northwest and unite the Atlantic and Pacific oceans. So vivid was his imagination that he made others see the advantages of such a railway system, and from there on the story is familiar enough to every school-boy. I would emphasize the part of the story that most people never mention–that Hill's Great Northern Railway system became a reality in his own imagination first. The railroad was built with steel rails and wooden cross ties, just as other railroads are built, and these things were paid for with capital that was secured in very much the same manner that capital for all railroads is secured, but if you want the real story of James J. Hill's success you must go back to that little country railway station where he worked at $30.00 a month and there pick up the little threads that he wove into a mighty railroad, with materials no more visible than the thoughts which he organized in his imagination.

What a mighty power is imagination, the workshop of the soul, in which thoughts are woven into railroads and skyscrapers and mills and factories and all manner of material wealth.

"I hold it true that thoughts are things;
They're endowed with bodies and breath and wings;

And that we send them forth to fill
The world with good results or ill.
That which we call our secret thought
Speeds forth to earth's remotest spot,
Leaving its blessings or its woes,
Like tracks behind it as it goes.
We build our future, thought by thought,
For good or ill, yet know it not,
Yet so the universe was wrought.
Thought is another name for fate;
Choose, then, thy destiny and wait,
For love brings love and hate brings hate."

If your imagination is the mirror of your soul, then you have a perfect right to stand before that mirror and see yourself as you wish to be. You have the right to see reflected in that magic mirror the mansion you intend to own, the factory you intend to manage, the bank of which you intend to be president, the station in life you intend to occupy. Your imagination belongs to you! Use it! The more you use it the more efficiently it will serve you.

At the east end of the great Brooklyn Bridge, in New York City, an old man conducts a cobbler shop. When the engineers began driving stakes and marking the foundation place for that great steel structure this man shook his head and said "It can't be done!" Now he looks out from his dingy little shoe-repair shop, shakes his head and asks himself: "How did they do it?"

He saw the bridge grow before his very eyes and still he lacks the imagination to analyze that which he saw. The engineer who planned the bridge saw it a reality long before a single shovel of dirt had been removed for the foundation stones. The bridge became a reality in his imagination because he had trained that imagination to weave new combinations out of old ideas.

Through recent experiments in the department of electricity one of our great educational institutions of America has discovered how to put flowers to sleep and wake them up again, with electric "sunlight." This discovery makes possible the growth of vegetables and flowers without the aid of sunshine. In a few more years the city dweller will be raising a crop of vegetables on his back porch, with the aid of a few boxes of dirt and a few electric lights, with some new vegetable maturing every month of the year.

This new discovery, plus a little imagination, plus Luther Burbank's discoveries in the field of horticulture, and lo! The city dweller will not only grow vegetables all the year around, within the confines of his back porch, but he will grow bigger vegetables than any which the modern gardener grows in the open sunlight.

In one of the cities on the coast of California all of the land that was suitable for building lots had been developed and put into use. On one side of the city there were some steep hills that could not be used for building purposes, and on the other side the land was unsuitable for buildings because it was so low that the back-water covered it once a day.

A man of imagination came to this city. Men of imagination usually have keen minds, and this man was no exception. The first day of his arrival he saw the possibilities for making money out of real estate. He secured an option on those hills that were unsuitable for use because of their steepness. He also secured an option on the ground that was unsuitable for use because of the back-water that covered it daily. He secured these options at a very low price because the ground was supposed to be without substantial value.

With the use of a few tons of explosives he turned those steep hills into loose dirt. With the aid of a few tractors and some road scrapers he leveled the ground down and turned it into beautiful building lots, and with the aid of a few mules and carts he dumped the surplus dirt on the low ground and raised it above the water level, thereby turning it into beautiful building lots.

He made a substantial fortune, for what?

For removing some dirt from where it was not needed to where it was needed! For mixing some useless dirt with imagination!

The people of that little city gave this man credit for being a genius; and he was–the same sort of genius that any one of them could have been had he used his imagination as this man used his.

In the field of chemistry it is possible to mix two or more chemical ingredients in such proportions that the mere act of mixing gives each of the ingredients a tremendous amount of energy that it did not possess. It is also possible to mix certain chemical ingredients in such proportions that all the ingredients of the combination take on an entirely different nature, as in the case of H_2O, which is a mixture of two parts hydrogen and one part oxygen, creating water.

Chemistry is not the only field in which a combination of various physical materials can be so assembled that each takes on a greater value, or the result is a product entirely foreign in nature to that of its component parts. The man who blew up those useless hills of dirt and stone and removed the surplus from where it was not needed over to the low-land, where it was needed, gave that dirt and stone a value that it did not have before.

A ton of pig-iron is worth but little. Add to that pig-iron carbon, silicon, manganese, sulphur and phosphorus, in the right proportions, and you have transformed it into steel, which is of much greater value. Add still other substances, in the right proportion, including some skilled labor, and that same ton of steel is transformed into watch-springs worth a small fortune. But, in all these transformation processes the one ingredient that is worth most is the one that has no material form–imagination!

Here lie great piles of loose brick, lumber, nails and glass. In its present form it is worse than useless for it is a nuisance and an eye-sore. But mix it with the architect's imagination and add some skilled labor and lo! It becomes a beautiful mansion worth a king's ransom.

On one of the great highways between New York and Philadelphia stood an old ramshackle, time-worn barn, worth less than fifty dollars. With the aid of a little lumber and some cement, plus imagination, this old barn has been turned into a beautiful automobile supply station that earns a small fortune for the man who supplied the imagination.

Across the street from my office is a little print-shop that earns coffee and rolls for its owner and his helper, but no more. Less than a dozen blocks away stands one of the most modern printing plants in the world, whose owner spends most of his time traveling and has far more wealth than he will ever use. Twenty-two years ago those two printers were in business together.

The one who owns the big print-shop had the good judgment to ally himself with a man who mixed imagination with printing. This man of imagination is a writer of advertisements and he keeps the printing plant with which he is associated supplied with more business than it can handle by analyzing its clients' business, creating attractive advertising features and supplying the necessary printed material with which to make these features of service. This plant receives top-notch prices for its printing because the imagination mixed with that printing produces a product that most printers cannot supply.

In the city of Chicago the level of a certain boulevard was raised, which spoiled a row of beautiful residences because the side-walk was raised to the level of the second story windows. While the property owners were bemoaning their ill-fortune a man of imagination came along, purchased the property for a "song," converted the second stories into business property, and now enjoys a handsome income from his rentals.

As you read these lines please keep in mind all that was stated in the beginning of this lesson; especially the fact that the greatest and most profitable thing you can do with your imagination is the act of rearranging old ideas in new combinations.

If you properly use your imagination it will help you convert your failures and mistakes into assets of priceless value; it will lead you to discovery of a truth known only to those who use their imagination; namely, that the greatest reverses and misfortunes of life often open the door to golden opportunities.

One of the finest and most highly paid engravers in the United States was formerly a mail-carrier. One day he was fortunate enough to be on a street car that met with an accident and had one of his legs cut off. The street railway company paid him $5,000.00 for his leg. With this money he paid his way through school and became an engraver. The product of his hands, plus his imagination, is worth much more than he could earn with his legs, as a mail-carrier. He discovered that he had imagination when it became necessary to redirect his efforts, as a result of the streetcar accident.

You will never know what is your capacity for achievement until you learn how to mix your efforts with imagination. The products of your hands, minus imagination, will yield you but a small return, but those selfsame hands, when properly guided by imagination, can be made to earn you all the material wealth you can use.

There are two ways in which you can profit by imagination. You can develop this faculty in your own mind, or you can ally yourself with those who have already developed it. Andrew Carnegie did both. He not only made use of his own fertile imagination, but he gathered around him a group of other men who also possessed this essential quality, for his definite purpose in life called for specialists whose imagination ran in numerous directions. In that group of men that constituted Mr. Carnegie's "master mind" were men whose imaginations were confined to the field of chemistry. He had other men in the group whose imaginations were confined to finances. He had still others whose imaginations were confined to salesmanship, one of whom was Charles M. Schwab, who is said to have been the most able salesman on Mr. Carnegie's staff.

If you feel that your own imagination is inadequate you should form an alliance with someone whose imagination is sufficiently developed to supply your deficiency. There are various forms of alliance. For example, there is the alliance of marriage and the alliance of a business partnership and the alliance of friendship and the alliance of employer and employee. Not all men have the capacity to serve their own best interests as employers, and those who haven't this capacity may profit by allying themselves with men of imagination who have such capacity.

It is said that Mr. Carnegie made more millionaires of his employees than any other employer in the steel business. Among these was Charles M. Schwab, who displayed evidence of the soundest sort of imagination by his good judgment in allying himself with Mr. Carnegie. It is no disgrace to serve in the capacity of employee. To the contrary, it often proves to be the most profitable side of an alliance since not all men are fitted to assume the responsibility of directing other men.

Perhaps there is no field of endeavor in which imagination plays such an important part as it does in salesmanship. The master salesman sees the merits of the goods he sells or the service he is rendering, in his own imagination, and if he fails to do so he will not make the sale.

A few years ago a sale was made which is said to have been the most far-reaching and important sale of its kind ever made. The object of the sale was not merchandise, but the freedom of a man who was confined in the Ohio penitentiary and the development of a prison reform system that promises a sweeping change in the method of dealing with unfortunate men and women who have become entangled in the meshes of the law.

That you may observe just how imagination plays the leading part in salesmanship I will analyze this sale for you, with due apologies for personal references, which cannot be avoided without destroying much of the value of the illustration. A few years ago I was invited to speak before the inmates of the Ohio penitentiary.

When I stepped upon the platform I saw in the audience before me a man whom I had known as a successful businessman, more than ten years previously. That man was B___, whose pardon I later secured, and the story of whose release has been spread upon the front page of practically every newspaper in the United States. Perhaps you will recall it.

After I had completed my address I interviewed Mr. B____and found out that he had been sentenced for forgery, for a period of twenty years. After he had told me his story I said:

"I will have you out of here in less than sixty days!"

With a forced smile he replied: "I admire your spirit but question your judgment. Why, do you know that at least twenty influential men have tried every means at their command to get me released, without success? It can't be done!"

I suppose it was that last remark–It can't be done–that challenged me to show him that it could be done. I returned to New York City and requested my wife to pack her trunks and get ready for an indefinite stay in the city of Columbus, where the Ohio penitentiary is located.

I had a definite purpose in mind! That purpose was to get B___ out of the Ohio penitentiary. Not only did I have in mind securing his release, but I intended to do it in such a way that his release would erase from his breast the scarlet letter of "convict" and at the same time reflect credit upon all who helped to bring about his release. Not once did I doubt that I would bring about his release, for no salesman can make a sale if he doubts that he can do it. My wife and I returned to Columbus and took up permanent headquarters.

The next day I called on the governor of Ohio and stated the object of my visit in about these words:

"Governor: I have come to ask you to release B___from the Ohio penitentiary. I have sound reason for asking his release and I hope you will give him his freedom at once, but I have come prepared to stay until he is released, no matter how long that may be.

"During his imprisonment B____ has inaugurated a system of correspondence instruction in the Ohio penitentiary, as you of course know. He has influenced 1729 of the 2518 prisoners of the Ohio penitentiary to take up courses of instruction. He has managed to beg sufficient textbooks and lesson materials with which to keep these men at work on their lessons, and has done this without a penny of expense to the state of Ohio. The warden and the chaplain of the penitentiary tell me that he has carefully observed the prison rules. Surely a man who can influence 1729 men to turn their efforts towards their efforts toward self-betterment cannot be a very bad sort of fellow.

"I have come to ask you to release B___because I wish to place him at the head of a prison school that will give the 160,000 inmates of the other penitentiaries of the United States a chance to profit by his influence. I am prepared to assume full responsibility for his conduct after his release.

"That is my case, but, before you give me your answer, I want you to know that I am not unmindful of the fact that your enemies will probably criticize you if you release him; in fact if you release him it may cost you many votes if you run for office again."

With his fist clinched and his broad jaw set firmly Governor Vic Donahey of Ohio said:

"If that is what you want with B___I will release him if it costs me five thousand votes. However, before I sign the pardon I want you to see the Clemency Board and secure its favorable recommendation. I want you also to secure the favorable recommendation of the warden and the chaplain of the Ohio penitentiary. You know a governor is amenable to the Court of Public Opinion, and these gentlemen are the representatives of that Court."

The sale had been made! And the whole transaction had required less than five minutes.

The next day I returned to the governor's office, accompanied by the chaplain of the Ohio penitentiary, and notified the governor that the Clemency Board, the Warden and the Chaplain all joined in recommending the release. Three days later the pardon was signed and B walked through the big iron gates, a free man.

I have cited the details to show you that there was nothing difficult about the transaction. The groundwork for the release had all been prepared before I came upon the scene. B___had done that, by his good conduct and the service he had rendered those 1729 prisoners. When he created the world's first prison correspondence school system he created the key that unlocked the prison doors for himself. Why, then, had the others who asked for his release failed to secure it? They failed because they used no imagination!

Perhaps they asked the governor for B___'s release on the ground that his parents were prominent people, or on the ground that he was a college graduate and not a bad sort of fellow. They failed to supply the governor of Ohio with a sufficient motive to justify him in granting a pardon, for had this not been so he would undoubtedly have released

B___long before I came upon the scene and asked for his release.

Before I went to see the governor I went over all the facts and in my own imagination I saw myself in the governor's place and made up my mind what sort of a presentation would appeal most strongly to me if I were in reality in his place.

When I asked for B___'s release I did so in the name of the 160,000 unfortunate men and women inmates of the prisons of the United States who would enjoy the benefits of the correspondence school system that he had created. I said nothing about his prominent parents. I said nothing about my friendship with him during former years. I said nothing about his being a deserving fellow. All these matters might have been used as sound reasons for his release, but they seemed insignificant when compared with the bigger and sounder reason that his release would be of help to 160,000 other people who would feel the influence of his correspondence school system after his release.

When the governor of Ohio came to a decision I doubt not that B___was of secondary importance as far as his decision was concerned. The governor no doubt saw a possible benefit, not to B___alone, but to 160,000 other men and women who needed the influence that B___could supply, if released.

And that was imagination!

It was also salesmanship! In speaking of the incident after it was over, one of the men who had worked diligently for more than a year in trying to secure B___'s freedom, asked:

"How did you do it?"

And I replied: "It was the easiest task I ever performed, because most of the work had been done before I took hold of it. In fact I didn't do it B___did it himself."

This man looked at me in bewilderment. He did not see that which I am here trying to make clear; namely, that practically all difficult tasks are easily performed if one approaches them from the right angle. There were two important factors entering B___'s release. The first was the fact that he had supplied the material for a good case before I took it in charge; and the second was the fact that before I called on the governor of Ohio I so completely convinced myself that I had a right to ask for B___'s release that I had no difficulty in presenting my case effectively.

Go back to what was stated in the beginning of this lesson, on the subject of telepathy, and apply it to this case. The governor could tell, long before I had stated my mission, that I knew I had a good case. If my brain did not telegraph this thought to his brain, then the look of self-confidence in my eyes and the positive tone of my voice made obvious my belief in the merits of my case.

Again I apologize for these personal references with the explanation that I have used them only because the whole of America was familiar with the B___case that I have described. I disclaim all credit for the small part I played in the case, for I did nothing except use my imagination as an assembly room in which to piece together the factors out of which the sale was made. I did nothing except that which any salesman of imagination could have done.

It requires considerable courage to prompt one to use the personal pronoun as freely as it has been used in relating the facts connected with this case, but justification lies in the value of application of the principle of imagination to a case with which nearly everybody is familiar.

I cannot recall an incident in my entire life in connection with which the soundness of the fifteen factors that enter into this Reading Course was more clearly manifested than it was in securing the release of B___.

It is but another link in a long chain of evidence that proves to my entire satisfaction the power of imagination as a factor in salesmanship. There are endless millions of approaches to every problem, but there is only one best approach. Find this one best approach and your problem is easily solved. No matter how much merit your goods may have, there are millions of wrong ways in which to offer them. Your imagination will assist you in finding the right way.

In your search for the right way in which to offer your merchandise or your services, remember this peculiar trait of mankind:

Men will grant favors that you request for the benefit of a third person when they would not grant them if requested for your benefit.

Compare this statement with the fact that I asked the governor of Ohio to release B___, not as a favor to me, and not as a favor to B___, but, for the benefit of 160,000 unfortunate inmates of the prisons of America.

Salesmen of imagination always offer their wares in such terminology that the advantages of those wares to the prospective purchaser are obvious. It is seldom that any man makes a purchase of merchandise or renders another a favor just to accommodate the salesman. It is a prominent trait of human nature that prompts us all to do that which advances our own interests. This is a cold, indisputable fact, claims of the idealist to the contrary notwithstanding.

To be perfectly plain, men are selfish!

To understand the truth is to understand how to present your case, whether you are asking for the release of a man from prison or offering for sale some commodity. In your own imagination so plan your presentation of your case that the strongest and most impelling advantages to the buyer are made plain.

This is imagination!

A farmer moved to the city, taking with him his well trained shepherd dog. He soon found that the dog was out of place in the city, so he decided to "get rid of him." (Note the words in quotation.) Taking the dog with him he went out into the country and rapped on the door of a farm-house. A man came hobbling to the door, on crutches.

The man with the dog greeted the man in the house in these words

"You wouldn't care to buy a fine shepherd dog, that I wish to get rid of, would you?"

The man on crutches replied, "No!" and closed the door.

The man with the dog called at half a dozen other farmhouses, asking the same question, and received the same answer. He made up his mind that no one wanted the dog and returned to the city. That evening he was telling of his misfortune, to a man of imagination. The man heard how the owner of the dog had tried in vain to "get rid of him."

"Let me dispose of the dog for you," said the man of imagination. The owner was willing. The next morning the man of imagination took the dog out into the country and stopped at the first farmhouse at which the owner of the dog had called the day before. The same old man hobbled out on crutches and answered the knock at the door.

The man of imagination greeted him in this fashion:

"I see you are all crippled with rheumatism. What you need is a fine dog to run errands for you. I have a dog here that has been trained to bring home the cows, drive away wild animals, herd the sheep and perform other useful services. You may have this dog for a hundred dollars."

"All right," said the crippled man, "I'll take him!"

That, too, was imagination!

No one wants a dog that someone else wants to "get rid of," but most anyone would like to own a dog that would herd sheep and bring home the cows and perform other useful services.

The dog was the same one that the crippled buyer had refused the day before, but the man who sold the dog was not the man who had tried to "get rid of him." If you use your imagination you will know that no one wants anything that someone else is trying to "get rid of."

Remember that which was said about the Law of Attraction through the operation of which "like attracts like." If you look and act the part of a failure you will attract nothing but failures.

Whatever your life-work may be, it calls for the use of imagination.

Niagara Falls was nothing but a great mass of roaring water until a man of imagination harnessed it and converted the wasted energy into electric current that now turns the wheels of industry. Before this man of imagination came along millions of people had seen and heard those roaring falls, but lacked the imagination to harness them.

The first Rotary Club of the world was born in the fertile imagination of Paul Harris, of Chicago, who saw in this child of his brain an effective means of cultivating prospective clients and the extension of his law practice. The ethics of the legal profession forbid advertising in the usual way, but Paul Harris' imagination found a way to extend his law practice without advertising in the usual way.

If the winds of Fortune are temporarily blowing against you, remember that you can harness them and make them carry you toward your definite purpose, through the use of your imagination. A kite rises against the wind–not with it!

Dr. Frank Crane was a struggling "third-rate" preacher until the starvation wages of the clergy forced him to use his imagination. Now he earns upward of a hundred thousand dollars a year for an hour's work a day, writing essays.

Bud Fisher once worked for a mere pittance, but he now earns seventy-five thousand dollars a year by making folks grin, with his Mutt and Jeff comic strip. No art goes into his drawings, therefore he must be selling his imagination.

Woolworth was a poorly paid clerk in a retail store–poorly paid, perhaps, because he had not yet found out that he had imagination. Before he died he built the tallest office building in the world and girdled the United States with Five and Ten Cent Stores, through the use of his imagination.

You will observe, by analyzing these illustrations, that a close study of human nature played an important part in the achievements mentioned. To make profitable use of your imagination you must make it give you a keen insight into the motives that cause men to do or refrain from doing a given act. If your imagination leads you to understand how quickly people grant your requests when those requests appeal to their self-interest, you can have practically anything you go after.

I saw my wife make a very clever sale to our baby not long ago. The baby was pounding the top of our mahogany library table with a spoon. When my wife reached for the spoon the baby refused to give it up, but being a woman of imagination she offered the baby a nice stick of red candy; he dropped the spoon immediately and centered his attention on the more desirable object.

That was imagination! It was also salesmanship. She won her point without using force.

I was riding in an automobile with a friend who was driving beyond the speed limit. An officer rode up on a motorcycle and told my friend he was under arrest for speeding. The friend smiled pleasantly at the officer and said: "I'm sorry to have brought you out in all this rain, but I wanted to make the ten o'clock train with my friend here, and I was hitting it up around thirty-five miles an hour."

"No, you were only going twenty-eight miles an hour," replied the officer, "and as long as you are so nice about it I will let you off this time if you will watch yourself hereafter."

And that, too, was imagination! Even a traffic cop will listen to reason when approached in the right manner, but woe unto the motorist who tries to bully the cop into believing his speedometer was not registering properly.

There is one form of imagination against which I would caution you. It is the brand which prompts some people to imagine that they can get something for nothing, or that they can force themselves ahead in the world without observing the rights of others.

There are more than 160,000 prisoners in the penal institutions of the United States, practically every one of whom is in prison because he imagined he could play the game of life without observing the rights of his fellow men.

There is a man in the Ohio penitentiary who has served more than thirty-five years of time for forgery, and the largest amount he ever got from his misapplication of imagination was twelve dollars.

There are a few people who direct their imaginations in the vain attempt to work out a way to show what happens when "an immovable body comes in contact with an irresistible force," but these types belong in the psychopathic hospitals.

There is also another form of misapplied imagination; namely, that of the young boy or girl who knows more about life than his or her "Dad." But this form is subject to modification with time. My own boys have taught me many things that my "Dad" tried, in vain, to teach me when I was their age.

Time and imagination (which is often but the product of time) teach us many things, but nothing of more importance than this:

That all men are much alike in many ways.

If you would know what your customer is thinking, Mr. Salesman, study yourself and find out what you would be thinking if you were in your customer's place.

Study yourself, find out what are the motives which actuate you in the performance of certain deeds and cause you to refrain from performing other deeds, and you will have gone far toward perfecting yourself in the accurate use of imagination.

The detective's biggest asset is imagination. The first question he asks, when called in to solve a crime is: "What was the motive?" If he can find out the motive he can usually find the perpetrator of the crime.

A man who had lost a horse posted a reward of five dollars for its return. Several days later a boy who was supposed to have been "weak-minded" came leading the horse home and claimed the reward. The owner was curious to know how the boy found the horse. "How did you ever think where to look for the horse?" he asked, and the boy replied, "Well, I just thought where I would have gone if I had been a horse and went there, and he had." Not so bad for a "weak-minded" fellow. Some who are not accused of being weak-minded go all the way through life without displaying as much evidence of imagination as did this boy.

If you want to know what the other fellow will do, use your imagination, put yourself in his place and find out what you would have done. That's imagination.

Every person should be somewhat of a dreamer. Every business needs the dreamer.

Every industry and every profession needs him. But, the dreamer must be, also, a doer; or else he must form an alliance with someone who can and does translate dreams into reality.

The greatest nation upon the face of this earth was conceived, born and nurtured through the early days of its childhood, as the result of imagination in the minds of men who combined dreams with action!

Your mind is capable of creating many new and useful combinations of old ideas, but the most important thing it can create is a definite chief aim that will give you that which you most desire.

Your definite chief aim can be speedily translated into reality after you have fashioned it in the cradle of your imagination. If you have faithfully followed the instructions set down for your guidance in Lesson Two you are now well on the road toward success, because you know what it is that you want, and you have a plan for getting that which you want.

The battle for the achievement of success is half won when one knows definitely what is wanted. The battle is all over except the "shouting" when one knows what is wanted and has made up his mind to get it, whatever the price may be.

The selection of a definite chief aim calls for the use of both imagination and decision!

The power of decision grows with use. Prompt decision in forcing the imagination to create a definite chief aim renders more powerful the capacity to reach decisions in other matters.

Adversities and temporary defeat are generally blessings in disguise, for the reason that they force one to use both imagination and decision. This is why a man usually makes a better fight when his back is to the wall and he knows there is no retreat. He then reaches the decision to fight instead of running.

The imagination is never quite so active as it is when one faces some emergency calling for quick and definite decision and action.

In these moments of emergency men have reached decisions, built plans, used their imagination in such a manner that they became known as geniuses. Many a genius has been born out of the necessity for unusual stimulation of the imagination, as the result of some trying experience which forced quick thought and prompt decision.

It is a well known fact that the only manner in which an over pampered boy or girl may be made to become useful is by forcing him or her to become self-sustaining. This calls for the exercise of both imagination and decision, neither of which would be used except out of necessity.

The late Dr. Harper, who was formerly president of the University of Chicago, was one of the most efficient college presidents of his time. He had a penchant for raising funds in large amounts. It was he who induced John D. Rockefeller to contribute millions of dollars to the support of the University of Chicago.

It may be helpful to the student of this philosophy to study Dr. Harper's technique, because he was a Leader of the highest order. Moreover, I have his own word for it that his leadership was never a matter of chance or accident, but always the result of carefully planned procedure.

The following incident will serve to show just how Dr. Harper made use of imagination in raising money in large sums:

He needed an extra million dollars for the construction of a new building. Taking inventory of the wealthy men of Chicago to whom he might turn for this large sum, he decided upon two men, each of whom was a millionaire, and both were bitter enemies.

One of these men was, at that time, the head of the Chicago Street Railway system.

Choosing the noon hour, when the office force and this man's secretary, in particular, would be apt to be out at lunch, Dr. Harper nonchalantly strolled into the office, and, finding no one on guard at the outer door, walked into the office of his intended "victim," whom he surprised by his appearance unannounced.

"My name is Harper," said the doctor, "and I am president of the University of Chicago. Pardon my intrusion, but I found no one in the outer office (which was no mere accident) so I took the liberty of walking on in.

"I have thought of you and your street railway system many many times. You have built up a wonderful system, and I understand that you have made lots of money for your efforts. I never think of you, however, without its occurring to me that one of these days you will be passing out into the Great Unknown, and after you are gone there will be nothing left as a monument to your name, because others will take over your money, and money has a way of losing its identity very quickly, as soon as it changes hands.

"I have often thought of offering you the opportunity to perpetuate your name by permitting you to build a new Hall out on the University grounds, and naming it after you. I would have offered you this opportunity long ago had it not been for the fact that one of the members of our Board wishes the honor to go to Mr. X___(the streetcar head's enemy). Personally, however, I have always favored you and I still favor you, and if I have your permission to do so I am going to try to swing the opposition over to you.

"I have not come to ask for any decision today, however, as I was just passing and thought it a good time to drop in and meet you. Think the matter over and if you wish to talk to me about it again, telephone me at your leisure.

"Good day, sir! I am happy to have had this opportunity of meeting you." With this he bowed himself out without giving the head of the streetcar company a chance to say either yes or no. In fact the streetcar man had very little chance to do any talking. Dr. Harper did the talking. That was as he planned it to be. He went into the office merely to plant the seed, believing that it would germinate and spring into life in due time.

His belief was not without foundation. He had hardly returned to his office at the University when the telephone rang. The streetcar man was on the other end of the wire. He asked for an appointment with Dr. Harper, which was granted, and the two met in Dr. Harper's office the next morning, and the check for a million dollars was in Dr. Harper's hands an hour later.

Despite the fact that Dr. Harper was a small, rather insignificant-looking man it was said of him that "he had a way about him that enabled him to get everything he went after."

And as to this "way" that he was reputed to have had–what was it?

It was nothing more nor less than his understanding of the power of Imagination. Suppose he had gone to the office of the streetcar head and asked for an appointment. Sufficient time would have elapsed between the time he called and the time when he would have actually seen his man, to have enabled the latter to anticipate the reason for his call, and also to formulate a good, logical excuse for saying, "No!"

Suppose, again, he had opened his interview with the streetcar man something like this: "The University is badly in need of funds and I have come to you to ask your help. You have made lots of money and you owe something to the community in which you have made it. (Which, perhaps, was true.) If you will give us a million dollars we will place your name on a new Hall that we wish to build."

What might have been the result?

In the first place, there would have been no motive suggested that was sufficiently appealing to sway the mind of the streetcar man. While it may have been true that he "owed something to the community from which he had made a fortune," he probably would not have admitted that fact. In the second place, he would have enjoyed the position of being on the offensive instead of the defensive side of the proposal.

But Dr. Harper, shrewd in the use of Imagination as he was, provided for just such contingencies by the way he stated his case. First, he placed the streetcar man on the defensive by informing him that it was not certain that he (Dr. Harper) could get the permission of his Board to accept the money and name the Hall after the streetcar man. In the second place, he intensified the desire of the streetcar man to have his name on that building because of the thought that his enemy and competitor might get the honor if it got away from him. Moreover (and this was no accident, either), Dr. Harper had made a powerful appeal to one of the most common of all human weaknesses by showing this streetcar man how to perpetuate his own name.

All of which required a practical application of the Law of Imagination.

Dr. Harper was a Master Salesman. When he asked men for money he always paved the way for success by planting in the mind of the man of whom he asked it a good sound reason why the money should be given; a reason which emphasized some advantage accruing to the man as the result of the gift. Often this would take on the form of a business advantage. Again it would take on the nature of an appeal to that part of man's nature which prompts him to wish to perpetuate his name so it will live after him. But, always, the request for money was carried out according to a plan that had been carefully thought out, embellished and smoothed down with the use of Imagination.

While the Law of Success philosophy was in the embryonic stage, long before it had been organized into a systematic course of instruction and reduced to textbooks, the author was lecturing on this philosophy in a small town in Illinois.

One of the members of the audience was a young life insurance salesman who had but recently taken up that line of work. After hearing what was said on the subject of Imagination he began to apply what he had heard to his own problem of selling life insurance. Something was said, during the lecture, about the value of allied effort, through which men may enjoy greater success by co-operative effort, through a working arrangement under which each "boosts" the interests of the other.

Taking this suggestion as his cue, the young man in question immediately formulated a plan whereby he gained the co-operation of a group of businessmen who were in no way connected with the insurance business.

Going to the leading grocer in his town he made arrangements with that grocer to give a thousand dollar insurance policy to every customer purchasing no less than fifty dollars worth of groceries each month. He then made it a part of his business to inform people of this arrangement and brought in many new customers. The grocery man had a large neatly lettered card placed in his store, informing his customers of this offer of free insurance, thus helping himself by offering all his customers an inducement to do ALL their trading in the grocery line with him.

This young life insurance man then went to the leading gasoline filling station owner in the town and made arrangements with him to insure all customers who purchased all their gasoline, oil and other motor supplies from him.

Next he went to the leading restaurant in the town and made a similar arrangement with the owner. Incidentally, this alliance proved to be quite profitable to the restaurant man, who promptly began an advertising campaign in which he stated that his food was so pure, wholesome and good that all who ate at his place regularly would be apt to live much longer, therefore he would insure the life of each regular customer for $1,000.00.

The life insurance salesman then made arrangements with a local builder and real estate man to insure the life of each person buying property from him, for an amount sufficient to pay off the balance due on the property in case the purchaser died before payments were completed.

The young man in question is now the General Agent for one of the largest life insurance companies in the United States, with headquarters in one of the largest cities in Ohio, and his income now averages well above $25,000.00 a year.

The turning-point in his life came when he discovered how he might make practical use of the Law of Imagination.

There is no patent on his plan. It may be duplicated over and over again by other life insurance men who know the value of imagination. Just now, if I were engaged in selling life insurance, I think I should make use of this plan by allying myself with a group of automobile distributors in each of several cities, thus enabling them to sell more automobiles and at the same time providing for the sale of a large amount of life insurance, through their efforts.

Financial success is not difficult to achieve after one learns how to make practical use of creative imagination. Someone with sufficient initiative and leadership, and the necessary imagination, will duplicate the fortunes being made each year by the owners of Five and Ten Cent Stores, by developing a system of marketing the same sort of goods now sold in these stores, with the aid of vending machines. This will save a fortune in clerk hire, insure against theft, and cut down the overhead of store operation in many other ways. Such a system can be conducted just as successfully as food can be dispensed with the aid of automatic vending machines.

The seed of the idea has been here sown. It is yours for the taking!

Someone with an inventive turn of the mind is going to make a fortune and at the same time save thousands of lives each year, by perfecting an automatic railroad crossing "control" that will reduce the number of automobile accidents on crossings.

The system, when perfected, will work somewhat after this fashion: A hundred yards or so before reaching the railroad crossing the automobile will cross a platform somewhat on the order of a large scale platform used for weighing heavy objects, and the weight of the automobile will lower a gate and ring a gong. This will force the automobile to slow down. After the lapse of one minute the gate will again rise and the car may continue on its way. Meanwhile, there will have been plenty of time for observation of the track in both directions, to make sure that no trains are approaching. Imagination, plus some mechanical skill, will give the motorist this much needed safeguard, and make the man who perfects the system all the money he needs and much more besides.

Some inventor who understands the value of imagination and has a working knowledge of the radio principle, may make a fortune by perfecting a burglar alarm system that will signal police headquarters and at the same time switch on lights and ring a gong in the place about to be burglarized, with the aid of apparatus similar to that now used for broadcasting.

Any farmer with enough imagination to create a plan, plus the use of a list of all automobile licenses issued in his state, may easily work up a clientele of motorists who will come to his farm and purchase all the vegetables he can produce and all the chickens he can raise, thus saving him the expense of hauling his products to the city.

By contracting with each motorist for the season the farmer may accurately estimate the amount of produce he should provide. The advantage to the motorist, accruing under the arrangement, is that he will be sure of direct-from-the-farm produce, at less cost than he could purchase it from local dealers.

The roadside gasoline filling station owner can make effective use of imagination by placing a lunch stand near his filling station, and then doing some attractive advertising along the road in each direction, calling attention to his "barbecue," "home-made sandwiches" or whatever else he may wish to specialize on. The lunch stand will cause the motorists to stop, and many of them will purchase gasoline before starting on their way again.

These are simple suggestions, involving no particular amount of complication in connection with their use, yet it is just such uses of imagination that bring financial success.

The Piggly-Wiggly self-help store plan, which made millions of dollars for its originator, was a very simple idea which anyone could have adopted, yet consider able imagination was required to put the idea to work in a practical sort of way.

The more simple and easily adapted to a need an idea is, the greater is its value, as no one is looking for ideas which are involved with great detail or in any manner complicated.

Imagination is the most important factor entering into the art of selling. The Master Salesman is always one who makes systematic use of imagination. The outstanding merchant relies upon imagination for the ideas which make his business excel.

Imagination may be used effectively in the sale of even the smallest articles of merchandise, such as ties, shirts, hosiery, etc. Let us proceed to examine just how this may be done.

I walked into one of the best known haberdasheries in the city of Philadelphia, for the purpose of put chasing some shirts and ties.

As I approached the tie counter a young man stepped forward and inquired:

"Is there something you want?"

Now if I had been the man behind the counter I would not have asked that question. He ought to have known, by the fact that I had approached the tie counter, that I wanted to look at ties.

I picked up two or three ties from the counter, examined them briefly, then laid down all but one light blue which somewhat appealed to me. Finally I laid this one down, also, and began to look through the remainder of the assortment.

The young man behind the counter then had a happy idea. Picking up a gaudy-looking yellow tie he wound it around his fingers to show how it would look when tied, and asked:

"Isn't this a beauty?"

Now I hate yellow ties, and the salesman made no particular hit with me by suggesting that a gaudy yellow tie is pretty. If I had been in that salesman's place I would have picked up the blue tie for which I had shown a decided preference, and I would have wound it around my fingers so as to bring out its appearance after being tied. I would have known what my customer wanted by watching the kinds of ties that he picked up and examined. Moreover, I would have known the particular tie that he liked best by the time he held it in his hands. A man will not stand by a counter and fondle a piece of merchandise which he does not like. If given the opportunity, any customer will give the alert salesman a clue as to the particular merchandise which should be stressed in an effort to make a sale.

I then moved over to the shirt counter. Here I was met by an elderly gentleman who asked:

"Is there something I can do for you today?"

Well, I thought to myself that if he ever did anything for me it would have to be today, as I might never come back to that particular store again. I told him I wanted to look at shirts, and described the style and color of shirt that I wanted.

The old gentleman made quite a hit with me when he replied by saying: "I am sorry, sir, but they are not wearing that style this season, so we are not showing it."

I said I knew "they" were not wearing the style for which I had asked, and for that very reason, among others, I was going to wear it providing I could find it in stock.

If there is anything which nettles a man–especially that type of man who knows exactly what he wants and describes it the moment he walks into the store–it is to be told that "they are not wearing it this season."

Such a statement is an insult to a man's intelligence, or to what he thinks is his intelligence, and in most cases it is fatal to a sale. If I were selling goods I might think what I pleased about a customer's taste, but I surely would not be so lacking in tact and diplomacy as to tell the customer that I thought he didn't know his business. Rather I would prefer to manage tactfully to show him what I believed to be more appropriate merchandise than that for which he had called, if what he wanted was not in stock.

One of the most famous and highly paid writers in the world has built his fame and fortune on the sole discovery that it is profitable to write about that which people already know and with which they are already in accord. The same rule might as well apply to the sale of merchandise.

The old gentleman finally pulled down some shirt boxes and began laying out shirts which were not even similar to the shirt for which I had asked. I told him that none of these suited, and as I started to walk out he asked if I would like to look at some nice suspenders.

Imagine it! To begin with I do not wear suspenders, and, furthermore, there was nothing about my manner or bearing to indicate that I might like to look at suspenders.

It is proper for a salesman to try to interest a customer in wares for which he makes no inquiry, but judgment should be used and care taken to offer something which the salesman has reason to believe the customer may want.

I walked out of the store without having bought either shirts or ties, and feeling somewhat resentful because I had been so grossly misjudged as to my tastes for colors and styles.

A little further down the street I went into a small, one-man shop which had shirts and ties on display in the window.

Here I was handled differently!

The man behind the counter asked no unnecessary or stereotyped questions. He took one glance at me as I entered the door, sized me up quite accurately and greeted me with a very pleasant "Good morning, sir!"

He then inquired, "Which shall I show you first, shirts or ties?" I said I would look at the shirts first. He then glanced at the style of shirt I was wearing asked my size, and began laying out shirts of the very type and color for which I was searching, without my saying another word. He laid out six different styles and watched to see which I would pick up first. I looked at each shirt, in turn, and laid them all back on the counter, but the salesman observed that I examined one of the shirts a little more closely than the others, and that I held it a little longer. No sooner had I laid this shirt down than the salesman picked it up and began to explain how it was made. He then went to the tie counter and came back with three very beautiful blue ties, of the very type for which I had been looking, tied each and held it in front of the shirt, calling attention to the perfect harmony between the colors of the ties and the shirt.

Before I had been in the store five minutes I had purchased three shirts and three ties, and was on my way with the package under my arm, feeling that here was a store to which I would return when I needed more shirts and ties.

I learned, afterwards, that the merchant who owns the little shop where I made these purchases pays a monthly rental of $500.00 for the small store, and makes a handsome income from the sale of nothing but shirts, ties and collars. He would have to go out of business, with a fixed charge of $500.00 a month for rent, if it were not for his knowledge of human nature which enables him to make a very high percentage of sales to all who come into his store.

I have often observed women when they were trying on hats, and have wondered why salespeople did not read the prospective buyer's mind by watching her manner of handling the hats.

A woman goes into a store and asks to be shown some hats. The salesperson starts bringing out hats and the prospective buyer starts trying them on. If a hat suits her, even in the slightest sort of way, she will keep it on a few seconds, or a few minutes, but if she does not like it she will pull it right off her head the moment the salesperson takes her hands off the hat.

Finally, when the customer is shown a hat that she likes she will begin to announce that fact, in terms which no well informed salesperson will fail to understand, by arranging her hair under the hat, or pulling it down on her head to just the angle which she likes best, and by looking at the hat from the rear, with the aid of a hand-mirror. The signs of admiration are unmistakable. Finally, the customer will remove the hat from her head, and begin to look at it closely; then she may lay it aside and permit another hat to be tried on her, in which event the clever salesperson will lay aside the hat just removed, and at the opportune time she will bring it back and ask the customer to try it on again. By careful observation of the customer's likes and dislikes a clever saleswoman may often sell as many as three or four hats to the same customer, at one sitting, by merely watching what appeals to the customer and then concentrating upon the sale of that.

The same rule applies in the sale of other merchandise. The customer will, if closely observed, clearly indicate what is wanted, and, if the clue is followed, very rarely will a customer walk out without buying.

I believe it a conservative estimate when I say that fully seventy-five per cent of the "walk-outs," as the non-purchasing customers are called, are due to lack of tactful showing of merchandise.

Last Fall I went into a hat store to purchase a felt hat. It was a busy Saturday afternoon and I was approached by a young "extra" rush-hour salesman who had not yet learned how to size people up at a glance. For no good reason whatsoever the young man pulled down a brown derby and handed it to me, or rather tried to hand it to me. I thought he was trying to be funny, and refused to take the hat into my hands, saying to him, in an attempt to return his compliment and be funny in turn, "Do you tell bedtime stories also?" He looked at me in surprise, but didn't take the cue which I had offered him.

If I had not observed the young man more closely than he had observed me, and sized him up as an earnest but inexperienced "extra," I would have been highly insulted, for if there is anything I hate it is a derby of any sort, much less a brown derby. One of the regular salesmen happened to see what was going on, walked over and snatched the brown derby out of the young man's hands, and, with a smile on his face intended as a sort of sop to me, said, "What the hell are you trying to show this gentleman, anyway?"

That spoiled my fun, and the salesman who had immediately recognized me as a gentleman sold me the first hat he brought out.

The customer generally feels complimented when a salesman takes the time to study the customer's personality and lay out merchandise suited to that personality. I went into one of the largest men's clothing stores in New York City, a few years ago, and asked for a suit, describing exactly what was wanted, but not mentioning price.

The young man, who purported to be a salesman, said he did not believe they carried such a suit, but I happened to see exactly what I wanted hanging on a model, and called his attention to the suit. He then made a hit with me by saying, "Oh, that one over there? That's a high-priced suit!"

His reply amused me; it also angered me, so I inquired of the young man what he saw about me which indicated that I did not come in to purchase a high-priced suit? With embarrassment he tried to explain, but his explanations were as bad as the original offense, and I started toward the door, muttering something to myself about "dumbbells." Before I reached the door I was met by another salesman who had sensed by the way I walked and the expression on my face that I was none too well pleased.

With tact well worth remembering, this salesman engaged me in conversation while I unburdened my woes and then managed to get me to go back with him and look at the suit. Before I left the store I purchased the suit I came in to look at, and two others which I had not intended purchasing.

That was the difference between a salesman and one who drove customers away. Moreover, I later introduced two of my friends to this same salesman and he made sizable sales to each of them.

I was once walking down Michigan Boulevard, in Chicago, when my eye was attracted to a beautiful gray suit in the window of a men's store. I had no notion of buying the suit, but I was curious to know the price, so I opened the door, and, without entering, merely pushed my head inside and asked the first man I saw how much the suit in the window was.

Then followed one of the cleverest bits of sales maneuvering I have ever observed. The salesman knew he could not sell me the suit unless I came into the store, so he said, "Will you not step inside, sir, while I find out the price of the suit?"

Of course he knew the price, all the time, but that was his way of disarming me of the thought that he intended trying to sell me the suit. Of course I had to be as polite as the salesman, so I said, "Certainly," and walked inside.

The salesman said, "Step right this way, sir, and I will get the information for you."

In less than two minutes I found myself standing in front of a case, with my coat off, getting ready to try on a coat like the one I had observed in the window.

After I was in the coat, which happened to fit almost perfectly (which was no accident, thanks to the accurate eyes of an observing salesman) my attention was called to the nice, smooth touch of the material. I rubbed my hand up and down the arm of the coat, as I had seen the salesman do while describing the material, and, sure enough, it was a very fine piece of material. By this time I had again asked the price, and when I was told that the suit was only fifty dollars I was agreeably surprised, because I had been led to believe that it might have been priced much higher. However, when I first saw the suit in the window my guess was that it was priced at about thirty-five dollars, and I doubt that I would have paid that much for it had I not fallen into the hands of a man who knew how to show the suit to best advantage. If the first coat tried on me had been about two sizes too large, or a size too small, I doubt that any sale would have been made, despite the fact that all ready-to-wear suits sold in the better stores are altered to fit the customer.

I bought that suit "on the impulse of the moment," as the psychologist would say, and I am not the only man who buys goods on that same sort of impulse. A single slip on the part of the salesman would have lost him the sale of that suit. If he had replied, "Fifty dollars," when I asked the price I would have said, "Thank you," and have gone my way without looking at the suit.

Later in the season I purchased two more suits from this same salesman, and if I now lived in Chicago the chances are that I would buy still other suits from him, because he always showed me suits that were in keeping with my personality.

The Marshall Field store, in Chicago, gets more for merchandise than does any other store of its kind in the country. Moreover, people knowingly pay more at this store, and feel better satisfied than if they bought the merchandise at another store for less money.

Why is this?

Well, there are many reasons, among them the fact that anything purchased at the Field store which is not entirely satisfactory may be returned and exchanged for other merchandise, or the purchase price may be refunded, just as the customer wishes. An implied guarantee goes with every article sold in the Field store.

Another reason why people will pay more at the Field store is the fact that the merchandise is displayed and shown to better advantage than it is at most other stores.

The Field window-displays are truly works of art, no less than if they were created for the sake of art alone, and not merely to sell merchandise. The same is true of the goods displayed in the store. There is harmony and proper grouping of merchandise throughout the Field establishment, and this creates an "atmosphere" that is more–much more–than merely an imaginary one.

Still another reason why the Field store can get more for merchandise than most other merchants is due to the careful selection and supervision of salespeople. One would seldom find a person employed in the Field store whom one would not be willing to accept as a social equal, or as a neighbor. Not a few men have made the acquaintance of girls in the Field store who later became their wives.

Merchandise purchased in the Field store is packed or wrapped more artistically than is common in other stores, which is still another reason why people go out of their way and pay higher prices to trade there.

While we are on the subject of artistic wrapping of merchandise I wish to relate the experience of a friend of mine which will not fail to convey a very definite meaning to those engaged in the business of selling, as it shows how imagination may be used even in wrapping merchandise.

This friend had a very fine silver cigarette case which he had carried for years, and of which he was very proud because it was a gift from his wife.

Constant usage had banged the case up rather badly. It had been bent, dented, the hinges warped, etc., until he decided to take it to Caldwell the jeweler, in Philadelphia, to be repaired. He left the case and asked them to send it to his office when it was ready.

About two weeks later a splendid-looking new delivery wagon with the Caldwell name on it drew up in front of his office, and a nice-looking young man in a neat uniform stepped out with a package that was artistically wrapped and tied with a ribbon tape string.

The package happened to be delivered to my friend on his birthday, and, having forgotten about leaving the cigarette case to be repaired, and observing the beauty and size of the package that was handed to him, he naturally imagined that someone had sent him a birthday present.

His secretary and other workers in his office gathered around his desk to watch him open up his "present." He cut the ribbon and removed the outer covering. Under this was a covering of tissue paper, fastened with beautiful gold seals bearing the Caldwell initials and trademark. This paper was removed and behold! A most beautiful plush-lined box met his eyes. The box was opened, and, after removing the tissue paper packing, there was a cigarette case which he recognized, after careful examination, as the one he had left to be repaired, but it did not look like the same case, thanks to the imagination of the Caldwell manager.

Every dent had been carefully straightened out. The hinges had been trued and the case had been polished and cleaned so it shone as it did when it was first purchased. Simultaneously a prolonged "Oo-o-o-o-o-o-h!" of admiration came from the onlookers, including the owner of the cigarette case. And the bill! Oh, it was a plenty, and yet the price charged for the repair did not seem too high. As a matter of fact everything that entered into the transaction from the packing of the case, with the fine tissue paper cover, the gold seals, the ribbon tape string, the delivery of the package by a neatly uniformed boy, from a well-appointed new delivery wagon, was based upon carefully calculated psychology which laid the foundation for a high price for the repair.

People, generally, do not complain of high prices providing the "service" or embellishment of the merchandise is such as to pave the way for high prices. What people do complain of, and rightly so, is high prices and "sloppy" service. To me there was a great lesson in this cigarette case incident, and I think there is a lesson in it for any person who makes a business of selling any sort of merchandise. The goods you are selling may actually be worth all you are asking for them, but if you do not carefully study the subjects of advantageous display and artistic packing you may be accused of overcharging your customers.

On Broad Street, in the city of Philadelphia, there is a fruit shop where those who patronize the store are met at the door by a man in uniform who opens the door for them. He does nothing else but merely open the door, but he does it with a smile (even though it be a carefully studied and rehearsed smile) which makes the customer feel welcome even before he gets inside of the store. This fruit merchant specializes on specially prepared baskets of fruit. Just outside the store is a big blackboard on which are listed the sailing dates of the various ocean liners leaving New York City. This merchant caters to people who wish baskets of fruit delivered on board departing boats on which friends are sailing. If a man's sweetheart, or perhaps his wife or a very dear friend, happens to be sailing on a certain date he naturally wants the basket of fruit he purchases for her to be embellished with frills and "trimmings." Moreover, he is not necessarily looking for something "cheap" or even inexpensive.

All of which the fruit merchant capitalizes! He gets from $10.00 to $25.00 for a basket of fruit which one could purchase just around the corner, not more than a block away, for from $3.00 to $7.50, with the exception that the latter would not be embellished with the seventy-five cents' worth of frills which the former contains. This merchant's store is a small affair, no larger than the average small fruit-stand store, but he pays, a rent of at least $15,000.00 a year for the place and makes more money than half a hundred ordinary fruit stands combined, merely because he knows how to display and deliver his wares so they appeal to the vanity of the buyers. This is but another proof of the value of imagination.

The American people–and this means all of them, not merely the so-called rich–are the most extravagant spenders on earth, but they insist on "class" when it comes to appearances such as wrapping and delivery and other embellishments which add no real value to the merchandise they buy. The merchant who understands this, and has learned how to mix IMAGINATION with his merchandise, may reap a rich harvest in return for his knowledge.

And a great many are doing it, too.

The salesman who understands the psychology of proper display, wrapping and delivery of merchandise, and who knows how to show his wares to fit the whims and characteristics of his customers, can make ordinary merchandise bring fancy prices, and what is more important still, he can do so and still retain the patronage of his customers more readily than if he sold the same merchandise without the "studied" appeal and the artistic wrapping and delivery service.

In a "cheap" restaurant, where coffee is served in heavy, thick cups and the silverware is tarnished or dirty, a ham sandwich is only a ham sandwich, and if the restaurant keeper gets fifteen cents for it he is doing well; but just across the street, where the coffee is served in dainty thin cups, on neatly covered tables, by neatly dressed young women, a much smaller ham sandwich will bring a quarter, to say nothing of the cost of the tip to the waitress. The only difference in the sandwiches is merely in appearances; the ham comes from the same butcher and the bread from the same baker, whether purchased from the former or the latter restaurant. The difference in price is very considerable, but the difference in the merchandise is not a difference of either quality or quantity so much as it is of "atmosphere," or appearances.

People love to buy "appearance" or atmosphere! Which is merely a more refined way of saying that which P. T. Barnum said about "one being born every minute."

It is no overstatement of fact to say that a master of sales psychology could go into the average merchant's store, where the stock of goods was worth, let us say, $50,000.00, and at very slight additional expense make the stock bring $60,000.00 to $75,000.00.

He would do nothing except coach the salespeople on the proper showing of the merchandise, after having purchased a small amount of more suitable fixtures, perhaps, and repacked the merchandise in more suitable coverings and boxes.

A man's shirt, packed one to the box, in the right sort of a box, with a piece of ribbon and a sheet of, tissue paper added for embellishment, can be made to bring a dollar or a dollar and a half more than the same shirt would bring without the more artistic packing. I know this is true, and I have proved it more times than I can recall, to convince some skeptical merchant who had not studied the effect of "proper displays."

Conversely stated, I have proved, many times, that, the finest shirt made cannot be sold for half its value if it is removed from its box and placed on a bargain counter, with inferior looking shirts, both of which examples prove that people do not know what they are buying - that they go more by appearances than they do by actual analysis of the merchandise they purchase.

This is noticeably true in the purchase of automobiles. The American people want, and DEMAND, style in the appearance of automobiles. What is under the hood or in the rear axle they do not know and really do not care, as long as the car looks the part.

Henry Ford required nearly twenty years of experience to learn the truth of the statement just made, and even then, despite all of his analytical ability, he only acknowledged the truth when forced to do so by his competitors. If it were not true that people buy "appearances" more than they buy "reality" Ford never would have created his new automobile. That car is the finest sort of example of a psychologist who appeals to the tendency which people have to purchase "appearance," although, of course, it must be admitted that in this particular example the real value of the car actually exists.

Lesson Seven: ENTHUSIASM

Enthusiasm is a state of mind that inspires and arouses one to put action into the task at hand. It does more than this–it is contagious, and vitally affects not only the enthusiast, but all with whom he comes in contact.

Enthusiasm bears the same relationship to a human being that steam does to the locomotive–it is the vital moving force that impels action. The greatest leaders of men are those who know how to inspire enthusiasm in their followers. Enthusiasm is the most important factor entering into salesmanship. It is, by far, the most vital factor that enters into public speaking.

If you wish to understand the difference between a man who is enthusiastic and one who is not, compare Billy Sunday with the average man of his profession. The finest sermon ever delivered would fall upon deaf ears if it were not backed with enthusiasm by the speaker.

HOW ENTHUSIASM WILL AFFECT YOU

Mix enthusiasm with your work and it will not seem hard or monotonous. Enthusiasm will so energize your entire body that you can get along with less than half the usual amount of sleep and at the same time it will enable you to perform from two to three times as much work as you usually perform in a given period, without fatigue.

For many years I have done most of my writing at night. One night, while I was enthusiastically at work over my typewriter, I looked out of the window of my study, just across the square from the Metropolitan tower, in New York City, and saw what seemed to be the most peculiar reflection of the moon on the tower. It was of a silvery gray shade, such as I had never seen before. Upon closer inspection I found that the reflection was that of the early morning sun and not that of the moon. It was daylight! I had been at work all night, but I was so engrossed in my work that the night had passed as though it were but an hour. I worked at my task all that day and all the following night without stopping, except for a small amount of light food.

Two nights and one day without sleep, and with but little food, without the slightest evidence of fatigue, would not have been possible had I not kept my body energized with enthusiasm over the work at hand.

Enthusiasm is not merely a figure of speech; it is a vital force that you can harness and use with profit. Without it you would resemble an electric battery without electricity. Enthusiasm is the vital force with which you recharge your body and develop a dynamic personality. Some people are blessed with natural enthusiasm, while others must acquire it. The procedure through which it may be developed is simple. It begins by the doing of the work or rendering of the service which one likes best. If you should be so situated that you cannot conveniently engage in the work which you like best, for the time being, then you can proceed along another line very effectively by adopting a definite chief aim that contemplates your engaging in that particular work at some future time.

Lack of capital and many other circumstances over which you have no immediate control may force you to engage in work which you do not like, but no one can stop you from determining in your own mind what your definite chief aim in life shall be, nor can anyone stop you from planning ways and means for translating this aim into reality, nor can anyone stop you from mixing enthusiasm with your plans.

Happiness, the final object of all human effort, is a state of mind that can be maintained only through the hope of future achievement. Happiness lies always in the future and never in the past. The happy person is the one who dreams of heights of achievement that are yet unattained. The home you intend to own, the money you intend to earn and place in the bank, the trip you intend to take when you can afford it, the position in life you intend to fill when you have prepared yourself, and the preparation, itself–these are the things that produce happiness. Likewise, these are the materials out of which your definite chief aim is formed; these are the things over which you may become enthusiastic, no matter what your present station in life may be.

More than twenty years ago I became enthusiastic over an idea. When the idea first took form in my mind I was unprepared to take even the first step toward its transformation into reality. But I nursed it in my mind -I became enthusiastic over it as I looked ahead, in my imagination, and saw the time when I would be prepared to make it a reality.

The idea was this: I wanted to become the editor of a magazine, based upon the Golden Rule, through which I could inspire people to keep up courage and deal with one another squarely.

Finally my chance came! And, on Armistice Day, 1918, I wrote the first editorial for what was to become the material realization of a hope that had lain dormant in my mind for nearly a score of years.

With enthusiasm I poured into that editorial the emotions which I had been developing in my heart over a period of more than twenty years. My dream had come true. My editorship of a national magazine had become a reality.

As I have stated, this editorial was written with enthusiasm. I took it to a man of my acquaintance and with enthusiasm I read it to him. The editorial ended in these words:

"At last my twenty-year-old dream is about to come true. It takes money, and a lot of it, to publish a national magazine, and I haven't the slightest idea where I am going to get this essential factor, but this is worrying me not at all because I know I am going to get it somewhere!" As I wrote those lines, I mixed enthusiasm and faith with them.

I had hardly finished reading this editorial when the man to whom I read it–the first and only person to whom I had shown it–said:

"I can tell you where you are going to get the money, for I am going to supply it."

And he did!

Yes, enthusiasm is a vital force; so vital, in fact, that no man who has it highly developed can begin even to approximate his power of achievement.

Before passing to the next step in this lesson, I wish to repeat and to emphasize the fact that you may develop enthusiasm over your definite chief aim in life, no matter whether you are in position to achieve that purpose at this time or not. You may be a long way from realization of your definite chief aim, but if you will kindle the fire of enthusiasm in your heart, and keep it burning, before very long the obstacles that now stand in the way of your attainment of that purpose will melt away as if by the force of magic, and you will find yourself in possession of power that you did not know you possessed.

HOW YOUR ENTHUSIASM WILL AFFECT OTHERS

We come, now, to the discussion of one of the most important subjects of this Reading Course, namely, suggestion.

In the preceding lessons we have discussed the subject of Auto-suggestion, which is self-suggestion. You saw, in Lesson Three, what an important part Auto-suggestion played.

Suggestion is the principle through which your words and your acts and even your state of mind influence others. That you may comprehend the far-reaching power of suggestion, let me refer to the Introductory Lesson, in which the principle of telepathy is described. If you now understand and accept the principle of telepathy (the communication of thought from one mind to another without the aid of signs, symbols or sounds) as a reality, you of course understand why enthusiasm is contagious, and why it influences all within its radius.

When your own mind is vibrating at a high rate, because it has been stimulated with enthusiasm, that vibration registers in the minds of all within its radius, and especially in the minds of those with whom you come in close contact. When a public speaker "senses" the feeling that his audience is "en rapport" with him he merely recognizes the fact that his own enthusiasm has influenced the minds of his listeners until their minds are vibrating in harmony with his own.

When the salesman "senses" the fact that the "psychological" moment for closing a sale has arrived, he merely feels the effect of his own enthusiasm as it influences the mind of his prospective buyer and places that mind "en rapport" (in harmony) with his own.

The subject of suggestion constitutes so vitally an important part of this lesson, and of this entire course, that I will now proceed to describe the three mediums through which it usually operates; namely, what you say, what you do and what you think!

When you are enthusiastic over the goods you are selling or the services you are offering, or the speech you are delivering, your state of mind becomes obvious to all who hear you, by the tone of your voice. Whether you have ever thought of it in this way or not, it is the tone in which you make a statement, more than it is the statement itself, that carries conviction or fails to convince. No mere combination of words can ever take the place of a deep belief in a statement that is expressed with burning enthusiasm. Words are but devitalized sounds unless colored with feeling that is born of enthusiasm.

Here the printed word fails me, for I can never express with mere type and paper the difference between words that fall from unemotional lips, without the fire of enthusiasm back of them, and those which seem to pour forth from a heart that is bursting with eagerness for expression. The difference is there, however.

Thus, what you say, and the way in which you say it, conveys a meaning that may be just the opposite to what is intended. This accounts for many a failure by the salesman who presents his arguments in words which seem logical enough, but lack the coloring that can come only from enthusiasm that is born of sincerity and belief in the goods he is trying to sell. His, words said one thing, but the tone of his voice suggested something entirely different; therefore, no sale was made.

That which you say is an important factor in the operation of the principle of suggestion, but not nearly so important as that which you do. Your acts will count for more than your words, and woe unto you if the two fail to harmonize.

If a man preaches the Golden Rule as a sound rule of conduct, his words will fall upon deaf ears if he does not practice that which he preaches. The most effective sermon that any man can preach on the soundness of the Golden Rule is that which he preaches, by suggestion, when he applies this rule in his relationships with his fellow men.

If a salesman of Ford automobiles drives up to his prospective purchaser in a Buick, or some other make of car, all the arguments he can present in behalf of the Ford will be without effect. Once I went into one of the offices of the Dictaphone Company to look at a dicta phone (dictating machine). The salesman in charge presented a logical argument as to the machine's merits, while the stenographer at his side was transcribing letters from a shorthand notebook. His arguments in favor of a dictating machine, as compared with the old method of dictating to a stenographer, did not impress me, because his actions were not in harmony with his words.

Your thoughts constitute the most important of the three ways in which you apply the principle of suggestion, for the reason that they control the tone of your words and, to some extent at least, your actions. If your thoughts and your actions and your words harmonize, you are bound to influence those with whom you come in contact, more or less toward your way of thinking.

We will now proceed to analyze the subject of suggestion and to show you exactly how to apply the principle upon which it operates. As we have already seen, suggestion differs from Auto-suggestion only in one way–we use it, consciously or unconsciously, when we influence others, while we use Auto-suggestion as a means of influencing ourselves.

Before you can influence another person through suggestion, that person's mind must be in a state of neutrality; that is, it must be open and receptive to your method of suggestion. Right here is where most salesmen fail–they try to make a sale before the mind of the prospective buyer has been rendered receptive or neutralized. This is such a vital point in this lesson that I feel impelled to dwell upon it until there can be no doubt that you understand the principle that I am describing.

When I say that the salesman must neutralize the mind of his prospective purchaser before a sale can be made I mean that the prospective purchaser's mind must be credulous. A state of confidence must have been established and it is obvious that there can be no set rule for either establishing confidence or neutralizing the mind to a state of openness. Here the ingenuity of the salesman must supply that which cannot be set down as a hard and fast rule.

I know a life insurance salesman who sells nothing but large policies, amounting to $100,000.00 and upward. Before this man even approaches the subject of insurance with a prospective client he familiarizes himself with the prospective client's complete history, including his education, his financial status, his eccentricities if he has any, his religious preferences and other data too numerous to be listed. Armed with this information, he manages to secure an introduction under conditions which permit him to know the Prospective client in a social as well as a business way. Nothing is said about the sale of life insurance during his first visit, nor his second, and sometimes he does not approach the subject of insurance until he has become very well acquainted with the prospective client.

All this time, however, he is not dissipating his efforts. He is taking advantage of these friendly visits for the purpose of neutralizing his prospective client's mind; that is, he is building up a relationship of confidence so that when the time comes for him to talk life insurance that which he says will fall upon ears that willingly listen. Some years ago I wrote a book entitled How to Sell Your Services. Just before the manuscript went to the publisher, it occurred to me to request some of the well-known men of the United States to write letters of endorsement to be published in the book. The printer was then waiting for the manuscript; therefore, I hurriedly wrote a letter to some eight or ten men, in which I briefly outlined exactly what I wanted, but the letter brought back no replies. I had failed to observe two important prerequisites for success–I had written the letter so hurriedly that I had failed to inject the spirit of enthusiasm into it, and, I had neglected so to word the letter that it had the effect of neutralizing the minds of those to whom it was sent; therefore, I had not paved the way for the application of the principle of suggestion.

After I discovered my mistake, I then wrote a letter that was based upon strict application of the principle of suggestion, and this letter not only brought back replies from all to whom it was sent, but many of the replies were masterpieces and served, far beyond my fondest hopes, as valuable supplements to the book. For the purpose of comparison, to show you how the principle of suggestion may be used in writing a letter, and what an important part enthusiasm plays in giving the written word "flesh," the two letters are here reproduced. It will not be necessary to indicate which letter failed, as that will be quite obvious:

My dear Mr. Ford:

I am just completing a manuscript for a new book entitled How to Sell Your Services. I anticipate the sale of several hundred thousand of these books and I believe those who purchase the book would welcome the opportunity of receiving a message from you as to the best method of marketing personal services.

Would you, therefore, be good enough to give me a few minutes of your time by writing a brief message to be published in my book? This will be a big favor to me personally and I know it would be appreciated by the readers of the book. Thanking you in advance for any consideration you may care to show me, I am,

Yours very truly,

....

Hon. Thomas R. Marshall,
Vice-President of the United States,
Washington, D. C.

My dear Mr. Marshall:

Would you care for the opportunity to send a message of encouragement, and possibly a word of advice, to a few hundred thousand of your fellow men who have failed to make their mark in the world as successfully as you have done?

I have about completed a manuscript for a book to be entitled How to Sell Your Services. The main point made in the book is that service rendered is cause and the pay envelope is effect; and that the latter varies in proportion to the efficiency of the former.

The book would be incomplete without a few words of advice from a few men who, like yourself, have come up from the bottom to enviable positions in the world. Therefore, if you will write me of your views as to the most essential points to be borne in mind by those who are offering personal services for sale I will pass your message on through my book, which will insure its getting into hands where it will do a world of good for a class of earnest people who are struggling to find their places in the world's work.

I know you are a busy man, Mr. Marshall, but please bear in mind that by simply calling in your secretary and dictating a brief letter you will be sending forth an important message to possibly half a million people. In money this will not be worth to you the two cent stamp that you will place on the letter, but, if estimated from the viewpoint of the good it may do others who are less fortunate than yourself, it may be worth the difference between success and failure to many a worthy person who will read your message believe in it, and be guided by it.

Very cordially yours,

Now, let us analyze the two letters and find out why one failed in its mission while the other succeeded. This analysis should start with one of the most important fundamentals of salesmanship, namely motive. In the first letter it is obvious that the motive is entirely one of self-interest. The letter states exactly what is wanted, but the wording of it leaves a doubt as to why the request is made or whom it is intended, to benefit. Study the sentence in the second paragraph, "This will be a big favor to me personally, etc." Now it may seem to be a peculiar trait, but the truth is that most people will not grant favors just to please others. If I ask you to render a service that will benefit me, without bringing you some corresponding advantage, you will not show much enthusiasm in granting that favor; you may refuse altogether if you have a plausible excuse for refusing. But if I ask you to render a service that will benefit a third person, even though the service must be rendered through me; and if that service is of such a nature that it is likely to reflect credit on you, the chances are that you will render the service willingly.

We see this psychology demonstrated by the man who pitches a dime to the beggar on the street, or perhaps refuses even the dime, but willingly hands over a hundred or a thousand dollars to the charity worker who is begging in the name of others.

But the most damaging suggestion of all is contained in the last and most important paragraph of the letter, "Thanking you in advance for any consideration you may care to show me." This sentence strongly suggests that the writer of the letter anticipates a refusal of his request. It clearly indicates lack of enthusiasm. It paves the way for a refusal of the request. There is not one single word in the entire letter that places in the mind of a man to whom it is sent a satisfactory reason why he should comply with the request. On the other hand, he can clearly see that the object of the letter is to secure from him a letter of endorsement that will help sell the book. The most important selling argument–in fact, the only selling argument available in connection with this request, has been lost because it was not brought out and established as the real motive for making the request. This argument was but faintly mentioned in the sentence, "I believe those who purchase the book would welcome the opportunity of receiving a message from you as to the best method of marketing personal services."

The opening paragraph of the letter violates an important fundamental of salesmanship because it clearly suggests that the object of the letter is to gain some advantage for its writer, and does not even hint at any corresponding advantage that may accrue to the person to whom it is sent. Instead of neutralizing the mind of the recipient of the letter, as it should do, it has just the opposite effect; it causes him to close his mind against all argument that follows; it puts him in a frame of mind that makes it easy for him to say no. It reminds me of a salesman–or, perhaps I should say, a man who wanted to be a salesman–who once approached me for the purpose of selling me a subscription to the Saturday Evening Post. As he held a copy of the magazine in front of me he suggested the answer I should make by this question:

"You wouldn't subscribe for the Post to help me out, would you?"

Of course I said no! He had made it easy for me to say no. There was no enthusiasm back of his words, and gloom and discouragement were written all over his face. He needed the commission he would have made on my subscription had I purchased; no doubt about that–but he suggested nothing that appealed to my self-interest motive, therefore he lost a sale. But the loss of this one sale was not the sad part of his misfortune; the sad part was that this same attitude was causing him to lose all other sales which he might have made had he changed his approach.

A few weeks later another subscription agent approached me. She was selling a combination of six magazines, one of which was the Saturday Evening Post, but how different was her approach. She glanced at my library table, on which she saw several magazines, then at my bookshelves, and exclaimed with enthusiasm:

"Oh! I see you are a lover of books and magazines."

I proudly pleaded guilty to the charge. Observe the word "proudly," for it has an important bearing on this incident. I laid down the manuscript that I was reading when this saleswoman came in, for I could see that she was a woman of intelligence. Just how I came to see this I will leave to your imagination. The important point is that I laid down the manuscript and actually felt myself wanting to hear what she had to say.

With the aid of eleven words, plus a pleasant smile, plus a tone of genuine enthusiasm, she had neutralized my mind sufficiently to make me want to hear her. She had performed her most difficult task, with those few words, because I had made up my mind when she was announced that I would keep my manuscript in my hands and thereby convey to her mind, as politely as I could, the fact that I was busy and did not wish to be detained.

Being a student of salesmanship and of suggestion, I carefully watched to see what her next move would be. She had a bundle of magazines under her arm and I expected she would unroll it and begin to urge me to purchase, but she didn't. You will recall that I said she was selling a combination of six magazines; not merely trying to sell them.

She walked over to my bookshelves, pulled out a copy of Emerson's Essays, and for the next ten minutes she talked about Emerson's essay on Compensation so interestingly that I lost sight of the roll of magazines that she carried. (She was neutralizing my mind some more.)

Incidentally, she gave me a sufficient number of new ideas about Emerson's works to provide material for an excellent editorial.

Then she asked me which magazines I received regularly, and after I told her she smiled as she began to unroll her bundle of magazines and laid them on the table in front of me. She analyzed her magazines one by one, and explained just why I should have each of them. The Saturday Evening Post would bring me the cleanest fiction; Literary Digest would bring me the news of the world in condensed form, such as a busy man like myself would demand; the American Magazine would bring me the latest biographies of the men who were leading in business and industry, and so on, until she had covered the entire list.

But I was not responding to her argument as freely as she thought I should have, so she slipped me this gentle suggestion:

"A man of your position is bound to be well-informed and, if he isn't, it will show up in his own work!"

She spoke the truth! Her remark was both a compliment and a gentle reprimand. She made me feel somewhat sheepish because she had taken inventory of my reading matter–and six of the leading magazines were not on my list. (The six that she was selling.)

Then I began to "slip" by asking her how much the six magazines would cost. She put on the finishing touches of a well-presented sales talk by this tactful reply: "The cost? Why, the cost of the entire number is less than you receive for a single page of the typewritten manuscript that you had in your hands when I came in."

Again she spoke the truth. And how did she happen to guess so well what I was getting for my manuscript? The answer is, she didn't guess–she knew! She made it a part of her business to draw me out tactfully as to the nature of my work (which in no way made me angry). She became so deeply interested in the manuscript which I had laid down when she came in, that she actually induced me to talk about it. (I am no saying, of course, that this required any great amount of skill or coaxing, for have I not said that it was my manuscript?) In my remarks about that manuscript, I suspect I admitted that I was receiving $250.00 for the fifteen pages; yes, I am sure I was careless enough to admit that I was being well paid for my work.

Perhaps she induced me to make the admission. At any rate, the information was valuable to her and she made effective use of it at the psychological moment. For all I know it was a part of her plan to observe carefully all that she saw and heard, with the object of finding out just what my weaknesses were and what I was most interested in discussing. Some salesmen take the time to do this; some do not. She was one of those who did.

Yes, she went away with my order for the six magazines; also my twelve dollars. But that was not all the benefit she derived from tactful suggestion plus enthusiasm; she got my consent to canvass my office, and before she left she had five other orders from my employees.

At no time during her stay did she leave the impression that I was favoring her by purchasing her magazines. Just to the contrary, she distinctly impressed me with the feeling that she was rendering me a favor. This was tactful suggestion. Before we get away from this incident, I wish to make an admission–when she drew me into conversation she did it in such a way that I talked with enthusiasm. There were two reasons for this. She was one of them; and the other one was the fact that she managed to get me to talk about my own work! Of course I am not suggesting that you should be meddlesome enough to smile at my carelessness as you read this; or that you should gather from this incident the impression that this tactful saleswoman actually led me to talk of my own work for the purpose of neutralizing my mind so that I would listen to her, when she was ready to talk of her magazines, as patiently as she had listened to me. However, if you should be clever enough to draw a lesson from her method, there is no way for me to stop you from doing so.

As I have stated, when I talked I mixed enthusiasm with my conversation. Perhaps I caught the spirit of enthusiasm from this clever saleswoman, when she made that opening remark as she came into my study. Yes, I am sure this is where I caught it, and, I am just as sure that her enthusiasm was not a matter of accident. She had trained herself to look for something in her prospective purchaser's office, or his work, or his conversation, over which she could express enthusiasm.

Remember, suggestion and enthusiasm go hand in hand!

I can remember, as though it were yesterday, the feeling that came over me when that would-be salesman pushed that Saturday Evening Post in front of me, as he remarked:

"You wouldn't subscribe for the Post to help me out, would you?"

His words were chilled, they were lifeless; they lacked enthusiasm; they registered an impression in my mind, but that impression was one of coldness. I wanted to see the man go out at the door at which he had come in. Mind you, I am not naturally unsympathetic, but the tone of his voice, the look on his face, his general bearing suggested that he was there to ask a favor and not to offer one.

Suggestion is one of the most subtle and powerful principles of psychology. You are making use of it in all that you do and say and think, but, unless you understand the difference between negative suggestion and positive suggestion, you may be using it in such a way that it is bringing you defeat instead of success.

Science has established the fact that through the negative use of suggestion life may be extinguished.

Some years ago, in France, a criminal was condemned to death, but before the time for his execution an experiment was performed on him which conclusively proved that through the principle of suggestion death, could be produced.

The criminal was brought to the guillotine and his head was placed under the knife, after he had been blindfolded. A heavy, sharp edged plank was then dropped on his neck, producing a shock similar to that of a sharp edged knife. Warm water was then gently poured on his neck and allowed to trickle slowly down his spine, to imitate the flow of warm blood. In seven minutes the doctors pronounced the man dead. His imagination, through the principle of suggestion, had actually turned the sharp edged plank into a guillotine blade and stopped his heart from beating.

In the little town where I was raised, there lived an old lady who constantly complained that she feared death from cancer. During her childhood she had seen a woman who had cancer and the sight had so impressed itself upon her mind that she began to look for the symptoms of cancer in her own body. She was sure that every little ache and pain was the beginning of her long-looked-for symptom of cancer. I have seen her place her hand on her breast and have heard her exclaim, "Oh, I am sure I have a cancer growing here. I can feel it." When complaining of this imaginary disease, she always placed her hand on her left breast, where she believed the cancer was attacking her.

For more than twenty years she kept this up.

A few weeks ago she died-with cancer on her left breast! If suggestion will actually turn the edge of a plank into a guillotine blade and transform healthy body cells into parasites out of which cancer will develop, can you not imagine what it will do in destroying disease germs, if properly directed? Suggestion is the law through which mental healers work what appear to be miracles. I have personally witnessed the removal of parasitical growths known as warts, through the aid of suggestion, within forty-eight hours.

You-the reader of this lesson-can be sent to bed with imaginary sickness of the worst sort, in two hours time or less, through the use of suggestion. If you should start down the street and three or four people in whom you had confidence should meet you and each exclaim that you look ill you would be ready for a doctor. This brings to mind an experience that I once had with a life insurance salesman. I had made application for a policy, but was undecided as to whether I would take ten or twenty thousand dollars.

Meanwhile, the agent had sent me to the life insurance company's doctor to be examined. The following day I was called back for another examination. The second time the examination was more searching, and the doctor carried a worried look on his face. The third day I was called back again, and this time two consulting physicians were there to look me over. They gave me the most searching examination I had ever received or even heard of.

The next day the agent called on me and addressed me as follows:

"I do not wish to alarm you! But the doctors who examined you do not agree on your analysis. You have not yet decided whether you will take ten or twenty thousand dollars' worth of insurance, and I do not think it fair for me to give you a report on your medical examination until you make this decision, because if I did you might feel that I was urging you to take the larger amount"

Then I spoke up and said: "Well, I have already decided to take the full amount." True enough; I had decided to take the full twenty thousand dollar policy. I decided the moment the agent planted the suggestion in my mind that perhaps I had some constitutional weakness that would make it hard for me to get as much insurance as I wanted.

"Very well," said the agent, "now that you have decided I feel it my duty to tell you that two of the doctors believe you have the tubercular germ in your system, while the other two disagree with them." The trick had been turned. Clever suggestion had pushed me over the fence of indecision and we were all satisfied.

Where does enthusiasm come in, do you ask? Never mind, it "came in" all right, but if you wish to know who brought it you will have to ask the life insurance agent and his four medical accomplices, for I am sure they must have had a hearty laugh at my expense. But the trick was all right. I needed the insurance anyway.

Of course, if you happen to be a life insurance agent you will not grab this idea and work it out on the next prospective client who is slow in making up his mind about taking a policy. Of course you will not!

A few months ago I received one of the most effective pieces of advertising I ever saw. It was a neat little book in which a clever automobile insurance salesman had reprinted press dispatches that he had gathered from all over the country, in which it was shown that sixty-five automobiles had been stolen in a single day. On the back page of the book was this highly suggestive statement:

"Your car may be the next one to go. Is it insured?" At the bottom of the page was the salesman's name and address; also his telephone number. Before I had finished reading the first two pages of the book I called the salesman on the telephone and made inquiry about rates. He came right over to see me, and you know the remainder of the story.

Go back, now, to the two letters and let us analyze the second one, which brought the desired replies from all to whom it was sent. Study, carefully, the first paragraph and you will observe that it asks a question which can be answered in but one way. Compare this opening paragraph with that of the first letter, by asking yourself which of the two would have impressed you most favorably. This paragraph is worded as it is for a two-fold purpose; first, it is intended to serve the purpose of neutralizing the mind of the reader so he will read the remainder of the letter in an open-minded attitude; and, second, it asks a question which can be answered in but one way, for the purpose of committing the reader to a viewpoint which harmonizes with the nature of the service that he is to be requested to render in subsequent paragraphs of the letter. In the second lesson of this course you observed that Andrew Carnegie refused to answer my question, when I asked him to what he attributed his success, until he had asked me to define the word success. He did this to avoid misunderstanding. The first paragraph of the letter we are analyzing is so worded that it states the object of the letter and at the same time practically forces the reader to accept that object as being sound and reasonable.

Any person who would answer the question asked in this paragraph of the letter under discussion, in the negative, would, by the same answer, convict himself on the charge of selfishness, and no man wants to face himself with a guilty conscience on such a charge. Just as the farmer first plows his ground, then fertilizes it, and perhaps harrows it and prepares it to receive the seed, in order that he may be sure of a crop, so does this paragraph fertilize the mind of the reader and prepare it for the seed which is to be placed there through the subtle suggestion that the paragraph contains.

Study, carefully, the second paragraph of the letter and you will observe that it carries a statement of fact which the reader can neither question nor deny! It provides him with no reason for argument because it is obviously based upon a sound fundamental. It takes him the second step of the psychological journey that leads straight toward compliance with the request that is carefully clothed and covered up in the third paragraph of the letter, but you will notice that the third paragraph begins by paying the reader a nice little compliment that was not designed to make him angry. "Therefore, if you will write me of your views as to the most essential points to be borne in mind by those who are offering personal services for sale," etc. Study the wording of this sentence, together with the setting in which it has been placed, and you will observe that it hardly appears to be a request at all, and certainly there is nothing about it to suggest that the writer of the letter is requesting a favor for his personal benefit. At most, it can be construed merely as a request for a favor for others.

Now study the closing paragraph and notice how tactfully concealed is the suggestion that if the reader should refuse the request he is placing himself in the awkward position of one who does not care enough about those who are less fortunate than himself to spend a two cent stamp and a few minutes of time for their benefit.

From start to finish the letter conveys its strongest impressions by mere suggestion, yet this suggestion is so carefully covered that it is not obvious except upon careful analysis of the entire letter.

The whole construction of the letter is such that if the reader lays it aside without complying with the request it makes he will have to reckon with his own conscience! This effect is intensified by the last sentence of the last paragraph and especially by the last thirteen words of that sentence, "who will read your message, believe in it, and be guided by it."

This letter brings the reader up with a bang and turns his own conscience into an ally of the writer; it corners him, just as a hunter might corner a rabbit by driving it into a carefully prepared net.

The best evidence that this analysis is correct is the fact that the letter brought replies from every person to whom it was sent, despite the fact that every one of these men was of the type that we speak of as being a man of affairs–the type that is generally supposed to be too busy to answer a letter of this nature. Not only did the letter bring the desired replies, but the men to whom it was sent replied in person, with the exception of the late Theodore Roosevelt, who replied under the signature of a secretary.

John Wanamaker and Frank A. Vanderlip wrote two of the finest letters I have ever read, each a masterpiece that might well have adorned the pages of a more dignified volume than the one for which the letters were requested. Andrew Carnegie also wrote a letter that was well worth consideration by all who have personal services for sale. William Jennings Bryan wrote a fine letter, as did, also, the late Lord Northcliffe. None of these men wrote merely to please me, for I was unknown to all of them, with the exception of four. They did not write to please me–they wrote to please themselves and to render a worthy service. Perhaps the wording of the letter had something to do with this, but, as to that, I make no point other than to state that all of these men whom I have mentioned, and most others of their type, are generally the most willing men to render service for others when they are properly approached.

I wish to take advantage of this appropriate opportunity to state that all of the really big men whom I have had the pleasure of knowing have been the most willing and courteous men of my acquaintance when it came to rendering service that was of benefit to others. Perhaps that was one reason why they were really big men. The human mind is a marvelous piece of machinery!

One of its outstanding characteristics is noticed in the fact that all impressions which reach it, either through outside suggestion or Auto-suggestion, are recorded together in groups which harmonize in nature. The negative impressions are stored away, all in one portion of the brain, while the positive impressions are stored in another portion. When one of these impressions (or past experiences) is called into the conscious mind, through the principle of memory, there is a tendency to recall with it all others of a similar nature, just as the raising of one link of a chain brings up other links with it. For example, anything that causes a feeling of doubt to arise in a person's mind is sufficient to call forth all of his experiences which caused him to become doubtful. If a man is asked by a stranger to cash a check, immediately he remembers having cashed checks that were not good, or of having heard of others who did so. Through the law of association all similar emotions, experiences and sense impressions that reach the mind are filed away together, so that the recalling of one has a tendency to bring back to memory all the others.

To arouse a feeling of distrust in a person's mind has a tendency to bring to the surface every doubt-building experience that person ever had. For this reason successful salesmen endeavor to keep away from the discussion of subjects that may arouse the buyer's "chain of doubt impressions" which he has stored away by reason of previous experiences. The successful salesman quickly learns that "knocking" a competitor or a competing article may result in bringing to the buyer's mind certain negative emotions growing out of previous experiences which may make it impossible for the salesman to "neutralize" the buyer's mind.

This principle applies to and controls every sense impression that is lodged in the human mind. Take the feeling of fear, for example; the moment we permit a single emotion that is related to fear to reach the conscious mind, it calls with it all of its unsavory relations. A feeling of courage cannot claim the attention of the conscious mind while a feeling of fear is there. One or the other must dominate. They make poor roommates because they do not harmonize in nature. Like attracts like. Every thought held in the conscious mind has a tendency to draw to it other thoughts of a similar nature. You see, therefore, that these feelings, thoughts and emotions growing out of past experiences, which claim the attention of the conscious mind, are backed by a regular army of supporting soldiers of a similar nature, that stand ready to aid them in their work.

Deliberately place in your own mind, through the principle of Auto-suggestion, the ambition to succeed through the aid of a definite chief aim, and notice how quickly all of your latent or undeveloped ability in the nature of past experiences will become stimulated and aroused to action in your behalf. Plant in a boy's mind, through the principle of suggestion, the ambition to become a successful lawyer or doctor or engineer or business man or financier, and if you plant that suggestion deeply enough, and keep it there, by repetition, it will begin to move that boy toward the achievement of the object of that ambition.

If you would plant a suggestion "deeply," mix it generously with enthusiasm; for enthusiasm is the fertilizer that will insure its rapid growth as well as its permanency.

When that kind-hearted old gentleman planted in my mind the suggestion that I was a "bright boy" and that I could make my mark in the world if I would educate myself, it was not so much what he said, as it was the way in which he said it that made such a deep and lasting impression on my mind. It was the way in which he gripped my shoulders and the look of confidence in his eyes that drove his suggestion so deeply into my subconscious mind that it never gave me any peace until I commenced taking the steps that led to the fulfillment of the suggestion.

This is a point that I would stress with all the power at my command. It is not so much what you say as it is the TONE and MANNER in which you say it that makes a lasting impression.

It naturally follows, therefore, that sincerity of purpose, honesty and earnestness must be placed back of all that one says if one would make a lasting and favorable impression.

Whatever you successfully sell to others you must first sell to yourself!

Not long ago I was approached by an agent of the government of Mexico who sought my services as a writer of propaganda for the administration in charge at that time. His approach was about as follows:

"Whereas, **Senor** has a reputation as an exponent of the Golden Rule philosophy; and whereas, **Senor** is known throughout the United States as an independent who is not allied with any political faction, now, therefore, would **Senor** be gracious enough to come to Mexico, study the economic and political, affairs of that country, then return to the United States and write a series of articles to appear in the newspapers, recommending to the people of America the immediate recognition of Mexico by the government of the United States, etc."

For this service, I was offered more money than I shall, perhaps, ever possess during my entire life; but I refused the commission, and for a reason that will fail to impress anyone except those who understand the principle which makes it necessary for all who would influence others to remain on good terms with their own conscience. I could not write convincingly of Mexico's cause for the reason that I did not believe in that cause; therefore, I could not have mixed sufficient enthusiasm with my writing to have made it effective, even though I had been willing to prostitute my talent and dip my pen into ink that I knew to be muddy.

I will not endeavor further to explain my philosophy on this incident for the reason that those who are far enough advanced in the study of Auto-suggestion will not need further explanation, while those who are not far enough advanced would not and could not understand.

No man can afford to express, through words or acts, that which is not in harmony with his own belief, and if he does so he must pay by the loss of his ability to influence others.

Please read, aloud, the foregoing paragraph! It is worth emphasizing by repetition, for lack of observation of the principle upon which it is based constitutes the rocks and reefs upon which many a man's definite chief aim dashes itself to pieces. I do not believe that I can afford to try to deceive anyone, about anything, but I know that I cannot afford to try to deceive myself. To do so would destroy the power of my pen and render my words ineffective. It is only when I write with the fire of enthusiasm burning in my heart that my writing impresses others favorably; and it is only when I speak from a heart that is bursting with belief in my message, that I can move my audience to accept that message.

I would also have you read, aloud, the foregoing paragraph. Yes, I would have you commit it to memory. Even more than this, I would have you write it out and place it where it may serve as a daily reminder of a principle, nay, a law as immutable as the law of gravitation, without which you can never become a power in your chosen lifework.

There have been times, and many of them, when it appeared that if I stood by this principle it would mean starvation!

There have been times when my closest friends and business advisers have strongly urged me to shade my philosophy for the sake of gaining a needed advantage here and there, but somehow I have managed to cling to it, mainly, I suppose, for the reason that I have preferred peace and harmony in my own heart to the material gain that I might have had by a forced compromise with my conscience. Strange as it may seem, my deliberations and conclusions on this subject of refusing to strangle my own conscience have seldom been based upon what is commonly called "honesty." That which I have done in the matter of refraining from writing or speaking anything that I did not believe has been solely a question of honor between my conscience and myself. I have tried to express that which my heart dictated because I have aimed to give my words "flesh." It might be said that my motive was based more upon self-interest than it was on a desire to be fair with others, although I have never desired to be unfair with others, so far as I am able to analyze myself.

No man can become a master salesman if he compromises with falsehood. Murder will out, and even though no one ever catches him red-handed in expressing that which he does not believe, his words will fail in the accomplishment of their purpose because he cannot give them "flesh," if they do not come from his heart, and if they are not mixed with genuine, unadulterated enthusiasm.

I would also have you read, aloud, the foregoing paragraph, for it embraces a great law that you must understand and apply before you can become a person of influence in any undertaking.

In making these requests, for the sake of emphasis, I am not trying to take undue liberties with you. I am giving you full credit for being an adult, a thinker, an intelligent person, yet I know how likely you are to skip over these vital laws without being sufficiently impressed by them to make them a part of your own workaday philosophy. I know your weakness because I know my own. It has required the better part of twenty-five years of ups and downs–mostly downs–to impress these basic truths upon my own mind so that they influenced me. I have tried both them and their opposites; therefore, I can speak, not as one who merely believes in their soundness, but as one who knows.

And what do I mean by "these truths"?

So that you cannot possibly misunderstand my meaning, and so that these words of warning cannot possibly convey an abstract meaning, I will state that by "these truths" I mean this:

You cannot afford to suggest to another person, by word of mouth or by an act of yours, that which you do not believe.

Surely that is plain enough.

And, the reason you cannot afford to do so, is this:

If you compromise with your own conscience, it will not be long before you will have no conscience; for your conscience will fail to guide you, just as an alarm clock will fail to awaken you if you do not heed it.

Surely, that is plain enough, also.

And how do I happen to be an authority on this vital subject, do you ask?

I am an authority because I have experimented with the principle until I know how it works!

"But," you may ask, "how do I know that you are telling the truth?"

The answer is that you will know only by experimenting for yourself, and by observing others who faithfully apply this principle and those who do not apply it.

If my evidence needs backing, then consult any man whom you know to be a person who has "tried to get by" without observing this principle, and if he will not or cannot give you the truth you can get it, nevertheless, by analyzing the man.

There is but one thing in the world that gives a man real and enduring power, and that is character! Reputation, bear in mind, is not character. Reputation is that which people are believed to be; character is that which people are! If you would be a person of great influence, then be a person of real character.

Character is the philosopher's lodestone through which all who have it may turn the base metals of their life into pure gold. Without character you have nothing; you are nothing; and you can be nothing, except a pile of flesh and bone and hair, worth perhaps twenty-five dollars. Character is something that you cannot beg or steal or buy.

You can get it only by building it; and you can build it by your own thoughts and deeds, and in no other way.

Through the aid of Auto-suggestion, any person can build a sound character, no matter what his past has been. As a fitting close for this lesson, I wish to emphasize the fact that all who have character have enthusiasm and personality sufficient to draw to them others who have character.

You will now be instructed as to how you shall proceed in developing enthusiasm, in the event that you do not already possess this rare quality.

The instructions will be simple, but you will be unfortunate if you discount their value on that account.

First: Complete the remaining lessons of this course, because other important instructions which are to be co-ordinated with this one will be found in subsequent lessons.

Second: If you have not already done so, write out your definite chief aim in clear, simple language, and follow this by writing out the plan through which you intend to transform your aim into reality.

Third: Read over the description of your definite chief aim each night, just before retiring, and as you read, see yourself (in your imagination) in full possession of the object of your aim. Do this with full faith in your ability to transform your definite chief aim into reality. Read aloud, with all the enthusiasm at your command, emphasizing every word. Repeat this reading until the small still voice within you tells you that your purpose will be realized. Sometimes you will feel the effects of this voice from within the first time you read your definite chief aim; while at other times, you may have to read it a dozen or fifty times before the assurance comes, but do not stop until you feel it.

If you prefer to do so you may read your definite chief aim as a prayer.

The remainder of this lesson is for the person who has not yet learned the power of faith and who knows little or nothing of the principle of Auto-suggestion.

One of the greatest powers for good, upon the face of this earth, is faith. To this marvelous power may be traced miracles of the most astounding nature. It offers peace on earth to all who embrace it.

Faith involves a principle that is so far-reaching in its effect that no man can say what are its limitations, or if it has limitations. Write into the description of your definite chief aim a statement of the qualities that you intend to develop in yourself, and the station in life that you intend to attain, and have faith, as you read this description each night, that you can transform this purpose into reality. Surely, you cannot miss the suggestion contained in this lesson.

To become successful you must be a person of action. Merely to "know" is not sufficient. It is necessary both to know and do.

Enthusiasm is the mainspring of the mind which urges one to put knowledge into action.

Billy Sunday is the most successful evangelist this country has ever known. For the purpose of studying his technique and checking up on his psychological methods the author of this course went through three campaigns with Reverend Sunday.

His success is based very largely upon one word–ENTHUSIASM!

By making effective use of the law of suggestion Billy Sunday conveys his own spirit of enthusiasm to the minds of his followers and they become influenced by it. He sells his sermons by the use of exactly the same sort of strategy employed by many Master Salesmen.

Enthusiasm is as essential to a salesman as water is to a duck!

All successful sales managers understand the psychology of enthusiasm and make use of it, in various ways, as a practical means of helping their men produce more sales.

Practically all sales organizations have get-together meetings at stated times, for the purpose of revitalizing the minds of all members of the sales force, and injecting the spirit of enthusiasm, which can be best done en masse, through group psychology.

Sales meetings might properly be called "revival" meetings, because their purpose is to revive interest and arouse enthusiasm which will enable the salesman to take up the fight with renewed ambition and energy.

During his administration as Sales Manager of the National Cash Register Company Hugh Chalmers (who later became famous in the motorcar industry) faced a most embarrassing situation which threatened to wipe out his position as well as that of thousands of salesmen under his direction.

The company was in financial difficulty. This fact had become known to the salesmen in the field and the effect of it was to cause them to lose their Enthusiasm. Sales began to dwindle until finally the conditions became so alarming that a general meeting of the sales organization was called, to be held at the company's plant in Dayton, Ohio.

Salesmen were called in from all over the country.

Mr. Chalmers presided over the meeting. He began by calling on several of his best salesmen to get on their feet and tell what was wrong out in the field that orders had fallen off. One by one they got up, as called, and each man had a most terrible tale of grief to unfold: Business conditions were bad, money was scarce, people were holding off buying until after Presidential election, etc. As the fifth man began to enumerate the difficulties which had kept him from making his usual quota of sales Mr. Chalmers jumped up on top of a table, held up his hands for silence, and said "STOP! I order this convention to come to a close for ten minutes while I get my shoes shined."

Then turning to a small colored boy who sat near by he ordered the boy to bring his shoe-shine outfit and shine his shoes, right where he stood, on top of the table.

The salesmen in the audience were astounded! Some of them thought that Mr. Chalmers had suddenly lost his mind. They began to whisper among themselves.

Meanwhile, the little colored boy shined first one and then the other shoe, taking plenty of time and doing a first-class job.

After the, job was finished Mr. Chalmers handed the boy a dime, then went ahead with his speech:

"I want each of you," said he, "to take a good look at this little colored boy. He has the concession for shoe shining throughout our plant and offices. His predecessor was a white boy, considerably older than himself, and despite the fact that the company subsidized him with a salary of $5.00 a week he could not make a living in this plant, where thousands of people are employed.

"This little colored boy not only makes a good living, without any subsidy from the company, but he is actually saving money out of his earnings each week, working under the same conditions, in the same plant, for the same people.

"Now I wish to ask you a question: Whose fault was it that the white boy did not get more business? Was it his fault, or the fault of his buyers?"

In a mighty roar from the crowd the answer came back:

"IT WAS THE BOY'S FAULT, OF COURSE!"

"Just so," replied Chalmers, "and now I want to tell you this, that you are selling Cash Registers in the same territory, to the same people, with exactly the same business conditions that existed a year ago, yet you are not producing the business that you were then. Now whose fault is that? Is it yours, or the buyer's?"

And again the answer came back with a roar:

"IT IS OUR FAULT, OF COURSE!"

"I am glad that you are frank to acknowledge your faults," Chalmers continued, "and I now wish to tell you what your trouble is: You have heard rumors about this company being in financial trouble and that has killed off your enthusiasm so that you are not making the effort that you formerly made. If you will go back into your territories with a definite promise to send in five orders each during the next thirty days this company will no longer be in financial difficulty, for that additional business will see us clear. Will you do it?"

They said they would, and they did!

That incident has gone down in the history of the National Cash Register Company under the name of Hugh Chalmers' Million Dollar Shoe Shine, for it is said that this turned the tide in the company's affairs and was worth millions of dollars.

Enthusiasm knows no defeat! The Sales Manager who knows how to send out an army of enthusiastic salespeople may set his own price on his services, and what is more important even than this, he can increase the earning capacity of every person under his direction; thus, his enthusiasm benefits not only himself but perhaps hundreds of others.

Enthusiasm is never a matter of chance. There are certain stimuli which produce enthusiasm, the most important of these being as follows:

- 1. Occupation in work which one loves best.
- 2. Environment where one comes in contact with others who are enthusiastic and optimistic.
- 3. Financial success.
- 4. Complete mastery and application, in one's daily work, of the Fifteen Laws of Success.
- 5. Good health.
- 6. Knowledge that one has served others in some helpful manner.
- 7. Good clothes, appropriate to the needs of one's occupation.

All of these seven sources of stimuli are self-explanatory with the exception of the last. The psychology of clothes is understood by very few people, and for this reason it will be here explained in detail. Clothes constitute the most important part of the embellishment which every person must have in order to feel self-reliant, hopeful and enthusiastic.

THE PSYCHOLOGY OF GOOD CLOTHES

When the good news came from the theater of war, on November the eleventh, 1918, my worldly possessions amounted to but little more than they did the day I came into the world.

The war had destroyed my business and made it necessary for me to make a new start!

My wardrobe consisted of three well-worn business suits and two uniforms which I no longer needed.

Knowing all too well that the world forms its first and most lasting impressions of a man by the clothes he wears, I lost no time in visiting my tailor.

Happily, my tailor had known me for many years, therefore he did not judge me entirely by the clothes I wore. If he had I would have been "sunk."

With less than a dollar in change in my pocket, I picked out the cloth for three of the most expensive suits I ever owned, and ordered that they be made up for me at once.

The three suits came to $375.00!

I shall never forget the remark made by the tailor as he took my measure. Glancing first at the three bolts of expensive cloth which I had selected, and then at me, he inquired:

"Dollar-a-year man, eh?"

"No," said I, "if I had been fortunate enough to get on the dollar-a-year payroll I might now have enough money to pay for these suits."

The tailor looked at me with surprise. I don't think he got the joke.

One of the suits was a beautiful dark gray; one was a dark blue; the other was a light blue with a pin stripe.

Fortunately I was in good standing with my tailor, therefore he did not ask when I was going to pay for those expensive suits.

I knew that I could and would pay for them in due time, but could I have convinced him of that? This was the thought which was running through my mind, with hope against hope that the question would not be brought up.

I then visited my haberdasher, from whom I purchased three less expensive suits and a complete supply of the best shirts, collars, ties, hosiery and underwear that he carried.

My bill at the haberdasher's amounted to a little over $300.00.

With an air of prosperity I nonchalantly signed the charge ticket and tossed it back to the salesman, with instructions to deliver my purchase the following morning. The feeling of renewed self-reliance and success had begun to come over me, even before I had attired myself in my newly purchased outfit.

I was out of the war and $675.00 in debt, all in less than twenty-four hours.

The following day the first of the three suits ordered from the haberdasher was delivered. I put it on at once, stuffed a new silk handkerchief in the outside pocket of my coat, shoved the $50.00 I had borrowed on my ring down into my pants pocket, and walked down Michigan Boulevard, in Chicago, feeling as rich as Rockefeller.

Every article of clothing I wore, from my underwear out, was of the very best. That it was not paid for was nobody's business except mine and my tailor's and my haberdasher's.

Every morning I dressed myself in an entirely new outfit, and walked down the same street, at precisely the same hour. That hour "happened" to be the time when a certain wealthy publisher usually walked down, the same street, on his way to lunch.

I made it my business to speak to him each day, and occasionally I would stop for a minute's chat with him.

After this daily meeting had been going on for about a week I met this publisher one day, but decided I would see if he would let me get by without speaking.

Watching him from under my eyelashes I looked straight ahead, and started to pass him when he stopped and motioned me over to the edge of the sidewalk, placed his hand on my shoulder, looked me over from head to foot, and said: "You look damned prosperous for a man who has just laid aside a uniform. Who makes your clothes?"

"Well," said I, "Wilkie & Sellery made this particular suit."

He then wanted to know what sort of business I was engaged in. That "airy" atmosphere of prosperity which I had been wearing, along with a new and different suit every day, had got the better of his curiosity. (I had hoped that it would.)

Flipping the ashes from my Havana perfecto, I said, "Oh, I am preparing the copy for a new magazine that I am going to publish."

"A new magazine, eh?" he queried, "and what are you going to call it?"

"It is to be named Hill's Golden Rule."

"Don't forget," said my publisher friend, "that I am in the business of printing and distributing magazines. Perhaps I can serve you, also."

That was the moment for which I had been waiting. I had that very moment, and almost the very spot of ground on which we stood, in mind when I was purchasing those new suits.

But, is it necessary to remind you, that conversation never would have taken place had this publisher observed me walking down that street from day to day, with a "whipped-dog" look on my face, an unpressed suit on my back and a look of poverty in my eyes.

An appearance of prosperity attracts attention always, with no exceptions whatsoever.

Moreover, a look of prosperity attracts "favorable attention," because the one dominating desire in every human heart is to be prosperous.

My publisher friend invited me to his club for lunch. Before the coffee and cigars had been served he had "talked me out of the contract for printing and distributing my magazine. I had even "consented" to permit him to supply the capital, without any interest charge.

For the benefit of those who are not familiar with the publishing business may I not offer the information that considerable capital is required for launching a new nationally distributed magazine.

Capital, in such large amounts, is often hard to get, even with the best of security. The capital necessary for launching Hill's Golden Rule Magazine, which you may have read, was well above $30,000.00, and every cent of it was raised on a "front" created mostly by good clothes. True, there may have been some ability back of those clothes, but many millions of men have ability who never have anything else, and who are never heard of outside of the limited community in which they live. This is a rather sad truth!

To some it may seem an unpardonable extravagance for one who was "broke" to have gne in debt for $675.00 worth of clothes, but the psychology back of that investment more than justified it.

The appearance of prosperity not only made a favorable impression on those to whom I had to look for favors, but of more importance still was the effect that proper attire HAD ON ME.

I not only knew that correct clothes would impress others favorably, but I knew also that good clothes would give me an atmosphere of self-reliance, without which I could not hope to regain my lost fortunes.

I got my first training in the psychology of good clothes from my friend Edwin C. Barnes, who is a close business associate of Thomas A. Edison. Barnes afforded considerable amusement for the Edison staff when, some twenty-odd years ago, he rode into West Orange on a freight train (not being able to raise sufficient money for passenger fare) and announced at the Edison offices that he had come to enter into a partnership with Mr. Edison.

Nearly everybody around the Edison plant laughed at Barnes, except Edison himself. He saw something in the square jaw and determined face of young Barnes which most of the others did not see, despite the fact that the young man looked more like a tramp than he did a future partner of the greatest inventor on earth.

Barnes got his start, sweeping floors in the Edison offices!

That was all he sought–just a chance to get a toehold in the Edison organization. From there on he made history that is well worth emulation by other young men who wish to make places for themselves.

Barnes has now retired from active business, even though he is still a comparatively young man, and spends most of his time at his two beautiful homes in Bradentown, Florida, and Damariscotta, Maine. He is a multimillionaire, prosperous and happy.

I first became acquainted with Barnes during the early days of his association with Edison, before he had "arrived."

In those days he had the largest and most expensive collection of clothes I had ever seen or heard of one man owning. His wardrobe consisted of thirty-one suits, one for each day of the month. He never wore the same suit two days in succession.

Moreover, all his suits were of the most expensive type. (Incidentally, his clothes were made by the same tailors who made those three suits for me.)

He wore socks which cost six dollars per pair.

His shirts and other wearing apparel cost in similar proportion. His cravats were specially made, at a cost of from five to seven dollars and a half each.

One day, in a spirit of fun, I asked him to save some of his old suits which he did not need, for me. He informed me that he hadn't a single suit which he did not need!

He then gave me a lesson on the psychology of clothes which is well worth remembering. "I do not wear thirty-one suits of clothes," said he, "entirely for the impression they make on other people; I do it mostly for the impression they have on me."

Barnes then told me of the day when he presented himself at the Edison plant, for a position. He said he had to walk around the plant a dozen times before he worked up enough courage to announce himself, because he knew that he looked more like a tramp than he did a desirable employee.

Barnes is said to be the most able salesman ever connected with the great inventor of West Orange. His entire fortune was made through his ability as a salesman, but he has often said that he never could have accomplished the results which have made him both wealthy and famous had it not been for his understanding of the psychology of clothes.

I have met many salesman in my time. During the past ten years I have personally trained and directed the efforts of more than 3,000 salespeople, both men and women, and I have observed that, without a single exception, the star producers were all people who understood and made good use of the psychology of clothes.

I have seen a few well-dressed people who made no outstanding records as salesmen, but I have yet to see the first poorly dressed man who became a star producer in the field of selling.

I have studied the psychology of clothes for so long, and I have watched its effect on people in so many different walks of life, that I am fully convinced there is a close connection between clothes and success.

Personally I feel no need of thirty-one suits of clothes, but if my personality demanded a wardrobe of this size I would manage to get it, no matter how much it might cost.

To be well dressed a man should have at least ten suits of clothes. He should have a different suit for each of the seven days of the week, a full dress suit and a Tuxedo, for formal evening occasions, and a cutaway for formal afternoon occasions.

For summer wear he should have an assortment of at least four appropriate light suits, with blue coat and white flannel trousers for informal afternoon and evening occasions.

If he plays golf he should have at least one golf suit.

This, of course, is for the man who is a notch or two above the "mediocre" class. The man who is satisfied with mediocrity needs but few clothes.

It may be true, as a well-known poet has said, that "clothes do not make the man," but no one can deny the fact that good clothes go a very long way toward giving him a favorable start.

A man's bank will generally loan him all the money he wants when he does not need it–when he is prosperous, but never go to your bank for a loan with a shabby-looking suit on your back and a look of poverty in your eyes, for if you do you'll get the gate.

Success attracts success! There is no escape from this great universal law; therefore, if you wish to attract success make sure that you look the part of success, whether your calling is that of day laborer or merchant prince.

For the benefit of the more "dignified" students of this philosophy who may object to resorting to "stunt" stimuli or "trick clothing" as a means of achieving success, it may be profitably explained that practically every successful man on earth has discovered some form of stimulus through which he can and does drive himself on to greater effort.

It may be shocking to members of the Anti-Saloon League, but it is said to be true, nevertheless, that James Whitcomb Riley wrote his best poems when he was under the influence of alcohol. His stimulus was liquor. (The author wishes it distinctly understood that he does not recommend the use of alcoholic or narcotic stimuli, for any purpose whatsoever, as either will eventually destroy both body and mind of all who use them.) Under the influence of alcohol Riley became imaginative, enthusiastic and an entirely different person, according to close personal friends of his.

Edwin Barnes spurred himself into the necessary action to produce outstanding results, with the aid of good clothes.

Some men rise to great heighs of achievement as the result of love for some woman. Connect this with the brief suggestion to the subject which was made in the Introductory Lesson and you will, if you are a person who knows the ways of men, be able to finish the discussion of this particular phase of enthusiasm stimulus without further comment by the author which might not be appropriate for the younger minds that will assimilate this philosophy.

Underworld characters who are engaged in the dangerous business of highway robbery, burglary, etc., generally "dope" themselves for the occasion of their operations, with cocaine, morphine and other narcotics. Even in this there is a lesson which shows that practically all men need temporary or artificial stimuli to drive them to greater effort than that normally employed in the ordinary pursuits of life.

SUCCESSFUL PEOPLE HAVE DISCOVERED WAYS AND MEANS WHICH THEY BELIEVE BEST SUITED TO THEIR OWN NEEDS, TO PRODUCE STIMULI WHICH CAUSE THEM TO RISE TO HEIGHTS OF ENDEAVOR ABOVE THE ORDINARY.

One of the most successful writers in the world employs an orchestra of beautifully dressed young women who play for him while he writes. Seated in a room that has been artistically decorated to suit his own taste, under lights that have been colored, tinted and softened, these beautiful young ladies, dressed in handsome evening gowns, play his favorite music. To use his own words, "I become drunk with enthusiasm, under the influence of this environment, and rise to heights I never know or feel on other occasions. It is then that I do my work. The thoughts pour in on me as if they were dictated by an unseen and unknown power."

This author gets much of his inspiration from music and art. Once a week he spends at least an hour in an art museum, looking at the works of the masters.

On these occasions, again using his own words, "I get enough enthusiasm from one hour's visit in the museum of art to carry me for two days."

Edgar Allan Poe wrote "The Raven" when, it is reported, he was more than half intoxicated. Oscar Wilde wrote his poems under the influence of a form of stimulus which cannot be appropriately mentioned in a course of this nature.

Henry Ford (so it is believed by this author, who admits that this is merely the author's opinion) got his real start as the result of his love for his charming life-companion. It was she who inspired him, gave him faith in himself, and kept him keyed up so that he carried on in the face of adversities which would have killed off a dozen ordinary men.

These incidents are cited as evidence that men of outstanding achievement have, by accident or design, discovered ways and means of stimulating themselves to a high state of enthusiasm.

Associate that which has been here stated with what was said concerning the law of the "Master Mind," in the Introductory Lesson, and you will have an entirely new conception of the modus operandi through which that law may be applied. You will also have a somewhat different understanding of the real purpose of "allied effort, in a spirit of perfect harmony," which constitutes the best-known method of bringing into use the Law of the Master Mind.

At this point it seems appropriate to call your attention to the manner in which the lessons of this course blend. You will observe that each lesson covers the subject intended to be covered, and in addition to this it overlaps and gives the student a better understanding of some other lesson or lessons of the course.

In the light of what has been said in this lesson, for example, the student will better understand the real purpose of the Law of the Master Mind; that purpose being, in the main, a practical method of stimulating the minds of all who participate in the group constituting the Master Mind.

Times too numerous to be here described this author has gone into conference with men whose faces showed the signs of care, who had the appearance of worry written all over them, only to see those same men straighten up their shoulders, tilt their chins at a higher angle, soften their faces with smiles of confidence, and get down to business with that sort of ENTHUSIASM which knows no defeat.

The change took place the moment harmony of purpose was established. If a man goes about the affairs of life in the same day-in and day-out, prosaic, lackadaisical spirit, devoid of enthusiasm, he is doomed to failure. Nothing can save him until he changes his attitude and learns how to stimulate his mind and body to unusual heights of enthusiasm AT WILL!

The author is unwilling to leave this subject without having stated the principle here described in so many different ways that it is bound to be understood and also respected by the students of this course, who, all will remember, are men and women of all sorts of natures, experiences and degrees of intelligence. For this reason much repetition is essential.

Your business in life, you are reminded once again, is to achieve success!

With the stimulus you will experience from studying this philosophy, and with the aid of the ideas you will gather from it, plus the personal co-operation of the author who will give you an accurate inventory of your outstanding qualities, you should be able to create a DEFINITE PLAN that will lift you to great heights of achievement. However, there is no plan that can produce this desirable result without the aid of some influence that will cause you to arouse yourself, in a spirit of enthusiasm, to where you will exert greater than the ordinary effort which you put into your daily occupation.

You are now ready for the lesson on Self-control!

As you read that lesson you will observe that it has a vital bearing on this lesson, just as this lesson has a direct connection with the preceding lessons on A Definite Chief Aim, Self-confidence, Initiative and Leadership and Imagination.

The next lesson describes the Law which serves as the Balance Wheel of this entire philosophy.

THE SEVEN DEADLY HORSEMEN–An After-the-Lesson Visit With the Author

The "seven horsemen" are Intolerance, Greed, Revenge, Egotism, Suspicion, Jealously and "?"

The worst enemy that any man has is the one that walks around under his own hat. If you could see yourself as others see you the enemies that you harbor in your own personality might be discovered and thrown out. The Seven Enemies named in this essay are the commonest which ride millions of men and women to failure without being discovered. Weigh yourself carefully and find out how many of the Seven you are harboring.

Seven deadly warriors! From birth until death every human being must give battle to these enemies. Your success will be measured very largely by the way you manage your battle against these swift riders.

You will say, of course, that it is only imagination. But the swift riders of destruction are REAL.

If these enemies rode openly, on real horses, they would not be dangerous, because they could be rounded up and put out of commission. But, they ride unseen, in the minds of men. So silently and subtly do they work that most people never recognize their presence.

Take inventory of yourself and find out how many of these seven horsemen you are harboring.

The most dangerous and the commonest of the riders is INTOLERANCE. You will be fortunate if you discover this enemy and protect yourself against it. This cruel warrior, INTOLERANCE, has killed more people, destroyed more friendships, brought more misery and suffering into the world and caused more wars than all of the other six horsemen that you see in this picture.

Until you master INTOLERANCE you will never become an accurate thinker. This enemy of mankind closes up the mind and pushes reason and logic and FACTS into the background. If you find yourself hating those whose religious viewpoint is different from your own you may be sure that the most dangerous of the seven deadly horsemen still rides in your brain.

Next REVENGE and GREED!

These riders travel side by side. Where one is found the other is always close at hand.

GREED warps and twists man's brain so that he wants to build a fence around the earth and keep everyone else on the outside of it. This is the enemy that drives man to accumulate millions upon top of millions of dollars which he does not need and can never use. This is the enemy that causes man to twist the screw until he has wrung the last drop of blood from his fellow man.

And, thanks to REVENGE which rides alongside of GREED, the unfortunate person who gives brain-room to these cruel twins is not satisfied to merely take away his fellow man's earthly belongings; he wants to destroy his reputation in the bargain.

"Revenge is a naked sword-
It has neither hilt nor guard.
Would'st thou wield this brand of the Lord:
Is thy grasp then firm and hard?
But the closer thy clutch of the blade,
The deadlier blow thou would'st deal,
Deeper wound in thy hand is made-
It is thy blood reddens the steel.
And when thou hast dealt the blow-
When the blade from thy hand has flown-
Instead of the heart of the foe
Thou may'st find it sheathed in thine own."

If you would know how deadly are ENVY and GREED, study the history of every man who has set out to become RULER OF THIS WORLD!

If you do not wish to undertake so ambitious a program of research, then study the people around YOU; those who have tried and those who are now trying to "feather their own nests" at the cost of others. GREED and REVENGE stand at the crossroads of life, where they turn aside to failure and misery every person who would take the road that leads to success. It is a part of your business not to permit them to interfere with you when you approach one of these crossroads.

Both individuals and nations rapidly decline where GREED and ENVY ride in the minds of those who dominate. Take a look at Mexico and Spain if you wish to know what happens to the envious and the greedy.

Most important of all, take a look at YOURSELF and make sure that these two deadly enemies are not riding in your brain!

Turn your attention, now, to two more twins of destruction–EGOTISM and SUSPICION. Observe that they, also, ride side by side. There is no hope of success for the person who suffers either from too much self-love or lack of confidence in others.

Someone who likes to manipulate figures has estimated that the largest club in the world is the "IT CAN'T BE DONE CLUB." It is claimed that there are approximately ninety-nine million members of this club in the United States of America alone.

If you have no FAITH in other people you have not the seed of success in you. SUSPICION is a prolific germ. If permitted to get a start it rapidly multiplies itself until it leaves no room for FAITH.

Without faith no man may enjoy enduring success.

Running, like a golden cord of illumination throughout the Bible, is the admonition to have FAITH. Before civilization lost itself in its mad rush for dollars men understood the power of FAITH.

Believe in people if you would have them believe in you. Kill off SUSPICION. If you do not it will kill you off.

If you would have power, cultivate FAITH in mankind!

EGOTISM thrives where SUSPICION exists. Interest yourself in others and you will be too busy to indulge in self-love. Observe those around you who begin every sentence with the personal pronoun, "I," and you will notice that they are suspicious of other people.

The man who can forget himself while engaging in useful service to other people is never cursed with SUSPICION. Study those about you who are both SUSPICIOUS and EGOTISTICAL and see how many of this type you can name who are successful in whatever work they may be engaged in.

And, while making this study of OTHERS, study, also, yourself!

Be sure that you are not bound down by EGOTISM and SUSPICION.

Bringing up the rear of this deadly group of riders you see two horsemen: One is JEALOUSY and the name of the other has been purposely omitted.

Each reader of this article may take inventory of himself and give the seventh rider a name that fits whatever he finds in his own mind.

Some will name this rider DISHONESTY. Others will name it PROCRASTINATION. A few will have the courage to name it UNCONTROLLED SEX DESIRE. As for you, name it whatever you please, but be sure to give it a name.

Perhaps your own imagination will supply an appropriate name as a fellow-traveler for JEALOUSY.

You will be better prepared to give the unnamed rider a name if you know that

JEALOUSY is a form of insanity! Facts are sometimes cruel things to face. It is a fact that

JEALOUSY is a form of insanity, known to the medical fraternity as "dementia praecox."

> "O jealousy,
> Thou ugliest fiend of hell!
> Thy deadly venom Preys on my vitals, turns the healthful hue
> Of my fresh cheek to haggard sallowness,
> And drinks my spirit up!"

You will notice that JEALOUSY rides just back of SUSPICION. Some who read this will say that JEALOUSY and SUSPICION should have ridden side by side, as one often leads to the other in man's mind.

JEALOUSY is the most common form of insanity. It rides in the minds of both men and women, sometimes with a real cause, but more often without any cause whatsoever.

This deadly rider is a great friend of the divorce lawyers!

It also keeps detective agencies busy night and day.

It takes its regular toll of murder. It breaks up home and makes widows of mothers and orphans of innocent little children. Peace and happiness can never be YOURS as long as this rider remains unharnessed in your brain.

Man and wife may go through life together in poverty and still be very happy, if both are free from this child of insanity known as JEALOUSY. Examine yourself carefully and if you find any evidence of JEALOUSY in your mind begin, at once, to master it.

JEALOUSY rides in many forms.

When it first begins to creep into the brain it manifests itself in something after this fashion:

"I wonder where she is and what she is doing while I am away?"

Or, "I wonder if he does not see another woman when he is away from me?"

When these questions begin to arise in your mind do not call in a detective. Instead, go to the psychopathic hospital and have yourself examined, because more than likely you are suffering from a mild form of insanity.

Get your foot on JEALOUSY'S neck before it gets its clutches on your throat.

After you have read this essay, lay it aside and THINK about it.

At first you may say, "This does not apply to me. I have no imaginary horsemen in my brain." And, you may be right–ONE OUT OF EVERY TEN MILLION COULD SAY THIS AND BE RIGHT! The other nine million nine hundred and ninety-nine thousand nine hundred and ninety-nine would be wrong.

Do not fool yourself! You may be in that larger class. The purpose of this article is to get you to see yourself as YOU ARE! If you are suffering failure and poverty and misery in any of their forms you are sure to discover one or more of these deadly riders in your brain.

Make no mistake about it–those who have all they want, including happiness and good health, have driven the seven horsemen out of their brains.

Come back to this essay a month from now, after you have had time to analyze yourself carefully. Read it again and it may bring you face to face with FACTS that will emancipate you from a horde of cruel enemies that now ride within your brain without your knowing it.

Lesson Eight: SELF-CONTROL

In the preceding lesson you learned of the value of enthusiasm. You also learned how to generate enthusiasm and how to transmit its influence to others, through the principle of suggestion.

You come, now, to the study of self-control, through which you may direct your enthusiasm to constructive ends. Without self-control enthusiasm resembles the unharnessed lightning of an electrical storm–it may strike anywhere; it may destroy life and property.

Enthusiasm is the vital quality that arouses you to action, while self-control is the balance wheel that directs your action so that it will build up and not tear down. To be a person who is well "balanced," you must be a person in whom enthusiasm and self-control are equalized. A survey which I have just completed of the 160,000 adult inmates of the penitentiaries of the United States discloses the startling fact that ninety-two per cent of these unfortunate men and women are in prison because they lacked the necessary self-control to direct their energies constructively.

Read the foregoing paragraph again; it is authentic, it is startling! It is a fact that the majority of a man's griefs come about through lack of self-control. The holy scriptures are full of admonition in support of self-control. They even urge us to love our enemies and to forgive those who injure us. The law of non-resistance runs, like a golden cord, throughout the Bible.

Study the records of those whom the world calls great, and observe that every one of them possesses this quality of self-control!

For example, study the characteristics of our own immortal Lincoln. In the midst of his most trying hours he exercised patience, poise and self-control. These were some of the qualities which made him the great man that he was. He found disloyalty in some of the members of his cabinet; but, for the reason that this disloyalty was toward him, personally, and because those in whom he found it had qualities which made them valuable to his country, Lincoln exercised self-control and disregarded the objectionable qualities.

How many men do you know who have self-control to equal this? In language more forceful than it was polished, Billy Sunday exclaimed from the pulpit: "There is something as rotten as hell about the man who is always trying to show some other fellow up!" I wonder if the "devil" didn't yell, "Amen, brother!" when Billy made that statement?

However, self-control becomes an important factor in this Reading Course on the Law of Success, not so much because lack of it works hardships on those who become its victims, as for the reason that those who do not exercise it suffer the loss of a great power which they need in their struggle for achievement of their definite chief aim. If you neglect to exercise self-control, you are not only likely to injure others, but you are sure to injure yourself!

During the early part of my public career I discovered what havoc lack of self-control was playing in my life, and this discovery came about through a very commonplace incident. (I believe it not out of place here to digress by making the statement that most of the great truths of life are wrapped up in the ordinary, commonplace events of every-day life.)

This discovery taught me one of the most important lessons I have ever learned. It came about in this way:

One day, in the building in which I had my office, the janitor and I had a misunderstanding. This led to a most violent form of mutual dislike between us. As a means of showing his contempt for me, this janitor would switch off the electric lights of the building when he knew that I was there alone at work in my study. This happened on several occasions until I finally decided to "strike back." My opportunity came one Sunday when I came to my study to prepare an address that I had to deliver the following night. I had hardly seated myself at my desk when off went the lights.

I jumped to my feet and ran toward the basement of the building where I knew I would find the janitor. When I arrived, I found him busily engaged, shoveling coal into the furnace, and whistling as though nothing unusual had happened.

Without ceremony I pitched into him, and for five minutes I hurled adjectives at him which were hotter than the fire that he was feeding. Finally, I ran out of words and had to slow down. Then he straightened himself up, looked back over his shoulder, and in a calm, smooth tone of voice that was full of poise and self-control, and with a smile on his face that reached from ear to ear, he said:

"Why, you-all's just a little bit excited this morning, ain't you?"

That remark cut as though it had been a stiletto.

Imagine my feelings as I stood there before an illiterate man who could neither read nor write, but who, despite this handicap, had defeated me in a duel that had been fought on grounds–and with a weapon–of my own choice.

My conscience pointed an accusing finger at me. I knew that not only had I been defeated but, what was worse, I knew that I was the aggressor and that I was in the wrong, which only served to intensify my humiliation.

Not only did my conscience point an accusing finger at me, but it placed some very embarrassing thoughts in my mind; it mocked me and it tantalized me. There I stood, a boasted student of advanced psychology, an exponent of the Golden Rule philosophy, having at least a fair acquaintance with the works of Shakespeare, Socrates, Plato, Emerson and the Bible; while facing me stood a man who knew nothing of literature or of philosophy, but who had, despite this lack of knowledge, whipped me in a battle of words.

I turned and went back to my office as rapidly as I could go. There was nothing else for me to do. As I began to think the matter over I saw my mistake, but, true to nature, I was reluctant to do that which I knew must be done to right the wrong. I knew that I would have to apologize to that man before I could place myself at peace in my own heart, much less with him. Finally, I made up my mind to go back down to the basement and suffer this humility which I knew I had to undergo. The decision was not easily reached, nor did I reach it quickly.

I started down, but I walked more slowly than I had when I went down the first trip. I was trying to think how I would make the second approach so as to suffer the least humiliation possible.

When I got to the basement I called to the janitor to come over to the door. In a calm, kindly tone of voice he asked:

"What do you wish this time?"

I informed him that I had come back to apologize for the wrong I had done, if he would permit me to do so. Again that smile spread all over his face as he said:

"For the love of the Lord, you don't have to apologize. Nobody heard you except these four walls and you and me. I ain't going to tell it and I know you ain't going to tell it, so just forget it."

And that remark hurt more than his first one, for he had not only expressed a willingness to forgive me, but he had actually indicated his willingness to help me cover the incident up, so it would not become known and do me an injury.

But I walked over to him and took him by the hand. I shook with more than my hand–I shook with my heart–and as I walked back to my office I felt good for having summoned the courage with which to right the wrong I had done.

This is not the end of the story. It is only the beginning! Following this incident, I made a resolution that I would never again place myself in a position in which another man, whether he be an illiterate janitor or a man of letters, could humiliate me because I had lost my self-control.

Following that resolution, a remarkable change began to take place in me. My pen began to take on greater power. My spoken words began to carry greater weight. I began to make more friends and fewer enemies among men of my acquaintance. The incident marked one of the most important turning-points of my life. It taught me that no man can control others unless he first controls himself. It gave me a clear conception of the philosophy back of these words, "Whom the gods would destroy, they first make mad." It also gave me a clear conception of the law of non-resistance and helped me interpret many passages of the Holy Scriptures, bearing on the subject of this law, as I had never before interpreted them.

This incident placed in my hands the pass-key to a storehouse of knowledge that is illuminating and helpful in all that I do, and, later in life, when enemies sought to destroy me, it gave me a powerful weapon of defense that has never failed me.

Lack of self-control is the average salesman's most damaging weakness. The prospective buyer says something that the salesman does not wish to hear, and, if he has not this quality of self-control, he will "strike back" with a counter remark that is fatal to his sale.

In one of the large department stores of Chicago I witnessed an incident that illustrated the importance of self-control. A long line of women were in front of the "complaint" desk, telling their troubles and the store's faults to the young woman in charge. Some of the women were angry and unreasonable and some of them made very ugly remarks.

The young woman at the desk received the disgruntled women without the slightest sign of resentment at their remarks. With a smile on her face she directed these women to the proper departments with such charming grace and poise that I marveled at her self-control.

Standing just back of her was another young woman who was making notations on slips of paper and passing them in front of her, as the women in the line unburdened their troubles. These slips of paper contained the gist of what the women in the line were saying, minus the "vitriolic coloring" and the anger.

The smiling young woman at the desk who was "hearing" the complaints was stone deaf! Her assistant supplied her with all the necessary facts, though those slips of paper.

I was so impressed with the plan that I sought the manager of the store and interviewed him. He informed me that he had selected a deaf woman for one of the most trying and important positions in the store for the reason that he had not been able to find any other person with sufficient self-control to fill the place.

As I stood and watched that line of angry women, I observed what pleasant effect the smile of the young woman at the desk had upon them. They came before her growling like wolves and went away as meek and quiet as sheep. In fact some of them had "sheepish" looks on their faces as they left, because the young woman's self-control had made them ashamed of themselves.

Ever since I witnessed that scene, I have thought of the poise and self-control of that young woman at the desk every time I felt myself becoming irritated at remarks which I did not like, and often I have thought that everybody should have a set of "mental ear muffs" which they could slip over their ears at times. Personally, I have developed the habit of "closing" my ears against much of the idle chatter such as I used to make it my business to resent. Life is too short and there is too much constructive work to be done to justify us in "striking back" at everyone who says that which we do not wish to hear.

In the practice of law I have observed a very clever trick that trial lawyers use when they wish to get a statement of facts from a belligerent witness who answers questions with the proverbial "I do not remember" or "I do not know." When everything else fails, they manage to make such a witness angry; and in this state of mind they cause him to lose his self-control and make statements that he would not have made had he kept a "cool" head.

Most of us go through life with our "weather eye" cast skyward in quest of trouble. We usually find that for which we are looking. In my travels I have been a student of men whom I have heard in "Pullman car conversation," and I have observed that practically nine out of every ten have so little self-control that they will "invite" themselves into the discussion of almost any subject that may be brought up. But few men are contented to sit in a smoking compartment and listen to a conversation without joining in and "airing" their views.

Once I was traveling from Albany to New York City. On the way down, the "Smoking Car Club" started a conversation about the late Richard Croker, who was then chief of Tammany Hall. The discussion became loud and bitter. Everyone became angry except one old gentleman who was agitating the argument and taking a lively interest in it. He remained calm and seemed to enjoy all the mean things the others said about the "Tiger" of Tammany Hall. Of course, I supposed that he was an enemy of the Tammany Chief, but he wasn't!

He was Richard Croker, himself!

This was one of his clever tricks through which he found out what people thought of him and what his enemies' plans were.

Whatever else Richard Croker might have been, he was a man of self-control. Perhaps that is one reason why he remained undisputed boss of Tammany Hall as long as he did. Men who control themselves usually boss the job, no matter what it may be. Please read, again, the last sentence of the preceding paragraph, for it carries a subtle suggestion that might be of profit to you. This is a commonplace incident, but it is in just such incidents that the great truths of life are hidden-hidden because the settings are ordinary and commonplace.

Not long ago I accompanied my wife on a "bargain hunting" bee. Our attention was attracted by a crowd of women who were elbowing each other out of the way in front of a petticoat counter at which "bargains" were being offered. One lady who looked to be about forty-five years of age crawled on her hands and knees through the crowd and "bobbed" up in front of a customer who had engaged the attention of the saleswoman ahead of her. In a loud, high-pitched tone of voice she demanded attention. The saleswoman was a diplomat who understood human nature; she also possessed self-control, for she smiled sweetly at the intruder and said: "Yes, Miss; I will be with you in a moment!"

The intruder calmed herself!

I do not know whether it was the "Yes, Miss," or the sweet tone in which it was said

that modified her attitude; but it was one or the other; perhaps it was both. I do know, however, that the saleswoman was rewarded for her self-control by the sale of three petticoats, and the happy "Miss" went away feeling much younger for the remark.

Roast turkey is a very popular dish, but overeating of it cost a friend of mine, who is in the printing business, a fifty thousand dollar order. It happened the day after Thanksgiving, when I called at his office for the purpose of introducing him to a prominent Russian who had come to the United States to publish a book. The Russian spoke broken English and it was therefore hard for him to make himself easily understood. During the interview he asked my printer friend a question which was mistaken as a reflection upon his ability as a printer. In an unguarded moment he countered with this remark:

"The trouble with you Bolsheviks is that you look with suspicion on the remainder of the world just because of your own short-sightedness."

My "Bolshevik" friend nudged me on the elbow and whispered:

"The gentleman seems to be sick. We shall call again, when he is feeling better."

But, he never called again. He placed his order with another printer, and I learned afterward that the profit on that order was more than $10,000.00!

Ten thousand dollars seems a high price to pay for a plate of turkey, but that is the price that it cost my printer friend; for he offered me an apology for his conduct on the ground that his turkey dinner had given him indigestion and therefore he had lost his self-control.

One of the largest chain store concerns in the world has adopted a unique, though effective, method of employing salespeople who have developed the essential quality of self-control which all successful salespeople must possess. This concern has in its employ a very clever woman who visits department stores and other places where salespeople are employed and selects certain ones whom she believes to possess tact and self-control; but, to be sure of her judgment, she approaches these salespeople and has them show her their wares. She asks all sorts of questions that are designed to try their patience. If they stand the test, they are offered better positions; if they fail in the test, they have merely allowed a good opportunity to pass by without knowing it.

No doubt all people who refuse or neglect to exercise self-control are literally turning opportunity after opportunity away without knowing it. One day I was standing at the glove counter of a large retail store talking to a young man who was employed there.

He was telling me that he had been with the store four years, but on account of the "short-sightedness" of the store, his services had not been appreciated and he was looking for another position. In the midst of this conversation a customer walked up to him and asked to see some hats. He paid no attention to the customer's inquiry until he had finished telling me his troubles, despite the fact that the customer was obviously becoming impatient. Finally, he returned to the customer and said: "This isn't the hat department." When the customer inquired as to where he might find that department the young man replied: "Ask the floor-walker over there; he will direct you."

For four years this young man had been standing on top of a fine opportunity but he did not know it. He could have made a friend of every person whom he served in that store and these friends could have made him one of the most valuable men in the store, because they would have come back to trade with him. "Snappy" answers to inquiring customers do not bring them back.

One rainy afternoon an old lady walked into a Pittsburgh department store and wandered around in an aimless sort of way, very much in the manner that people who have no intention of buying often do. Most of the salespeople gave her the "once over" and busied themselves by straightening the stock on their shelves so as to avoid being troubled by her. One of the young men saw her and made it his business to inquire politely if he might serve her. She informed him that she was only waiting for it to stop raining; that she did not wish to make any purchases. The young man assured her that she was welcome, and by engaging her in conversation made her feel that he had meant what he said. When she was ready to go he accompanied her to the street and raised her umbrella for her. She asked for his card and went on her way.

The incident had been forgotten by the young man when, one day, he was called into the office by the head of the firm and shown a letter from a lady who wanted a salesman to go to Scotland and take an order for the furnishings for a mansion. That lady was Andrew Carnegie's mother; she was also the same woman whom the young man had so courteously escorted to the street many months previously.

In the letter, Mrs. Carnegie specified that this young man was the one whom she desired to be sent to take her order. That order amounted to an enormous sum, and the incident brought the young man an opportunity for advancement that he might never have had except for his courtesy to an old lady who did not look like a "ready sale." Just as the great fundamental laws of life are wrapped up in the commonest sort of every-day experiences that most of us never notice, so are the real opportunities often hidden in the seemingly unimportant transactions of life.

Ask the next ten people whom you meet why they have not accomplished more in their respective lines of endeavor, and at least nine of them will tell you that opportunity does not seem to come around their way. Go a step further and analyze each of these nine accurately by observing their actions for one single day, and the chances are that you will find that every one of them is turning away the finest sort of opportunities every hour of the day.

One day I went to visit a friend who was associated with a Commercial School, in the capacity of solicitor. When I asked him how he was getting along he replied: "Rotten! I see a large number of people but I am not making enough sales to give me a good living. In fact my account with the school is overdrawn and I am thinking about changing positions as there is no opportunity here."

It happened that I was on my vacation and had ten days' time that I could use as I wished, so I challenged his remark that he had no opportunity by telling him that I could turn his position into $250.00 in a week's time and show him how to make it worth that every week thereafter. He looked at me in amazement and asked me not to joke with him over so serious a matter. When he was finally convinced that I was in earnest he ventured to inquire how I would perform the "miracle."

Then I asked him if he had ever heard of organized effort, to which he replied: "What do you mean by organized effort?" I informed him that I had reference to the direction of his efforts in such a manner that he would enroll from five to ten students with the same amount of effort that he had been putting into the enrollment of one or of none. He said he was willing to be shown, so I gave him instructions to arrange for me to speak before the employees of one of the local department stores. He made the appointment and I delivered the address. In my talk I outlined a plan through which the employees could not only increase their ability so that they could earn more money in their present positions, but it also offered them an opportunity to prepare themselves for greater responsibilities and better positions. Following my talk, which of course was designed for that purpose, my friend enrolled eight of those employees for night courses in the Commercial School which he represented.

The following night he booked me for a similar address before the employees of a laundry, and following the address he enrolled three more students, two of them young women who worked over the washing machines at the hardest sort of labor. Two days later he booked me for an address before the employees of one of the local banks, and following the address he enrolled four more students, making a total of fifteen students, and the entire time consumed was not more than six hours, including the time required for the delivery of the addresses and the enrollment of the students. My friend's commission on the transactions was a little over four hundred dollars!

These places of employment were within fifteen minutes' walk of this man's place of business, but he had never thought of looking there for business. Neither had he ever thought of allying himself with a speaker who could assist him in "group" selling. That man now owns a splendid Commercial School of his own, and I am informed that his net income last year was over $10,000.00.

"No opportunities" come your way? Perhaps they come but you do not see them. Perhaps you will see them in the future as you are preparing yourself, through the aid of this Reading Course on the Law of Success, so that you can recognize an opportunity when you see it. The sixth lesson of this course is on the subject of imagination, which was the chief factor that entered into the transaction that I have just related. Imagination, plus a Definite Plan, plus Self-confidence, plus Action, were the main factors that entered into this transaction. You now know how to use all of these, and before you shall have finished this lesson you will understand how to direct these factors through self-control.

Now let us examine the scope of meaning of the term self-control, as it is used in connection with this course, by describing the general conduct of a person who possesses it. A person with well-developed self-control does not indulge in hatred, envy, jealousy, fear, revenge, or any similar destructive emotions. A person with well-developed self-control does not go into ecstasies or become ungovernably enthusiastic over anything or anybody.

Greed and selfishness and self-approval beyond the point of accurate self-analysis and appreciation of one's actual merits, indicate lack of self-control in one of its most dangerous forms. Self-confidence is one of the important essentials of success, but when this faculty is developed beyond the point of reason it becomes very dangerous. Self-sacrifice is a commendable quality, but when it is carried to extremes, it, also, becomes one of the dangerous forms of lack of self-control.

You owe it to yourself not to permit your emotions to place your happiness in the keeping of another person. Love is essential for happiness, but the person who loves so deeply that his or her happiness is placed entirely in the hands of another, resembles the little lamb who crept into the den of the nice, gentle little wolf and begged to be permitted to lie down and go to sleep, or the canary bird that persisted in playing with the cat's whiskers.

A person with well-developed self-control will not permit himself to be influenced by the cynic or the pessimist; nor will he permit another person to do his thinking for him. A person with well-developed self-control will stimulate his imagination and his enthusiasm until they have produced action, but he will then control that action and not permit it to control him.

A person with well-developed self-control will never, under any circumstances, slander another person or seek revenge for any cause whatsoever.

A person with self-control will not hate those who do not agree with him; instead, he will endeavor to understand the reason for their disagreement, and profit by it. We come, now, to a form of lack of self-control which causes more grief than all other forms combined; it is the habit of forming opinions before studying the facts. We will not analyze this particular form in detail, in this lesson, for the reason that it is fully covered in Lesson Eleven, on accurate thought, but the subject of self-control could not be covered without at least a passing reference to this common evil to which we are all more or less addicted.

No one has any right to form an opinion that is not based either upon that which he believes to be facts, or upon a reasonable hypothesis; yet, if you will observe yourself carefully, you will catch yourself forming opinions on nothing more substantial than your desire for a thing to be or not to be.

Another grievous form of lack of self-control is the "spending" habit. I have reference, of course, to the habit of spending beyond one's needs. This habit has become so prevalent since the close of the world war that it is alarming. A well-known economist has prophesied that three more generations will transform the United States from the richest country in the world to the poorest if the children are not taught the savings habit, as a part of their training in both the schools and the homes. On every hand, we see people buying automobiles on the installment plan instead of buying homes. Within the last fifteen years the automobile "fad" has become so popular that literally tens of thousands of people are mortgaging their futures to own cars.

A prominent scientist, who has a keen sense of humor, has prophesied that not only will this habit grow lean bank accounts, but, if persisted in, it will eventually grow babies whose legs will have become transformed into wheels.

This is a speed-mad, money-spending age in which we are living, and the uppermost thought in the minds of most of us is to live faster than our neighbors. Not long ago the general] manager of a concern that employs 600 men and women became alarmed over the large number of his employees who were becoming involved with "loan sharks," and decided to put an end to this evil. When he completed his investigation, he found that only nine per cent of his employees had savings accounts, and of the other ninety-one per cent who had no money ahead, seventy-five per cent were in debt in one form or another, some of them being hopelessly involved financially. Of those who were in debt 210 owned automobiles.

We are creatures of imitation. We find it hard to resist the temptation to do that which we see others doing. If our neighbor buys a Buick, we must imitate him and if we cannot scrape together enough to make the first payment on a Buick we must, at least, have a Ford. Meanwhile, we take no heed of the morrow. The old-fashioned "rainy-day nest egg" has become obsolete. We live from day to day. We buy our coal by the pound and our flour in five pound sacks, thereby paying a third more for it than it ought to cost, because it is distributed in small quantities.

Of course this warning does not apply to you!

It is intended only for those who are binding themselves in the chains of poverty by spending beyond their earning capacity, and who have not yet heard that there are definite laws which must be observed by all who would attain success.

The automobile is one of the modern wonders of the world, but it is more often a luxury than it is a necessity, and tens of thousands of people who are now "stepping on the gas" at a lively pace are going to see some dangerous skidding when their "rainy days" arrive.

It requires considerable self-control to use the street cars as a means of transportation when people all around us are driving automobiles, but all who exercise this self-control are practically sure to see the day when many who are now driving cars will be either riding the streetcars or walking.

It was this modem tendency to spend the entire income which prompted Henry Ford to safeguard his employees with certain restrictions when he established his famous $5.00 a day minimum wage scale.

Twenty years ago, if a boy wanted a wagon, he fashioned the wheels out of boards and had the pleasure of building it himself. Now, if a boy wants a wagon, he cries for it–and gets it!

Lack of self-control is being developed in the oncoming generations by their parents who have become victims of the spending habit. Three generations ago, practically any boy could mend his own shoes with the family cobbling outfit. Today the boy takes his shoes to the corner shoe-shop and pays $1.75 for heels and half soles, and this habit is by no means confined to the rich and well-to-do classes.

I repeat–the spending habit is turning America into a nation of paupers! I am safe in assuming that you are struggling to attain success, for if you were not you would not be reading this course. Let me remind you, then, that a little savings account will attract many an opportunity to you that would not come your way without it. The size of the account is not so important as is the fact that you have established the savings habit, for this habit marks you as a person who exercises an important form of self-control.

The modem tendency of those who work for a salary is to spend it all. If a man who receives $3,000.00 a year and manages to get along on it fairly well, receives an increase of $1,000.00 a year, does he continue to live on $3,000.00 and place the increased portion of his income in the savings bank? No, not unless he is one of the few who have developed the savings habit. Then, what does he do with this additional $1,000.00? He trades in the old automobile and buys a more expensive one, and at the end of the year he is poorer on a $4,000.00 income than he was the previous year on a $3,000.00 income.

This is a "modern, twentieth century model" American that I am describing, and you will be lucky if, upon close analysis, you do not find yourself to be one of this class. Somewhere between the miser who hoards every penny he gets his hands on, in an old sock, and the man who spends every cent he can earn or borrow, there is a "happy medium," and if you enjoy life with reasonable assurance of average freedom and contentment, you must find this half-way point and adopt it as a part of your self-control program.

Self-discipline is the most essential factor in the development of personal power, because it enables you to control your appetite and your tendency to spend more than you earn and your habit of "striking back" at those who offend you and the other destructive habits which cause you to dissipate your energies through non-productive effort that takes on forms too numerous to be catalogued in this lesson.

Very early in my public career I was shocked when I learned how many people there are who devote most of their energies to tearing down that which the builders construct. By some queer turn of the wheel of fate one of these destroyers crossed my path by making it his business to try to destroy my reputation. At first, I was inclined to "strike back" at him, but as I sat at my typewriter late one night, a thought came to me which changed my entire attitude toward this man. Removing the sheet of paper that was in my typewriter, I inserted another one on which I stated this thought, in these words:

You have a tremendous advantage over the man who does you an injury: you have it within your power to forgive him, while he has no such advantage over you.

As I finished writing those lines, I made up my mind that I had come to the point at which I had to decide upon a policy that would serve as a guide concerning my attitude toward those who criticize my work or try to destroy my reputation. I reached this decision by reasoning something after this fashion: Two courses of action were open to me. I could waste much of my time and energy in striking back at those who would try to destroy me, or I could devote this energy to furthering my life-work and let the result of that work serve as my sole answer to all who would criticize my efforts or question my motives. I decided upon the latter as being the better policy and adopted it.

"By their deeds you shall know them!"

If your deeds are constructive and you are at peace with yourself, in your own heart, you will not find it necessary to stop and explain your motives, for they will explain themselves.

The world soon forgets its destroyers. It builds its monuments to and bestows its honors upon none but its builders. Keep this fact in mind and you will more easily reconcile yourself to the policy of refusing to waste your energies by "striking back" at those who offend you.

Every person who amounts to anything in this world comes to the point, sooner or later, at which he is forced to settle this question of policy toward his enemies, and if you want proof that it pays to exercise sufficient self-control to refrain from dissipating your vital energies by "striking back" then study the records of all who have risen to high stations in life and observe how carefully they curbed this destructive habit.

It is a well known fact that no man ever reached a high station in life without opposition of a violent nature from jealous and envious enemies. The late President Warren G. Harding and ex-President

Wilson and John H. Patterson of the National Cash Register Company and scores of others whom I could mention, were victims of this cruel tendency, of a certain type of depraved man, to destroy reputation. But these men wasted no time explaining or "striking back" at their enemies. They exercised self-control.

I do not know but that these attacks on men who are in public life, cruel and unjust and untruthful as they often are, serve a good purpose. In my own case, I know that I made a discovery that was of great value to me, as a result of a series of bitter attacks which a contemporary journalist launched against me. I paid no attention to these attacks for four or five years, until finally they became so bold that I decided to override my policy and "strike back" at my antagonist. I sat down at my typewriter and began to write. In all of my experience as a writer I do not believe I ever assembled such a collection of biting adjectives as those which I used on this occasion. The more I wrote, the more angry I became, until I had written all that I could think of on the subject. As the last line was finished, a strange feeling came over me–it was not a feeling of bitterness toward the man who had tried to injure me–it was a feeling of compassion, of sympathy, of forgiveness.

I had unconsciously psycho-analyzed myself by releasing, over the keys of my typewriter, the repressed emotions of hate and resentment which I had been unintentionally gathering in my subconscious mind over a long period of years. Now, if I find myself becoming very angry, I sit down at my typewriter and "write it out of my system," then throw away the manuscript, or file it away as an exhibit for my scrapbook to which I can refer back in the years to come–after the evolutionary processes have carried me still higher in the realm of understanding.

Repressed emotions, especially, the emotion of hatred, resemble a bomb that has been constructed of high explosives, and unless they are handled with as much understanding of their nature as an expert would handle a bomb, they are as dangerous. A bomb may be rendered harmless by explosion in an open field, or by disintegration in a bath of the proper sort. Also, a feeling of anger or hatred may be rendered harmless by giving expression to it in a manner that harmonizes with the principle of psychoanalysis.

Before you can achieve success in the higher and broader sense you must gain such thorough control over yourself that you will be a person of poise.

You are the product of at least a million years of evolutionary change. For countless generations preceding you Nature has been tempering and refining the materials that have gone into your make-up. Step by step, she has removed from the generations that have preceded you the animal instincts and baser passions until she has produced, in you, the finest specimen of animal that lives. She has endowed you, through this slow evolutionary process, with reason and poise and "balance" sufficient to enable you to control and do with yourself whatever you will.

No other animal has ever been endowed with such self-control as you possess. You have been endowed with the power to use the most highly organized form of energy known to man, that of thought. It is not improbable that thought is the closest connecting link there is between the material, physical things of this world and the world of Divinity.

You have not only the power to think but, what is a thousand times more important still, you have the power to control your thoughts and direct them to do your bidding! We are coming, now, to the really important part of this lesson. Read slowly and meditatively! I approach this part of this lesson almost with fear and trembling, for it brings us face to face with a subject which but few men are qualified to discuss with reasonable intelligence.

I repeat, you have the power to control your thoughts and make them do your bidding! Your brain may be likened to a dynamo, in this respect, that it generates or sets into motion the mysterious energy called thought. The stimuli that start your brain into action are of two sorts; one is Autosuggestion and the other is Suggestion. You can select the material out of which your thinking is produced, and that is Auto-suggestion (or self-suggestion). You can permit others to select the material out of which your thinking is produced and that is Suggestion. It is a humiliating fact that most thought is produced by the outside suggestions of others, and it is more humiliating, still, to have to admit that the majority of us accept this suggestion without either examining it or questioning its soundness. We read the daily papers as though every word were based upon fact. We are swayed by the gossip and idle chatter of others as though every word were true.

Thought is the only thing over which you have absolute control, yet, unless you are the proverbial exception, which is about one out of every ten thousand, you permit other people to enter the sacred mansion of your mind and there deposit, through suggestion, their troubles and woes, adversities and falsehoods, just as though you did not have the power to close the door and keep them out.

You have within your control the power to select the material that constitutes the dominating thoughts of your mind, and just as surely as you are reading these lines, those thoughts which dominate your mind will bring you success or failure, according to their nature.

The fact that thought is the only thing over which you have absolute control is, within itself, of most profound significance, as it strongly suggests that thought is your nearest approach to Divinity, on this earthly plane. This fact also carries another highly impressive suggestion; namely, that thought is your most important tool; the one with which you may shape your worldly destiny according to your own liking. Surely, Divine Providence did not make thought the sole power over which you have absolute control without associating with that power potentialities which, if understood and developed, would stagger the imagination.

Self-control is solely a matter of thought-control!

Please read the foregoing sentence aloud; read it thoughtfully and meditate over it before reading further, because it is, without doubt, the most important single sentence of this entire course.

You are studying this course, presumably because you are earnestly seeking truth and understanding sufficient to enable you to attain some high station in life.

You are searching for the magic key that will unlock the door to the source of power; and yet you have the key in your own hands, and you may make use of it the moment you learn to control your thoughts.

Place in your own mind, through the principle of Auto-suggestion, the positive, constructive thoughts which harmonize with your definite chief aim in life, and that mind will transform those thoughts into physical reality and hand them back to you, as a finished product.

This is thought-control!

When you deliberately choose the thoughts which dominate your mind and firmly refuse admittance to outside suggestion, you are exercising self-control in its highest and most efficient form. Man is the only living animal that can do this.

How many millions of years Nature has required in which to produce this animal no one knows, but every intelligent student of psychology knows that the dominating thoughts determine the actions and the nature of the animal.

The process through which one may think accurately is a subject that has been reserved for Lesson Eleven, of this course. The point we wish clearly to establish, in this lesson, is that thought, whether accurate or inaccurate, is the most highly organized functioning power of your mind; and that you are but the sum total of your dominating or most prominent thoughts.

If you would be a master salesman, whether of goods and wares or of personal services, you must exercise sufficient self-control to shut out all adverse arguments and suggestions. Most salesmen have so little self-control that they hear the prospective purchaser say "no" even before he says it. Not a few salesmen hear this fatal word "no" even before they come into the presence of their prospective purchaser. They have so little self-control that they actually suggest to themselves that their prospective purchaser will say "no" when asked to purchase their wares.

How different is the man of self-control! He not only suggests to himself that his prospective purchaser will say "yes," but if the desired "yes" is not forthcoming, he stays on the job until he breaks down the opposition and forces a "yes." If his prospective purchaser says "no," he does not hear it. If his prospective purchaser says "no"–a second, and a third, and a fourth time–does not hear it, for he is a man of self-control and he permits no suggestions to reach his mind except those which he desires to influence him.

The master salesman, whether he be engaged in selling merchandise, or personal services, or sermons, or public addresses, understands how to control his own thoughts.

Instead of being a person who accepts, with meek submission, the suggestions of others, he is a person who persuades others to accept his suggestions. By controlling himself and by placing only positive thoughts in his own mind, he thereby becomes a dominating personality, a master salesman.

This, too, is self-control!

A master salesman is one who takes the offensive, and never the defensive side of an argument, if argument arises.

Please read the foregoing sentence again!

If you are a master salesman you know that it is necessary for you to keep your prospective purchaser on the defensive, and you also know that it will be fatal to your sale if you permit him to place you on the defensive and keep you there. You may, and of course you will at times, be placed in a position in which you will have to assume the defensive side of the conversation for a time, but it is your business to exercise such perfect poise and self-control that you will change places with your prospective purchaser without his noticing that you have done so, by placing him back on the defensive.

This requires the most consummate skill and self-control!

Most salesmen sweep this vital point aside by becoming angry and trying to scare the prospective purchaser into submission, but the master salesman remains calm and serene, and usually comes out the winner.

The word "salesman" has reference to all people who try to persuade or convince others by logical argument or appeal to self-interest. We are all salesmen; or, at least, we should be, no matter what form of service we are rendering or what sort of goods we are offering.

The ability to negotiate with other people without friction and argument is the outstanding quality of all successful people. Observe those nearest you and notice how few there are who understand this art of tactful negotiation. Observe, also, how successful are the few who understand this art, despite the fact that they may have less education than those with whom they negotiate.

It is a knack that can be cultivated.

The art of successful negotiation grows out of patient and painstaking self-control.

Notice how easily the successful salesman exercises self-control when he is handling a customer who is impatient. In his heart such a salesman may be boiling over, but you will see no evidence of it in his face or manner or words.

He has acquired the art of tactful negotiation!

A single frown of disapproval or a single word denoting impatience will often spoil a sale, and no one knows this better than the successful salesman. He makes it his business to control his feelings, and as a reward he sets his own salary mark and chooses his own position.

To watch a person who has acquired the art of successful negotiation is a liberal education, within itself. Watch the public speaker who has acquired this art; notice the firmness of his step as he mounts the platform; observe the firmness of his voice as he begins to speak; study the expression on his face as he sweeps his audience with the mastery of his argument. He has learned how to negotiate without friction.

Watch the physician who has acquired this art, as he walks into the sick room and greets his patient with a smile. His bearing, the tone of his voice, the look of assurance on his face, all mark him as one who has acquired the art of successful negotiation, and the patient begins to feel better the moment he enters the sick room.

Watch the foreman of the works who has acquired this art, and observe how his very presence spurs his men to greater effort and inspires them with confidence and enthusiasm.

Watch the lawyer who has acquired this art, and observe how he commands the respect and attention of the court, the jury and his fellow-practitioners. There is something about the tone of his voice, the posture of his body, and the expression on his face which causes his opponent to suffer by comparison. He not only knows his case, but he convinces the court and the jury that he knows, and as his reward he wins his cases and claims big retaining fees.

And all of this is predicated upon self-control!

And self-control is the result of thought-control!

Deliberately place in your own mind the sort of thoughts that you desire there, and keep out of your mind those thoughts which others place there through suggestion, and you will become a person of self-control.

This privilege of stimulating your mind with suggestions and thoughts of your own choosing is your prerogative power that Divine Providence gave you, and if you will exercise this holy right there is nothing within the bounds of reason that you cannot attain. "Losing your temper," and with it your case, or your argument, or your sale, marks you as one who has not yet familiarized himself with the fundamentals upon which self-control is based, and the chief one of these fundamentals is the privilege of choosing the thoughts that dominate the mind.

A student in one of my classes once asked how one went about controlling one's thoughts when in a state of intense anger, and I replied: "In exactly the same way that you would change your manner and the tone of your voice if you were in a heated argument with a member of your family and heard the door bell ring, warning you that company was about to visit you. You would control yourself because you would desire to do so."

If you have ever been in a similar predicament, where you found it necessary to cover up your real feelings and change the expression on your face quickly, you know how easily it can be done, and you also know that it can be done because one wants to do it! Back of all achievement, back of all self-control, back of all thought control, is that magic something called DESIRE!

It is no misstatement of fact to say that you are limited only by the depth of your desires!

When your desires are strong enough you will appear to possess superhuman powers to achieve. No one has ever explained this strange phenomenon of the mind, and perhaps no one ever will explain it, but if you doubt that it exists you have but to experiment and be convinced.

If you were in a building that was on fire, and all the doors and windows were locked, the chances are that you would develop sufficient strength with which to break down the average door, because of your intense desire to free yourself.

If you desire to acquire the art of successful negotiation, as you undoubtedly will when you understand its significance in relation to your achievement of your definite chief aim, you will do so, providing your desire is intense enough.

Napoleon desired to become emperor of France and did rule. Lincoln desired to free the slaves, and he accomplished it. The French desired that "they shall not pass," at the beginning of the world war, and they didn't pass! Edison desired to produce light with electricity, and he produced it–although he was many years in doing so. Roosevelt desired to unite the Atlantic and Pacific oceans, through the Panama Canal, and he did it. Demosthenes desired to become a great public speaker, and despite the handicap of serious impediment of speech, he transformed his desire into reality. Helen Keller desired to speak, and despite the fact that she was deaf, dumb and blind, she now speaks. John H. Patterson desired to dominate in the production of cash registers, and he did it. Marshall Field desired to be the leading merchant of his time, and he did. Shakespeare desired to become a great playwright, and, despite the fact that he was only a poor itinerant actor, he made his desire come true. Billy Sunday desired to quit playing baseball and become a master preacher, and he did. James J. Hill desired to become an empire builder; and, despite the fact that he was only a poor telegraph operator, he transformed that desire into reality.

Don't say, "It can't be done," or that you are different from these and thousands of others who have achieved noteworthy success in every worthy calling. If you are "different," it is only in this respect: they desired the object of their achievement with more depth and intensity than you desire yours.

Plant in your mind the seed of a desire that is constructive by making the following your creed and the foundation of your code of ethics:

"I wish to be of service to my fellow men as I journey through life. To do this I have adopted this creed as a guide to be followed in dealing with my fellow-beings:

"To train myself so that never, under any circumstances, will I find fault with any person, no matter how much I may disagree with him or how inferior his work may be, as long as I know he is sincerely trying to do his best.

"To respect my country, my profession and myself. To be honest and fair with my fellow men, as I expect them to be honest and fair with me. To be a loyal citizen of my country. To speak of it with praise, and act always as a worthy custodian of its good name. To be a person whose name carries weight wherever it goes.

"To base my expectations of reward on a solid foundation of service rendered. To be willing to pay the price of success in honest effort. To look upon my work as an opportunity to be seized with joy and made the most of, and not as a painful drudgery to be reluctantly endured.

"To remember that success lies within myself–in my own brain. To expect difficulties and to force my way through them.

"To avoid procrastination in all its forms, and never, under any circumstances, put off until tomorrow any duty that should be performed today.

"Finally, to take a good grip on the joys of life, so I may be courteous to men, faithful to friends, true to God–a fragrance in the path I tread."

The energy which most people dissipate through lack of self-control would, if organized and used constructively, bring all the necessities and all the luxuries desired. The time which many people devote to "gossiping" about others would, if controlled and directed constructively, be sufficient to attain the object of their definite chief aim (if they had such an aim).

All successful people grade high on self-control! All "failures" grade low, generally zero, on this important law of human conduct.

Study the comparative analysis chart in the Introductory Lesson, and observe the self-control gradings of Jesse James and Napoleon.

Study those around you and observe, with profit, that all the successful ones exercise self-control, while the "failures" permit their THOUGHTS, WORDS and DEEDS to run wild!

One very common and very destructive form of lack of self-control is the habit of talking too much. People of wisdom, who know what they want and are bent on getting it, guard their conversation carefully. There can be no gain from a volume of uninvited, uncontrolled, loosely spoken words.

It is nearly always more profitable to listen than it is to speak. A good listener may, once in a great while, hear something that will add to his stock of knowledge. It requires self-control to become a good listener, but the benefits to be gained are worth the effort.

"Taking the conversation away from another person" is a common form of lack of self-control which is not only discourteous, but it deprives those who do it of many valuable opportunities to learn from others.

After completing this lesson you should go back to the self-analysis chart, in the Introductory Lesson, and re-grade yourself on the Law of Self-control. Perhaps you may wish to reduce your former grading somewhat.

Self-control was one of the marked characteristics of all successful leaders whom I have analyzed, in gathering material for this course. Luther Burbank said that, in his opinion, self-control was the most important of the Fifteen Laws of Success. During all his years of patient study and observation of the evolutionary processes of vegetable life he found it necessary to exercise the faculty of self-control, despite the fact that he was dealing with inanimate life.

John Burroughs, the naturalist, said practically the same thing; that self-control stood near the head of the list, in importance, of the Fifteen Laws of Success. The man who exercises complete self-control cannot be permanently defeated, as Emerson has so well stated in his essay on Compensation, for the reason that obstacles and opposition have a way of melting away when confronted by the determined mind that is guided to a definite end with complete self-control.

Every wealthy man whom I have analyzed (referring to those who have become wealthy through their own efforts) showed such positive evidence that self-control had been one of his strong points that I reached the conclusion that no man can hope to accumulate great wealth and keep it without exercising this necessary quality. The saving of money requires the exercise of self-control of the highest order, as, I hope, has been made quite clear in the fourth lesson of this course. I am indebted to Edward W. Bok for the following rather colorful description of the extent to which he found it necessary to exercise self-control before he achieved success and was crowned with fame as one of the great journalists of America:

WHY I BELIEVE IN POVERTY AS THE RICHEST EXPERIENCE THAT CAN COME TO A BOY

I make my living trying to edit the Ladies' Home Journal. And because the public has been most generous in its acceptance of that periodical, a share of that success has logically come to me. Hence a number of my very good readers cherish an opinion that often I have been tempted to correct, a temptation to which I now yield. My correspondents express the conviction variously, but this extract from a letter is a fair sample:

"It is all very easy for you to preach economy to us when you do not know the necessity for it: To tell us how, as for example in my own case, we must live within my husband's income of eight hundred dollars a year, when you have never known what it is to live on less than thousands. Has it occurred to you, born with the proverbial silver spoon in your mouth, that theoretical writing is pretty cold and futile compared to the actual hand-to-mouth struggle that so many of us live, day by day and year in and year out–an experience that you know not of?"

"An experience that you know not of!"

Now, how far do the facts square with this statement?

Whether or not I was born with the proverbial silver spoon in my mouth, I cannot say. It is true that I was born of well-to-do parents. But when I was six years old my father lost all his means, and faced life at forty-five, in a strange country, without even necessaries. There are men and their wives who know what that means, for a man to try to "come back" at forty-five, and in a strange country!

I had the handicap of not knowing one word of the English language. I went to a public school and learned what I could. And sparse morsels they were! The boys were cruel, as boys are. The teachers were impatient, as tired teachers are.

My father could not find his place in the world. My mother who had always had servants at her beck and call, faced the problems of housekeeping that she had never learned nor been taught. And there was no money.

So, after school hours, my brother and I went home, but not to play. After-school hours meant for us to help a mother who daily grew more frail under the burdens that she could not carry. Not for days, but for years, we two boys got up in the gray cold winter dawn when the beds feel so warm to growing boys, and we sifted the coal ashes of the day- before's fire for a stray lump or two of unburned coal, and with what we had or could find we made the fire and warmed up the room. Then we set the table for the scant breakfast, went to school, and directly after school we washed the dishes, swept and scrubbed the floors. Living in a three-family tenement, each third week meant that we scrubbed the entire three flights of stairs from the third story to the first, as well as the doorsteps and the sidewalk outside. The latter work was the hardest; for we did it on Saturdays, with the boys of the neighborhood looking on none too kindly, so we did it to the echo of the crack of the ball and bat on the adjoining lot!

In the evening when the other boys could sit by the lamp or study their lessons, we two boys went out with a basket and picked up wood and coal in the adjoining lots, or went after the dozen or so pieces of coal left from the ton of coal put in that afternoon by one of the neighbors, with the spot hungrily fixed in mind by one of us during the day, hoping that the man who carried in the coal might not be too careful in picking up the stray lumps!

"An experience that you know not of!" Don't I?

At ten years of age I got my first job, washing the windows of a baker's shop at fifty cents a week. In a week or two I was allowed to sell bread and cakes behind the counter after school hours for a dollar a week–handing out freshly baked cakes and warm, delicious-smelling bread, when scarcely a crumb had passed my mouth that day!

Then on Saturday mornings I served a route for a weekly paper, and sold my remaining stock on the street. It meant from sixty to seventy cents for that day's work.

I lived in Brooklyn, New York, and the chief means of transportation to Coney Island at that time was the horse car. Near where we lived the cars would stop to water the horses, the men would jump out and get a drink of water, but the women had no means of quenching their thirst. Seeing this lack I got a pail, filled it with water and a bit of ice, and, with a glass, jumped on each car on Saturday afternoon and all day Sunday, and sold my wares at a cent a glass. And when competition came, as it did very quickly when other boys saw that a Sunday's work meant two or three dollars, I squeezed a lemon or two in my pail, my liquid became "lemonade" and my price two cents a glass, and Sunday meant five dollars to me.

Then, in turn, I became a reporter during the evenings, an office boy day-times, and learned stenography at midnight.

My correspondent says she supports her family of husband and child on eight hundred dollars a year, and says I have never known what that means. I supported a family of three on six dollars and twenty-five cents a week-less than one-half of her yearly income. When my brother and I, combined, brought in eight hundred dollars a year we felt rich!

I have for the first time gone into these details in print so that you may know, at first hand, that the editor of the Ladies' Home journal is not a theorist when he writes or prints articles that seek to preach economy or that reflect a hand-to-hand struggle on a small or an invisible income. There is not a single step, not an inch, on the road of direct poverty that I do not know of or have not experienced. And, having experienced every thought, every feeling and every hardship that come to those who travel that road, I say today that I rejoice with every boy who is going through the same experience.

Nor am I discounting or forgetting one single pang of the keen hardships that such a struggle means. I would not today exchange my years of the keenest hardship that a boy can know or pass through for any single experience that could have come to me. I know what it means to earn–not a dollar, but to earn two cents. I know the value of money as I could have learned it or known it in no other way. I could have been trained for my life-work in no surer way. I could not have arrived at a truer understanding of what it means to face a day without a penny in hand, not a loaf of bread in the cupboard, not a piece of kindling wood for the fire–with nothing to eat, and then be a boy with the hunger of nine and ten, with a mother frail and discouraged!

"An experience that you know not of!" Don't I?

And yet I rejoice in the experience, and I repeat: I envy every boy who is in that condition and going through it. But–and here is the pivot of my strong belief in poverty as an undisguised blessing to a boy–I believe in poverty as a condition to experience, to go through, and then to get out of: not as a condition to stay in. "That's all very well," some will say; "easy enough to say, but how can you get out of it?" No one can definitely tell another that. No one told me. No two persons can find the same way out. Each must find his way for himself. That depends on the boy. I was determined to get out of poverty, because my mother was not born in it, could not stand it and did not belong in it. This gave me the first essential: a purpose. Then I backed up the purpose with effort and willingness to work and to work at anything that came my way, no matter what it was, so long as it meant "the way out." I did not pick and choose; I took what came and did it in the best way I knew how; and when I didn't like what I was doing I still did it well while I was doing it, but I saw to it that I didn't do it any longer than I had to do it. I used every rung in the ladder as a rung to the one above. It meant effort, but out of the effort and the work came the experience; the upbuilding, the development; the capacity to understand and sympathize; the greatest heritage that can come to a boy. And nothing in the world can give that to a boy, so that it will burn into him, as will poverty.

That is why I believe so strongly in poverty, the greatest blessing in the way of the deepest and fullest experience that can come to a boy. But, as I repeat: always as a condition to work out of, not to stay in.

Before you can develop the habit of perfect self-control you must understand the real need for this quality. Also, you must understand the advantages which self-control provides those who have learned how to exercise it.

By developing self-control you develop, also, other qualities that will add to your personal power. Among other laws which are available to the person who exercises self-control is the Law of Retaliation.

You know what "retaliate" means!

In the sense that we are using here it means to "return like for like," and not merely to avenge or to seek revenge, as is commonly meant by the use of this word. If I do you an injury you retaliate at first opportunity. If I say unjust things about you, you will retaliate in kind, even in greater measure!

On the other hand, if I do you a favor you will reciprocate even in greater measure if possible.

Through the proper use of this law I can get you to do whatever I wish you to do. If I wish you to dislike me and to lend your influence toward damaging me, I can accomplish this result by inflicting upon you the sort of treatment that I want you to inflict upon me through retaliation.

If I wish your respect, your friendship and your co-operation I can get these by extending to you my friendship and co-operation.

On these statements I know that we are together. You can compare these statements with your own experience and you will see how beautifully they harmonize. How often have you heard the remark, "What a wonderful personality that person has."

How often have you met people whose personalities you coveted?

The man who attracts you to him through his pleasing personality is merely making use of the Law of Harmonious Attraction, or the Law of Retaliation, both of which, when analyzed, mean that "like attracts like."

If you will study, understand and make intelligent use of the Law of Retaliation you will be an efficient and successful salesman. When you have mastered this simple law and learned how to use it you will have learned all that can be learned about salesmanship.

The first and probably the most important step to be taken in mastering this law is to cultivate complete self-control. You must learn to take all sorts of punishment and abuse without retaliating in kind. This self-control is a part of the price you must pay for mastery of the Law of Retaliation.

When an angry person starts in to vilify and abuse you, justly or unjustly, just remember that if you retaliate in a like manner you are being drawn down to that person's mental level, therefore that person is dominating you!

On the other hand, if you refuse to become angry, if you retain your self-composure and remain calm and serene you retain all your ordinary faculties through which to reason. You take the other fellow by surprise. You retaliate with a weapon with the use of which he is unfamiliar, consequently you easily dominate him.

Like attracts like! There's no denying this!

Literally speaking, every person with whom you come in contact is a mental looking-glass in which you may see a perfect reflection of your own mental attitude. As an example of direct application of the Law of Retaliation, let us cite an experience that I recently had with my two small boys, Napoleon Junior and James.

We were on our way to the park to feed the birds and squirrels. Napoleon junior had bought a bag of peanuts and James had bought a box of "Crackerjack." James took a notion to sample the peanuts. Without asking permission he reached over and made a grab for the bag. He missed and Napoleon Junior "retaliated" with his left fist which landed rather briskly on James' jaw.

I said to James: "Now, see here, son, you didn't go about getting those peanuts in the right manner. Let me show you how to get them." It all happened so quickly that I hadn't the slightest idea when I spoke what I was going to suggest to James, but I sparred for time to analyze the occurrence and work out a better way, if possible, than that adopted by him.

Then I thought of the experiments we had been making in connection with the Law of Retaliation, so I said to James: "Open your box of "Crackerjack' and offer your little brother some and see what happens." After considerable coaxing I persuaded him to do this. Then a remarkable thing happened–a happening out of which I learned my greatest lesson in salesmanship! Before Napoleon would touch the "Crackerjack" he insisted on pouring some of his peanuts into James' overcoat pocket. He "retaliated in kind!" Out of this simple experiment with two small boys I learned more about the art of managing them than I could have learned in any other manner. Incidentally, my boys are beginning to learn how to manipulate this Law of Retaliation which saves them many a physical combat.

None of us have advanced far beyond Napoleon Junior and James as far as the operation and influence of the Law of Retaliation is concerned. We are all just grownup children and easily influenced through this principle. The habit of "retaliating in kind" is so universally practiced among us that we can properly call this habit the Law of Retaliation. If a person presents us with a gift we never feel satisfied until we have "retaliated" with something as good or better than that which we received. If a person speaks well of us we increase our admiration for that person, and we "retaliate" in return!

Through the principle of retaliation we can actually convert our enemies into loyal friends. If you have an enemy whom you wish to convert into a friend you can prove the truth of this statement if you will forget that dangerous millstone hanging around your neck, which we call "pride" (stubbornness). Make a habit of speaking to this enemy with unusual cordiality. Go out of your way to favor him in every manner possible. He may seem immovable at first, but gradually he will give way to your influence and "retaliate in kind!" The hottest coals of fire ever heaped upon the head of one who has wronged you are the coals of human kindness.

One morning in August, 1863, a young clergyman was called out of bed in a hotel at Lawrence, Kansas. The man who called him was one of Quantrell's guerrillas, and he wanted him to hurry downstairs and be shot. All over the border that morning people were being murdered. A band of raiders had ridden in early to perpetrate the Lawrence massacre.

The guerrilla who called the clergyman was impatient. The latter, when fully awake, was horrified by what he saw going on through his window. As he came downstairs the guerrilla demanded his watch and money, and then wanted to know if he was an abolitionist. The clergyman was trembling. But he decided that if he was to die then and there it would not be with a lie on his lips. So he said that he was, and followed up the admission with a remark that immediately turned the whole affair into another channel.

He and the guerrilla sat down on the porch, while people were being killed through the town, and had a long talk. It lasted until the raiders were ready to leave. When the clergyman's guerrilla mounted to join his confederates he was strictly on the defensive. He handed back the New Englander's valuables, apologized for disturbing him and asked to be thought well of.

That clergyman lived many years after the Lawrence massacre. What did he say to the guerrilla? What was there in his personality that led the latter to sit down and talk?

What did they talk about?

"Are you a Yankee abolitionist?" the guerrilla had asked. "Yes, I am," was the reply, "and you know very well that you ought to be ashamed of what you're doing"

This drew the matter directly to a moral issue. It brought the guerrilla up roundly. The clergyman was only a stripling beside this seasoned border ruffian. But he threw a burden of moral proof on to the raider, and in a moment the latter was trying to demonstrate that he might be a better fellow than circumstances would seem to indicate.

After waking this New Englander to kill him on account of his politics, he spent twenty minutes on the witness stand trying to prove an alibi. He went into his personal history at length. He explained matters from the time when he had been a tough little kid who wouldn't say his prayers, and became quite sentimental in recalling how one thing had led to another, and that to something worse, until–well, here he was, and "a mighty bad business to be in, pardner." His last request in riding away was: "Now, pardner, don't think too hard of me, will you?"

The New England clergyman made use of the Law of Retaliation, whether he knew it at that time or not. Imagine what would have happened had he come downstairs with a revolver in his hand and started to meet physical force with physical force!

But he didn't do this! He mastered the guerrilla because he fought him with a force that was unknown to the brigand.

Why is it that when once a man begins to make money the whole world seems to beat a pathway to his door?

Take any person that you know who enjoys financial success and he will tell you that he is being constantly sought, and that opportunities to make money are constantly being urged upon him!

"To him that hath shall be given, but to him that hath not shall be taken away even that which he hath."

This quotation from the Bible used to seem ridiculous to me, yet how true it is when reduced to its concrete meaning.

Yes, "to him that hath shall be given!" If he "hath" failure, lack of self-confidence, hatred or lack of self-control, to him shall these qualities be given in still greater abundance! But, if he "hath" success, self-confidence, self-control, patience, persistence and determination, to him shall these qualities be increased!

Sometimes it may be necessary to meet force with force until we overpower our opponent or adversary, but while he is down is a splendid time to complete the "retaliation" by taking him by the hand and showing him a better way to settle disputes.

Like attracts like! Germany sought to bathe her sword in human blood, in a ruthless escapade of conquest. As a result she has drawn the "retaliation in kind" of most of the civilized world.

It is for you to decide what you want your fellow men to do and it is for you to get them to do it through the Law of Retaliation!

The Divine Economy is automatic and very simple: we receive only that which we give."

How true it is that "we receive only that which we give"! It is not that which we wish for that comes back to us, but that which we give.

I implore you to make use of this law, not alone for material gain, but, better still, for the attainment of happiness and good-will toward men.

This, after all, is the only real success for which to strive.

SUMMARY

In this lesson we have learned a great principle–probably the most important major principle of psychology! We have learned that our thoughts and actions toward others resemble an electric magnet which attracts to us the same sort of thought and the same sort of action that we, ourselves, create.

We have learned that "like attracts like," whether in thought or in expression of thought through bodily action. We have learned that the human mind responds, in kind, to whatever thought impressions it receives. We have learned that the human mind resembles mother earth in that it will reproduce a crop of muscular action which corresponds, in kind, to the sensory impressions planted in it. We have learned that kindness begets kindness and unkindness and injustice beget unkindness and injustice.

We have learned that our actions toward others, whether of kindness or unkindness, justice or injustice, come back to us, even in a larger measure! We have learned that the human mind responds in kind, to all sensory impressions it receives, therefore we know what we must do to influence any desired action upon the part of another. We have learned that "pride" and "stubbornness" must be brushed away before we can make use of the Law of Retaliation in a constructive way. We have not learned what the Law of Retaliation is, but we have learned how it works and what it will do; therefore, it only remains for us to make intelligent use of this great principle.

You are now ready to proceed with Lesson Nine, where you will find other laws which harmonize perfectly with those described in this lesson on Self-control. It will require the strongest sort of self-control to enable the beginner to apply the major law of the next lesson, on the Habit of Doing More Than Paid For, but experience will show that the development of such control is more than justified by the results growing out of such discipline.

THE EVOLUTION OF TRANSPORTATION–An After-the-Lesson Visit With the Author

Nothing is permanent except change. Life resembles a great kaleidoscope before which Time is ever shifting, changing and rearranging both the stage setting and the players. New friends are constantly replacing the old. Everything is in a state of flux. In every heart is the seed of both rascality and justice. Every human being is both a criminal and a saint, depending upon the expediency of the moment as to which will assert itself. Honesty and dishonesty are largely matters of individual viewpoint. The weak and the strong, the rich and the poor, the ignorant and the well-informed are exchanging places continuously.

Know YOURSELF and you know the entire human race. There is but one real achievement, and that is the ability to THINK ACCURATELY. We move with the procession, or behind it, but we cannot stand still.

Nothing is permanent except change!

The law of evolution is working out improvements in the methods of travel. At the beginning of history the method of transportation was crude. Man was not satisfied with this slow process. Those two little words "not satisfied," have been the starting point of all advancement. Think of them as you read this article.

The history of transportation grew tep-by-step as man's brain began to expand. It was a long step forward when man discovered how to hitch a bullock to a wagon and thereby escape the toil of pulling the load. That was practical utility. But, when the stage-coach was ushered into use that was both utility and style.

Still man was "not satisfied" and this dissatisfaction created the crude locomotive that you see in the picture.

Now all these methods of travel have been discarded except in certain uncivilized (or uncommercialized) parts of the world. The man drawing the cart, the bullock drawing the cart, the stage-coach and the crude locomotive all belong to ages that have passed.

Compare current modes of transportation with those of the past and you may have a fair idea of the enormous expansion that has taken place in the brain and mind of man. Man now moves about more rapidly than in the past. From the first type of locomotive there has been evolved a powerful machine capable of hauling a hundred cars of freight, compared with the one small light car that could be drawn with the original. Automobiles that travel at the speed of seventy-five miles an hour are now as common as were the two-wheel carts in ages past. Moreover, they are within the means of all who want them.

And still man's mind was "not satisfied." Travel on the earth was too slow. Turning his eyes upward he watched the birds soaring high in the elements and became "DETERMINED" to excel them. Study, also, the word "determined," for whatever man becomes determined to do man does! Within the brief period of fifteen years man has mastered the air and now travels in the airplane at the rate of a hundred and fifty miles an hour.

Not only has man made the air carry him at amazingly rapid speed, but he has harnessed the ether and made it carry his words all the way around the earth in the fractional part of a second.

We have been describing the PAST and the PRESENT!

Someday we may see the next step forward that man will take in methods of travel; a machine that will fly in the air, run on the ground and swim in the water, at the discretion of man.

The purpose of this essay is to provide food for THOUGHT!

Any influence that causes one to think causes one, also, to grow stronger mentally. Mind stimulants are essential for growth. From the days of the man-drawn cart to the present days of air mastery the only progress that any man has made has been the result of some influence that stimulated his mind to greater than normal action.

The two great major influences that cause the mind of man to grow are the urge of necessity and the urge of desire to create. Some minds develop only after they have undergone failure and defeat and other forms of punishment which arouse them to greater action. Other minds wither away and die under punishment, but grow to unbelievable heights when provided with the opportunity to use their imaginative forces in a creative way.

Study the evolution of transportation and you will observe one outstanding fact worth remembering, namely, that the whole story has been one of development and advancement that grew out of necessity. The entire period described as "THE PAST" was one wherein the urge was that of necessity.

In the period described as "THE PRESENT" the urge has been a combination of both necessity and the desire to create. The period described as "THE FUTURE" will be one in which the strong desire to create will be the sole urge that will drive man's mind on and on to heights as yet undreamed of.

It is a long distance from the days of the man-drawn cart to the present, when man has harnessed the lightning of the clouds and made it turn machinery that will perform as much service in a minute as ten thousand men could perform in a day. But, if the distance has been long the development of man's mind has been correspondingly great, and that development has been sufficient to eventually do the work of the world with machines operated by Nature's forces and not by man's muscles.

The evolutionary changes in the methods of transportation have created other problems for man's mind to solve. The automobile drove man to build better roads and more of them. The automobile and the speedy locomotive, combined, have created dangerous crossings which claim thousands of lives annually. Man's mind must now respond to the urge of "necessity" and meet this emergency.

Keep this essay and remember this prophecy:

Within five years every railroad crossing in the country will be amply protected against automobile accidents, and, the automobile, itself, will manipulate the system that will do the protecting; a system that will be fool-proof and effective; a system that will work whether the driver of the automobile is asleep or awake, drunk or sober.

Come, now, for a brief glimpse at the machinery of the imagination of man, as it works under the stimulant of desire to create.

Some imaginative man; perhaps some fellow who never did anything else of note and who will never do anything worth while again; will create a system of railroad crossing protection that will be operated by the weight of the passing automobile. Within the required distance from the crossing a platform similar to the platform of a large freight scale will cover an entire section of the roadway. As soon as an automobile mounts this platform the weight of the machine will lower a gate, ring a gong and flash a red light in front of the motorist. The gate will rise in one minute, allowing the motorist to pass over the track, thus forcing him to "stop, look and listen."

If you have a highly imaginative mind YOU maybe the one who will create this system and collect the royalties from its sale.

To be practical the imaginative mind should be always on the alert for ways and means of diverting waste motion and power into useful channels. Most automobiles are far too heavy in comparison with the load they carry. This weight can be utilized by making it provide the motorist with railroad crossing protection.

Remember, the purpose of this essay is to give you merely the seed of suggestion; not the finished product of an invention ready to set up and render service. The value to you, of this suggestion, lies in the possibility of THOUGHT that you may devote to it, thereby developing and expanding your own mind.

Study yourself and find out to which of the two great major urges to action your mind responds most naturally–the urge of necessity or the desire to create. If you have children, study them and determine to which of these two motives they respond most naturally. Millions of children have had their imagination dwarfed and retarded by parents who removed as much as possible of the urge of necessity. By "making it easy" for your child you may be depriving the world of a genius. Bear in mind the fact that most of the progress that man has made came as the result of bitter, biting NECESSITY!

You need no proof that methods of transportation have undergone a continuous process of evolution. So marked has the change been that the old one-lung type of automobile now provokes a laugh wherever it is found on the street.

The law of evolution is always and everywhere at work, changing, tearing down and rebuilding every material element on this earth and throughout the universe. Towns, cities and communities are undergoing constant change. Go back to the place where you lived twenty years ago and you will recognize neither the place nor the people.

New faces will have made their appearance. The old faces will have changed. New buildings will have taken the place of the old. Everything will appear differently because everything will be different.

The human mind is also undergoing constant change. If this were not true we would never grow beyond the child-mind age. Every seven years the mind of a normal person becomes noticeably developed and expanded. It is during these periodical changes of the mind that bad habits may be left off and better habits cultivated. Fortunate for the human being that his mind is undergoing a continuous process of orderly change.

The mind that is driven by the urge of necessity, or out of love to create, develops more rapidly than does the mind that is never stimulated to greater action than that which is necessary for existence.

The imaginative faculty of the human mind is the greatest piece of machinery ever created. Out of it has come every man-made machine and every man-made object.

Back of the great industries and railroads and banking houses and commercial enterprises is the all-powerful force of IMAGINATION!

Force your mind to THINK! Proceed by combining old ideas into new plans. Every great invention and every outstanding business or industrial achievement that you can name is, in final analysis, but the application of a combination of plans and ideas that have been used before, in some other manner.

"Back of the beating hammer
By which the steel is wrought,
Back of the workshop's clamor
The seeker may find the Thought;
The thought that is ever Master
Of iron and steam and steel,
That rises above disaster
And tramples it under heel.

"The drudge may fret and tinker
Or labor with lusty blows,
But back of him stands the Thinker,
The clear-eyed man who knows;
For into each plow or saber,
Each piece and part and whole,
Must go the brains of labor,
Which gives the work a soul.

"Back of the motor's humming,
Back of the bells that ring,
Back of the hammer's drumming,
Back of the cranes that swing,
There is the Eye which scans them,
Watching through stress and strain,
There is the Mind which plans them–
Back of the brawn, the Brain.

"Might of the roaring boiler,
Force of the engine's thrust,
Strength of the sweating toiler,

Greatly in these we trust;
But back of them stands the schemer,
The Thinker who drives things through,
Back of the job–the Dreamer
Who's making the dream come true."

Six months or a year from now come back and read this essay again and you will observe how much more you will get from it than you did at first reading. TIME gives the law of evolution a chance to expand your mind so it can see and understand more.

Lesson Nine: HABIT OF DOING MORE THAN PAID FOR

It may seem to be a departure from the subject of this lesson to start the lesson with a discussion of love, but, if you will reserve your opinion until you have completed the lesson, you may be ready to agree that the subject of love could not have been omitted without impairing the value of the lesson.

The word "love" is here used in an all-embracing sense!

There are many objects, motives and people which arouse one's love-nature. There is some work which we do not like, some that we do like moderately, and, under certain conditions, there may be work which we actually LOVE!

Great artists, for example, generally love their work. The day laborer, on the other hand, usually not only dislikes his work, but may actually hate it.

Work which one does merely for the sake of earning a living is seldom liked. More often it is disliked, or even hated.

When engaged in work which he loves, a man may labor for an unbelievably long period of hours without becoming fatigued. Work that a man dislikes or hates brings on fatigue very quickly.

A man's endurance, therefore, depends very largely on the extent to which he likes, dislikes or loves that which he is doing.

We are here laying the foundation, as you will of course observe, for the statement of one of the most important laws of this philosophy, viz.:

A man is most efficient and will more quickly and easily succeed when engaged in work that he loves, or work that he performs in behalf of some person whom he loves.

Whenever the element of love enters into any task that one performs, the quality of the work becomes immediately improved and the quantity increased, without a corresponding increase in the fatigue by the work.

Some years ago a group of socialists, or perhaps they called themselves "co-operators," organized a colony in Louisiana, purchased several hundred acres of farm land, and started to work out an ideal which they believed would give them greater happiness in life and fewer of the worried through a system that provided each person with work at the sort of labor he liked best.

Their idea was to pay no wages to anyone. Each person did the work he liked best, or that for which he might be best equipped, and the products of their combined labors became the property of all. They had their own dairy, their own brick-making plant, their own cattle, poultry, etc. They had their own schools and a printing plant through which they published a paper.

A Swedish gentleman from Minnesota joined the colony, and at his own request he was placed at work in the printing plant. Very soon he complained that he did not like the work, so he was changed and put to work on the farm, operating a tractor. Two days of this was all he could stand, so he again applied for a transfer, and was assigned to the dairy. He could not get along with the cows, so he was once more changed, to the laundry, where he lasted but one day. One by one he tried every job on the works, but liked none of them. It had begun to look as if he did not fit in with the co-operative idea of living, and he was about to withdraw when someone happened to think of one job he had not yet tried–in the brick plant, so he was given a wheelbarrow and put to work wheeling bricks from the kilns and stacking them in piles, in the brick yard. A week's time went by and no complaint was registered by him. When asked if he liked his job he replied, "This ban chust the job I like."

Imagine anyone preferring a job wheeling bricks! However, that job suited the Swede's nature, he worked alone, at a task which called for no thought, and placed upon him no responsibility, which was just what he wanted.

He remained at the job until all the bricks had been wheeled out and stacked, then withdrew from the colony because there was no more brick work to be done. "The nice quiet job ban finished, so I yank I ban go back to Minney-so-tie," and back to "Minney-so-tie" he went!

When a man is engaged in work that he loves it is no hardship for him to do more work and better work than that for which he is paid, and for this very reason every man owes it to himself to do his best to find the sort of work he likes best.

I have a perfect right to offer this advice to the students of this philosophy for the reason that I have followed it, myself, without reason to regret having done so.

This seems to be an appropriate place to inject a little personal history concerning both the author and the Law of Success philosophy, the purpose of which is to show that labor performed in a spirit of love for the sake of the labor, itself, never has been and never will be lost.

This entire lesson is devoted to the offering of evidence that it really pays to render more service and better service than one is paid to render. What an empty and useless effort this would be if the author had not, himself, practiced this rule long enough to be able to say just how it works out.

For over a quarter of a century I have been engaged in the labor of love out of which this philosophy has been developed, and I am perfectly sincere when I repeat that which I have stated elsewhere in this course, that I have been amply paid for my labors, by the pleasure I have had as I went along, even if I received nothing more.

My labors on this philosophy made it necessary, many years ago, for me to choose between immediate monetary returns, which I might have enjoyed by directing my efforts along purely commercial lines, and remuneration that comes in later years, and which is represented by both the usual financial standards and other forms of pay which can be measured only in terms of accumulated knowledge that enables one to enjoy the world about him more keenly.

The man who engages in work that he loves best does not always have the support, in his choice, of his closest friends and relatives.

Combating negative suggestions from friends and relatives has required an alarming proportion of my energies, during the years that I have been engaged in research work for the purpose of gathering, organizing, classifying and testing the material which has gone into this course.

These personal references are made solely for the purpose of showing the students of this philosophy that seldom, if ever, can one hope to engage in the work one loves best without meeting with obstacles of some nature. Generally, the chief obstacles in the way of one engaging in the sort of work one loves best is that it may not be the work which brings the greatest remuneration at the start.

To offset this disadvantage, however, the one who engages in the sort of work he loves is generally rewarded with two very decided benefits, namely; first, he usually finds in such work the greatest of all rewards, HAPPINESS, which is priceless, and secondly, his actual reward in money, when averaged over a life-time of effort, is generally much greater, for the reason that labor which is performed in a spirit of love is usually greater in quantity and finer in quality than that which is performed solely for money.

The most embarrassing and, I might without any intention of disrespect say, the most disastrous opposition to my choice of a life-work came from my wife. This, perhaps, will explain why I have made frequent references, in many of the lessons of this course, to the fact that a man's wife may either "make" or "break" him, according to the extent to which she gives or withholds co-operation and encouragement in connection with his chosen work.

My wife's idea was that I should accept a salaried position that would insure a regular monthly income, because I had shown, by the few salaried positions I had held, that I had marketable ability which should command an income of from $6,000.00 to $10,000.00 a year without any very great effort on my part.

In a way I saw my wife's viewpoint and was in sympathy with it, because we had young growing children coming on who needed clothes and education, and a regular salary, even though it were not large, seemed to be a necessity.

Despite this logical argument, however, I chose to override my wife's counsel. Came, then, to her rescue, the combined forces of her family and mine, and collectively they charged me, head-on, with what amounted to a command to right-about-face and settle down on a salary basis.

Studying other people might be all right for a man who had the time to spend in this "unprofitable" manner, they reasoned, but for a young married man with a growing family this seemed hardly the thing to do.

But I remained adamant! I had made my choice and I was determined to stand by it. The opposition did not yield to my viewpoint, but gradually, of course, it melted away. Meanwhile, the knowledge that my choice had worked at least a temporary hardship on my family, combined with the thought that my dearest friends and relatives were not in harmony with me, greatly increased my labors.

Fortunately, not all of my friends believed my choice unwise!

There were a few friends who not only believed I was following a course that would ultimately bring me out somewhere near the top of the mountain of useful achievement, but, in addition to believing in my plans, they actually went out of their way to encourage me not to be whipped by either adversity or the opposition of relatives.

Of this small group of faithful ones who gave me encouragement at a time when it was badly needed, perhaps one man should have the fullest credit, and this man is Edwin C. Barnes, a business associate of Thomas A. Edison.

Mr. Barnes became interested in my chosen work nearly twenty years ago, and I owe it to him to state here that had it not been for his unwavering faith in the soundness of the Law of Success philosophy I would have yielded to the persuasion of my friends and sought the way of least resistance via the salary route.

This would have saved me much grief and an almost endless amount of criticism, but it would have wrecked the hopes of a life-time, and in the end I would in all probability have lost, also, the finest and most desirable of all things, HAPPINESS! For I have been extremely happy in my work, even during the periods when the remuneration it brought me could be measured by nothing but a mountain of debts which I could not for the moment pay.

Perhaps this may explain, to some extent, why the subject of slavery through debt was so extensively emphasized in Lesson Four, on the Habit of Saving.

We want that lesson to "sink in."

Edwin Barnes not only believed in the soundness of the Law of Success philosophy, but his own financial success had demonstrated, as had also his close business relationship with the greatest inventor on earth, that he had the right to speak with authority on the subject of the laws through which success may be achieved.

I began my work of research with the belief that success could be attained, by anyone with reasonable intelligence and a real desire to succeed, by following certain (then by me unknown) rules of procedure. I wanted to know what these rules were and how they could be applied.

Mr. Barnes believed as I did. Moreover, he was in a position to know that the astounding achievements of his business associate, Mr. Edison, came about entirely through the application of some of the principles which later were tested and included as a part of this philosophy. From his way of thinking it seemed that the accumulation of money, enjoying peace of mind and finding happiness could be brought about by the application of never-varying laws which anyone might master and apply.

That was my belief, also. That belief has now been transformed into not merely a provable, but a PROVED reality, as I hope every student of this course will have reason to understand when the course shall have been mastered.

Please keep in mind that during all these years of research I was not only applying the law covered by this lesson, by DOING MORE THAN PAID FOR, but, I was going much further than this by doing work for which I did not, at the time I was doing it, hope ever to receive pay.

Thus, out of years of chaos, adversity and opposition this philosophy was finally completed and reduced to manuscripts, ready for publication.

For a time nothing happened!

I was resting on my oars, so to speak, before taking the next step toward placing the philosophy in the hands of people who I had reason to believe would welcome it.

"God moves in a mysterious way, His wonders to perform!"

During the earlier years of my experience I thought these words to be empty and meaningless, but I have since modified my belief considerably.

I was invited to deliver an address in Canton, Ohio. My coming had been well advertised and there was reason to expect that I would have a large audience. To the contrary, conflicting meetings being held by two large groups of businessmen reduced my audience to the lucky number of "thirteen."

It has always been my belief that a man should do his best, regardless of how much he receives for his services, or the number of people he may be serving or the class of people served. I went at my subject as though the hall were filled. Somehow there arose in me a sort of feeling of resentment on account of the way the "wheel of fate" had turned against me, and if I ever made a convincing speech I made it that night.

Down deep in my heart, however, I thought I had failed!

I did not know until the next day that I was making history the night before that was destined to give the Law of Success philosophy its first real impetus.

One of the men who sat in my audience, as one of the "thirteen," was the late Don R. Mellett, who was then the publisher of the Canton Daily News, brief reference to whom I made in the Introductory Lesson of this course.

After I had finished speaking I slipped out at the back door and returned to my hotel, not wanting to face any of my "thirteen" victims on the way out.

The next day I was invited to Mr. Mellett's office.

Inasmuch as it was he who had taken the initiative by inviting me in to see him I left it to him to do most of the talking. He began in something like this fashion:

"Would you mind telling me your entire life-story, from the days of your early childhood on up to the present?"

I told him I would do so if he could stand the burden of listening to so long a narrative. He said he could, but before I began he cautioned me not to omit the unfavorable side.

"What I wish you to do," said he, "is to mix the fat with the lean and let me take a look at your very soul, not from its most favorable side, but from all sides."

For three hours I talked while Mellett listened!

I omitted nothing. I told him of my struggles, of my mistakes, of my impulses to be dishonest when the tides of fortune swept against me too swiftly, and of my better judgment which prevailed in the end, but only after my conscience and I had engaged in prolonged combat. I told him how I conceived the idea of organizing the Law of Success philosophy, how I had gone about gathering the data that had gone into the philosophy, of the tests I had made which resulted in the elimination of some of the data and the retention of other parts of it.

After I had finished Mellett said: "I wish to ask you a very personal question, and I hope you will answer it as frankly as you have told the remainder of your story. Have you accumulated any money from your efforts, and, if not, do you know why you have not?"

"No!" I replied. "I have accumulated nothing but experience and knowledge and a few debts, and the reason, while it may not be sound, is easily explained. The truth is that I have been so busy all these years in trying to eliminate some of my own ignorance so I could intelligently gather and organize the data that have gone into the Law of Success philosophy, that I have had neither the opportunity nor the inclination to turn my efforts to making money."

The serious look on Don Mellett's face, much to my surprise, softened into a smile as he laid his hand on my shoulder and said:

"I knew the answer before you stated it, but I wondered if you knew it. You probably know that you are not the only man who has had to sacrifice immediate monetary remuneration for the sake of gathering knowledge, for in truth your experience has been that of every philosopher from the time of Socrates down to the present."

Those words fell as the sound of music upon my ears!

I had made one of the most embarrassing admissions of my life; I had laid my soul bare, admitting temporary defeat at almost every cross-road which I had passed in my struggles, and I had capped all this off by admitting that an exponent of the Law of Success was, himself, a temporary failure!

How incongruous it seemed! I felt stupid, humiliated and embarrassed as I sat in front of the most searching pair of eyes and the most inquisitive man I had ever met.

The absurdity of it all came over me like a flash–THE PHILOSOPHY OF SUCCESS, CREATED AND BROADCASTED BY A MAN WHO WAS OBVIOUSLY A FAILURE!

This thought struck me so forcibly that I expressed it in words.

"What?" Mellett exclaimed, "a failure?

"Surely you know the difference between failure and temporary defeat," he continued.

"No man is a failure who creates a single idea, much less an entire philosophy, that serves to soften the disappointments and minimize the hardships of generations yet unborn."

I wondered what was the object of this interview. My first conjecture was that Mellett wanted some facts on which to base an attack, in his newspaper, on the Law of Success philosophy. Perhaps this thought grew out of some of my previous experiences with newspaper men, a few of whom had been antagonistic toward me. At any rate, I decided at the outset of the interview to give him the facts, without embellishment come from it what would.

Before I left Mellett's office we had become business partners, with the understanding that he would resign as publisher of the Canton Daily News and take over the management of all my affairs, as soon as this could be arranged.

Meanwhile, I began writing a series of Sunday feature-page editorials which were published in the Canton Daily News, based upon the Law of Success philosophy.

One of these editorials (the one entitled "Failure," which appears in the back of one of the lessons of this course) came to the attention of judge Elbert H. Gary, who was at that time the Chairman of the Board of the United States Steel Corporation. This resulted in the opening of communication between Mellett and Judge Gary, which, in turn, led to judge Gary's offer to purchase the Law of Success course for the use of the employees of the Steel Corporation, in the manner described in the Introductory Lesson.

The tides of fortune had begun to turn in my favor!

The seeds of service which I had been sowing over a long period of toilsome years, by DOING MORE THAN PAID FOR, were beginning to germinate at last!

Despite the fact that my partner was assassinated before our plans had much more than started, and Judge Gary died before the Law of Success philosophy could be rewritten so it conformed to his requirements, the "love's labor lost" on that fateful night, when I spoke to an audience of thirteen in Canton, Ohio, started a chain of events which now move rapidly without thought or effort on my part.

It is no abuse of confidences to enumerate here a few of the events which show that no labor of love is ever performed at a total loss, and that those who render more service and better service than that for which they are paid sooner or later receive pay for much more than they actually do.

As this lesson is ready to go to the publisher some of the following well-known concerns are considering favorably the purchase of the Law of Success course for all their employees, while others have actually arranged for the purchase of the course:

Mr. Daniel Willard, President of the Baltimore & Ohio Railroad Co.
Indian Refining Company
Standard Oil Company
New York Life Insurance Company
The Postal Telegraph Commercial-Cable Company
The Pierce-Arrow Motor Car Company
The Cadillac Motor Car Company
And some fifty other concerns of a similar size.

In addition to this, a newly organized club for boys, similar in nature to the Y. M. C. A., has contracted for the use of the Law of Success course as the basis of its educational program, and estimates that it will distribute more than 100,000 courses of the philosophy within the next two years.

Quite aside from these sources of distribution, the Ralston University Press, of Meriden, Conn., has contracted to publish and distribute the course to individuals throughout the United States, and perhaps in some foreign countries. How many courses they will distribute cannot be accurately estimated, but when one stops to consider the fact that they have a mailing list of approximately

800,000 people who have faith in anything they offer for sale, it seems very reasonable to suppose that their distribution will place tens of thousands of courses in the hands of men and women who are earnestly searching for the knowledge conveyed by the Law of Success philosophy.

Perhaps it is unnecessary, but I wish to explain that my only object in here relating the story of how the Law of Success philosophy has gained the recognition described is to show how the law upon which this lesson is based actually works out in the practical affairs of life.

If I could have made this analysis without the use of the personal pronoun I would have done so.

With this background of history concerning the Law of Success philosophy as a whole, and this lesson in particular, you are better prepared to accept as sound the law on which this lesson is based.

There are more than a score of sound reasons why you should develop the habit of performing more service and better service than that for which you are paid, despite the fact that a large majority of the people are not rendering such service.

There are two reasons, however, for rendering such service, which transcend, in importance, all the others; namely,

First: By establishing a reputation as being a person who always renders more service and better service than that for which you are paid, you will benefit by comparison with those around you who do not render such service, and the contrast will be so noticeable that there will be keen competition for your services, no matter what your life-work may be.

It would be an insult to your intelligence to offer proof of the soundness of this statement, because it is obviously sound. Whether you are preaching sermons, practicing law, writing books, teaching school, or digging ditches, you will become more valuable and you will be able to command greater pay the minute you gain recognition as a person who does more than that for which he is paid.

Second: By far the most important reason why you should render more service than that for which you are paid, a reason that is basic and fundamental in nature, may be described in this way: Suppose that you wished to develop a strong right arm, and suppose that you tried to do so by tying the arm to your side with a rope, thus taking it out of use and giving it a long rest. Would disuse bring strength, or would it bring atrophy and weakness, resulting, finally, in your being compelled to have the arm removed?

You know that if you wished a strong right arm you could develop such an arm only by giving it the hardest sort of use. Take a look at the arm of a blacksmith if you wish to know how an arm may be made strong. Out of resistance comes strength. The strongest oak tree of the forest is not the one that is protected from the storm and hidden from the sun, but it is the one that stands in the open, where it is compelled to struggle for its existence against the winds and rains and the scorching sun.

It is through the operation of one of Nature's unvarying laws that struggle and resistance develop strength, and the purpose of this lesson is to show you how to harness this law and so use it that it will aid you in your struggle for success. By performing more service and better service than that for which you are paid, you not only exercise your service-rendering qualities, and thereby develop skill and ability of an extraordinary sort, but you build reputation that is valuable. If you form the habit of rendering such service you will become so adept in your work that you can command greater remuneration than those who do not perform such service. You will eventually develop sufficient strength to enable you to remove yourself from any undesirable station in life, and no one can or will desire to stop you.

If you are an employee you can make yourself so valuable, through this habit of performing more service than that for which you are paid, that you can practically set your own wages and no sensible employer will try to stop you. If your employer should be so unfortunate as to try to withhold from you the compensation to which you are entitled, this will not long remain as a handicap because other employers will discover this unusual quality and offer you employment.

The very fact that most people are rendering as little service as they can possibly get by with serves as an advantage to all who are rendering more service than that for which they are paid, because it enables all who do this to profit by comparison. You can "get by" if you render as little service as possible, but that is all you will get; and when work is slack and retrenchment sets in, you will be one of the first to be dismissed.

For more than twenty-five years I have carefully studied men with the object of ascertaining why some achieve noteworthy success while others with just as much ability do not get ahead; and it seems significant that every person whom I have observed applying this principle of rendering more service than that for which he was paid, was holding a better position and receiving more pay than those who merely performed sufficient service to "get by" with.

Personally I never received a promotion in my life that I could not trace directly to recognition that I had gained by rendering more service and better service than that for which I was paid.

I am stressing the importance of making this principle a habit as a means of enabling an employee to promote himself to a higher position, with greater pay, for the reason that this course will be studied by thousands of young men and young women who work for others. However, the principle applies to the employer or to the professional man or woman just the same as to the employee.

Observance of this principle brings a two-fold reward. First, it brings the reward of greater material gain than that enjoyed by those who do not observe it; and, second, it brings that reward of happiness and satisfaction which come only to those who render such service. If you receive no pay except that which comes in your pay envelope, you are underpaid, no matter how much money that envelope contains.

My wife has just returned from the Public Library with a book for me to read. The book is entitled "Observation; Every Man His Own University," by Russell H. Conwell. By chance I opened this book at the beginning of the chapter entitled Every Man's University, and, as I read it through, my first impulse was to recommend that you go to the Public Library and read the entire book; but, upon second thought, I will not do this; instead, I will recommend that you purchase the book and read it, not once but a hundred times, because it covers the subject of this lesson as though it had been written for that purpose; covers it in a far more impressive manner than I could do it.

The following quotation from the chapter entitled Every Man's University will give you an idea of the golden nugget of truth to be found throughout the book:

> "The intellect can be made to look far beyond the range of what men and women ordinarily see, but not all the colleges in the world can alone confer this power–this is the reward of self-culture; each must acquire it for himself; and perhaps this is why the power of observing deeply and widely is so much oftener found in those men and those women who have never crossed the threshold of any college but the University of Hard Knocks."

Read that book as a part of this lesson, because it will prepare you to profit by the philosophy and psychology upon which the lesson is built.

We will now analyze the law upon which this entire lesson is founded, namely–

THE LAW OF INCREASING RETURNS!

Let us begin our analysis by showing how Nature employs this law in behalf of the tillers of the soil. The farmer carefully prepares the ground, then sows his wheat and waits while the Law of Increasing Returns brings back the seed he has sown, plus a many-fold increase.

But for this Law of Increasing Returns, man would perish, because he could not make the soil produce sufficient food for his existence. There would be no advantage to be gained by sowing a field of wheat if the harvest yield did not return more than was sown.

With this vital "tip" from Nature, which we may gather from the wheat fields, let us proceed to appropriate this Law of Increasing Returns and learn how to apply it to the service we render, to the end that it may yield returns in excess of and out of proportion to the effort put forth.

First of all, let us emphasize the fact that there is no trickery or chicanery connected with this Law, although quite a few seem not to have learned this great truth, judging by the number who spend all of their efforts either trying to get something for nothing, or something for less than its true value.

It is to no such end that we recommend the use of the Law of Increasing Returns, for no such end is possible, within the broad meaning of the word success.

Another remarkable and noteworthy feature of the Law of Increasing Returns is the fact that it may be used by those who purchase service with as great returns as it can be by those who render service, for Proof of which we have but to study the effects of Henry Ford's famous Five-Dollar-a-day minimum wage scale which he inaugurated some years ago.

Those who are familiar with the facts say that Mr. Ford was not playing the part of a philanthropist when he inaugurated this minimum wage scale; but, to the contrary, he was merely taking advantage of a sound business principle which has probably yielded him greater returns, in both dollars and goodwill, than any other single policy ever inaugurated at the Ford plant.

By paying more wages than the average, he received more service and better service than the average!

At a single stroke, through the inauguration of that minimum wage policy, Ford attracted the best labor on the market and placed a premium upon the privilege of working in his plant.

I have no authentic figures at hand bearing on the subject, but I have sound reason to conjecture that for every five dollars Ford spent, under this policy, he received at least seven dollars and fifty cents' worth of service. I have, also, sound reason to believe that this policy enabled Ford to reduce the cost of supervision, because employment in his plant became so desirable that no worker would care to run the risk of losing his position by "soldiering" on the job or rendering poor service.

Where other employers were forced to depend upon costly supervision in order to get the service to which they were entitled, and for which they were paying, Ford got the same or better service by the less expensive method of placing a premium upon employment in his plant.

Marshall Field was probably the leading merchant of his time, and the great Field store, in Chicago, stands today as a monument to his ability to apply the Law of Increasing Returns.

A customer purchased an expensive lace waist at the Field store, but did not wear it. Two years later she gave it to her niece as a wedding present. The niece quietly returned the waist to the Field store and exchanged it for other merchandise, despite the fact that it had been out for more than two years and was then out of style.

Not only did the Field store take back the waist, but, what is of more importance it did so without argument!

Of course there was no obligation, moral or legal, on the part of the store to accept the return of the waist at that late date, which makes the transaction all the more significant.

The waist was originally priced at fifty dollars, and of course it had to be thrown on the bargain counter and sold for whatever it would bring, but the keen student of human nature will understand that the Field store not only did not lose anything on the waist, but it actually profited by the transaction to an extent that cannot be measured in mere dollars.

The woman who returned the waist knew that she was not entitled to a rebate; therefore, when the store gave her that to which she was not entitled the transaction won her as a permanent customer. But the effect of the transaction did not end here; it only began; for this woman spread the news of the "fair treatment" she had received at the Field store, far and near. It was the talk of the women of her set for many days, and the Field store received more advertising from the transaction than it could have purchased in any other way with ten times the value of the waist.

The success of the Field store was built largely upon Marshall Field's understanding of the Law of Increasing Returns, which prompted him to adopt, as a part of his business policy, the slogan, "The customer is always right."

When you do only that for which you are paid, there is nothing out of the ordinary to attract favorable comment about the transaction; but, when you willingly do more than that for which you are paid, your action attracts the favorable attention of all who are affected by the transaction, and goes another step toward establishing a reputation that will eventually set the Law of Increasing Returns to work in your behalf, for this reputation will create a demand for your services, far and wide.

Carol Downes went to work for W. C. Durant, the automobile manufacturer, in a minor position. He is now Mr. Durant's right-hand man, and the president of one of his automobile distributing companies. He promoted himself into this profitable position solely through the aid of the Law of Increasing Returns, which he put into operation by rendering more service and better service than that for which he was paid.

In a recent visit with Mr. Downes I asked him to tell me how he managed to gain promotion so rapidly. In a few brief sentences he told the whole story.

"When I first went to work with Mr. Durant," said he, "I noticed that he always remained at the office long after all the others had gone home for the day, and I made it my business to stay there, also. No one asked me to stay, but I thought someone should be there to give Mr. Durant any assistance he might need. Often he would look around for someone to bring him a letter file, or render some other trivial service, and always he found me there ready to serve him. He got into the habit of calling on me; that is about all there is to the story."

"He got into the habit of calling on me!"

Read that sentence again, for it is full of meaning of the richest sort.

Why did Mr. Durant get into the habit of calling on Mr. Downes? Because Mr. Downes made it his business to be on hand where he would be seen. He deliberately placed himself in Mr. Durant's way in order that he might render service that would place the Law of Increasing Returns back of him.

Was he told to do this? No!

Was he paid to do it? Yes! He was paid by the opportunity it offered for him to bring himself to the attention of the man who had it within his power to promote him.

We are now approaching the most important part of this lesson, because this is an appropriate place at which to suggest that you have the same opportunity to make use of the Law of Increasing Returns that Mr. Downes had, and you can go about the application of the Law in exactly the same way that he did, by being on hand and ready to volunteer your services in the performance of work which others may shirk because they are not paid to do it.

Stop! Don't say it-don't even think it if you have the slightest intention of springing that old timeworn phrase entitled, "But my employer is different."

Of course he is different. All men are different in most respects, but they are very much alike in this–they are somewhat selfish; in fact they are selfish enough not to want a man such as Carol Downes to cast his lot with their competitor, and this very selfishness may be made to serve you as an asset and not as a liability if–You have the good judgment to make yourself so useful that the person to whom you sell your services cannot get along without you.

One of the most advantageous promotions I ever received came about through an incident which seemed so insignificant that it appeared to be unimportant. One Saturday afternoon, a lawyer, whose office was on the same floor as that of my employer, came in and asked if I knew where he could get a stenographer to do some work which he was compelled to finish that day.

I told him that all of our stenographers had gone to the ball game, and that I would have been gone had he called five minutes later, but that I would be very glad to stay and do his work as I could go to a ball game any day and his work had to be done then.

I did the work for him, and when he asked how much he owed me I replied, "Oh, about a thousand dollars, as long as it is you; if it were for anyone else, I wouldn't charge anything." He smiled, and thanked me.

Little did I think, when I made that remark, that he would ever pay me a thousand dollars for that afternoon's work, but he did. Six months later, after I had entirely forgotten the incident, he called on me again, and asked how much salary I was receiving. When I told him, he informed me that he was ready to pay me that thousand dollars which I had laughingly said I would charge him for the work I had performed for him, and he did pay it by giving me a position at a thousand dollars a year increase in salary.

Unconsciously, I had put the Law of Increasing Returns to work in my behalf that afternoon, by giving up the ball game and rendering a service which was obviously rendered out of a desire to be helpful and not for the sake of a monetary consideration.

It was not my duty to give up my Saturday afternoon, but–It was my privilege!

Furthermore, it was a profitable privilege, because it yielded me a thousand dollars in cash and a much more responsible position than the one I had formerly occupied.

It was Carol Downes' duty to be on hand until the usual quitting time, but it was his privilege to remain at his post after the other workers had gone, and that privilege properly exercised brought him greater responsibilities and a salary that yields him more in a year than he would have made in a lifetime in the position he occupied before he exercised the privilege.

I have been thinking for more than twenty-five years of this privilege of performing more service and better service than that for which we are paid, and my thoughts have led me to the conclusion that a single hour devoted each day to rendering service for which we are not paid, can be made to yield bigger returns than we received from the entire remainder of the day during which we are merely performing our duty.

(We are still in the neighborhood of the most important part of this lesson, therefore, think and assimilate as you pass over these pages.)

The Law of Increasing Returns is no invention of mine, nor do I lay claim to the discovery of the principle of rendering more service and better service than paid for, as a means of utilizing this Law.

I merely appropriated them, after many years of careful observation of those forces which enter into the attainment of success, just as you will appropriate them after you understand their significance.

You might begin this appropriation process now by trying an experiment which may easily open your eyes and place back of your efforts powers that you did not know you possessed.

Let me caution you, however, not to attempt this experiment in the same spirit in which a certain woman experimented with that passage which says something to the effect that if you have faith the size of a grain of mustard, and say to yonder mountain be removed to some other place, it will be removed. This woman lived near a high mountain that she could see from her front door; therefore, as she retired that night she commanded the mountain to remove itself to some other place.

Next morning she jumped out of bed, rushed to the door and looked out, but lo! the mountain was still there. Then she said:

"Just as I had expected! I knew it would be there."

I am going to ask you to approach this experiment with full faith that it will mark one of the most important turning-points of your entire life. I am going to ask you to make the object of this experiment the removal of a mountain that is standing where your temple of success should stand, but where it never can stand until you have removed the mountain.

You may never have noticed the mountain to which I refer, but it is standing there in your way just the same, unless you have already discovered and removed it.

"And what is this mountain?" you ask!

It is the feeling that you have been cheated unless you receive material pay for all the service you render.

That feeling may be unconsciously expressing itself and destroying the very foundation of your temple of success in scores of ways that you have not observed.

In the very lowly bred type of humanity, this feeling usually seeks outward expression in terms something like this:

"I am not paid to do this and I'll be blankety-blankety-blank if I'll do it!"

You know the type to which reference is made; you have met with it many times, but you have never found a single person of this type who was successful, and you never will.

Success must be attracted through understanding and application of laws which are as immutable as is the law of gravitation. It cannot be driven into the corner and captured as one would capture a wild steer. For this reason you are requested to enter into the following experiment with the object of familiarizing yourself with one of the most important of these laws; namely, the Law of Increasing Returns.

The experiment:

During the next six months make it your business to render useful service to at least one person every day, for which you neither expect nor accept monetary pay.

Go at this experiment with faith that it will uncover for your use one of the most powerful laws that enter into the achievement of enduring success, and you will not be disappointed.

The rendering of this service may take on any one of more than a score of forms. For example, it may be rendered personally to one or more specific persons; or it may be rendered to your employer, in the nature of work that you perform after hours.

Again, it may be rendered to entire strangers whom you never expect to see again. It matters not to whom you render this service so long as you render it with willingness, and solely for the purpose of benefitting others.

If you carry out this experiment in the proper attitude of mind, you will discover that which all others who have become familiar with the law upon which it is based have discovered; namely, that-You can no more render service without receiving compensation than you can withhold the rendering of it without suffering the loss of reward.

"Cause and effect, means and ends, seed and fruit, cannot be severed," says Emerson; "for the effect already blooms in the cause, the end pre-exists in the means, the fruit in the seed."

"If you serve an ungrateful master, serve him the more. Put God in your debt. Every stroke shall be repaid. The longer the payment is withholden, the better for you; for compound interest on compound interest is the rate and usage of this exchequer."

"The law of Nature is, Do the thing and you shall have the power; but they who do not the thing have not the power."

"Men suffer all their life long, under the foolish superstition that they can be cheated. But it is as impossible for a man to be cheated by anyone but himself, as for a thing to be, and not to be, at the same time. There is a third silent party to all our bargains. The nature and soul of things takes on itself the guaranty of fulfillment of every contract, so that honest service cannot come to loss."

Before you begin the experiment that you have been requested to undertake, read Emerson's essay on Compensation, for it will go a very long way toward helping you to understand why you are making the experiment.

Perhaps you have read Compensation before. Read it again! One of the strange phenomena that you will observe about this essay may be found in the fact that every time you read it you will discover new truths that you did not notice during previous readings.

A few years ago I was invited to deliver the graduation address before the students of an eastern college. During my address I dwelt at length, and with all the emphasis at my command, on the importance of rendering more service and better service than that for which one is paid.

After the address was delivered, the president and the secretary of the college invited me to luncheon. While we were eating, the secretary turned to the president and said:

"I have just found out what this man is doing. He is putting himself ahead in the world by first helping others to get ahead."

In that brief statement he had epitomized the most important part of my philosophy on the subject of success.

It is literally true that you can succeed best and quickest by helping others to succeed.

Some ten years ago, when I was engaged in the advertising business, I built my entire clientele by the application of the fundamentals upon which this lesson is founded. By having my name placed on the follow-up lists of various mail order houses, I received their sales literature. When I received a sales letter or a booklet or a folder which I believed I could improve I went right to work on it and made the improvement, then sent it back to the firm that had sent it to me, with a letter stating that this was but a trifling sample of what I could do-that there were plenty of other good ideas where that one came from-and, that I would be glad to render regular service for a monthly fee.

Invariably this brought an order for my services.

On one occasion I remember that the firm was dishonest enough to appropriate my idea and use it without paying me for it, but this turned out to be an advantage to me, in this way: A member of the firm who was familiar with the transaction started another business and as a result of the work I had done for his former associates, for which I was not paid, he engaged me to serve him, on a basis that paid me more than double the amount I would have realized from his original firm.

Thus the Law of Compensation gave back to me, and with compound interest added, that which I had lost by rendering service to those who were dishonest.

If I were looking for a profitable field of employment today, I could find it by again putting into action this plan of rewriting sales literature as a means of creating a market for my services. Perhaps I would find others who would appropriate my ideas without paying for them, but by and large people would not do this for the simple reason that it would be more profitable to them to deal fairly with me and thereby avail themselves of my continued services.

Several years ago I was invited to deliver a lecture before the students of the Palmer School, at Davenport, Iowa. My manager completed arrangements for me to accept the invitation under the regular terms in effect at that time, which were $100.00 for the lecture and my traveling expenses.

When I arrived at Davenport, I found a reception committee awaiting me at the depot and that evening I was given one of the warmest welcomes I had ever received during my public career, up to that time. I met many delightful people from whom I gathered many valuable facts that were of benefit to me; therefore, when I was asked to make out my expense account so the school could give me a check, I told them that I had received my pay, many times over, by that which I had learned while I was there. I refused my fee and returned to my office, in Chicago, feeling well repaid for the trip. The following morning Dr. Palmer went before the two thousand students of his school and announced what I had said about feeling repaid by what I had learned, and added:

"In the twenty years that I have been conducting this school I have had scores of speakers address the student body, but this is the first time I ever knew a man to refuse his fee because he felt that he had been repaid for his services in other ways. This man is the editor of a national magazine and I advise every one of you to subscribe for that magazine, because such a man as this must have much that each of you will need when you go into the field and offer your services."

By the middle of that week I had received more than $6,000.00 for subscriptions to the magazine of which I was editor, and during the following two years these same two thousand students and their friends sent in more than $50,000.00 for subscriptions. Tell me, if you can, how or where I could have invested $100.00 as profitably as this, by refusing to accept my $100.00 fee and thereby setting the Law of Increasing Returns to work in my behalf?

We go through two important periods in this life; one is that period during which we are gathering, classifying and organizing knowledge, and the other is that period during which we are struggling for recognition. We must first learn something, which requires more effort than most of us are willing to put into the job; but, after we have learned much that can be of useful service to others, we are still confronted with the problem of convincing them that we can serve them.

One of the most important reasons why we should always be not only ready but willing to render service, is the fact that every time we do so, we gain thereby another opportunity to prove to someone that we have ability; we go just one more step toward gaining the necessary recognition that we must all have.

Instead of saying to the world, "Show me the color of your money and I will show you what I can do," reverse the rule and say, "Let me show you the color of my service so that I may take a look at the color of your money if you like my service."

In 1917 a certain woman who was then nearing the fifty-year milepost of life, was working as a stenographer, at fifteen dollars a week. Judging by the salary she must have been none too competent in that work.

Now note this change:

Last year, this same woman cleared a little over $100,000.00 on the lecture platform.

What bridged that mighty chasm between these two earning capacities? you ask, and I answer:

The habit of performing more service and better service than that for which she was paid, thereby taking advantage of the Law of Increasing Returns.

This woman is well known throughout the country, as she is now a prominent lecturer on the subject of Applied Psychology.

Let me show you how she harnessed the Law of Increasing Returns. First, she goes into a city and delivers a series of fifteen free lectures. All may attend who will, without money and without price. During the delivery of these fifteen lectures she has the opportunity of "selling herself to her audience, and at the end of the series she announces the formation of a class for which she charges twenty-five dollars per student.

That's all there is to her plan!

Where she is commanding a small fortune for a year's work there are scores of much more proficient lecturers who are barely getting enough from their work to pay their expenses, simply because they have not yet familiarized themselves with the fundamentals upon which this lesson is based, as she has done.

Now, I would like to have you stop right here and answer this question:

If a fifty-year-old woman, who has no extraordinary qualifications, can harness the Law of Increasing Returns and make it raise her from the position as stenographer at fifteen dollars a week to that of lecturer at over $100,000.00 a year–why cannot you apply this same law so that it will give you advantages that you do not now possess?

Never mind what is to come in the remainder of this lesson until you have answered this question and answered it AS IT SHOULD BE ANSWERED!

You are struggling, either meekly or earnestly, to make a place for yourself in the world. Perhaps you are exerting enough effort to bring you success of the highest order, if that effort were coupled with and supported by the Law of Increasing Returns.

For this reason, you owe it to yourself to find out just how you can apply this law to best advantage.

Now go back to that question, again; for I am determined that you shall not pass it by lightly,without giving yourself the benefit of at least trying to answer it.

In other words, there is no mistaking the fact that you are being brought face to face with a question that vitally affects your future, and, if you evade it, the fault will be with you.

You may lay this lesson aside after you have read it, and it is your privilege to do so, without making any attempt to profit by it; but, if you do so, you will never again be able to look at yourself in a mirror without being haunted by the feeling that–YOU HAVE DELIBERATELY CHEATED YOURSELF!

Perhaps this is telling the truth in an undiplomatic way; but, when you purchased this course on the Law of Success, you did so because you wanted facts, and you are getting them, without the embellishment of apology.

After you have finished this lesson, if you will go back and review the lessons on Initiative and Leadership and Enthusiasm, you will better understand those lessons.

Those lessons and this one clearly establish the necessity of taking the initiative, following it with aggressive action and doing more than you are paid to do. If you will burn the fundamentals of these three lessons into your consciousness you will be a changed person, and I make this statement regardless of who you are or what your calling may be.

If this plain language has made you angry, I am glad; for it indicates that you can be moved! Now, if you would profit by the counsel of one who has made many more mistakes than you ever made, and for that reason learned a few of the fundamental truths of life, harness this anger and focus it on yourself until it drives you forth to render the service of which you are capable.

If you will do this you can collect a king's ransom as your reward.

Now let us turn our attention to still another important feature of this habit of performing more service and better service than that for which we are paid; namely, the fact that we can develop this habit without asking for permission to do so. Such service may be rendered through your own initiative, without the consent of any person. You do not have to consult those to whom you render the service, for it is a privilege over which you have entire control.

There are many things you could do that would tend to promote your interests, but most of them require the co-operation or the consent of others. If you render less service than that for which you are paid you must do so by leave of the purchaser of the service, or the market for your service will soon cease.

I want you to get the full significance of this right of prerogative, which you have, to render more service and better service than that for which you are paid, for this places squarely upon your shoulders the responsibility of rendering such service, and if you fail to do so, you haven't a plausible excuse to offer or an "alibi upon which to fall back, if you fail in the achievement of your definite chief aim in life.

One of the most essential yet the hardest truths that I have had to learn, is that every person should be his own hardest task-master.

We are all fine builders of "alibis" and creators of "excuses" in support of our shortcomings.

We are not seeking facts and truths as they are, but, as we wish them to be. We prefer honeyed words of flattery to those of cold, unbiased truth, wherein lies the weakest spot of the man-animal.

Furthermore, we are up in arms against those who dare to uncover the truth for our benefit.

One of the most severe shocks I received in the early part of my public career was the knowledge that men are still being crucified for the high crime of telling the truth. I recall an experience I had some ten years ago, with a man who had written a book advertising his business school. He submitted this book to me and paid me to review it and give him my candid opinion of it. I reviewed the book with painstaking care, then did my duty by showing him wherein I believed the book was weak.

Here I learned a great lesson, for that man became so angry that he has never forgiven me for allowing him to look at his book through my eyes. When he asked me to tell him frankly what "criticism" I had to offer of the book, what he really meant was that I should tell him what I saw in the book that I could "compliment."

That's human nature for you!

We court flattery more than we do the truth. I know, because I am human.

All of which is in preparation for the "unkindest cut of all" that I am duty-bound to inflict upon you; namely, to suggest that you have not done as well as you might have done for the reason that you have not applied a sufficient amount of truth set out in Lesson Eight, on Self-control, to charge yourself with your own mistakes and shortcomings.

To do this takes self-control and plenty of it.

If you paid some person who had the ability and the courage to do it, a hundred dollars to strip you of your vanity and conceit and love for flattery, so that you might see the weakest part of your make-up, the price would be reasonable enough.

We go through life stumbling and falling and struggling to our knees, and struggling and falling some more, making asses of ourselves, and going down, finally, in defeat, largely because we either neglect or flatly refuse to learn the truth about ourselves. Since I have come to discover some of my own weaknesses through my work of helping others discover theirs, I blush with shame when I take a retrospective view of life and think how ridiculous I must have seemed in the eyes of those who could see me as I wouldn't see myself.

We parade before the enlarged shadows of our own vanity and imagine that those shadows are our real selves, while the few knowing souls with whom we meet stand in the background and look at us with pity or with scorn. Hold on a minute. I am not through with you yet.

You have paid me to delve into the depths of your real self and give you an introspective inventory of what is there, and I am going to do the job right, as nearly as I can.

Not only have you been fooling yourself as to the real cause of your failures of the past, but you have tried to hang these causes on the door of someone else. When things did not go to suit you, instead of accepting full responsibility for the cause, you have said, "Oh, hang this job! I don't like the way 'they' are treating me, so I'm going to quit!"

Don't deny it!

Now let me whisper a little secret in your ear–a secret which I have had to gather from grief and heartaches and unnecessary punishment of the hardest sort–

Instead of "quitting" the job because there were obstacles to master and difficulties to be overcome, you should have faced the facts and then you would have known that life, itself, is just one long series of mastery of difficulties and obstacles. The measure of a man may be taken very accurately by the extent to which he adapts himself to his environment and makes it his business to accept responsibility for every adversity with which he meets, whether the adversity grows out of a cause within his control or not.

Now, if you feel that I have "panned" you rather severely, have pity on me, O Fellow-Wayfarer, for you surely must know that I have had to punish myself more sorely than I have punished you before I learned the truth that I am here passing on to you for your use and guidance.

I have a few enemies–thank God for them!–for they have been vulgar and merciless enough to say some things about me that forced me to rid myself of some of my most serious shortcomings; mainly those which I did not know I possessed. I have profited by the criticism of these enemies without having to pay them for their services in dollars, although I have paid in other ways.

However, it was not until some years ago that I caught sight of some of my most glaring faults which were brought to my attention as I studied Emerson's essay on Compensation, particularly the following part of it:

"Our strength grows out of our weakness.

"Not until we are pricked, and stung, and sorely shot at, awakens the indignation which arms itself with secret forces. A great man is always willing to be little. While he sits on the cushion of advantage he goes to sleep. When he is pushed, tormented, defeated, he has a chance to learn something; he has been put on his wits, on his manhood; he has gained facts; learned his ignorance; is cured of the insanity of conceit; has got moderation and real skill. The wise man always throws himself on the side of his assailants. It is more his interest than it is theirs to find his weak point. Blame is safer than praise. I hate to be defended in a newspaper. As long as all that is said is said against me, I feel a certain assurance of success. But as soon as honeyed words of praise are spoken of me, I feel as one that lies unprotected before his enemies."

Study this, the philosophy of the immortal Emerson, for it may serve as a modifying force that will temper your metal and prepare you for the battles of life, as carbon tempers the steel.

If you are a very young person, you need to study it all the more, for it often requires the stern realities of many years of experience to prepare one to assimilate and apply this philosophy.

Better that you should understand these great truths as a result of my undiplomatic presentation of them than to be forced to gather them from the less sympathetic sources of cold experience. Experience is a teacher that knows no favorites. When I permit you to profit by the truths I have gathered from the teachings of this cold and unsympathetic teacher called "experience," I am doing my best to show you favoritism, which reminds me, somewhat, of the times when my father used to "do his duty" by me, in the woodshed, always starting with this bit of encouraging philosophy:

"Son, this hurts me worse than it does you."

Thus we approach the close of this lesson without having exhausted the possibilities of the subject; nay, without having more than scratched the surface of it.

There comes to my mind the story of a romance of long ago through which I can leave in your mind the main import of this lesson. This story had its setting in the city of Antioch, in ancient Rome, two thousand Years ago, when the great city of Jerusalem and all the land of Judea were under the oppressive heel of Rome.

The star figure of the story was a young Jew by the name of Ben Hur, who was falsely accused of crime and sentenced to hard labor, at the galley's oar. Chained to a bench in the galley, and being forced to tug wearily at the oars, Ben Hur developed a powerful body. Little did his tormentors know that out of his punishment would grow the strength with which he would one day gain his freedom. Perhaps Ben Hur, himself, had no such hopes.

Then came the day of the chariot races: the day that was destined to break the chains that bound Ben Hur to the oars of the galley and give him his freedom.

One span of horses was without a driver. In desperation the owner sought the aid of the young slave because of his mighty arms, and begged him to take the place of the missing driver.

As Ben Hur picked up the reins, a mighty cry went up from the onlookers.

"Look! Look! Those arms! Where did you get them?" they howled, and Ben Hur answered:

"At the galley's oar!"

The race was on. With those mighty arms Ben Hur calmly drove that charging span of horses on to victory; victory that won for him his freedom.

Life, itself, is a great chariot race, and the victory goes only to those who have developed the strength of character and determination and will-power to win.

What matters it that we develop this strength through cruel confinement at the galley's oar, as long as we use it so that it brings us, finally, to victory and freedom.

It is an unvarying law that strength grows out of resistance. If we pity the poor blacksmith who swings a five pound hammer all day long, we must also admire the wonderful arm that he develops in doing it.

"Because of the dual constitution of all things, in labor as in life, there can be no cheating," says Emerson. "The thief steals from himself. The swindler swindles himself. For the real price of labor is knowledge and virtue, whereof wealth and creditare signs. The signs, like paper money, may be counterfeited or stolen, but that which they represent; namely, knowledge and virtue, cannot be counterfeited or stolen."

Henry Ford receives fifteen thousand letters a week from people who are begging for a part of his wealth; yet how few of these poor ignorant souls understand that Ford's real wealth is not measured by the dollars he has in the bank, nor the factories he owns, but by the reputation he has gained through the rendering of useful service at a reasonable price.

And how did he gain that reputation?

Certainly not by rendering as little service as possible and collecting for it all he could filch from the purchasers.

The very warp and woof of Ford's business philosophy is this:

"Give the people the best product at the lowest price possible."

When other automobile manufacturers raise their prices, Ford lowers his. When other employers lower wages, Ford increases them. What has happened? This policy has placed the Law of Increasing Returns back of Ford so effectively that he has become the richest and most powerful man in the world.

Oh, you foolish and short-sighted seekers after wealth, who are returning from the daily chase empty-handed, why do you not take a lesson from men like Ford? Why do you not reverse your philosophy and give in order that you may get?

Life is but a short span of years at best. Like a candle we are lighted, flicker for a moment, and then go out! If we were placed here for the purpose of laying up treasures for use in a life that lies beyond the dark shadow of Death, may it not be possible that we can best collect these treasures by rendering all the service we can, to all the people we can, in a loving spirit of kindness and sympathy?

I hope you agree with this philosophy.

Here this lesson must end, but it is by no means completed. Where I lay down the chain of thought it is now your duty to take it up and develop it, in your own way, and to your own benefit.

By the very nature of the subject of this lesson it can never be finished, for it leads into the heart of all human activities. Its purpose is to cause you to take the fundamentals upon which it is based and use them as a stimulus that will cause your mind to unfold, thereby releasing the latent forces that are yours.

This lesson was not written for the purpose of teaching you, but it was intended as a means of causing you to teach yourself one of the great truths of life. It was intended as a source of education, in the true sense of educing, drawing out, developing from within, those forces of mind which are available for your use.

When you deliver the best service of which you are capable, striving each time to excel all your previous efforts, you are making use of the highest form of education.

Therefore, when you render more service and better service than that for which you are paid, you, more than anyone else, are profiting by the effort.

It is only through the delivery of such service that mastery in your chosen field of endeavor can be attained. For this reason you should make it a part of your definite chief aim to endeavor to surpass all previous records in all that you do. Let this become a part of your daily habits, and follow it with the same regularity with which you eat your meals.

Make it your business to render more service and better service than that for which you are paid, and lo! Before you realize what has happened, you will find that THE WORLD IS WILLINGLY PAYING YOU FOR MORE THAN YOU DO!

Compound interest upon compound interest is the rate that you will be paid for such service. Just how this pyramiding of gains takes place is left entirely to you to determine.

Now, what are you going to do with that which you have learned from this lesson? And when? And how? And why? This lesson can be of no value to you unless it moves you to adopt and use the knowledge it has brought you.

Knowledge becomes POWER only through organization and USE! Do not forget this.

You can never become a Leader without doing more than you are paid for, and you cannot become successful without developing leadership in your chosen occupation.

THE MASTER MIND–An After-the-Lesson Visit With the Author

A Power That Can Bring You Whatever You Want On This Earth

Success is achieved through the application of power.

There are two kinds of Power, physical power, produced by Nature, with the aid of organized raindrops pouring over Niagara Falls. Man has harnessed this form of power and power that is produced through the *harmonious* co-ordination of THOUGHT in the minds of men. Observe that the word "harmonious" has been emphasized.

With the aid of the MIND man has discovered many interesting facts about the earth on which he lives, the air and the ether that fill the endless space about him, and the millions of other planets and heavenly bodies that float through space.

With the aid of a little mechanical contrivance (which his MIND conceived) called a "spectroscope," man has discovered, at a distance of 93,000,000 miles, the nature of the substances of which the sun is made.

We have lived through the stone age, the iron age, the copper age, the religious fanatic age, the scientific research age, the industrial age and we enter, now, the age of THOUGHT.

Out of the spoils of the dark ages through which man has passed he has saved much material that is sound food for THOUGHT. While for more than ten thousand years the battle between IGNORANCE, SUPERSTITION and FEAR on the one side, and INTELLIGENCE on the other, has raged, man has picked up some useful knowledge.

Among other fragments of useful knowledge gathered by man, he has discovered and classified the 83 elements of which all physical matter consists. By study and analysis and comparison man has discovered the "bigness" of the material things in the universe as they are represented by the suns and stars, some of them over ten million times as large as the earth on which he lives. On the other hand, man has discovered the "littleness" of things by reducing matter to molecules, atoms, and finally, to the smallest known particle, the electron. An atom is so inconceivably small that a grain of sand contains millions of them.

The molecule is made up of atoms, which are said to be little particles of matter that revolve around each other in one continuous circuit, at lightning speed, very much as the earth and other planets whirl around the sun in an endless circuit. The atom, in turn, is made up of electrons which are constantly in rapid motion; thus it is said that in every drop of water and every grain of sand the entire principle upon which the whole universe operates, is duplicated.

How marvelous! How stupendous! How do we know these things to be true? Through the aid of the MIND.

You may gather some slight idea of the magnitude of it all the next time you eat a beefsteak, by remembering that the steak on your plate, the plate itself, and the table on which you are eating and the silverware with which you are eating are all, in final analysis, made of exactly the same material, electrons.

In the physical or material world, whether one is looking at the largest star that floats through the heavens or the smallest grain of sand to be found on earth, the object under observation is but an organized collection of molecules, atoms and electrons. (An electron is an inseparable form of power, made up of a positive and a negative pole.) Man knows much about the physical facts of the universe!

The next great scientific discovery will be the fact, which already exists, that every human brain is both a broadcasting and a receiving station; that every thought vibration released by the brain may be picked up and interpreted by all other brains that are in harmony, or in "tune" with the rate of vibration of the broadcasting brain.

How did man acquire the knowledge that he possesses concerning the physical laws of this earth? How did he learn what has taken place before his time, and during his uncivilized period? He gathered this knowledge by turning back the pages of Nature's Bible and there viewing the unimpeachable evidence of millions of years of struggle among animals of a lower intelligence. By turning back the great stone pages man has uncovered the bones, skeletons, footprints and other unmistakable evidence which Mother Nature has held for his inspection throughout unbelievable periods of time.

Now man is about to turn his attention to another section of Nature's Bible–the one wherein has been written a history of the great mental struggle that has taken place in the realm of THOUGHT. This page is represented by the boundless ether which has picked up and still carries every thought vibration that was ever released from the mind of man.

This great page in Nature's Bible is one that no human being has been able to tamper with. Its records are positive, and soon they may be clearly interpreted. No interpolations by man have been permitted. Of the authenticity of the story written on this page there can be no doubt.

Thanks to EDUCATION (meaning the unfolding,educing, drawing out, developing from within of the human mind) Nature's Bible is now being interpreted.

The story of man's long, perilous struggle upward has been written on the pages of this, the greatest of all Bibles.

All who have partly conquered the Six Basic Fears described in another "author's visit" in this series, and who have successfully conquered SUPERSTITION and IGNORANCE, may read the records that have been written in Nature's Bible. To all others this privilege is denied. For this reason there are probably fewer than one thousand people in the entire world at this time who are in, even the primary grade as far as the reading of this Bible is concerned.

In the entire world there are probably fewer than one hundred people, today, who know anything about or have ever heard of the chemistry of the mind, through which two or more minds-

-MAY BE BLENDED, IN A SPIRIT OF PERFECT HARMONY, IN SUCH A MANNER THAT THERE IS BORN A THIRD MIND POSSESSING THE SUPERHUMAN POWER TO READ THE STORY OF THE VIBRATION OF THOUGHT AS IT HAS BEEN WRITTEN AND NOW EXISTS IN THE IMPERISHABLE RECORDS OF THE ETHER.

The newly-discovered radio principle has shut the mouths of the Doubting Thomases and sent the scientist scurrying into new fields of experimentation. When they emerge from this field of research they will show us that the mind as we understand it today, as compared to the mind of tomorrow, is about the same as comparing the intelligence of a polliwog to that of a professor of biology who has read the entire life-line of animal life, from the amoeba on up to man.

Come for a short visit with a few of the POWERFUL men now living who are making use of power created through the blending, in a spirit of harmony, of two or more minds.

We will begin with three well-known men, who are known to be men of great achievement in their respective fields of endeavor. Their names are Henry Ford, Thomas A. Edison and Harvey Firestone.

Of the three Henry Ford is the most POWERFUL, having reference to economic power. Mr. Ford is the most powerful man now living on earth, and is believed to be the most powerful who ever lived. So great is his power that he may have anything of a physical nature that he desires, or its equivalent. Millions of dollars, to him, are but playthings, no harder to acquire than the grains of sand with which the child builds sand-tunnels.

Mr. Edison has such a keen insight into Mother Nature's Bible that he has harnessed and combined for the good of man, more of Nature's laws than any other man who ever lived. It was he who brought together the point of a needle and a piece of wax in such a way that they record and preserve the human voice. It was he who first made the lightning serve to light our houses and streets, through the aid of the incandescent light. It was he who made the camera record and produce all sorts of motion, through the modem moving picture apparatus.

Mr. Firestone's industrial achievement is so well-known that it needs no comment. He has made dollars multiply themselves so rapidly that his name has become a by-word wherever automobiles are operated.

All three men began their business and professional careers with no capital and but little schooling of the nature usually referred to as "education."

Perhaps Mr. Ford's beginning was, by far, the most humble of the three. Cursed with poverty, retarded by lack of even the most elementary form of schooling, and handicapped by ignorance in many forms, he has mastered all of these in the inconceivably short period of twenty-five years.

Thus might we briefly describe the achievements of three well-known, successful men of POWER!

But, we have been dealing with EFFECT only!

The true philosopher wishes to know something of the cause which produced these desirable EFFECTS.

It is a matter of public knowledge that Mr. Ford, Mr. Edison and Mr. Firestone are close personal friends; that they go away to the woods once a year for a period of recuperation and rest.

But, it is not generally known–it is doubtful if these three men, themselves, even know it-

-THAT THERE EXISTS BETWEEN THE THREE MEN A BOND OF HARMONY OUT OF WHICH HAS GROWN A MASTER MIND THAT IS BEING USED BY EACH OF THE THREE. A MIND OF SUPERHUMAN ABILITY, THAT HAS IRE CAPACITY TO "TUNE IN" ON FORCES WITH WHICH MOST MEN ARE TO NO EXTENT FAMILIAR.

Let us repeat the statement that out of the blending and harmonizing of two or more minds (twelve or thirteen minds appear to be the most favorable number) may be produced a mind which has the capacity to "tune in" on the vibrations of the ether and pick up, from that source, kindred thoughts, on any subject.

Through the principle of harmony of minds, Ford, Edison and Firestone have created a Master Mind that now supplements the efforts of each of the three, and WHETHER CONSCIOUSLY OR UNCONSCIOUSLY, THIS "MASTER MIND" IS THE CAUSE OF THE SUCCESS OF EACH OF THE THREE.

There is no other answer to their attainment of great power, and their far-reaching success in their respective fields of endeavor, and this is true despite the fact that neither of them may be conscious of the power they have created, or the manner in which they have done so.

In the city of Chicago live six powerful men known as the Big Six. These six men are said to be the most powerful group of men in the middle west. It is said that their combined income totals more than twenty-five million dollars a year.

Every man in the group began in the most humble of circumstances.

Their names are:

Wm. Wrigley, Jr., who owns the Wrigley Chewing Gum business, and whose income is said to be over fifteen million dollars a year. John R. Thompson, who owns the chain of Thompson self-help lunch rooms throughout the country. Mr. Lasker, who owns the Lord & Thomas Advertising Agency. Mr. McCullough,who owns the largest express business in the world. And, Mr. Ritchie and Mr. Hertz, who own the Yellow Taxicab business of the country.

There is nothing startling about a man who does nothing more than become a millionaire, as a rule. However, there is something connected with the financial success of these particular millionaires that is more than startling, for it is well-known that there exists between them a bond of friendship out of which has grown the condition of harmony that produces a Master Mind.

These six men, whether by accident or design, have blended their minds in such a way that the mind of each has been supplemented by a superhuman power known as a "Master Mind," and that mind has brought each of them more worldly gain than any person could possibly use to advantage.

Despite the fact that one of the thirteen (Judas) broke the chain of harmony, sufficient seed was sown during the period of harmony that originally existed between these thirteen people, to insure the continuation of THE GREATEST AND MOST FAR-REACHING PHILOSOPHY KNOWN TO THE INHABITANTS OF THIS EARTH.

Many millions of people believe themselves to possess WISDOM. Many of these do possess wisdom, in certain elementary stages, but no man may possess real wisdom without the aid of the power known as a Master Mind, and such a mind cannot be created except through the principle of blending, in harmony, of two or more minds. Through many years of practical experimentation it has been found that thirteen minds, when blended in a spirit of perfect harmony, produce the most practical results.

Upon this principle, whether consciously or unconsciously, is founded all of the great industrial and commercial successes that are so abundant in this age.

The word "merger" is becoming one of the most popular words in newspaper parlance, because hardly a day goes by that one may not read of some big industrial, commercial, financial or railroad merger. Slowly the world is beginning to learn (in a very few minds only) that through friendly alliance and cooperation great POWER may be developed.

The successful business and industrial and financial enterprises are those managed by leaders who either consciously or unconsciously apply the principle of co-ordinated effort described in this article. If you would be a great leader in any undertaking, surround yourself with other minds that can be blended in a spirit of co-operation so that they act and function as one.

If you can grasp this principle and apply it you may have, for your efforts, whatever you want on this earth!

Lesson Ten: PLEASING PERSONALITY

What is an ATTRACTIVE personality?

Of course the answer is: A personality that attracts.

But what causes a personality to attract? Let us proceed to find out. Your personality is the sum total of your characteristics and appearances which distinguish you from all others. The clothes you wear, the lines in your face, the tone of your voice, the thoughts you think, the character you have developed by those thoughts–all constitute parts of your personality.

Whether your personality is attractive or not is another matter.

By far the most important part of your personality is that which is represented by your character, and is therefore the part that is not visible. The style of your clothes and their appropriateness undoubtedly constitute a very important part of your personality, for it is true that people form first impressions of you from your outward appearance.

Even the manner in which you shake hands forms an important part of your personality, and goes a very long way toward attracting or repelling those with whom you shake hands.

This art can be cultivated.

The expression of your eyes also forms an important part of your personality, for there are people, and they are more numerous than one might imagine, who can look through your eyes into your heart and see that which is written there by the nature of your most secret thoughts.

The vitality of your body–sometimes called personal magnetism–also constitutes an important part of your personality.

Now let us proceed to arrange these outward mediums through which the nature of our personality is expressed, so that it will attract and not repel.

There is one way in which you can so express the composite of your personality that it will always attract, even though you may be as homely as the circus "fat woman," and this is by–

Taking a keen heart-interest in the other fellow's "game" in life.

Let me illustrate exactly what is meant, by relating an incident that happened some years ago, from which I was taught a lesson in master salesmanship.

One day an old lady called at my office and sent in her card with a message saying that she must see me personally. No amount of coaxing by secretaries could induce her to disclose the nature of her visit, therefore I made up my mind that she was some poor old soul who wanted to sell me a book, and remembering that my own mother was a woman, I decided to go out to the reception room and buy her book, whatever it might be.

Please follow every detail thoughtfully, for you, too, may learn a lesson in master salesmanship from this incident.

As I walked down the hallway from my private office, this old lady, who was standing just outside of the railing that led to the main reception room, began to smile.

I had seen many people smile, but never before had I seen one who smiled so sweetly as did this lady. It was one of those contagious smiles, because I caught the spirit of it and began to smile also.

As I reached the railing the old lady extended her hand to shake hands with me. Now, as a rule, I do not become too friendly on first acquaintance when a person calls at my office, for the reason that it is very hard to say "no" if the caller should ask me to do that which I do not wish to do.

However, this dear old lady looked so sweetly innocent and harmless that I extended my hand and she began to shake it! Whereupon, I discovered that she not only had an attractive smile, but she also had a magnetic handshake. She took hold of my hand firmly, but not too firmly, and the very manner in which she went about it telegraphed he thought to my brain that it was she who was doing the honors. She made me feel that she was really and truly glad to shake my hand, and I believe that she was. I believe that her handshake came from the heart as well as from the hand.

I have shaken hands with many thousands of people during my public career, but I do not recall having ever done so with anyone who understood the art of doing it as well as this old lady did. The moment she touched my hand I could feel myself "slipping," and I knew that whatever it was that she had come after she would go away with it, and that I would aid and abet her all I could toward this end.

In other words, that penetrating smile and that warm hand-shake had disarmed me and made me a "willing victim." At a single stroke this old lady had shorn me of that false shell into which I crawl when salesmen come around selling or trying to sell that which I do not want. To go back to an expression which you found quite frequently in previous lessons of this course, this gentle visitor had "neutralized" my mind and made me want to listen.

Ah, but here is the stumbling point at which most salespeople fall and break their necks, figuratively speaking, for it is as useless to try to sell a man something until you have first made him want to listen, as it would be to command the earth to stop rotating.

Note well how this old lady used a smile and a handshake as the tools with which to pry open the window that led to my heart; but the most important part of the transaction is yet to be related.

Slowly and deliberately, as if she had all the time there was in the universe (which she did have, as far as I was concerned at that moment) the old lady began to crystallize the first step of her victory into reality by saying:

"I just came here to tell you (what seemed to me to be a long pause) that I think you are doing the most wonderful work of any man in the world today."

Every word was emphasized by a gentle, though firm squeeze of my hand, and she was looking through my eyes and into my heart as she spoke.

After I regained consciousness (for it became a standing joke among my assistants at the office that I fainted dead away), I reached down and unlocked the little secret latch that fastened the gate and said:

"Come right in, dear lady–come right into my private office," and with a gallant bow that would have done credit to the cavaliers of olden times, I bade her come in and "sit awhile."

As she entered my private office, I motioned her to the big easy-chair back of my desk while I took the little hard-seated chair which, under ordinary circumstances, I would have used as a means of discouraging her from taking up too much of my time.

For three-quarters of an hour I listened to one of the most brilliant and charming conversations I have ever heard, and my visitor was doing all of the conversing. From the very start she had assumed the initiative and taken the lead, and, up to the end of that first three-quarters of an hour, she found no inclination, on my part, to challenge her right to it.

I repeat, lest you did not get the full import of it, that I was a willing listener!

Now comes the part of the story which would make me blush with embarrassment, if it were not for the fact that you and I are separated by the pages of this book; but I must summon the courage with which to tell you the facts because the entire incident would lose its significance if I failed to do this.

As I have stated, my visitor entranced me with brilliant and captivating conversation for three-quarters of an hour. Now, what do you suppose she was talking about all that time?

No! You are wrong.

She was not trying to sell me a book, nor did she once use the personal pronoun "I."

However, she was not only trying, but actually selling me something, and that something was myself.

She had no sooner been seated in that big cushioned chair than she unrolled a package which I had mistaken for a book that she had come to sell me, and sure enough, there was a book in the package–in fact, several of them; for she had a complete year's file of the magazine of which I was then editor (Hill's Golden Rule). She turned the pages of those magazines and read places that she had marked here and there, assuring me, in the meanwhile, that she had always believed the philosophy back of that which she was reading.

Then, after I was in a state of complete mesmerism, and thoroughly receptive, my visitor tactfully switched the conversation to a subject which, I suspect, she had in mind to discuss with me long before she presented herself at my office; but–and this is another point at which most salespeople blunder–had she reversed the order of her conversation and begun where she finished, the chances are that she never would have had the opportunity to sit in that big easy-chair.

During the last three minutes of her visit, she skillfully laid before me the merits of some securities that she was selling. She did not ask me to purchase, but the way in which she told me of the merits of the securities (plus the way in which she had so impressively told me of the merits of my own "game") had the psychological effect of causing me to want to purchase; and, even though I made no purchase of securities from her, she made a sale–because I picked up the telephone and introduced her to a man to whom she later sold more than five times the amount that she had intended selling me.

If that same woman, or another woman, or a man who had the tact and personality that she possessed should call on me, I would again sit down and listen for three-quarters of an hour.

We are all human, and we are all more or less vain!

We are all alike in this respect–we will listen with intense interest to those who have the tact to talk to us about that which lies closest to our hearts; and then, out of a sense of reciprocity, we will also listen with interest when the speaker finally switches the conversation to the subject which lies closest to his or her heart. And at the end, we will not only "sign on the dotted line" but we will say, "What a wonderful personality!"

In the city of Chicago, some years ago, I was conducting a school of salesmanship for a securities house which employed more than 1,500 salespeople. To keep the ranks of that big organization filled, we had to train and employ six hundred new salespeople every week. Of all the thousands of men and women who went through that school, there was but one man who grasped the significance of the principle I am here describing the first time he heard it analyzed.

This man had never tried to sell securities and frankly admitted, when he entered the salesmanship class, that he was not a salesman. Let's see whether he was or not.

After he had finished his training, one of the "star" salesmen took a notion to play a practical joke on him, believing him to be a credulous person who would believe all that he heard. So this "star" gave him an inside "tip" as to where he would be able to sell some securities without any great effort. This star would make the sale himself, so he said; but the man to whom he referred as being a likely purchaser was an ordinary artist who would purchase with so little urging that he, being a "star," did not wish to waste his time on him.

The newly made salesman was delighted to receive the "tip," and, forthwith, he was on his way to make the sale. As soon as he was out of the office, the "star" gathered the other "stars" around him and told of the joke he was playing. For in reality the artist was a very wealthy man and the "star," himself had spent nearly a month trying to sell him, but without success. It then developed that all of the "stars" of that particular group had called on this same artist but had failed to interest him.

The newly made salesman was gone about an hour and a half. When he returned he found the "stars" waiting for him with smiles on their faces.

To their surprise, the newly made salesman also wore a broad smile on his face. The "stars" looked at each other inquiringly, for they had expected that this "green" man would not return in a joyful mood.

"Well, did you sell to your man?" inquired the originator of this "joke."

"Certainly," replied the uninitiated one, "and I found that artist to be all you said he was–a perfect gentleman and a very interesting man."

Reaching into his pocket he pulled out an order and a check for $2,000.00.

The "stars" wanted to know how he did it.

"Oh, it wasn't difficult," replied the newly-made salesman; "I just walked in and talked to him a few minutes and he brought up the subject of the securities himself, and said he wanted to purchase; therefore, I really did not sell to him–he purchased of his own accord."

When I heard of the transaction, I called the newly-made salesman in and asked him to describe, in detail, just how he made the sale, and I will relate it just as he told it.

When he reached the artist's studio, he found him at work on a picture. So engaged in his work was the artist that he did not see the salesman enter, so the salesman walked over to where he could see the picture and stood there looking at it without saying a word.

Finally the artist saw him; then the salesman apologized for the intrusion and began to talk–about the picture that the artist was painting!

He knew just enough about art to be able to discuss the merits of the picture with some intelligence and he was really interested in the subject.

He liked the picture and frankly told the artist so, which, of course, made the artist very angry!

For nearly an hour those two men talked of nothing but art, particularly that picture that stood on the artist's easel. Finally, the artist asked the salesman his name and his business, and the salesman (yes, the master salesman) replied, "Oh, never mind my business or my name. I am more interested in you and your art!"

The artist's face beamed with a smile of joy.

Those words fell as sweet music upon his ears. But, not to be outdone by his polite visitor, he insisted on knowing what mission had brought him to his studio.

Then, with an air of genuine reluctance, this master salesman–this real "star"– introduced himself and told his business.

Briefly he described the securities he was selling, and the artist listened as if he enjoyed every word that was spoken. After the salesman had finished the artist said:

"Well, well! I have been very foolish. Other salesmen from your firm have been here trying to sell me some of those securities, but they talked nothing but business; in fact, they annoyed me so that I had to ask one of them to leave. Now let me see–what was that fellow's name–oh, yes, it was Mr. Perkins." (Perkins was the "star" who had thought of this clever trick to play on the newly made salesman.) "But you present the matter so differently, and now I see how foolish I have been, and I want you to let me have $2,000.00 worth of those securities."

Think of that–"You present the matter so differently!"

And how did this newly made salesman present the matter so differently? Putting the question another way, what did this master salesman really sell that artist? Did he sell him securities?

No! He sold him his own picture which he was painting on his own canvas.

The securities were but an incident.

Don't overlook this point. That master salesman had remembered the story of the old lady who entertained me for three-quarters of an hour by talking about that which was nearest my heart, and it had so impressed him that he made up his mind to study his prospective purchasers and find out what would interest them most, so he could talk about that.

This "green," newly-made salesman earned $7,900.00 in commissions the first month he was in the field, leading the next highest man by more than double, and the tragedy of it was that not one person out of the entire organization of 1,500 salespeople took the time to find out how and why he became the real "star" of the organization–a fact which I believe fully justifies the rather biting reprimand suggested in Lesson Nine to which you may have taken offense.

A Carnegie, or a Rockefeller, or a James J. Hill, or a Marshall Field accumulates a fortune through the application of the selfsame principles that are available to all the remainder of us, but we envy them their wealth without ever thinking of studying their philosophy and appropriating it to our own use.

We look at a successful man in the hour of his triumph, and wonder how he did it, but we overlook the importance of analyzing his methods and we forget the price he had to pay in careful, well-organized preparation which had to be made before he could reap the fruits of his efforts.

Throughout this course on the Law of Success, you will not find a single new principle.

Every one of them is as old as civilization itself. Yet you will find but few people who seem to understand how to apply them.

The salesman who sold those securities to that artist was not only a master salesman, but he was a man with an attractive personality. He was not much to look at; perhaps that is why the "star" conceived the idea of playing that cruel joke on him; but even a homely person may have a very attractive personality in the eyes of those whose handiwork he has praised.

Of course, there are some who will get the wrong conception of the principle I am here trying to make clear, by drawing the conclusion that any sort of cheap flattery will take the place of genuine heart interest. I hope that you are not one of these. I hope that you are one of those who understand the real psychology upon which this lesson is based, and that you will make it your business to study other people closely enough to find something about them or their work that you really admire. Only in this way can you develop a personality that will be irresistibly attractive.

Cheap flattery has just the opposite effect to that of constituting an attractive personality. It repels instead of attracting. It is so shallow that even the ignorant easily detect it.

Perhaps you have observed–and if you have not I wish you to do so–that this lesson emphasizes at length the importance of making it your business to take a keen interest in other people and in their work, business or profession. This emphasis was by no means an accident.

You will quickly observe that the principles upon which this lesson is based are very closely related to those which constitute the foundation of Lesson Six, on Imagination.

Also, you will observe that this lesson is based upon much the same general principles as those which form the most important part of Lesson Thirteen, on Co-operation.

Let us here introduce some very practical suggestions as to how the laws of Imagination, Co-operation and Pleasing Personality may be blended or coordinated to profitable ends, through the creation of usable ideas.

Every thinker knows that "ideas" are the beginning of all successful achievement. The question most often asked, however, is, "How can I learn to create ideas that will earn money?"

In part we will answer this question in this lesson by suggesting some new and novel ideas, any of which might be developed and made very profitable by almost anyone, in practically any locality.

IDEA NUMBER ONE

The world war has deprived Germany of her enormous trade in toys. Before the war we bought most of our toys from Germany. We are not likely to buy any more toys from German manufacturers in our time, or for a long while afterward.

Toys are in demand, not alone in the United States, but in foreign countries, many of which will not buy toys from Germany. Our only competitor is Japan and her toys are of so poor a quality that her competition means nothing.

But what sort of toys shall I manufacture and where will I get the capital with which to carry on the business, you will ask?

First, go to a local toy dealer and find out just which class of toys sells most rapidly. If you do not feel competent to make improvements on some of the toys now on the market, advertise for an inventor "with an idea for a marketable toy" and you will soon find the mechanical genius who will supply this missing link in your undertaking.

Have him make you a working model of just what you want, then go to some small manufacturer, woodworker, machine shop or the like, and arrange to have your toys manufactured.

You now know just what your toy will cost, so you are ready to go to some big jobber, wholesaler or distributor and arrange for the sale of your entire product.

If you are an able salesman you can finance this whole project on the few dollars required with which to advertise for the inventor. When you find this man you can probably arrange with him to work out a model for you during his spare evening hours, with a promise that you will give him a better job when you are manufacturing your own toys. He will probably give you all the time you want in which to pay him for his labor; or he may do the work in return for an interest in the business.

You can get the manufacturer of your toys to wait for his money until you are paid by the firm to which you sell them, and if necessary, you can assign to him the invoices for the toys sold and let the money come direct to him.

Of course if you have an unusually pleasing and convincing personality and considerable ability to organize, you will be able to take the working model of your toy to some man of means and, in return for an interest in the business, secure the capital with which to do your own manufacturing.

If you want to know what will sell, watch a crowd of children at play, study their likes and dislikes, find out what will amuse them and you will probably get an idea on which to build your toy. It requires no genius to invent! Common sense is all that is necessary. Simply find out what the people want and then produce it. Produce it well- better than anyone else is doing. Give it a touch of individuality. Make it distinctive.

We spend millions of dollars annually for toys with which to entertain our children.

Make your new toy useful as well as interesting. Make it educational if possible. If it entertains and teaches at the same time it will sell readily and live forever. If your toy is in the nature of a game make it teach the child something about the world in which it lives- geography, arithmetic, English, physiology, etc. Or, better still, produce a toy that will cause the child to run, jump or in some other way exercise. Children love to move about and moving about is of benefit to them, especially when stimulated by the play motive.

An indoor baseball game would be a ready seller, especially in the cities. Work out an arrangement for attaching the ball to a string that will be suspended from the ceiling so one child may throw the ball against the wall and then stand back and strike it with a bat as it rebounds. A one-child baseball game, in other words.

PLAN NUMBER TWO

This will be of interest only to the man or woman who has the self-confidence and the ambition to "run the risk" of making a big income, which, we may add, most people have not.

It is a suggestion that could be put into practical operation by at least forty or fifty people in every large city throughout the United States, and by a smaller number in the smaller cities.

It is intended for the man or woman who can write or will learn to write advertising copy, sales literature, follow-up letters, collection letters and the like, using the ability to write which we will suppose that you possess.

To make practical and profitable use of this suggestion you will need the co- operation of a good advertising agency and from one to five firms or individuals who do enough advertising to warrant their appropriations going through an agency.

You should go to the agency first and make arrangements with it to employ you and pay you seven per cent on the gross expenditures of all accounts which you bring to it; this seven per cent to compensate you for getting the account and for writing the copy and otherwise serving the client in the management of his advertising appropriation. Any reliable agency will gladly give you this amount for all the business you will bring.

Then you go to a firm or individual whose advertising account you wish to handle and say in effect that you wish to go to work without compensation. Tell what you can do and what you intend to do for that particular firm that will help it sell more goods. If the firm employs an advertising manager you are to become virtually his assistant without pay, on one condition: namely, that the advertising appropriation is to be placed through the agency with which you have the connection. Through this arrangement the firm or individual whose account you thus secure will get the benefit of your personal services, without cost, and pay no more for placing its advertising through your agency than it would through any other. If your canvass is convincing and you really take the time to prepare your case, you will get your account without much argument.

You can repeat this transaction until you have as many accounts as you can handle advantageously, which, under ordinary conditions, will be not more than ten or twelve; probably less if one or more of your clients spends upwards of $25,000.00 a year in advertising.

If you are a competent writer of advertising copy and have the ability to create new and profitable ideas for your clients you will be able to hold their business from year to year. You of course understand that you are not to accept more accounts than you can handle individually. You should spend a portion of your time in the place of business of each of your clients. In fact, you should have a desk and working equipment right on the grounds so you can get firsthand information as to your clients' sales problems, as well as accurate information as to their goods and wares.

Through this sort of effort you will give the advertising agency a reputation for effective service such as it would get in no other way, and you will please your clients because they will see satisfactory returns from your efforts. As long as you keep the agency and the clients whom you serve satisfied your job is safe and you will make money. A reasonable expectation of returns under this plan would be a gross business of $250,000.00 a year, on which your seven per cent would amount to $17,500.00.

A man or woman of unusual ability could run the figure much higher than this, up to, say, an income of $25,000.00 a year, while the tendency would be, however, to drop down to around $5,000.00 to $7,500.00, which are the figures that the "average" man or woman might reasonably expect to earn.

You can see that the plan has possibilities. It supplies independent work and gives you one hundred per cent of your earning power. It is better than a position as advertising manager, even if the position paid the same money, because it practically places you in a business of your own–one in which your name is constantly developing a survival value.

PLAN NUMBER THREE

This plan can be put into operation by almost any man or woman of average intelligence, and with but little preparation. Go to any first-class printer and make arrangements with him to handle all the business you bring to him, allowing you a commission of say ten per cent on the gross amount. Then go to the largest users of printed matter and get samples of everything in the way of printing that they use.

Form a partnership or working arrangement with a commercial artist who will go over all this printed matter and wherever suitable or appropriate he will improve the illustrations or make illustrations where none were used before, making a rough pencil sketch which can be pasted to the original printed matter.

Then, if you are not a writer of copy, form a working arrangement with someone who is and get him or her to go over the copy of the printed matter and improve it in every respect possible.

When the work is complete go back to the firm from whom you get the printed matter, taking with you quotations on the work and show what can be done in the way of improvement. Say nothing about your quotations, however, until you have shown how much you could improve the printed matter. You will probably get the entire business of that firm by giving that sort of service in connection with every job of printing it has done.

If you perform your service properly you will soon have all the business that your commercial artist, your copy writer and you can handle. It ought to be good for $5,000.00 a year a piece for you.

Any profits that you earn from the work of others in connection with any of these plans will be a legitimate profit–a profit to which you will be entitled in return for your ability to organize and bring together the necessary talent and ability with which to perform satisfactory service.

If you go into the toy business you will be entitled to a profit on the work of those who make the toys because it will be through your ability that employment for them is available.

It is more than likely that your brains and your ability, when added to that of those who work with you or for you, will greatly increase their earning capacity–even to the extent that they can well afford to see you make a small amount from their efforts because they will be still earning much more than they could earn without your guidance!

You are willing to take any of these plans and make a profit out of them, are you not?

You see nothing wrong on your part, do you? If you are an employee, working for some other person or firm, may it not be possible that the head of that firm or that individual, with his ability to organize, finance, etc., is increasing your own earning capacity right now?

You want to get out of the employee class and become an employer. We do not blame you for that. Nearly every normal person wants to do the same. The one best first step to take is to serve the firm or individual for whom you are working just as you would wish to be served if you were that individual or the head of that firm.

Who are the big employers of help today? Are they the rich men's sons who fell heir to employer ship? Not on your life! They are the men and women who came up from the ranks of the most lowly sort of labor; men and women who have had no greater opportunity than you have. They are in the positions that they hold because their superior ability has enabled them intelligently to direct others. You can acquire that ability if you will try.

Right in the town or city where you live there are people who probably could benefit by knowing you, and who could undoubtedly benefit you in return. In one section of the city lives John Smith who wishes to sell his grocery store and open a moving picture theater. In another section of the city is a man who has a moving picture theater that he would like to trade for a grocery store.

Can you bring them together?

If you can, you will serve both and earn a nice remuneration.

In your town or city are people who want the products raised on the farms in the surrounding community. On those farms are fanners who raise farm products and who want to get them into the hands of those who live in town. If you can find a way of carrying the farm products direct from the farm to the city or town consumer you will enable the farmer to get more for his products and the consumer to get those products for less, and still there will be a margin to pay you for your ingenuity in shortening the route between producer and consumer.

In business there are, broadly speaking, two classes of people–the Producers and the Consumers. The tendency of the times is to find some way of bringing these two together without so many intermediaries. Find a way to shorten the route between producer and consumer and you will have created a plan that will help these two classes and handsomely profit you.

The laborer is worthy of his hire. If you can create such a plan you are entitled to a fair proportion of that which you save for the consumer, and also a fair proportion of that which you make for the producer.

Let us warn you that whatever plan you create as a means of making money, you had better see that it slices off a little of the cost to the consumer instead of adding a little to that cost.

The business of bringing producer and consumer together is a profitable business when it is conducted fairly to both, and without a greedy desire to get all there is in sight!

The American public is wonderfully patient with profiteers who impose upon it, but there is a pivotal point beyond which even the shrewdest of them dare not go. It may be all right to corner the diamond market and run up enormously high the price of those white rocks which are dug out of the ground in Africa without trouble, but when the prices of food and clothing and other necessities begin to soar skyward there is a chance of someone getting into the bad graces of the American public.

If you crave wealth and are really brave enough to shoulder the burdens which go with it, reverse the usual method of acquiring it by giving your goods and wares to the world at the lowest possible profit you can afford instead of exacting all that you can with safety. Ford has found it profitable to pay his workers, not as little as he can get them for, but as much as his profits will permit. He has also found it profitable to reduce the price of his automobile to the consumer while other manufacturers (many of whom have long since failed) continued to increase their price.

There may be some perfectly good plans through the operation of which you could squeeze the consumer and still manage to keep out of jail, but you will enjoy much more peace of mind and in all probability more profits in the long run if your plan, when you complete it, is built along the Ford lines.

You have heard John D. Rockefeller abused considerably, but most of this abuse has been prompted by sheer envy upon the part of those who would like to have his money but who haven't the inclination to earn it. Regardless of your opinion of Rockefeller, do not forget that he began as a humble bookkeeper and that he gradually climbed to the top in the accumulation of money because of his ability to organize and direct other and less able men intelligently. This author can remember when he had to pay twenty-five cents for a gallon of lamp oil and walk two miles through the hot sun and carry it home in a tin can in the bargain. Now, Rockefeller's wagon will deliver it at the back door, in the city or on the farm, at a little over half that sum.

Who has a right to begrudge Rockefeller his millions as long as he has reduced the price of a needed commodity? He could just as easily have increased the price of lamp oil to half a dollar, but we seriously doubt that he would be a multi-millionaire today if he had done so.

There are a lot of us who want money, but ninety-nine out of every hundred who start to create a plan through which to get money give all their thought to the scheme through which to get hold of it and no thought to the service to be given in return for it. A Pleasing Personality is one that makes use of Imagination and Co-operation. We have cited the foregoing illustrations of how ideas may be created to show you how to co-ordinate the laws of Imagination, Co-operation and a Pleasing Personality.

Analyze any man who does not have a Pleasing Personality and you will find lacking in that man the faculties of Imagination and Co-operation also.

This brings us to a suitable place at which to introduce one of the greatest lessons on personality ever placed on paper. It is also one of the most effective lessons on salesmanship ever written, for the subjects of attractive personality and salesmanship must always go hand in hand; they are inseparable. I have reference to Shakespeare's masterpiece, Mark Antony's speech at the funeral of Caesar. Perhaps you have read this oration, but it is here presented with interpretations in parentheses which may help you to gather a new meaning from it.

The setting for that oration was something like the following:

Caesar is dead, and Brutus, his slayer, is called on to tell the Roman mob, that has gathered at the undertaker's, why he put Caesar out of the way. Picture, in your imagination, a howling mob that was none too friendly to Caesar, and that already believed that Brutus had done a noble deed by murdering him.

Brutus takes the platform and makes a short statement of his reasons for killing Caesar. Confident that he has won the day he takes his seat. His whole demeanor is that of one who believes his word will be accepted without question; it is one of haughtiness.

Mark Antony now takes the platform, knowing that the mob is antagonistic to him because he is a friend of Caesar. In a low, humble tone of voice Antony begins to speak:

> Antony: "For Brutus' sake, I am beholding to you."
> Fourth Citizen: "What does he say of Brutus?"
> Third Citizen: "He says, for Brutus' sake, he finds himself beholding to us all."
> Fourth Citizen: '"Twere best he speak no harm of Brutus here."
> First Citizen: "This Caesar was a tyrant."
> Third Citizen: "Nay, that's certain; we are blest that Rome is rid of him."
> Second Citizen: "Peace! Let us hear what Antony can say."

(Here you will observe, in Antony's opening sentence, his clever method of "neutralizing" the minds of his listeners.)

Antony: "You gentle Romans, –"

(About as "gentle" as a gang of Bolsheviks in a revolutionary labor meeting.)

All: "Peace, ho! Let us hear him."

(Had Antony begun his speech by "knocking" Brutus, the history of Rome would have been different.)

Antony: "Friends, Romans, Countrymen, lend me your ears;
I come to bury Caesar, not to praise him."

(Allying himself with what he knew to be the state of mind of his listeners.)

"The evil that men do lives after them;
The good is oft interred with their bones;
So let it be with Caesar. The noble Brutus
Hath told you Caesar was ambitious;
If it were so, it was a grievous fault;
And grievously bath Caesar answered it.
Here, under leave of Brutus and the rest, –
For Brutus is an honorable man;
So are they all, all honorable men–
Come I to speak at Caesar's funeral.
He was my friend–faithful, and just to me;
But Brutus says he was ambitious;
And Brutus is an honorable man;
He hath brought many captives home to Rome,
Whose ransoms did the general coffers fill;
Did this in Caesar seem ambitious?
When the poor have cried, Caesar hath wept;
Ambition should be made of sterner stuff;
Yet Brutus says he was ambitious;
And Brutus is an honorable man.
You all did see that on the Lupercal
I thrice presented him a kingly crown,
Which he did thrice refuse. Was this ambition?
Yet Brutus says he was ambitious;
And, surely, he is an honorable man.
I speak not to disprove what Brutus spoke,
But here I am to speak what I do know.
You all did love him once, not without cause;
What cause withholds you then to mourn for him?
O judgment! thou art fled to brutish beasts,

And men have lost their reason. Bear with me,
My heart is in the coffin there with Caesar,
And I must pause till it come back to me."

(At this point Antony paused to give his audience a chance to discuss hurriedly, among themselves, his opening statements. His object in doing this was to observe what effect his words were having, just as a master salesman always encourages his prospective purchaser to talk so he may know what is in his mind.)

First Citizen: "Me thinks there is much in his sayings"
Second Citizen: "If thou consider rightly of the matter, Caesar has had great wrong."
Third Citizen: "Has he, masters? I fear there will be worse come in his place."
Fourth Citizen: "Mark'd ye his words? He would not take the crown? Therefore 'tis certain he was not ambitious."
First Citizen: "If it be found so, someone will dear abide it."
Second Citizen: "Poor soul! His eyes are red as fire with weeping."
Third Citizen: "There's not a nobler man in Rome than Antony."
Fourth Citizen: "Now mark him, he begins again to speak ."
Antony: "But yesterday the word of Caesar might
Have stood against the world; now lies he there,
And none so poor to do him reverence.
O masters (appealing to their vanity) if I were disposed to stir Your hearts and minds to mutiny and rage, I should do Brutus wrong and Cassius wrong, Who, you all know, are honorable men."

(Observe how often Antony has repeated the term "honorable." Observe, also, how cleverly he brings in the first suggestion that, perhaps, Brutus and Cassius may not be as honorable as the Roman mob believes them to be. This suggestion is carried in the words "mutiny" and "rage" which he here uses for the first time, after his pause gave him time to observe that the mob was swinging over toward his side of the argument. Observe how carefully he is "feeling" his way and making his words fit that which he knows to be the frame of mind of his listeners.)

Antony: "I will not do them wrong; I rather choose
To wrong the dead, to wrong myself and you,
Than I will wrong such honorable men."

(Crystallizing his suggestion into hatred of Brutus and Cassius, he then appeals to their curiosity and begins to lay the foundation for his climax–a climax which he knows will win the mob because he is reaching it so cleverly that the mob believes it to be its own conclusion.)

Antony: "But here's a parchment, with the seal of Caesar;
I found it in his closet; 'tis his will;

Let but the commons hear this testament,
Which, pardon me, I do not mean to read -"

(Tightening up on his appeal to their curiosity by making them believe he does not intend to read the will.)

"And they would go and kiss dead Caesar's wounds
And dip their napkins in his sacred blood,
Yea, beg a hair of him for memory,
And, dying, mention it within their wills,
Bequeathing it as a rich legacy
Unto their issue."

(Human nature always wants that which is difficult to get, or that of which it is about to be deprived. Observe how craftily Antony has awakened the interest of the mob and made them want to hear the reading of the will, thereby preparing them to hear it with open minds. This marks his second step in the process of "neutralizing" their minds.)

All: "The will, the will! We will hear Caesar's will."
Antony: "Have patience, gentle friends, I must not read it;
It is not meet you know how Caesar loved you.
You are not wood, you are not stones, but men;
And, being men, hearing the will of Caesar,
It will inflame you; (Exactly what he wishes to do)
It will make you mad;
'Tis good you know not that you are his heirs,
For if you should, O what will come of it!"
Fourth Citizen: "Read the will; we'll hear it,
Antony: You shall read us the will; Caesar's will."
Antony: "Will you be patient? Will you stay awhile?
I have o'ershot myself to tell you of it;
I fear I wrong the honorable men
Whose daggers have stabb'd Caesar, I do fear it."

("Daggers" and "stabb'd" suggest cruel murder. Observe how cleverly Antony injects this suggestion into his speech, and observe, also, how quickly the mob catches its significance, because, unknown to the mob, Antony has carefully prepared their minds to receive this suggestion.)

Fourth Citizen: "They were traitors, honorable men!"
All: "The will! The testament!"
Second Citizen: "They were villains, murderers; the will!"

(Just what Antony would have said in the beginning, but he knew it would have a more desirable effect if he planted the thought in the minds of the mob and permitted them to say it themselves.)

Antony: "You will compel me then to read the will?
Then make a ring about the corpse of Caesar,
And let me show you him that made the will.
Shall I descend, and will you give me leave?"

(This was the point at which Brutus should have begun to look for a back door through which to make his escape.)

All: "Come down."
Second Citizen: "Descend."
Third Citizen: "Room for Antony, most noble Antony."
Antony: "Nay, press not so upon me, stand far off."

(He knew this command would make them want to draw nearer, which is what he wanted them to do.)

All: "Stand back. Room."
Antony: "If you have tears, prepare to shed them now.
You all do know this mantle;
remember
The first time ever Caesar put it on;
'Twas on a summer's evening, in his tent,
That day he overcame the Nervii;
Look, in this place ran Cassius' dagger through;
See what a rent the envious Casca made;
Through this the well-beloved Brutus stabb'd;
And as he plucked his cursed steel away,
Mark how the blood of Caesar followed it,
As rushing out of doors, to be resolved
If Brutus so unkindly knock'd or no;
For Brutus, as you know, was Caesar's angel;
Judge, O you gods, how dearly Caesar loved him!
This was the most unkindest cut of all;
For, when the noble Caesar saw him stab,
Ingratitude, more strong than traitor's arms,
Quite vanquish'd him; then burst his mighty heart;
And, in his mantle muffling up his face,
Even at the base of Pompey's statue,
Which all the while ran blood, great Caesar fell.
O, what a fall was there, my countrymen!
Then I, and you, and all of us fell down
While bloody treason flourish'd over us.
O, now you weep, and I perceive you feel
The dint of pity; these are gracious drops.

Kind soul, why weep you when you but behold
Our Caesar's vesture wounded? Look you here;
Here is himself, marr'd, as you see, with traitors."

(Observe how Antony now uses the words "traitors" quite freely, because he knows that it is in harmony with that which is in the minds of the Roman mob.)

First Citizen: "O piteous spectacle!"
Second Citizen: "O woeful day!"
Third Citizen: "O woeful day!"
First Citizen: "O most bloody sight!"
Second Citizen: "We will be revenged."

(Had Brutus been a wise man instead of a braggart he would have been many miles from the scene by this tune.)

All: "Revenge! About! Seek! Burn! Fire! Kill! Slay! Let not a traitor live!"

(Here Antony takes the next step toward crystallizing the frenzy of the mob into action; but, clever salesman that he is, does not try to force this action.)

Antony: "Stay, countrymen."
First Citizen: "Peace there! Hear the noble Antony."
Second Citizen: "We'll hear him, we'll follow him, we'll die with him."

(From these words Antony knows that he has the mob with him. Observe how he takes advantage of this psychological moment–the moment for which all master salesmen wait.)

Antony: "Good friends, sweet friends,
let me not stir you up to such a sudden flood of mutiny.
They that have done this deed are honorable.
What private griefs they have, alas, I know not,
That made them do it; they were wise and honorable,
And will, no doubt, with reasons answer you.
I come not, friends, to steal away your hearts:
I am no orator as Brutus is;
But, as you know me all, a plain, blunt man,
That love my friend; and that they know full well
That gave me public leave to speak of him;
For I have neither wit, nor words, nor worth,
Action, nor utterance, nor the power of speech,
To stir men's blood; I only speak right on;
I tell you that which you yourselves do know;
Show you sweet Caesar's wounds, poor, poor, dumb mouths.

And bid them speak for me; but were I Brutus,
And Brutus Antony, there an Antony
Would ruffle up your spirits, and put a tongue
In every wound of Caesar that should move
The stones of Rome to rise and mutiny."
All: "We'll mutiny."
First Citizen: "We'll burn the house of Brutus."
Third Citizen: "Away, then! Come, seek the conspirators."
Antony: "Yet hear me, countrymen; yet hear me speak!"
All: "Peace, ho! Hear Antony. Most noble Antony!"
Antony: "Why, friends, you go to do you know not what;
Wherein hath Caesar thus deserved your love?
Alas, you know not; I must tell you, then;
You have forgot the will I told you of."

(Antony is now ready to play his trump card; he is ready to reach his climax. Observe how well he has marshaled his suggestions, step by step, saving until the last his most important statement, the one on which he relied for action. In the great field of salesmanship and in public speaking many a man tries to reach this point too son, tries to "rush" his audience or his prospective purchaser, and thereby loses his appeal.)

All: "Most true; the will! Let's stay and hear the will."
Antony: "Here is the will, and under Caesar's seal.
To every Roman citizen he gives,
To every several man, seventy-five drachmas."
Second Citizen: "Most noble Caesar! we'll revenge his death."
Third Citizen: "O royal Caesar!"
Antony: "Hear me with patience."
All: "Peace, ho!"
Antony: "Moreover, he hath left you all his walks,
His private arbors and new planted orchards,
On this side Tiber; he hath left them you,
And to your heirs forever; common pleasures,
To walk abroad and recreate yourself.
Here was a Caesar! When comes such another?"
First Citizen: "Never, never. Come, away, away!
We'll burn his body in the holy place,
And with the brands fire the traitors' houses.
Take up the body."
Second Citizen: "Go fetch fire."
Third Citizen: "Pluck down benches."
Fourth Citizen: "Pluck down forms, windows, anything."

And that was Brutus' finish!

He lost his case because he lacked the personality and the good judgment with which to present his argument from the viewpoint of the Roman mob, as Mark Antony did. His whole attitude clearly indicated that he thought pretty well of himself, that he was proud of his deed. We have all seen people, in this day and time, who somewhat resemble Brutus in this respect, but, if we observe closely, we notice that they do not accomplish very much.

Suppose that Mark Antony had mounted the platform in a "strutting" attitude, and had begun his speech in this wise:

"Now let me tell you Romans something about this man Brutus–he is a murderer at heart and"–he would have gone no further, for the mob would have howled him down.

Clever salesman and practical psychologist that he was, Mark Antony so presented his case that it appeared not to be his own idea at all, but that of the Roman mob itself.

Go back to the lesson on initiative and leadership and read it again, and as you read, compare the psychology of it with that of Mark Antony's speech. Observe how the "you" and not "I" attitude toward others was emphasized. Observe, if you please, how this same point is emphasized throughout this course, and especially in Lesson Seven, on enthusiasm.

Shakespeare was, by far, the most able psychologist and writer known to civilization; for that reason, all of his writings are based upon unerring knowledge of the human mind. Throughout this speech, which he placed in the mouth of Mark Antony, you will observe how carefully he assumed the "you" attitude; so carefully that the Roman mob was sure that its decision was of its own making.

I must call your attention, however, to the fact that Mark Antony's appeal to the self-interest of the Roman mob was of the crafty type, and was based upon the stealth with which dishonest men often make use of this principle in appealing to the cupidity and avarice of their victims. While Mark Antony displayed evidence of great self-control in being able to assume, at the beginning of his speech, an attitude toward Brutus that was not real, at the same time it is obvious that his entire appeal was based upon his knowledge of how to influence the minds of the Roman mob through flattery.

The two letters reproduced in Lesson Seven of this course illustrate, in a very concrete way, the value of the "you" and the fatality of the "I" appeal. Go back and read these letters again and observe how the more successful of the two follows closely the Mark Antony appeal, while the other one is based upon an appeal of just the opposite nature. Whether you are writing a sales letter, or preaching a sermon or writing an advertisement or a book, you will do well to follow the same principles employed by Mark Antony in his famous speech.

Now let us turn our attention to the study of ways and means through which one may develop a pleasing personality.

Let us start with the first essential, which is character, for no one may have a pleasing personality without the foundation of a sound, positive character. Through the principle of telepathy you "telegraph" the nature of your character to those with whom you come in contact, which is responsible for what you have often called an "intuitive" feeling that the person whom you had just met but about whom you did not know very much, was not trustworthy.

You may embellish yourself with clothes of the neatest and latest design, and conduct yourself in a most pleasing manner as far as outside appearances go, but if there is greed, and envy, and hatred, and jealousy, and avarice, and selfishness in your heart, you will never attract any, except those characters which harmonize with your own. Like attracts like, and you may be sure therefore, that those who are attracted to you are those whose inward natures parallel your own.

You may embellish yourself with an artificial smile that belies your feelings, and you may practice the art of handshaking so that you can imitate, perfectly, the handshake of the person who is adept at this art, but if these outward manifestations of an attractive personality lack that vital factor called earnestness of purpose, they will repel instead of attract.

How, then, may one build character?

The first step in character building is rigid self-discipline.

In both the second and eighth lessons of this course, you will find the formula through which you may shape your character after any pattern that you choose, but I repeat it here, as it is based upon a principle that will bear much repetition, as follows:

First: Select those whose characters were made up of the qualities which you wish to build into your own character, and then proceed, in the manner described in Lesson Two, to appropriate these qualities through the aid of Auto-suggestion. Create in your imagination a council table and gather your characters around it each night, first having written out a clear, concise statement of the particular qualities that you wish to appropriate from each. Then proceed to affirm or suggest to yourself, in outspoken, audible words, that you are developing the desired qualities in yourself. As you do this close your eyes and see in your imagination the figures seated around your imaginary table, in the manner described in Lesson Two.

Second: Through the principles described in Lesson Eight on self-control, control your thoughts and keep your mind vitalized with thoughts of a positive nature. Let the dominating thought of your mind be a picture of the person that you intend to be; the person that you are deliberately building through this procedure. At least a dozen times a day, when you have a few minutes to yourself, shut your eyes and direct your thoughts to the figures which you have selected to sit at your imaginary council table, and feel, with a faith that knows NO LIMITATION, that you are actually growing to resemble in character those figures of your choice.

Third: Find at least one person each day, and more if possible, in whom you see some good quality that is worthy of praise, and praise it. Remember, however, that this praise must not be in the nature of cheap, insincere flattery; it must be genuine. Speak your words of praise with such earnestness that they will impress those to whom you speak. Then watch what happens. You will have rendered those whom you praise a decided benefit of great value to them, and you will have gone just one more step in the direction of developing the habit of looking for and finding the good qualities in others. I cannot overemphasize the far-reaching effects of this habit of praising, openly and enthusiastically, the good qualities in others; for this habit will soon reward you with a feeling of self-respect and manifestation of gratitude from others that will modify your entire personality. Here, again, the law of attraction enters, and those whom you praise will see in you the qualities that you see in them. Your success in the application of this formula will be in exact proportion to your faith in its soundness.

I do not merely believe that it is sound–I know that it is–and the reason I know is that I have used it successfully and I have also taught others how to use it successfully. Therefore, I have a right to promise you that you can use it with equal success. Furthermore, you can, with the aid of this formula, develop an attractive personality so speedily that you will surprise all who know you. The development of such a personality is entirely within your own control, a fact which gives you a tremendous advantage and at the same time places upon you the responsibility if you fail or neglect to exercise your privilege.

I now wish to direct your attention to the reason for speaking aloud the affirmation that you are developing the desired qualities which you have selected as the materials out of which to develop an attractive personality. This procedure has two desirable effects, namely–

First: It sets into motion the vibration through which the thought back of your words reaches and imbeds itself in your subconscious mind, where it takes root and grows until it becomes a great moving force in your outward, physical activities, leading in the direction of transformation of the thought into reality.

Second: It develops in you the ability to speak with force and conviction which will lead, finally, to great ability as a public speaker. No matter what your calling in life may be, you should be able to stand upon your feet and speak convincingly, as this is one of the most effective ways of developing an attractive personality.

Put feeling and emotion into your words as you speak, and develop a deep, rich tone of voice. If your voice is inclined to be high pitched, tone it down until it is soft and pleasing. You can never express an attractive personality to best advantage through a harsh or shrill voice. You must cultivate your voice until it becomes rhythmical and pleasing to the ear.

Remember that speech is the chief method of expressing your personality, and for this reason it is to your advantage to cultivate a style that is both forceful and pleasing. I do not recall a single outstanding attractive personality that was not made up, in part, of ability to speak with force and conviction.

Study the prominent men and women of today, wherever you find them, and observe the significant fact that the more prominent they are, the more efficient are they in speaking forcefully. Study the outstanding figures of the past in politics and statesmanship and observe that the most successful ones were those who were noted for their ability to speak with force and conviction.

In the field of business, industry and finance, it seems significant also that the most prominent leaders are men and women who are able public speakers.

In fact, no one may hope to become a prominent leader in any noteworthy undertaking without developing the ability to speak with forcefulness that carries conviction. While the salesman may never deliver a public address, he will profit nevertheless if he develops the ability to do so, because this ability increases his power to talk convincingly in ordinary conversation.

Let us now summarize the chief factors which enter into the development of an attractive personality, as follows:

First: Form the habit of interesting yourself in other people, and make it your business to find their good qualities and speak of them in terms of praise.

Second: Develop the ability to speak with force and conviction, both in your ordinary conversational tones and before public gatherings where you must use more volume.

Third: Clothe yourself in a style that is becoming to your physical build and the work in which you are engaged.

Fourth: Develop a positive character, through the aid of the formula outlined in this lesson.

Fifth: Learn how to shake hands so that you express warmth of feeling and enthusiasm through this form of greeting.

Sixth: Attract other people to you by first "attracting yourself" to them.

Seventh: Remember that your only limitation, within reason, is the one which YOU set up in YOUR OWN mind.

These seven points cover the most important factors that enter into the development of an attractive personality, but it seems hardly necessary to suggest that such a personality will not develop of its own accord. It will develop if you submit yourself to the discipline herein described with a firm determination to transform yourself into the person that you would like to be.

As I study this list of seven important factors that enter into the development of an attractive personality, I feel moved to direct your attention to the second and the fourth as being the most important.

If you will cultivate those finer thoughts and feelings and actions out of which a positive character is built, and then learn to express yourself with force and conviction, you will have developed an attractive personality–for it will be seen that out of this attainment will come the other qualities here outlined.

There is a great power of attraction back of the person who has a positive character, and this power expresses itself through unseen as well as visible sources. The moment you come within speaking distance of such a person, even though not a word is spoken, the influence of the "unseen power within" makes itself felt.

Every "shady" transaction in which you engage, every negative thought that you think, and every destructive act in which you indulge, destroys just so much of that "subtle something" within you that is known as character.

"There is full confession in the glances of our eyes; in our smiles; in salutations; in the grasp of the hands. His sin bedaubs him, mars all his good impression. Men know not why they do not trust him, but they do not trust him. His vice glasses his eye, demeans his cheek, pinches the nose, sets the mark of beast on the back of the head, and writes, 'O fool! Fool!' on the forehead of a king." (Emerson.)

I would direct your attention, now, to the first of the seven factors that enter into the development of an attractive personality. You have observed that all through this lesson I have gone into lengthy detail to show the material advantages of being agreeable to other people.

However, the biggest advantage of all lies not in the possibility of monetary or material gain which this habit offers, but in the beautifying effect that it has upon the character of all who practice it.

Acquire the habit of making yourself agreeable and you profit both materially and mentally; for you will never be as happy in any other way as you will be when you know that you are making others happy.

Remove the chips from your shoulders and quit challenging men to engage you in useless arguments! Remove the smoked glasses through which you see what you believe to be the "blueness" of life and behold the shining sunlight of friendliness in its stead. Throw away your hammer and quit knocking, for surely you must know that the big prizes of life go to the builders and not the destroyers.

The man who builds a house is an artist; the man who tears it down is a junkman. If you are a person with a grievance, the world will listen to your vitriolic "ravings," providing it does not "see you coming"; but, if you are a person with a message of friendliness and optimism, it will listen because it wishes to do so.

No person with a grievance can be also a person with an attractive personality!

The art of being agreeable–

–Just that one simple trait–

–is the very foundation of all successful salesmanship.

I drive my automobile five miles into the outskirts of the city to purchase gasoline which I could procure within two blocks of my own garage because the man who runs the filling station is an artist; he makes it his business to be agreeable. I go there, not because he has cheaper gasoline, but because I enjoy the vitalizing effect of his attractive personality!

I buy shoes at Fiftieth Street and Broadway, in New York, not because I cannot find other good shoes at the same price, but for the reason that Mr. Cobb, the manager of that particular Regal Store, has an attractive personality. While he is fitting me with shoes, he makes it his business to talk to me on subjects which he knows to be close to my heart.

I do my banking at the Harriman National Bank, at Forty-fourth Street and Fifth Avenue, not because there are not scores of other good banks much nearer my place of business; but for the reason that the tellers, and the cashiers, and the lobby detective, and Mr. Harriman, and all of the others with whom I come in contact, make it their business to be agreeable. My account is small but they receive me as though it were large.

I greatly admire John D. Rockefeller, Jr., not because he is the son of one of the world's richest men, but for the better reason that he, too, has acquired the art of being agreeable.

In the little city of Lancaster, Pennsylvania, lives M. T. Garvin, a very successful merchant whom I would travel hundreds of miles to visit, not because he is a wealthy merchant, but for the reason that he makes it his business to be agreeable. However, I have no doubt that his material success is closely related to this noble art of affability which he has acquired.

I have in my vest pocket a Parker fountain pen, and my wife and children have pens of the same brand, not because there are not other good fountain pens, but for the reason that I have been attracted to George S. Parker on account of his habit of being agreeable.

My wife takes the Ladies' Home Journal, not because there are not other good magazines of a similar nature, but for the reason that we became attracted to the journal several years ago, while Edward Bok was its editor, because he had acquired the art of being agreeable.

O ye struggling pilgrims, who are searching for the rainbow's end; ye drawers of water and hewers of wood, tarry for a moment by the wayside and learn a lesson from the successful men and women who have succeeded because they acquired the art of being agreeable!

You can win, for a time, through ruthlessness and stealth; you can garner in more of this world's goods than you will need by sheer force and shrewd strategy, without taking the time or going to the trouble of being agreeable; but, sooner or later, you will come to that point in life at which you will feel the pangs of remorse and the emptiness of your well-filled purse.

I never think of power and position and wealth that was attained by force, without feeling–very deeply–the sentiment expressed by a man whose name I dare not mention, as he stood at the tomb of Napoleon:

"A little while ago I stood by the grave of the old Napoleon–a magnificent tomb of gilt and gold, fit almost for a deity dead–and gazed upon the sarcophagus of rare and nameless marble, where rest at last the ashes of that restless man. I leaned over the balustrade and thought about the career of the greatest soldier of the modem world. I saw him at Toulon. I saw him walking upon the banks of the Seine contemplating suicide. I saw him putting down the mob in the streets of Paris. I saw him at the head of the army in Italy. I saw him crossing the bridge at Lodi with the tri-color in his hand. I saw him in Egypt, in the shadows of the pyramids; I saw him conquer the Alps and mingle the eagles of France with the eagles of the crags. I saw him at Marengo, at Ulm and at Austerlitz. I saw him in Russia, when the infantry of the snow and the cavalry of the wild blast scattered his legions like winter's withered leaves. I saw him at Leipsic in defeat and disaster–driven by a million bayonets back upon Paris–clutched like a wild beast–banished to Elba. I saw him escape and re-take an empire by the force of his genius. I saw him upon the frightful field of Waterloo, where chance and fate combined to wreck the fortunes of their former king. And I saw him at St. Helena, with his hands crossed behind him, gazing out upon the sad and solemn sea.

I thought of the widows and orphans he had made, of the tears that had been shed for his glory, and of the only woman who ever loved him, pushed from his heart by the cold hand of ambition. And I said I would rather have been a French peasant and worn wooden shoes; I would rather have lived in a hut with a vine growing over the door, and the grapes growing purple in the amorous kisses of the autumn sun; I would rather have been that poor peasant, with my wife by my side knitting as the day died out of the sky, with my children upon my knees and their arms about me; I would rather have been this man and gone down to the tongueless silence of the dreamless dust, than to have been that imperial personation of force and murder, known as Napoleon the Great."

I leave with you, as a fitting climax for this lesson, the thought of this deathless dissertation on a man who lived by the sword of force and died an ignominious death, an outcast in the eyes of his fellow men, a sore to the memory of civilization, a failure because–

He did not acquire the art of being agreeable! Because he could not or would not subordinate "self "for the good of his followers.

Lesson Eleven: ACCURATE THOUGHT

This is at one and the same time the most important, the most interesting and the most difficult to present lesson of this entire course on the Law of Success. It is important because it deals with a principle which runs through the entire course. It is interesting for the same reason. It is difficult to present for the reason that it will carry the average student far beyond the boundary line of his common experiences and into a realm of thought in which he is not accustomed to dwell.

Unless you study this lesson with an open mind, you will miss the very key-stone to the arch of this course, and without this stone you can never complete your Temple of Success.

This lesson will bring you a conception of thought which may carry you far above the level to which you have risen by the evolutionary processes to which you have been subjected in the past; and, for this reason, you should not be disappointed if, at first reading, you do not fully understand it. Most of us disbelieve that which we cannot understand, and it is with knowledge of this human tendency in mind that I caution you against closing your mind if you do not grasp all that is in this lesson at the first reading.

For thousands of years men made ships of wood, and of nothing else. They used wood because they believed that it was the only substance that would float; but that was because they had not yet advanced far enough in their thinking process to understand the truth that steel will float, and that it is far superior to wood for the building of ships. They did not know that anything could float which was lighter than the amount of water is displaced, and until they learned of this great truth they went on making ships of wood.

Until some twenty-five years ago, most men thought that only the birds could fly, but now we know that man can not only equal the flying of the birds, but he can excel it. Men did not know, until quite recently, that the great open void known as the air is more alive and more sensitive than anything that is on the earth. They did not know that the spoken word would travel through the ether with the speed of a flash of lightning, without the aid of wires. How could they know this when their minds had not been unfolded sufficiently to enable them to grasp it? The purpose of this lesson is to aid you in so unfolding and expanding your mind that you will be able to think with accuracy, for this unfoldment will open to you a door that leads to all the power you will need in completing your Temple of Success.

All through the preceding lessons of this course you observed that we have dealt with principles which any one could easily grasp and apply. You will also observe that these principles have been so presented that they lead to success as measured by material wealth. This seemed necessary for the reason that to most people the word success and the word money are synonymous terms. Obviously, the previous lessons of this course were intended for those who look upon worldly things and material wealth as being all that there is to success.

Presenting the matter in another way, I was conscious of the fact that the majority of the students of this course would feel disappointed if I pointed out to them a roadway to success that leads through other than the doorways of business, and finance, and industry; for it is a matter of common knowledge that most men want success that is spelled $UCCE$$!

Very well–let those who are satisfied with this standard of success have it; but some there are who will want to go higher up the ladder, in search of success which is measured in other than material standards, and it is for their benefit in particular that this and the subsequent lessons of this course are intended.

Accurate thought involves two fundamentals which all who indulge in it must observe.

First, to think accurately you must separate facts from mere information. There is much "information" available to you that is not based upon facts. Second, you must separate facts into two classes; namely, the important and the unimportant, or, the relevant and the irrelevant.

Only by so doing can you think clearly.

All facts which you can use in the attainment of your definite chief aim are important and relevant; all that you cannot use are unimportant and irrelevant. It is mainly the neglect of some to make this distinction which accounts for the chasm which separates so widely people who appear to have equal ability, and who have had equal opportunity. Without going outside of your own circle of acquaintances you can point to one or more persons who have had no greater opportunity than you have had, and who appear to have no more, and perhaps less, ability than you, who are achieving far greater success.

And you wonder why!

Search diligently and you will discover that all such people have acquired the habit of combining and using the important facts which affect their line of work. Far from working harder than you, they are perhaps working less and with greater ease. By virtue of their having learned the secret of separating the important facts from the unimportant, they have provided themselves with a sort of fulcrum and lever with which they can move with their little fingers loads that you cannot budge with the entire weight of your body.

The person who forms the habit of directing his attention to the important facts out of which he is constructing his Temple of Success, thereby provides himself with a power which may be likened to a trip-hammer which strikes a ten-ton blow as compared to a jack-hammer which strikes a one-pound blow!

If these similes appear to be elementary you must keep in mind the fact that some of the students of this course have not yet developed the capacity to think in more complicated terms, and to try to force them to do so would be the equivalent of leaving them hopelessly behind.

That you may understand the importance of distinguishing between facts and mere information, study that type of man who is guided entirely by that which he hears; the type who is influenced by all the "whisperings of the winds of gossip"; that accepts, without analysis, all that he reads in the newspapers and judges others by what their enemies and competitors and contemporaries say about them.

Search your circle of acquaintances and pick out one of this type as an example to keep before your mind while we are on this subject. Observe that this man usually begins his conversation with some such term as this –"I see by the papers," or "they say." The accurate thinker knows that the newspapers are not always accurate in their reports, and he also knows that what "they say" usually carries more falsehood than truth. If you have not risen above the "I see by the papers," and the "they say" class, you have still far to go before you become an accurate thinker. Of course, much truth and many facts travel in the guise of idle gossip and newspaper reports; but the accurate thinker will not accept as such all that he sees and hears.

This is a point which I feel impelled to emphasize, for the reason that it constitutes the rocks and reefs on which so many people flounder and go down to defeat in a bottomless ocean of false conclusions.

In the realm of legal procedure, there is a principle which is called the law of evidence; and the object of this law is to get at the facts. Any judge can proceed with justice to all concerned, if he has the facts upon which to base his judgment, but he may play havoc with innocent people if he circumvents the law of evidence and reaches a conclusion or judgment that is based upon hearsay information.

The law of Evidence varies according to the subject and circumstances with which it is used, but you will not go far wrong if, in the absence of that which you know to be facts, you form your judgments on the hypothesis that only that part of the evidence before you which furthers your own interests without working any hardship on others is based upon facts.

This is a crucial and important point in this lesson; therefore, I wish to be sure that you do not pass it by lightly. Many a man mistakes, knowingly or otherwise, expediency or fact; doing a thing, or refraining from doing it, for the sole reason that his action furthers his own interest without consideration as to whether it interferes with the rights of others.

No matter how regrettable, it is true that most thinking of today, far from being accurate, is based upon the sole foundation of expediency. It is amazing to the more advanced student of accurate thought, how many people there are who are "honest" when it is profitable to them, but find myriads of facts (?) to justify themselves in following a dishonest course when that course seems to be more profitable or advantageous.

No doubt you know people who are like that.

The accurate thinker adopts a standard by which he guides himself, and he follows that standard at all times, whether it works always to his immediate advantage, or carries him, now and then, through the fields of disadvantage (as it undoubtedly will).

The accurate thinker deals with facts, regardless of how they affect his own interests, for he knows that ultimately this policy will bring him out on top, in full possession of the object of his definite chief aim in life. He understands the soundness of the philosophy that the old philosopher, Croesus, had in mind when he said:

"There is a wheel on which the affairs of men revolve, and its mechanism is such that it prevents any man from being always fortunate."

The accurate thinker has but one standard by which he conducts himself, in his intercourse with his fellow men, and that standard is observed by him as faithfully when it brings him temporary disadvantage as it is when it brings him outstanding advantage; for, being an accurate thinker, he knows that, by the law of averages, he will more than regain at some future time that which he loses by applying his standard to his own temporary detriment.

You might as well begin to prepare yourself to understand that it requires the staunchest and most unshakable character to become an accurate thinker, for you can see that this is where the reasoning of this lesson is leading.

There is a certain amount of temporary penalty attached to accurate thinking; there is no denying this fact; but, while this is true, it is also true that the compensating reward, in the aggregate, is so overwhelmingly greater that you will gladly pay this penalty.

In searching for facts it is often necessary to gather them through the sole source of knowledge and experience of others. It then becomes necessary to examine carefully both the evidence submitted and the person from whom the evidence comes; and when the evidence is of such a nature that it affects the interest of the witness who is giving it, there will be reason to scrutinize it all the more carefully, as witnesses who have an interest in the evidence that they are submitting often yield to the temptation to color and pervert it to protect that interest.

If one man slanders another, his remarks should be accepted, if of any weight at all, with at least a grain of the proverbial salt of caution; for it is a common human tendency for men to find nothing but evil in those whom they do not like. The man who has attained to the degree of accurate thinking that enables him to speak of his enemy without exaggerating his faults, and minimizing his virtues, is the exception and not the rule.

Some very able men have not yet risen above this vulgar and self-destructive habit of belittling their enemies, competitors and contemporaries. I wish to bring this common tendency to your attention with all possible emphasis, because it is a tendency that is fatal to accurate thinking.

Before you can become an accurate thinker, you must understand and make allowance for the fact that the moment a man or a woman begins to assume leadership in any walk of life, the slanderers begin to circulate "rumors" and subtle whisperings reflecting upon his or her character.

No matter how fine one's character is or what service he may be engaged in rendering to the world, he cannot escape the notice of those misguided people who delight in destroying instead of building. Lincoln's political enemies circulated the report that he lived with a colored woman. Washington's political enemies circulated a similar report concerning him. Since both Lincoln and Washington were southern men, this report was undoubtedly regarded by those who circulated it as being at one and the same time the most fitting and degrading one they could imagine.

But we do not have to go back to our first President to find evidence of this slanderous nature with which men are gifted, for they went a step further, in paying their tributes to the late President Harding, and circulated the report that he had negro blood in his veins.

When Woodrow Wilson came back from Paris with what he believed to be a sound plan for abolishing war and settling international disputes, all except the accurate thinker might have been led to believe, by the reports of the "they say" chorus, that he was a combination of Nero and Judas Iscariot. The little politicians, and the cheap politicians, and the "interest-paid" politicians, and the plain ignorants who did no thinking of their own, all joined in one mighty chorus for the purpose of destroying the one and only man in the history of the world who offered a plan for abolishing war. The slanderers killed both Harding and Wilson–murdered them with vicious lies. They did the same to Lincoln, only in a somewhat more spectacular manner, by inciting a fanatic to hasten his death with a bullet.

Statesmanship and politics are not the only fields in which the accurate thinker must be on guard against the "they say" chorus. The moment a man begins to make himself felt in the field of industry or business, this chorus becomes active. If a man makes a better mouse-trap than his neighbor, the world will make a beaten path to his door, no doubt about that; and in the gang that will trail along will be those who come, not to commend, but to condemn and to destroy his reputation. The late John H. Patterson, president of the National Cash Register Company, is a notable example of what may happen to a man who builds a better cash register than that of his neighbor; yet, in the mind of the accurate thinker, there is not one scintilla of evidence to support the vicious reports that Mr. Patterson's competitors circulated about him.

As for Wilson and Harding, we may only judge how posterity will view them by observing how it has immortalized the names of Lincoln and Washington. Truth, alone, endures. All else must pass on with Time.

The object of these references is not to eulogize those who stand in no particular need of eulogy; but, it is to direct your attention to the fact that "they say" evidence is always subject to the closest scrutiny; and all the more so when it is of a negative or destructive nature. No harm can come from accepting, as fact, hearsay evidence that is constructive; but its opposite, if accepted at all, should be subjected to the closest inspection possible under the available means of applying the law of evidence.

As an accurate thinker, it is both your privilege and your duty to avail yourself of facts, even though you must go out of your way to get them. If you permit yourself to be swayed to and fro by all manner of information that comes to your attention, you will never become an accurate thinker; and if you do not think accurately, you cannot be sure of attaining the object of your definite chief aim in life.

Many a man has gone down to defeat because, due to his prejudice and hatred, he underestimated the virtues of his enemies or competitors. The eyes of the accurate thinker see facts–not the delusions of prejudice, hate and envy.

An accurate thinker must be something of a good sportsman–in that he is fair enough (with himself at least) to look for virtues as well as faults in other people, for it is not without reason to suppose that all men have some of each of these qualities.

"I do not believe that I can afford to deceive others–I know I cannot afford to deceive myself!"

This must be the motto of the accurate thinker.

With the supposition that these "hints" are sufficient to impress upon your mind the importance of searching for facts until you are reasonably sure that you have found them, we will take up the question of organizing, classifying and using these facts. Look, once more, in the circle of your own acquaintances and find a person who appears to accomplish more with less effort than do any of his associates. Study this man and you observe that he is a strategist in that he has learned how to arrange facts so that he brings to his aid the Law of Increasing Returns which we described in a previous lesson.

The man who knows that he is working with facts goes at his task with a feeling of self-confidence which enables him to refrain from temporizing, hesitating or waiting to make sure of his ground. He knows in advance what the outcome of his efforts will be; therefore, he moves more rapidly and accomplishes more than does the man who must "feel his way" because he is not sure that he is working with facts.

The man who has learned of the advantages of searching for facts as the foundation of his thinking has gone a very long way toward the development of accurate thinking, but the man who has learned how to separate facts into the important and the unimportant has gone still further. The latter may be compared to the man who uses a trip-hammer, and thereby accomplishes at one blow more than the former, who uses a tack-hammer, can accomplish with ten thousand blows.

Let us analyze, briefly, a few men who have made it their business to deal with the important or relevant facts pertaining to their life-work.

If it were not for the fact that this course is being adapted to the practical needs of men and women of the present workaday world, we would go back to the great men of the past–Plato, Aristotle, Epictetus, Socrates, Solomon and Moses–and direct attention to their habit of dealing with facts. However, we can find examples nearer our own generation that will serve our purpose to better advantage at this particular point. Inasmuch as this is an age in which money is looked upon as being the most concrete proof of success, let us study a man who has accumulated almost as much of it as has any other man in the history of the world–John D. Rockefeller.

Mr. Rockefeller has one quality that stands out, like a shining star, above all of his other qualities; it is his habit of dealing only with the relevant facts pertaining to his life-work. As a very young man (and a very poor young man, at that) Mr. Rockefeller adopted, as his definite chief aim, the accumulation of great wealth. It is not my purpose, nor is it of any particular advantage, to enter into Mr. Rockefeller's method of accumulating his fortune other than to observe that his most pronounced quality was that of insisting on facts as the basis of his business philosophy. Some there are who say that Mr. Rockefeller was not always fair with his competitors. That may or may not be true (as accurate thinkers we will leave the point undisturbed), but no one (not even his competitors) ever accused Mr. Rockefeller of forming "snap-judgments" or of underestimating the strength of his competitors. He not only recognized facts that affected his business, wherever and whenever he found them, but he made it his business to search for them until he was sure he had found them.

Thomas A. Edison is another example of a man who has attained to greatness through the organization, classification and use of relevant facts. Mr. Edison works with natural laws as his chief aids; therefore, he must be sure of his facts before he can harness those laws. Every time you press a button and switch on an electric light, remember that it was Mr. Edison's capacity for organizing relevant facts which made this possible.

Every time you hear a phonograph, remember that Mr. Edison is the man who made it a reality, through his persistent habit of dealing with relevant facts.

Every time you see a moving picture, remember that it was born of Mr. Edison's habit of dealing with important and relevant facts.

In the field of science relevant facts are the tools with which men and women work.

Mere information, or hearsay evidence, is of no value to Mr. Edison; yet he might have wasted his life working with it, as millions of other people are doing.

Hearsay evidence could never have produced the incandescent electric light, the phonograph or the moving picture, and if it had, the phenomenon would have been an "accident." In this lesson we are trying to prepare the student to avoid "accidents."

The question now arises as to what constitutes an important and relevant fact.

The answer depends entirely upon what constitutes your definite chief aim in life, for an important and relevant fact is any fact which you can use, without interfering with the rights of others, in the attainment of that purpose.

All other facts, as far as you are concerned, are superfluous and of minor importance at most.

However, you can work just as hard in organizing, classifying and using unimportant and irrelevant facts as you can in dealing with their opposites, but you will not accomplish as much.

Up to this point we have been discussing only one factor of accurate thought, that which is based upon deductive reasoning. Perhaps this is the point at which some of the students of this course will have to think along lines with which they are not familiar, for we come, now, to the discussion of thought which does much more than gather, organize and combine facts.

Let us call this creative thought!

That you may understand why it is called creative thought it is necessary briefly to study the process of evolution through which the thinking man has been created.

Thinking man has been a long time on the road of evolution, and he has traveled a very long way. In the words of judge T. Troward (in *Bible Mystery and Bible Meaning),* "Perfected man is the apex of the Evolutionary Pyramid, and this by a necessary sequence."

Let us trace thinking man through the five evolutionary steps through which we believe he has traveled, beginning with the very lowest; namely-

1. The Mineral Period. Here we find life in its lowest form, lying motionless and inert; a mass of mineral substances, with no power to move.
2. Then comes the Vegetable Period. Here we find life in a more active form, with intelligence sufficient to gather food, grow and reproduce, but still unable to move from its fixed moorings.
3. Then comes the Animal Period. Here we find life in a still higher and more intelligent form, with ability to move from place to place.
4. Then comes the Human or Thinking Man Period, where we find life in its highest known form; the highest, because man can think, and because thought is the highest known form of organized energy. In the realm of thought man knows no limitations. He can send his thoughts to the stars with the quickness of a flash of lightning. He can gather facts and assemble them in new and varying combinations. He can create hypotheses and translate them into physical reality, through thought. He can reason both inductively and deductively.
5. Then comes the Spiritual Period. On this plane the lower forms of life, described in the previously mentioned four periods, converge and become infinitude in nature. At this point thinking man has unfolded, expanded and grown until he has projected his thinking ability into infinite intelligence. As yet, thinking man is but an infant in this fifth period, for he has not learned how to appropriate to his own use this infinite intelligence called Spirit. Moreover, with a few rare exceptions, man has not yet recognized thought as the connecting link which gives him access to the power of infinite intelligence. These exceptions have been such men as Moses, Solomon, Plato, Aristotle, Socrates, Confucius and a comparatively small number of others of their type. Since their time we have had many who partly uncovered this great truth; yet the truth, itself, is as available now as it was then.

To make use of creative thought, one must work very largely on faith, which is the chief reason why more of us do not indulge in this sort of thought. The most ignorant of the race can think in terms of deductive reasoning, in connection with matters of a purely physical and material nature, but to go a step higher and think in terms of infinite intelligence is another question. The average man is totally at sea the moment he gets beyond that which he can comprehend with the aid of his five physical senses of seeing, hearing, feeling, smelling and tasting. Infinite intelligence works through none of these agencies and we cannot invoke its aid through any of them.

How, then, may one appropriate the power of infinite intelligence is but a natural question.

And the answer is:

Through creative thought!

To make clear the exact manner in which this is done I will now call your attention to some of the preceding lessons of this course through which you have been prepared to understand the meaning of creative thought.

In the second lesson, and to some extent in practically every other lesson that followed it, up to this one, you have observed the frequent introduction of the term "Autosuggestion." (Suggestion that you make to yourself.) We now come back to that term again, because Auto-suggestion is the telegraph line, so to speak, over which you may register in your subconscious mind a description or plan of that which you wish to create or acquire in physical form.

It is a process you can easily learn to use.

The subconscious mind is the intermediary between the conscious thinking mind and infinite intelligence, and you can invoke the aid of infinite intelligence only through the medium of the subconscious mind, by giving it clear instructions as to what you want. Here you become familiar with the psychological reason for a definite chief aim. If you have not already seen the importance of creating a definite chief aim as the object of your life-work, you will undoubtedly do so before this lesson shall have been mastered.

Knowing, from my own experience as a beginner in the study of this and related subjects, how little I understood such terms as "Subconscious Mind" and "Auto-suggestion" and "Creative Thought," I have taken the liberty, throughout this course, of describing these terms through every conceivable simile and illustration, with the object of making their meaning and the method of their application so clear that no student of this course can possibly fail to understand. This accounts for the repetition of terms which you will observe throughout the course, and at the same time serves as an apology to those students who have already advanced far enough to grasp the meaning of much that the beginner will not understand at first reading.

The subconscious mind has one outstanding characteristic to which I will now direct your attention; namely, it records the suggestions which you send it through Autosuggestion, and invokes the aid of infinite intelligence in translating these suggestions into their natural physical form, through natural means which are in no way out of the ordinary. If is important that you understand the foregoing sentence, for, if you fail to understand it, you are likely to fail, also, to understand the importance of the very foundation upon which this entire course is built–that foundation being the principle of infinite intelligence, which may be reached and appropriated at will through aid of the law of the "Master Mind" described in the Introductory Lesson.

Study carefully, thoughtfully and with meditation, the entire preceding paragraph. The subconscious mind has another outstanding characteristic– it accepts and acts upon all suggestions that reach it, whether they are constructive or destructive, and whether they come from the outside or from your own conscious mind.

You can see, therefore, how essential it is for you to observe the law of evidence and carefully follow the principles laid down in the beginning of this lesson, in the selection of that which you will pass on to your sub-conscious mind through Autosuggestion. You can see why one must search diligently for facts, and why one cannot afford to lend a receptive ear to the slanderer and the scandal monger–for to do so is the equivalent of feeding the subconscious mind with food that is poison and ruinous to creative thought.

The subconscious mind may be likened to the sensitive plate of a camera on which the picture of any object placed before the camera will be recorded. The plate of the camera does not choose the sort of picture to be recorded on it; it records anything which reaches it through the lens. The conscious mind may be likened to the shutter which shuts off the light from the sensitized plate, permitting nothing to reach the plate for record except that which the operator wishes to reach it. The lens of the camera may be likened to Auto-suggestion, for it is the medium which carries the image of the object to be registered, to the sensitized plate of the camera. And infinite intelligence may be likened to the one who develops the sensitized plate, after a picture has been recorded on it, thus bringing the picture into physical reality.

The ordinary camera is a splendid instrument with which to compare the whole process of creative thought. First comes the selection of the object to be exposed before the camera. This represents one's definite chief aim in life. Then comes the actual operation of recording a clear outline of that purpose, through the lens of Autosuggestion, on the sensitized plate of the subconscious mind. Here infinite intelligence steps in and develops the outline of that purpose in a physical form appropriate to the nature of the purpose. The part which you must play is clear!

You select the picture to be recorded (definite chief aim). Then you fix your conscious mind upon this purpose with such intensity that it communicates with the subconscious mind, through Auto-suggestion, and registers that picture. You then begin to watch for and to expect manifestations of physical realization of the subject of that picture.

Bear in mind the fact that you do not sit down and wait, nor do you go to bed and sleep, with the expectation of awaking to find that infinite intelligence has showered you with the object of your definite chief aim. You go right ahead, in the usual way, doing your daily work in accordance with the instructions laid down in Lesson Nine of this course, with full faith and confidence that natural ways and means for the attainment of the object of your definite purpose will open to you at the proper time and in a suitable manner.

The way may not open suddenly, from the first step to the last, but it may open one step at a time. Therefore, when you are conscious of an opportunity to take the first step, take it without hesitation, and do the same when the second, and the third, and all subsequent steps, essential for the attainment of the object of your definite chief aim, are manifested to you.

Infinite intelligence will not build you a home and deliver that home to you, ready to enter; but infinite intelligence will open the way and provide the necessary means with which you may build your own house.

Infinite intelligence will not command the cashier of your bank to place a definite sum of money to your credit, just because you suggested this to your subconscious mind; but infinite intelligence will open to you the way in which you may earn or borrow that money and place it to your own credit.

Infinite intelligence will not throw out the present incumbent of the White House and make you President in his place; but infinite intelligence would most likely proceed, under the proper circumstances, to influence you to prepare yourself to fill that position with credit and then help you to attain it through the regular method of procedure.

Do not rely upon the performance of miracles for the attainment of the object of your definite chief aim; rely upon the power of infinite intelligence to guide you, through natural channels, and with the aid of natural laws, for its attainment. Do not expect infinite intelligence to bring to you the object of your definite chief aim; instead, expect infinite intelligence to direct you toward that object.

As a beginner, do not expect infinite intelligence to move quickly in your behalf; but, as you become more adept in the use of the principle of Auto-suggestion, and as you develop the faith and understanding required for its quick realization, you can create a definite chief aim and witness its immediate translation into physical reality. You did not walk the first time you tried, but now, as an adult (an adept at walking), you walk without effort. You also look down at the little child as it wobbles around, trying to walk, and laugh at its efforts. As a beginner in the use of creative thought, you may be compared to the little child who is learning to take its first step.

I have the best of reasons for knowing that this comparison is accurate, but I will not state them. I will let you find out your own reason, in your own way. Keep in mind, always, the principle of evolution through the operation of which everything physical is eternally reaching upward and trying to complete the cycle between finite and infinite intelligences.

Man, himself, is the highest and most noteworthy example of the working of the principle of evolution. First, we find him down in the minerals of the earth, where there is life but no intelligence. Next, we find him raised, through the growth of vegetation (evolution), to a much higher form of life, where he enjoys sufficient intelligence to feed himself. Next, we find him functioning in the animal period, where he has a comparatively high degree of intelligence, with ability to move around from place to place. Lastly, we find him risen above the lower species of the animal kingdom, to where he functions as a thinking entity, with ability to appropriate and use infinite intelligence.

Observe that he did not reach this high state all at one bound. He climbed–step-by-step, perhaps through many reincarnations.

Keep this in mind and you will understand why you cannot reasonably expect infinite intelligence to circumvent the natural laws and turn man into the storehouse of all knowledge and all power until he has prepared himself to use this knowledge and power with higher than finite intelligence.

If you want a fair example of what may happen to a man who suddenly comes into control of power, study some newly-rich or someone who has inherited a fortune.

Money-power in the hands of John D. Rockefeller is not only in safe hands, but it is in hands where it is serving mankind throughout the world, blotting out ignorance, destroying contagious disease and serving in a thousand other ways of which the average individual knows nothing.

But place John D. Rockefeller's fortune in the hands of some young lad who has not yet finished high school and you might have another story to tell, the details of which your own imagination and your knowledge of human nature will supply.

I will have more to say on this subject in Lesson Fourteen.

If you have ever done any farming, you understand that certain preparations are necessary before a crop can be produced from the ground. You know, of course, that grain will not grow in the woods, that it requires sunshine and rain for its growth.

Likewise, you understand that the farmer must plow the soil and properly plant the grain.

After all this has been done, he then waits on Nature to do her share of the work; and she does it in due time, without outside help.

This is a perfect simile which illustrates the method through which one may attain the object of one's definite chief aim. First comes the preparing of the soil to receive the seed, which is represented by faith and infinite intelligence and understanding of the principle of Auto-suggestion and the subconscious mind through which the seed of a definite purpose may be planted. Then comes a period of waiting and working for the realization of the object of that purpose. During this period, there must be continuous, intensified faith, which serves as the sunshine and the rain, without which the seed will wither and die in the ground. Then comes realization, harvest-time.

And a wonderful harvest can be brought forth.

I am fully conscious of the fact that much of that which I am stating will not be understood by the beginner, at the first reading, for I have in mind my own experiences at the start. However, as the evolutionary process carries on its work (and it will do so, make no mistake about this) all the principles described in this and in all other lessons of this course, will become as familiar to you as did the multiplication table after you had mastered it; and, what is of greater importance still, these principles will work with the same unvarying certainty as does the principle of multiplication.

Each lesson of this course has provided you with definite instructions to follow. The instructions have been simplified as far as possible, so anyone can understand them.

Nothing has been left to the student except to follow the instructions and supply the faith in their soundness without which they would be useless.

In this lesson you are dealing with four major factors to which I would again direct your attention with the request that you familiarize yourself with them. They are: Autosuggestion, the Subconscious Mind, Creative Thought and Infinite Intelligence. These are the four roadways over which you must travel in your upward climb in quest of knowledge. Observe that you control three of these. Observe, also–and this is especially emphasized– that upon the manner in which you traverse these three roadways will depend the time and place at which they will converge into the fourth, or infinite intelligence.

You understand what is meant by the terms Auto-suggestion and Subconscious Mind. Let us make sure that you understand, also, what is meant by the term Creative Thought. This means thought of a positive, non-destructive, creative nature. The object of Lesson Eight, on Self-control, was to prepare you to understand and successfully apply the principle of Creative Thought. If you have not mastered that lesson you are not ready to make use of Creative Thought in the attainment of your definite chief aim.

Let me repeat a simile already used by saying that your subconscious mind is the field or the soil in which you sow the seed of your definite chief aim. Creative Thought is the instrument with which you keep that soil fertilized and conditioned to awaken that seed into growth and maturity. Your subconscious mind will not germinate the seed of your definite chief aim nor will infinite intelligence translate that purpose into physical reality if you fill your mind with hatred, and envy, and jealousy, and selfishness and greed. These negative or destructive thoughts are the weeds which will choke out the seed of your definite purpose.

Creative thought presupposes that you will keep your mind in a state of expectancy of attainment of the object of your definite chief aim; that you will have full faith and confidence in its attainment in due course and in due order.

If this lesson does that which it was intended to do, it will bring you a fuller and deeper realization of the third lesson of this course, on Self-confidence. As you begin to learn how to plant the seed of your desires in the fertile soil of your subconscious mind, and how to fertilize that seed until it springs into life and action, you will then have reason, indeed, to believe in yourself.

And, after you have reached this point in the process of your evolution, you will have sufficient knowledge of the real source from which you are drawing your power, to give full credit to infinite intelligence for all that you had previously credited to your Self-confidence.

Auto-suggestion is a powerful weapon with which one may rise to heights of great achievement, when it is used constructively. Used in a negative manner, however, it may destroy all possibility of success, and if so used continuously it will actually destroy health.

Careful comparison of the experiences of leading physicians and psychiatrists disclosed the startling information that approximately seventy-five per cent of those who are ill are suffering from hypochondria, which is a morbid state of mind causing useless anxiety about one's health.

Stated in plain language, the hypochondriac is a person who believes he or she is suffering with some sort of imaginary disease, and often these unfortunates believe they have every disease of which they ever heard the name.

Hypochondriacal conditions are generally super induced by auto-intoxication, or poisoning through failure of the intestinal system to throw off the waste matter. The person who suffers with such a toxic condition is not only unable to think with accuracy, but suffers from all sorts of perverted, destructive, illusory thoughts. Many sick people have tonsils removed, or teeth pulled, or the appendix taken out, when their trouble could have been removed with an internal bath and a bottle of Citrate of Magnesia (with due apologies to my friends, the physicians, one of the leading of whom gave me this information).

Hypochondria is the beginning of most cases of insanity!

Dr. Henry R. Rose is authority for the following typical example of the power of Autosuggestion: "'If my wife dies I will not believe there is a God.' His wife was ill with pneumonia, and this is the way he greeted me when I reached his home. She had sent for me because the doctor had told her she could not recover. (Most doctors know better than to make a statement such as this in the presence of a patient.) She had called her husband and two sons to her bedside and bidden them goodbye. Then she asked that I, her minister, be sent for. I found the husband in the front room sobbing and the sons doing their best to brace her up. When I went into her room she was breathing with difficulty, and the trained nurse told me she was very low.

"I soon found that Mrs. N___had sent for me to look after her two sons after she was gone. Then I said to her: 'You mustn't give up. YOU ARE NOT GOING TO DIE! You have always been a strong and healthy woman and I do not believe God wants you to die and leave your boys to me or anyone else.'

"I talked to her along this line and then read the 103d Psalm and made a prayer in which I prepared her to get well rather than to enter eternity. I told her to put her faith in God and throw her mind and will against every thought of dying. Then I left her, saying, 'I will come again, and I will then find you much better.'

"This was on Sunday morning. I called that afternoon. Her husband met me with a smile. He said that the moment I had gone his wife called him and the boys into the room and said: 'Dr. Rose says that I am not going to die; that I am going to get well, and I am.'

"She did get well. But what did it? Two things: Auto-suggestion, super induced by the suggestion I had given her, and faith on her part. I came just in the nick of time, and so great was her faith in me that I was able to inspire faith in herself. It was that faith that tipped the scales and brought her through the pneumonia. No medicine can cure pneumonia. The physicians admit that. There are cases of pneumonia, perhaps, that nothing can cure. We all sadly agree to that, but there are times, as in this case, when the mind, if worked upon and worked with in just the right way, will turn the tide. While there is life there is hope; but hope must rule supreme and do the good that hope was intended to do.

"Here is another remarkable case showing the power of the human mind when used constructively. A physician asked me to see Mrs. H___. He said there was nothing organically wrong with her, but she just wouldn't eat. Having made up her mind that she could not retain anything on her stomach, she had quit eating, and was slowly starving herself to death. I went to see her and found, first, that she had no religious belief. She had lost her faith in God. I also found that she had no confidence in her power to retain food. My first effort was to restore her faith in the Almighty and to get her to believe that He was with her and would give her power. Then I told her that she could eat anything she wanted. True, her confidence in me was great and my statement impressed her. She began to eat from that day! She was out of her bed in three days, for the first time in weeks. She is a normal, healthy and happy woman today.

"What did it? The same forces as those described in the preceding case; outside suggestion (which she accepted in faith and applied, through self-suggestion) and inward confidence.

"There are times when the mind is sick and it makes the body sick. At such times it needs a stronger mind to heal it by giving it direction and especially by giving it confidence and faith in itself. This is called suggestion. It is transmitting your confidence and power to another, and with such force as to make the other believe as you wish and do as you will. It need not be hypnotism. You can get wonderful results with the patient wide awake and perfectly rational. The patient must believe in you and you must understand the workings of the human mind in order to meet the arguments and questions of the patient. Each one of us can be a healer of this sort and thus help our fellow men.

"It is the duty of every person to read some of the best books on the forces of the human mind and learn what amazing things the mind can do to keep people well and happy. We see the terrible things that wrong thinking does to people, even going to such lengths as to make them positively insane. It is high time we found out the good things the mind can do, not only to cure mental disorders, but physical diseases as well."

You should delve deeper into this subject.

I do not say the mind can cure everything. There is no reliable evidence that certain forms of cancer have been cured by thinking or faith or any mental or religious process. If you would be cured of cancer you must take it at the very beginning and treat it surgically. There is no other way, and it would be criminal to suggest that there is. But the mind can do much with so many types of human indisposition and disease that we ought to rely upon it more often than we do.

Napoleon, during his campaign in Egypt, went among his soldiers who were dying by the hundreds of the black plague. He touched one of them and lifted a second, to inspire the others not to be afraid, for the awful disease seemed to spread as much by the aid of the imagination as in any other way. Goethe tells us that he himself went where there was malignant fever and never contracted it because he put forth his will. These giants among men knew something WE ARE SLOWLY BEGINNING TO FIND OUT–the power of Auto-suggestion! This means the influence we have upon ourselves by believing we cannot catch a disease or be sick. There is something about the operation of the automatic or subconscious mind by which it rises above disease germs and bids defiance to them when we resolve not to let the thought of them frighten us, or when we go in and out among the sick, even the contagiously sick, without thinking anything about it.

"Imagination will kill a cat," so runs the old adage. It certainly will kill a man, or, on the other hand, it will help him rise to heights of achievement of the most astounding nature, providing he uses it as the basis of self-confidence. There are authentic cases on record of men having actually died because they imagined they were cut by a knife across the jugular vein, when in reality a piece of ice was used and water was allowed to drip so they could hear it and imagine their blood was running out. They had been blindfolded before the experiment was begun. No matter how well you may be when you start for work in the morning, if everyone you meet should say to you, "How ill you look; you should see a doctor," it will not be long before you begin to feel ill, and if this keeps up a few hours you will arrive at home in the evening as limp as a rag and ready for a doctor. Such is the power of the imagination or Auto-suggestion.

The imaginative faculty of the human mind is a marvelous piece of mental machinery, but it may, and usually does, play queer tricks on us unless we keep constantly on guard and control it.

If you allow your imagination to "expect the worst" it will play havoc with you. Young medical students not infrequently become frightened and believe they have every disease on the medical calendar, as the result of medical lectures and class-room discussions of the various diseases.

As has been stated, hypochondria may often be super induced by toxic poisoning, through improper elimination of the waste matter of the body; also, it may be brought on by false alarm, through improper use of the imagination. In other words, the hypochondriacal condition may have as its cause a real physical basis, or it may arise entirely as the result of allowing the imagination to run wild. Physicians are pretty well agreed upon this point!

Dr. Schofield describes the case of a woman who had a tumor. They placed her on the operating table and gave her anesthetics, when lo! The tumor immediately disappeared, and no operation was necessary. But when she came back to consciousness the tumor returned. The physician then learned that she had been living with a relative who had a real tumor, and that her imagination was so vivid that she had imagined this one upon herself. She was placed on the operating table again, given anesthetics and then she was strapped around the middle so that the tumor could not artificially return. When she revived she was told that a successful operation had been performed but that it would be necessary to wear the bandage for several days. She believed the doctor, and when the bandage was finally removed the tumor did not return. No operation whatever had been performed. She had simply relieved her subconscious mind of the thought that she had a tumor and her imagination had nothing to work upon save the idea of health, and, as she had never really been sick, of course she remained normal.

The mind may be cured of imaginary ills in exactly the same manner that it became diseased with those ills, by Auto-suggestion. The best time to work on a faulty imagination is at night, just as you are ready to go to sleep, for then the automatic or subconscious mind has everything its own way, and the thoughts or suggestions you give it just as your conscious or "day" mind is about to go off duty will be taken up and worked on during the night.

This may seem impossible, but you can easily test the principle by the following procedure: You wish to get up at seven o'clock tomorrow morning, or at some hour other than your regular time to awaken. Say to yourself, as you are about ready to go to sleep, "I must arise at seven o'clock tomorrow without fail." Repeat this several times, at the same time impressing the fact upon your mind that you must actually arise at the precise moment mentioned. Turn this thought over to your subconscious mind with absolute confidence that you will awaken at seven o'clock, and when that hour arrives your subconscious mind will awaken you. This test has been successfully made hundreds of times. The subconscious mind will awaken you, at any hour you demand, just as if someone came to your bed and tapped you on the shoulder. But you must give the command in no uncertain or indefinite terms.

Likewise, the subconscious mind may be given any other sort of orders and it will carry them out as readily as it will awaken you at a given hour. For example, give the command, as you are about to go to sleep each night, for your subconscious mind to develop self-confidence, courage, initiative or any other quality, and it will do your bidding.

If the imagination of man can create imaginary ills and send one to bed with those ills, it can also, and just as easily, remove the cause of those ills.

Man is a combination of chemical equivalents the value of which is said to be about twenty-six dollars, with the exception, of course, of that stupendous power called the human mind. In the aggregate the mind seems to be a complicated machine, but in reality, as far as the manner in which it may be used is concerned, it is the nearest thing to perpetual motion that is known. It works automatically when we are asleep; it works both automatically and in conjunction with the will, or voluntary section, when we are awake.

The mind is deserving of the minutest possible analysis in this lesson because the mind is the energy with which all thinking is done. To learn how to THINK ACCURATELY, the teaching of which is the sole object of this lesson, one must thoroughly understand:

First: That the mind can be controlled, guided and directed to creative, constructive ends.

Second: That the mind can be directed to destructive ends, and, that it may, voluntarily, tear down and destroy unless it is with plan and deliberation controlled and directed constructively.

Third: That the mind has power over every cell of the body, and can be made to cause every cell to do its intended work perfectly, or it may, through neglect or wrong direction, destroy the normal functionary purposes of any or all cells.

Fourth: That all achievement of man is the result of thought, the part which his physical body plays being of secondary importance, and in many instances of no importance whatsoever except as a housing place for the mind.

Fifth: That the greatest of all achievements, whether in literature, art, finance, industry, commerce, transportation, religion, politics or scientific discoveries, are usually the results of ideas conceived in one man's brain but ACTUALLY TRANSFORMED INTO REALITY BY OTHER MEN, through the combined use of their minds and bodies. (Meaning that the conception of an idea is of greater importance than the transformation of that idea into more material form, because relatively few men can conceive useful ideas, while there are hundreds of millions who can develop an idea and give it material form after it has been conceived.)

Sixth: The majority of all thoughts conceived in the minds of men are not ACCURATE, being more in the nature of "opinions" or "snap-judgments." When Alexander the Great sighed because he had no more worlds (as he believed) that could be conquered he was in a frame of mind similar to that of the present-day "Alexanders" of science, industry, invention, etc., whose "accurate thoughts" have conquered the air and the sea, explored practically every square mile of the little earth on which we live, and wrested from Nature thousands of "secrets" which, a few generations ago, would have been set down as "miracles" of the most astounding and imponderable sort.

In all this discovery and mastery of mere physical substances is it not strange, indeed, that we have practically neglected and overlooked the most marvelous of all powers, the human mind?

All scientific men who have made a study of the human mind readily agree on this–that the surface has not yet been scratched in the study of the wonderful power which lies dormant in the mind of man, waiting, as the oak tree sleeps in the acorn, to be aroused and put to work. Those who have expressed themselves on the subject are of the opinion that the next great cycle of discovery lies in the realm of the human mind. The possible nature of these discoveries has been suggested, in many different ways, in practically every lesson of this course, particularly in this and the following lessons of the course.

If these suggestions appear to lead the student of this philosophy into deeper water than he or she is accustomed to, bear in mind the fact that the student has the privilege of stopping at any depth desired, until ready, through thought and study, to go further. The author of this course has found it necessary to take the lead, and to keep far enough ahead, as it were, to induce the student to go at least a few paces ahead of the normal average range of human thought. It is not expected that any beginner will, at first, try to assimilate and put into use all that has been included in this philosophy. But, if the net result of the course is nothing more than to sow the seed of constructive thought in the mind of the student the author's work will have been completed. Time, plus the student's own desire for knowledge, will do the rest.

This is an appropriate place to state frankly that many of the suggestions passed on through this course would, if literally followed, lead the student far beyond the necessary bounds and present needs of what is ordinarily called business philosophy. Stated differently, this course goes more deeply into the functioning processes of the human mind than is necessary as far as the use of this philosophy as a means of achieving business or financial success is concerned.

However, it is presumed that many students of this course will wish to go more deeply into the study of mind power than may be required for purely material achievement, and the author has had in mind these students throughout the labor of organizing and writing this course.

SUMMARY OF PRINCIPLES INVOLVED IN ACCURATE THINKING

We have discovered that the body of man is not singular, but plural–that it consists of billions on top of billions of living, intelligent, individual cells which carry on a very definite, well-organized work of building, developing and maintaining the human body.

We have discovered that these cells are directed, in their respective duties, by the subconscious or automatic action of the mind; that the subconscious section of the mind can be, to a very large extent, controlled and directed by the conscious or voluntary section of the mind.

We have found that any idea or thought which is held in the mind, through repetition, has a tendency to direct the physical body to transform such thought or idea into its material equivalent. We have found that any order that is PROPERLY given to the subconscious section of the mind (through the law of Auto-suggestion) will be carried out unless it is sidetracked or countermanded by another and stronger order. We have found that the subconscious mind does not question the source from which it receives orders, nor the soundness of those orders, but it will proceed to direct the muscular system of the body to carry out any order it receives.

This explains the necessity for guarding closely the environment from which we receive suggestions, and by which we are subtly and quietly influenced at times and in ways of which we do not take cognizance through the conscious mind. We have found that every movement of the human body is controlled by either the conscious or the subconscious section of the mind; that not a muscle can be moved until an order has been sent out by one or the other of these two sections of the mind, for the movement.

When this principle is thoroughly understood we understand, also, the powerful effect of any idea or thought which we create through the faculty of IMAGINATION and hold in the conscious mind until the subconscious section of the mind has time to take over that thought and begin the work of transforming it into its material counterpart. When we understand the principle through which any idea is first placed in the conscious mind, and held there until the subconscious section of the mind picks it up and appropriates it, we have a practical working knowledge of the Law of Concentration, covered by next lesson (and, it might be added, we have also a thorough understanding of the reason why the Law of Concentration is necessarily a part of this philosophy).

When we understand this working relationship between the imagination, the conscious mind and the subconscious section of the mind, we can see that the very first step in the achievement of any definite chief aim is to create a definite picture of that which is desired. This picture is then placed in the conscious mind, through the Law of Concentration, and held there (through the formulas described in next lesson) until the subconscious section of the mind picks it up and translates it into its ultimate and desired form.

Surely this principle has been made clear. It has been stated and restated, over and over, not only for the purpose of thoroughly describing it, but, of greater importance, to IMPRESS UPON THE MIND OF THE STUDENT THE PART IT PLAYS IN ALL HUMAN ACHIEVEMENT.

THE VALUE OF ADOPTING A CHIEF AIM

This lesson on Accurate Thought not only describes the real purpose of a definite chief aim, but it explains in simple terms the principles through which such an aim or purpose may be realized. We first create the objective toward which we are striving, through the imaginative faculty of the mind, then transfer an outline of this objective to paper by writing out a definite statement of it in the nature of a definite chief aim. By daily reference to this written statement the idea or thing aimed for is taken up by the conscious mind and handed over to the subconscious mind, which, in turn, directs the energies of the body to transform the desire into material form.

DESIRE

Strong, deeply rooted desire is the starting point of all achievement. Just as the electron is the last unit of matter discernible to the scientist, DESIRE is the seed of all achievement; the starting place, back of which there is nothing, or at least there is nothing of which we have any knowledge.

A definite chief aim, which is only another name for DESIRE, would be meaningless unless based upon a deeply seated, strong desire for the object of the chief aim. Many people "wish" for many things, but a wish is not the equivalent of a strong DESIRE, and therefore wishes are of little or no value unless they are crystallized into the more definite form of DESIRE.

It is believed by men who have devoted years of research to the subject, that all energy and matter throughout the universe respond to and are controlled by the Law of Attraction which causes elements and forces of a similar nature to gather around certain centers of attraction. It is through the operation of this same universal Law of

Attraction that constant, deeply seated, strong DESIRE attracts the physical equivalent or counterpart of the thing desired, or the means of securing it.

We have learned, then, if this hypothesis is correct, that all cycles of human achievement work somewhat after this fashion: First, we picture in our conscious minds, through a definite chief aim (based upon a strong desire), some objective; we then focus our conscious mind upon this objective, by constant thought of it and belief in its attainment, until the subconscious section of the mind takes up the picture or outline of this objective and impels us to take the necessary physical action to transform that picture into reality.

SUGGESTION AND AUTO-SUGGESTION

Through this and other lessons of the Law of Success course the student has learned that sense impressions arising out of one's environment, or from statements or actions of other people, are called suggestions, while sense impressions that we place in our own minds are placed there by self-suggestion, or Autosuggestion.

All suggestions coming from others, or from environment, influence us only after we have accepted them and passed them on to the subconscious mind, through the principle of Auto-suggestion, thus it is seen that suggestion becomes, and must become, Autosuggestion before it influences the mind of the one receiving it.

Stated in another way, no one may influence another without the consent of the one influenced, as the influencing is done through one's own power of Auto-suggestion. The conscious mind stands, during the hours when one is awake, as a sentinel, guarding the subconscious mind and warding off all suggestions which try to reach it from the outside, until those suggestions have been examined by the conscious mind, passed upon and accepted. This is Nature's way of safeguarding the human being against intruders who would otherwise take control of any mind desired at will.

It is a wise arrangement.

THE VALUE OF AUTO-SUGGESTION IN ACCOMPLISHING THE OBJECT OF YOUR DEFINITE CHIEF AIM

One of the greatest uses to which one may direct the power of Auto-suggestion is that of making it help accomplish the object of one's definite chief aim in life. The procedure through which this may be accomplished is very simple. While the exact formula has been stated in Lesson Two, and referred to in many other lessons of the course, the principle upon which it is based will be here, again, described, viz.:

Write out a clear, concise statement of that which you intend to accomplish, as your definite chief aim, covering a period of, let us say, the next five years. Make at least two copies of your statement, one to be placed where you can read it several times a day, while you are at work, and the other to be placed in the room where you sleep, where it can be read several times each evening before you go to sleep and just after you arise in the morning.

The suggestive influence of this procedure (impractical though it may seem) will soon impress the object of your definite chief aim on your subconscious mind and, as if by a stroke of magic, you will begin to observe events taking place which will lead you nearer and nearer the attainment of that object.

From the very day that you reach a definite decision in your own mind as to the precise thing, condition or position in life that you deeply desire, you will observe, if you read books, newspapers and magazines, that important news items and other data bearing on the object of your definite chief aim will begin to come to your attention; you will observe, also, that opportunities will begin to come to you that will, if embraced, lead you nearer and nearer the coveted goal of your desire. No one knows better than the author of this course how impossible and impractical this may seem to the person who is not informed on the subject of mind operation; however, this is not an age favorable to the doubter or the skeptic, and the best thing for any person to do is to experiment with this principle until its practicality has been established.

To the present generation it may seem that there are no more worlds to conquer in the field of mechanical invention, but every thinker (even those who are not accurate thinkers) will concede that we are just entering a new era of evolution, experiment and analysis as far as the powers of the human mind are concerned.

The word "impossible" means less now than ever before in the history of the human race. There are some who have actually removed this word from their vocabularies, believing that man can do anything he can imagine and BELIEVE HE CAN DO! We have learned, for sure, that the universe is made up of two substances: matter and energy. Through patient scientific research we have discovered what we believe to be good evidence that everything that is or ever has been in the way of matter, when analyzed to the finest point, can be traced back to the electron, which is nothing but a form of energy. On the other hand, every material thing that man has created began in the form of energy, through the seed of an idea that was released through the imaginative faculty of the human mind. In other words, the beginning of every material thing is energy and the ending of it is energy.

All matter obeys the command of one form or another of energy. The highest known form of energy is that which functions as the human mind. The human mind, therefore, is the sole directing force of everything man creates, and what he may create with: this force in the future, as compared with that which he has created with it in the past, will make his past achievements seem petty and small.

We do not have to wait for future discoveries in connection with the powers of the human mind for evidence that the mind is the greatest force known to mankind. We know, now, that any idea, aim or purpose that is fixed in the mind and held there with a will to achieve or attain its physical or material equivalent, puts into motion powers that cannot be conquered.

Buxton said: "The longer I live the more certain I am that the great difference between men, between the feeble and the powerful, the great and the insignificant, is energy -invincible determination-a purpose once fixed, and then death or victory. That quality will do anything that can be done in this world-and no talents, no circumstances, no opportunities will make a two-legged creature a man without it."

Donald G. Mitchell has well said: "Resolve is what makes a man manifest. Not puny resolve; not crude determinations; not errant purposes-but that strong and indefatigable will which treads down difficulties and danger, as a boy treads down the heaving frostlands of winter, which kindles his eye and brain with proud pulse beat toward the unattainable. WILL MAKES MEN GIANTS!"

The great Disraeli said: "I have brought myself, by long meditation, to the conviction that a human being with a settled purpose must accomplish it, and that nothing can resist a will which will stake even existence upon its fulfillment."

Sir John Simpson said: "A passionate DESIRE and an unwearied will can perform impossibilities, or what may seem to be such to the cold, timid and feeble."

And John Foster adds his testimony when he says: "It is wonderful how even the casualties of life seem to bow to a spirit that will not bow to them, and yield to subserve a design which they may, in their first apparent tendency, threaten to frustrate. When a firm, decisive spirit is recognized, it is curious to see how the space clears around a man and leaves him room and freedom."

Abraham Lincoln said of General Grant: "The great thing about Grant is his cool persistency of purpose. He is not easily excited, and he has got the grip of a bulldog. When he once gets his teeth in, nothing can shake him off."

It seems appropriate to state here that a strong desire, to be transformed into reality, must be backed with persistency until it is taken over by the subconscious mind. It is not enough to feel very deeply the desire for achievement of a definite chief aim, for a few hours or a few days, and then forget all about that desire. The desire must be placed in the mind and held there, with PERSISTENCE THAT KNOWS NO DEFEAT, until the automatic or subconscious mind takes it over. Up to this point you must stand back of the desire and push it; beyond this point the desire will stand back of you and push you on to achievement.

Persistence may be compared to the dropping of water which finally wears away the hardest stone. When the final chapter of your life shall have been completed it will be found that your persistence, or lack of this sterling quality, played an important part in either your success or your failure.

This author watched the Tunney-Dempsey fight, in Chicago. He also studied the psychology leading up to and surrounding their previous bout. Two things helped Tunney defeat Dempsey, on both occasions, despite the fact that Dempsey is the stronger of the two men, and, as many believe, the better fighter. And these two things, which spelled Dempsey's doom, were, first, his own lack of self-confidence–the fear that Tunney might defeat him; and, second, Tunny's complete self-reliance and his belief that he would whip Dempsey.

Tunney stepped into the ring, with his chin in the air, an atmosphere of self-assurance and certainty written in his every movement. Dempsey walked in, with a sort of uncertain stride, eying Tunney in a manner that plainly queried, "I wonder what you'll do to me?"

Dempsey was whipped, in his own mind, before he entered the ring. Press agents and propagandists had done the trick, thanks to the superior thinking ability of his opponent, Tunney.

And so the story goes, from the lowest and most brutal of occupations, prize-fighting, on up to the highest and most commendable professions. Success is won by the man who understands how to use his power of thought.

Throughout this course much stress has been laid upon the importance of environment and habit out of which grow the stimuli that put the "wheels" of the human mind into operation. Fortunate is the person who has found how to arouse or stimulate his or her mind so that the powers of that mind will function constructively, as they may be made to do when placed back of any strong, deeply seated desire.

Accurate thinking is thinking that makes intelligent use of all the powers of the human mind, and does not stop with the mere examination, classification and arranging of ideas. Accurate thought creates ideas and it may be made to transform these ideas into their most profitable, constructive form.

The student will perhaps be better prepared to analyze, without a feeling of skepticism and doubt, the principles laid down in this lesson if the fact is kept in mind that the conclusions and hypotheses here enumerated are not solely those of the author. I have had the benefit of close co-operation from some of the leading investigators in the field of mental phenomena, and conclusions reached, as stated in this entire course, are those of many different minds.

In the lesson on Concentration, you will be further instructed in the method of applying the principle of Auto-suggestion. In fact, throughout the course, the principle of gradual unfoldment has been followed, paralleling that of the principle of evolution as nearly as possible. The first lesson laid the foundation for the second, and the second prepared the way for the third, and so on. I have tried to build this course just as Nature builds a man–by a series of steps each of which lifts the student just another step higher and nearer the apex of the pyramid which the course, as a whole, represents.

The purpose in building this course in the manner outlined is one that cannot be described in words, but that purpose will become obvious and clear to you as soon as you shall have mastered the course, for its mastery will open to you a source of knowledge which cannot be imparted by one man to another, but is attainable only by educing, drawing out and expanding, from within one's own mind. The reason this knowledge cannot be imparted by one to another is the same as that which makes it impossible for one person to describe colors to a blind person who has never seen colors.

The knowledge of which I write became obvious to me only after I had diligently and faithfully followed the instructions which I have laid down in this course for your guidance and enlightenment; therefore, I speak from experience when I say that there are no illustrations, similes or words with which to describe this knowledge adequately. It can only be imparted from within.

With this vague "hint" as to the reward which awaits all who earnestly and intelligently search for the hidden passageway to knowledge to which I refer, we will now discuss that phase of accurate thought which will take you as high as you can go–except through the discovery and use of the secret passageway to which I have alluded.

Thoughts are things!

It is the belief of many that every completed thought starts an unending vibration with which the one who releases it will have to contend at a later time; that man, himself, is but the physical reflection of thought that was put into motion by infinite intelligence.

The only hope held out to mankind in the entire Bible is of a reward which may be attained in no way except by constructive thought. This is a startling statement, but if you are even an elementary student and interpreter of the Bible you understand that it is a true statement.

If the Bible is plain on any one point above all others, it is on the fact that thought is the beginning of all things of a material nature.

At the beginning of every lesson of this course you will observe this motto:

"You can do it if you BELIEVE you can!"

This sentence is based upon a great truth which is practically the major premise of the entire Bible teaching. Observe the emphasis which is placed upon the word BELIEVE.

Back of this word "believe" lies the power with which you can vitalize and give life to the suggestions that you pass on to your subconscious mind, through the principle of Auto-suggestion, with the aid of the law of the Master Mind. Do not miss this point.

You cannot afford to miss it, as it is the very beginning, the middle and the end of all the power you will ever have.

All thought is creative! However, not all thought is constructive or positive. If you think thoughts of misery and poverty and see no way to avoid these conditions, then your thoughts will create those very conditions and curse you with them. But reverse the order, and think thoughts of a positive, expectant nature and your thoughts will create those conditions.

Thought magnetizes your entire personality and attracts to you the outward, physical things that harmonize with the nature of your thoughts. This has been made clear in practically every lesson preceding this one, yet it is repeated here, and will be repeated many times more in the lessons that follow. The reason for this constant repetition is that nearly all beginners in the study of mind operation overlook the importance of this fundamental and eternal truth.

When you plant a definite chief aim in your subconscious mind you must fertilize it with full belief that infinite intelligence will step in and mature that purpose into reality in exact accordance with the nature of the purpose. Anything short of such belief will bring you disappointment.

When you suggest a definite chief aim which embodies some definite desire, in your subconscious mind, you must accompany it with such faith and belief in the ultimate realization of that purpose that you can actually see yourself in possession of the object of the purpose. Conduct yourself in the exact manner in which you would if you were already in possession of the object of your definite purpose, from the moment you suggest it to your subconscious mind.

Do not question; do not wonder if the principles of Auto-suggestion will work; do not doubt, but believe!

Surely this point has been sufficiently emphasized to impress upon your mind its importance. Positive belief in the attainment of your definite purpose is the very germ with which you fertilize the "egg of your thought" and if you fail to give it this fertilization, you might as well expect an unfertilized hen-egg to produce a chicken as to expect the attainment of the object of your definite chief aim.

You never can tell what a thought will do
In bringing you hate or love;
For thoughts are things, and their airy wings
Are swifter than a carrier dove.
They follow the law of the universe,-
Each thought creates its kind,
And they speed o'er the track to bring you back
Whatever went out from your mind.

Thoughts are things! This is a great truth which,when you understand it, will bring you as close to the door of that secret passageway to knowledge, previously mentioned, as is possible for another person to bring you. When you grasp this fundamental truth you will soon find that door and open it.

The power to think as you wish to think is the only power over which you have absolute control.

Please read and study the foregoing sentence until you grasp its meaning. If it is within your power to control your thoughts the responsibility then rests upon you as to whether your thoughts will be of the positive or the negative type, which brings to mind one of the world's most famous poems:

Out of the night that covers me,
Black as the pit from pole to pole,
I thank whatever gods may be
For my unconquerable soul.

In the fell clutch of circumstance
I have not winced or cried aloud.
Under the bludgeonings of chance
My head is bloody, but unbowed.

Beyond this place of wrath and tears
Looms but the horror of the shade,
And yet the menace of the years
Finds, and shall find, me unafraid.

It matters not how strait the gate,
How charged with punishments the scroll,
I am the master of my fate,
I am the captain of my soul.-Henley

Henley did not write this poem until after he had discovered the door to that secret passageway which I have mentioned.

You are the "master of your fate" and the "captain of your soul," by reason of the fact that you control your own thoughts, and, with the aid of your thoughts, you may create whatever you desire.

As we approach the close of this lesson, let us pull aside the curtain that hangs over the gateway called death and take a look into the Great Beyond. Behold a world peopled with beings who function without the aid of physical bodies. Look closely and, whether for weal or for woe, observe that you look at a world peopled with beings of your own creation, which correspond exactly to the nature of your own thoughts as you expressed them before death. There they are, the children of your own heart and mind, patterned after the image of your own thoughts.

Those which were born of your hatred and envy and jealousy and selfishness and injustice toward your fellow men will not make very desirable neighbors, but you must live with them just the same, for they are your children and you cannot turn them out.

You will be unfortunate, indeed, if you find there no children which were born of love, and justice, and truth, and kindness toward others.

In the light of this allegorical suggestion, the subject of accurate thought takes on a new and a much more important aspect, doesn't it?

If there is a possibility that every thought you release during this life will step out, in the form of a living being, to greet you after death, then you need no further reason for guarding all your thoughts more carefully than you would guard the food that you feed your physical body.

I refer to this suggestion as "allegorical" for a reason that you will understand only after you shall have passed through the door of that secret passageway to knowledge that I have heretofore mentioned.

To ask me how I know these things, before you pass through that door, would be as useless as it would be for a man who has never seen with his physical eyes to ask me what the color red looks like.

I am not urging you to accept this viewpoint. I am not even arguing its soundness. I am merely fulfilling my duty and discharging my responsibility by giving you the suggestion. You must carry it out to a point at which you can accept or reject it, in your own way, and of your own volition.

The term "accurate thought" as used in this lesson refers to thought which is of your own creation. Thought that comes to you from others, through either suggestion or direct statement, is not accurate thought within the meaning and purpose of this lesson, although it may be thought that is based upon facts.

I have now carried you to the apex of the pyramid of this lesson on accurate thought. I can take you no further. However, you have not gone the entire distance; you have but started. From here on you must be your own guide, but, if you have not wholly missed the great truth upon which the lesson is founded, yarn will not have difficulty in finding your own way.

Let me caution you, however, not to become discouraged if the fundamental truth of this lesson does not dawn upon you at first reading. It may require weeks or even months of meditation for you to comprehend fully this truth, but it is worth working for.

The principles laid down in the beginning of this lesson you can easily understand and accept, because they are of the most elementary nature. However, as you began to follow the chain of thought along toward the close of the lesson, you perhaps found yourself being carried into waters too deep for you to fathom.

Perhaps I can throw one final ray of light on the subject by reminding you that the sound of every voice, and of every note of music, and of every other nature that is being released at the time you are reading these lines is floating through the ether right where you are. To hear these sounds you need but the aid of a modern radio outfit.

Without this equipment as a supplement to your own sense of hearing you are powerless to hear these sounds.

Had this same statement been made twenty years ago, you would have believed the one who made it to be insane or a fool. But you now accept the statement without question, because you know it is true.

Thought is a much higher and more perfectly organized form of energy than is mere sound; therefore, it is not beyond the bounds of reason to suppose that every thought now being released and every thought that has ever been released is also in the ether (or somewhere else) and may be interpreted by those who have the equipment with which to do it.

And, what sort of equipment is necessary? you ask.

That will be answered when you shall have passed through the door that leads to the secret passageway to knowledge. It cannot be answered before. The passageway can be reached only through the medium of your own thoughts. This is one reason why all the great philosophers of the past admonished man to know himself. "Know thyself is and has been the cry of the ages.

One of the unanswerable mysteries of God's work is the fact that this great discovery is always self-discovery. The truth for which man is eternally searching is wrapped up in his own being; therefore, it is fruitless to search far afield in the wilderness of life or in the hearts of other men to find it. To do so brings you no nearer that which you are seeking, but takes you further away from it.

And, it may be–who knows but you?–that even now, as you finish this lesson, you are nearer the door that leads to the secret passageway to knowledge than you have ever been before.

With your mastery of this lesson will come a fuller understanding of the principle referred to in the Introductory Lesson as the "Master Mind." Surely you now understand the reason for friendly co-operative alliance between two or more people.

This alliance "steps up" the minds of those who participate in it, and permits them to contact their thought-power with infinite intelligence.

With this statement the entire Introductory Lesson should have a new meaning for you.

This lesson has familiarized you with the main reason why you should make use of the law of the Master Mind by showing you the height to which this law may be made to carry all who understand and use it.

By this time you should understand why a few men have risen to great heights of power and fortune, while others all around them remained in poverty and want. If you do not now understand the cause for this, you will by the time you master the remaining lessons of this course.

Do not become discouraged if complete understanding of these principles does not follow your first reading of this lesson. This is the one lesson of the entire course which cannot be fully assimilated by the beginner through one reading. It will give up its rich treasures of knowledge only through thought, reflection and meditation. For this reason you are instructed to read this lesson at least four times, at intervals of one week apart.

You are also instructed to read, again, the Introductory Lesson, that you may more accurately and definitely understand the law of the Master Mind and the relationship between this law and the subjects covered by this lesson on accurate thought.

The Master Mind is the principle through which you may become an accurate thinker!

Is not this statement both plain and significant?

FAILURE–An After-the-Lesson Visit With the Author

The Great Success Lessons That Can Be Learned From Reverses

An all-wise Providence has arranged the affairs of mankind so that every person who comes into the age of reason must bear the cross of FAILURE in one form or another.

The heaviest and most cruel of all the crosses, POVERTY!

Hundreds of millions of people living on this earth today find it necessary to struggle under the burden of this cross in order to enjoy the three bare necessities of life, a place to sleep, something to eat and clothes to wear.

Carrying the cross of POVERTY is no joke!

But, it seems significant that the greatest and most successful men and women who ever lived found it necessary to carry this cross before they "arrived."

FAILURE is generally accepted as a curse. But few people ever understand that failure is a curse only when it is accepted as such. But few ever learn the truth that FAILURE is seldom permanent.

Go back over your own experiences for a few years and you will see that your failures generally turned out to be blessings in disguise. Failure teaches men lessons which they would never learn without it. Moreover, it teaches in a language that is universal.

Among the great lessons taught by failure is that of HUMILITY.

No man may become great without feeling himself humble and insignificant when compared to the world about him and the stars above him and the harmony with which Nature does her work.

For every rich man's son who becomes a useful, constructive worker in behalf of humanity, there are ninety-nine others rendering useful service who come up through POVERTY and misery. This seems more than a coincidence!

Most people who believe themselves to be failures are not failures at all. Most conditions which people look upon as failure are nothing more than temporary defeat.

If you pity yourself and feel that you are a failure, think how much worse off you would be if you had to change places with others who have real cause for complaint.

In the city of Chicago lives a beautiful young woman. Her eyes are a light blue. Her complexion is extremely fair. She has a sweet charming voice. She is educated and cultured. Three days after graduating in one of the colleges of the East she discovered that she had negro blood in her veins.

The man to whom she was engaged refused to marry her. The negroes do not want her and the whites will not associate with her. During the remainder of her life she must bear the brand of permanent FAILURE.

Remember, this is PERMANENT failure!

As this essay is being written news comes of a beautiful girl baby who was born to an unwed girl and taken into an orphanage, there to be brought up mechanically, without ever knowing the influence of a mother's love. All through life this unfortunate child must bear the brunt of another's mistake which can never be corrected.

How fortunate are YOU, no matter what may be your imaginary failures, that you are not this child.

If you have a strong body and a sound mind you have much for which you ought to be thankful. Millions of people all about you have no such blessings.

Careful analysis of one hundred men and women whom the world has accepted as being "great" shows that they were compelled to undergo hardship and temporary defeat and failure such as YOU probably have never known and never will know.

Woodrow Wilson went to his grave altogether too soon, the victim of cruel slander and disappointment, believing, no doubt, that he was a FAILURE. TIME, the great miracle worker that rights all wrongs and turns failure into success, will place the name of Woodrow Wilson at the top of the page of the really great.

Few now living have the vision to see that out of Wilson's "FAILURE" will come, eventually, such a powerful demand for universal peace that war will be an impossibility.

Lincoln died without knowing that his "FAILURE" gave sound foundation to the greatest nation on this earth.

Columbus died, a prisoner in chains, without ever knowing that his "FAILURE" meant the discovery of the great nation which Lincoln and Wilson helped to preserve, with their "FAILURES."

Do not use the word FAILURE carelessly.

Remember, carrying a burdensome cross temporarily is not FAILURE. If you have the real seed of success within you, a little adversity and temporary defeat will only serve to nurture that seed and cause it to burst forth into maturity.

When Divine Intelligence wants a great man or woman to render some needed service in the world, the fortunate one is tested out through some form of FAILURE. If you are undergoing what you believe to be failure, have patience; you may be passing through your testing time.

No capable executive would select, as his lieutenants, those whom he had not tested for reliability, loyalty, perseverance and other essential qualities.

Responsibility, and all that goes with it in the way of remuneration, always gravitates to the person who will not accept temporary defeat as permanent failure.

"The test of a man is the fight he makes,
The grit that he daily shows;
The way he stands on his feet and takes
Fate's numerous bumps and blows,
A coward can smile when there's naught to fear,
When nothing his progress bars;
But it takes a man to stand up and cheer
While some other fellow stars.
"It isn't the victory, after all,
But the fight that a brother makes;
The man who, driven against the wall,
Still stands up erect and takes
The blows of fate with his head held high:
Bleeding, and bruised, and pale,
Is the man who'll win in the by and by,
For he isn't afraid to fail.
"It's the bumps you get, and the jolts you get,
And the shocks that your courage stands,
The hours of sorrow and vain regret,
The prize that escapes your hands,
That test your mettle and prove your worth;
It isn't the blows you deal,
But the blows you take on the good old earth,
That show if your stuff is real."

Failure often places one in a position where unusual effort must be forthcoming. Many a man has wrung victory from defeat, fighting with his back to the wall, where he could not retreat.

Caesar had long wished to conquer the British. He quietly sailed his soldier-laden ships to the British island, unloaded his troops and supplies, then gave the order to burn all the ships. Calling his soldiers about him he said: "Now it is win or perish. We have no choice."

They won! Men usually win when they make up their minds to do so.

Burn your bridges behind you and observe how well you work when you KNOW THAT YOU HAVE NO RETREAT.

A streetcar conductor got a leave of absence while he tried out a position in a great mercantile business. "If I do not succeed in holding my new position," he remarked to a friend, "I can always come back to the old job."

At the end of the month he was back, completely cured of all ambition to do anything except work on a streetcar. Had he resigned instead of asking for a leave of absence he might have made good in the new job.

The Thirteen Club movement, which is now spreading over the entire country, was born as the result of a shocking disappointment experienced by its founder. That shock was sufficient to open the mind to a broader and more comprehensive view of the needs of the age, and this discovery led to the creation of one of the most outstanding influences of this generation.

The Fifteen Laws of Success, upon which this course is based, grew out of twenty years of hardship and poverty and failure such as rarely come to one person in an entire lifetime.

Surely those of you who have followed this series of lessons from the beginning must have read between the lines and back of them a story of struggle which has meant self-discipline and self-discovery such as never would have been known without this hardship.

Study the roadway of life, in the picture at the beginning of this essay, and observe that everyone who travels that road carries a cross. Remember, as you take inventory of your own burdens, that Nature's richest gifts go to those who meet FAILURE without flinching or whining. Nature's ways are not easily understood. If they were, no one could be tested for great responsibility, with FAILURE!

"When Nature wants to make a man,
And shake a man,
And wake a man;
When Nature wants to make a man
To do the Future's will;
When she tries with all her skill
And she yearns with all her soul
To create him large and whole...
With what cunning she prepares him!
How she goads and never spares him!
How she whets him, and she frets him,
And in poverty begets him....
How she often disappoints
How she often anoints,
With what wisdom she will hide him,
Never minding what betide him

Though his genius sob with slighting
And his pride may not forget!
Bids him struggle harder yet.
Makes him lonely
So that only
God's high messages shall reach him,
So that she may surely teach him
What the Hierarchy planned.
Though he may not understand
Gives him passions to command.
How remorselessly she spurs him
With terrific ardor stirs him
When she poignantly prefers him!

* * *

Lo, the crisis! Lo, the shout
That must call the leader out.
When the people need salvation
Doth he come to lead the nation....
Then doth Nature show her plan
When the world has found–A MAN!"

There is no FAILURE. That which looks to be failure is usually nothing but temporary defeat. Make sure that you do not accept it as PERMANENT!

Lesson Twelve: CONCENTRATION

This lesson occupies a key-stone position in this course, for the reason that the psychological law upon which it is based is of vital importance to every other lesson of the course.

Let us define the word concentration, as it is here used, as follows: "Concentration is the act of focusing the mind upon a given desire until ways and means for its realization have been worked out and successfully put into operation." Two important laws enter into the act of concentrating the mind on a given desire. One is the law of Auto-suggestion and the other is the law of habit. The former having been fully described in a previous lesson of this course, we will now briefly describe the law of habit.

Habit grows out of environment–out of doing the same thing in the same way over and over again–out of repetition–out of thinking the same thoughts over and over–and, when once formed, it resembles a cement block that has hardened in the mold–in that it is hard to break.

Habit is the basis of all memory training, a fact which you may easily demonstrate in remembering the name of a person whom you have just met, by repeating that name over and over until you have fixed it permanently and plainly in your mind. "The force of education is so great that we may mold the minds and manners of the young into whatever shape we please and give the impressions of such habits as shall ever afterwards remain." –Atterbury.

Except on rare occasions when the mind rises above environment, the human mind draws the material out of which thought is created from the surrounding environment, and habit crystallizes this thought into a permanent fixture and stores it away in the subconscious mind where it becomes a vital part of our personality which silently influences our actions, forms our prejudices and our biases, and controls our opinions. A great philosopher had in mind the power of habit when he said: "We first endure, then pity, and finally embrace," in speaking of the manner in which honest men come to indulge in crime.

Habit may be likened to the grooves on a phonograph record, while the mind may be likened to the needle point that fits into that groove. When any habit has been well-formed (by repetition of thought or action) the mind attaches itself to and follows that habit as closely as the phonograph needle follows the groove in the wax record, no matter what may be the nature of that habit.

We begin to see, therefore, the importance of selecting our environment with the greatest of care, because environment is the mental feeding ground out of which the food that goes into our minds is extracted.

Environment very largely supplies the food and materials out of which we create thought, and habit crystallizes these into permanency. You of course understand that "environment" is the sum total of sources through which you are influenced by and through the aid of the five senses of seeing, hearing, smelling, tasting and feeling.

"Habit is force which is generally recognized by the average thinking person, but which is commonly viewed in its adverse aspect to the exclusion of its favorable phase. It has been well said that all men are 'the creatures of habit,' and that 'habit is a cable; we weave a thread of it each day and it becomes so strong that we cannot break it.'

"If it be true that habit becomes a cruel tyrant, ruling and compelling men against their will, desire, and inclination–and this is true in many cases–the question naturally arises in the thinking mind whether this mighty force cannot be harnessed and controlled in the service of men, just as have other forces of Nature. If this result can be accomplished, then man may master habit and set it to work, instead of being a slave to it and serving it faithfully though complaining. And the modern psychologists tell us in no uncertain tones that habit may certainly be thus mastered, harnessed and set to work, instead of being allowed to dominate one's actions and character. And thousands of people have applied this new knowledge and have turned the force of habit into new channels, and have compelled it to work their machinery of action, instead of being allowed to run to waste, or else permitted to sweep away the structures that men have erected with care and expense, or to destroy fertile mental fields.

"A habit is a 'mental path' over which our actions have traveled for some time, each passing making the path a little deeper and a little wider. If you have to walk over a field or through a forest, you know how natural it is for you to choose the clearest path in preference to the less worn ones, and greatly in preference to stepping out across the field or through the woods and making a new path. And the line of mental action is precisely the same. It is movement along the lines of least resistance–passage over the well-worn path. Habits are created by repetition and are formed in accordance to a natural law, observable in all animate things and some would say in inanimate things as well. As an instance of the latter, it is pointed out that a piece of paper once folded in a certain way will fold along the same lines the next time. And all users of sewing machines, or other delicate pieces of machinery, know that as a machine or instrument is once 'broken in' so will it tend to run thereafter. The same law is also observable in the case of musical instruments. Clothing or gloves form into creases according to the person using them, and these creases once formed will always be in effect, notwithstanding repeated pressings. Rivers and streams of water cut their courses through the land, and thereafter flow along the habit-course. The law is in operation everywhere.

"These illustrations will help you to form the idea of the nature of habit, and will aid you in forming new mental paths–new mental creases. And–remember this always–the best (and one might say the only) way in which old habits may be removed is to form new habits to counteract and replace the undesirable ones. Form new mental paths over which to travel, and the old ones will soon become less distinct and in time will practically fill up from disuse. Every time you travel over the path of the desirable mental habit, you make the path deeper and wider, and make it so much easier to travel it thereafter. This mental path-making is a very important thing, and I cannot urge upon you too strongly the injunction to start to work making the desirable mental paths over which you wish to travel. Practice, practice, practice–be a good path-maker."

The following are the rules of procedure through which you may form the habits you desire:

First: At the beginning of the formation of a new habit put force and enthusiasm into your expression. Feel what you think. Remember that you are taking the first steps toward making the new mental path; that it is much harder at first than it will be afterwards. Make the path as clear and as deep as you can, at the beginning, so that you can readily see it the next time you wish to follow it.

Second: Keep your attention firmly concentrated on the new path-building, and keep your mind away from the old paths, lest you incline toward them. Forget all about the old paths, and concern yourself only with the new ones that you are building to order.

Third: Travel over your newly made paths as often as possible. Make opportunities for doing so, without waiting for them to arise through luck or chance. The oftener you go over the new paths the sooner will they become well worn and easily traveled. Create plans for passing over these new habit-paths, at the very start.

Fourth: Resist the temptation to travel over the older, easier paths that you have been using in the past. Every time you resist a temptation, the stronger do you become, and the easier will it be for you to do so the next time. But every time you yield to the temptation, the easier does it become to yield again, and the more difficult it becomes to resist the next time. You will have a fight on at the start, and this is the critical time. Prove your determination, persistency and will-power now, at the very beginning. Fifth: Be sure that you have mapped out the right path, as your definite chief aim, and then go ahead without fear and without allowing yourself to doubt. "Place your hand upon the plow, and look not backward." Select your goal, then make good, deep, wide mental paths leading straight to it.

As you have already observed, there is a close relationship between habit and Autosuggestion (self-suggestion). Through habit, an act repeatedly performed in the same manner has a tendency to become Permanent, and eventually we come to perform the act automatically or unconsciously. In playing a piano, for example, the artist can play a familiar piece while his or her conscious mind is on some other subject.

Auto-suggestion is the tool with which we dig a mental path; Concentration is the hand that holds that tool; and Habit is the map or blueprint which the mental path follows.

An idea or desire, to be transformed into terms of action or physical reality, must be held in the conscious mind faithfully and persistently until habit begins to give it permanent form.

Let us turn our attention, now, to environment.

As we have already seen, we absorb the material for thought from our surrounding environment. The term "environment" covers a very broad field. It consists of the books we read, the people with whom we associate, the community in which we live, the nature of the work in which we are engaged, the country or nation in which we reside, the clothes we wear, the songs we sing, and, most important of all, the religious and intellectual training we receive prior to the age of fourteen years.

The purpose of analyzing the subject of environment is to show its direct relationship to the personality we are developing, and the importance of so guarding it that its influence will give us the materials out of which we may attain our definite chief aim in life.

The mind feeds upon that which we supply it, or that which is forced upon it, through our environment; therefore, let us select our environment, as far as possible, with the object of supplying the mind with suitable material out of which to carry on its work of attaining our definite chief aim.

If your environment is not to your liking, change it!

The first step is to create in your own mind an exact, clear and well-rounded out picture of the environment in which you believe you could best attain your definite chief aim, and then concentrate your mind upon this picture until you transform it into reality.

In Lesson Two, of this course, you learned that the first step you must take, in the accomplishment of any desire, is to create in your mind a dear, well defined picture of that which you intend to accomplish. This is the first principle to be observed in your plans for the achievement of success, and if you fail or neglect to observe it, you cannot succeed, except by chance.

Your daily associates constitute one of the most important and influential parts of your environment, and may work for your progress or your retrogression, according to the nature of those associates. As far as possible, you should select as your most intimate daily associates those who are in sympathy with your aims and ideals–especially those represented by your definite chief aim–and whose mental attitude inspires you with enthusiasm, self-confidence, determination and ambition.

Remember that every word spoken within your hearing, every sight that reaches your eyes, and every sense impression that you receive through any of the five senses, influences your thought as surely as the sun rises in the east and sets in the west. This being true, can you not see the importance of controlling, as far as possible, the environment in which you live and work? Can you not see the importance of reading books that deal with subjects which are directly related to your definite chief aim? Can you not see the importance of talking with people who are in sympathy with your aims, and, who will encourage you and spur you on toward their attainment?

We are living in what we call a "twentieth century civilization." The leading scientists of the world are agreed that Nature has been millions of years in creating, through the process of evolution, our present civilized environment.

How many hundreds of centuries the so-called Indians had lived upon the North American continent, without any appreciable advance toward modem civilization, as we understand it, we have no way of ascertaining. Their environment was the wilderness, and they made no attempt whatsoever to change or improve that environment; the change took place only after new races from afar came over and forced upon them the environment of progressive civilization in, which we are living today.

Observe what has happened within the short period of three centuries. Hunting grounds have been transformed into great cities, and the Indian has taken on education and culture, in many instances, that equal the accomplishment of his white brothers. (In Lesson Fifteen, we discuss the effects of environment from a worldwide viewpoint, and describe, in detail, the principal of social heredity which is the chief source through which the effects of environment may be imposed upon the minds of the young.)

The clothes you wear influence you; therefore, they constitute a part of your environment. Soiled or shabby clothes depress you and lower your self-confidence, while clean clothes, of an appropriate style, have just the opposite effect.

It is a well-known fact that an observant person can accurately analyze a man by seeing his workbench, desk or other place of employment. A well-organized desk indicates a well-organized brain. Show me the merchant's stock of goods and I will tell you whether he has an organized or disorganized brain, as there is a close relationship between one's mental attitude and one's physical environment.

The effects of environment so vitally influence those who work in factories, stores and offices, that employers are gradually realizing the importance of creating an environment that inspires and encourages the workers.

One unusually progressive laundryman, in the city of Chicago, has plainly outdone his competitors, by installing in his workroom a player-piano, in charge of a neatly dressed young woman who keeps it going during the working hours. His laundrywomen are dressed in white uniforms, and there is no evidence about the place that work is drudgery. Through the aid of this pleasant environment, this laundryman turns out more work, earns more profits, and pays better wages than his competitors can pay.

This brings us to an appropriate place at which to describe the method through which you may apply the principles directly and indirectly related to the subject of concentration.

Let us call this method the-MAGIC KEY TO SUCCESS!

In presenting you with this "Magic Key" let me first explain that it is no invention or discovery of mine.

It is the same key that is used, in one form or another, by the followers of New Thought and all other sects which are founded upon the positive philosophy of optimism.

This Magic Key constitutes an irresistible power which all who will may use.

It win unlock the door to riches!

It will unlock the door to fame!

And, in many instances, it will unlock the door to physical health.

It will unlock the door to education and let you into the storehouse of all your latent ability. It will act as a pass-key to any position in life for which you are fitted.

Through the aid of this Magic Key we have unlocked the secret doors to all of the world's great inventions.

Through its magic powers all of our great geniuses of the past have been developed.

Suppose you are a laborer, in a menial position, and desire a better place in life. The Magic Key will help you attain it! Through its use Carnegie, Rockefeller, Hill, Harriman, Morgan and scores of others of their type have accumulated vast fortunes of material wealth.

It will unlock prison doors and turn human derelicts into useful, trustworthy human beings. It will turn failure into success and misery into happiness.

You ask- "What is this Magic Key?"

And I answer with one word-concentration!

Now let me define concentration in the sense that it is here used. First, I wish it to be clearly understood that I have no reference to occultism, although I will admit that all the scientists of the world have failed to explain the strange phenomena produced through the aid of concentration.

Concentration, in the sense in which it is here used, means the ability, through fixed habit and practice, to keep your mind on one subject until you have thoroughly familiarized yourself with that subject and mastered it. It means the ability to control your attention and focus it on a given problem until you have solved it.

It means the ability to throw off the effects of habits which you wish to discard, and the power to build new habits that are more to your liking. It means complete self-mastery. Stating it in another way, concentration is the ability to think as you wish to think; the ability to control your thoughts and direct them to a definite end; and the ability to organize your knowledge into a plan of action that is sound and workable.

You can readily see that in concentrating your mind upon your definite chief aim in life, you must cover many closely related subjects which blend into each other and complete the main subject upon which you are concentrating.

Ambition and desire are the chief factors which enter into the act of successful concentration. Without these factors the Magic Key is useless, and the main reason why so few people make use of this key is that most people lack ambition, and desire nothing in particular.

Desire whatever you may, and if your desire is within reason and if it is strong enough the Magic Key of concentration will help you attain it. There are learned men of science who would have us believe that the wonderful power of prayer operates through the principle of concentration on the attainment of a deeply-seated desire.

Nothing was ever created by a human being which was not first created in the imagination, through desire, and then transformed into reality through concentration.

Now, let us put the Magic Key to a test, through the aid of a definite formula.

First, you must put your foot on the neck of skepticism and doubt! No unbeliever ever enjoyed the benefits of this Magic Key. You must believe in the test that you are about to make.

We will assume that you have thought something about becoming a successful writer, or a powerful public speaker, or a successful business executive, or an able financier.

We will take public speaking as the subject of this test, but remember that you must follow instructions to the letter.

Take a plain sheet of paper, ordinary letter size, and write on it the following:

I am going to become a powerful public speaker because this will enable me to render the world useful service that is needed–and because it will yield me a financial return that will provide me with the necessary material things of life.

I will concentrate my mind upon this desire for ten minutes daily, just before retiring at night and just after arising in the morning, for the purpose of determining just how I shall proceed to transform it into reality.

I know that I can become a powerful and magnetic speaker, therefore I will permit nothing to interfere with my doing so.

Signed..

Sign this pledge, then proceed to do as you have pledged your word that you would do.

Keep it up until the desired results have been realized.

Now, when you come to do your concentrating, this is the way to go about it: Look ahead one, three, five or even ten years, and see yourself as the most powerful speaker of your time. See, in your imagination, an appropriate income. See yourself in your own home that you have purchased with the proceeds from your efforts as a speaker or lecturer. See yourself in possession of a nice bank account as a reserve for old age. See yourself as a person of influence, due to your great ability as a public speaker. See yourself engaged in a life-calling in which you will not fear the loss of your position.

Paint this picture clearly, through the powers of your imagination, and lo! It will soon become transformed into a beautiful picture of deeply-seated desire. Use this desire as the chief object of your concentration and observe what happens.

You now have the secret of the Magic Key!

Do not underestimate the power of the Magic Key because it did not come to you clothed in mysticism, or because it is described in language which all who will may understand. All great truths are simple in final analysis, and easily understood; if they are not they are not great truths.

Use this Magic Key with intelligence, and only for the attainment of worthy ends, and it will bring you enduring happiness and success. Forget the mistakes you have made and the failures you have experienced. Quit living in the past, for do you not know that your yesterdays never return? Start all over again, if your previous efforts have not turned outwell, and make the next five or ten years tell a story of success that will satisfy your most lofty ambitions.

Make a name for yourself and render the world a great service, through ambition, desire and concentrated effort!

You can do it if you BELIEVE you can!

Thus endeth the Magic Key.

. . . . . .

The presence of any idea or thought in your consciousness tends to produce an "associated" feeling and to urge you to appropriate or corresponding action. Hold a deeply-seated desire in your consciousness, through the principle of concentration, and if you do it with full faith in its realization your act attracts to your aid powers which the entire scientific world has failed to understand or explain with a reasonable hypothesis.

When you become familiar with the powers of concentration you will then understand the reason for choosing a definite chief aim as the first step in the attainment of enduring success.

Concentrate your mind upon the attainment of the object of a deeply-seated desire and very soon you will become a lodestone that attracts, through the aid of forces which no man can explain, the necessary material counterparts of that desire, a statement of fact which paves the way for the description of a principle which constitutes the most important part of this lesson, if not, in fact, the most important part of the entire course, viz.:

When two or more people ally themselves, in a spirit of perfect harmony, for the purpose of attaining a definite end, if that alliance is faithfully observed by all of whom it is composed, the alliance brings, to each of those of whom it is composed, power that is superhuman and seemingly irresistible in nature.

Back of the foregoing statement is a law, the nature of which science has not yet determined, and it is this law that I have had in mind in connection with my repeated statements concerning the power of organized effort which you will notice throughoutthis course.

In chemistry we learn that two or more elements may be so compounded that the result is something entirely different in nature, from any of the individual elements. For example, ordinary water, known in chemistry under the formula of H_2O, is a compound consisting of two atoms of hydrogen and one atom of oxygen, but water is neither hydrogen nor oxygen. This "marrying" of elements creates an entirely different substance from that of either of its component parts.

The same law through which this transformation of physical elements takes place may be responsible for the seemingly superhuman powers resulting from the alliance of two or more people, in a perfect state of harmony and understanding, for the attainment of a given end.

This world, and all matter of which the other planets consist, is made up of electrons (an electron being the smallest known analyzable unit of matter, and resembling, in nature, what we call electricity, or a form of energy). On the other hand, thought, and that which we call the "mind," is also a form of energy; in fact, it is the highest form of energy known. Thought, in other words, is organized energy, and it is not improbable that thought is exactly the same sort of energy as that which we generate with an electric dynamo, although of a much more highly organized form.

Now, if all matter, in final analysis, consists of groups of electrons, which are nothing more than a form of energy which we call electricity, and if the mind is nothing but a form of highly organized electricity, do you not see how it is possible that the laws which affect matter may also govern the mind?

And if combining two or more elements of matter, in the proper proportion and under the right conditions, will produce something entirely different from those original elements (as in the case of H_2O), do you not see how it is possible so to combine the energy of two or more minds that the result will be a sort of composite mind that is totally different from the individual minds of which it consists?

You have undoubtedly noticed the manner in which you are influenced while in the presence of other people. Some people inspire you with optimism and enthusiasm.

Their very presence seems to stimulate your own mind to greater action, and, this not only "seems" to be true, but it is true. You have noticed that the presence of others had a tendency to lower your vitality and depress you; a tendency which I can assure you was very real!

What, do you imagine, could be the cause of these changes that come over us when we come within a certain range of other people, unless it is the change resulting from the blending or combining of their minds with our own, through the operation of a law that is not very well understood, but resembles (if, in fact, it is not the same law) the law through which the combining of two atoms of hydrogen and one atom of oxygen produces water?

I have no scientific basis for this hypothesis, but I have given it many years of serious thought and always I come to the conclusion that it is at least a sound hypothesis, although I have no possible way, as yet, of reducing it to a provable hypothesis.

You need no proof, however, that the presence of some people inspires you, while the presence of others depresses you, as you know this to be a fact. Now it stands to reason that the person who inspires you and arouses your mind to a state of greater activity gives you more power to achieve, while the person whose presence depresses you and lowers your vitality, or causes you to dissipate it in useless, disorganized thought, has just the opposite effect on you. You can understand this much without the aid of a hypothesis and without further proof than that which you have experienced time after time.

Come back, now, to the original statement that:

"When two or more people ally themselves, in a spirit of perfect harmony, for the purpose of attaining a definite end, if that alliance is faithfully observed by all of whom it is composed, the alliance brings, to each of those of whom it is composed, power that is superhuman and seemingly irresistible in nature."

Study, closely, the emphasized part of the foregoing statement, for there you will find the "mental formula" which, if not faithfully observed, destroys the effect of the whole.

One atom of hydrogen combined with one atom of oxygen will not produce water, nor will an alliance in name only, that is not accompanied by "a spirit of perfect harmony" (between those forming the alliance) produce "power that is superhuman and seemingly irresistible in nature."

I have in mind a family of mountain-folk who, for more than six generations, have lived in the mountainous section of Kentucky, Generation after generation of this family came and went without any noticeable improvement of a mental nature, each generation following in the footsteps of its ancestors. They made their living from the soil, and as far as they knew, or cared, the universe consisted of a little spot of territory known as Letcher County. They married strictly in their own "set," and in their own community.

Finally, one of the members of this family strayed away from the flock, so to speak, and married a well-educated and highly cultured woman from the neighbor state of Virginia. This woman was one of those types of ambitious people who had learned that the universe extended beyond the border line of Letcher County, and covered, at least, the whole of the southern states. She had heard of chemistry, and of botany, and of biology, and of pathology, and of psychology, and of many other subjects that were of importance in the field of education. When her children began to come along to the age of understanding, she talked to them of these subjects; and they, in turn, began to show a keen interest in them.

One of her children is now the president of a great educational institution, where most of these subjects, and many others of equal importance, are taught. Another one of them is a prominent lawyer, while still another is a successful physician.

Her husband (thanks to the influence of her mind) is a well-known dental surgeon, and the first of his family, for six generations, to break away from the traditions by which the family had been bound.

The blending of her mind with his gave him the needed stimulus to spur him on and inspired him with ambition such as he would never have known without her influence.

For many years I have been studying the biographies of those whom the world calls 'great', and it seems to me more than a mere coincidence that in every instance where the facts were available the person who was really responsible for the greatness was in the background, behind the scenes, and seldom heard of by the hero-worshiping public.

Not infrequently is this "hidden power" a patient little wife who has inspired her husband and urged him on to great achievement, as was true in the case I have just described.

Henry Ford is one of the modem miracles of this age, and I doubt that this country, or any other, ever produced an industrial genius of his equal. If the facts were known (and perhaps they are known) they might trace the cause of Mr. Ford's phenomenal achievements to a woman of whom the public hears but little–his wife!

We read of Ford's achievements and of his enormous income and imagine him to be blessed with matchless ability, and he is–ability of which the world would never have heard had it not been for the modifying influence of his wife, who has co-operated with him, during all the years of his struggle, "in a spirit of perfect harmony, for the purpose of attaining a definite end."

I have in mind another genius who is well-known to the entire civilized world, Thomas A. Edison. His inventions are so well-known that they need not be named. Every time you press a button and turn on an electric light, or hear a phonograph playing, you should think of Edison, for it was he who perfected both the incandescent light and the modem phonograph. Every time you see a moving picture you should think of Edison, for it was his genius, more than that of any other person, who made this great enterprise possible.

But, as in the case of Henry Ford, back of Mr. Edison stands one of the most remarkable women in America–his wife! No one outside of the Edison family, and perhaps a very few intimate personal friends of theirs, knows to what extent her influence has made Edison's achievements possible. Mrs. Edison once told me that Mr. Edison's outstanding quality, the one which, above all others, was his greatest asset, was that of-Concentration!

When Mr. Edison starts a line of experiment or research or investigation; he never "lets go" until he either finds that for which he is looking or exhausts every possible effort to do so.

Back of Mr. Edison stand two great powers; one is concentration and the other is M Mrs. Edison!

Night after night Mr. Edison has worked with such enthusiasm that he required but three or four hours of sleep. (Observe what was said about the sustaining effects of enthusiasm in Lesson Seven of this course.)

Plant a tiny apple seed in the right sort of soil, at the right time of the year, and gradually it will burst forth into a tiny sprig, and then it will expand and grow into an apple tree. That tree does not come from the soil, nor does it come from the elements of the air, but from both of these sources, and the man has not yet lived who could explain the law that attracts from the air and the soil the combination of cells of which that apple tree consists.

The tree does not come out of the tiny apple seed, but, that seed is the beginning of the tree.

When two or more people ally themselves, "in a spirit of perfect harmony, for the purpose of attaining a definite end," the end, itself, or the desire back of that end, may be likened to the apple seed, and the blending of the forces of energy of the two or more minds may be likened to the air and the soil out of which come the elements that form the material objects of that desire.

The power back of the attraction and combination of these forces of the mind can no more be explained than can the power back of the combination of elements out of which an apple tree "grows."

But the all-important thing is that an apple tree will "grow" from a seed thus properly planted, an great achievement will follow the systematic blending of two or more minds with a definite object in view.

In Lesson Thirteen you will see this principle of allied effort carried to proportions which almost stagger the imagination of all who have not trained themselves to think in terms of organized thought!

This course, itself, is a very concrete illustration of the principle underlying that which we have termed organized effort, but you will observe that it requires the entire sixteen lessons to complete the description of this principle. Omit a single one of the sixteen lessons and the omission would affect the whole as the removal of one link would affect the whole of a chain.

As I have already stated in many different ways, and for the purpose of emphasis, I now repeat: there is a well-founded hypothesis that when one concentrates one's mind upon a given subject, facts of a nature that is closely related to that subject will "pour" in from every conceivable source. The theory is that a deeply seated desire, when once planted in the right sort of "mental soil," serves as a center of attraction or magnet that attracts to it everything that harmonizes with the nature of the desire.

Dr. Elmer Gates, of Washington, D. C, is perhaps one of the most competent psychologists in the world. He is recognized both in the field of psychology and in other directly and indirectly related fields of science, throughout the world, as being a man of the highest scientific standing.

Come with me, for a moment, and study his methods!

After Dr. Gates has followed a line of investigation as far as possible through the usual channels of research, and has availed himself of all the recorded facts at his command, on a given subject, he then takes a pencil and a tablet and "sits" for further information, by concentrating his mind on that subject until thoughts related to it begin to FLOW IN UPON HIM. He writes down these thoughts, as they come (from he knows not where).

He told me that many of his most important discoveries came through this method. It was more than twenty years ago that I first talked with Dr. Gates on this subject. Since that time, through the discovery of the radio principle, we have been provided with reasonable hypothesis through which to explain the results of these "sittings," viz.:

The ether, as we have discovered through the modern radio apparatus, is in a constant state of agitation. Sound waves are floating through the ether at all times, but these waves cannot be detected, beyond a short distance from their source, except by the aid of properly attuned instruments.

Now, it seems reasonable to suppose that thought, being the most highly organized form of energy known, is constantly sending waves through the ether, but these waves, like those of sound, can only be detected and correctly interpreted by a properly attuned mind.

There is no doubt that when Dr. Gates sat down in a room and placed himself in a quiet, passive state of mind, the dominating thoughts in his mind served as a magnetic force that attracted the related or similar thought waves of others as they passed through the ether about him.

Taking the hypothesis just a step further, it has occurred to me many times since the discovery of the modern radio principle, that every thought that has ever been released in organized form, from the mind of any human being, is still in existence in the form of a wave in the ether, and is constantly passing around and around in a great endless circle; that the act of concentrating one's mind upon a given subject with intensity sends out thought- waves which reach and blend with those of a related or similar nature, thereby establishing a direct line of communication between the one doing the concentrating and the thoughts of a similar nature which have been previously set into motion.

Going still a step further, may it not be possible for one so to attune his mind and harmonize the rate of vibration of thought with the rate of vibration of the ether that all knowledge that has been accumulated through the organized thoughts of the past is available?

With these hypotheses in mind, go back to Lesson Two, of this course, and study Carnegie's description of the "master mind" through which he accumulated his great fortune.

When Carnegie formed an alliance between more than a score of carefully selected minds, he created, by that means of compounding mind power, one of the strongest industrial forces that the world has ever witnessed. With a few notable (and very disastrous) exceptions, the men constituting the "master mind" which Carnegie created thought and acted as one!

And, that "master mind" (composed of many individual minds) was concentrated upon a single purpose, the nature of which is familiar to everyone who knew Mr. Carnegie; particularly those who were competing with him in the steel business.

If you have followed Henry Ford's record, even slightly, you undoubtedly have observed that concentrated effort has been one of the outstanding features of his career.

Nearly thirty years ago he adopted a policy of standardization as to the general type of automobile that he would build, and he consistently maintained that policy until the change in public demand forced him, in 1927, to change it.

A few years ago, I met the former chief engineer of the Ford plant, and he told me of an incident that happened during the early stages of Mr. Ford's automobile experience which very clearly points to concentrated effort as being one of his prominent fundamentals of economic philosophy.

On this occasion the engineers of the Ford plant had gathered in the engineering office for the purpose of discussing a proposed change in the design of the rear axle construction of the Ford automobile. Mr. Ford stood around and listened to the discussion until each man had had his "say"; then he walked over to the table, tapped the drawing of the proposed axle with his finger, and said:

"Now listen! The axle we are using does the work for which it was intended, and does it well, and there's going to be no more change in that axle!"

He turned and walked away, and from that day until this the rear axle construction of the Ford automobile has remained substantially the same. It is not improbable that Mr. Ford's success in building and marketing automobiles has been due, very largely, to his policy of consistently concentrating his efforts back of one plan, with but one definite purpose in mind at a time.

A few years ago I read Edward Bok's book, The Man From Maine, which is the biography of his father-in-law, Mr. Cyrus H. K. Curtis, the owner of the Saturday Evening Post, the Ladies' Home Journal, and several other publications. All through the book I noticed that the outstanding feature of Mr. Curtis' philosophy was that of concentration of effort back of a definite purpose.

During the early days of his ownership of the Saturday Evening Post, when he was pouring money into a losing venture by the hundreds of thousands of dollars, it required concentrated effort that was backed by courage such as but few men possess, to enable him to "carry on."

Read The Man From Maine. It is a splendid lesson on the subject of concentration, and supports, to the smallest detail, the fundamentals upon which this lesson is based. The Saturday Evening Post is now one of the most profitable magazines in the world, but its name would have been long since forgotten had not Mr. Curtis concentrated his attention and his fortune on the one definite purpose of making it a great magazine.

We have seen what an important part environment and habit play in connection with the subject of concentration. We shall now discuss, briefly, a third subject which is no less related to the subject of concentration than are the other two, namely, memory. The principles through which an accurate, unfaltering memory may be trained are few, and comparatively simple; viz.:

1. Retention: The receiving of a sense impression through one or more of the five senses, and the recording of this impression, in orderly fashion, in the mind. This process may be likened to the recording of a picture on the sensitized plate of a camera or Kodak.

2. Recall: The reviving or recalling into the conscious mind of those sense impressions which have been recorded in the subconscious mind. This process may be compared to the act of going through a card index and pulling out a card on which information had been previously recorded.

3. Recognition: The ability to recognize a sense impression when it is called into the conscious mind, and to identify it as being a duplicate of the original impression, and to associate it with the original source from which it came when it was first recorded. This process enables us to distinguish between "memory" and "imagination." These are the three principles that enter into the act of remembering. Now let us make application of these principles and determine how to use them effectively, which may be done as follows:

First: When you wish to be sure of your ability to recall a sense impression, such as a name, date or place, be sure to make the impression vivid by concentrating your attention upon it to the finest detail. An effective way to do this is to repeat, several times, that which you wish to remember. Just as a photographer must give an "exposure" proper time to record itself on the sensitized plate of the camera, so must we give the subconscious mind time to record properly and clearly any sense impression that we wish to be able to recall with readiness.

Second: Associate that which you wish to remember with some other object, name, place or date with which you are quite familiar, and which you can easily recall when you wish, as, for example, the name of your home town, your close friend, the date of your birth, etc., for your mind will then file away the sense impression that you wish to be able to recall, with the one that you can easily recall, so that when bringing forth one into the conscious mind it brings, also, the other one with it.

Third: Repeat that which you wish to remember, a number of times, at the same time concentrating your mind upon it, just as you would fix your mind on a certain hour at which you wished to arise in the morning, which, as you know, insures your awakening at that precise hour. The common failing of not being able to remember the names of other people, which most of us have, is due entirely to the fact that we do not properly record the name in the first place. When you are introduced to a person whose name you wish to be able to recall at will, repeat that name four or five times, first making sure that you understood the name correctly. If the name is similar to that of some person whom you know well, associate the two names together, thinking of both as you repeat the name of the one whose name you wish to be able to recall.

If someone gives you a letter to be mailed, look at the letter, then increase its size, in your imagination, and see it hanging over a letter-box. Fix in your mind a letter approximately the size of a door, and associate it with a letter box, and you will observe that the first letter box you pass on the street will cause you to recall that big, odd-looking letter, which you have in your pocket.

Suppose that you were introduced to a lady whose name was Elizabeth Shearer, and you wished to be able to recall her name at will. As you repeat her name associate with it a large pair of scissors, say ten feet in length, and Queen Elizabeth, and you will observe that the recalling of either the large pair of scissors or the name of Queen Elizabeth will help you recall, also, the name of Elizabeth Shearer.

If you wish to be able to remember the name of Lloyd Keith, just repeat the name several times and associate with it the name of Lloyd George and Keith's Theater, either of which you can easily recall at will.

The law of association is the most important feature of a well-trained memory, yet it is a very simple law. All you have to do to make use of it is to record the name of that which you wish to remember with the name of that which you can readily remember, and the recalling of one brings with it the other.

Nearly ten years ago a friend gave me his residence telephone number, in Milwaukee, Wisconsin, and although I did not write it down I remember it today as well as I did the day he gave it to me. This is the way that I recorded it:

The number and exchange were Lakeview 2651.

At the time he gave me the number we were standing at the railroad station, in sight of Lake Michigan; therefore, I used the lake as an associated object with which to file the name of the telephone exchange. It so happened that the telephone number was made up of the age of my brother, who was 26, and my father, who was 51, therefore I associated their names with the number, thus insuring its recall. To recall the telephone exchange and number, therefore, I had only to think of Lake Michigan, my brother and my father.

An acquaintance of mine found himself to be suffering from what is ordinarily called a "wandering mind." He was becoming "absent-minded" and unable to remember. Let him tell you, in his own words which follow, how he overcame this handicap:

"I am fifty years old. For a decade I have been a department manager in a large factory.

At first my duties were easy, then the firm had a rapid expansion of business which gave me added responsibilities. Several of the young men in my department developed unusual energy and ability–at least one of them had his eye on my job.

"I had reached the age in life when a man likes to be comfortable and, having been with the company a long time, I felt that I could safely settle back into an easy berth.

The effect of this mental attitude was well nigh disastrous to my position.

"About two years ago I noticed that my power of concentration was weakening and my duties were becoming irksome. I neglected my correspondence until I looked with dread upon the formidable pile of letters; reports accumulated and subordinates were inconvenienced by the delay. I sat at my desk with my mind wandering elsewhere.

"Other circumstances showed plainly that my mind was not on my work. I forgot to attend an important meeting of the officers of the company. One of the clerks under me caught a bad mistake made in an estimate on a carload of goods, and, of course, saw to it that the manager learned of the incident.

"I was thoroughly alarmed at the situation, and asked for a week's vacation to think things over. I was determined to resign, or find the trouble and remedy it. A few days of earnest introspection at an out-of-the-way mountain resort convinced me that I was suffering from a plain case of mind wandering. I was lacking in concentration; my physical and mental activities at the desk had become desultory. I was careless and shiftless and neglectful–all because my mind was not alertly on the job. When I had diagnosed my case with satisfaction to myself I next sought the remedy. I needed a complete new set of working habits, and I made a resolve to acquire them.

"With paper and pencil I outlined a schedule to cover the working day: first, the morning mail; then, the orders to be filled; dictation; conference with subordinates and miscellaneous duties; ending with a clean desk before I left.

"'How is habit formed?' I asked myself mentally. 'By repetition,' came back the answer. 'But I have been doing these things over and over thousands of times,' the other fellow in me protested. 'True, but not in orderly concentrated fashion,' replied the echo.

"I returned to the office with mind in leash, but restless, and placed my new working schedule in force at once. I performed the same duties with the same zest and as nearly as possible at the same time every day. When my mind started to slip away I quickly brought it back.

"From a mental stimulus, created by will-power, I progressed in habit building. Day after day, I practiced concentration of thought. When I found repetition becoming comfortable, then I knew that I had won."

Your ability to train your memory, or to develop any desired habit, is a matter, solely, of being able to fix your attention on a given subject until the outline of that subject has been thoroughly impressed upon the "sensitized plate" of your mind.

Concentration, itself, is nothing but a matter of control of the attention!

You will observe that by reading a line of print with which you are not familiar, and which you have never seen before, and then closing your eyes, you can see that line as plainly as though you were looking at it on the printed page. In reality, you are "looking at it," not on the printed page, but on the sensitized plate of your own mind. If you try this experiment and it does not work the first time it is because you did not concentrate your attention on the line closely enough! Repeat the performance a few times and finally you will succeed.

If you wish to memorize poetry, for example, you can do so very quickly by training yourself to fix your attention on the lines so closely that you can shut your eyes and see them in your mind as plainly as you see them on the printed page.

So important is this subject of control of attention that I feel impelled to emphasize it in such a way that you will not pass it by lightly. I have reserved reference to this important subject until the last, as a climax to this lesson, for the reason that I consider it, by far, the most important part of the lesson.

The astounding results experienced by those who make a practice of "crystal-gazing" are due, entirely, to their ability to fix attention upon a given subject for an unbroken period far beyond the ordinary.

Crystal-gazing is nothing but concentrated attention!

I have already hinted at that which I will now state as my belief, namely, that it is possible, through the aid of concentrated attention, for one so to attune one's mind to the vibration of the ether that all the secrets in the world of unfathomed and uncharted mental phenomena may become as open books which may be read at will.

What a thought this is to ponder over!

I am of the opinion, and not without substantial evidence to support me, that it is possible for one to develop the ability of fixing the attention so highly that one may "tune in" and understand that which is in the mind of any person. But this is not all, nor is it the most important part of a hypothesis at which I have arrived after many years of careful research, for I am satisfied that one may just as easily go a step further and "tune in" on the universal mind in which all knowledge is stored where it may be appropriated by all who master the art of coming after it.

To a highly orthodox mind these statements may seem very irrational; but, to the student (and, so far, there are but few people in the world who are more than mere students, of an elementary grade, of this subject) who has studied this subject with any appreciable degree of understanding, these hypotheses seem not only possible, but absolutely probable.

But put the hypothesis to a test of your own!

You can select no better subject upon which to try an experiment than that which you have selected as your definite chief aim in life.

Memorize your definite chief aim so you can repeat it without looking at the written page, then make a practice of fixing your attention on it at least twice a day, proceeding as follows:

Go into some quiet place where you will not be disturbed; sit down and completely relax your mind and your body; then close your eyes and place your fingers in your ears, thereby excluding the ordinary sound waves and all of the light waves. In that position repeat your definite chief aim in life, and as you do so see yourself, in your imagination, in full possession of the object of that aim. If a part of your aim is the accumulation of money, as it undoubtedly is, then see yourself in possession of that money. If a part of the object of your definite aim is the ownership of a home, then see a picture of that home, in your imagination, just as you expect to see it in reality. If a part of your definite aim is to become a powerful and influential public speaker, then see yourself before an enormous audience, and feel yourself playing upon the emotions of that audience as a great violinist would play upon the strings of the violin.

As you approach the end of this lesson, there are two things which you might do, viz.

First: You might begin, now, to cultivate the ability to fix attention, at will, on a given subject, with a feeling that this ability, when fully developed, would bring you the object of your definite chief aim in life; or,

Second: You might tilt your nose in the air and with the smile of a cynic say to yourself–"Bosh" and thereby mark yourself a fool!

Take your choice!

This lesson was not written as an argument, nor as the subject of a debate. It is your privilege to accept it, in whole or in part, or reject it, just as you please.

But at this place I wish to state, however, that this is not an age of cynicism or doubt.

An age that has conquered the air above us and the sea beneath us, that has enabled us to harness the air and turn it into a messenger that will carry the sound of our voice halfway around the earth in the fractional part of a second, certainly is not an age that lends encouragement to the "doubting Thomases" or the "I-don't-believe-it Joneses."

The human family has passed through the "Stone Age" and the "Iron Age" and the "Steel Age," and unless I have greatly misinterpreted the trend of the times it is now entering the "Mind Power Age," which will eclipse, in stupendous achievement, all the other "ages" combined.

Learn to fix your attention on a given subject, at will, for whatever length of time you choose, and you will have learned the secret passageway to power and plenty!

This is concentration!

You will understand, from this lesson, that the object of forming an alliance between two or more people, and thereby creating a "Master Mind," is to apply the Law of Concentration more effectively than it could be applied through the efforts of but one person.

The principle referred to as the "Master Mind" is nothing more nor less than group concentration of mind power upon the attainment of a definite object or end. Greater power comes through group mind concentration because of the "stepping up" process produced through the reaction of one mind upon another or others.

PERSUASION VS. FORCE

Success, as has been stated in dozens of different ways throughout this course, is very largely a matter of tactful and harmonious negotiation with other people. Generally speaking, the man who understands how to "get people to do things" he wants done may succeed in any calling.

As a fitting climax for this lesson, on the Law of Concentration, we shall describe the principles through which men are influenced; through which cooperation is gained; through which antagonism is eliminated and friendliness developed. Force sometimes gets what appear to be satisfactory results, but force, alone, never has built and never can build enduring success.

The world war has done more than anything which has happened in the history of the world to show us the futility of force as a means of influencing the human mind. Without going into details or recounting the instances which could be cited, we all know that force was the foundation upon which German philosophy has been built during the past forty years. The doctrine that might makes right was given a worldwide trial and it failed.

The human body can be imprisoned or controlled by physical force, but it is not so with the human mind. No man on earth can control the mind of a normal, healthy person if that person chooses to exercise his God-given right to control his own mind. The majority of people do not exercise this right. They go through the world, thanks to our faulty educational system, without having discovered the strength which lies dormant in their own minds. Now and then something happens, more in the nature of an accident than anything else, which awakens a person and causes him to discover where his real strength lies and how to use it in the development of industry or one of the professions. Result: a genius is born!

There is a given point at which the human mind stops rising or exploring unless something out of the daily routine happens to "push" it over this obstacle. In some minds this point is very low and in others it is very high. In still others it varies between low and high. The individual who discovers a way to stimulate his mind artificially, arouse it and cause it to go beyond this average stopping point frequently, is sure to be rewarded with fame and fortune if his efforts are of a constructive nature.

The educator who discovers a way to stimulate any mind and cause it to rise above this average stopping point without any bad reactionary effects, will confer a blessing on the human race second to none in the history of the world. We, of course, do not have reference to physical stimulants or narcotics. These will always arouse the mind for a time, but eventually they ruin it entirely. We have reference to a purely mental stimulant, such as that which comes through intense interest, desire, enthusiasm, love, etc., the factors out of which a "Master Mind" may be developed. The person who makes this discovery will do much toward solving the crime problem.

You can do almost anything with a person when you learn how to influence his mind. The mind may be likened to a great field. It is a very fertile field which always produces a crop after the kind of seed which is sown in it. The problem, then, is to learn how to select the right sort of seed and how to sow that seed so that it takes root and grows quickly. We are sowing seed in our minds daily, hourly, nay, every second, but we are doing it promiscuously and more or less unconsciously. We must learn to do it after a carefully prepared plan, according to a well-laid out design! Haphazardly sown seed in the human mind brings back a haphazard crop! There is no escape from this result.

History is full of notable cases of men who have been transformed from law-abiding, peaceful, constructive citizens to roving, vicious criminals. We also have thousands of cases wherein men of the low, vicious, so-called criminal type have been transformed into constructive, law-abiding citizens. In every one of these cases the transformation of the human being took place in the mind of the man. He created in his own mind, for one reason or another, a picture of what he desired and then proceeded to transform that picture into reality. As a matter of fact, if a picture of any environment, condition or thing be pictured in the human mind and if the mind be focused or concentrated on that picture long enough and persistently enough, and backed up with a strong desire for the thing pictured, it is but a short step from the picture, to the realization of it in physical or mental form.

The world war brought out many startling tendencies of the human mind which corroborate the work which the psychologist has carried on in his research into the workings of the mind. The following account of a rough, uncouth, unschooled, undisciplined young mountaineer is an excellent case in point:

FOUGHT FOR HIS RELIGION; NOW GREAT WAR HERO

Rotarians Plan to Present Farm to Arvin York, Unlettered Tennessee Squirrel Hunter

BY GEORGE W. DIXON

How Arvin Cullom York, an unlettered Tennessee squirrel hunter, became the foremost hero of the American Expeditionary Forces in France, forms a romantic chapter in the history of the world war.

York is a native of Fentress County. He was born and reared among the hardy mountaineers of the Tennessee woods. There is not even a railroad in Fentress County. During his earlier years he was reputed to be a desperate character. He was what was known as a gunman. He was a dead shot with a revolver, and his prowess with the rifle was known far and wide among the plain people of the Tennessee hills.

One day a religious organization pitched its tent in the community in which York and his parents lived. It was a strange sect that came to the mountains looking for converts, but the methods of the evangels of the new cult were full of fire and emotionalism. They denounced the sinner, the vile character and the man who took advantage of his neighbor. They pointed to Christianity as an example that all should follow.

ALVIN GETS RELIGION

Alvin Cullom York startled his neighbors one night by flinging himself down at the mourners' bench. Old men stirred in their seats and women craned their necks, as York wrestled with his sins in the shadows of the Tennessee mountains.

York became an ardent apostle of the new religion. He became an exhorter, a leader in the religious life of the community and, although his marksmanship was as deadly as ever, no one feared him who walked in the path of righteousness.

When the news of the war reached that remote section of Tennessee and the mountaineers were told that they were going to be "conscripted," York grew sullen and disagreeable. He didn't believe in killing human beings, even in war. His Bible taught him, "Thou shalt not kill." To his mind this was literal and final. He was branded as a "conscientious objector."

The draft officers anticipated trouble. They knew that his mind was made up, and they would have to reach him in some manner other than by threats of punishment.

WAR IN A HOLY CAUSE

They went to York with a Bible and showed him that the war was in a holy cause- the cause of liberty and human freedom. They pointed out that men like himself were called upon by the Higher Powers to make the world free; to protect innocent women and children from violation; to make life worth living for the poor and oppressed; to overcome the "beast" pictured in the Scriptures. It was a fight between the hosts of righteousness and the hordes of Satan. The devil was trying to conquer the world through his chosen agents, the Kaiser and his generals.

York's eyes blazed with a fierce light. His big hands closed like a vise. His strong jaws snapped. "The Kaiser," he hissed between his teeth, "The beast! The destroyer of women and children! I'll show him where he belongs if I ever get within gunshot of him!"

He caressed his rifle, kissed his mother goodbye and told her he would see her again when the Kaiser had been put out of business.

He went to the training camp and drilled with scrupulous care and strict obedience to orders.

His skill at target practice attracted attention. His comrades were puzzled at his high scores. They had not reckoned that a backwoods squirrel hunter would make fine material for a sniper in the front-line trenches.

York's part in the war is now history. General Pershing has designated him as the foremost individual hero of the war. He won every decoration, including the Congressional Medal, the Croix de Guerre, the Legion of Honor. He faced the Germans without fear of death. He was fighting to vindicate his religion, for the sanctity of the home; the love of women and children. Fear was not in his code or his vocabulary. His daring electrified more than a million men and set the world to talking about this strange, unlettered hero from the hills of Tennessee.

Here we have a case of a young mountaineer who, had he been approached from just a slightly different angle, undoubtedly would have resisted conscription and, likely as not, would have become so embittered toward his country that he would have become an outlaw, looking for an opportunity to strike back at the first chance.

Those who approached him knew something of the principles through which the human mind works. They knew how to manage young York by first overcoming the resistance that he had worked up in his own mind. This is the very point at which thousands of men, through improper understanding of these principles, are arbitrarily classed as criminals and treated as dangerous, vicious people. Through suggestion these people could have been handled as effectively as young York was handled, and developed into useful, productive human beings.

In your search for ways and means of understanding and manipulating your own mind so you can persuade it to create that which you desire in life, let us remind you that, without a single exception, anything which irritates you and arouses you to anger, hatred, dislike, or cynicism, is destructive and very bad for you.

You can never get the maximum or even a fair average of constructive action out of your mind until you have learned to control it and keep it from becoming stimulated through anger or fear!

These two negatives, anger and fear, are positively destructive to your mind, and as long as you allow them to remain you can be sure of results which are unsatisfactory and away below what you are capable of producing.

In our discussion of environment and habit we learned that the individual mind is amenable to the suggestions of environment; that the minds of the individuals of a crowd blend with one another conforming to the suggestion of the prevailing influence of the leader or dominating figure. Mr. J. A. Fisk gives us an interesting account of the influence of mental suggestion in the revival meeting, which bears out the statement that the crowd mind blends into one, as follows:

MENTAL SUGGESTION IN THE REVIVAL

Modern psychology has firmly established the fact that the greater part of the phenomena of the religious "revival" are psychical rather than spiritual in their nature, and abnormally psychical at that. The leading authorities recognize the fact that the mental excitement attendant upon the emotional appeals of the "revivalist" must be classified with the phenomena, of hypnotic suggestion rather than with that of true, religious experience. And those who have made a close study of the subject believe that instead of such excitement tending to elevate the mind and exalt the spirit of the individual, it serves to weaken and degrade the mind and prostitute the spirit by dragging it in the mud of abnormal psychic frenzy and emotional excess. In fact, by some careful observers, familiar with the respective phenomena, the religious "revival" meeting is classed with the public hypnotic "entertainment" as a typical example of psychic intoxication and hysterical excess.

David Starr Jordan, chancellor emeritus of Leland Stanford University, says: "Whisky, cocaine and alcohol bring temporary insanity, and so does a revival of religion." The late Professor William James, of Harvard University, the eminent psychologist, says: "Religious revivalism is more dangerous to the life of society than drunkenness."

It should be unnecessary to state that in this lesson the term "revival" is used in the narrower signification indicating the typical religious emotional excitement known by the term in question, and is not intended to apply to the older and respected religious experience designated by the same term, which was so highly revered among the Puritans, Lutherans and others in the past.

In order to understand the principle of the operation of mental suggestion in the revival meeting, we must first understand something of what is known as the psychology of the crowd. Psychologists are aware that the psychology of a crowd, considered as a whole, differs materially from that of the separate individuals composing that crowd. There is a crowd of separate individuals, and a composite crowd in which the emotional natures of the units seem to blend and fuse. The change from the first-named crowd to the second arises from the influence of earnest attention, or deep emotional appeals or common interest. When this change occurs the crowd becomes a composite individual, the degree of whose intelligence and emotional control is but little above that of its weakest member. This fact, startling as it may appear to the average reader, is well-known and is admitted by the leading psychologists of the day, and many important essays and books have been written thereupon. The predominant characteristics of this "composite-mindedness" of a crowd are the evidences of extreme suggestibility, response to appeals of emotion, vivid imagination, and action arising from imitation–all of which are mental traits universally manifested by primitive man. In short, the crowd manifests atavism, or reversion to early racial traits.

Dials, in his Psychology of the Aggregate Mind of an Audience, holds that the mind of an assemblage listening to a powerful speaker undergoes a curious process called "fusion," by which the individuals in the audience, losing their personal traits for the time being, to a greater or less degree, are reduced, as it were, to a single individual, whose characteristics are those of an impulsive youth of twenty, imbued in general with high ideals, but sacking in reasoning, power and will. Tarde, the French psychologist, advances similar views.

Professor Joseph Jastrow, in his Fact and Fable in Psychology, says: "In the production of this state of mind a factor as yet unmentioned plays a leading role, the power of mental contagion. Error, like truth, flourishes in crowds. At the heart of sympathy each finds a home... No form of contagion is so insidious in its outset, so difficult to check in its advance, so certain to leave germs that may at any moment reveal their pernicious power, as a mental contagion–the contagion of fear, of panic, of fanaticism, of lawlessness, of superstition, of error....In brief, we must add to the many factors which contribute to deception, the recognized lowering of critical ability, of the power of accurate observation, indeed, of rationality, which merely being one of a crowd induces. The conjurer finds it easy to perform to a large audience, because, among other reasons, it is easier to arouse their admiration and sympathy, easier to make them forget themselves and enter into the uncritical spirit of wonderland. It would seem that in some respects the critical tone of an assembly, like the strength of a chain, is that of its weakest member."

Professor Le Bon, in his The Crowd, says:

> "The sentiments and ideas of all the persons in the gathering take one and the same direction, and their conscious personality vanishes. A collective mind is formed, doubtless transitory, by presenting very clearly marked characteristics. The gathering has become what, in the absence of a better expression, I will call an organized crowd, or, if the term be considered preferable, a psychological crowd. It forms a single being, and is subjected to the law of the mental unity of crowds...The most striking peculiarity presented by a psychological crowd is the following: Whoever be the individuals that compose it, however like or unlike be their mode of life, their occupation, their character, or their intelligence, the fact that they have been transformed into a crowd puts them in Possession of a sort of collective mind which makes them feel, think and act in a manner quite different from that in which each individual of them would feel, think and act were he in a state of isolation. There are certain ideas and feelings which do not come into being, or do not transform themselves into acts, except in the case of the individuals forming a crowd....In crowds it is stupidity and not mother wit that is accumulated. In the collective mind the intellectual aptitudes of the individuals, and in consequence their individuality, is weakened....The most careful observations seem to prove that an individual immersed for some length of time in a crowd in action soon finds himself in a special state, which most resembles the state of fascination in which the hypnotized

> individual finds himself....The conscious personality has entirely vanished, will and discernment are lost. All feelings and thoughts are bent in the direction determined by the hypnotizer.... Under the influence of a suggestion he will undertake the accomplishment of certain acts with irresistible impetuosity. This impetuosity is the more irresistible in the case of crowds, from the fact that, the suggestion being the same for all the individuals of the crowd, it gains in strength by reciprocity. Moreover, by the mere fact that he forms part of an organized crowd, a man descends several rungs in the ladder of civilization. Isolated, he may be a cultured individual; in a crowd, he is a barbarian–that is, a creature acting by instinct. He possesses the spontaneity, the violence, the ferocity, and also the enthusiasm and heroism of primitive beings, whom he further tends to resemble by the facility with which he allows himself to be induced to commit acts contrary to his most obvious interests and his best-known habits. An individual in a crowd is a grain of sand amid other grains of sand, which the wind stirs up at will."

Professor Davenport, in his Primitive Traits in Religious Revivals, says:

> "The mind of the crowd is strangely like that of primitive man. Most of the people in it may be far from primitive in emotion, in thought, in character; nevertheless, the result tends always to be the same. Stimulation immediately begets action. Reason is in abeyance. The cool, rational speaker has little chance beside the skillful emotional orator. The crowd thinks in images, and speech must take this form to be accessible to it. The images are not connected by any natural bond, and they take each other's place like the slides of a magic lantern. It follows from this, of course, that appeals to the imagination have paramount influence....The crowd is united and governed by emotion rather than by reason. Emotion is the natural bond, for men differ much less in this respect than in intellect. It is also true that in a crowd of a thousand men the amount of emotion actually generated and existing is far greater than the sum which might conceivably be obtained by adding together the emotions of the individuals taken by themselves. The explanation of this is that the attention of the crowd is always directed either by the circumstances of the occasion or by the speaker to certain common ideas–as 'salvation' in religious gatherings...and every individual in the gathering is stirred with emotion, not only because the idea or the shibboleth stirs him, but also because he is conscious that every other individual in the gathering believes in the idea or the shibboleth, and is stirred by it, too. And this enormously increases the volume of his own emotion and consequently the total volume of emotion in the crowd. As in the case of the primitive mind, imagination has unlocked the floodgates of emotion, which on occasion may become wild enthusiasm or demoniac frenzy."

The student of suggestion will see that not only are the emotional members of a revival audience subject to the effect of the "composite-mindedness" arising from the "psychology of the crowd" and are thereby weakened in resistive power, but that they are also brought under the influence of two other very potent forms of mental suggestion. Added to the powerful suggestion of authority exercised by the revivalist, which is exerted to its fullest along lines very similar to that of the professional hypnotist, is the suggestion of imitation exerted upon each individual by the combined force of the balance of the crowd.

As Durkheim observed in his psychological investigations, the average individual is "intimidated by the mass" of the crowd around him, or before him, and experiences that peculiar psychological influence exerted by the mere number of people as against his individual self. Not only does the suggestible person find it easy to respond to the authoritative suggestions of the preacher and the exhortations of his helpers, but he is also brought under the direct fire of the imitative suggestions of those on all sides who are experiencing emotional activities and who are manifesting them outwardly. Not only does the voice of the shepherd urge forward, but the tinkle of the bellwether's bell is also heard, and the imitative tendency of the flock, which causes one sheep to jump because one ahead of him does so (and so on until the last sheep has jumped), needs but the force of the example of a leader to start into motion the entire flock. This is not an exaggeration– human beings, in times of panic, fright, or deep emotion of any kind, manifest the imitative tendency of the sheep, and the tendency of cattle and horses to "stampede" under imitation.

To the student experienced in the experimental work of the psychological laboratory there is the very closest analogy observed in the respective phenomena of the revival and hypnotic suggestion. In both cases the attention and interest is attracted by the unusual procedure; the element of mystery and awe is induced by words and actions calculated to inspire them; the senses are tired by monotonous talk in an impressive and authoritative tone; and finally the suggestions are projected in a commanding, suggestive manner familiar to all students of hypnotic suggestion. The subjects in both cases are prepared for the final suggestions and commands, by previously given minor suggestions, such as: "Stand up," or "Look this way," etc., in the case of the hypnotist; and by: "All those who think so-and-so, stand up," and "All who are willing to become better, stand up," etc., in the case of the revivalist. The impressionable subjects are thus accustomed to obedience to suggestion by easy stages. And, finally, the commanding suggestion: "Come right up–right up–this way–right up–come, I say, come, come, COME!"etc., which takes the impressed ones right off their feet and rushes them to the front, are, almost precisely the same in the hypnotic experiment or seance, on the one hand, and the sensational revival, on the other. Every good revivalist would make a good hypnotic operator, and every good hypnotic operator would make a good revivalist if his mind were turned in that direction.

In the revival, the person giving the suggestions has the advantage of breaking down the resistance of his audience by arousing their sentiments and emotions. Tales depicting the influence of mother, home and heaven; songs like "Tell Mother, I'll Be There"; and personal appeals to the revered associations of one's past and early life tend to reduce one to the state of emotional response, and render him most susceptible to strong, repeated suggestions along the same line. Young people and hysterical women are especially susceptible to this form of emotional suggestion. Their feelings are stirred, and the will is influenced by the preaching, the songs, and the personal appeals of the co-workers of the revivalist.

The most sacred sentimental memories are reawakened for the moment and old conditions of mind are reinduced. "Where Is My Wandering Boy Tonight?" brings forth tears to many a one to whom the memory of the mother is sacred, and the preaching that the mother is dwelling in a state of bliss beyond the skies, from which the unconverted child is cut off unless he professes faith, serves to move many to action for the time being. The element of fear is also invoked in the revival–not so much as formerly, it is true, but still to a considerable extent and more subtly. The fear of a sudden death in an unconverted condition is held over the audience, and, "Why not now–why not tonight?" is asked

him, accompanied by the hymn; "Oh, Why Do You Wait, Dear Brother?"
As Davenport says:

> "It is well known that the employment of symbolic images immensely increases the emotion of an audience. The vocabulary of revivals abounds in them–the cross, the crown, the angel band, hell, heaven. Now vivid imagination and strong feeling and belief are states of mind favorable to suggestion as well as to impulsive action. It is also true that the influence of a crowd largely in sympathy with the ideas suggested is thoroughly coercive or intimidative upon the individual sinner. There is considerable professed conversion which results in the beginning from little more than this form of social pressure, and which may never develop beyond it. Finally, the inhibition of all extraneous ideas is encouraged in revival assemblies both by prayer and speech. There is, therefore, extreme sensitiveness to suggestion. When to these conditions of negative consciousness on the part of an audience there has been added a conductor of the meetings who has a high hypnotic potential, such as Wesley or Finney, or who is only a thoroughly persuasive and magnetic personality, such as Whitefield, there may easily be an influence exerted upon certain individuals of a crowd which closely approaches the abnormal or thoroughly hypnotic. When this point is not reached there is still a great amount of highly acute though normal suggestibility to be reckoned with." The persons who show signs of being influenced are then "labored with" by either the revivalist or his co-workers. They are urged to surrender their will, and "Leave it all to the Lord." They are told to "Give yourself to God, now, right now, this minute"; or to "Only believe now, and you shall be saved" etc. They are exhorted and prayed with; arms are placed around their shoulders, and every art of emotional persuasive suggestion is used to make the sinner "give up."

Starbuck in his The Psychology of Religion relates a number of instances of the experiences of converted persons at revivals. One person wrote as follows:

> "My will seemed wholly at the mercy of others, particularly of the revivalist M___. There was absolutely no intellectual element. It was pure feeling. There followed a period of ecstasy. I was bent on doing good and was eloquent in appealing to others. The state of moral exaltation did not continue. It was followed by a complete relapse from orthodox religion."

Davenport has the following to say in reply to the claim that the old methods of influencing converts at a revival have passed away with the crude theology of the past:

> "I lay particular stress upon this matter here, because, while the employment of irrational fear in revivals has largely passed away, the employment of the hypnotic method has not passed away. There has rather been a recrudescence and a conscious strengthening of it because the old prop of terror is gone. And it cannot be too vigorously emphasized that such a force is not a 'spiritual' force in any high and clear sense at all, but is rather uncanny and psychic and obscure. And the method itself needs to be greatly refined before it can ever be of any spiritual benefit whatever. It is thoroughly primitive and belongs with the animal and instinctive means of fascination. In this bald, crude form, the feline employs it upon the helpless bird and

the Indian medicine-man upon the ghost-dance votary. When used, as it has often been, upon little children who are naturally highly suggestible, it has no justification whatever and is mentally and morally injurious in the highest degree. I do not see how violent emotional throes and the use of suggestion in its crude forms can be made serviceable even in the cases of hardened sinners, and certainly with large classes of the population the employment of this means is nothing but psychological malpractice. We guard with intelligent care against quackery in physiological obstetrics. It would be well if a sterner training and prohibition hedged about the spiritual obstetrician, whose function it is to guide the far more delicate process of the new birth."

Some who favor the methods of the revival, but who also recognize the fact that mental suggestion plays a most important part in the phenomena thereof, hold that the objections similar to those here advanced are not valid against the methods of the revival, inasmuch as mental suggestion, as is well-known, may be used for good purposes as well as bad–for the benefit and uplifting of people as well as in the opposite direction. This being admitted, these good folks argue that mental suggestion in the revival is a legitimate method or "weapon of attack upon the stronghold of the devil." But this argument is found to be defective when examined in its effects and consequences. In the first place, it would seem to identify the emotional, neurotic and hysterical mental states induced by revival methods with the spiritual uplift and moral regeneration which is the accompaniment of true religious experience. It seeks to place the counterfeit on a par with the genuine–the baleful glare of the rays of the psychic moon with the invigorating and animating rays of the spiritual sun. It seeks to raise the hypnotic phase to that of the "spiritual-mindedness" of man. To those who are familiar with the two classes of phenomena, there is a difference as wide as that between the poles existing between them.

But what do the authorities say of the revival of the future–the new revival–the real revival? Let Professor Davenport speak for the critics–he is well adapted for the task. He says:

"There will be, I believe, far less use of the revival meeting as a crass coercive instrument for overriding the will and overwhelming the reason of the individual man. The influence of public religious gatherings will be more indirect, more unobtrusive. It will be recognized that hypnotization and forced choices weaken the soul, and there will be no attempt to press to decision in so great a matter under the spell of excitement and contagion and suggestion. . . . The converts may be few. They may be many. They will be measured, not by the capacity of the preacher for administrative hypnotism, but rather by the capacity for unselfish friendship of every Christian man and woman. But of this I think we may be confident–the days of religious effervescence and passional unrestraint are dying. The days of intelligent, undemonstrative and self-sacrificing piety are dawning. To do justly, to love mercy, to walk humbly with God–these remain the cardinal tests of the divine in man."

The Law of Concentration is one of the major principles which must be understood and applied intelligently by all who would successfully experiment with the principle described in this course as the "Master Mind."

The foregoing comments, by leading authorities of the world, will give you a better understanding of the Law of Concentration as it is often used by those who wish to "blend" or "fuse" the minds of a crowd so they will function as a single mind.

You are now ready for the lesson on Co-operation, which will take you further into the methods of applying the psychological laws upon which this philosophy of success is based.

Lesson Thirteen: CO-OPERATION

CO-OPERATION is the beginning of all organized effort. As was stated in the second lesson of this course, Andrew Carnegie accumulated a gigantic fortune through the cooperative efforts of a small group of men numbering not more than a score. You, too, can learn how to use this principle.

There are two forms of Co-operation to which your attention will be directed in this lesson; namely:

First, the Co-operation between people who group themselves together or form alliances for the purpose of attaining a given end, under the principles known as the Law of the Master Mind.

Second, the Co-operation between the conscious and the subconscious minds, which forms a reasonable hypothesis of man's ability to contact, communicate with and draw upon infinite intelligence.

To one who has not given serious thought to this subject, the foregoing hypothesis may seem unreasonable; but follow the evidence of its soundness, and study the facts upon which the hypothesis is based, and then draw your own conclusions. Let us begin with a brief review of the physical construction of the body: "We know that the whole body is traversed by a network of nerves which serve as the channels of communication between the indwelling spiritual ego, which we call mind, and the functions of the external organism.

"This nervous system is dual. One system, known as the Sympathetic, is the channel for all those activities which are not consciously directed by our volition, such as the operation of the digestive organs, the repair of the daily wear and tear of the tissues, and the like.

"The other system, known as the Voluntary or Cerebro-spinal system, is the channel through which we receive conscious perception from the physical senses and exercise control over the movements of the body. This system has its center in the brain, while the other has its center in the ganglionic mass at the back of the stomach known as the solar plexus, and sometimes spoken of as the abdominal brain. The cerebro-spinal system is the channel of our volitional or conscious mental action, and the sympathetic system is the channel of that mental action which unconsciously supports the vital functions of the body.

"Thus the cerebro-spinal system is the organ of the conscious mind and the sympathetic is that of the subconscious mind.

"But the interaction of conscious and subconscious minds requires a similar interaction between the corresponding systems of nerves, and one conspicuous connection by which this is provided is the "vagus" nerve. This nerve passes out of the cerebral region as a portion of the voluntary system, and through it we control the vocal organs; then it passes onward to the thorax, sending out branches to the heart and lungs; and finally, passing through the diaphragm, it loses the outer coating which distinguishes the nerves of the voluntary system and becomes identified with those of the sympathetic system, so forming a connecting link between the two and making the man physically a single entity.

"Similarly different areas of the brain indicate their connection with the objective and subjective activities of the mind respectively, and, speaking in a general way, we may assign the frontal portion of the brain to the former, and the posterior portion to the latter, while the intermediate portion partakes of the character of both.

"The intuitional faculty has its correspondence in the upper area of the brain, situated between the frontal and the posterior portions, and, physiologically speaking, it is here that intuitive ideas find entrance. These, at first, are more or less unformed and generalized in character, but are, nevertheless, perceived by the conscious mind; otherwise, we should not be aware of them at all. Then the effort of Nature is to bring these ideas into more definite and usable shape, so the conscious mind lays hold on them and induces a corresponding vibratory current in the voluntary system of nerves, and this in turn induces a similar current in the involuntary system, thus handing the idea over to the subjective mind. The vibratory current which had first descended from the apex of the brain to the frontal brain and thus through the voluntary system to the solar plexus is now reversed and ascends from the solar plexus through the sympathetic system to the posterior brain, this return current indicating the action of the subjective mind."

If we were to remove the surface portion of the apex of the brain we should find immediately below it the shining belt of brain substance called the "corpus callous." This is the point of union between the subjective and objective, and, as the current returns from the solar plexus to this point, it is restored to the objective portion of the brain in a fresh form which it has acquired by the silent alchemy of the subjective mind. Thus the conception which was at first only vaguely recognized is restored to the objective mind in a definite and workable form, and then the objective mind, acting through the frontal brain–the area of comparison and analysis–proceeds to work upon a clearly perceived idea and to bring out the potentialities that are latent in it (Judge T. Toward, in The Edinburgh Lectures on Mental Science).

The term "subjective mind" is the same as the term "subconscious mind," and the term "objective mind" is the same as the term "conscious mind." Please understand these different terms.

By studying this dual system through which the body transmits energy, we discover the exact points at which the two systems are connected, and the manner in which we may transmit a thought from the conscious to the subconscious mind. This Co-operative dual nervous system is the most important form of co-operation known to man; for it is through the aid of this system that the principle of evolution carries on its work of developing accurate thought, as described in Lesson Eleven.

When you impress any idea on your subconscious mind, through the principle of Autosuggestion, you do so with the aid of this dual nervous system: and when your subconscious mind works out a definite plan of any desire with which you impress it, the plan is delivered back to your conscious mind through this same dual nervous system.

This Co-operative system of nerves literally constitutes a direct line of communication between your ordinary conscious mind and infinite intelligence.

Knowing, from my own previous experience as a beginner in the study of this subject, how difficult it is to accept the hypothesis here described, I will illustrate the soundness of the hypothesis in a simple way that you can both understand and demonstrate for yourself.

Before going to sleep at night impress upon your mind the desire to arise the next morning at a given hour, say at four A.M., and if your impression is accompanied by a positive determination to arise at that hour, your subconscious mind will register the impression and awaken you at precisely that time. Now the question might well be asked:

"If I ran impress my subconscious mind with the desire to arise at a specified time and it will awaken me at that time, why do I not form the habit of impressing it with other and more important desires?"

If you will ask yourself this question, and insist upon an answer, you will find yourself very near, if not on the pathway that leads to the secret door to knowledge, as described in Lesson Eleven.

We will now take up the subject of Co-operation between men who unite, or group themselves together for the purpose of attaining a given end. In the second lesson of this course we referred to this sort of cooperation as organized effort.

This course touches some phase of co-operation in practically every lesson. This result was inevitable for the reason that the object of the course is to help the student develop power, and power is developed only through organized effort.

We are living in an age of co-operative effort. Nearly all successful businesses are conducted under some form of co-operation. The same is true in the field of industry and finance, as well as in the professional field.

Doctors and lawyers have their alliances for mutual aid and protection in the form of Bar Associations and Medical Associations.

The bankers have both local and national Associations for their mutual aid and advancement.

The retail merchants have their Associations for the same purpose.

The automobile owners have grouped themselves into Clubs and Associations.

The Printers have their Associations; the plumbers have theirs and the coal dealers have theirs. Co-operation is the object of all these Associations.

The laboring men have their unions and those who supply the working capital and superintend the efforts of laboring men have their alliances, under various names.

Nations have their co-operative alliances, although they do not appear to have yet discovered the full meaning of "co-operation." The attempt of the late President Wilson to perfect the League of Nations, followed by the efforts of the late President Harding to perfect the same idea under the name of the World Court, indicates the trend of the times in the direction of co-operation.

It is slowly becoming obvious to man that those who most efficiently apply the principle of co-operative effort survive longest, and, that this principle applies from the lowest form of animal life to the highest form of human endeavor.

Mr. Carnegie, and Mr. Rockefeller, and Mr. Ford have taught the business man the value of co-operative effort; that is, they have taught all who cared to observe, the principle through which they accumulated vast fortunes.

Co-operation is the very foundation of all successful leadership. Henry Ford's most tangible asset is the well-organized agency force that he has established. This organization not only provides him with an outlet for all the automobiles he can manufacture, but, of greater importance still, it provides him with financial power sufficient to meet any emergency that may arise, a fact which he has already demonstrated on at least one occasion.

As a result of his understanding of the value of the co-operative principle Ford has removed himself from the usual position of dependence upon financial institutions and at the same time provided himself with more commercial power than he can possibly use.

The Federal Reserve Bank System is another example of co-operative effort which practically insures the United States against a money panic.

The chain-store systems constitute another form of commercial co-operation that provides advantage through both the purchasing and the distributing end of the business.

The modern department store, which is the equivalent of a group of small stores operating under one roof, one management and one overhead expense, is another illustration of the advantage of co-operative effort in the commercial field.

In Lesson Fifteen you will observe the possibilities of co-operative effort in its highest form and at the same time you will see the important part that it plays in the development of power.

As you have already learned, power is organized effort. The three most important factors that enter into the process of organizing effort are:

Concentration,
Co-operation and
Co-ordination.

HOW POWER IS DEVELOPED THROUGH CO-OPERATION

As we have already seen, power is organized effort or energy. Personal power is developed by developing, organizing and co-ordinating the faculties of the mind. This may be accomplished by mastering and applying the fifteen major principles upon which this course is founded. The necessary procedure through which these principles may be mastered is thoroughly described in the sixteenth lesson. The development of personal power is but the first step to be taken in the development of the potential power that is available through the medium of allied effort, or cooperation, which may be called group power.

It is a well-known fact that all men who have amassed large fortunes have been known as able "organizers." By this is meant that they possessed the ability to enlist the cooperative efforts of other men who supplied talent and ability which they, themselves, did not possess.

The chief object of this course is so to unfold the principles of organized and cooperative or allied effort that the student will comprehend their significance and make them the basis of his philosophy.

Take, as an example, any business or profession that you choose and you will observe, by analysis, that it is limited only by lack of application of organized and co-operative effort. As an illustration, consider the legal profession.

If a law firm consists of but one type of mind it will be greatly handicapped, even though it may be made up of a dozen able men of this particular type. The complicated legal system calls for a greater variety of talent than any one man could possibly provide.

It is evident, therefore, that mere organized effort is not sufficient to insure outstanding success; the organization must consist of individuals each of whom supplies some specialized talent which the other members of the organization do not possess.

A well-organized law firm would include talent that was specialized in the preparation of cases; men of vision and imagination who understood how to harmonize the law and the evidence of a case under a sound plan. Men who have such ability are not always possessed of the ability to try a case in court; therefore, men who are proficient in court procedure must be available. Carrying the analysis a step further, it will be seen that there are many different classes of cases which call for men of various types of specialized ability in both the preparation and the trial of these cases. A lawyer who had prepared himself as a specialist in corporation law might be wholly unprepared to handle a case in criminal procedure.

In forming a law partnership, the man who understood the principles of organized, cooperative effort, would surround himself with talent that was specialized in every branch of law and legal procedure in which he intended to practice. The man who had no conception of the potential power of these principles would probably select his associates by the usual "hit or miss" method, basing his selections more upon personality or acquaintanceship than consideration of the particular type of legal talent that each possessed.

The subject of organized effort has been covered in the preceding lessons of this course, but it is again brought up in connection with this lesson for the purpose of indicating the necessity of forming alliances or organizations consisting of individuals who supply all of the necessary talent that may be needed for the attainment of the object in mind.

In nearly all commercial undertakings, there is a need for at least three classes of talent; namely, buyers, salesmen and those who are familiar with finance. It will be readily seen that when these three classes of men organize and co-ordinate their efforts they avail themselves, through this form of co-operation, of power which no single individual of the group possesses.

Many a business fails because all of the men back of it are salesmen, or financial men or buyers. By nature, the most able salesmen are optimistic, enthusiastic and emotional; while able financial men, as a rule, are unemotional, deliberate and conservative. Both classes are essential to the success of a commercial enterprise; but either class will prove too much of a load for any business, without the modifying influence of the other class.

It is generally conceded that James J. Hill was the most efficient railroad builder that America ever produced; but it is equally well-known that he was not a civil engineer, nor a bridge builder, nor a locomotive engineer, nor a mechanical engineer, nor a chemist, although these highly specialized classes of talent are essential in railroad building. Mr. Hill understood the principles of organized effort and co-operation; therefore, he surrounded himself with men who possessed all this necessary ability which he lacked.

The modern department store is a splendid example of organized, co-operative effort. Each merchandising department is under the management of one who understands the purchasing and marketing of the goods carried in that department.

Back of all these department managers is a general staff consisting of specialists in buying, selling, financing, and the management of units, or groups, of people. This form of organized effort places back of each department both buying and selling power such as that department could not afford if it were separated from the group and had to be operated under its own overhead, in a separate location.

The United States of America is one of the richest and most powerful nations of the world. Upon analysis, it will be seen that this enormous power has grown out of the cooperative efforts of the states of the Union.

It was for the purpose of saving this power that the immortal Lincoln made up his mind to erase the Mason and Dixon line. The saving of the Union was of far greater concern to him than was the freedom of the slaves of the South. Had this not been so, the present status of the United States as a power among the nations of the world would be far different from what it is.

It was this same principle of co-operative effort that Woodrow Wilson had in mind when he created his plan for a League of Nations. He foresaw the need of such a plan as a medium for preventing war between nations; just as Lincoln foresaw it as a medium for harmonizing the efforts of the people of the United States, thereby preserving the Union.

Thus it is seen that the principle of organized, co-operative effort through the aid of which the individual may develop personal power, is the selfsame principle that must be employed in developing group power.

Andrew Carnegie easily dominated the steel business during his active connection with that industry, for the reason that he took advantage of the principle of organized, cooperative effort by surrounding himself with highly specialized financial men, chemists, sales managers, buyers of raw materials, transportation experts and others whose services were essential to that industry. He organized this group of "co-operators" into what he called a "Master Mind."

Any great university affords an excellent example of the necessity of organized, cooperative effort. The professorate is made up of men and women of highly specialized, though vastly different, ability. One department is presided over by experts in literature; another department by expert mathematicians; another department by experts in chemistry; another department by experts in economic philosophy; another department by experts in medicine; another, by experts in law, etc. The university, as a whole, is the equivalent of a group of colleges each of which is directed by experts in its own line, whose efficiency is greatly increased through allied or co-operative effort that is directed by a single head.

Analyze power, no matter where, or in what form, it may be found, and you will find organization and co-operation as the chief factors back of it. You will find these two principles in evidence in the lowest form of vegetation no less than in the highest form of animal, which is man.

Off the coast of Norway is the most famous and irresistible maelstrom in the world.

This great whirlpool of ceaseless motion has never been known to give up any victim who was caught in its circling embrace of foaming water.

No less sure of destruction are those unfortunate souls who are caught in the great maelstrom of life toward which all who do not understand the principle of organized, co-operative effort are traveling. We are living in a world in which the law of the survival of the fittest is everywhere in evidence. Those who are "fit" are those who have power, and power is organized effort.

Unfortunate is the person who either through ignorance, or because of egotism, imagines that he can sail this sea of life in the frail bark of independence. Such a person will discover that there are maelstroms more dangerous than any mere whirlpool of unfriendly waters. All natural laws and all of Nature's plans are based upon harmonious, co-operative effort, as all who have attained high places in the world have discovered.

Wherever people are engaged in unfriendly combat, no matter what may be its nature, or its cause, one may observe the nearness of one of these maelstroms that awaits the combatants.

Success in life cannot be attained except through peaceful, harmonious, co-operative effort. Nor can success be attained single-handed or independently. Even though a man live as a hermit in the wilderness, far from all signs of civilization, he is, nevertheless, dependent upon forces outside of himself for an existence. The more he becomes a part of civilization the more dependent upon co-operative effort he becomes.

Whether a man earns his living by days' work or from the interest on the fortune he has amassed, he will earn it with less opposition through friendly co-operation with others. Moreover, the man whose philosophy is based upon co-operation instead of competition will not only acquire the necessities and the luxuries of life with less effort, but he will enjoy an extra reward in happiness such as others will never feel.

Fortunes that are acquired through co-operative effort inflict no scars upon the hearts of their owners, which is more than can be said of fortunes that are acquired through conflict and competitive methods that border on extortion.

The accumulation of material wealth, whether the object is that of bare existence or luxury, consumes most of the time that we put into this earthly struggle. If we cannot change this materialistic tendency of human nature, we can, at least, change the method of pursuing it by adopting co-operation as the basis of the pursuit.

Co-operation offers the two-fold reward of providing one with both the necessities and the luxuries of life and the peace of mind which the covetous never know. The avaricious and covetous person may amass a great fortune in material wealth; there is no denying this fact; but he will have sold his soul for a mess of pottage in the bargain.

Let us keep in mind the fact that all success is based upon power, and power grows out of knowledge, that has been organized and expressed in terms of ACTION.

The world pays for but one kind of knowledge, and that is the kind which is expressed in terms of constructive service. In addressing the graduating class of a business college one of the best known bankers in America said:

"You ought to feel proud of your diplomas, because they are evidence that you have been preparing yourselves for action in the great field of business.

"One of the advantages of a business college training is that it prepares you for action!

Not to belittle other methods of education, but to exalt the modern business college method, I am reminded to say that there are some colleges in which the majority of the students are preparing for practically everything else except action.

"You came to this business college with but one object in view, and that object is to learn to render service and earn a living. The latest style of clothing has been of little interest to you because you have been preparing yourself for work in which clothes of the latest style will play no important part. You did not come here to learn how to pour tea at an afternoon party nor to become masters at affecting friendliness while inwardly feeling envy for those who wear finer gowns and drive costly motor cars–you came here to learn how to work!"

In the graduating class before which this man spoke were thirteen boys, all of whom were so poor that they had barely enough money with which to pay their way. Some of them were paying their own way by working before and after school hours. That was twenty-five years ago. Last summer, I met the president of the business college which these boys attended and he gave me the history of each one of them, from the time that they graduated until the time when I talked to him. One of them is the president of one of the big wholesale drug companies, and a wealthy man; one is a successful lawyer; two own large business colleges of their own; one is a professor in the department of economics in one of the largest universities in America; one is the president of one of the large automobile manufacturing companies; two are presidents of banks, and wealthy men; one is the owner of a large department store; one is the vice-president of one of the great railway systems of the country; one is a well-established Certified Public Accountant; one is dead; and the thirteenth is compiling this Reading Course on the Law of Success.

Eleven successes out of a class of thirteen boys is not a bad record, thanks to the spirit of action developed by that business college training.

It is not the schooling you have had that counts; it is the extent to which you express that which you learned from your schooling through well-organized and intelligently directed action.

By no means would I belittle higher education, but I would offer hope and encouragement to those who have had no such education, provided they express that which they know, be it ever so little, in intensive action, along constructive lines. One of the greatest Presidents who ever occupied the White House had but little schooling, but he did such a good job of expressing what knowledge he acquired by that little schooling, through properly directed action, that his name has been inseparably woven into the history of the United States.

Every city, town and hamlet has its population of those well known characters called "ne'er-do-wells," and if you will analyze these unfortunate people, you will observe that one of their outstanding features is procrastination.

Lack of action has caused them to slip backward until they got into a "rut," where they will remain unless, through accident, they are forced out into the open road of struggle where unusual action will become necessary.

Don't let yourself get into such a condition.

Every office, and every shop, and every bank, and every store, and every other place of employment has its outstanding victims of procrastination who are doing the goose-step down the dusty road of failure because they have not developed the habit of expressing themselves in action.

You can pick out these unfortunates all about you if you will begin to analyze those with whom you come in contact each day. If you will talk to them you will observe that they have built up a false philosophy somewhat of this nature: "I am doing all I am paid to do, and I am getting by." Yes, they are "getting by"–but that is all they are getting.

Some years ago, at a time when labor was scarce and wages unusually high, I observed scores of able-bodied men lying about in the parks of Chicago, doing nothing. I became curious to know what sort of an alibi they would offer for their conduct, so I went out one afternoon and interviewed seven of them.

With the aid of a generous supply of cigars and cigarettes and a little loose change I bought myself into the confidence of those whom I interviewed and thereby gained a rather intimate view of their philosophy. All gave exactly the same reason for being there, without employment. They said: "The world will not give me a chance!!!" The exclamation points are my own. Think of it–the world would not "give them a chance." Of course the world wouldn't give them a chance.

It never gives anyone a chance. A man who wants a chance may create it through action, but if he waits for someone to hand it to him on a silver platter he will meet with disappointment.

I fear that this excuse that the world does not give a man a chance is quite prevalent, and I strongly suspect that it is one of the commonest causes of poverty and failure.

The seventh man that I interviewed on that well-spent afternoon was an unusually fine looking specimen, physically. He was lying on the ground asleep, with a newspaper over his face. When I lifted the paper from his face, he reached up, took it out of my hands, put it back over his face and went right on sleeping.

Then I used a little strategy by removing the paper from his face and placing it behind me, where he could not get it. He then sat up on the ground and I interviewed him.

That fellow was a graduate from two of the great universities of the east, with a master's degree from one, and a Ph.D. from the other.

His story was pathetic.

He had held job after job, but always his employer or his fellow employee "had it in for him." He hadn't been able to make them see the value of his college training. They wouldn't "give him a chance."

Here was a man who might have been at the head of some great business, or the outstanding figure in one of the professions had he not built his house upon the sands of procrastination and held to the false belief that the world should pay him for what he knew!

Luckily, most college graduates do not build upon such flimsy foundations, because no college on earth can crown with success the man who tries to collect for that which he knows instead of that which he can do with what he knows.

The man to whom I have referred was from one of the best known families of Virginia. He traced his ancestry back to the landing of the Mayflower. He threw back his shoulders, pounded himself on the breast with his fist and said: "Just think of it, sir! I am a son of one of the first families of old Virginia!"

My observations lead me to believe that being the son of a "first family" is not always fortunate for either the son or the family. Too often these sons of "first families" try to slide home from third base on their family names. This may be only a peculiar notion of mine, but I have observed that the men and women who are doing the world's work have but little time, and less inclination, to brag about their ancestry.

Not long ago I took a trip back to southwest Virginia, where I was born. It was the first time I had been there in over twenty years. It was a sad sight to compare the sons of some of those who were known as "first families" twenty years ago, with the sons of those who were but plain men who made it their business to express themselves in action of the most intensive nature.

The comparison reflected no credit upon the "first family" boys! It is with no feeling of exaltation that I express my gratitude for not having been brought into the world by parents who belonged to the "first family" class. That, of course, was not a matter of choice with me, and if it had been perhaps I, too, would have selected parents of the "first family" type.

Not long ago I was invited to deliver an address in Boston, Mass. After my work was finished, a reception committee volunteered to show me the sights of the city, including a trip to Cambridge, where we visited Harvard University. While there, I observed many sons of "first families"-some of whom were equipped with Packards.

Twenty years ago I would have felt proud to be a student at Harvard, with a Packard car, but the illuminating effect of my more mature years has led me to the conclusion that had I had the privilege of going to Harvard I might have done just as well without the aid of a Packard.

I noticed some Harvard boys who had no Packards. They were working as waiters in a restaurant where I ate, and as far as I could see they were missing nothing of value because they owned no Packards; nor did they seem to be suffering by comparison with those who could boast of the ownership of parents of the "first family" type.

All of which is no reflection upon Harvard University-one of the great universities of the world-nor upon the "first families" who send boys to Harvard. To the contrary, it is intended as a bit of encouragement to those unfortunates who, like myself, have but little and know but little, but express what little they know in terms of constructive, useful action.

The psychology of inaction is one of the chief reasons why some towns and cities are dying with the dry-rot!

Take the city of X, for example. You'll recognize the city by its description, if you are familiar with this part of the country. Sunday blue-laws have closed up all the restaurants on Sunday. Railroad trains must slow down to twelve miles an hour while passing through the city. "Keep off the grass" signs are prominently displayed in the parks. Unfavorable city ordinances of one sort or another have driven the best industries to other cities. On every hand one may see evidence of restraint. The people of the streets show signs of restraint in their faces, and in their manner, and in their walk.

The mass psychology of the city is negative.

The moment one gets off the train at the depot, this negative atmosphere becomes depressingly obvious and makes one want to take the next train out again. The place reminds one of a graveyard and the people resemble walking ghosts.

They register no signs of action!

The bank statements of the banking institutions reflect this negative, inactive state of mind. The stores reflect it in their show windows and in the faces of their salespeople. I went into one of the stores to buy a pair of hose. A young woman with bobbed hair who would have been a "flapper" if she hadn't been too lazy, threw out a box of hose on the counter. When I picked up the box, looked the hose over and registered a look of disapproval on my face, she languidly yawned:

"They're the best you can get in this dump!"

"Dump!" She must have been a mind reader, for "dump" was the word that was in my mind before she spoke. The store reminded me of a rubbish dump; the city reminded me of the same. I felt the stuff getting into my own blood. The negative psychology of the people was actually reaching out and gathering me in.

Maine is not the only state that is afflicted with a city such as the one I have described. I could name others, but I might wish to go into politics some day; therefore, I will leave it to you to do your own analyzing and comparing of cities that are alive with action and those that are slowly dying with the dry-rot of inaction.

I know of some business concerns that are in this same state of inaction, but I will omit their names. You probably know some, too.

Many years ago Frank A. Vanderlip, who is one of the best-known and most capable bankers in America, went to work for the National City Bank, of New York City.

His salary was above the average from the start, for the reason that he was capable and had a record of successful achievement that made him a valuable man.

He was assigned to a private office that was equipped with a fine mahogany desk and an easy chair. On the top of the desk was an electric push button that led to a secretary's desk outside.

The first day went by without any work coming to his desk. The second, and third, and fourth days went by without any work. No one came in or said anything to him.

By the end of the week he began to feel uneasy. (Men of action always feel uneasy when there is no work in sight.)

The following week Mr. Vanderlip went into the president's office and said, "Look here, you are paying me a big salary and giving me nothing to do and it is grating on my nerves!"

The president looked up with a lively twinkle in his keen eyes.

"Now I have been thinking," Mr. Vanderlip continued, "while sitting in there with nothing to do, of a plan for increasing the business of this bank."

The president assured him that both "thinking" and "plans" were valuable, and asked him to continue with his interview.

"I have thought of a plan," Mr. Vanderlip went on, "that will give the bank the benefit of my experience in the bond business. I propose to create a bond department for this bank and advertise it as a feature of our business."

"What! This bank advertise?" queried the president. "Why, we have never advertised since we began business. We have managed to get along without it."

"Well, this is where you are going to begin advertising," said Mr. Vanderlip, "and the first thing you are going to advertise is this new bond department that I have planned."

Mr. Vanderlip won! Men of action usually win–that is one of their distinctive features. The National City Bank also won, because that interview was the beginning of one of the most progressive and profitable advertising campaigns ever carried on by any bank, with the result that the National City Bank became one of the most powerful financial institutions of America.

There were other results, also, that are worth naming. Among them the result that Mr. Vanderlip grew with the bank, as men of action usually grow in whatever they help to build, until finally he became the president of that great banking house. In the lesson on Imagination you learned how to recombine old ideas into new plans, but no matter how practical your plans may be they will be useless if they are not expressed in action. To dream dreams and see visions of the person you would like to be or the station in life you would like to obtain are admirable provided you transform your dreams and visions into reality through intensive action.

There are men who dream, but do nothing more. There are others who take the visions of the dreamers and translate them into stone, and marble, and music, and good books, and railroads, and steamships. There are still others who both dream and transform these dreams into reality. They are the dreamer-doer types.

There is a psychological as well as an economic reason why you should form the habit of intensive action. Your body is made up of billions of tiny cells that are highly sensitive and amenable to the influence of your mind. If your mind is of the lethargic, inactive type, the cells of your body become lazy and inactive also. Just as the stagnant water of an inactive pond becomes impure and unhealthful, so will the cells of an inactive body become diseased.

Laziness is nothing but the influence of an inactive mind on the cells of the body. If you doubt this, the next time you feel lazy take a Turkish bath and have yourself well-rubbed down, thereby stimulating the cells of your body by artificial means, and see how quickly your laziness disappears. Or, a better way than this, turn your mind toward some game of which you are fond and notice how quickly the cells of your body will respond to your enthusiasm and your lazy feeling will disappear.

The cells of the body respond to the state of mind in exactly the same manner that the people of a city respond to the mass psychology that dominates the city. If a group of leaders engage in sufficient action to give a city the reputation of being a "live-wire" city, this action influences all who live there. The same principle applies to the relationship between the mind and the body. An active, dynamic mind keeps the cells of which the physical portions of the body consist, in a constant state of activity.

The artificial conditions under which most inhabitants of our cities live have led to a physical condition known as auto-intoxication, which means self-poisoning through the inactive state of the intestines. Most headaches may be cured in an hour's time by simply cleansing the lower intestines with an enema.

Eight glasses of water a day and a reasonable amount of physical action popularly known as "exercise" will take the place of the enema. Try it for a week and then you will not have to be urged to keep it up, for you will feel like a new person, unless the nature of your work is such that you get plenty of physical exercise and drink plenty of water in the regular course of your duties.

On two pages of this book enough sound advice could be recorded to keep the average person healthy and ready for action during sixteen of the twenty-four hours of the day, but the advice would be so simple that most people would not follow it.

The amount of work that I perform every day and still keep in good physical condition is a source of wonderment and mystery to those who know me intimately, yet there is no mystery to it, and the system I follow does not cost anything.

Here it is, for your use if you want it:

First: I drink a cup of hot water when I first get up in the morning, before I have breakfast.

Second: My breakfast consists of rolls made of whole wheat and bran, breakfast cereal, fruit, soft-boiled eggs once in a while, and coffee. For luncheon I eat vegetables (most any kind), whole wheat bread and a glass of buttermilk. Supper, a well-cooked steak once or twice a week, vegetables, especially lettuce, and coffee.

Third: I walk an average of ten miles a day: five miles into the country and five miles back, using this period for meditation and thought. Perhaps the thinking is as valuable, as a health builder, as the walk.

Fourth: I lie across a straight bottom chair, flat on my back, with most of my weight resting on the small of my back, with my head and arms relaxed completely, until they almost touch the floor. This gives the nervous energy of my body an opportunity to balance properly and distribute itself, and ten minutes in this position will completely relieve all signs of fatigue, no matter how tired I may be.

Fifth: I take an enema at least once every ten days, and more often if I feel the need of it, using water that is a little below blood temperature, with a tablespoonful of salt in it, chest and knee position.

Sixth: I take a hot shower bath, followed immediately by a cold shower, every day, usually in the morning when I first get up. These simple things I do for myself. Mother Nature attends to everything else necessary for my health.

I cannot lay too much stress upon the importance of keeping the intestines clean, for it is a well-known fact that the city dwellers of today are literally poisoning themselves to death by neglecting to cleanse their intestines with water. You should not wait until you are constipated to take an enema. When you get to the stage of constipation you are practically ill and immediate relief is absolutely essential, but if you will give yourself the proper attention regularly, just as you attend to keeping the outside of your body clean, you will never be bothered with the many troubles which constipation brings.

For more than fifteen years no single week ever passed without my having a headache.

Usually I administered a dose of aspirin and got temporary relief. I was suffering with auto-intoxication and did not know it, for the reason that I was not constipated.

When I found out what my trouble was I did two things, both of which I recommend to you; namely, I quit using aspirin and I cut down my daily consumption of food nearly one half.

Just a word about aspirin–a word which those who profit by its sale will not like–it affords no permanent cure of headache. All it does might be compared to a lineman that cuts the telegraph wire while the operator is using that wire in a call for aid from the fire department to save the burning building in which he is located. Aspirin cuts or "deadens" the line of nerve communication that runs from the stomach or the intestinal region, where auto-intoxication is pouring poison into the blood, to the brain, where the effect of that poison is registering its call in the form of intense pain.

Cutting the telegraph line over which a call for the fire department is being sent does not put out the fire; nor does it remove the cause to deaden, with the aid of a dose of aspirin, the nerve line over which a headache is registering a call for help.

You cannot be a person of action if you permit yourself to go without proper physical attention until auto-intoxication takes your brain and kneads it into an inoperative mass that resembles a ball of putty. Neither can you be a person of action if you eat the usual devitalized concoction called "white bread" (which has had all the real food value removed from it) and twice as much meat as your system can digest and properly dispose of.

You cannot be a person of action if you run to the pill bottle every time you have, or imagine you have, an ache or a pain, or swallow an aspirin tablet every time your intestines call on your brain for a douche bag of water and a spoonful of salt for cleansing purposes.

You cannot be a person of action if you overeat and under-exercise.

You cannot be a person of action if you read the patent medicine booklets and begin to imagine yourself ailing with the symptoms described by the clever advertisement writer who has reached your pocket book through the power of suggestion.

I have not touched a drug for more than five years, and I have not been either sick or ailing during that time, in spite of the fact that I perform more work each day than most men of my profession. I have enthusiasm, endurance and action because I eat the sort of simple food that contains the body-building elements that I require, and look after the eliminative processes as carefully as I bathe my body.

If these simple and frank admissions appeal to you as being based upon common sense, take them and put them to the test, and if they serve you as well as they are serving me, both of us will have profited by the courage I had to summon to list them as a part of this lesson.

Usually, when anyone except a physician offers suggestions on the care of the body, he is immediately catalogued as a "long-haired crank," and I will admit that the analysis is often correct. In this instance, I make no stronger recommendations than this: That you try an enema the next time you have a headache, and if any of the other suggestions appeal to you give them a trial until you are satisfied that they are either sound or unsound.

Before leaving the subject, perhaps I should explain that water which is barely lukewarm should be used for the enema for the reason that this causes the muscles of the intestines to contract, which, in turn, forces the poisonous matter out of the pores of the mucous linings. This exercises those muscles and eventually, it will so develop them that they will do their work in the natural way, without the aid of the enema. A warm water enema is very detrimental for the reason that it relaxes the muscles of the intestines, which, in time, causes them to cease functioning altogether, producing what is ordinarily referred to as the "enema habit."

With due apologies to my friends, the physicians and osteopaths and chiropractors and other health builders, I will now invite you back to that part of the subject of this lesson over which there can be no conflict of opinion as to the soundness of my counsel.

There is another enemy which you must conquer before you can become a person of action, and that is the worry habit.

Worry, and envy, and jealousy, and hatred, and doubt, and fear are all states of mind which are fatal to action.

Any of these states of mind will interfere with, and in some instances destroy altogether, the digestive process through which the food is assimilated and prepared for distribution through the body. This interference is purely physical, but the damage does not stop here, because these negative states of mind destroy the most essential factor in the achievement of success; namely, desire to achieve.

In the second lesson of this course you learned that your definite chief aim in life should be supported by a burning desire for its realization. You can have no burning desire for achievement when you are in a negative state of mind, no matter what the cause of that state of mind may be.

To keep myself in a positive frame of mind I have discovered a very effective "gloom-chaser." That may not be a very dignified way of expressing my meaning, but since the subject of this lesson is action and not dignity I will make it serve. The "gloom-chaser" to which I refer is a hearty laugh. When I feel "out of sorts" or inclined to argue with somebody over something that is not worthy of discussion, I know that I need my "gloom-chaser," and I proceed to get away where I will disturb no one and have a good hearty laugh. If I can find nothing really funny about which to laugh I simply have a forced laugh. The effect is the same in both cases.

Five minutes of this sort of mental and physical exercise–for it is both–will stimulate action that is free from negative tendencies.

Do not take my word for it–try it!

Not long ago I heard a phonograph record entitled, as I recall it, The Laughing Fool, which should be available to all whose dignity forbids them to indulge in a hearty laugh for their health's sake. This record was all that its name implies. It was made by a man and a woman; the man was trying to play a cornet and the woman was laughing at him. She laughed so effectively that she finally made the man laugh, and the suggestion was so pronounced that all who heard it usually joined in and had a good laugh, whether they felt like it or not.

"As a man thinketh in his heart, so is he."

You cannot think fear and act courageously. You cannot think hatred and act in a kindly manner toward those with whom you associate. The dominating thoughts of your mind–meaning by this, the strongest and deepest and most frequent of your thoughts–influence the physical action of your body.

Every thought put into action by your brain reaches and influences every cell in your body. When you think fear your mind telegraphs this thought down to the cells that form the muscles of your legs and tells those muscles to get into action and carry your away as rapidly as possible. A man who is afraid runs away because his legs carry him, and they carry him because the fear thought in his mind instructed them to do so, even though the instructions were given unconsciously.

In the first lesson of this course you learned how thought travels from one mind to another, through the principle of telepathy, but, what is a million times more important to you to understand, they register themselves on the cells of your own body and affect those cells in a manner that harmonizes with the nature of the thoughts.

To understand this principle is to understand the soundness of the statement: "As a man thinketh in his heart, so is he."

Action, in the sense that the term is used in this lesson, is of two forms. One is physical and the other is mental. You can be very active with your mind while your body is entirely inactive, except as to the involuntary action of the vital organs. Or you can be very active with both body and mind.

In speaking of men of action, either or both of two types may be referred to. One is the caretaker type and the other is the promoter or salesman type. Both of these types are essential in modem business, industry and finance. One is known as a "dynamo" while the other is often referred to as a "balance wheel."

Once in a great while you will find a man who is both a dynamo and a balance wheel, but such well-balanced personalities are rare. Most successful business organizations that assume great size are made up of both of these types.

The "balance wheel" who does nothing but compile facts and figures and statistics is just as much a man of action as the man who goes upon the platform and sells an idea to a thousand people by the sheer power of his active personality. To determine whether a man is a man of action or not it is necessary to analyze both his mental and his physical habits.

In the first part of this lesson I said that "the world pays you for what you do and not for what you know." That statement might easily be misconstrued. What the world really pays you for is what you do or what you can get others to do.

A man who can induce others to co-operate and do effective teamwork, or inspire others so that they become more active, is no less a man of action than the man who renders effective service in a more direct manner.

In the field of industry and business there are men who have the ability so to inspire and direct the efforts of others that all under their direction accomplish more than they could without this directing influence. It is a well-known fact that Carnegie so ably directed the efforts of those who constituted his personal staff that he made many wealthy men of those who would never have become wealthy without the directing genius of his brain. The same may be said of practically all great leaders in the field of industry and business–the gain is not all on the side of the leaders. Those under their direction often profit most by their leadership.

It is a common practice for a certain type of man to berate his employers because of their opposite stations in a financial sense. It is usually true that such men would be infinitely worse off without these employers than they are with them.

In the first lesson of this course the value of allied effort was particularly emphasized for the reason that some men have the vision to plan while others have the ability to carry plans into action although they do not possess the imagination or the vision to create the plans they execute.

It was his understanding of this principle of allied effort that enabled Andrew Carnegie to surround himself with a group of men that was made up of those who could plan and those who could execute. Carnegie had in his group of assistants some of the most efficient salesmen in the world, but if his entire staff had been made up of men who could do nothing but sell he could never have accumulated the fortune that he did. If his entire staff had been made up of salesmen only he would had action in abundance, but action, in the sense that it is used in this lesson, must be intelligently guided.

One of the best known law firms in America is made up of two lawyers, one of whom never appears in court. He prepares the firm's cases for trail and the other member of the firm goes to court and tried them. Both are men of intense action, but they express it in different ways.

There can be as much action in preparation, in most undertakings, as in execution.

In finding your own place in the world, you could analyze yourself and find out whether you are a "dynamo" or a "balance wheel," and select a definite chief aim for yourself that harmonizes with your native ability. If you are in business with others, you should analyze them as well as yourself, and endeavor to see that each person takes the part for which his temperament and native ability best fit him.

Stating it another way, people may be classified under two headings: one is the promoter and the other is the caretaker. The promoter type makes an able salesman and organizer. The caretaker type makes an excellent conserver of assets after they have been accumulated.

Place the caretaker type in charge of a set of books and he is happy, but place him on the outside selling and he is unhappy and will be a failure at his job. Place the promoter in charge of a set of books and he will be miserable. His nature demands more intense action. Action of the passive type will not satisfy his ambitions, and if he is kept at work which does not give him the action his nature demands he will be a failure. It very frequently turns out that men who embezzle funds in their charge are of the promoter type and they would not have yielded to temptation had their efforts been confined to the work for which they are best fitted.

Give a man the sort of work that harmonizes with his nature and the best there is in him will exert itself. One of the outstanding tragedies of the world is the fact that most people never engage in the work for which they are best fitted by nature.

Too often the mistake is made, in the selection of a life-work, of engaging in the work which seems to be the most profitable from a monetary viewpoint, without consideration of native ability. If money alone brought success this procedure would be all right, but success in its highest and noblest form calls for peace of mind and enjoyment and happiness which comes only to the man who has found the work that he likes best.

The main purpose of this course is to help you analyze yourself and determine what your native ability best fits you to do. You should make this analysis by carefully studying the chart that accompanies the Introductory Lesson before you select your definite chief aim.

We come, now, to the discussion of the principle through which action may be developed. To understand how to become active requires understanding of how not to procrastinate.

These suggestions will give you the necessary instructions:

First: Form the habit of doing each day the most distasteful tasks first. This procedure will be difficult at first, but after you have formed the habit you will take pride in pitching into the hardest and most undesirable part of your work first.

Second: Place this sign in front of you where you can see it in your daily work, and put a copy in your bedroom, where it will greet you as you retire and when you arise: "Do not tell them what you can do; show them!"

Third: Repeat the following words, aloud, twelve times each night just before you go to sleep: "Tomorrow I will do everything that should be done, when it should be done, and as it should be done. I will perform the most difficult tasks first because this will destroy the habit of procrastination and develop the habit of action in its place."

Fourth: Carry out these instructions with faith in their soundness and with belief that they will develop action, in body and in mind, sufficient to enable you to realize your definite chief aim.

The outstanding feature of this course is the simplicity of the style in which it is written. All great fundamental truths are simple, in final analysis, and whether one is delivering an address or writing a course of instruction, the purpose should be to convey impressions and statements of fact in the clearest and most concise manner possible.

Before closing this lesson, permit me to go back to what was said about the value of a hearty laugh as a healthful stimulant to action, and add the statement that singing produces the same effect, and in some instances is far preferable to laughing.

Billy Sunday is one of the most dynamic and active preachers in the world, yet it has been said that his sermons would lose much of their effectiveness if it were not for the psychological effect of his song services.

It is a well-known fact that the German army was a winning army at the beginning, and long after the beginning of the world war; and it has been said that much of this was due to the fact that the German army was a singing army. Then came the khaki-clad doughboys from America, and they, too, were singers. Back of their singing was an enduring faith in the cause for which they were fighting. Soon the Germans began to quit singing, and as they did so the tide of war began to turn against them.

During the war I helped devise ways and means of speeding production in industrial plants that were engaged in manufacturing war supplies. By actual test, in a plant employing 3,000 men and women, the production was increased forty-five per cent in less than thirty days after we had organized the workers into singing groups and installed orchestras and bands that played at ten-minute intervals such stirring songs as "Over There," and "Dixie;" and "There'll Be a Hot Time in the Old Town Tonight." The workers caught the rhythm of the music and speeded up their work accordingly. Properly selected music would stimulate any class of workers to greater action, a fact which does not seem to be understood by all who direct the efforts of large numbers of people.

In all my travels I have found but one business firm whose managers made use of music as a stimulant for their workers. This was the Filene Department Store, in Boston, Mass. During the summer months this store provides an orchestra that plays the latest dance music for half an hour before opening time, in the morning. The salespeople use the aisles of the store for dancing and by the time the doors are thrown open they are in an active state of mind and body that carries them through the entire day.

Incidentally, I have never seen more courteous or efficient salespeople than those employed by the Filene store. One of the department managers told me that every person in his department performed more service and with less real effort, as a result of the morning music program.

A singing army is a winning army, whether on the field of battle, in warfare, or behind the counters in a department store. There is a book entitled Singing Through Life With God by George Wharton James, which I recommend to all who are interested in the psychology of song.

If I were the manager of an industrial plant in which the work was heavy and monotonous, I would install some sort of musical program that would supply every worker with music. On lower Broadway, in New York City, an ingenious Greek has discovered how to entertain his customers and at the same time speed up the work of his helpers by the use of a phonograph. Every boy in the place keeps time with the music as he draws the cloth across the shoes, and seems to get considerable fun out of his work in doing so. To speed up the work the proprietor has but to speed up the phonograph.

Any form of group effort, where two or more people form a co-operative alliance for the purpose of accomplishing a definite purpose, becomes more powerful than mere individual effort.

A football team may win consistently and continuously, by well co-ordinated teamwork, even though the members of the team may be unfriendly and out of harmony in many ways outside of their actual work on the ball ground.

A group of men composing a board of directors may disagree with one another; they may be unfriendly, and in no way in sympathy with one another, and still carry on a business which appears to be very successful.

A man and his wife may live together, accumulate a fair-sized or even a great fortune, rear and educate a family, without the bond of harmony which is essential for the development of a Master Mind.

But all of these alliances might be made more powerful and effective if based upon a foundation of perfect harmony, thus permitting the development of a supplemental power known as the Master Mind.

Plain co-operative effort produces power; there can be no doubt about this; but cooperative effort that is based upon complete harmony of purpose develops superpower. Let every member of any co-operative group set his heart upon the achievement of the same definite end, in a spirit of perfect harmony, and the way has been paved for the development of a Master Mind, providing all members of the group willingly subordinate their own personal interests for the attainment of the objective for which the group is aiming.

The United States of America has become one of the most powerful nations on earth, largely because of the highly organized co-operative effort between the states. It will be helpful to remember that these United States were born as the result of one of the most powerful Master Minds ever created. The members of this Master Mind were the signers of the Declaration of Independence.

The men who signed that document either consciously or unconsciously put into operation the power known as the "Master Mind," and that power was sufficient to enable them to defeat all the soldiers who were sent into the field against them. The men who fought to make the Declaration of Independence endure did not fight for money, alone; they fought for a principle-the principle of freedom, which is the highest known motivating force.

A great leader, whether in business, finance, industry or statesmanship, is one who understands how to create a motivating objective which will be accepted with enthusiasm by every member of his group of followers. In politics a "live issue" is everything!

By "live issue" is meant some popular objective toward the attainment of which the majority of the voters can be rallied. These "issues" generally are broadcast in the form of snappy slogans, such as "Keep Cool with Coolidge," which suggested to the minds of the voters that to keep Coolidge was the equivalent of keeping prosperity. It worked! During Lincoln's election campaign the cry was, "Stand back of Lincoln and preserve the Union." It worked. Woodrow Wilson's campaign managers, during his second campaign, coined the slogan, "He kept us out of war," and it worked.

The degree of power created by the co-operative effort of any group of people is measured, always, by the nature of the motive which the group is laboring to attain. This may be profitably home in mind by all who organize group effort for any purpose whatsoever. Find a motive around which men may be induced to rally in a highly emotionalized, enthusiastic spirit of perfect harmony and you have found the starting point for the creation of a Master Mind.

It is a well-known fact that men will work harder for the attainment of an ideal than they will for mere money. In searching for a "motive" as the basis for developing cooperative group effort it will be profitable to bear this fact in mind.

At the time of the writing of this lesson there is much adverse agitation and general criticism directed against the railroads of the country. Who is back of this agitation this author does not know, but he does know that the very fact that such agitation exists could and should be made the motivating force around which the railroad officials might rally the hundreds of thousands of railroad employees who earn their living by railroading, thereby creating a power that would effectively eliminate this adverse criticism.

The railroads are the very backbone of the country. Tie up all railroad service and the people of the larger cities would starve before food could reach them. In this fact may be found a motive around which a large majority of the public could be caused to rally in support of any plan for self-protection which the railroad officials might wish to carry out.

The power represented by all of the railroad employees and a majority of the public who patronize the railroads is sufficient to protect the railroads against all manner of adverse legislation and other attempts to depreciate their properties, but the power is only potential until it is organized and placed definitely back of a specific motive.

Man is a queer animal. Give him a sufficiently vitalized motive and the man of but average ability, under ordinary circumstances, will suddenly develop superpower. What man can and will accomplish to please the woman of his choice (providing the woman knows how to stimulate him to action) has ever been a source of wonderment to students of the human mind.

There are three major motivating forces to which man responds in practically all of his efforts. These are:

1. The motive of self-preservation
2. The motive of sexual contact

3. The motive of financial and social power

Stated more briefly, the main motives which impel men to action are money, sex and self-preservation. Leaders who are seeking a motivating force out of which to secure action from a following may find it under one or more of these three classifications.

As you have observed, this lesson is very closely related to the Introductory Lesson and Lesson Two which cover the Law of the Master Mind. It is possible for groups to function co-operatively, without thereby creating a Master Mind, as, for example, where people co-operate merely out of necessity, without the spirit of harmony as the basis of their efforts. This sort of co-operation may produce considerable power, but nothing to compare with that which is possible when every person in an alliance subordinates his or her own individual interests and co-ordinates his or her efforts with those of all other members of the alliance, in perfect harmony.

The extent to which people may be induced to co-operate, in harmony, depends upon the motivating force which impels them to action. Perfect harmony such as is essential for creating a Master Mind can be obtained only when the motivating force of a group is sufficient to cause each member of the group completely to forget his or her own personal interests and work for the good of the group, or for the sake of attaining some idealistic, charitable or philanthropic objective.

The three major motivating forces of mankind have been here stated for the guidance of the Leader who wishes to create plans for securing cooperation from followers who will throw themselves into the carrying out of his plans in a spirit of unselfishness and perfect harmony.

Men will not rally to the support of a leader in such a spirit of harmony unless the motive that impels them to do so is one that will induce them to lay aside all thoughts of themselves.

We do well that which we love to do, and fortunate is the Leader who has the good judgment to bear this fact in mind and so lay his plans that all his followers are assigned parts that harmonize with this law.

The leader who gets all there is to be had from his followers does so because he has set up in the mind of each a sufficiently strong motive to get each to subordinate his own interests and work in a perfect spirit of harmony with all other members of the group. Regardless of who you are, or what your definite chief aim may be, if you plan to attain the object of your chief aim through the co-operative efforts of others, you must set up in the minds of those whose co-operation you seek a motive strong enough to insure their full, undivided, unselfish co-operation, for you will then be placing back of your plans the power of the Law of the Master Mind.

You are now ready to take up Lesson Fourteen, which will teach you how to make working capital out of all mistakes, errors and failures which you have experienced, and also how to profit by the mistakes and failures of others.

The president of one of the great railway systems of the United States said, after reading the next lesson, that "this lesson carries a suggestion which, if heeded and understood, will enable any person to become a master in his chosen life-work."

For reasons which will be plain after you have read the next lesson, it is the author's favorite lesson of this course.

YOUR STANDING ARMY–An After-the-Lesson Visit With the Author

Power comes from organized effort. There are fifteen forces which enter into all organized effort. Master these fifteen forces and you may have whatever you want in life. Others will be helpless to defeat your plans. Make these fifteen forces your own and you will be an accurate thinker.

If you are a normal person you long for material success.

Success and POWER are always found together. You cannot be sure of success unless you have power. You cannot have power unless you develop it through fifteen essential qualities.

Each of these fifteen qualities may be likened to the commanding officer of a regiment of soldiers. Develop these qualities in your own mind and you will have POWER.

The most important of the fifteen commanding officers in this army is DEFINITE PURPOSE.

Without the aid of a definite purpose the remainder of the army would be useless to you. Find out, as early in life as possible, what your major purpose in life shall be. Until you do this you are nothing but a drifter, subject to control by every stray wind of circumstance that blows in your direction.

Millions of people go through life without knowing what it is they want.

All have a purpose, but only two out of every hundred have a DEFINITE purpose.

Before you decide whether your purpose is DEFINITE or not, look up the meaning of the word in the dictionary.

NOTHING IS IMPOSSIBLE TO THE PERSON WHO KNOWS WHAT IT IS HE WANTS AND MAKES UP HIS MIND TO ACQUIRE IT!

Columbus had a DEFINITE PURPOSE and it became a reality. Lincoln's major DEFINITE PURPOSE was to free the black slaves of the South and he turned that purpose into reality. Roosevelt's major purpose, during his first term of office, was to build the Panama Canal. He lived to see that purpose realized. Henry Ford's DEFINITE PURPOSE was to build the best popular-priced automobile on earth. That purpose, backed persistently, has made him the most powerful man on earth. Burbank's DEFINITE PURPOSE was to improve plant life. Already that purpose has made possible the raising of enough food on ten square miles of land to feed the entire world.

Twenty years ago Edwin C. Barnes formed a DEFINITE PURPOSE in his mind. That purpose was to become the business partner of Thomas A. Edison. At the time his purpose was chosen Mr. Barnes had no qualification entitling him to a partnership with the world's greatest inventor. Despite this handicap he became the partner of the great Edison. Five years ago he retired from active business, with more money than he needs or can use, wealth that he accumulated in partnership with Edison. NOTHING IS IMPOSSIBLE TO THE MAN WITH A DEFINITE PURPOSE! Opportunity, capital, co-operation from other men and all other essentials for success gravitate to the man who knows what he wants!

Vitalize your mind with a DEFINITE PURPOSE and immediately your mind becomes a magnet which attracts everything that harmonizes with that purpose.

James J. Hill, the great railroad builder, was a poorly paid telegraph operator. Moreover, he had reached the age of forty and was still ticking away at the telegraph key without any outward appearances of success.

Then something of importance happened! Of importance to Hill and to the people of the United States. He formed the DEFINITE PURPOSE of building a railroad across the great waste desert of the West. Without reputation, without capital, without encouragement from others, James J. Hill got the capital and built the greatest of all the railroad systems of the United States.

Woolworth was a poorly paid clerk in a general store. In his mind's eye he saw a chain of novelty stores specializing on five and ten cent sales. That chain of stores became his DEFINITE PURPOSE. He made that purpose come true, and with it more millions than he could use.

Cyrus H. K. Curtis selected, as his DEFINITE PURPOSE, the publishing of the world's greatest magazine. Starting with nothing but the name "Saturday Evening Post," and opposed by friends and advisers who said "It couldn't be done," he transformed that purpose into reality.

Martin W. Littleton is the most highly paid lawyer in the world. It is said that he will accept no retainer under $50,000.00. When he was twelve years old he had never been inside of a school room. He went to hear a lawyer defend a murderer. That speech so impressed him that he grabbed hold of his father's hand and said, "Some day I am going to be the best lawyer in the United States and make speeches like that man."

"Fine chance for an ignorant mountain youth to become a great lawyer," someone might say, but remember that NOTHING IS IMPOSSIBLE TO THE MAN WHO KNOWS WHAT HE WANTS AND MAKES UP HIS MIND TO GET IT.

Remember, that no one of these soldiers alone is powerful enough to insure success. Remove a single one of them and the entire army would be weakened.

The powerful man is the man who has developed, in his own mind, the entire fifteen qualities represented by the fifteen commanding officers shown in the picture. Before you can have power you must have a DEFINITE PURPOSE; you must have SELF-CONFIDENCE with which to back up that purpose; you must have INITIATIVE and LEADERSHIP with which to exercise your self-confidence; you must have IMAGINATION in creating your definite purpose and in building the plans with which to transform that purpose into reality and put your plans into action. You must mix ENTHUSIASM with your action or it will be insipid and without "kick." You must exercise SELF-CONTROL. You must form the habit of DOING MORE THAN PAID FOR. You must cultivate a PLEASING PERSONALITY. You must acquire the HABIT OF SAVING. You must become an ACCURATE THINKER, remembering, as you develop this quality, that accurate thought is based upon FACTS and not upon hearsay evidence or mere information. You must form the habit of CONCENTRATION by giving your undivided attention to but one task at a time. You must acquire the habit of CO-OPERATION and practice it in all your plans. You must profit by FAILURE, your own and that of others. You must cultivate the habit of TOLERANCE. Last, but by no means the least important, you must make the GOLDEN RULE the foundation of all you do that affects other people.

Keep this picture where you can see it each day and, one by one, call these fifteen soldiers out of the line and study them. Make sure that the counterpart of each is developed in your own mind.

All Efficient Armies Are Well-disciplined!

The army which you are building in your own mind must, also, be disciplined. It must obey your command at every step.

When you call out of the line the thirteenth soldier, "FAILURE," remember that nothing will go as far toward developing discipline as will failure and temporary defeat. While you are comparing yourself with this soldier determine whether or not you have been profiting by your own failures and temporary defeat.

FAILURE comes to all at one time or another. Make sure, when it comes your way, that you will learn something of value from its visit. Make sure, also, that it would not visit you if there was not room for it in your make-up.

To make progress in this world you must rely solely upon the forces within your own mind for your start. After this start has been made you may turn to others for aid, but the first step must be taken without outside aid.

After you have made this "start," it will surprise you to observe how many willing people you will encounter who will volunteer to assist you.

Success is made up of many facts and factors, chiefly of the fifteen qualities represented by these fifteen soldiers. To enjoy a well-balanced and rounded out success one must appropriate as much or as little of each of these fifteen qualities as may be missing in one's own inherited ability.

When you came into this world you were endowed with certain inborn traits, the result of millions of years of evolutionary changes, through thousands of generations of ancestors.

Added to these inborn traits you acquired many other qualities, according to the nature of your environment and the teaching you received during your early childhood. You are the sum total of that which was born in you and that which you have picked up from your experiences, what you have thought and what you have been taught, since birth.

Through the law of chance one in a million people will receive, through inborn heredity and from knowledge acquired after birth, all of the fifteen qualities named in the picture above.

All who are not fortunate enough to have thus acquired the essentials for SUCCESS must develop them within themselves.

The first step in this "development" process is to realize what qualities are missing in your naturally acquired equipment. The second step is the strongly planted DESIRE to develop yourself where you are now deficient.

Prayer sometimes works, while at other times it does not work.

It always works when backed with unqualified FAITH. This is a truth which no one will deny, yet, it is a truth which no one can explain. All we know is that prayer works when we BELIEVE it will work. Prayer without FAITH is nothing but an empty collection of words.

A DEFINITE PURPOSE may be transformed into reality only when one BELIEVES it can be done. Perhaps the selfsame law that turns the prayer based upon FAITH into reality transforms, also, a DEFINITE PURPOSE that is founded upon belief into reality.

It can do no harm if you make your DEFINITE PURPOSE in life the object of your daily prayer. And, as you pray remember that prayer based upon FAITH always works. Develop in your own mind all of the fifteen qualities, from a DEFINITE PURPOSE to the GOLDEN RULE, and you will find the application of FAITH is not difficult.

Take inventory of yourself. Find out how many of the fifteen qualities you now possess. Add to this inventory the missing qualities until you have, in your mind, the entire fifteen. You will then be ready to measure your success in whatever terms you DESIRE.

The qualities represented by the fifteen soldiers shown in this picture are the brick and the mortar and the building material with which you must build your Temple of Success. Master these fifteen qualities and you may play a perfect symphony of success in any undertaking, just as one who has mastered the fundamentals of music may play any piece at sight.

Make these fifteen qualities your own and you will be an EDUCATED person, because you will have the power to get whatever you want in life without violating the rights of others.

> "All worlds are man's, to conquer and to rule
> This is the glory of his life.
> But this its iron law: first must he school

Himself. Here 'gins and ends all strife."

Lesson Fourteen: FAILURE

Under ordinary circumstances the term "failure" is a negative term. In this lesson, the word will be given a new meaning, because the word has been a very much misused one; and, for that reason, it has brought unnecessary grief and hardship to millions of people.

In the outset, let us distinguish between "failure" and "temporary defeat." Let us see if that which is so often looked upon as "failure" is not, in reality, but "temporary defeat." Moreover, let us see if this temporary defeat is not usually a blessing in disguise, for the reason that it brings us up with a jerk and redirects our energies along different and more desirable lines.

In Lesson Nine of this course, we learned that strength grows out of resistance; and we shall learn, in this lesson, that sound character is usually the handiwork of reverses, and setbacks, and temporary defeat, which the uninformed part of the world calls "failure."

Neither temporary defeat nor adversity amounts to failure in the mind of the person who looks upon it as a teacher that will teach some needed lesson. As a matter of fact, there is a great and lasting lesson in every reverse, and in every defeat; and, usually, it is a lesson that could he learned in no other way than through defeat.

Defeat often talks to us in a "dumb language" that we do not understand. If this were not true, we would not make the same mistakes over and over again without profiting by the lessons that they might teach us. If it were not true, we would observe more closely the mistakes which other people make and profit by them.

The main object of this lesson is to help the student understand and profit by this "dumb language" in which defeat talks to us.

Perhaps I can best help you to interpret the meaning of defeat by taking you back over some of my own experiences covering a period of approximately thirty years. Within this period, I have come to the turning-point, which the uninformed call "failure," seven different times. At each of these seven turning-points I thought I had made a dismal failure; hut now I know that what looked to be a failure was nothing more than a kindly, unseen hand, that halted me in my chosen course and with great wisdom forced me to redirect my efforts along more advantageous pathways.

I arrived at this decision, however, only after I had taken a retrospective view of my experiences and had analyzed them in the light of many years of sober and meditative thought.

FIRST TURNING-POINT

After finishing a course in a business college, I secured a position as stenographer and bookkeeper which I held for the ensuing five years. As a result of having practiced the habit of performing more work and better work than that for which I was paid, as described in Lesson Nine of this course, I advanced rapidly until I was assuming responsibilities and receiving a salary far out of proportion to my age. I saved my money, and my bank account amounted to several thousand dollars. My reputation spread rapidly and I found competitive bidders for my services.

To meet these offers from competitors my employer advanced me to the position of General Manager of the mines where I was employed. I was quickly getting on top of the world, and I knew it!

Ah! But that was the sad part of my fate–I knew it!

Then the kindly hand of Fate reached out and gave me a gentle nudge. My employer lost his fortune and I lost my position. This was my first real defeat; and, even though it came about as a result of causes beyond my control, I should have learned a lesson from it; which, of course, I did, but not until many years later.

SECOND TURNING-POINT

My next position was that of Sales Manager for a large lumber manufacturing concern in the South. I knew nothing about lumber, and but little about sales management; but I had learned that it was beneficial to render more service than that for which I was paid, and I had also learned that it paid to take the initiative and find out what ought to be done without someone telling me to do it. A good sized bank account, plus a record of steady advancement in my previous position, gave me all the self-confidence I needed, with some to spare, perhaps.

My advancement was rapid, my salary having been increased twice during the first year. I did so well in the management of sales that my employer took me into partnership with him. We began to make money and I began to see myself on top of the world again!

To stand "on top of the world" gives one a wonderful sensation; but it is a very dangerous place to stand, unless one stands very firmly, because the fall is so long and hard if one should stumble.

I was succeeding by leaps and bounds!

Up to that time it had never occurred to me that success could be measured in terms other than money and authority. Perhaps this was due to the fact that I had more money than I needed and more authority than I could manage safely at that age.

Not only was I "succeeding," from my viewpoint of success, but I knew I was engaged in the one and only business suited to my temperament. Nothing could have induced me to change into another line of endeavor. That is–nothing except that which happened, which forced me to change.

The unseen hand of Fate allowed me to strut around under the influence of my own vanity until I had commenced to feel my importance. In the light of my more sober years, I now wonder if the Unseen Hand does not purposely permit us foolish human beings to parade ourselves before our own minors of vanity until we come to see how vulgarly we are acting and become ashamed of ourselves. At any rate, I seemed to have a clear track ahead of me; there was plenty of coal in the bunker; there was water in the tank; my hand was on the throttle–I opened it wide and sped along at a rapid pace. Alas! Fate awaited me just around the comer, with a stuffed club that was not stuffed with cotton. Of course I did not see the impending crash until it came. Mine was a sad story, but not unlike that which many another might tell if he would be frank with himself.

Like a stroke of lightning out of a clear sky, the 1907 panic swept down upon me; and, overnight, it rendered me an enduring service by destroying my business and relieving me of every dollar that I possessed.

This was my first serious defeat! I mistook it, then, for failure; but it was not, and before I complete this lesson I will tell you why it was not.

THIRD TURNING-POINT

It required the 1907 panic, and the defeat that it brought me, to divert and redirect my efforts from the lumber business to the study of law. Nothing on earth, except defeat, could have brought about this result; thus, the third turning-point of my life was ushered in on the wings of that which most people would call "failure," which reminds me to state again that every defeat teaches a needed lesson to those who are ready and willing to be taught.

When I entered law school, it was with the firm belief that I would emerge doubly prepared to catch up with the end of the rainbow and claim my pot of gold; for I still had no other conception of success except that of money and power.

I attended law school at night and worked as an automobile salesman during the day. My sales experience in the lumber business was turned to good advantage. I prospered rapidly, doing so well (still featuring the habit of performing more service and better service than that for which I was paid) that the opportunity came to enter the automobile manufacturing business. I saw the need for trained automobile mechanics, therefore I opened an educational department in the manufacturing plant and began to train ordinary machinists in automobile assembling and repair work. The school prospered, paying me over a thousand dollars a month in net profits.

Again I was beginning to near the end of the rainbow. Again I knew I had at last found my niche in the world's work; that nothing could swerve me from my course or divert my attention from the automobile business.

My banker knew that I was prospering, therefore he loaned me money with which to expand. A peculiar trait of bankers–a trait which may be more or less developed in the remainder of us also–is that they will loan us money without any hesitation when we are prosperous!

My banker loaned me money until I was hopelessly in his debt, then he took over my business as calmly as if it had belonged to him, which it did!

From the station of a man of affairs who enjoyed an income of more than a thousand dollars a month, I was suddenly reduced to poverty.

Now, twenty years later, I thank the hand of Fate for this forced change; but at that time I looked upon the change as nothing but failure.

The rainbow's end had disappeared, and with it the proverbial pot of gold which is supposed to be found at its end. It was many years afterwards that I learned the truth that this temporary defeat was probably the greatest single blessing that ever came my way, because it forced me out of a business that in no way helped me to develop knowledge of self or of others, and directed my efforts into a channel which brought me a rich experience of which I was in need.

For the first time in life I began to ask myself if it were not possible for one to find something of value other than money and power at the rainbow's end. This temporary questioning attitude did not amount to open rebellion, mind you, nor did I follow it far enough to get the answer. It merely came as a fleeting thought, as do so many other thoughts to which we pay no attention, and passed out of my mind. Had I known as much then as I now know about the Law of Compensation, and had I been able to interpret experiences as I can now interpret them, I would have recognized that event as a gentle nudge from the hand of Fate.

After putting up the hardest fight of my life, up to that time, I accepted my temporary defeat as failure and thus was ushered in my next and fourth turning-point, which gave me an opportunity to put into use the knowledge of law that I had acquired.

FOURTH TURNING-POINT

Because I was my wife's husband and her people had influence, I secured the appointment as assistant to the chief counsel for one of the largest coal companies in the world. My salary was greatly out of proportion to those usually paid to beginners, and still further out of proportion to what I was worth; but pull was pull, and I was there just the same. It happened that what I lacked in legal skill I more than made up through the application of the principle of performing more service than that for which I was paid, and by taking the initiative and doing that which should have been done without being told to do it.

I was holding my position without difficulty. I practically had a soft berth for life had I cared to keep it.

Without consultation with my friends, and without warning, I resigned!

This was the first turning-point that was of my own selection. It was not forced upon me. I saw the old man Fate coming and beat him to the door. When pressed for a reason for resigning, I gave what seemed to me to be a very sound one, but I had trouble convincing the family circle that I had acted wisely.

I quit that position because the work was too easy and I was performing it with too little effort. I saw myself drifting into the habit of inertia. I felt myself becoming accustomed to taking life easily and I knew that the next step would be retrogression. I had so many friends at court that there was no particular impelling urge that made it necessary for me to keep moving. I was among friends and relatives, and I had a position that I could keep as long as I wished it, without exerting myself. I received an income that provided me with all the necessities and some of the luxuries, including a motor car and enough gasoline to keep it running.

What more did I need?

"Nothing!" I was beginning to say to myself.

This was the attitude toward which I felt myself slipping. It was an attitude which, for some reason that is still unknown to me, startled me so sharply that I made what many believed to be an irrational move by resigning. However ignorant I might have been in other matters at the time, I have felt thankful ever since for having had sense enough to realize that strength and growth come only through continuous effort and struggle, that disuse brings atrophy and decay.

This move proved to be the next most important turning-point of my life, although it was followed by ten years of effort which brought almost every conceivable grief that the human heart can experience. I quit my job in the legal field, where I was getting along well, living among friends and relatives, where I had what they believed to be an unusually bright and promising future ahead of me. I am frank to admit that it has been an ever-increasing source of wonderment to me as to why and how I gathered the courage to make the move that I did. As far as I am able to interpret the event, I arrived at my decision to resign more because of a "hunch," or a sort of "prompting" which I then did not understand, than by logical reasoning.

I selected Chicago as my new field of endeavor. I did this because I believed Chicago to be a place where one might find out if one had those sterner qualities which are so essential for survival in a world of keen competition. I made up my mind that if I could gain recognition, in any honorable sort of work, in Chicago, it would prove that I had the sort of material in my make-up that might be developed into real ability. That was a queer process of reasoning; at least it was an unusual process for me to indulge in at that time, which reminds me to state that we human beings often take unto ourselves credit for intelligence to which we are not entitled. I fear we too often assume credit for wisdom and for results that accrue from causes over which we have absolutely no control.

While I do not mean to convey the impression that I believe all of our acts to be controlled by causes beyond our power to direct, yet I strongly urge you to study and correctly interpret those causes which mark the most vital turning-points of your life; the points at which your efforts are diverted–from the old into new channels–in spite of all that you can do. At least refrain from accepting any defeat as failure until you shall have had time to analyze the final result.

My first position in Chicago was that of advertising manager of a large correspondence school. I knew but little about advertising, but my previous experience as a salesman, plus the advantage gained by rendering more service than that for which I was paid, enabled me to make an unusual showing.

The first year I earned $5,200.00.

I was "coming back" by leaps and bounds. Gradually the rainbow's end began to circle around me, and I saw, once more, the shining pot of gold almost within my reach.

History is full of evidence that a feast usually precedes a famine. I was enjoying a feast but did not anticipate the famine that was to follow. I was getting along so well that I thoroughly approved of myself.

Self-approval is a dangerous state of mind.

This is a great truth which many people do not learn until the softening hand of Time has rested upon their shoulders for the better part of a life-time. Some never do learn it, and those who do are those who finally begin to understand the "dumb language" of defeat.

I am convinced that one has but few, if any, more dangerous enemies to combat than that of self-approval. Personally I fear it more than defeat.

This brings me to my fifth turning-point, which was also of my own choice.

FIFTH TURNING-POINT

I had made such a good record as advertising manager of the correspondence school that the president of the school induced me to resign my position and go into the candy manufacturing business with him. We organized the Betsy Ross Candy Company and I became its first president, thus beginning the next most important turning-point of my life.

The business grew rapidly until we had a chain of stores in eighteen different cities. Again I saw my rainbow's end almost within my reach. I knew that I had at last found the business in which I wished to remain for life. The candy business was profitable and, because I looked upon money as being the only evidence of success, I naturally believed I was about to corner success.

Everything went smoothly until my business associate and a third man, whom we had taken into the business, took a notion to gain control of my interest in the business without paying for it.

Their plan was successful, in a way, but I balked more stiffly than they had anticipated I would; therefore, for the purpose of "gentle persuasion," they had me arrested on a false charge and then offered to withdraw the charge on condition that I turn over to them my interest in the business.

I had commenced to learn, for the first time, that there was much cruelty, and injustice, and dishonesty in the hearts of men.

When the time for a preliminary hearing came, the complaining witnesses were nowhere to be found. But I had them brought and forced them to go on the witness stand and tell their stories, which resulted in my vindication, and a damage suit against the perpetrators of the injustice.

This incident brought about an irreparable breach between my business associates and myself, which finally cost me my interest in the business, but that was but slight when compared to that which it cost my associates; for they are still paying, and no doubt will continue to pay as long as they live.

My damage suit was brought under what is known as a "tort" action, through which damages were claimed for malicious damage to character. In Illinois, where the action was brought, judgment under a tort action gives the one in favor of whom the judgment is rendered the right to have the person against whom it is obtained placed in jail until the amount of the judgment has been paid.

In due time I got a heavy judgment against my former business associates. I could then have had both of them placed behind the bars.

For the first time in my life I was brought face to face with the opportunity to strike back at my enemies in a manner that would hurt. I had in my possession a weapon with "teeth" in it–a weapon placed there by the enemies, themselves.

The feeling that swept over me was a queer one!

Would I have my enemies jailed, or would I take advantage of this opportunity to extend them mercy, thereby proving myself to be made of a different type of material?

Then and there was laid, in my heart, the foundation upon which the Sixteenth Lesson of this course is built, for I made up my mind to permit my enemies to go free–as free as they could be made by my having extended them mercy and forgiveness.

But long before my decision had been reached the hand of Fate had commenced to deal roughly with these misguided fellow men who had tried, in vain, to destroy me. Time, the master worker, to which we must all submit sooner or later, had already been at work on my former business associates, and it had dealt with them less mercifully than I had done. One of them was later sentenced to a long term in the penitentiary, for another crime that he had committed against some other person, and the other one had, meanwhile, been reduced to pauperism.

We can circumvent the laws which men place upon statute books, but the Law of Compensation never!

The judgment which I obtained against these men stands on the records of the Superior Court, of Chicago, as silent evidence of vindication of my character; but it serves me in a more important way than that–it serves as a reminder that I could forgive enemies who had tried to destroy me, and for this reason, instead of destroying my character, I suspect that the incident served to strengthen it.

Being arrested seemed, at the time, a terrible disgrace, even though the charge was false. I did not relish the experience, and I would not wish to go through a similar experience again, but I am bound to admit that it was worth all the grief it cost me, because it gave me the opportunity to find out that revenge was not a part of my makeup.

Here I would direct your attention to a close analysis of the events described in this lesson, for if you observe carefully you can see how this entire course of study has been evolved out of these experiences. Each temporary defeat left its mark upon my heart and provided some part of the material of which this course has been built. We would cease to fear or to run away from trying experiences if we observed, from the biographies of men of destiny, that nearly every one of them was sorely tried and run through the mill of merciless experience before he "arrived." This leads me to wonder if the band of Fate does not test "the metal of which we are made" in various and sundry ways before placing great responsibilities upon our shoulders. Before approaching the next turning-point of my life, may I now call your attention to the significant fact that each turning-point carried me nearer and nearer my rainbow's end, and brought me some useful knowledge which became, later, a permanent part of my philosophy of life.

SIXTH TURNING-POINT

We come, now, to the turning-point which probably brought me nearer the rainbow's end than any of the others had, because it placed me in a position where I found it necessary to bring into use all the knowledge I had acquired up to that time, concerning practically every subject with which I was acquainted, and gave me opportunity for self-expression and development such as rarely comes to a man so early in life. This turning-point came shortly after my dreams of success in the candy business had been shattered, when I turned my efforts to teaching Advertising and Salesmanship as a department of one of the colleges of the Middle West.

Some wise philosopher has said that we never learn very much about a given subject until we commence teaching it to others. My first experience as a teacher proved this to be true. My school prospered from the very beginning. I had a resident class and also a correspondence school through which I was teaching students in nearly every English-speaking country. Despite the ravages of war, the school was growing rapidly and I again saw the end of the rainbow within sight.

Then came the second military draft which practically destroyed my school, as it caught most of those who were enrolled as students. At one stroke I charged off more than $75,000.00 in tuition fees and at the same time contributed my own service to my country.

Once more I was penniless!

Unfortunate is the person who has never had the thrill of being penniless at one time or another; for, as Edward Bok has truthfully stated, poverty is the richest experience that can come to a man; an experience which, however, he advises one to get away from as quickly as possible.

Again I was forced to redirect my efforts, but, before I proceed to describe the next and last important turning-point, I wish to call your attention to the fact that no single event described up to this point is, within itself, of any practical significance. The six turning-points that I have briefly described meant nothing to me, taken singly, and they will mean nothing to you if analyzed singly. But take these events collectively and they form a very significant foundation for the next turning-point, and constitute reliable evidence that we human beings are constantly undergoing evolutionary changes as a result of the experiences of life with which we meet, even though no single experience may seem to convey a definite, usable lesson.

I feel impelled to dwell at length on the point which I am here trying to make clear, because I have now reached the point in my career at which men go down in permanent defeat or rise, with renewed energies, to heights of attainment of stupendous proportions, according to the manner in which they interpret their past experiences and use those experiences as the basis of working plans. If my story stopped here it would be of no value to you, but there is another and a more significant chapter yet to be written, covering the seventh and most important of all the turning-points of my life. It must have been obvious to you, all through my description of the six turning-points already outlined, that I had not really found my place in the world. It must have been obvious to you that most, if not all, of my temporary defeats were due mainly to the fact that I had not yet discovered the work into which I could throw my heart and soul. Finding the work for which one is best fitted and which one likes best is very much like finding the one person whom one loves best; there is no rule by which to make the search, but when the right niche is contacted one immediately recognizes it.

SEVENTH TURNING-POINT

Before I finish I will describe the collective lessons that I learned from each of the seven turning-points of my life, but first let me describe the seventh and last of these turning-points. To do so, I must go back to that eventful day–November Eleven, Nineteen Hundred and Eighteen!

That was Armistice Day, as everyone knows. The war had left me without a penny, as I have already stated, but I was happy to know that the slaughter had ceased and reason was about to reclaim civilization once more.

As I stood in front of my office window and looked out at the howling mob that was celebrating the end of the war, my mind went back into my yesterdays, especially to that eventful day when that kind old gentleman laid his band on my shoulder and told me that if I would acquire an education I could make my mark in the world. I had been acquiring that education without knowing it. Over a period of more than twenty years I had been going to school in the University of Hard Knocks, as you must have observed from my description of the various turning-points of my life. As I stood in front of that window my entire past, with its bitter and its sweet, its ups and its downs, passed before me in review.

The time had come for another turning-point!

I sat down to my typewriter and, to my astonishment, my hands began to play a regular tune upon the keyboard. I had never written so rapidly or so easily before. I did not plan or think about that which I was writing–I just wrote that which came into my mind!

Unconsciously, I was laying the foundation for the most important turning-point of my life; for, when I had finished, I had prepared a document through which I financed a national magazine that gave me contact with people throughout the English-speaking world. So greatly did that document influence my own career, and the lives of tens of thousands of other people, that I believe it will be of interest to the students of this course; therefore, I am reproducing it, just as it appeared in Hill's Golden Rule magazine, where it was first published, as follows:

"A PERSONAL VISIT WITH YOUR EDITOR"

I am writing on Monday, November eleventh, 1918. Today will go down in history as the greatest holiday.

On the street, just outside of my office window,the surging crowds of people are celebrating the downfall of an influence that has menaced civilization for the past four years.

The war is over!

Soon our boys will be coming back home from the battlefields of France.

The lord and master of Brute Force is nothing but a shadowy ghost of the past!

Let each of us take unto himself the great lesson that this world war has taught; namely, only that which is based upon justice and mercy toward all–the weak and the strong, the rich and the poor, alike can survive. All else must pass on.

Out of this war will come a new idealism–an idealism that will be based upon the Golden Rule philosophy; an idealism that will guide us, not to see how much we can "do our fellow man for"; but how much we can do for him that will ameliorate his hardships and make him happier as he tarries by the wayside of life.

Emerson embodied this idealism in his great essay, the Law of Compensation.

The time for practicing the Golden Rule philosophy is upon us. In business as well as in social relationships he who neglects or refuses to use this philosophy as the basis of his dealings will but hasten the time of his failure.

And, while I am intoxicated with the glorious news of the war's ending, is it not fitting that I should attempt to do something to help preserve for the generations yet to come, one of the great lessons to be learned from William Hohenzollern's effort to rule the earth by force?

I can best do this by going back twenty-two years for my beginning. Come with me, won't you?

It was a bleak November morning, probably not far from the eleventh of the month, that I got my first job as a laborer in the coal mine regions of Virginia, at wages of a dollar a day.

A dollar a day was a big sum in those days; especially to a boy of my age. Of this, I paid fifty cents a day for my board and room.

Shortly after I began work, the miners became dissatisfied and commenced talking about striking. I listened eagerly to all that was said. I was especially interested in the organizer who had organized the union. He was one of the smoothest speakers I had ever heard, and his words fascinated me. He said one thing, in particular, that I have never forgotten; and, if I knew where to find him, I would look him up today and thank him warmly for saying it. The philosophy which I gathered from his words has had a most profound and enduring influence upon me.

Perhaps you will say that most labor agitators are not very sound philosophers; and I would agree with you if you said so. Maybe this one was not a sound philosopher, but surely the philosophy he expounded on this occasion was sound.

Standing on a dry goods box, in the corner of an old shop where he was holding a meeting, he said:

"Men, we are talking about striking. Before you vote I wish to call your attention to something that will benefit you if you will heed what I say. "You want more money for your work; and I wish to see you get it, because I believe you deserve it.

"May I not tell you how to get more money and still retain the good-will of the owner of this mine?

"We can call a strike and probably force them to pay more money, but we cannot force them to do this and like it. Before we call a strike, let us be fair with the owner of the mine and with ourselves; let us go to the owner and ask him if he will divide the profits of his mine with us fairly.

"If he says 'yes,' as he probably will, then let us ask him how much he made last month and, if he will divide among us a fair proportion of any additional profits he may make if we all jump in and help him earn more next month.

"He, being human, like each of us, will no doubt say–'Why, certainly boys; go to it and I'll divide with you.' It is but natural that he would say that, boys.

"After he agrees to the plan, as I believe he will if we make him see that we are in earnest, I want every one of you to come to work with a smile on your face for the next thirty days. I want to bear you whistling a tune as you go into the mines. I want you to go at your work with the feeling that you are one of the partners in this business.

"Without hurting yourself you can do almost twice as much work as you are dong; and if you do more work, you are sure to help the owner of this mine make more money.

And if he makes more money he will be glad to divide a part of it with you. He will do this for sound business reasons if not out of a spirit of fair play.

"He will retaliate as surely as there is a God above us. If he doesn't, I'll be personally responsible to you, and if you say so I'll help blow this mine into smithereens!

"That's how much I think of the plan, boys! Are you with me?"

They were, to the man!

Those words sank into my heart as though they had been burned there with a red-hot iron.

The following month every man in the mines received a bonus of twenty per cent of his month's earnings. Every month thereafter each man received a bright red envelope with his part of the extra earnings in it. On the outside of the envelope were these printed words:

Your part of the profits from the work which you did that you were not paid to do.

I have gone through some pretty tough experiences since those days of twenty-odd years ago, but I have always come out on top–a little wiser, a little happier, and a little better prepared to be of service to my fellow men, owing to my having applied the principle of performing more work than I was actually paid to perform.

It may be of interest to you to know that the last position I held in the coal business was that of Assistant to the Chief Counsel for one of the largest companies in the world. It is a considerable jump from the position of common laborer in the coal mines to that of Assistant to the Chief Counsel of one of the largest companies–a jump that I never could have made without the aid of this principle of performing more work than I was paid to perform.

I wish I had the space in which to tell you of the scores of times that this idea of performing more work than I was paid to perform has helped me over rough spots.

Many have been the times that I have placed an employer so deeply in my debt, through the aid of this principle, that I got whatever I asked for, without hesitation or quibbling; without complaint or hard feelings; and, what is more important, without the feeling that I was taking unfair advantage of my employer.

I believe most earnestly that anything a man acquires from his fellow man without the full consent of the one from whom it is acquired, will eventually burn a hole in his pocket, or blister the palms of his hands, to say nothing of gnawing at his conscience until his heart aches with regret.

As I said in the beginning, I am writing on the morning of the Eleventh of November, while the crowds are celebrating the great victory of right over wrong!

Therefore, it is but natural that I should turn to the silence of my heart for some thought to pass on to the world today–some thought that will help keep alive in the minds of Americans the spirit of idealism for which they have fought and in which they entered the world war.

I find nothing more appropriate than the philosophy which I have related, because I earnestly believe it was the arrogant disregard of this philosophy that brought Germany–the Kaiser and his people–grief. To get this philosophy into the hearts of those who need it I shall publish a magazine to be called Hill's Golden Rule.

It takes money to publish national magazines, and I haven't very much of it at this writing; but before another month shall have passed, through the aid of the philosophy that I have tried to emphasize here, I shall find someone who will supply the necessary money and make it possible for me to pass on to the world the simple philosophy that lifted me out of the dirty coal mines and gave me a place where I can be of service to humanity. The philosophy which will raise you, my dear reader, whoever you may be and whatever you may be doing, into whatever position in life you may make up your mind to attain.

Every person has, or ought to have, the inherent desire to own something of monetary value. In at least a vague sort of way, every person who works for others (and this includes practically all of us) looks forward to the time when he will have some sort of a business or a profession of his own.

The best way to realize that ambition is to perform more work than one is paid to perform. You can get along with but little schooling; you can get along with but little capital; you can overcome almost any obstacle with which you are confronted, if you are honestly and earnestly willing to do the best work of which you are capable, regardless of the amount of money you receive for it....

(Note: It is the afternoon of November the twenty-first, just ten days since I wrote the foregoing editorial. I have just read it to George B. Williams, of Chicago, a man who came up from the bottom through the aid of the philosophy of which I have written, and he has made the publication of Hill's Golden Rule magazine possible.)

It was in this somewhat dramatic manner that a desire which had lain dormant in my mind for nearly twenty years became translated into reality. During all that time I had wanted to become the editor of a newspaper. Back more than thirty years ago, when I was a very small boy, I used to "kick" the press for my father when he was publishing a small weekly newspaper, and I grew to love the smell of printer's ink.

Perhaps this desire was subconsciously gaining momentum all those years of preparation, while I was going through the experiences outlined in the turning-points of my life, until it had finally to burst forth in terms of action; or it may be that there was another plan, over which I had no control, that urged me on and on, never giving me any rest in any other line of work, until I began the publication of my first magazine. That point can be passed for the moment. The important thing to which I would direct your attention is the fact that I found my proper niche in the world's work and I was very happy over it

Strangely enough, I entered upon this work with never a thought of looking for either the end of the rainbow or the proverbial pot of gold which is supposed to be found at its end. For the first time in my life, I seemed to realize, beyond room for doubt, that there was something else to be sought in life that was worth more than gold; therefore,

I went at my editorial work with but one main thought in mind– and I pause while you ponder over this thought

And that thought was to render the world the best service of which I was capable, whether my efforts brought me a penny in return or not!

The publication of Hill's Golden Rule magazine brought me in contact with the thinking class of people all over the country. It gave me my big chance to be heard.

The message of optimism and good-will among men that it carried became so popular that I was invited to go on a country-wide speaking tour during the early part of 1920, during which I had the privilege of meeting and talking with some of the most progressive thinkers of this generation. Contact with these people went a very long way toward giving me the courage to keep on doing the good work that I had started.

This tour was a liberal education, within itself, because it brought me in exceedingly close contact with people in practically all walks of life, and gave me a chance to see that the United States of America was a pretty large country.

Comes, now, a description of the climax of the seventh turning-point of my life.

During my speaking tour I was sitting in a restaurant in Dallas, Texas, watching the hardest downpour of rain that I have ever seen. The water was pouring down over the plate-glass window in two great streams, and Playing backward and forward from one of these streams to the other were little streams, making what resembled a great ladder of water.

As I looked at this unusual scene, the thought"flashed into my mind" that I would have a splendid lecture if I organized all that I had learned from the seven turning-points of my life and all I had learned from studying the lives of successful men, and offered it under the title of the "Magic Ladder to Success."

On the back of an envelope I outlined the fifteen points out of which this lecture was built, and later I worked these points into a lecture that was literally built from the temporary defeats described in the seven turning-points of my life.

All that I lay claim to knowing that is of value is represented by these fifteen points; and the material out of which this knowledge was gathered is nothing more or less than the knowledge that was forced upon me through experiences which have undoubtedly been classed, by some, as failures!

The reading course, of which this lesson is a part, is but the sum total of that which I gathered through these "failures." If this course proves to be of value to you, as I hope it will, you may give the credit to those "failures" described in this lesson.

Perhaps you will wish to know what material, monetary benefits I have gained from these turning-points, for you probably realize that we are living in an age in which life is an irksome struggle for existence and none too pleasant for those who are cursed with poverty.

All right! I'll be frank with you.

To begin with, the estimated income from the sale of this course is all that I need, and this, despite the fact that I have insisted that my publishers apply the Ford philosophy and sell the course at a popular price that is within the reach of all who want it.

In addition to the income from the sale of the course (which, please bear in mind, is but the sale of knowledge I have gathered through "failure"), I am now engaged in writing a series of illustrated editorials that is to be syndicated and published in the newspapers of the country. These editorials are based upon these same fifteen points as outlined in this course.

The estimated net income from the sale of the editorials is more than enough to care for my needs.

In addition to this I am now engaged in collaboration with a group of scientists, psychologists and businessmen, in writing a postgraduate course which will soon be available to all students who have mastered this more elementary course, covering not only the fifteen laws here outlined, from a more advanced viewpoint, but including still other laws which have but recently been discovered.

I have mentioned these facts only because I know what a common thing it is for all of us to measure success in terms of dollars, and to refuse, as unsound, all philosophy that does not foot up a good bank balance.

Practically all the past years of my life I have been poor–exceedingly poor–as far as bank balances were concerned. This condition has been, very largely, a matter of choice with me, because I have been putting the best of my time into the toilsome job of throwing off some of my ignorance and gathering in some of the knowledge of life of which I felt myself in need.

From the experiences described in these seven turning-points of my life, I have gathered a few golden threads of knowledge that I could have gained in no other way than through defeat!

My own experiences have led me to believe that the "dumb language" of defeat is the plainest and most effective language in the world, once one begins to understand it. I am almost tempted to say that I believe it to be the universal language in which Nature cries out to us when we will listen to no other language.

I am glad that I have experienced much defeat!

It has had the effect of tempering me with the courage to undertake tasks that I would never have begun had I been surrounded by protecting influences.

Defeat is a destructive force only when it is accepted as failure! When accepted as teaching some needed lesson it is always a blessing.

I used to hate my enemies!

That was before I learned how well they were serving me by keeping me everlastingly on the alert lest some weak spot in my character provide an opening through which they might damage me.

In view of what I have learned of the value of enemies, if I had none I would feel it my duty to create a few. They would discover my defects and point them out to me, whereas my friends, if they saw my weaknesses at all, would say nothing about them.

Of all Joaquin Miller's poems none expressed a nobler thought than did this one:

"All honor to him who shall win a prize,"
The world has cried for a thousand years;
But to him who tries, and who fails, and dies,
I give great honor, and glory, and tears.

Give glory and honor and pitiful tears
To all who fail in their deeds sublime;
Their ghosts are many in the van of years,
They were born with Time, in advance of Time.
Oh, great is the hem who wins a name;
But greater many, and many a time,
Some pale-faced fellow who dies in shame
And lets God finish the thought sublime.

And great is the man with a sword undrawn,
And good is the man who refrains from wine;
But the man who fails and yet still fights on,
In, he is the twin-brother of mine.

There can be no failure for the man who "still fights on." A man has never failed until he accepts temporary defeat as failure. There is a wide difference between temporary defeat and failure; a difference I have tried to emphasize throughout this lesson. In her poem entitled When Nature Wants a Man, Angela Morgan expressed a great truth in support of the theory set out in this lesson, that adversity and defeat are generally blessings in disguise.

When Nature wants to drill a man,
And thrill a man,
And skill a man.
When Nature wants to mold a man
To play the noblest part;
When she yearns with all her heart
To create so great and bold a man
That all the world shall praise-
Watch her method, watch her ways!
How she ruthlessly perfects
Whom she royally elects;
How she hammers him and hurts him,
And with mighty blows converts him
Into trial shapes of clay which only Nature understands-
While his tortured heart is crying and he lifts beseeching hands!
How she bends, but never breaks,
When his good she undertakes...
How she uses whom she chooses
And with every purpose fuses him,
By every art induces him
To try his splendor out-
Nature knows what she's about.
When Nature wants to take a man,
And shake a man,

And wake a man;
When Nature wants to make a man
To do the Future's will;
When she tries with all her skill
And she yearns with all her soul
To create him large and whole...
With what cunning she prepares him!
How she goads and never spares him,
How she whets him, and she frets him,
And in poverty begets him...
How she often disappoints
Whom she sacredly anoints,
With what wisdom she will hide him,
Never minding what betide him
Though his genius sob with slighting and his pride may not forget!
Bids him struggle harder yet.
Makes him lonely
So that only
God's high messages shall reach him,
So that she may surely teach him
What the Hierarchy planned.
Though he may not understand,
Gives him passions to command.
How remorselessly she spurs him
With terrific ardor stirs him
When she poignantly prefers him!

When Nature wants to name a man
And fame a man
And tame a man;
When Nature wants to shame a man
To do his heavenly best...
When she tries the highest test
That she reckoning may bring-
When she wants a god or king!
How she reins him and restrains him
So his body scarce contains him
While she fires him
And inspires him!
Keeps him yearning, ever burning for a tantalizing goal-
Lures and lacerates his soul.
Sets a challenge for his spirit,
Draws it higher when he's near it-

Makes a jungle, that he clear it;
Makes a desert that he fear it
And subdue it if he can–
So doth Nature make a man.
Then, to test his spirit's wrath
Hurls a mountain in his path–
Puts a bitter choice before him
And relentlessly stands o'er him.
"Climb, or perish!" so she says....
Watch her purpose, watch her ways!
Nature's plan is wondrous kind
Could we understand her mind...
Fools are they who call her blind.
When his feet are torn and bleeding
Yet his spirit mounts unheeding,
All his higher powers speeding,
Blazing newer paths and fine;
When the force that is divine
Leaps to challenge every failure and his ardor still is sweet
And love and hope are burning in the presence of defeat...
Lo, the crisis! Lo, the shout
That must call the leader out.
When the people need salvation
Doth he come to lead the nation...
Then doth Nature show her plan
When the world has found– a MAN!

(From 'Forward, March P' The John Lane Company.)

I am convinced that failure is Nature's plan through which she hurdle-jumps men of destiny and prepares them to do their work. Failure is Nature's great crumble in which she burns the dross from the human heart and so purifies the metal of the man that it can stand the test of hard usage.

I have found evidence to support this theory in the study of the records of scores of great men, from Socrates on down the centuries to the well-known men of achievement of our modern times. The success of each man seemed to be in almost exact ratio to the extent of the obstacles and difficulties he had to surmount.

No man ever arose from the knock-out blow of defeat without being stronger and wiser for the experience. Defeat talks to us in a language all its own; a language to which we must listen whether we like it or not.

Of course one must have considerable courage to look upon defeat as a blessing in disguise; but the attainment of any position in life, that is worth having, requires a lot of "sand," which brings to mind a poem that harmonizes with the philosophy of this lesson.

I observed a locomotive in the railroad yards one day,

It was waiting in the roundhouse where the locomotives stay;
It was panting for the journey, it was coaled and fully manned,
And it had a box the fireman was filling full of sand.

It appears that locomotives cannot always get a grip
On their slender iron pavement, 'cause the wheels are apt to slip;
And when they reach a slippery spot, their tactics they command,
And to get a grip upon the rail, they sprinkle it with sand.

It's about the way with travel along life's slippery track-
If your load is rather heavy, you're always slipping back;
So, if a common locomotive you completely understand,
You'll provide yourself in starting with a good supply of sand.

If your track is steep and hilly and you have a heavy grade,
If those who've gone before you have the rails quite slippery made,
If you ever reach the summit of the upper tableland,
You'll find you'll have to do it with a liberal use of sand.

If you strike some frigid weather and discover to your cost,
That you're liable to slip upon a heavy coat of frost,
Then some prompt decided action will be called into demand,
And you'll slip 'way to the bottom if you haven't any sand.

You can get to any station that is on life's schedule seen,
If there's fire beneath the boiler of ambition's strong machine,
And you'll reach a place called Flushtown at a rate of speed that's grand,
If for all the slippery places you've a good supply of sand.

It can do you no harm if you memorize the poems quoted in this lesson and make the philosophy upon which they are based a part of your own.

'Tis the human touch in this world that counts,
The touch of your hand and mine,
Which means far more to the fainting heart,
Than shelter and bread and wine;
For shelter is gone when the night is o'er,
And bread lasts only a day,
But the touch of the hand and the sound of the voice,
Sing on in the soul alway.-Spencer M. Tree

As I near the end of this lesson on Failure, there comes to mind a bit of philosophy taken from the works of the great Shakespeare, which I wish to challenge because I believe it to be unsound. It is stated in the following quotation:

> There is a tide in the affairs of men
> Which, taken at the flood, leads on to fortune;
> Omitted, all the voyage of their life
> Is bound in shallows, and in miseries.
> On such a full sea are we now afloat;
> And we must take the current when it serves,
> Or lose our ventures.

Fear and admission of failure are the ties which cause us to be "bound in shallows, and in miseries." We can break these ties and throw them off. Nay, we can turn them to advantage and make them serve as a tow-line with which to pull ourselves ashore if we observe and profit by the lessons they teach.

> Who ne'er has suffered, he has lived but half,
> Who never failed, he never strove or sought,
> Who never wept is stranger to a laugh,
> And he who never doubted never thought.

As I near the end of this, my favorite lesson of this course, I close my eyes for a moment and see before me a great army of men and women whose faces show the lines of care and despair.

Some are in rags, having reached the last stage of that long, long trail which men call failure!

Others are in better circumstances, but the fear of starvation shows plainly on their faces; the smile of courage has left their lips; and they, too, seem to have given up the battle.

The scene shifts!

I look again and I am carried backward into the history of man's struggle for a place in the sun, and there I see, also, the "failures" of the past–failures that have meant more to the human race than all the so-called successes recorded in the history of the world.

I see the homely face of Socrates as he stood at the very end of that trail called failure, waiting, with upturned eyes, through those moments which must have seemed like an eternity, just before he drank the cup of hemlock that was forced upon him by his tormentors.

I see, also, Christopher Columbus, a prisoner in chains, which was the tribute paid him for his sacrifice in having set sail on an unknown and uncharted sea, to discover an unknown continent.

I see, also, the face of Thomas Paine, the man whom the English sought to capture and put to death as the real instigator of the American Revolution. I see him lying in a filthy prison, in France, as he waited calmly, under the shadow of the guillotine, for the death which he expected would be meted out to him for his part in behalf of humanity.

Oh, to be such a failure. Oh, to go down in history, as these men did, as one who was brave enough to place humanity above the individual and principle above pecuniary gain.

On such "failures" rest the hopes of the world.

> Oh, men, who are labeled "failures" –up, rise up! again and do!
> Somewhere in the world of action is room; there is room for you.
> No failure was e'er recorded, in the annals of truthful men,

Except of the craven-hearted who fails, nor attempts again.
The glory is in the doing, and not in the trophy won;
The walls that are laid in darkness may laugh to the kiss of the sun.
Oh, weary and worn and stricken, oh, child of fate's cruel gales!
I sing-that it haply may cheer him-I sing to the man who fails.

Be thankful for the defeat which men call failure, because if you can survive it and keep on trying it gives you a chance to prove your ability to rise to the heights of achievement in your chosen field of endeavor.

No one has the right to brand you as a failure except yourself.

If, in a moment of despair, you should feel inclined to brand yourself as a failure, just remember those words of the wealthy philosopher, Croesus, who was advisor to Cyrus, king of the Persians:

> "I am reminded, O king, and take this lesson to heart, that there is a wheel on which the affairs of men revolve and its mechanism is such that it prevents any man from being always fortunate."

What a wonderful lesson is wrapped up in those words-a lesson of hope and courage and promise.

Who of us has not seen "off days, when everything seemed to go wrong? These are the days when we see only the flat side of the great wheel of life.

Let us remember that the wheel is always turning. If it brings us sorrow today, it will bring us joy tomorrow. Life is a cycle of varying events-fortunes and misfortunes.

We cannot stop this wheel of fate from turning, but we can modify the misfortune it brings us by remembering that good fortune will follow, just as surely as night follows day, if we but keep faith with ourselves and earnestly and honestly do our best.

In his greatest hours of trial the immortal Lincoln was heard, often, to say: "And this, too, will soon pass."

If you are smarting from the effects of some temporary defeat which you find it hard to forget, let me recommend this stimulating little poem, by Walter Malone.

OPPORTUNITY

They do me wrong who say I come no more
When once I knock and fail to find you in;
For every day I stand outside your door,
And bid you wake, and rise to fight and win.
Wail not for precious chances passed away;
Weep not for golden ages on the wane;
Each night I burn the records of the day;
At sunrise every soul is born again.
Laugh like a boy at splendors that have sped,
To vanished joys be blind and deaf and dumb;
My judgments seal the dead past with its dead,
But never bind a moment yet to come.
Though deep in mire wring not your hands and
weep,

I lend my arm to all who say, "I can!"
No shamefaced outcast ever sank so deep
But yet might rise and be again a man!
Dost thou behold thy lost youth all aghast?
Dost reel from righteous retribution's blow?
Then turn from blotted archives of the past
And find the future's pages white as snow.
Art thou a mourner? Rouse thee from thy spell;
Art thou a sinner? Sin may be forgiven;
Each morning gives thee wings to flee from hell,
Each night a star to guide thy feet to heaven.

Lesson Fifteen: TOLERANCE

There are two significant features about intolerance, and your attention is directed to these at the beginning of this lesson.

These features are:

First: Intolerance is a form of ignorance which must be mastered before any form of enduring success may be attained. It is the chief cause of all wars. It makes enemies in business and in the professions. It disintegrates the organized forces of society in a thousand forms, and stands, like a mighty giant, as a barrier to the abolition of war. It dethrones reason and substitutes mob psychology in its place.

Second: Intolerance is the chief disintegrating force in the organized religions of the world, where it plays havoc with the greatest power for good there is on this earth; by breaking up that power into small sects and denominations which spend as much effort opposing each other as they do in destroying the evils of the world.

But this indictment against intolerance is general. Let's see how it affects you, the individual. It is, of course, obvious that anything which impedes the progress of civilization stands, also, as a barrier to each individual; and, stating it conversely, anything that beclouds the mind of the individual and retards his mental, moral and spiritual development, retards, also, the progress of civilization.

All of which is an abstract statement of a great truth; and, inasmuch as abstract statements am neither interesting nor highly informative, let us proceed to illustrate more concretely the damaging effects of intolerance.

I will begin this illustration by describing an incident which I have mentioned quite freely in practically every public address that I have delivered within the past five years; but, inasmuch as the cold printed page has a modifying effect which makes possible the misinterpretation of the incident here described, I believe it necessary to caution you not to read back of the lines a meaning which I had no intention of placing there. You will do yourself an injustice if you either neglect or intentionally refuse to study this illustration in the exact words and with the exact meaning which I have intended those words to convey- a meaning as clear as I know how to make the English language convey it.

As you read of this incident, place yourself in my position and see if you, also, have not had a parallel experience, and, if so, what lesson did it teach you?

One day I was introduced to a young man of unusually fine appearance. His clear eye, his warm handclasp, the tone of his voice and the splendid taste with which he was groomed marked him as a young man of the highest intellectual type. He was of the typical young American college student type, and as I ran my eyes over him, hurriedly studying his personality, as one will naturally do under such circumstances, I observed a Knights of Columbus pin on his vest.

Instantly, I released his hand as if it were a piece of ice!

This was done so quickly that it surprised both him and me. As I excused myself and started to walk away, I glanced down at the Masonic pin that I wore on my own vest, then took another look at his Knights of Columbus pin, and wondered why a couple of trinkets such as these could dig such a deep chasm between men who knew nothing of each other.

All the remainder of that day I kept thinking of the incident, because it bothered me. I had always taken considerable pride in the thought that I was tolerant with all men; but here was a spontaneous outburst of intolerance which proved that down in my subconscious mind existed a complex that was influencing me toward narrow-mindedness.

This discovery so shocked me that I began a systematic process of psycho-analysis through which I searched into the very depths of my soul for the cause of my rudeness. I asked myself over and over again:

"Why did you abruptly release that young man's hand and turn away from him, when you knew nothing about him?"

Of course the answer led me, always, back to that Knights of Columbus pin that he wore. But that was not a real answer and therefore it did not satisfy me.

As I began to reach out in this direction and that, for knowledge, my mind began to unfold and broaden with such alarming rapidity that I practically found it necessary to: Wipe the slate of what I believed to be my previously gathered knowledge, and to unlearn much that I had previously believed to be truth. Comprehend the meaning of that which I have just stated!

Imagine yourself suddenly discovering that most of your philosophy of life had been built of bias and prejudice, making it necessary for you to acknowledge that, far from being a finished scholar, you were barely qualified to become an intelligent student! That was exactly the position in which I found myself, with respect to many of what I believed to be sound fundamentals of life; but of all the discoveries to which this research led, none was more important than that of the relative importance of physical and social heredity, for it was this discovery that disclosed the cause for my action when I turned away from a man whom I did not know, on the occasion that I have described.

It was this discovery that disclosed to me how and where I acquired my views of religion, of politics, of economics and many other equally important subjects, and I both regret and rejoice to state that I found most of my views on these subjects without support by even a reasonable hypothesis, much less sound facts or reason. I then recalled a conversation between the late Senator Robert L. Taylor and myself, in which we were discussing the subject of politics. It was a friendly discussion, as we were of the same political faith, but the Senator asked me a question for which I never forgave him until I began the research to which I have referred.

"I see that you are a very staunch Democrat," said he, "and I wonder if you know why you are?"

I thought of the question for a few seconds, then blurted out this reply: "I am a Democrat because my father was one, of course!" With a broad grin on his face the Senator then nailed me with this rejoinder: "Just as I thought! Now wouldn't you be in a bad fix if your father had been a horse-thief?"

It was many years later, after I began the research work herein described, that I understood the real meaning of Senator Taylor's joke. Too often we hold opinions that are based upon no sounder foundation than that of what someone else believes. That you may have a detailed illustration of the far-reaching effects of one of the important principles uncovered by the incident to which I have referred, and-

That you may learn how and where you acquired your philosophy of life, in general; That you may trace your prejudices and your biases to their original source; That you may discover, as I discovered, how largely you are the result of the training you received before you reached the age of fifteen years.

I will now quote the full text of a plan which I submitted to Mr. Edward Bok's Committee, The American Peace Award, for the abolition of war. This plan covers not only the most important of the principles to which I refer, but, as you will observe, it shows how the principle of organized effort, as outlined in Lesson Two of this course, may be applied to one of the most important of the world's problems, and at the same time gives you a more comprehensive idea of how to apply this principle in the attainment of your definite chief aim.

HOW TO ABOLISH WAR–The Background

Before offering this plan for the prevention of war, it seems necessary to sketch briefly a background that will clearly describe the principle which constitutes the warp and the woof of the plan.

The causes o f war may be properly omitted for the reason that they have but little, if any, relation to the principle through which war may be prevented.

The beginning of this sketch deals with two important factors which constitute the chief controlling forces of civilization. One is physical heredity and the other is social heredity.

The size and form of the body, the texture of the skin, the color of the eyes, and the functioning power of the vital organs are all the result of physical heredity; they are static and fixed and cannot be changed, for they are the result of a million years of evolution; but by far the most important part of what we are is the result of social heredity, and came to us from the effects of our environment and early training.

Our conception of religion, politics, economics, philosophy and other subjects of a similar nature, including war, is entirely the result of those dominating forces of our environment and training.

The Catholic is a Catholic because of his early training, and the Protestant is a Protestant for the same reason; but this is hardly stating the truth with sufficient emphasis, for it might be properly said that the Catholic is a Catholic and the Protestant is a Protestant because he cannot help it! With but few exceptions the religion of the adult is the result of his religious training during the years between four and fourteen when his religion was forced upon him by his parents or those who had control of his schooling.

A prominent clergyman indicated how well he understood the principle of social heredity when he said: "Give me the control of the child until it is twelve years old and you can teach it any religion you may please after that time, for I will have planted my own religion so deeply in its mind that no power on earth could undo my work."

The outstanding and most prominent of man's beliefs are those which were forced upon him, or which he absorbed of his own volition, under highly emotionalized conditions, when his mind was receptive. Under such conditions the evangelist can plant the idea of religion more deeply and permanently during an hour's revival service than he could through years of training under ordinary conditions, when the mind was not in an emotionalized state.

The people of the United States have immortalized Washington and Lincoln because they were the leaders of the nation during times when the minds of the people were highly emotionalized, as the result of calamities which shook the very foundation of our country and vitally affected the interests of all the people. Through the principle of social heredity, operating through the schools (American history), and through other forms of impressive teaching, the immortality of Washington and Lincoln is planted in the minds of the young and in that way kept alive.

The three great organized forces through which social heredity operates are:

The schools and the public press.

Any ideal that has the active co-operation of these three forces may, during the brief period of one generation, be forced upon the minds of the young so effectively that they cannot resist it.

In 1914 the world awoke one morning to find itself aflame with warfare on a scale previously unheard of, and the outstanding feature of importance of that world-wide calamity was the highly organized German armies. For more than three years these armies gained ground so rapidly that world domination by Germany seemed certain.

The German military machine operated with efficiency such as had never before been demonstrated in warfare. With "kultur" as her avowed ideal, modern Germany swept the opposing armies before her as though they were leaderless, despite the fact that the allied forces outnumbered her own on every front.

The capacity for sacrifice in the German soldiers, in support of the ideal of "kultur," was the outstanding surprise of the war; and that capacity was largely the result of the work of two men. Through the German educational system, which they controlled, the psychology which carried the world into war in 1914 was created in the definite form of "kultur." These men were Adalbert Falk, Prussian Minister of Education until 1879, and the German Emperor William II.

The agency through which these men produced this result was social heredity: the imposing of an ideal on the minds of the young, under highly emotionalized conditions.

"Kultur," as a national ideal, was fixed in the minds of the young of Germany, beginning first in the elementary schools and extending on up through the high schools and universities. The teachers and professors were forced to implant the ideal of "kultur" in the minds of the students, and out of this teaching, in a single generation, grew the capacity for sacrifice of the individual for the interest of the nation which surprised the modern world.

As Benjamin Kidd so well stated the case: "The aim of the state of Germany was everywhere to orientate public opinion through the heads of both its spiritual and temporal departments, through the bureaucracy, through the officers of the army, through the State direction of the press; and, last of all, through the State direction of the entire trade and industry of the nation, so as to bring the idealism of the whole people to a conception of and to a support of the national policy of modem Germany."

Germany controlled the press, the clergy and the schools; therefore, is it any wonder that she grew an army of soldiers, during one generation, which represented to a man her ideal of "kultur"? Is it any wonder that the German soldiers faced certain death with fearless impunity, when one stops to consider the fact that they had been taught, from early childhood, that this sacrifice was a rare privilege?

Turn, now, from this brief description of the modus operandi through which Germany prepared her people for war, to another strange phenomenon, Japan. No western nation, with the exception of Germany, has so clearly manifested its understanding of the far-reaching influence of social heredity, as has Japan. Within a single generation Japan has advanced from her standing as a fourth-rate nation to the ranks of nations that are the recognized powers of the civilized world. Study Japan and you will find that she forces upon the minds of her young, through exactly the same agencies employed by

Germany, the ideal of subordination of individual rights for the sake of accumulation of power by the nation.

In all of her controversies with China, competent observers have seen that back of the apparent causes of the controversies was Japan's stealthy attempt to control the minds of the young by controlling the schools. If Japan could control the minds of the young of China, she could dominate that gigantic nation within one generation.

If you would study the effect of social heredity as it is being used for the development of a national ideal by still another nation of the West, observe what has been going on in Russia since the ascendency to power of the Soviet government of Russia which is now patterning the minds of the young to conform with a national ideal, the nature of which it requires no master analyst to interpret. That ideal, when fully developed during the maturity of the present generation, will represent exactly that which the Soviet government wishes it to represent.

Of all the flood of propaganda concerning the soviet government of Russia that has been poured into this country through the tens of thousands of columns of newspaper space devoted to it since the close of the war, the following brief dispatch is by far the most significant:

> "RUSS REDS ORDER BOOKS. Contracts being let in Germany for 20,000,000 volumes. Educational propaganda is aimed chiefly at children.
>
> "(By GEORGE WITTS)
>
> "Special Cable to the Chicago Daily News Foreign Service. Berlin, Germany,
>
> November 9th, 1920.
>
> "Contracts for printing 20,000,000 books in the Russian language, chiefly for children, are being placed in Germany on behalf of the soviet government by Grschebin, a well known Petrograd publisher and a friend of Maxim Gorky. Grschebin first went to England, but was received with indifference when he broached the subject to the British government. The Germans, however, not only welcomed him eagerly but submitted prices so low that they could not possibly be under bidden in any other country. The Ullsteins, Berlin newspaper and book publishers, have agreed to print several million of the books at less than cost."

This shows what is going on over there.

Far from being shocked by this significant press dispatch, the majority of the newspapers of America did not publish it, and those that did give it space placed it in an obscure part of the paper, in small type. Its real significance will become more apparent some twenty-odd years from now, when the Soviet government of Russia will have grown an army of soldiers who will support, to the man, whatever national ideal the soviet government sets up.

The possibility of war exists as a stern reality today solely because the principle of social heredity has not only been used as a sanctioning force in support of war, but it has actually been used as a chief agency through which the minds of men have been deliberately prepared for war. For evidence with which to support this statement, examine any national or world history and observe how tactfully and effectively war has been glorified and so described that it not only did not shock the mind of the student, but it actually established a plausible justification of war.

Go into the public squares of our cities and observe the monuments that have been erected to the leaders of war. Observe the posture of these statues as they stand as living symbols to glorify men who did nothing more than lead armies on escapades of destruction. Notice how well these statues of warriors, mounted on charging steeds, serve as agencies through which to stimulate the minds of the young and prepare them for the acceptance of war, not only as a pardonable act, but as a distinctly desirable source of attainment of glory, fame and honor. At the time of this writing some well-meaning ladies are having the image of Confederate Soldiers carved in the deathless granite on the face of Stone Mountain, in Georgia, in figures a hundred feet tall, thus seeking to perpetuate the memory of a lost "cause" that never was a "cause" and therefore the sooner forgotten, the better.

If these references to far-away Russia, Japan and Germany seem unimpressive and abstract, then let us study the principle of social heredity as it is now functioning on a highly developed scale here in the United States; for it may be expecting too much of the average of our race to suppose that they will be interested in that which is taking place outside of the spot of ground that is bounded on the north by Canada, on the east by the Atlantic, on the west by the Pacific and on the south by Mexico.

We, too, are setting up in the minds of our young a national ideal, and this ideal is being so effectively developed, through the principle of social heredity, that it has already become the dominating ideal of the nation.

This ideal is the desire for wealth!

The first question we ask about a new acquaintance is not, "Who are you?" but, "What have you?" And the next question we ask is, "How can we get that which you have?" Our ideal is not measured in terms of warfare, but in terms of finance and industry and business. Our Patrick Henrys and our George Washingtons and our Abraham Lincoln of a few generations ago are now represented by the able leaders who manage our steel mills and our coal mines and our timber lands and our banking institutions and our railroads.

We may deny this indictment if we choose, but the facts do not support the denial. The outstanding problem of the American people today is the spirit of unrest upon the part of the masses who find the struggle for existence becoming harder and harder because the most competent brains of the country are engaged in the highly competitive attempt to accumulate wealth and to control the wealth-producing machinery of the nation.

It is not necessary to dwell at length upon this description of our dominating ideal, or to offer evidence in support of its existence, for the reason that its existence is obvious and as well understood by the most ignorant as it is by those who make a pretense of thinking accurately.

So deeply-seated has this mad desire for money become that we are perfectly willing for the other nations of the world to cut themselves to pieces in warfare so long as they do not interfere with our scramble for wealth; nor is this the saddest part of the indictment that we might render against ourselves, for we are not only willing for other nations to engage in warfare, but there is considerable reason to believe that those of us who profit by the sale of war supplies actually encourage this warfare among other nations.

THE PLAN

War grows out of the desire of the individual to gain advantage at the expense of his fellow men, and the smoldering embers of this desire are fanned into a flame through the grouping of these individuals who place the interests of the group above those of other groups.

War cannot be stopped suddenly!

It can be eliminated only by education, through the aid of the principle of subordination of the individual interests to the broader interests of the human race as a whole.

Man's tendencies and activities, as we have already stated, grow out of two great forces. One is physical heredity, and the other is social heredity. Through physical heredity, man inherits those early tendencies to destroy his fellow man out of self-protection. This Practice is a holdover from the age when the struggle for existence was so great that only the physically strong could survive.

Gradually men began to learn that the individual could survive under more favorable circumstances by allying himself with others, and out of that discovery grew our modern society, through which groups of people have formed states, and these groups, in turn, have formed nations. There is but little tendency toward warfare between the individuals of a particular group or nation, for they have learned, through the principle of social heredity, that they can best survive by subordinating the interest of the individual to that of the group.

Now, the problem is to extend this principle of grouping so that the nations of the world will subordinate their individual interests to those of the human race as a whole. This can be brought about only through the principle of social heredity. By forcing upon the minds of the young of all races the fact that war is horrible and does not serve either the interest of the individual engaging in it or the group to which the individual belongs.

The question then arises, "How can this be done?" Before we answer this question, let us again define the term "social heredity" and find out what its possibilities are.

Social heredity is the principle through which the young of the race absorb from their environment, and particularly from their earlier training by parents, teachers and religious leaders, the beliefs and tendencies of the adults who dominate them.

No League of Nations and no mere agreement between nations can abolish war as long as there is the slightest evidence of sanction of war in the hearts of the people. Universal peace between nations will grow out of a movement that will be begun and carried on, at first, by a comparatively small number of thinkers. Gradually this number will grow until it will be composed of the leading educators, clergymen and publicists of the world, and these, in turn, will so deeply and permanently establish peace as a world ideal that it will become a reality.

This desirable end may be attained in a single generation under the right sort of leadership; but, more likely, it will not be attained for many generations to come, for the reason that those who have the ability to assume this leadership are too busy in their pursuit of worldly wealth to make the necessary sacrifice for the good of generations yet unborn.

War can be eliminated, not by appeal to reason, but by appeal to the emotional side of humanity. This appeal must be made by organizing and highly emotionalizing the people of the different nations of the world in support of a universal plan for peace, and this plan must be forced upon the minds of the oncoming generations with the same diligent care that we now force upon the minds of our young the ideal of our respective religions.

The majority of the people of the world want peace, wherein lies the possibility of its attainment!

In Schopenhauer's bitter arraignment of woman, he unconsciously stated a truth upon which the hope of civilization rests, when he declared that the race is always to her more than the individual. In terms that are uncompromising, Schopenhauer charges woman with being the natural enemy of man because of this inborn trait of placing the interests of the race above those of the individual.

It seems a reasonable prophecy to suggest that civilization passed into a new era, beginning with the world war, in which woman is destined to take into her own hands the raising of the ethical standards of the world. This is a hopeful sign, because it is woman's nature to subordinate the interests of the present to those of the future. It is woman's nature to implant, in the mind of the young, ideals that will accrue to the benefit of generations yet unborn, while man is motivated generally by expediency of the present.

In Schopenhauer's vicious attack upon woman, he has stated a great truth concerning her nature: a truth which might well be utilized by all who engage in the worthy work of establishing universal peace as a world ideal.

The women's clubs of the world are destined to play a part in world affairs other than that of gaining suffrage for women.

LET CIVILIZATION REMEMBER THIS!

Those who do not want peace are the ones who profit by war. In numbers, this class constitutes but a fragment of the power of the world, and could be swept aside as though it did not exist, if the multitude who do not want war were organized with the high ideal of universal peace as their objective.

In closing, it seems appropriate to apologize for the unfinished state of this essay, but it may be pardonable to suggest that the bricks and the mortar, and the foundation stones, and all the other necessary materials for the construction of the temple of universal peace have been here assembled, where they might be rearranged and transformed into this high ideal as a world reality.

Let us now proceed to apply the principle of social heredity to the subject of business economy, and ascertain whether or not it can be made of practical benefit in the attainment of material wealth.

If I were a banker I would procure a list of all the births in the families within a given distance of my place of business, and every child would receive an appropriate letter, congratulating it on its arrival in the world at such an opportune time, in such a favorable community; and from that time on it would receive from my bank a birthday reminder of an appropriate nature. When it arrived at the storybook age, it would receive from my bank an interesting story book in which the advantages of saving would be told in story form. If the child were a girl, it would receive doll "cut-out" books, with the name of my bank on the back of each doll, as a birthday gift. If it were a boy, it would receive baseball bats. One of the most important floors (or even a whole, nearby building) of my banking house would be set aside as a children's playroom; and it would be equipped with merry-go-rounds, sliding-boards, seesaws, scooters, games and sand piles, with a competent supervisor in charge to give the kiddies a good time. I would let that play-room become the popular habitat of the children of the community, where mothers might leave their youngsters in safety while shopping or visiting.

I would entertain those youngsters so royally that when they grew up and became bank depositors, whose accounts were worth while, they would be inseparably bound to my bank; and, meanwhile, I would, in no way, be lessening my chances of making depositors of the fathers and mothers of those children.

If I were the owner of a business school, I would begin cultivating the boys and girls of my community from the time they reached the fifth grade, on up through high school, so that by the time they were through high school and ready to choose a vocation, I would have the name of my business school well fixed in their minds.

If I were a grocer, or a department store owner, or a druggist, I would cultivate the children, thereby attracting both them and their parents to my place of business; for it is a well-known fact that there is no shorter route to the heart of a parent than that which leads through interest manifested in the offspring. If I were a department store owner, and used whole pages of newspaper space, as most of them do, I would run a comic strip at the bottom of each page, illustrating it with scenes in my playroom, and in this way induce the children to read my advertisements.

If I were a national advertiser, or the owner of a mail order house, I would find appropriate ways and means of establishing a point of contact with the children of the country; for, let me repeat, there is no better way of influencing the parent than that of "capturing" the child.

If I were a barber, I would have a room equipped exclusively for children, for this would bring me the patronage of both the children and their parents.

In the outskirts of every city there is an opportunity for a flourishing business for someone who will operate a restaurant and serve meals of the better "home-cooked" quality, and cater to families who wish to take the children and dine out occasionally. I would have the place equipped with well-stocked fishing ponds, and ponies, and all sorts of animals and birds in which children are interested, if I were operating it, and induce the children to come out regularly and spend the entire day. Why speak of gold mines when opportunities such as this are abundant?

These are but a few of the ways in which the principle of social heredity might be used to advantage in business,

Attract the children and you attract the parents!

If nations can build soldiers of war to order, by bending the minds of their young in the direction of war, businessmen can build customers to order through the same principle.

We come, now, to another important feature of this lesson through which we may see, from another angle, how power may be accumulated by co-operative, organized effort. We learned many lessons of value from the world war, outrageous and destructive as it was, but none of greater importance than that of the effect of organized effort. You will recall that the tide of war began to break in favor of the allied armies just after all armed forces were placed under the direction of Foch, which wrought about complete co-ordination of effort in the allied ranks.

Never before, in the history of the world, had so much power been concentrated in one group of men as that which was created through the organized effort of the allied armies. We come, now, to one of the most outstanding and significant facts to we found in the analysis of these allied armies, namely, that they were made up of the most cosmopolitan group of soldiers ever assembled on this earth.

Catholics and Protestants, Jews and Gentiles, blacks and whites, yellows and tans, and every race on earth were represented in those armies. If they had any differences on account of race or creed, they laid them aside and subordinated them to the cause for which they were fighting. Under the stress of war, that great mass of humanity was reduced to a common level where they fought shoulder to shoulder, side by side, without asking any questions as to each other's racial tendencies or religious beliefs.

If they could lay aside intolerance long enough to fight for their lives over there, why can we not do the same while we fight for a higher standard of ethics in business and finance and industry over here?

Is it only when civilized people are fighting for their lives that they have the foresight to lay aside intolerance and co-operate in the furtherance of a common end? If it were advantageous to the allied armies to think and act as one thoroughly coordinated body, would it we less advantageous for the people of a city or a community or an industry to do so?

Bring the illustration still nearer your own individual interests by an imaginary alliance between all of the employers and all of the employees of your city, for the purpose of reducing friction and misunderstandings, thereby enabling them to render better service at a lower cost to the public and greater profit to themselves.

We learned from the world war that we cannot destroy a part without weakening the whole; that when one nation or group of people is reduced to poverty and want, the remainder of the world suffers, also. Stated conversely, we learned from the world war that co-operation and tolerance are the very foundation of enduring success.

Surely the more thoughtful and observant individuals will not fail to profit (as individuals) by these great lessons which we learned from the world war.

I am not unmindful of the fact that you are probably studying this course for the purpose of profiting, in every way possible, from a purely personal viewpoint, by the principles upon which it is founded. For this very reason, I have endeavored to outline the application of these principles to as wide a scope of subjects as possible.

In this lesson, you have had opportunity to observe the application of the principles underlying the subjects of organized effort, tolerance and social heredity to an extent which must have given you much food for thought, and which must have given your imagination much room for profitable exercise.

I have endeavored to show you how these principles may be employed both in the furtherance of your own individual interests, in whatever calling you may be engaged, and for the benefit of civilization as a whole.

Whether your calling is that of preaching sermons, selling goods or personal services, practicing law, directing the efforts of others, or working as a day laborer, it seems not too much to hope that you will find in this lesson a stimulus to thought which may lead you to higher achievements. If, perchance, you are a writer of advertisements you will surely find in this lesson sufficient food for thought to add more power to your pen. If you have personal services for sale, it is not unreasonable to expect that this lesson will suggest ways and means of marketing those services to greater advantage.

In uncovering for you the source from which intolerance is usually developed, this lesson has led you, also, to the study of other thought-provoking subjects which might easily mark the most profitable turning-point of your life. Books and lessons, in themselves, are of but little value; their real value, if any, lies not in their printed pages, but in the possible action which they may arouse in the reader.

For example, when my proof-reader had finished reading the manuscript of this lesson, she informed me that it had so impressed her and her husband that they intended to go into the advertising business and supply banks with an advertising service that would reach the parents through the children. She believes the plan is worth $10,000.00 a year to her.

Frankly, her plan so appealed to me that I would estimate its value at a minimum of more than three times the amount she mentioned, and I doubt not that it could be made to yield five times that amount, if it were properly organized and marketed by an able salesman.

Nor is that all that this lesson has accomplished before passing from the manuscript stage. A prominent business college owner, to whom I showed the manuscript, has already begun to put into effect the suggestion which referred to the use of social heredity as a means of "cultivating" students; and he is sanguine enough to believe that a plan, similar to the one he intends using, could be sold to the majority of the 1500 business colleges in the United States and Canada, on a basis that would yield the promoter of the plan a yearly income greater than the salary received by the President of the United States.

And, as this lesson is being completed, I am in receipt of a letter from Dr. Charles F. Crouch, of Atlanta, Georgia, in which he informs me that a group of prominent business men in Atlanta have just organized the Golden Rule Club, the main object of which is to put into operation, on a nation-wide scale, the plan for the abolition of war, as outlined in this lesson. (A copy of that portion of this lesson dealing with the subject of abolition of war was sent to Dr. Crouch several weeks before the completion of the lesson.)

These three events, happening one after the other, within a period of a few weeks, have strengthened my belief that this is the most important lesson of the entire sixteen, but its value to you will depend entirely upon the extent to which it stimulates you to think and to act as you would not have done without its influence.

The chief object of this course and, particularly, of this lesson is to educate, more than it is to inform–meaning by the word "educate" to educe, to draw out! to develop from within; to cause you to use the power that lies sleeping within you, awaiting the awakening hand of some appropriate stimulus to arouse you to action.

In conclusion, may I not leave with you my personal sentiments on tolerance, in the following essay which I wrote, in the hour of my most trying experience, when an enemy was trying to ruin my reputation and destroy the results of a life-time of honest effort to do some good in the world.

A handsome wall hanger of this essay on Intolerance will be sent to each student of this course, along with the report on the Personal Analysis Questionnaire. This hanger is printed in two colors and personally autographed by the author of the Law of Success course.

TOLERANCE!

When the dawn of Intelligence shall have spread its wings over the eastern horizon of progress, and Ignorance and Superstition shall have left their last footprints on the sands of Time, it will be recorded in the book of man's crimes and mistakes that his most grievous sin was that of Intolerance!

The bitterest Intolerance grows out of racial and religious differences of opinion, as the result of early childhood training. How long, O Master of Human Destinies, until we poor mortals will understand the folly of trying to destroy one another because of dogmas and creeds and other superficial matters over which we do not agree?

Our allotted time on this earth is but a fleeting moment, at most!

Like a candle, we are lighted, shine for a moment and flicker out! Why can we not so live during this short earthly sojourn that when the Great Caravan called Death draws up and announces this visit about finished we will be ready to fold our tents, and, like the Arabs of the Desert, silently follow the Caravan out into the Darkness of the Unknown without fear and trembling?

I am hoping that I will find no Jews or Gentiles, Catholics or Protestants, Germans or Englishmen, Frenchmen or Russians, Blacks or Whites, Reds or Yellows, when I shall have crossed the Bar to the Other Side.

I am hoping I will find there only human Souls, Brothers and Sisters all, unmarked by race, creed or color, far I shall want to be done with Intolerance so I may lie down and rest an eon or two, undisturbed by the strife, ignorance, superstition and petty misunderstandings which mark with chaos and grief this earthly existence.

Lesson Sixteen: THE GOLDEN RULE

With this lesson we approach the apex of the pyramid of this course on the Law of Success.

This lesson is the Guiding Star that will enable you to use profitably and constructively the knowledge assembled in the preceding lessons.

There is more power wrapped up in the preceding lessons of this course than most men could trust themselves with; therefore, this lesson is a governor that will, if observed and applied, enable you to steer your ship of knowledge over the rocks and reefs of failure that usually beset the pathway of all who come suddenly into possession of power.

For more than twenty-five years I have been observing the manner in which men behave themselves when in possession of power, and I have been forced to the conclusion that the man who attains it in any other than by the slow, step-by-step process, is constantly in danger of destroying himself and all whom he influences. It must have become obvious to you, long before this, that this entire course leads to the attainment of power of proportions which may be made to perform the seemingly "impossible." Happily, it becomes apparent that this power can only be attained by the observance of many fundamental principles all of which converge in this lesson, which is based upon a law that both equals and transcends in importance every other law outlined in the preceding lessons.

Likewise, it becomes apparent to the thoughtful student that this power can endure only by faithful observance of the law upon which this lesson is based, wherein lies the "safety-valve" that protects the careless student from the dangers of his own follies; and protects, also, those whom he might endanger if he tried to circumvent the injunction laid down in this lesson.

To "prank" with the power that may be attained from the knowledge wrapped up in the preceding lessons of this course, without a full understanding and strict observance of the law laid down in this lesson, is the equivalent of "pranking" with a power which may destroy as well as create.

I am speaking, now, not of that which I suspect to be true, but, of that which I KNOW TO BE TRUE! The truth upon which this entire course, and this lesson in particular, is founded, is no invention of mine. I lay no claim to it except that of having observed its unvarying application in the every-day walks of life over a period of more than twenty-five years of struggle; and, of having appropriated as much of it as, in the light of my human frailties and weaknesses, I could make use of.

If you demand positive proof of the soundness of the laws upon which this course in general, and this lesson in particular, is founded, I must plead inability to offer it except through one witness, and that is yourself. You may have positive proof only by testing and applying these laws for yourself.

If you demand more substantial and authoritative evidence than my own, then I am privileged to refer you to the teachings and philosophy of Plato, Socrates, Epictetus, Confucius, Emerson and two of the more modern philosophers, James and Munsterberg, from whose works I have appropriated all that constitutes the more

important fundamentals of this lesson, with the exception of that which I have gathered from my own limited experience.

For more than four thousand years men have been preaching the Golden Rule as a suitable rule of conduct among men, but unfortunately the world has accepted the letter while totally missing the spirit of this Universal Injunction. We have accepted the Golden Rule philosophy merely as a sound rule of ethical conduct but we have failed to understand the law upon which it is based.

I have heard the Golden Rule quoted scores of times, but I do not recall having ever heard an explanation of the law upon which it is based, and not until recent years did I understand that law, from which I am led to believe that those who quoted it did not understand it.

The Golden Rule means, substantially, to do unto others as you would wish them to do unto you if your positions were reversed.

But why? What is the real reason for this kindly consideration of others? The real reason is this:

There is an eternal law through the operation of which we reap that which we sow. When you select the rule of conduct by which you guide yourself in your transactions with others, you will be fair and just, very likely, if you know that you are setting into motion, by that selection, a power that will run its course for weal or woe in the lives of others, returning, finally, to help or to hinder you, according to its nature.

"Whatsoever a man soweth that shall he also reap!"

It is your privilege to deal unjustly with others, but, if you understand the law upon which the Golden Rule is based, you must know that your unjust dealings will "come home to roost."

If you fully understood the principles described in Lesson Eleven, on accurate thought, it will be quite easy for you to understand the law upon which the Golden Rule is based. You cannot pervert or change the course of this law, but you can adapt yourself to its nature and thereby use it as an irresistible power that will carry you to heights of achievement which could not be attained without its aid.

This law does not stop by merely flinging back upon you your acts of injustice and unkindness toward others; it goes further than this–much further–and returns to you the results of every thought that you release.

Therefore, not alone is it advisable to "do unto others as you wish them to do unto you," but to avail yourself fully of the benefits of this great Universal Law you must "think of others as you wish them to think of you."

The law upon which the Golden Rule is based begins affecting you, either for good or evil, the moment you release a thought. It has amounted almost to a world-wide tragedy that people have not generally understood this law. Despite the simplicity of the law it is practically all there is to be learned that is of enduring value to man, for it is the medium through which we become the masters of our own destiny.

Understand this law and you understand all that the Bible has to unfold to you, for the Bible presents one unbroken chain of evidence in support of the fact that man is the maker of his own destiny; and, that his thoughts and acts are the tools with which he does the making.

During ages of less enlightenment and tolerance than that of the present, some of the greatest thinkers the world has ever produced have paid with their lives for daring to uncover this Universal Law so that it might be understood by all. In the light of the past history of the world, it is an encouraging bit of evidence, in support of the fact that men are gradually throwing off the veil of ignorance and intolerance, to note that I stand in no danger of bodily harm for writing that which would have cost me my life a few centuries ago.

While this course deals with the highest laws of the universe, which man is capable of interpreting, the aim, nevertheless, has been to show how these laws may be used in the practical affairs of life. With this object of practical application in mind, let us now proceed to analyze the effect of the Golden Rule through the following incident.

THE POWER OF PRAYER

"No," said the lawyer, "I shan't press your claim against that man; you can get someone else to take the case, or you can withdraw it; just as you please."

"Think there isn't any money in it?"

"There probably would be some little money in it, but it would come from the sale of the little house that the man occupies and calls his home! But I don't want to meddle with the matter, anyhow."

"Got frightened out of it, eh?"

"Not at all."

"I suppose likely the fellow begged hard to be let off?"

"Well, yes, he did."

"And you caved in, likely?"

"Yes."

"What in creation did you do?"

"I believe I shed a few tears."

"And the old fellow begged you hard, you say?"

"No, I didn't say so; he didn't speak a word to me."

"Well, may I respectfully inquire whom he did address in your hearing?"

"God Almighty."

"Ah, he took to praying, did he?"

"Not for my benefit, in the least. You see, I found the little house easily enough and knocked on the outer door, which stood ajar; but nobody heard me, so I stepped into the little hall and saw through the crack of a door a cozy sitting-room, and there on the bed, with her silver head high on the pillows, was an old lady who looked for all the world just like my mother did the last time I ever saw her on earth. Well, I was on the point of knocking, when she said: 'Come, father, now begin; I'm all ready.' And down on his knees by her side went an old, white-haired man, still older than his wife, I should judge, and I couldn't have knocked then, for the life of me. Well, he began. First, he reminded God they were still His submissive children, mother and he, and no matter what He saw fit to bring upon them they shouldn't rebel at His will. Of course 'twas going to be very hard for them to go out homeless in their old age, especially with poor mother so sick and helpless, and, oh! how different it all might have been if only one of the boys had been spared. Then his voice kind of broke, and a white hand stole from under the coverlet and moved softly over his snowy hair. Then he went on to repeat that nothing could be so sharp again as the parting with those three sons–unless mother and he should be separated.

"But, at last, he fell to comforting himself with the fact that the dear Lord knew that it was through no fault of his own that mother and he were threatened with the loss of their dear little home, which meant beggary and the alms-house–a place they prayed to be delivered from entering if it should be consistent with God's will. And then he quoted a multitude of promises concerning the safety of those who put their trust in the Lord. In fact, it was the most thrilling plea to which I ever listened. And at last, he prayed for God's blessing on those who were about to demand justice."

The lawyer then continued, more lowly than ever: "And I–believe–I'd rather go to the poor-house myself tonight than to stain my heart and hands with the blood of such a prosecution as that."

"Little afraid to defeat the old man's prayer, eh?"

"Bless your soul, man, you couldn't defeat it!" said the lawyer. "I tell you he left it all subject to the will of God; but he claimed that we were told to make known our desires unto God; but of all the pleadings I ever heard that beat all. You see, I was taught that kind of thing myself in my childhood. Anyway, why was I sent to hear that prayer? I am sure I don't know, but I hand the case over."

"I wish," said the client, twisting uneasily, "you hadn't told me about the old man's prayer."

"Why so?"

"Well, because I want the money the place would bring; but I was taught the Bible straight enough when I was a youngster and I'd hate to run counter to what you tell about. I wish you hadn't heard a word about it, and, another time, I wouldn't listen to petitions not intended for my ears." The lawyer smiled.

"My dear fellow," he said, "you're wrong again. It was intended for my ears, and yours, too; and God

Almighty intended it. My old mother used to sing about God's moving in a mysterious way, as I remember it."

"Well, my mother used to sing it, too," said the claimant, as he twisted the claim-papers in his fingers."You can call in the morning, if you like, and tell 'mother' and 'him' the claim has been met."

"In a mysterious way," added the lawyer, smiling.

Neither this lesson nor the course of which it is a part is based upon an appeal to maudlin sentiment, but there can be no escape from the truth that success, in its highest and noblest form, brings one, finally, to view all human relationships with a feeling of deep emotion such as that which this lawyer felt when he overheard the old man's prayer.

It may be an old-fashioned idea, but somehow I can't get away from the belief that no man can attain success in its highest form without the aid of earnest prayer! Prayer is the key with which one may open the secret doorway referred to in Lesson Eleven. In this age of mundane affairs, when the uppermost thought of the majority of people is centered upon the accumulation of wealth, or the struggle for a mere existence, it is both easy and natural for us to overlook the power of earnest prayer. I am not saying that you should resort to prayer as a means of solving your daily problems which press for immediate attention; no, I am not going that far in a course of instruction which will be studied largely by those who are seeking in it the road to success that is measured in dollars; but, may I not modestly suggest to you that you, at least, give prayer a trial after everything else fails to bring you a satisfying success? Thirty men, red-eyed and disheveled, lined up before the judge of the San Francisco police court. It was the regular morning company of drunks and dis-orderlies. Some were old and hardened; others hung their beads in shame. Just as the momentary disorder attending the bringing in of the prisoners quieted down, a strange thing happened. A strong, clear voice from below began singing:

"Last night I lay a-sleeping,
There came a dream so fair."

"Last night!"

It had been for them all a nightmare or a drunken stupor. The song was such a contrast to the horrible fact that no one could fail of a sudden shock at the thought the song suggested.

"I stood in old Jerusalem,
Beside the Temple there,"

the song went on. The judge had paused. He made a quiet inquiry. A former member of a famous opera company known all over the country was awaiting trial for forgery. It was he who was singing in his cell.

Meantime the song went on, and every man in the line showed emotion. One or two dropped on their knees; one boy at the end of the line, after a desperate effort at self-control, leaned against the wall, buried his face against his folded arms, and sobbed,

"Oh, mother, mother."

The sobs, cutting to the very heart the men who heard, and the song, still welling its way through the court-room, blended in the hush. At length one man protested. "Judge," said he, "have we got to submit to this? We're here to take our punishment, but this –" He, too, began to sob.

It was impossible to proceed with the business of the court; yet the court gave no order to stop the song. The police sergeant, after an effort to keep the men in line, stepped back and waited with the rest. The song moved on to its climax:

> "Jerusalem, Jerusalem!
> Sing, for the night is o'er!
> Hosanna, in the highest!
> Hosanna, for evermore!"

In an ecstasy of melody the last words rang out, and then there was silence. The judge looked into the faces of the men before him. There was not one who was not touched by the song; not one in whom some better impulse was not stirred. He did not call the cases singly–a kind word of advice, and he dismissed them all. No man was fined or sentenced to the workhouse that morning. The song had done more good than punishment could possibly have accomplished.

You have read the story of a Golden Rule lawyer and a Golden Rule judge. In these two commonplace incidents of every-day life you have observed how the Golden Rule works when applied.

A passive attitude toward the Golden Rule will bring no results; it is not enough merely to believe in the philosophy, while, at the same time, failing to apply it in your relationships with others. If you want results you must take an active attitude toward the Golden Rule. A mere passive attitude, represented by belief in its soundness, will avail you nothing.

Nor will it avail you anything to proclaim to the world your belief in the Golden Rule while your actions are not in harmony with your proclamation. Conversely stated, it will avail you nothing to appear to practice the Golden Rule, while, at heart, you are willing and eager to use this universal law of right conduct as a cloak to cover up a covetous and selfish nature. Murder will out. Even the most ignorant person will "sense" you for what you are.

> "Human character does evermore publish itself. It will not be concealed. It hates darkness–it rushes into light. ... I heard an experienced counselor say that he never feared the effect upon a jury of a lawyer who does not believe in his heart that his client ought to have a verdict. If he does not believe it, his unbelief will appear to the jury, despite all his protestations, and will become their unbelief. This is that law whereby a work of art, of whatever kind, sets us in the same state of mind wherein the artist was when he made it. That which we do not believe we cannot adequately say, though we may repeat the words ever so often. It was this conviction which Swedenborg expressed when he described a group of persons in the spiritual world endeavoring in vain to articulate a proposition which they did not believe; but they could not, though they twisted and folded their lips even to indignation.
>
> "A man passes for what he is worth. What he is engraves itself on his face, on his form, on his fortunes, in letters of light which all men may read but himself....If you would not be known to do anything, never do it. A man may play the fool in the drifts of a desert, but every grain of sand shall seem to see."–Emerson.

It is the law upon which the Golden Rule philosophy is based to which Emerson has reference in the foregoing quotation. It was this same law that he had in mind when he wrote the following:

> "Every violation of truth is not only a sort of suicide in the liar, but is a stab at the health of human society. On the most profitable lie the course of events presently lays a destructive tax; whilst frankness proves to be the best tactics, for it invites frankness, puts the parties on a convenient footing and makes their business a friendship. Trust men and they will be true to you; treat them greatly and they will show themselves great, though they make an exception in your favor to all their rules of trade."

The Golden Rule philosophy is based upon a law which no man can circumvent. This law is the same law that is described in Lesson Eleven, on Accurate Thought, through the operation of which one's thoughts are transformed into reality corresponding exactly to the nature of the thoughts.

"Once grant the creative power of our thought and there is an end of struggling for our own way, and an end of gaining it at some one else's expense; for, since by the terms of the hypothesis we can create what we like, the simplest way of getting what we want is, not to snatch it from somebody else, but to make it for ourselves; and, since there is no limit to thought there can be no need for straining, and for everyone to have his own way in this manner, would be to banish all strife, want, sickness, and sorrow from the earth."

"As this comes to be understood, co-operation will take the place of competition, with the result of removing all ground for enmity, whether between individuals, classes, or nations...." (The foregoing quotation is from Bible Mystery and Bible Meaning by the late Judge T. Troward, published by Robert McBride & Company, New York City. Judge Troward was the author of several interesting volumes, among them The Edinburgh Lectures, which is recommended to all students of this course.)

If you wish to know what happens to a man when he totally disregards the law upon which the Golden Rule philosophy is based, pick out any man in your community whom you know to live for the single dominating purpose of accumulating wealth, and who has no conscientious scruples as to how he accumulates that wealth. Study this man and you will observe that there is no warmth to his soul; there is no kindness to his words; there is no welcome to his face. He has become a slave to the desire for wealth; he is too busy to enjoy life and too selfish to wish to help others enjoy it. He walks, and talks, and breathes, but he is nothing but a human automaton. Yet there are many who envy such a man and wish that they might occupy his position, foolishly believing him to be a success.

There can never be success without happiness, and no man can be happy without dispensing happiness to others. Moreover, the dispensation must be voluntary and with no other object in view than that of spreading sunshine into the hearts of those whose hearts are heavy-laden with burdens.

George D. Herron had in mind the law upon which the Golden Rule philosophy is based when he said:

"We have talked much of the brotherhood to come; but brotherhood has always been the fact of our life, long before it became a modern and inspired sentiment. Only we have been brothers in slavery and torment, brothers in ignorance and its perdition, brothers in disease, and war, and want, brothers in prostitution and hypocrisy. What happens to one of us sooner or later happens to all; we have always been inescapably involved in common destiny. The world constantly tends to the level of the down most man in it; and that down most man is the world's real ruler, hugging it close to his bosom, dragging it down to his death. You do not think so, but it is true, and it ought to be true. For if there were some way by which some of us could get free, apart from others, if there were some way by which some of us could have heaven while others had hell, if there were some way by which part of the world could escape some form of the blight and peril and misery of disinherited labor, then indeed would our world be lost and damned; but since men have never been able to separate themselves from one another's woes and wrongs, since history is fairly stricken with the lesson that we cannot escape brotherhood of some kind, since the whole of life is teaching us that we are hourly choosing between brotherhood in suffering and brotherhood in good, it remains for us to choose the brotherhood of a co-operative world, with all its fruits thereof–the fruits of love and liberty."

The world war ushered us into an age of cooperative effort in which the law of "live and let live" stands out like a shining star to guide us in our relationships with each other. This great universal call for co-operative effort is taking on many forms, not the least important of which are the Rotary Clubs, the Kiwanis Clubs, the Lions Clubs and the many other luncheon clubs which bring men together in a spirit of friendly intercourse, for these clubs mark the beginning of an age of friendly competition in business. The next step will be a closer alliance of all such clubs in an out-and-out spirit of friendly co-operation.

The attempt by Woodrow Wilson and his contemporaries to establish the League of Nations, followed by the efforts of Warren G. Harding to give footing to the same cause under the name of the World Court, marked the first attempt in the history of the world to make the Golden Rule effective as a common meeting ground for the nations of the world.

There is no escape from the fact that the world has awakened to the truth in George D. Herron's statement that "we are hourly choosing between brotherhood in suffering and brotherhood in good." The world war has taught us–nay, forced upon us–the truth that a part of the world cannot suffer without injury to the whole world. These facts are called to your attention, not in the nature of a preachment on morality, but for the purpose of directing your attention to the underlying law through which these changes are being brought about. For more than four thousand years the world has been thinking about the Golden Rule philosophy, and that thought is now becoming transformed into realization of the benefits that accrue to those who apply it.

Still mindful of the fact that the student of this course is interested in a material success that can be measured by bank balances, it seems appropriate to suggest here that all who will may profit by shaping their business philosophy to conform with this sweeping change toward co-operation which is taking place all over the world.

If you can grasp the significance of the tremendous change that has come over the world since the close of the world war, and if you can interpret the meaning of all the luncheon clubs and other similar gatherings which bring men and women together in a spirit of friendly co-operation, surely your imagination will suggest to you the fact that this is an opportune time to profit by adopting this spirit of friendly co-operation as the basis of your own business or professional philosophy.

Stated conversely, it must be obvious to all who make any pretense of thinking accurately, that the time is at hand when failure to adopt the Golden Rule as the foundation of one's business or professional philosophy is the equivalent of economic suicide.

Perhaps you have wondered why the subject of honesty has not been mentioned in this course, as a prerequisite to success, and, if so, the answer will be found in this lesson. The Golden Rule philosophy, when rightly understood and applied, makes dishonesty impossible. It does more than this–it makes impossible all the other destructive qualities such as selfishness, greed, envy, bigotry, hatred and malice. When you apply the Golden Rule, you become, at one and the same time, both the judge and the judged–the accused and the accuser. This places one in a position in which honesty begins in one's own heart, toward one's self, and extends to all others with equal effect. Honesty based upon the Golden Rule is not the brand of honesty which recognizes nothing but the question of expediency.

It is no credit to be honest, when honesty is obviously the most profitable policy, lest one lose a good customer or a valuable client or be sent to jail for trickery. But when honesty means either a temporary or a permanent material loss, then it becomes an honor of the highest degree to all who practice it. Such honesty has its appropriate reward in the accumulated power of character and reputation enjoyed, by all who deserve it.

Those who understand and apply the Golden Rule philosophy are always scrupulously honest, not alone out of their desire to be just with others, but because of their desire to be just with themselves. They understand the eternal law upon which the Golden Rule is based, and they know that through the operation of this law every thought they release and every act in which they indulge has its counterpart in some fact or circumstance with which they will later be confronted.

Golden Rule philosophers are honest because they understand the truth that honesty adds to their own character that "vital something" which gives it life and power. Those who understand the law through which the Golden Rule operates would poison their own drinking water as quickly as they would indulge in acts of injustice to others, for they know that such injustice starts a chain of causation that will not only bring them physical suffering, but will destroy their characters, stain for ill their reputations and render impossible the attainment of enduring success.

The law through which the Golden Rule philosophy operates is none other than the law through which the principle of Auto-suggestion operates. This statement gives you a suggestion from which you should be able to make a deduction of a far-reaching nature and of inestimable value.

Test your progress in the mastery of this course by analyzing the foregoing statement and determining, before you read on, what suggestion it offers you.

Of what possible benefit could it be to you to know that when you do unto others as if you were the others, which is the sum and substance of the Golden Rule, you are putting into motion a chain of causation through the aid of a law which affects the others according to the nature of your act, and at the same time planting in your character, through your subconscious mind, the effects of that act?

This question practically suggests its own answer, but as I am determined to cause you to think this vital subject out for yourself I will put the question in still another form, viz.:

If all your acts toward others, and even your thoughts of others, are registered in your subconscious mind, through the principle of Auto-suggestion, thereby building your own character in exact duplicate of your thoughts and acts, can you not see how important it is to guard those acts and thoughts?

We are now in the very heart of the real reason for doing unto others as we would have them do unto us, for it is obvious that whatever we do unto others we do unto ourselves.

Stated in another way, every act and every thought you release modifies your own character in exact conformity with the nature of the act or thought, and your character is a sort of center of magnetic attraction which attracts to you the people and conditions that harmonize with it.

You cannot indulge in an act toward another person without having first created the nature of that act in your own thought, and you cannot release a thought without planting the sum and substance and nature of it in your own subconscious mind, there to become a part and parcel of your own character.

Grasp this simple principle and you will understand why you cannot afford to hate or envy another person. You will also understand why you cannot afford to strike back, in kind, at those who do you an injustice. Likewise, you will understand the injunction, "Return good for evil."

Understand the law upon which the Golden Rule injunction is based and you will understand, also, the law that eternally binds all mankind in a single bond of fellowship and renders it impossible for you to injure another person, by thought or deed, without injuring yourself; and, likewise, adds to your own character the results of every kind thought and deed in which you indulge.

Understand this law and you will then know, beyond room for the slightest doubt, that you are constantly punishing yourself for every wrong you commit and rewarding yourself for every act of constructive conduct in which you indulge.

It seems almost an act of Providence that the greatest wrong and the most severe injustice ever done me by one of my fellow men was done just as I began this lesson.

(Some of the students of this course will know what it is to which I refer.)

This injustice has worked a temporary hardship on me, but that is of little consequence compared to the advantage it has given me by providing a timely opportunity for me to test the soundness of the entire premise upon which this lesson is founded.

The injustice to which I refer left two courses of action open to me. I could have claimed relief by "striking back" at my antagonist, through both civil court action and criminal libel proceedings, or I could have stood upon my right to forgive him. One course of action would have brought me a substantial sum-of money and whatever joy and satisfaction there may be in defeating and punishing an enemy. The other course of action would have brought me self-respect which is enjoyed by those who have successfully met the test and discovered that they have evolved to the point at which they can repeat the Lord's Prayer and mean it!

I chose the latter course. I did so, despite the recommendations of close personal friends to "strike back," and despite the offer of a prominent lawyer to do my "striking" for me without cost.

But the lawyer offered to do the impossible, for the reason that no man can "strike back" at another without cost. Not always is the cost of a monetary nature, for there are other things with which one may pay that are dearer than money.

It would be as hopeless to try to make one who was not familiar with the law upon which the Golden Rule is based understand why I refused to strike back at this enemy as it would to try to describe the law of gravitation to an ape. If you understand this law you understand, also, why I chose to forgive my enemy.

In the Lord's Prayer we are admonished to forgive our enemies, but that admonition will fall on deaf ears except where the listener understands the law upon which it is based. That law is none other than the law upon which the Golden Rule is based. It is the law that forms the foundation of this entire lesson, and through which we must inevitably reap that which we sow. There is no escape from the operation of this law, nor is there any cause to try to avoid its consequences if we refrain from putting into motion thoughts and acts that are destructive.

That we may more concretely describe the law upon which this lesson is based, let us embody the law in a code of ethics such as one who wishes to follow literally the injunction of the Golden Rule might appropriately adopt, as follows.

MY CODE OF ETHICS

I. I believe in the Golden Rule as the basis of all human conduct; therefore, I will never do to another person that which I would not be willing for that person to do to me if our positions were reversed.

II. I will be honest, even to the slightest detail, in all my transactions with others, not alone because of my desire to be fair with them, but because of my desire to impress the idea of honesty on my own subconscious mind, thereby weaving this essential quality into my own character.

III. I will forgive those who are unjust toward me, with no thought as to whether they deserve it or not, because I understand the law through which forgiveness of others strengthens my own character and wipes out the effects of my own transgressions, in my subconscious mind.

IV. I will be just, generous and fair with others always, even though I know that these acts will go unnoticed and unrecorded, in the ordinary terms of reward, because I understand and intend to apply the law through the aid of which one's own character is but the sum total of one's own acts and deeds.

V. Whatever time I may have to devote to the discovery and exposure of the weaknesses and faults of others I will devote, more profitably, to the discovery and correction of my own.

VI. I will slander no person, no matter how much I may believe another person may deserve it, because I wish to plant no destructive suggestions in my own subconscious mind.

VII. I recognize the power of Thought as being an inlet leading into my brain from the universal ocean of life; therefore, I will set no destructive thoughts afloat upon that ocean lest they pollute the minds of others.

VIII. I will conquer the common human tendency toward hatred, and envy, and selfishness, and jealousy, and malice, and pessimism, and doubt, and fear; for I believe these to be the seed from which the world harvests most of its troubles.

IX. When my mind is not occupied with thoughts that tend toward the attainment of my definite chief aim in life, I will voluntarily keep it filled with thoughts of courage, and self-confidence, and good-will toward others, and faith, and kindness, and loyalty, and love for truth, and justice, for I believe these to be the seed from which the world reaps its harvest of progressive growth.

X. I understand that a mere passive belief in the soundness of the Golden Rule philosophy is of no value whatsoever, either to myself or to others; therefore, I will actively put into operation this universal rule for good in all my transactions with others.

XI. I understand the law through the operation of which my own character is developed from my own acts and thoughts; therefore, I will guard with care all that goes into its development.

XII. Realizing that enduring happiness comes only through helping others find it; that no act of kindness is without its reward, even though it may never be directly repaid, I will do my best to assist others when and where the opportunity appears.

You have noticed frequent reference to Emerson throughout this course. Every student of the course should own a copy of Emerson's Essays, and the essay on Compensation should be read and studied at least every three months. Observe, as you read this essay, that it deals with the same law as that upon which the Golden Rule is based.

There are people who believe that the Golden Rule philosophy is nothing more than a theory, and that it is in no way connected with an immutable law. They have arrived at this conclusion because of personal experience wherein they rendered service to others without enjoying the benefits of direct reciprocation.

How many are there who have not rendered service to others that was neither reciprocated nor appreciated? I am sure that I have had such an experience, not once, but many times, and I am equally sure that I will have similar experiences in the future, nor will I discontinue rendering service to others merely because they neither reciprocate nor appreciate my efforts.

And here is the reason:

When I render service to another, or indulge in an act of kindness, I store away in my subconscious mind the effect of my efforts, which may be likened to the "charging" of an electric battery. By and by, if I indulge in a sufficient number of such acts I will have developed a positive, dynamic character that will attract to me people who harmonize with or resemble my own character.

Those whom I attract to me will reciprocate the acts of kindness and the service that I have rendered others, thus the Law of Compensation will have balanced the scales of justice for me, bringing back from one source the results of service that I rendered through an entirely different source.

You have often heard it said that a salesman's first sale should be to himself, which means that unless he first convinces himself of the merits of his wares he will not be able to convince others. Here, again, enters this same Law of Attraction, for it is a well-known fact that enthusiasm is contagious, and when a salesman shows great enthusiasm over his wares he will arouse a corresponding interest in the minds of others.

You can comprehend this law quite easily by regarding yourself as a sort of human magnet that attracts those whose characters harmonize with your own. In thus regarding yourself as a magnet that attracts to you all who harmonize with your dominating characteristics and repels all who do not so harmonize, you should keep in mind, also, the fact that you are the builder of that magnet; also, that you may change its nature so that it will correspond to any ideal that you may wish to set up and follow.

And, most important of all, you should keep in mind the fact that this entire process of change takes place through thought!

Your character is but the sum total of your thoughts and deeds! This truth has been stated in many different ways throughout this course.

Because of this great truth it is impossible for you to render any useful service or indulge in any act of kindness toward others without benefiting thereby. Moreover, it is just as impossible for you to indulge in any destructive act or thought without paying the penalty in the loss of a corresponding amount of your own power.

Positive thought develops a dynamic personality. Negative thought develops a personality of an opposite nature. In many of the preceding lessons of this course, and in this one, definite instructions are given as to the exact method of developing personality through positive thought. These instructions are particularly detailed in Lesson Three, on Self-confidence. In that lesson you have a very definite formula to follow. All of the formulas provided in this course are for the purpose of helping you consciously to direct the power of thought in the development of a personality that will attract to you those who will be of help in the attainment of your definite chief aim.

You need no proof that your hostile or unkind acts toward others bring back the effects of retaliation. Moreover, this retaliation is usually definite and immediate. Likewise, you need no proof that you can accomplish more by dealing with others in such a way that they will want to co-operate with you. If you mastered the eighth lesson, on Self-control, you now understand how to induce others to act toward you as you wish them to act– through your own attitude toward them.

The law of "an eye for an eye and a tooth for a tooth" is based upon the self-same law as that upon which the Golden Rule operates. This is nothing more than the law of retaliation with which all of us are familiar. Even the most selfish person will respond to this law, because he cannot help it! If I speak ill of you, even though I tell the truth, you will not think kindly of me. Furthermore, you will most likely retaliate in kind. But, if I speak of your virtues you will think kindly of me, and when the opportunity appears you will reciprocate in kind in the majority of instances.

Through the operation of this law of attraction the uninformed are constantly attracting trouble and grief and hatred and opposition from others by their unguarded words and destructive acts.

Do unto others as you would have them do unto you!

We have heard that injunction expressed thousands of times, yet how many of us understand the law upon which it is based? To make this injunction somewhat clearer it might be well to state it more in detail, about as follows:

> Do unto others as you would have them do unto you, bearing in mind the fact that human nature has a tendency to retaliate in kind.

Confucius must have had in mind the law of retaliation when he stated the Golden Rule philosophy in about this way:

> Do not unto others that which you would not have them do unto you.

And he might well have added an explanation to the effect that the reason for his injunction was based upon the common tendency of man to retaliate in kind.

Those who do not understand the law upon which the Golden Rule is based are inclined to argue that it will not work, for the reason that men are inclined toward the principle of exacting "an eye for an eye and a tooth for a tooth," which is nothing more nor less than the law of retaliation. If they would go a step further in their reasoning they would understand that they are looking at the negative effects of this law, and that the self-same law is capable of producing positive effects as well.

In other words, if you would not have your own eye plucked out, then insure against this misfortune by refraining from plucking out the other fellow's eye. Go a step further and render the other fellow an act of kindly, helpful service, and through the operation of this same law of retaliation he will render you a similar service.

And, if he should fail to reciprocate your kindness–what then?

You have profited, nevertheless, because of the effect of your act on your own subconscious mind!

Thus by indulging in acts of kindness and applying, always, the Golden Rule philosophy, you are sure of benefit from one source and at the same time you have a pretty fair chance of profiting from another source.

It might happen that you would base all of your acts toward others on the Golden Rule without enjoying any direct reciprocation for a long period of time, and it might so happen that those to whom you rendered those acts of kindness would never reciprocate, but meantime you have been adding vitality to your own character and sooner or later this positive character which you have been building will begin to assert itself and you will discover that you have been receiving compound interest on compound interest in return for those acts of kindness which appeared to have been wasted on those who neither appreciated nor reciprocated them.

Remember that your reputation is made by others, but your character is made by you! You want your reputation to be a favorable one, but you cannot be sure that it will be for the reason that it is something that exists outside of your own control, in the minds of others. It is what others believe you to be. With your character it is different. Your character is that which you are, as the results of your thoughts and deeds. You control it. You can make it weak, good or bad. When you are satisfied and know in your mind that your character is above reproach you need not worry about your reputation, for it is as impossible for your character to be destroyed or damaged by anyone except yourself as it is to destroy matter or energy.

It was this truth that Emerson had in mind when he said: "A political victory, a rise of rents, the recovery of your sick or the return of your absent friend, or some other quite external event raises your spirits, and you think your days are prepared for you. Do not believe it. It can never be so. Nothing can bring you peace but yourself. Nothing can bring you peace but the triumph of principles."

One reason for being just toward others is the fact that such action may cause them to reciprocate, in kind, but a better reason is the fact that kindness and justice toward others develop positive character in all who indulge in these acts.

You may withhold from me the reward to which I am entitled for rendering you helpful service, but no one can deprive me of the benefit I will derive from the rendering of that service in so far as it adds to my own character.

We are living in a great industrial age. Everywhere we see the evolutionary forces working great changes in the method and manner of living, and rearranging the relationships between men, in the ordinary pursuit of life, liberty and a living.

This is an age of organized effort. On every hand we see evidence that organization is the basis of all financial success, and while other factors than that of organization enter into the attainment of success, this factor is still one of major importance.

This industrial age has created two comparatively new terms. One is called "capital" and the other "labor." Capital and labor constitute the main wheels in the machinery of organized effort. These two great forces enjoy success in exact ratio to the extent that both understand and apply the Golden Rule philosophy. Despite this fact, however, harmony between these two forces does not always prevail, thanks to the destroyers of confidence who make a living by sowing the seed of dissension and stirring up strife between employers and employees.

During the past fifteen years I have devoted considerable time to the study of the causes of disagreement between employers and employees. Also, I have gathered much information on this subject from other men who, likewise, have been studying this problem.

There is but one solution which will, if understood by all concerned, bring harmony out of chaos and establish a perfect working relationship between capital and labor. The remedy is no invention of mine. It is based upon a great universal law of Nature. This remedy has been well stated by one of the great men of this generation, in the following words:

"The question we propose to consider is exciting deep interest at the present time, but no more than its importance demands. It is one of the hopeful signs of the times that these subjects of vital interest to human happiness are constantly coming up for a hearing, are engaging the attention of the wisest men, and stirring the minds of all classes of people. The wide prevalence of this movement shows that a new life is beating in the heart of humanity, operating upon their faculties like the warm breath of spring upon the frozen ground and the dormant germs of the plant. It will make a great stir, it will break up many frozen and dead forms, it will produce great and, in some cases, it may be, destructive changes, but it announces the blossoming of new hopes, and the coming of new harvests for the supply of human wants and the means of greater happiness. There is great need of wisdom to guide the new forces coming into action. Every man is under the most solemn obligation to do his part in forming a correct public opinion and giving wise direction to popular will.

"The only solution for the problems of labor, of want, of abundance, of suffering and sorrow can only be found by regarding them from a moral and spiritual point of view. They must be seen and examined in a light that is not of themselves. The true relations of labor and capital can never be discovered by human selfishness. They must be viewed from a higher purpose than wages or the accumulation of wealth. They must be regarded from their bearing upon the purposes for which men was created. It is from this point of view I propose to consider the subject before us.

"Capital and labor are essential to each other. Their interests are so bound together that they cannot be separated. In civilized and enlightened communities they are mutually dependent. If there is any difference, capital is more dependent upon labor than labor upon capital. Life can be sustained without capital. Animals, with a few exceptions, have no property, and take no anxious thought for the morrow, and our Lord commends them to our notice as examples worthy of imitation. The savages live without capital. Indeed, the great mass of human beings live by their labor from day to day, from hand to mouth. But no man can live upon his wealth. He cannot eat his gold and silver; he cannot clothe himself with deeds and certificates of stock. Capital can do nothing without labor, and its only value consists in its power to purchase labor or its results. It is itself the product of labor. It has no occasion, therefore, to assume an importance that does not belong to it. Absolutely dependent, however, as it is upon labor for its value, it is an essential factor in human progress.

"The moment man begins to rise from a savage and comparatively independent state to a civilized and dependent one, capital becomes necessary. Men come into more intimate relations with one another. Instead of each one doing everything, men begin to devote themselves to special employments, and to depend upon others to provide many things for them while they engage in some special occupation. In this way labor becomes diversified. One man works in iron, another in wood; one manufactures cloth, another makes it into garments; some raise food to feed those who build houses and manufacture implements of husbandry. This necessitates a system of exchanges, and to facilitate exchanges roads must be made, and men must be employed to make them. As population increases and necessities multiply, the business of exchange becomes enlarged, until we have immense manufactories, railroads girding the earth with iron bends, steamships plowing every sea, and a multitude of men who cannot raise bread or make a garment, or do anything directly for the supply of their own wants.

"Now, we can see how we become more dependent upon others as our wants are multiplied and civilization advances. Each one works in his special employment, does better work, because he can devote his whole thought and time to a form of use for which he is specially fitted, and contributes more largely to the public good. While he is working for others, all others are working for him. Every member of the community is working for the whole body, and the whole body for every member. This is the law of perfect life, a law which rules everywhere in the material body. Every man who is engaged in any employment useful to body or mind is a philanthropist, a public benefactor, whether he raises corn on the prairie, cotton in Texas or India, mines coal in the chambers of the earth, or feeds it to engines in the hold of a steamship. If selfishness did not pervert and blast human motives, all men and women would be fulfilling the law of charity while engaged in their daily employment.

"To carry on this vast system of exchanges, to place the forest and the farm, the factory and the mine side by side, and deliver the products of all at every door, requires immense capital. One man cannot work his farm or factory, and build a railroad or a line of steamships. As raindrops acting singly cannot drive a mill or supply steam for an engine, but, collected in a vast reservoir, become the resistless power of Niagara, or the force which drives the engine and steamship like mighty shuttles from mountain to seacoast and from shore to shore, so a few dollars in a multitude of pockets are powerless to provide the means for these vast operations, but combined they move the world.

"Capital is a friend of labor and essential to its economical exercise and just reward. It can be, and often is, a terrible enemy, when employed for selfish purposes alone; but the great mass of it is more friendly to human happiness than is generally supposed. It cannot be employed without in some way, either directly or indirectly, helping the laborer. We think of the evils we suffer, but allow the good we enjoy to pass unnoticed. We think of the evils that larger means would relieve and the comforts they would provide, but overlook the blessings we enjoy that would have been impossible without large accumulations of capital. It is the part of wisdom to form a just estimate of the good we receive as well as the evils we suffer.

"It is a common saying at the present time, that the rich are growing richer and the poor poorer; but when all man's possessions are taken into the account there are good reasons for doubting this assertion. It is true that the rich are growing richer. It is also true that the condition of the laborer is constantly improving. The common laborer has conveniences and comforts which princes could not command a century ago. He is better clothed, has a greater variety and abundance of food, lives in a more comfortable dwelling, and has many more conveniences for the conduct of domestic affairs and the prosecution of labor than money could purchase but a few years ago. An emperor could not travel with the ease, the comfort, and the swiftness that the common laborer can today. He may think that he stands alone, with no one to help. But, in truth, he has an immense retinue of servants constantly waiting upon him, ready and anxious to do his bidding. It requires a vast army of men and an immense outlay of capital to provide a common dinner, such as every man and woman, with few exceptions, has enjoyed today.

"Think of the vast combination of means and men and forces necessary to provide even a frugal meal. The Chinaman raises your tea, the Brazilian your coffee, the East Indian your spices, the Cuban your sugar, the farmer upon the western prairies your bread and possibly your beef, the gardener your vegetables, the dairyman your butter and milk; the miner has dug from the hills the coal with which your food was cooked and your house was warmed, the cabinet-maker has provided you with chairs and tables, the cutler with knives and forks, the potter with dishes, the Irishman has made your tablecloth, the butcher has dressed your meat, the miller your flour.

"But these various articles of food, and the means of preparing and serving them, were produced at immense distances from you and from one another. Oceans had to be traversed, hills leveled, valleys filled, and mountains tunneled, ships must be built, railways constructed, and a vast army of men instructed and employed in every mechanical art before the materials for your dinner could be prepared and served. There must also be men to collect these materials, to buy and sell and distribute them. Everyone stands in his own place and does his own work, and receives his wages. But he is none the less working for you, and serving you as truly and effectively as he would be if he were in your special employment and received his wages from your hand. In the light of these facts, which everyone must acknowledge, we may be able to see more clearly the truth, that every man and woman who does useful work is a public benefactor, and the thought of it and the purpose of it will ennoble the labor and the laborer. We are all bound together by common ties. The rich and the poor, the learned and the ignorant, the strong and the weak, are woven together in one social and civic web. Harm to one is harm to all; help to one is help to all.

"You see what a vast army of servants it requires to provide your dinner. Do you not see that it demands a corresponding amount of capital to provide and keep this complicated machinery in motion? And do you not see that every man, woman and child is enjoying the benefit of it? How could we get our coal, our meat, our flour, our tea and coffee, sugar and rice? The laborer cannot build ships and sail them and support himself while doing it. The farmer cannot leave his farm and take his produce to the market. The miner cannot mine and transport his coal. The farmer in Kansas may be burning corn today to cook his food and warm his dwelling, and the miner may be hungry for the bread which the corn would supply, because they cannot exchange the fruits of their labor. Every acre of land, every forest and mine has been increased in value by railways and steamboats, and the comforts of life and the means of social and intellectual culture have been carried to the most inaccessible places.

"But the benefits of capital are not limited to supplying present wants and comforts. It opens new avenues for labor. It diversifies it and gives a wider field to everyone to do the kind of work for which he is best fitted by natural taste and genius. The number of employments created by railways, steamships, telegraph, and manufactories by machinery can hardly be estimated. Capital is also largely invested in supplying the means of intellectual and spiritual culture.

"Books are multiplied at constantly diminishing prices, and the best thought of the world, by means of our great publishing houses, is made accessible to the humblest workman. There is no better example of the benefits the common laborer derives from capital than the daily newspaper. For two or three cents the history of the world for twenty-four hours is brought to every door. The laborer, while riding to or from his work in a comfortable car, can visit all parts of the known world and get a truer idea of the events of the day than he could if he were bodily present. A battle in China or Africa, an earthquake in Spain, a dynamite explosion in London, a debate in Congress, the movements of men in public and private life for the suppression of vice, for enlightening the ignorant, helping the needy, and improving the people generally, are spread before him in a small compass, and bring him into contact and on equality, in regard to the world's history, with kings and queens, with saints and sages, and people in every condition in life. Do you ever think, while reading the morning paper, how many men have been running on your errands, collecting intelligence for you from all parts of the earth, and putting it into a form convenient for your use? It required the investment of millions of money and the employment of thousands of men to produce that paper and leave it at your door. And what did all this service cost you? A few cents.

"These are examples of the benefits which everyone derives from capital, benefits which could not be obtained without vast expenditures of money; benefits which come to us without our care and lay their blessings at our feet. Capital cannot be invested in any useful production without blessing a multitude of people. It sets the machinery of life in motion, it multiplies employment; it places the product of all climes at every door, it draws the people of all nations together; brings mind in contact with mind, and gives to every man and woman a large and valuable share of the product. These are facts which it would be well for everyone, however poor he may be, to consider.

"If capital is such a blessing to labor; if it can only be brought into use by labor, and derives all its value from it, how can there be any conflict between them? There could be none if both the capitalist and laborer acted from humane principles. But they do not. They are governed by inhuman principles. Each party seeks to get the largest returns for the least service. Capital desires larger profits, labor higher wages. The interests of the capitalist and the laborer come into direct collision. In this warfare capital has great advantages, and has been prompt to take them. It has demanded and taken the lion's share of the profits. It has despised the servant that enriched it. It has regarded the laborer as a menial, a slave, whose rights and happiness it was not bound to respect. It influences legislators to enact laws in its favor, subsidizes governments and wields its power for its own advantage. Capital has been a lord and labor a servant. While the servant remained docile and obedient, content with such compensation as its lord chose to give, there was no conflict. But labor is rising from a servile, submissive, and hopeless condition. It has acquired strength and intelligence; it has gained the idea that it has rights that ought to be respected, and begins to assert and combine to support them.

"Each party in this warfare regards the subject from its own selfish interests. The capitalist supposes that gain to labor is loss to him, and that he must look to his own interests first; that the cheaper the labor the larger his gains. Consequently it is for his interest to keep the price as low as possible. On the contrary, the laborer thinks that he loses what the capitalist gains, and, consequently, that it is for his interest to get as large wages as possible. From these opposite points of view their interests appear to be directly hostile. What one party gains the other loses; hence the conflict. Both are acting from selfish motives, and, consequently, must be wrong. Both parties see only half of the truth, and, mistaking that for the whole of it, they fall into a mistake ruinous to both. Each one stands on his own ground, and regards the subject wholly from his point of view and in the misleading light of his own selfishness. Passion inflames the mind and blinds the understanding; and when passion is aroused men will sacrifice their own interests to injure others, and both will suffer loss. They will wage continual warfare against each other; they will resort to all devices, and take advantage of every necessity to win a victory. Capital tries to starve the laborer into submission, like a beleaguered city; and hunger and want are most powerful weapons. Labor sullenly resists, and tries to destroy the value of capital by rendering it unproductive. If necessity or interest compels a truce, it is a sullen one, and maintained with the purpose of renewing hostilities as soon as there is any prospect of success. Thus laborers and capitalists confront each other like two armed hosts, ready at any time to renew the conflict. It will be renewed, without doubt, and continued with varying success until both parties discover that they are mistaken, that their interests are mutual, and can only be secured to the fullest extent by co-operation and giving to each the reward it deserves. The capitalist and the laborer must clasp hands across the bottomless pit into which so much wealth and work has been cast.

"How this reconciliation is to be effected is a question that is occupying the minds of many wise and good men on both sides at the present time. Wise and impartial legislation will, no doubt, be an important agent in restraining blind passion and protecting all classes from insatiable greed; and it is the duty of every man to use his best endeavors to secure such legislation both in state and national governments. Organizations of laborers for protecting their own rights and securing a better reward for their labor, will have a great influence. That influence will continue to increase as their temper becomes normal and firm, and their demands are based on justice and humanity. Violence and threats will effect no good. Dynamite, whether in the form of explosives or the more destructive force of fierce and reckless passion, will heal no wounds nor subdue any hostile feeling. Arbitration is, doubtless, the wisest and most practicable means now available to bring about amicable relations between these hostile parties and secure justice to both. Giving the laborer a share in the profits of the business has worked well in some cases, but it is attended with great practical difficulties which require more wisdom, self-control and genuine regard for the common interests of both parties than often can be found. Many devices may have a partial and temporary effect. But no permanent progress can be made in settling this conflict without restraining and finally removing its cause.

"Its real central cause is an inordinate love of self and the world, and that cause will continue to operate as long as it exists. It may be restrained and moderated, but it will assert itself when occasion offers. Every wise man must, therefore, seek to remove the cause, and as far as he can do it he will control effects. Purify the fountain, and you make the whole stream pure and wholesome.

"There is a principle of universal influence that must underlie and guide every successful effort to bring these two great factors of human good which now confront each other with hostile purpose, into harmony. It is no invention or discovery of mine. It embodies a higher than human wisdom. It is not difficult to understand or apply. The child can comprehend it and act according to it. It is universal in its application, and wholly useful in its effects. It will lighten the burdens of labor and increase its rewards. It will give security to capital and make it more productive. It is simply the Golden Rule, embodied in these words: 'Therefore all things whatsoever ye would that men should do to you, do ye even so to them: for this is the law and the prophets.'

"Before proceeding to apply this principle to the case in hand, let me call your special attention to it. It is a very remarkable law of human life which seems to have been generally overlooked by statesmen, philosophers and religious teachers. This rule embodies the whole of religion; it comprises all the precepts, commandments, and means of the future triumphs of good over evil, of truth over error, and the peace and happiness of men, foretold in the glorious visions of the prophets. Mark the words. It does not merely say that it is a wise rule; that it accords with the principles of the Divine order revealed in the law and the prophets. It embodies them all; it 'IS the law and the prophets.' It comprises love to God. It says we should regard Him as we desire to have Him regard us; that we should do to Him as we wish to have Him do to us. If we desire to have Him love us with all His heart, with all His soul, with all His mind, and with all His strength, we must love Him in the same manner. If we desire to have our neighbor love us as he loves himself, we must love him as we love ourself. Here, then, is the universal and Divine law of human service and fellowship. It is not a precept of human wisdom; it has its origin in the Divine nature, and its embodiment in human nature. Now, let us apply it to the conflict between labor and capital.

"You are a capitalist. Your money is invested in manufactures, in land, in mines, in merchandise, railways, and ships, or you loan it to others on interest. You employ, directly or indirectly, men to use your capital. You cannot come to a just conclusion concerning your rights and duties and privileges by looking wholly at your own gains. The glitter of the silver and gold will exercise so potent a spell over your mind that it will blind you to everything else. You can see no interest but your own. The laborer is not known or regarded as a man who has any interests you are bound to regard. You see him only as your slave, your tool, your means of adding to your wealth. In this light he is a friend so far as he serves you, an enemy so far as he does not. But change your point of view. Put yourself in his place; put him in your place. How would you like to have him treat you if you were in his place? Perhaps you have been there. In all probability you have, for the capitalist today was the laborer yesterday, and the laborer today will be the employer tomorrow. You know from lively and painful experience how you would like to be treated. Would you like to be regarded as a mere tool? As a means of enriching another? Would you like to have your wages kept down to the bare necessities of life? Would you like to be regarded with indifference and treated with brutality? Would you like to have your blood, your strength, your soul coined into dollars for the benefit of another? These questions are easy to answer. Everyone knows that he would rejoice to be treated kindly, to have his interests regarded, his rights recognized and protected. Everyone knows that such regard awakens a response in his own heart. Kindness begets kindness; respect awakens respect. Put yourself in his place. Imagine that you are dealing with yourself, and you will have no difficulty in deciding whether you should give the screw another turn, that you may wring a penny more from the muscles of the worker, or relax its pressure, and, if possible, add something to his wages, and give him respect for his service. Do to him as you would have him do to you in changed conditions.

"You are a laborer. You receive a certain sum for a day's work. Put yourself in the place of your employer. How would you like to have the men you employed work for you? Would you think it right that they should regard you as their enemy? Would you think it honest in them to slight their work, to do as little and to get as much as possible? If you had a large contract which must be completed at a fixed time or you would suffer great loss, would you like to have your workmen take advantage of your necessity to compel an increase of their wages? Would you think it right and wise in them to interfere with you in the management of your business? To dictate whom you should employ, and on what terms you should employ them? Would you not rather have them do honest work in a kind and good spirit? Would you not be much more disposed to look to their interests, to lighten their labor, to increase their wages when you could afford to do so, and look after the welfare of their families, when you found that they regarded yours? I know that it would be so. It is true that men are selfish, and that some men are so mean and contracted in spirit that they cannot see any interest but their own; whose hearts, not made of flesh but of silver and gold, are so hard that they are not touched by any human feeling, and care not how much others suffer if they can make a cent by it. But they are the exception, not the rule. We are influenced by the regard and devotion of others to our interests. The laborer who knows that his employer feels kindly toward him, desires to treat him justly and to regard his good, will do better work and more of it, and will be disposed to look to his employer's interests as well as his own.

"I am well aware that many will think this Divine and humane law of doing to others as we would have them do to us, is impracticable in this selfish and worldly age. If both parties would be governed by it, everyone can see how happy would be the results. But, it will be said, they will not. The laborer will not work unless compelled by want. He will take advantage of every necessity. As soon as he gains a little independence of his employer he becomes proud, arrogant and hostile. The employer will seize upon every means to keep the workmen dependent upon him, and to make as much out of them as possible. Every inch of ground which labor yields capital will occupy and entrench itself in it, and from its vantage bring the laborer into greater dependence and more abject submission. But this is a mistake. The history of the world testifies that when the minds of men are not embittered by intense hostility and their feelings outraged by cruel wrongs, they are ready to listen to calm, disinterested and judicious counsel. A man who employed a large number of laborers in mining coal told me that he had never known an instance to fail of a calm and candid response when he had appealed to honorable motives, as a man to man, both of whom acknowledged a common humanity. There is a recent and most notable instance in this city of the happy effect of calm, disinterested and judicious counsel in settling difficulties between employers and workmen that were disastrous to both.

"When the mind is inflamed by passion men will not listen to reason. They become blind to their own interests and regardless of the interests of others. Difficulties are never settled while passion rages. They are never settled by conflict. One party may be subdued by power; but the sense of wrong will remain; the fire of passion will slumber ready to break out again on the first occasion. But let the laborer or the capitalist feel assured that the other party has no wish to take any advantage, that there is a sincere desire and determination on both sides to be just and pay due regard to their common interests, and all the conflict between them would cease, as the wild waves of the ocean sink to calm when the winds are at rest. The laborer and the capitalist have a mutual and common interest. Neither can permanently prosper without the prosperity of the other. They are parts of one body. If labor is the arm, capital is the blood. Devitalize or waste the blood, and the arm loses its power. Destroy the arm, and the blood is useless. Let each care for the other, and both are benefitted. Let each take the Golden Rule as a guide, and all cause of hostility will be removed, all conflict will cease, and they will go hand in hand to do their work and reap their just reward."

If you have mastered the fundamentals upon which this lesson is based, you understand why it is that no public speaker can move his audience or convince men of his argument unless he, himself, believes that which he is saying.

You also understand why no salesman can convince his prospective purchaser unless he has first convinced himself of the merits of his goods.

Throughout this entire course one particular principle has been emphasized for the purpose of illustrating the truth that every personality is the sum total of the individual's thoughts and acts–that we come to resemble the nature of our dominating thoughts.

Thought is the only power that can systematically organize, accumulate and assemble facts and materials according to a definite plan. A flowing river can assemble dirt and build land, and a storm can gather and assemble sticks into a shapeless mass of debris, but neither storms nor river can think; therefore, the materials which they assemble are not assembled in organized, definite form.

Man, alone, has the power to transform his thoughts into physical reality; man, alone, can dream and make his dreams come true.

Man has the power to create ideals and rise to their attainment.

How did it happen that man is the only creature on earth that knows how to use the power of thought? It "happened" because man is the apex of the pyramid of evolution, the product of millions of years of struggle during which man has risen above the other creatures of the earth as the result of his own thoughts and their effects upon himself.

Just when, where and how the first rays of thought began to flow into man's brain no one knows, but we all know that thought is the power which distinguishes man from all other creatures; likewise, we all know that thought is the power that has enabled man to lift himself above all other creatures.

No one knows the limitations of the power of thought, or whether or not it has any limitations. Whatever man believes he can do he eventually does. But a few generations back the more imaginative writers dared to write of the "horseless carriage," and lo! It became a reality and is now a common vehicle. Through the evolutionary power of thought the hopes and ambitious of one generation become a reality in the next.

The power of thought has been given the dominating position throughout this course, for the reason that it belongs in that position. Man's dominating position in the world is the direct result of thought, and it must be this power that you, as an individual, will use in the attainment of success, no matter what may be your idea of what represents success.

You have now arrived at the point at which you should take inventory of yourself for the purpose of ascertaining what qualities you need to give you a well-balanced and rounded out personality.

Fifteen major factors entered into the building of this course. Analyze yourself carefully, with the assistance of one or more other persons if you feel that you need it, for the purpose of ascertaining in which of the fifteen factors of this course you are the weakest, and then concentrate your efforts upon those particular lessons until you have fully developed those factors which they represent.

PERSONAL ANALYSIS SERVICE

As a student of this course you are entitled to a continuation of the author's services for the purpose of making a complete Personal Analysis that will indicate your general efficiency and your understanding of the Fifteen Laws of Success.

To avail yourself of this service you must fill out the Personal Analysis Questionnaire, which accompanies the course, and mail it to the author, at the address shown on the Questionnaire.

You will, in due time, receive a graphic chart diagram which will show you, at a glance, the percentage to which you are entitled in connection with each of the Fifteen Laws. It will be both interesting and instructive to compare this analysis with the one which you, yourself, have made, through the aid of the chart shown in Lesson One. The Questionnaire should not be filled out until after you have read all the lessons of this course at least once. Answer the questions correctly, and frankly, as near as you can. The data contained in your answers will be strictly confidential, and will be seen by no one except the author of this philosophy.

Your analysis will be in the nature of a signed report, which may be used to great advantage in the marketing of your personal services, if you wish so to use it. This analysis will be the same, in every respect, as those for which the author made a charge of $25.00 during the years he was engaged in research in connection with the organization of this course, and it may, under some circumstances, be worth many times this amount to you, as similar analyses have been to scores of people whom the author has served.

No charge is made for this analysis, as it is a part of the service to which each student of this course is entitled upon completion of the sixteen lessons and the payment of the nominal tuition fee charged for the course.

INDECISION–An After-the-Lesson Visit With the Author

TIME!

Procrastination robs you of opportunity. It is a significant fact that no great leader was ever known to procrastinate. You are fortunate if AMBITION drives you into action, never permitting you to falter or turn back, once you have rendered a DECISION to go forward. Second-by-second, as the clock ticks off the distance TIME is running a race with YOU. Delay means defeat, because no man may ever make up a second of lost TIME. TIME is a master worker which heals the wounds of failure and disappointment and rights all wrongs and turns all mistakes into capital, but, it favors only those who kill off procrastination and remain in ACTION when decisions are to made. Life is a great checker-board. The player opposite you is TIME.

If you hesitate you will be wiped off the board. If you keep moving you may win. The only real capital is TIME, but it is capital only when used.

You may be shocked if you keep accurate account of the TIME you waste in a single day.

Wasted time is one of the chief causes of FAILURE!

One of the players is "TIME" and the other is Mr. Average Man; let us call him YOU.

Move by move Time has wiped off Mr. Average Man's men until he is finally cornered, where Time will get him, no matter which way he moves. INDECISION has driven him into the corner.

Ask any well-informed salesman and he will tell you that indecision is the outstanding weakness of the majority of people. Every salesman is familiar with that time-worn alibi, "I will think it over," which is the last trench line of defense of those who have not the courage to say either yes or no. Like the player in the picture above, they cannot decide which way to move. Meanwhile, Time forces them into a corner where they can't move.

The great leaders of the world were men and women of quick decision.

General Grant had but little to commend him as an able General except the quality of firm decision, but this was sufficient to offset all of his weaknesses. The whole story of his military success may be gathered from his reply to his critics when he said "We will fight it out along these lines if it takes all summer."

When Napoleon reached a decision to move his armies in a given direction, he permitted nothing to cause him to change that decision. If his line of march brought his soldiers to a ditch, dug by his opponents to stop him, be would give the order to charge the ditch until it had been filled with dead men and horses sufficient to bridge it.

The suspense of indecision drives millions of people to failure. A condemned man once said that the thought of his approaching execution was not so terrifying, once he had reached the decision in his own mind to accept the inevitable.

Lack of decision is the chief stumbling block of all revival meeting workers. Their entire work is to get men and women to reach a decision in their own minds to accept a given religious tenet. Billy Sunday once said, "Indecision is the devil's favorite tool."

Andrew Carnegie visualized a great steel industry, but that industry would not be what it is today had he not reached a decision in his own mind to transform his vision into reality.

James J. Hill saw, in his mind's eye, a great transcontinental railway system, but that railroad never would have become a reality had he not reached a decision to start the project.

Imagination, alone, is not enough to insure success.

Millions of people have imagination and build plans that would easily bring them both fame and fortune, but those plans never reach the DECISION stage.

Samuel Instil was an ordinary stenographer, in the employ of Thomas A. Edison. Through the aid of his imagination he saw the great commercial possibilities of electricity. But, he did more than see the possibilities-he reached a decision to transform the mere possibilities into realities, and today he is a multimillionaire electric light plant operator.

Demosthenes was a poor Greek lad who had a strong desire to be a great public speaker. Nothing unusual about that; others have "desired" this and similar ability without living to see their desires realized. But, Demosthenes added DECISION to DESIRE, and, despite the fact that he was a stammerer he mastered this handicap and made himself one of the great orators of the world.

Martin W. Littleton was a poor lad who never saw the inside of a school house until he was past twelve years of age. His father took him to hear a great lawyer defend a murderer, in one of the southern cities. The speech made such a profound impression on the lad's mind that he grabbed his father by the hand and said, "Father, one of these days I am going to become the ablest lawyer in America."

That was a DEFINITE DECISION!

Today Martin W. Littleton accepts no fee under $50,000.00, and it is said that he is kept busy all the time. He became an able lawyer because be reached a DECISION to do so.

Edwin C. Barnes reached a DECISION in his own mind to become the partner of Thomas A. Edison. Handicapped by lack of schooling, without money to pay his railroad fare, and with no influential friends to introduce him to Mr. Edison, young Barnes made his way to East Orange on a freight car and so thoroughly sold himself to Mr. Edison that he got his opportunity which led to a partnership. Today, just twenty years since that decision was reached, Mr. Barnes lives at Bradenton, Florida, retired, with all the money he needs.

Men of decision usually get all that they go after!

Well within the memory of this writer a little group of men met at Westerville, Ohio, and organized what they called the Anti-Saloon League. Saloon men treated them as a joke. People, generally, made fun of them. But, they had reached a decision.

That decision was so pronounced that it finally drove the powerful saloon men into the corner.

William Wrigley, Jr., reached a decision to devote his entire business career to the manufacture and sale of a five-cent package of chewing gum. He has made that decision bring him financial returns running into millions of dollars a year.

Henry Ford reached a decision to manufacture and sell a popular priced automobile that would be within the means of all who wished to own it. That decision has made Ford the most powerful man on earth and brought travel opportunity to millions of people.

All these men had two outstanding qualities: A DEFINITE PURPOSE and a firm DECISION to transform that purpose into reality.

The man of DECISION gets that which he goes after, no matter how long it takes, or how difficult the task. An able salesman wanted to meet a Cleveland banker. The banker would not see him. One morning this salesman waited near the banker's house until he saw him get into his automobile and start downtown. Watching his opportunity, the salesman drove his own automobile into the banker's, causing slight damage to the automobile. Alighting from his own car, he handed the banker his card, expressed regret on account of the damage done, but promised the banker a new car exactly like the one that had been damaged. That afternoon a new car was delivered to the banker, and out of that transaction grew a friendship that terminated, finally, in a business partnership which still exists.

The man of DECISION cannot be stopped!

The man of INDECISION cannot be started! Take your own choice.

"Behind him lay the gray Azores,
Behind the Gates of Hercules;
Before him not the ghosts of shores;
Before him only shore less seas.
The good mate said: 'Now must we pray,
For lo! the very stars are gone.
Brave Adm'r'l, speak; what shall I say?'
'Why, say: "Sail on and on!"'

When Columbus began his famous voyage he made one of the most far-reaching DECISIONS in the history of mankind. Had he not remained firm on that decision the freedom of America, as we know it today, would never have been known.

Take notice of those about you and observe this significant fact–THAT THE SUCCESSFUL MEN AND WOMEN ARE THOSE WHO REACH DECISIONS QUICKLY AND THEN STAND FIRMLY BY THOSE DECISIONS AFTER THEY ARE MADE.

If you are one of those who make up their minds today and change them again tomorrow you are doomed to failure. If you are not sure which way to move it is better to shut your eyes and move in the dark than to remain still and make no move at all.

The world will forgive you if you make mistakes, but it will never forgive you if you make no DECISIONS, because it will never hear of you outside of the community in which you live.

No matter who you are or what may be your lifework, you are playing checkers with TIME! It is always your next move. Move with quick DECISION and Time will favor you. Stand still and Time will wipe you off the board.

You cannot always make the right move, but, if you make enough moves you may take advantage of the law of averages and pile up a creditable score before the great game of LIFE is ended.

SELF-ANALYSIS TEST QUESTIONS

* Do you complain often of "feeling bad," and if so, what is the cause?
* Do you find fault with other people at the slightest provocation?
* Do you frequently make mistakes in your work, and if so, why?
* Are you sarcastic and offensive in your conversation?
* Do you deliberately avoid the association of anyone, and if so, why?
* Do you suffer frequently with indigestion? If so, what is the cause?
* Does life seem futile and the future hopeless to you? If so, why?
* Do you like your occupation? If not, why?
* Do you often feel self-pity, and if so why?
* Are you envious of those who excel you?
* To which do you devote most time, thinking of SUCCESS, or of FAILURE?
* Are you gaining or losing self-confidence as you grow older?
* Do you learn something of value from all mistakes?
* Are you permitting some relative or acquaintance to worry you? If so, why?
* Are you sometimes "in the clouds" and at other times in the depths of despondency?
* Who has the most inspiring influence upon you? What is the cause?
* Do you tolerate negative or discouraging influences which you can avoid?
* Are you careless of your personal appearance? If so, when and why?
* Have you learned how to "drown your troubles" by being too busy to be annoyed by them?
* Would you call yourself a "spineless weakling" if you permitted others to do your thinking for you?
* Do you neglect internal bathing until auto intoxication makes you ill-tempered and irritable?
* How many preventable disturbances annoy you, and why do you tolerate them?
* Do you resort to liquor, narcotics, or cigarettes to "quiet your nerves"? If so, why do you not try will-power instead?
* Does anyone "nag" you, and if so, for what reason?
* Do you have a DEFINITE MAJOR PURPOSE, and if so, what is it, and what plan have you for achieving it?
* Do you suffer from any of the Six Basic Fears? If so, which ones?
* Have you a method by which you can shield yourself against the negative influence of others?
* Do you make deliberate use of auto-suggestion to make your mind positive?
* Which do you value most, your material possessions, or your privilege of controlling your own thoughts?
* Are you easily influenced by others against your own judgment?
* Has today added anything of value to your stock of knowledge or state of mind?
* Do you face squarely the circumstances which make you unhappy, or sidestep the responsibility?
* Do you analyze all mistakes and failures and try to profit by them or, do you take the attitude that this is not your duty?

- Can you name three of your most damaging weaknesses? What are you doing to correct them?
- Do you encourage other people to bring their worries to you for sympathy?
- Do you choose, from your daily experiences, lessons or influences which aid in your personal advancement?
- Does your presence have a negative influence on other people as a rule?
- What habits of other people annoy you most?
- Do you form your own opinions or permit yourself to be influenced by other people?
- Have you learned how to create a mental state of mind with which you can shield yourself against all discouraging influences?
- Does your occupation inspire you with faith and hope?
- Are you conscious of possessing spiritual forces of sufficient power to enable you to keep your mind free from all forms of FEAR?
- Does your religion help you to keep your own mind positive?
- Do you feel it your duty to share other people's worries? If so, why?
- If you believe that "birds of a feather flock together" what have you learned about yourself by studying the friends whom you attract?
- What connection, if any, do you see between the people with whom you associate most closely, and any unhappiness you may experience?
- Could it be possible that some person whom you consider to be a friend is, in reality, your worst enemy, because of his negative influence on your mind?
- By what rules do you judge who is helpful and who is damaging to you?
- Are your intimate associates mentally superior or inferior to you?

- How much time out of every 24 hours do you devote to:
  a. your occupation
  b. sleep
  c. play and relaxation
  d. acquiring useful knowledge
  e. plain waste

Who among your acquaintances,

a. encourages you most
b. cautions you most
c. discourages you most
d. helps you most in other ways

- What is your greatest worry?
- Why do you tolerate it?
- When others offer you free, unsolicited advice, do you accept it without question, or analyze their motive?
- What, above all else, do you most DESIRE?
- Do you intend to acquire it?
- Are you willing to subordinate all other desires for this one?

- How much time daily do you devote to acquiring it?
- Do you change your mind often? If so, why?
- Do you usually finish everything you begin?
- Are you easily impressed by other people's business or professional titles, college degrees, or wealth?
- Are you easily influenced by what other people think or say of you?
- Do you cater to people because of their social or financial status?
- Whom do you believe to be the greatest person living?
- In what respect is this person superior to yourself?
- How much time have you devoted to studying and answering these questions?
-

(At least one day is necessary for the analysis and the answering of the entire list.)

If you have answered all these questions truthfully, you know more about yourself than the majority of people. Study the questions carefully, come back to them once each week for several months, and be astounded at the amount of additional knowledge of great value to yourself, you will have gained by the simple method of answering the questions truthfully. If you are not certain concerning the answers to some of the questions, seek the counsel of those who know you well, especially those who have no motive in flattering you, and see yourself through their eyes. The experience will be astonishing.

You have ABSOLUTE CONTROL over but one thing, and that is your thoughts. This is the most significant and inspiring of all facts known to man! It reflects man's Divine nature. This Divine prerogative is the sole means by which you may control your own destiny. If you fail to control your own mind, you may be sure you will control nothing else.

If you must be careless with your possessions, let it be in connection with material things. Your mind is your spiritual estate! Protect and use it with the care to which Divine Royalty is entitled. You were given a WILLPOWER for this purpose.

Unfortunately, there is no legal protection against those who, either by design or ignorance, poison the minds of others by negative suggestion. This form of destruction should be punishable by heavy legal penalties, because it may and often does destroy one's chances of acquiring material things which are protected by law.

Men with negative minds tried to convince Thomas A. Edison that he could not build a machine that would record and reproduce the human voice, "Because" they said, "no one else had ever produced such a machine." Edison did not believe them. He knew that the mind could produce ANYTHING THE MIND COULD CONCEIVE AND BELIEVE, and that knowledge was the thing that lifted the great Edison above the common herd.

Men with negative minds told F. W. Woolworth, he would go "broke" trying to run a store on five and ten cent sales. He did not believe them. He knew that he could do anything, within reason, if he backed his plans with faith. Exercising his right to keep other men's negative suggestions out of his mind, he piled up a fortune of more than a hundred million dollars.

Men with negative minds told George Washington he could not hope to win against the vastly superior forces of the British, but he exercised his Divine right to BELIEVE, therefore this book was published under the protection of the Stars and Stripes, while the name of Lord Corawallis has been all but forgotten.

Doubting Thomases scoffed scornfully when Henry Ford tried out his first crudely built automobile on the streets of Detroit. Some said the thing never would become practical. Others said no one would pay money for such a contraption.

FORD SAID, "I'LL BELT THE EARTH WITH DEPENDABLE MOTOR CARS," AND HE DID!

His decision to trust his own judgment has already piled up a fortune far greater than the next five generations of his descendants can squander. For the benefit of those seeking vast riches, let it be remembered that practically the sole difference between Henry Ford and a majority of the more than one hundred thousand men who work for him, is this-FORD HAS A MIND AND CONTROLS IT, THE OTHERS HAVE MINDS WHICH THEY DO NOT TRY TO CONTROL.

Henry Ford has been repeatedly mentioned, because he is an astounding example of what a man with a mind of his own, and a will to control it, can accomplish. His record knocks the foundation from under that time worn alibi, "I never had a chance." Ford never had a chance, either, but he CREATED AN OPPORTUNITY AND BACKED IT WITH PERSISTENCE UNTIL IT MADE HIM RICHER THAN CROESUS.

Mind control is the result of self-discipline and habit. You either control your mind or it controls you. There is no halfway compromise. The most practical of all methods for controlling the mind is the habit of keeping it busy with a definite purpose, backed by a definite plan. Study the record of any man who achieves noteworthy success, and you will observe that he has control over his own mind, moreover, that he exercises that control and directs it toward the attainment of definite objectives. Without this control, success is not possible.

www.ingramcontent.com/pod-product-compliance
Lightning Source LLC
LaVergne TN
LVHW031150200826
846147LV00014B/92